D0151616

Trash Talk

Trash Talk

An Encyclopedia of Garbage and Recycling around the World

ROBERT WILLIAM COLLIN

ABC-CLIO™

An Imprint of ABC-CLIO, LLC

Santa Barbara, California • Denver, Colorado

Library of Congress Cataloging-in-Publication Data

Collin, Robert W., 1957–
    Trash talk : an encyclopedia of garbage and recycling around the world /
Robert William Collin.
        pages cm
    Includes bibliographical references and index.
    ISBN 978-1-61069-508-4 (print : acid-free paper) — ISBN 978-1-61069-509-1 (e-book)
    1. Refuse and refuse disposal—Encyclopedias.   2. Recycling (Waste, etc.)—
Encyclopedias.   3. Refuse and refuse disposal—Social aspects—Encyclopedias.
4. Refuse and refuse disposal—Environmental aspects—Encyclopedias.   I. Title.
    TD791.C59 2015
    363.72'8503—dc23   2015008376

ISBN: 978-1-61069-508-4
EISBN: 978-1-61069-509-1

19 18 17 16 15   1 2 3 4 5

This book is also available on the World Wide Web as an eBook.
Visit www.abc-clio.com for details.

ABC-CLIO
An Imprint of ABC-CLIO, LLC

ABC-CLIO, LLC
130 Cremona Drive, P.O. Box 1911
Santa Barbara, California 93116-1911

This book is printed on acid-free paper ∞

Manufactured in the United States of America

Contents

Preface

"Garbage" is a broad term for visible wastes. Although most waste is unseen by many people, more and more of it dominates the world's urban landscapes, even in developed countries.

This encyclopedia is a focused examination of waste practices around the world. Waste is a personal and private act having public policy effects. A new global focus on sustainability, rising public health concerns, a robust international waste trade, and accumulating waste effects drives the discussion about waste into modern public policy debates. Cultural and geopolitical divides still suppress engaged communication on this important topic. Poor countries of the world may not be able to afford waste treatment and may also be on the receiving end of wastes from waste-producing countries. Waste is often dumped into the oceans of the world. Even wealthy cities in developed countries have only recently, and reluctantly, developed basic waste treatment facilities. New forms of wastes, such as e-wastes, are surging forward, propelled by rapid waste creation but little waste recycling and very little decomposition.

This encyclopedia's introduction provides a brief history of waste disposal and describes different kinds of "waste" from a modern perspective. Although historical documents treating waste disposal are few, the evidence of waste disposal practices becomes apparent when environmental and public health effects from wastes accumulate over time. The environmental interaction of wastes with air, water, and land is also more observable. The rapid environmental monitoring, public reports such as "State of Garbage" reports, and international agreements all attest to expanding venues and increasing social concern around garbage.

This volume includes several thematic essays that examine topics such as emerging waste issues, castes and waste in India, waste issues in a refugee camp, Native Americans and nuclear waste, climate justice, menstruation and waste, environmental justice, and human rights and waste. These currents frame the emerging international debate on waste. Because waste can be a vector, or pathway, for exposure to communicable diseases and environmental stressors, public health researchers and officials frame many of the waste issues. Environmental justice refers to the distribution of environmental benefits and burdens. Waste is generally considered an environmental burden, and when it is unequally distributed and concentrated in low-income or minority communities, it is an environmental injustice. Because of the nature of waste burden distribution, increased waste production, and increasing human population, these burdens continue to be concentrated in communities that cannot resist them. These communities are now actively resisting traditional waste distribution process. Sustainability proponents face significant ecological challenges in these communities because of the unequal distribution of waste. Their increasing concentrations can overload and erode ecological systems, such as in many U.S. cities. Public health issues, accumulating environmental effects of unequal waste distribution, and a surging growth in sustainability are emerging areas defining the rising profile of garbage.

This volume describes the specific waste management practices and statistics of 173 countries. Each entry introduces a country by discussing its basic geography and population. Current waste practices, recycling, air and water pollution, and greenhouse gas emissions (GHE) generally, as well as from wastes, are emphasized. Greenhouse gas emissions for each country are summarized by agricultural, energy, industrial, and waste sectors, and emissions within each sector are included. Most entries discuss the climate change effects of global warming and the climate adaptation plans. Many of these plans include infectious disease, sanitation, and hygiene planning. All this information is intended to give entry-level readers an environmental and human context for the complexities of modern waste issues from a global and local perspective and in a modern, practical, and comprehensive way. Outstanding characteristics for each country are noted. Any major issues specific to a particular nation are listed, such as war, natural disasters, technological advancement in waste treatment, and participation in global waste collaborations and industries. Organizing each entry according to its geographic, demographic, and environmental context and then describing current practices, waste pollution, the role of government, and major waste issues allows the reader to compare countries. Each entry concludes with suggestions for further reading in print and electronic sources, including the official website of the country. Sidebars on various topics also deal with concepts such as technological advancements, controversies, dynamic waste leaders, and the future of waste. These topics include space waste, processing of wastewater into drinking water, and waste-to- energy conversion. A glossary helps explain unknown terms and acronyms. A bibliography and index is provided at the end of the work.

Waste flows to land, air, and water to and from all of the countries of the world. Geography, population, environment, infectious diseases, climate changes, and climate change adaptation are part of this scope because of their effects on waste generation, exposure, transfer, and final disposal. The purpose of this encyclopedia is to give entry-level readers an environmental and human context for the complexities of modern waste issues from a global and local perspective.

Introduction

What Is Waste?

This is both a simple and complicated question. Generally, feces and urine are considered wastes. These wastes, along with food wastes and household garbage, are unavoidable: They must go somewhere. Wastes can also be dangerous chemicals, biomedical wastes, and some industrial byproducts. Some wastes can be reused or recycled. Other waste, such as nuclear waste, can last a long time and pose an ever-present threat to the environment. Wastes can change form over their lifetime in terms of environmental effects. The premise of landfills is that the dirt will essentially rot the wastes. Some wastes can be treated but leave a toxic residue, such as that produced by incineration. Whether waste dilution in land, air, and water is a solution to pollution is a controversial public policy issue in many countries. Nations that have small populations spread out over strong, diverse, and resilient ecosystems may not observe their waste effects, which could be within the ecological carrying capacity of such places. But even these places will have environmental effects from air and water pollution originating from other places. Nations that have large, concentrated populations observe more waste effects because there are more, and they accumulate in place unless moved.

Current Waste Classifications

Waste classification can be challenging to understand, because the materials in various waste categories shift in both policy and practice, but the main categories are hazardous wastes, including nuclear wastes; solid wastes; industrial wastes; agricultural wastes; and liquid wastes. Organizations, communities, and corporations seeking to increase recycling can do so by expanding the range or reusable applications. When the reusable applications of what was formerly waste are expanded, then more waste is considered recycled. A modern U.S. example of this is liquid wastes. By restricting the worst wastes to agricultural or industrial areas, it can be reused and is so measured even though environmental effects occur. The environmental effects remain the same on people and place regardless of government regulation.

On the international level, countries differ greatly in waste perceptions, definitions, policies, and practices. The economic and political history has current effects on waste policy and practice. Many countries have a limited role for government. Countries experiencing war and civil violence often have destroyed waste infrastructure. In wartorn countries, the apparatus for environmental and public health monitoring or observation may be damaged or destroyed, representing a loss to the global community.

Other countries may not prioritize waste policy. Waste infrastructure from high-end waste treatment plants all the way down to the safe and sanitary disposal of our own personal waste is expensive. It is expensive because it was not, and often is not, a policy priority. The recent trend of global urbanization was preceded by the slower and smaller urban beginnings. Because more waste is generated in a more densely populated area, global urbanization prioritizes waste policy. Because of accumulation of waste effects and the high cost of the infrastructure necessary for full treatment of wastes, many countries may prioritize emergency waste measures in urban areas only. Emergency wastes measures are often taken in response to outbreaks of diseases such as cholera and malaria, especially in wartorn countries. Poor countries often prioritize economic development based on industry and natural resource exportation. Both practices introduce hazardous wastes and create substantial environmental effects. Industrialization and natural resource effects often occur with rapid urban growth.

Language challenges also pose an enormous obstacle in international waste management. Some cultures and countries may not have a word for a certain chemical. All countries and cultures designate waste streams using different perceptions and priorities of risk. This allows for the manipulation of waste practices and policies, often dumping the worst wastes in poor or wartorn countries or in the ocean. Generally, the worst wastes are a category of hazardous wastes. The focus of many international environmental treaties is on hazardous wastes, with special attention to dumping them in disempowered countries.

Most of the data on waste is in an early stage of forming baselines. Because more waste is always being created and the scale and volume only increases, these baselines will accumulate information and continue to refine their methodologies. An example of this is the measurement of greenhouse gas emissions in the United States for carbon dioxide and nitrogen oxides. There is little information about the site-specific operating conditions of composting facilities. The United States now composts more than three times more wastes than in 1990. These emissions are dependent on the kind of the feedstock material combusted, the climate, and a range of operational and maintenance practices. The estimated range of uncertainty for these emissions is 50 percent, which is large. The same is true for emissions based on combustion, including incineration. Even the exact number of industrial waste facilities is not known yet. The increased social profile of garbage pushes environmental research and monitoring of wastes, and many of the currently unmeasured impacts and aspects of waste will be known in the future.

Hazardous Wastes

Hazardous wastes are roughly the worst wastes. Hazardous wastes can have powerful and destructive interactions with the environment. They can be combustible, corrosive, reactive to common chemicals, and toxic to life. Hazardous wastes are defined by government agencies at international, national, and local levels. Listing a material as toxic or hazardous is complicated, so listing parts of the waste stream as "hazardous" is very complicated. In the United States, waste must first be listed as a solid waste before it can be labeled a hazardous waste, though practices vary widely. In the United States, the main agency that oversees this is the Environmental Protection Agency (EPA). Other nations may have different rules, or no rules at all, regarding what is hazardous. Because hazardous waste disposal is usually the most expensive, much of it is illegally dumped in the ocean. The off shore waters of many countries are lined with accumulating toxic wastes, such as in the United States and Italy. Other countries are affected when large storms and tsunamis move these wastes across oceans.

Although the amount of global illegal dumping in the ocean and on land is not known, the actual practice of hazardous waste disposal is highly regulated for some of this waste stream in some countries and is unregulated in others. Over time, this tends to move hazardous waste disposal to the unregulated countries.

Wastes from common manufacturing and industrial processes, from commercial chemical products, and nuclear processes are hazardous. Batteries and pesticides are hazardous wastes. Electronic wastes, or e-wastes, are increasing rapidly in the face of no easy recycling and decreasing landfill space. Many international waste treaties and agreements specifically describe which wastes are hazardous and the process to become listed as a hazardous material.

Nuclear Wastes

Nuclear wastes are a special class of hazardous wastes. They create radiation that is very damaging to life for a long time. Radiation is measured in roentgen equivalent man (rem), a measure of living tissue damage. The cumulative rem dose determines bodily damage. 100 rems of exposure causes the first symptoms of nausea and loss of white blood cells. 300 rems can cause temporary hair loss, nerve damage, and gastrointestinal damage. 450 rems kill about half of people so exposed. 800 rems are usually fatal to everyone. Radiation exposure destroys white blood cells, lowering immunity to disease and destroying blood platelets. This prevents the blood from clotting and can cause hemorrhaging. The radiation exposure levels and environmental effects on plants and other animals are equally devastating.

Radioactive wastes generated from mining and milling uranium contain long-lived radionuclides. Tailings, or leftover material, from mining can be radioactive for about 80,000 years. Some of these wastes can leech into the ground and water and offgas into the air. Mill tailings from uranium mining contain heavy metals such as copper, arsenic, molybdenum, and vanadium. The radioactive waste stream from nuclear power generation also includes spent reactor fuel, wastes generated by chemical reprocessing of spent fuels, and waste generated by reactor operations. The cumulative power generated allows for estimates of the amount of waste generated. This is the foundation for the global inventory of nuclear waste. There are also radioactive wastes from decommissioning nuclear power plants and remediating radioactive wastes. The defense agencies and industries also create radioactive wastes in the production of weapons. Some estimates count 70,000 nuclear warheads in existence globally. This would produce approximately 400,000 tons of depleted uranium. Much defense nuclear waste information is classified as secret in most countries.

Solid Wastes

Most solid wastes in the United States and many countries is in some type of landfill. Dumping wastes outside of town in one location, then burying it, is based on the assumption that all these wastes will essentially rot into the land. Before the Industrial Revolution in the mid 1800s, the scale of environmental effects of the waste stream was more organic. Solid wastes are also a creature of classification and regulatory definition. Generally, solid wastes in municipal wastes from residential, commercial, and institutional sources are solid wastes. Private residences produce household wastes. Commercial wastes come from businesses, such as restaurants, stores, hotels, and warehouses. Institutional wastes come from schools, hospitals, and government buildings. Solid wastes include dried sewage sludge, the material produced by a sewage treatment plant and dewatered. Solid wastes include bulky wastes such as cars, trucks, appliances, and furniture. Construction and demolition wastes are mixtures of other wastes and vary widely. Usually they include tree limbs and stumps, brush, dirt, wood, asphalt, concrete, bricks, plaster, drywall, roofing material, insulation (no asbestos allowed), any metals (nonradioactive), all plastics, glass, carpeting, and anything else generally found on a construction or demolition site. Animal and food processing wastes are solid wastes. Wastes from canneries, meatpacking plants, and slaughterhouses, as well as the wastes excreted by the animal in the process and any carcasses, are animal and food processing wastes. This waste is treated differently if it is intended for reuse, composting, or recycling.

There are several other categories of solid wastes. Asbestos and incinerator ash are often in a class by themselves, though states can differ in their treatment of hazardous wastes. Another industrial category of solid wastes is waste from manufacturing, industrial development processes, and sometimes pesticides. In the United States and other countries, there are specialized industrial wastes landfills.

Like many countries, the United States moves most of its solid wastes to landfills. The practice is to pick up or move wastes to a waste transfer station that then hauls it to a landfill. The modern landfill is composed of cells. The size of the cell is theoretically based on the decomposition rate of the organic material. After a cell is full, it is covered and the next one filled, and so on, depending on the amount of space available. Landfill space is at a premium, because it is filling rapidly. Landfills receive about 70 percent of all solid wastes generated in the United States. The number of municipal solid waste (MSW) landfills decreased from about 6,326 in 1990 to about 2,000 in 2010. The number of closed or active industrial landfills is not known. It is estimated that about 1,300 landfills accept industrial, construction, and demolitions wastes in the United States. Landfill gases are only estimated for MSW landfills, not industrial landfills. With industrial landfills, waste treatment processes differ widely, with variable results and byproducts. There are additional uncounted environmental and community effects from industrial waste treatment.

In other countries, where there are few modern landfills, dumping areas also receive a high proportion of solid wastes. Global urbanization brings with it large communities on the fringe of cities, their inhabitants often referred to as squatters. These communities have few municipal services, and freshwater is often scarce. These dumping grounds of solid wastes are often harvested by squatting communities for anything valuable or edible. These communities produce wastes that are not treated. Waste treatment for squatting communities is one of the major policy challenges for waste management.

Some parts of this waste stream move through recovery or composting. Some of this waste stream is used in waste to energy conversion. MSW facilities and specialized industrial landfills are all presumed to be compliant with modern landfill protocols.

It is unknown exactly how much illegal dumping occurs. As landfill regulations increase, the cost of waste disposal increases. Many old dumps needed to be cleaned up, which also increases waste disposal costs. Illegal wastes dumping of all kinds of off reservation wastes are a problem on many western U.S. Native American reservations.

The presumption that all waste in the ground eventually rots is dependent on many factors. Aerobic bacteria first consume organic wastes. Organic wastes include food wastes, paper, and some plant wastes. Eventually the aerobic bacteria use available oxygen, and anaerobic bacteria begin the decomposition process. The organic is broken down into sugars, amino acids, and cellulose. After that, fermentation breaks down remaining materials into gases and organic compounds. These organic compounds form the basis of methanogenic bacteria. These bacteria change the fermented organic wastes into "stabilized" organic material and gases. These gases are about half carbon dioxide and half methane, which are greenhouse gas emissions. Methane generation and generation of other gases is affected by the total waste land filled annually over the operational life of the landfill, the climate, the material used to cover it, whether the methane is burned off or "flared," and the amount oxidized through the cover and emitted into the air.

The remaining organic materials are often referred to as "biosolids." These biosolids are considered treated wastes and suitable for use as fertilizer. The composition of the biosolids is premised on a purely organic waste stream. If the waste stream is contaminated with nonorganic waste material, the waste may not decompose fully and be passed on in the biosolids. Communities near large-scale agricultural biosolids applications feel the environmental effects of its use, and it is often a basis for controversy.

Classifications of solid wastes are more important as waste policies and practices develop. All the different kinds of solid waste require different environmental and economic considerations. How much of a particular waste stream can be recycled, and for how long? How long does it take consumer packaging to biodegrade in a landfill? Should the government subsidize treatment of any solid waste? Which one? Why? States can use the definition of waste to promote certain kinds of economic development and prevent others. The segregation of wastes into different waste streams is fairly recent in environmental policy. Places that disposed of waste often just put it all together and left it, burned, buried, or dumped it. One place that disposed of many waste streams set the foreground for modern redefinitions of solid wastes.

For example, in Texas, many waste streams were directed to deep well injection of wastes. A deep hole was dug, into which industrial, petrochemical, and other wastes were placed or pumped. Because of concern about groundwater pollution in underground aquifers, this practice has largely been stopped. Currently, waste from the exploration, development, or production of oil, natural gas, and geothermal sources is specifically not solid waste, by statute. It is considered special waste that the local MSW must accept by Texas law. These specific activities have significant environmental impacts. Currently there is a controversy over hydrofracturing, drilling deep underground, in several directions, to mine natural gas. Powerful solvents are forced at high pressure into holes in search for the gas. Significant wastes are left over from this, as well as from oil drilling operations. This will be part of the solid waste stream, though it is not organic and is a contaminant in the landfill process.

Texas is not unique in the United States or the world in accommodating economic growth using waste definitions. This type of regulation is difficult to enforce. Ultimately the decisions about waste are up to local government for implementation. With most kinds of basic waste streams, no decision on waste is a decision itself because of continuing environmental effects. Past waste decisions devaluing environmental effects created some of the tension around current waste decisions. Many communities the world over cannot afford a waste treatment plant, and even those that can afford one may not have one. However, rapidly declining water quality and increased population waste pressures are forcing more communities to find a way to minimize their environmental effects. As they seek these types of solutions, the issue becomes more complex. Not all waste is solid, and liquid waste streams can be large and powerful.

Liquid Wastes

The definition of liquid wastes usually applies to bulk liquids and includes any solid matter in the liquid. Wastes from septic tanks and liquid sewage sludge can be separate categories. Liquid wastes are difficult to recycle and reuse.

As industrialization and urban population increases, so, too, does demand for waste treatment and fresh water. Diseases such as typhoid remained constant until adequate sewage removal systems protected the public health. The treatment of sewage is the process of removing physical, biological, or chemical pollution. The goal is to produce treated effluent and a reusable solid waste that is contamination-free.

Biological oxygen demand, or BOD, defines wastewater. BOD measures the amount of putrescible organic matter in water. When large amounts of sewage enter the water, dissolved bacteria consume oxygen. A high BOD indicates high levels of sewage. High levels of sewage foster algae blooms. Sewage can have other oxygen-depleting ecological impacts.. Remaining low levels of dissolved oxygen stress aquatic life. BOD evaluates the oxygen needs of the bacteria as they decompose organic material. BOD is a measure of the strength of the environmental effects of sewage on aquatic ecosystems. BOD measurements need to be constant and accurate. This type of sewer waste monitoring is one of the more advanced methods used by governments and could be a part of evaluating environmental effects for sustainability issues.

Many liquids are separated from the general waste stream in the processes of cleaning raw wastes. Generally it is a process of removing solids. The remaining liquids are reused, treated, and/or discharged. Some drought-stricken cities are cleaning waste water to drink. However, it is far more often the case that sewage and wastewater are not treated at all.

The three basic levels of waste treatment are applied in Germany, for example. The first level is called the primary level and reduces part of the solids. The secondary level further reduces solids and removes some pollutants. The tertiary level removes remaining solids and reduces most pollutants to safer levels. This effluent can be discharged into fresh water or reused as gray water for other purposes. The European Union required all cities having more than 15,000 people to have secondary treatment by 2000. The goal was to have all urban centers served by secondary levels of sewage treatment. This is a common goal in many waste regulatory schemes but is seldom financed enough for implementation. Tertiary waste treatment systems are costly and require maintenance and monitoring. Even with one of the more advanced waste treatment regulations, thirty-two different kinds of pharmaceutical drug residue are found in German sewers.

The treatment of the leftovers from the biological treatment of wastes is called sewer sludge. This disposal of untreated sewage sludge was discontinued in 2005. About 2.1 million tons of sewer sludge was produced in 2008. Sewage sludge from German sewage treatment facilities contains high levels of phosphorus. It is recycled as fertilizer because of the phosphorus. Almost a third of the sewage sludge is recycled in agriculture, although this is a small part of the economy. About half the sewer sludge is incinerated.

This method of treating liquid wastes incurs front-end capital costs and high operational costs. Many countries, including the United States, use subsidies and programmatic support to develop these treatment systems. This system may not be adaptable to all areas. It relies on a minimum level of water flow that in arid places may not be met.

Waste is a term of art that has evolved over time. Most living creatures create some by products or wastes. In early human history, humans were the only primates to disdain excrement as waste. Other primate mothers eat the waste of their offspring, as do many mammals. Although historical documents about waste disposal are few, the evidence of waste disposal practices becomes apparent when waste environmental effects accumulate over time. Waste disposal is an indelible issue in every society.

Waste: Why It Matters

Waste is a growing problem, because it is increasing more quickly than its treatment and more quickly than the escalating rate of global urbanization. In 2002, about

2.9 billion people lived in urban areas and produced .64 kilograms of municipal solid waste per person per day (68 billion tons a year). In 2012, 3 billion people lived in cities and produced 1.2 kilograms per person per day (1.3 billion tons per year). It is estimated that in 2025 there will be 4.3 billion people living in cities producing 2.2 billion tons per year. Waste matters because of its accumulating effects on the environment and on public health. In real life, this waste will be generated in an environment of increasing temperatures, violent weather events, and ecosystem degradation.

Globally, about 2.6 billion people have absolutely no access to any sanitation. Human wastes surround about 40 percent of the global population. In the United States, more than 850 million gallons per year of untreated sewage is released from just the sewage overflows from combined sewer systems, among other sources. Climate changes, like temperature increases, are beginning as urban overcrowding and waste concentration increases. This increases the vectors for many infectious diseases. Predictions for the tropical undeveloped world are grim because of the lack of medical access and availability. Diseases do not know borders. Rapid population growth and international travel introduce diseases to other countries.

The environmental burdens of waste become expressed in the public health burdens that accompany waste. This includes a host of viruses, parasites, bacteria, and diseases such as cholera, *E. coli*, and *cryptosporidium*. One gram of human feces may contain about 10 million viruses, 1 million bacteria, 1,000 parasite cysts, and 100 worm eggs. Individuals with little or no sanitation can ingest 10 grams of feces per day through water, air, food, and articles of clothing. This is a leading cause of diarrhea, which is primarily water borne. Globally, many children die from diarrhea. Other emerging public health burdens are asthma, endocrine disruption, cancer, and heart problems and strokes, all leading to a decreased mortality. The lack of control over the increasing amount and pervasiveness of waste creates larger environmental and public health effects.

Waste transfer and terminal treatments are far behind waste creation when they exist at all. Water and sewage treatment facilities fall far behind the increasing volume of these wastes, especially as population increases. The emerging result is the increased pervasiveness of waste, in the air, in water, or on land. Cultural distaste for waste prevents meaningful communication, but as it becomes unavoidable, it provides fertile ground for controversy.

As waste becomes more pervasive, more people are exposed to it. Historically and today, some groups in society are more exposed to waste sites, transfer stations, and risks. Waste generation, and toxic waste are increasing, and landfill space is decreasing, especially with rising e-waste generation As more groups become exposed, waste technologies develop, communities organize, and governments develop public policies. These groups may agree or disagree with each other as waste policies develop. Nonetheless, waste generation increases. Controversies often focus on financing any part of the waste process, responsibility for pollution, health effects and their causes, and environmental accountability. The intensity and number of waste controversies continues to increase.

Most groups avoid wastes when they can. Some groups are required to prove scientifically that the wastes are harmful or noncontained, as the U.S. Navajo in the case of uranium mining by an international corporation and potential seepage into their main aquifer. Other groups are powerful through political saliency and wealth. They are not held to the same level of scientific proof as less powerful groups. Through control of the land, they avoid the negative aspects of waste. Rich or poor, weak or strong, environmental effects are the great leveling ground. Waste's environmental effects are omnipresent.

There is a growing consensus that certain wastes are harmful. For example, persistent organic pollutants (POPs) are powerful chemicals having adverse environmental and public health effects. They are a large international concern and are the focus of several international conventions. Many nations have strict rules about the importation, transit, and exportation of hazardous wastes for final disposition or recycling. Environmental groups challenge whether these rules are effective because of lax enforcement nationally and internationally, an incomplete list of chemicals that are hazardous, and the practice of ocean dumping of hazardous wastes. As strict as many rules are, they do not prohibit it in every case. Frequently the rules require the hazardous waste shipper, creator, warehouse, or disposal facility to get a permit. The permit allows the transactions to occur legally and helps monitor the amount. Usually there are permit fees, reporting requirements, and taxes. The permit alone does not decrease the harmful effectives of hazardous wastes. A common and highly regulated POP is polychlorinated biphenyls, or PCBs. Eleven other similar chemicals are designated for destruction, with more chemicals proposed. POPs' environmental effects include species population decreases, lowered resistance to diseases, and congenital abnormalities. They are spread all around the planet by winds and water. POPs generated in one country can have effects far away. They also persist in the environment, because they can pass from part of the food chain to another. The bioaccumulation of POPs weakens ecotones, such as the Arctic. There are other wastes that follow similar paths and have similar damages.

An increasing number of social policies confront the waste issues. Sustainability is emerging as a dominant global paradigm. However, one of the principles of sustainability is the precautionary principle, which stops an action if there is uncertainty about its environmental effects. Because wastes were seldom accounted for in the many decisions of communities, governments, and industry an increased awareness of wastes can initiate the application of the precautionary principle. One curious aspect of the precautionary principle is that it may not be possible to stop all waste streams even if there is a chance of irreparable damage. This heightens the call for advanced methods of waste treatment and ecological mitigation in those communities seeking sustainable development. Economic development often comes with a high waste impact requiring mitigation.

The reason waste matters now is that it is everywhere, and growing. Denial of a degree of personal responsibility is not possible and, in more places, denial of public responsibility is less possible.

Raw Garbage to Dumps to Waste Sites: The Waste Evolution

Garbage crises have always affected cities because there is a greater concentration of human wastes. Ancient approaches to wastes generally involve throwing garbage of all kinds out the window into the street. This practice persisted in many U.S. and European cities for thousands of years. One of the first garbage crisis occurred in ancient Athens, Greece. Because the city was prosperous, the waste thrown from windows and doors began to accumulate. It smelled bad, and created both public health and transportation issues. The Athenians passed a law requiring a municipal dump and forbade the disposal of garbage within one mile of Athens. However, very few cities in history followed this practice, with some notable exceptions. The Romans built efficient infrastructure to handle waste that included running water, indoor toilets, and a sewer system. However, much household waste was still deposited in the streets.

As is still the case in many urban areas, the layers of waste accumulated in the streets. People and animals such as rats, dogs, pigs, and horses ate it and in turn created more wastes. Rain was often a welcome relief, because it moved the open and closed sewers and natural water paths along. As time passed, these piles of waste grew larger, and cities simply built over it. Many ancient and some modern cities continue to grow upward on a pile of garbage.

It wasn't until the 1300s when the French reinitiated the legal requirement to have a municipal dump. The garbage piles were so high at the gates of Paris that it was difficult to prepare for potential attackers. They required that garbage be moved to locations that did not interfere with their defensive security. However, Parisians continued to throw garbage out the window inside the city. Without sewer systems, human and animal wastes continued to accumulate.

Large, heaping piles of stinking and rotting wastes attract rats in large numbers. Rats carried fleas that harbored the bubonic plague, which transferred it to humans. The plague was deadly for Europe, killing up to a third of the population from 1347 to 1351, and history. One way history was shaped, for example, was the population loss in the working class. This affected labor availability and depressed economic development. It also propelled the science of epidemiology into life-saving practical application by discovering waste and waterborne disease vectors.

Early U.S. Waste Practices

In the late 1800s and early 1900s, U.S. cities had inefficient waste practices. Human waste, animal wastes, garbage, and dead horses accumulated in the streets. There were approximately 120,000 horses in New York City before the advent of the automobile. These horses alone produced about 1,200 tons of excrement and 60,000 gallons of urine every day on the streets. Horses were worked to death and their carcasses left in the street. In 1880, 15,000 dead horses were left on the streets. Safe drinking water was not considered, so that waterborne diseases like cholera were as bad in New York City as in European cities in medieval times. New York City was considered an urban leader in the United States, setting the tone for municipal approaches to waste treatment. Up until 1872, garbage was simply dumped into the East River. Many communities the world over rely on water to move waste, either by dumping it into a river or the ocean, basing a sewer system on water to move waste, or relying on heavy rains or tides to flush it from the community.

Marauding herds of pigs were commonly used to eat some of the street garbage. Hundreds of communities owned hog farms where garbage was the food source. Hogs create their own waste. A large hog can produce the waste of four humans. This was often the backdrop to then emerging infrastructure development on wastes—sewers.

Modern Problems and Practices toward Waste

In the United States, the municipal waste stream was about 370 million tons in 2002, more waste per person than any other nation, averaging out to about 4.3 pounds of garbage per every person per day, or about 1.3 tons of garbage per person per year. Of this, most of it is buried in landfills—about two-thirds. About 27 percent is recycled or composted in some way. About 7 percent is incinerated. In the United States, there were over 16,000 waste disposal sites in 1970, along with many, many more illegal dumps. In 2011, there were 1,200 sanitary landfills. The old sites are closed, especially as new environmental regulations have mandated environmental protections. Sometimes their leaking wastes are so toxic that they become the focus of hazardous waste cleanup programs.

Abandoned hazardous waste sites pose one of significant human health risks and greatest environmental effects. In many countries, all wastes merge, and hazardous wastes enter the solid and liquid waste stream. Because of this, and because of accumulating hazardous wastes, it is likely there are many hazardous waste sites all over the world.

In countries such as the United States that highly regulate hazardous wastes, many industrial sites that have hazardous wastes found it cheaper to leave it on the site and try to pass the cleanup costs to the next owner. If no one buys it with the pollution, it is abandoned by owner. In the United States, the toxic waste program is called "Superfund," established by the Comprehensive Environmental Response, Compensation and Liability Act of 1980, or CERCLA. Most hazardous waste sites adversely affect surrounding groundwater. Many chemicals in hazardous waste sites can degrade landfill liners faster. With Superfund, hazardous waste sites are environmentally assessed and, if dangerous enough, placed on the National Priorities List (NPL). Superfund cleanups occasionally engage ecological risk assessment and cumulative effects assessment, one of the few programs to meaningfully do so.

Though Superfund is one of the first policy responses to the worst wastes, it does have controversial aspects. The main one is the underlying premise of liability without culpability. Even if the property owner did not cause or even know of the pollution, it could be responsible for cleanup costs. Superfund cleanup typically cost millions of dollars. Potentially responsible parties (PRPs) can submit an appropriate cleanup plan and do it themselves. PRPs can run into the hundreds, as with the current Superfund in Portland, Oregon. If no acceptable cleanup plan is proposed by the PRPs, the EPA does the cleanup and recovers costs from the PRPs. Liability for cleanup costs is complicated.

Superfund makes the creators, shippers, storers, and ultimately the property owner, in that order, liable. The issue is complicated by a concept of "joint and several liability" of these groups. Even if one of these groups is only 10 percent liable, the EPA could get the full amount of the costs of cleanup from the defendant, which would then sue the other groups for 90 percent of the judgment. This defendant will also go after the other members of the group that can pay their part of the costs for which they are legally liable. This is one reason why the litigation costs of Superfund are so high. The creators of hazardous wastes, the shippers of it, and those who store it are often difficult to locate or out of business. The property owner is always the easiest to find for the EPA to collect its cleanup costs, even if it is not 100 percent liable for the hazardous wastes. The current alternatives are for government to be responsible for waste cleanup and remediation or that waste stay in places untreated or partially treated.

Because of the growth and hazardousness of this waste stream, there are rapidly changing waste policies and new clean up programs. There is also an increase in illegal dumping on land, merger with solid and liquid waste streams, and ocean dumping off the continental coasts. Hazardous wastes are the subject of several prominent international treaties. The international and national hazardous waste policies of individual countries are noted where data is available. Because of differences in language, culture, and economic circumstance, the specific and precise meaning of hazardous wastes differs.

Air and Greenhouse Gas Emissions

Air pollution is a broad and often ambiguous term. Its meaning varies from place, time, and culture. Most of the world has few enforced environmental policies to abate air pollution. Surges in global population growth in places with high air emissions and little to no controls add to global air pollution. At the same time urbanization is increasing rapidly, intensifying the present and accumulative environmental effects.

The main focus of most international air pollution policy is to reduce carbon dioxide production and preserve Earth's ozone layer. The ozone layer is an essential part of the atmosphere, shielding us from deadly ultraviolet rays. In an effort to decrease global warming, greenhouse gas emissions are targeted. The consequences of global warming are many, and some are yet unknown. The temperature of the Earth is increasing, causing a decrease in snow cover in the poles and in high mountains. More violent weather is predicted for some places. Species extinction and altered migratory routes could be another environmental effect of airborne wastes. Greenhouse gas emissions are pollution pumped into the sky.

Greenhouse gas emissions refer to a set of chemicals known to erode the ozone layer that is a major cause of global warming. Greenhouse gas emissions that are subject to international law are carbon dioxide, ethane, nitrous oxide, and fluorinated gases. Most greenhouse gases are expressed in terms of carbon dioxide equivalents in metric tons for country comparison in each entry. The quality and number of air quality monitoring stations by government, communities and industry is rapidly increasing, but vast parts of the Earth remain unmonitored for any type of waste or pollution. As monitoring increases its range and scope, the far-reaching effects of air pollution are seen from pole to pole. Environmental air quality baselines are slowly moving forward but have yet to fully capture airborne waste streams in all parts of the biosphere. The international use and development of greenhouse gas monitoring and regulation is a foundational development in that direction.

Waste emissions account for 3 percent of all emissions globally, with significant variance, undercounting, and sometimes controversy. Most of the emissions are from unsanitary landfills and untreated sewage. Countries with coasts and rivers used for wastes are not accounted for in most models. Emissions from cesspools, latrines, and waste drainage canals are difficult to assess but do emit greenhouse gases. So does animal manure. With the rise of large herds of livestock comes a wave of manure, food waste, and greenhouse gas emissions. Attempts to report these are noted in country entries.

Even sanitary landfills use natural decomposition to "treat" trash and garbage, emitting methane, a greenhouse gas with a strong effect on ozone in the atmosphere. Small proportions of the world's landfills actually use this gas or burn it off. Most landfills eventually leach chemicals through the soils and into water sources. Sanitary landfills will have thick ground cover to last twenty to thirty years, a system to control leachate as hazardous wastes, and a way to capture methane. Most landfills in the world are not sanitary and can quickly leach into the ground water. With the rise of e-waste in many countries without sanitary landfills, this new wave of leachates may have public health impacts. Whatever is in the landfill will determine the leachate composition. If the leachate intrudes on local drinking water or irrigation sources, it can cause cancers, kidney and liver disease, or neurological damage if it contains pesticides or lead. It can affect fish, livestock, agricultural crops, and people. Some of the leachates can contain chemicals that bioaccumulate. Although controversial, there is concern that some leachates may be the cause of endocrine disruption.

Countries that are decreasing their landfill operations are generally decreasing their greenhouse gas emissions. Some are recovering the methane in waste-to-energy projects. Others increase their recycling and composting while reducing use and reusing goods. Sometimes countries will increase incineration, especially waste-to-energy incineration.

Greenhouse gas emissions can give an indication of the overall amount of untreated wastes. These are also sites for infectious diseases such as malaria, cholera, typhoid, and dysentery.

In terms of global greenhouse gas emissions the vast majority is carbon dioxide. Global carbon dioxide emissions continue to grow. China emitted about 23 percent of global greenhouse gas emissions, the United States about 19 percent, and the European Union about 13 percent. India, the Russian Federation, Japan, and Canada emitted about 18 percent of greenhouse gas emissions. There is a large category of other, about 28 percent. One category of greenhouse gas emissions is land use, land-use change, and forestry, which constitute about 17 percent of greenhouse gas emissions. Greenhouse gas emissions from here are mainly carbon dioxide from deforestation, opening up land for farming, fires from waste and field burning, and the organic decay of peat soils. All four sources are increasing. This estimate does not include carbon dioxide absorbed by ecosystems. This information is being developed and is fundamental for a global ecosystem analysis.

Much of the greenhouse gas emissions data is self-reported, and little is scientifically validated. It is likely that some airborne waste is underreported. One value of cumulative environmental effects is that chemicals that do accumulate become more easily observed and studied over time as they move through an ecosystem (including the human body). The scientific framework of greenhouse gas emissions is expanding use in global and local applications, though some measurements may be incomplete or initially inaccurate.

Carbon dioxide from fuel use is about 57 percent of global greenhouse gas emissions and carbon dioxide from deforestation and decay of biomass another 17 percent. Methane is 14 percent of total global greenhouse gas emissions. Nitrous oxide is 8 percent. F-gases are about 8 percent.

In the United States, about a third of greenhouse gas emissions come from human activities such as electricity production, especially in power plants that use coal and natural gas (Collin and Collin, Energy Choices). Transportation from cars, trucks, ships, trains, and airplanes emit about another 28 percent of greenhouse gas emissions in the United States. Airborne waste emissions from industry in the United States are about a fifth of the U.S. total. Businesses, homes, waste handling, and agriculture (cattle, agricultural soils, and rice production) emit about another third. Emissions in the United States increased by 1.6 percent in 2011, but greenhouse gas emissions from 2011 were 6.9 percent of 2005 levels.

Where data are available, the greenhouse gas emissions from various economic sectors of each country are included here. These data are emissions-driven and so only capture the emissions from a given country. They do not measure actual environmental impact of emissions from all airborne waste sources, because airborne wastes can migrate and accumulate far from their source.

Epidemiology and Infectious Diseases

Epidemiology studies the trends, causes, and effects of disease and other health conditions within a specific population. This science has its foundations in studying the connection between waste and disease. In 1854, Dr. John Snow discovered that cholera was associated with human feces in the drinking water in London, a city in which only five years earlier half a million people had died of cholera. In that case, the vector for the cholera was a water pump used by the residents of London.

Sewers were then developed on a large scale to separate wastewater from drinking water. The story of the London sewer construction is an epic tale of ingenuity and hard, dangerous work. Basic sewers existed since early history, but their capacity and functionality become limited as the amount and kinds of waste increased. Generally, sewers began as natural drainage basins or other water bodies. Over time, many communities would cover them. Gradually they would become contaminated as the increase and population and the cumulative effects of waste caused human feces to form in cesspools.

Sewers simply move wastes away from drinking water. They do not treat the wastes, and the wastes throughout most of history went untreated into water sources. Waste disposal remained a big problem. Many parts of the world did not learn the lessons of John Snow and the plague. The early U.S. colonialists and young U.S. cities did eventually incorporate and then develop some sewer systems.

Infectious diseases cause more death in the world than any other single thing. Contact with germs includes drinking, eating, breathing, and touching anything that has germs. One consequence of global warming is the spread of tropical diseases. As areas become warmer, more disease vectors open. Rapid urban population growth and poor sanitation practices compound the problem by providing hospitable environments for tropical diseases. Disease vectors follow increased global transportation access. In 2014, Ebola from Africa quickly became an international health crisis, partly because many nations were affected. As global warming causes human populations to migrate, waste will be increasingly handled in refugee camps such as those described by Faduma Ali in her essay. Without attention to the connection between global warming, waste, and diseases, proponents of sustainability face insurmountable challenges.

The average temperature of the world started to gradually increase in 1950. Airborne emissions from human activities contribute significantly to climate changes that increase the warming of the planet. Increased amounts of carbon dioxide and methane from many human activities erode the ozone layer, letting in more ultra violet radiation. Agricultural, energy, industrial, and waste emissions are some of the main sources and are discussed in each country entry.

Water and Wastes

Most human societies separate wastes from drinking water because of the personal and public health risks. Many diseases are waterborne and can thrive in waste-concentrated environments. The interaction of waste and water depends on many variables, such as quality and quantity of waste, ecological carrying capacity, social waste practices, and presence of other environmental effects. Outbreaks of cholera, typhoid fever, giardiasis, cryptosporidiosis, amebiasis, and amebae are the main diseases. Other tropical diseases, such as the Guinea worm, thrive in water. A host of intestinal disorders, parasites, and waste feeders/disease vectors (mosquitoes) are present in the waste/water environment. These diseases are communicable on a global scale. Rapid urbanization and population growth, combined with the increase in international travel to almost any location, increase potential vectors for all communicable diseases, causing generations of people to suffer short, miserable lives. When data is available, public health factors relevant to waste is included here.

The inputs of industrial development usually equal the product and the byproduct. Byproducts form the basis of the industrial waste stream. Industrial byproducts depend on the product produced and the processes for producing it. Some byproducts include metals that can have negative health effects and that are relatively easier to locate in the ecosystem. Earlier industrial development proceeded with no environmental regulation and still does so in many parts of the world. From the consumption of natural resources to the final disposition of all waste streams, this early form of industrial development had a large environmental footprint. Industrial wastes have accumulated over the last several centuries in many cities, often combined with water-based sewage systems.

As industrial development grew globally, the byproducts increased in quantity and environmental effects. Some waste can work its way up the food chain until we consume it. For example, in the 1960s, the Great Lakes had concentrations of dangerous wastes, including heavy metals. Via fish, these metals made their way up the food chain, affecting nursing mothers and their children. Other chemicals follow similar vectors. There is some concern when chemicals bioaccumulate in developing animals, including us.

Research is currently under way into the effects of the bioaccumulation of specific chemicals on developing human endocrine systems. Whether they present an actual risk is often disputed. Even when the past and current risks are known from these waste streams, little action is taken to remediate their environmental and community effects.

The reliance of many communities and industries on water-based waste removal forces the issue. The waste could be mine tailings laden with arsenic from leachates used in mining or wastewater from hydraulic fracturing for natural gas. As population increases drive demand for residential waste treatment based on water, the quality and quantity of fresh drinking water can decrease. As quantities of freshwater decline, the focus on actual waste treatment and control increases. In the United States, it is estimated that there are about 4–32 million cases of acute gastrointestinal illness per year from public drinking water sources—and the United States has one of the best public drinking water systems in the world. However, there are many data gaps in estimating the magnitude and burden of waterborne disease, as well as the role of waste. Cultural attitudes toward waste and the perception that the supply of fresh water is limitless have stunted research in this area.

Fresh water is generally necessary for adequate sanitation and personal hygiene. Globally, about 780 million people do not have any access to an improved water source. This can include a piped household water connection, protected dug well, protected spring, and rainwater collection. About 2.5 billion more people lack access to improved sanitation. Unimproved sanitation means that drinking water has come from unprotected wells and springs and from surface water sources, including rivers, lakes, dams, ponds, creeks, canals, and irrigation channels. Surface water sources can easily become contaminated from sewage, animal wastes, settling airborne wastes, industrial wastes, and agricultural pesticide and fertilizer runoff. Surface water sources also present vectors for waterborne diseases from insects that breed in stagnant water, such as mosquitoes carrying malaria. In the United States, about 90 percent of drinking water comes from public water systems. Generally a public water system must have at least fifteen service connections or serve twenty-five people. There are communities having more people that do not have public water systems in the United States and globally. Freshwater is a shrinking resource, in part thanks to garbage and waste. The amount of socioeconomic drought is increasing. This drought measures the extent and severity of episodic drought conditions. It occurs when available freshwater supplies do not equal or surpass aggregate water withdrawals. High levels of water reuse without treatment allow freshwater to be contaminated with garbage and wastes. Population increases, inefficient agricultural use of water, and increased energy use can increase chances of socioeconomic drought.

Oceans

The Earth's oceans hold 97 percent of its total water; only 0.02 percent of water is found in lakes, channels, and seas. The oceans have always been the final disposition for most wastes. Covering 70 percent of the Earth and generally downhill from land, the oceans were thought to be an endlessly resilient waste repository. Solid, liquid, and hazardous wastes all mix together along the coastlines of the continents. Agriculture and urban runoff means that the wastes run downstream into the oceans. These are called "nonpoint sources," which are not completely regulated. These wastes include pesticides, fertilizers, and petrochemicals. Estimates of the source of ocean pollution from land range from 70 percent to 90 percent.

The effects of ocean pollution are widespread. It blocks sunlight that disrupts life at the base level in the food chain. It can use up available oxygen and suffocate shellfish and other fishes. It can bioaccumulate up the food chain to spread through the ecosystem. Ocean runoff is a partial cause of hazardous algae blooms, which take oxygen out of the water, killing fish. Garbage has accumulated in the oceans for centuries. The increasing amount of long-lasting garbage is now forming large areas of garbage around vast oceanic whirlpools called gyres.

The five largest gyres where floating litter concentrates are in the north and south Atlantic, north and south Pacific, and Indian oceans. There are other smaller gyres in Alaska and Antarctica. Ocean currents, wind, and Earth's rotational forces form gyres, large ocean areas with a circular geostrophic current. Trash, especially plastic, is accumulating in these areas. The North Pacific Gyre is about double the size of the United States, though its size fluctuates. It is generally between Hawaii and California. There are east and west versions of the North Pacific Gyre that are sometimes connected north of Hawaii. The western part is between Japan and Hawaii. The long-lasting plastic absorbs other pollutants, such as pesticides, fertilizers, persistent organic pollutants (POPs), and polycyclic aromatic hydrocarbons (PAHs). These plastics, adversely affect about 267 species, including many endangered species. It is estimated that the plastics in the ocean adversely affect 86 percent of all sea turtles, 44 percent of all seabirds, and 43 percent of all marine mammals.

Ocean acidification from air pollution is increasing, by 25 percent over the last two centuries. Carbon dioxide, a greenhouse gas, is absorbed by oceans and disrupts ecosystems. When it is absorbed in the water, carbonic acid is formed. About 22 million tons of carbon dioxide is absorbed every day. As oil and gas drilling, mining, and transit routes grow to encompass the Polar Regions there is concern that air pollution will increase. The Arctic Ocean is beginning to be explored and drilled for oil, natural gas, and minerals. As the arctic ice recedes to create more year-round shipping lanes, this will increase. Generally more oil drilling operations bring more spills and hazardous wastes. Shipping transports about 90 percent of all global goods, generates about 4 percent of global carbon dioxide emissions, and dumps sewage and garbage directly overboard in coastal areas.

Recycling

Recycling is an evolving term with different meanings and processes in different countries. The recent policies of recycling are meant to lessen environmental effects, generally by reducing landfill disposal. Garbage sorters and sanitation workers may find items and materials they can reuse and therefore recycle. Squatters who recycle the waste of city dumps/waste sites surround many of the increasingly urban areas of the world. Modern recycling generally requires an analysis of the waste stream for materials that can be profitably removed. For a material to be profitably removed, it is better to separate waste streams early and have a wide range of applications for it. Organizations, communities, governments, and corporations seeking to increase recycling can do so by expanding the range or reusable applications. Recycling or reusing materials and wastes generally reduces environmental effects. Some materials, such as glass, can be recycled over and over; others, like paper, have a recycling life of about five to eight generations.

By differentiating types of waste early in the waste stream, it is easier to pull out materials to recycle—both materials that can be recycled with some treatment and hazardous materials. A prefecture in Japan requires residents to separate recyclable into forty-two waste streams, for example. Most U.S. recycling waste division is between glass, brush, recycling (paper), hazardous wastes, and household wastes. Whether the biological waste output is recycled depends on the practices of the local community. If the sewage goes through a waste treatment process it can be considered recycled. When the reusable applications of what was formerly waste are expanded, more waste is considered recycled. A modern U.S. example of this is with liquid wastes. By restricting the worst wastes to agricultural or industrial areas, it can be reused and is measured as such even though environmental effects occur. The environmental effects remain the same on people and place regardless of government regulation.

Plastics in Arctic Ice

Plastics last a very long time and are pervasive in the environment. Wastewater plants do not remove microplastics. The huge amount of illegal ocean-dumping of waste is evidenced by its increasing and undeniable presence. Plastic ends up in the ocean and becomes part of the massive amounts of ocean trash. Most of it degrades into smaller pieces that absorb pollution and can be eaten by more marine animals. Crustaceans such as crabs eat these pieces, which become stuck in their gills. Because many other land and marine animals eat crabs, this introduces microplastic into important ecological niches.

The arctic ice holds tons of small, often brightly colored, pieces of microplastic. It is unknown what pollutants, or how much of them, has been absorbed. As ice melts, large amounts of this plastic will be released into the oceans. The arctic ice is steadily retreating and is expected to be ice-free year-round by 2100.

In most countries, consumption of goods and materials is increasing faster than recycling rates per capita and overall. Many new electronic materials and packaging materials are not easily recyclable and continue to fuel the waste stream in increasing numbers.

In the United States, only about 10 percent of recyclable plastics are collected for recycling and processing inside the United States. The United States, like other industrialized countries, exports low-quality wastes to countries that will pay for it or take it for a cost lower than disposal costs. Many of these countries do not recycle the wastes and instead dump it in illegal land sites or in the ocean. Because the wastes are low-quality, they contain more toxic and hazardous chemicals. China receives about half of this and then separates it and moves it to specialized recycling facilities. E-wastes are rapidly increasing as the costs of technology decrease and become widely available. The U.S. e-waste flow sends televisions and computer monitors to Mexico and circuit boards to Canada, Germany, Japan, and Sweden, where they are melted down. The rest of the exported e-wastes goes to China, India, Pakistan, and Nigeria.

Recycling is part of an integrated waste management strategy. It is part of reducing use and reusing goods. Many communities in developing countries reuse or recycle as part of a cultural tradition. In developed countries, material consumption is a value often associated with status, which can cause more waste. Formal recycling programs, complete municipal waste collection and disposition, and environmental monitoring and enforcement help control this increased waste flow.

Role of Government in Waste

Local Roles

Waste first and foremost is the province of local governance. The primary effect of waste is on the local ecosystem, which in an urban area can encompass millions of people. Many communities subsidize waste disposal, treatment, economic development, and research. Some communities prioritize recycling and public spaces. Some poor school districts accept wastes to fund their schools, such as in Virginia. The politics and controversies about waste transfer and siting involves all aspects of government and in the United States involve federal, state, and local agencies. The dynamics around the give and take of wastes only increase, playing out in local government first and last.

Almost all environmental decisions are local when they are implemented. In addition to control of sewage and solid wastes, local government is also responsible for a number of unfunded mandates from regional, state, or national governments. Trash is one of the obvious results of lack of funding for communities.

Many countries lack national leadership in the struggles and controversies around greenhouse gas emissions. The reduction of greenhouse gases is ultimately one of accurate local observation and control of local environmental behavior. Many cities have in fact reduced their greenhouse gas emissions. New York City reduced city-wide greenhouse gas emissions by 19 percent from 2005 to 2012. On September 2014, a group of 228 mayors of cities signed the "Compact of Mayors" and agreed to aim for a 2 billion metric ton reduction in greenhouse gases. It is estimated that cities could reduce emissions by 8 billion metric tons by 2050. This was announced at the United Nations Climate Summit, where there are many global city networks such as the Climate Leadership Group and United Cities and Local Governments.

State and Regional Roles

Garbage policy is made at all levels of government. Many countries have federal or national agencies that are divided into regions. The U.S. EPA has ten regions. Some countries have no regions, only a national governmental agency. Many countries have regions separated by urban and rural areas. Rural areas are basically those areas that are not urban. Urbanity is measured by population density, which is noted in the entries. In some countries regions can represent areas of past and present tribal lands.

National Roles

The relationship and power of government to the people and environment in each country is different. In the United States, the Environmental Protection Agency (EPA) started in 1970 and is the lead federal environmental agency. Federal government environmental agencies or ministries are relatively new.

The focus on waste in environmental agencies at the federal level is newer. Because of the local production of waste, it was informally presumed that local governments would handle it because they had to. In many countries, including the United States, the federal agency is reluctant to intervene in state and local government although they generally have preeminent power. Many environmental protection agencies at every level also have economic development as part of their mission, which can be at cross-purposes with waste regulation because the cost of effective waste treatment can deter economic development.

The prevailing policy emphasis in national waste management is clean drinking water, safe and sanitary bathrooms, and sewage treatment. Many federal governments, including that of the United States, subsidize wastewater treatment plants. Some nongovernmental organizations (NGOs) are specifically working on these issues, as in India. They may work with national campaigns for sanitation.

Air pollution in urban areas also receives national attention, in part because of international treaties on greenhouse emissions. Industry is often concentrated in urban areas. Residential and commercial vehicle emissions are also concentrated there.

International Roles

There is a robust international trade in waste. It is difficult to know the exact scale of how waste is traded. Few countries keep records, definitions of different kinds of waste vary widely, and most industrial and hazardous waste streams are self-reported—if at all. The amount of waste dumped directly into the oceans over the last 500 years has begun to test its ecological limits. In the recent past, the idea that there could be oceans without fish was unthinkable. Now that fishing has moved into a harvesting, as opposed to hunting, mode with large-scale techno-logically advanced efficiency, it is now a consideration. Labels for waste matter in terms of international regulations. Although the United States exports only about 3 percent of toxic wastes, it may be a labeling loophole. Hazardous waste is more expensive to trade because of health dangers, storage and shipping requirements, and other regulatory requirements. Since there is weak enforcement of interna-tional and national waste laws, there are large amounts of hazardous wastes being traded and dumped into oceans, lakes, rivers, streams, and creeks, as well as on and in land. The number, regulation, political resistance, and community mobili-zation of hazardous wastes increased land-based dumping and final disposal costs, moving hazardous waste to ocean-based trading and dumping. The ocean coasts of most industrialized countries contain toxic sites. The increasing violent storms predicted from global warming and climate change models will move these toxic materials around Earth. Global monitoring in real time can find toxic and hazard-ous wastes with greater and greater accuracy.

The lack of accounting for toxic wastes, or many other wastes, makes recycling and waste separation difficult. This affects the international recycling industry, because it increases their costs. Some industrialized countries exported hazardous wastes as recyclable. There is an emerging international movement to repatriate hazardous wastes to the country of origin. Italy would retrieve its toxic waste from Lebanon and Nigeria; Germany from Albania and Romania; South Korea from China; the United States from China, Bangladesh, and India; and Japan from the Philippines. As population and wastes have increased, so has ocean dumping. And technology will soon reveal sites of toxicity and the transit routes of waste traders. As the controversy around wastes increases globally, some countries are making efforts to set standards, usually starting with modest reporting requirements. Many of these efforts focus on the transit and final disposition of hazardous wastes. Other countries have no waste regulation of any kind. Unfortunately, these countries are the recipients of illegally exported toxic materials.

International agreements define the roles of countries and set international stan-dards designed to lessen environmental effects of waste. There are many treaties, conventions, and other international agreements between countries. The amount of international engagement differs greatly by country. So far most countries have not fully ratified most treaties. The treaties that involve waste are noted when the country is a signatory to a treaty or convention.

There is global environmental concern about waste, especially its greenhouse gas emissions. The United Nations and other organizations focus on global warm-ing, and greenhouse gas emissions are a large part of that. When countries agree to perform in a certain way, they do it with a treaty. Treaties have "protocols," or activities that signatories are expected to develop. Treaties including waste issues are included here. Countries that agree to these treaties often have data on some aspects of waste. Most countries have not ratified many of the major treaties, but the countries having the most environmental effects either have ratified many of them or are in the process of doing so. Treaties represent years of diplomatic nego-tiations and applied scientific research. Whether a country is a signatory to a treaty or not, international treaties perform important educational functions on a global level by raising awareness of environmental effects locally and globally.

Several more treaties and international agreements affect wastes. All the treaties involving greenhouse gas emissions are essentially about wastes in the air. Most treaties allow solid and liquid waste disposal and cover primarily hazardous wastes. Many allow wastes to be disposed with a permit. There is no real international legal enforcement mechanism for international treaties and agreements. However, they represent a rising global approach to wastes that seeks to deter dumping hazardous wastes in the ocean and the saturation of the atmosphere with green house gases.

Global Security Issues and Infectious Diseases

The 2014 outbreak of Ebola raised international concerns about the threat to international travel and public health. President Obama formed the Global Health Security Agenda to work with the World Health Organization to develop consensus about how to handle infectious disease spread. Forty-four countries are members of the agenda. One of its main goals is to provide public health systems that deter infectious diseases, reducing risks of outbreaks and epidemics. There are major concerns from the U.S. Department of Defense because of scientific, economic, and demographic trends that are magnifying the risk of infectious disease outbreaks. Many world leaders consider the risk of infectious diseases to be geopolitically destabilizing. Political destabilization can create civil unrest and war. When this happens, all waste infrastructures suffer and the risk of infectious diseases increases. In many places, health care workers are the most exposed and may leave when an outbreak threatens. The fewer health care workers who remain on the job, the greater is the individual exposure and risk of infection for those who remain.

The increase in security for infectious diseases encompasses new activities. The United States will aid other countries with their immunization programs and provide technical assistance to improve biological security, which helps countries store, transport, secure, and study diseases. Many developed countries have the epidemiological ability to quickly follow the DNA and rate of gene mutation to trace the vectors of infectious diseases to their source. This is necessary to prevent the spread of the disease. The United States will also provide emergency assistance to help countries build emergency response centers.

Part I
Thematic Essays

Emerging Public Health and Waste Issues: A Case Study from Oregon

Ben Duncan

This essay focuses on approaches to public health that include waste drawing a parallel to the control strategies of the nineteenth and twentieth centuries. That era focused on a new understanding of the contribution of microbes that cause disease to the contemporary effects of waste and human health and the need for strategies that reignite a focus on sanitation and waste as a contributor to human health risks. The understanding of the relationships between industrialization, urbanization, and overcrowding in poor housing without waste disposal systems and safe water supplies resulted in approaches that focused on population-based public health. It is this origin that is critical in understanding the future of disease reduction, particularly in parts of the world where these same overlays (industrialization, urbanization, overcrowding, lack of sewer and public water supplies) is compounded by the effects of global climate change. Race and class issues are now part of emerging public health issues at the local level. Multnomah County, Oregon, has developed some proactive steps to engage these new issues.

The modern contributors to infectious disease and global warming require a renewed focus on the environmental conditions, policies, practices, and behaviors that affect population-wide health outcomes. Although the focus here is on "waste" and its contribution to disease, its intersectionality with urbanization, deforestation, war, famine, social injustices, and the associated desperation that drives this vicious cycle of environmental degradation for short-term survival should not be lost on the reader.

The need to develop public health approaches informed by environmental and social justice principles and practices is to mitigate negative affects, particularly on those most vulnerable, including people who earn a low income, people of color, people who have pre-existing health conditions, elderly people, people who have limited mobility, and people who are homeless.

Public "health equity" represented the strength of a public health and social justice framework for addressing not simply health outcomes that we were measuring (e.g., asthma rates, cardiovascular illness, low-birth weight, years of potential life lost) but also the root causes of disease: poverty, racism and discrimination, environmental conditions, and lack of power and voice in decisions and practices affecting communities' lives.

The health of our communities feels the downstream effects of waste generation. The distribution of environmental burdens experienced by communities of color is disproportionate to the benefits they receive. How does public health lead in local and global efforts to combat both the effects of waste generation and disposal (downstream) and address the root causes that not only contribute to the perpetuation of climate and environmental harm but that also represent societal decisions affecting downstream outcomes in disease and infirmity?

Historical Context

The U.S. Centers for Disease Control and Prevention provide a relevant U.S. historical perspective and timeline that outlines the establishment of public health. Most developed nations have an equivalent center that will recount their public health history. In less developed nations, it is more difficult to discern public health histories. Many such nations suffer from diseases at a much higher level.

In the United States in 1900, the three leading causes of death were pneumonia, tuberculosis (TB), and diarrhea and enteritis, which caused a third of all deaths. The highest mortality was children. Forty percent were children younger than 5.

The nineteenth-century urbanization that accompanied industrialization and immigration led to overcrowding in poor housing. Public water supplies and waste disposal systems were woefully inadequate. This is the current condition of many urban areas in less developed countries. These conditions result in repeated outbreaks of cholera, dysentery, TB, typhoid fever, influenza, yellow fever, and malaria. By 1900 in the United States, the incidence of many of these diseases began to decline because of public health improvements and sewer and water systems. These improvements, including sewage, water treatment, food safety, trash disposal, and behavioral messaging, contributed to this decline. Handwashing is an example of behavioral messaging as relevant today as it was then, being one of the most important public health practices for reducing the spread of illness. In the United States, reducing overcrowding through land use regulation and the introduction and widespread application of medical treatments reduced diseases such as tuberculosis., cholera, and diarrhea.

Globally, the same approaches that resulted in disease prevention in the United States are necessary to address the prevalence of preventable deaths related to water, trash, and sanitation, including diarrhea, which still results in death throughout the world.

Social Determinants of Health

Public health is defined as what our society does collectively to ensure conditions for people to be healthy. These conditions are the social determinants of health—a set of factors that affect population health outcomes and what environmental justice communities have described as the places we live, work, play, and pray. Exploring the public health role in addressing waste requires a focus on using models that get at the root or source of the problem. In this discussion, it's also important to call out and acknowledge the direct connection and consideration of history. Pollution may alter our genetic structure. The field of epigenetics is teaching us more and more about generational effects from exposure that show up long after exposure occurred. In the United States, the legacy and effects of institutional and systemic racism have generational effects. Another area to explore is what has prevented us often from using approaches that we know would benefit those communities, particularly low-income communities and communities of color. This intentional and unintentional environmental harming of communities carries with it a legacy of health effects affecting subsequent generations.

This understanding that the effects of racism, discrimination, oppression, and lack of power occur in many communities are a challenge to public health. Multnomah County, Oregon, is the smallest but most populous county in Oregon. It is also one of the most diverse. The county office of diversity and equity has had to deal with environmental justice issues directly. Its definition now incorporates action, inclusion, and planning. It also includes an evaluation of these efforts.

By defining racial equity in this way, we lay out a vision for how public health models can shift how we address and approach waste and return to the roots of public health as a discipline deeply connected to social reform movements and for recognizing the social and political changes necessary to address diseases. Public health approaches to waste require a commitment to racial equity and must address changes from an individual level as well as the political level.

The Public Health Approach

As part of a national movement within public health stressing the intersection of the framing of social determinants with an emphasis on health equity and racial and ethnic health disparities, Multnomah County developed the Health Equity Initiative. Essential public health services are applied through a racial justice framework.

These provide the directive and authority for public health to play a critical role in addressing issues around waste. It also provides the possibility to combine frameworks that support racial equity analysis, meaningful involvement of communities affected by environmental harm in the development of solutions, using self-efficacy theory to motivate behavior change and, perhaps most notably in the challenging and complexity of waste in all its forms, the authority to develop and enforce policies that ensure health protection for all communities. The vision of eliminating the root causes of racial and ethnic health disparities in the United States should also remind us that throughout the world, communities are situated in various spaces without resources to the power and control to affect the choices, or lack thereof, that they can make to mitigate against environmental harm and disease. Whether because of climate change, exposure to pollution, access to clean water, or sewage and waste management systems, the disparate and cumulative effect is that those who are most marginalized and oppressed in societies bears the brunt of social policies and systems that result in poor health outcomes.

The socioecological model design, to address issues at multiple levels, looking at the individual, interpersonal, community, and society, has the potential to allow multiple strategies to combine to address waste issues in holistic ways. Although having many applications throughout various disciplines, in the case of health promotion, some researchers proposed that addressing chronic illness required both an individual and social context understanding. It suggests that changes in social environments produce changes in individuals, and that to create these changes in environments, communities must be supported and empowered.

We have the ability to shift individual behavior change, even as we acknowledge that it takes a lot of energy and collective social commitment. The case study that is still playing out with smoking is analogous to the strategies that need to be combined to normalize waste reduction strategies at an individual level. Using the smoking analogy, the second level of the socioecological model, the interpersonal, meant that in order to effectively communicate messages and increase the efficacy of individuals to stop smoking, messaging moved toward second hand smoke—the interpersonal harm caused by one individual act. What is the metaphor for waste? What messages can we develop around the effects on families?

Smoking reduction strategies used the connection at the individual and institutional level to motivate individual changes, but perhaps the most critical strategies were in the community policy arena. Indoor smoking bans and increased taxes and cost have influenced the social decline, particularly in younger populations who are not starting to smoke

Public Health and Trash

Recognizing that public health and sanitation have historical roots encourages us to examine how the conditions that led to practices and policies regarding sanitation and sewage need to be examined in the context of how we manage waste now. Because the United States is the leading trash producer per capita in the world, how we deal with our municipal waste has important ramifications for health outcomes.

Solid waste at its core is a public health issue. Although generally in the United States we think only about our waste when our garbage isn't picked up or when our toilets are clogged, the risks associated with trash—including vectorborne disease from rodents and insects and water and land contamination—are considerable and include new and emerging science related to health hazards of being in proximity to landfills. Although most research isn't conclusive, public health epidemiological research has the opportunity to explore how the chemicals both being put into landfills, and the chemicals coming out of landfills, can affect health, controlling for the many variables that lead to negative health outcomes. The challenges, of course, with understanding the linkages between proximity to landfills, as with many other public health risk assessments, relate to the relatively low dose of exposure over long periods of time and the cumulative risk of exposure through other contributors.

But at a very localized level, we know that the risks associated with trash—and the relationship of having household trash removed in a timely way—can be seen in multifamily housing communities. Multnomah County, in its PACE-EH (Protocol for Assessing Community Excellence in Environmental Health), engaged low-income renters in multifamily housing properties to understand the priority environmental health issues the communities were experiencing. In this work, the community identified three distinct areas of hazard—mold, lead, and trash—and a fourth overarching issue, "feeling ignored," that underscores the importance of public health approaches understanding the fundamental overlay of race, class, and oppression with empowerment.

What we saw in this example was that families who were living in substandard housing to begin with had paint peeling that was exposing children to lead and fans that didn't work or windows that leaked, leading to mold growth. Trash bins were not sufficient to handle the household waste of the multiple families, so issues with rats and cockroaches existed. These housing properties, consisting of low-income people, predominantly people of color, were also in close proximity to both highways and industrial areas of north and northeast Portland. Families had asthma, a product of genetics and environment that was exacerbated by the "triggers" in the homes, and felt helpless because of the lack of response and lack of control to change the conditions.

Public health, understanding the intersections of "triggers" (rats, cockroaches, mold, dust, and dander) and substandard housing, is able to link policy and practice to address the effects of trash (and, in this case, move "upstream" to address issues around housing inspections and code enforcement, indoor air quality education, landlord–tenant law education, and partnership with community-based organizations) as well as the "downstream" ability to care and treat clients with asthma with proper medication and guidance on control.

This public health approach relied on the idea that communities understand the issues that affect them. Communities evaluate their own environments and the public health efforts focus on generating resources, political will, and community empowerment to address the identified issues. It provides the opportunity for communities to own their expertise with the support of governmental agencies to develop the infrastructure and the policies that support change. For the PACE-EH process, the primary factors contributing to the success of the efforts were

1. PACE-EH assessment identifying affordable housing and mold, lead, trash, and feeling ignored as community concerns
2. A clear and concise operating framework focusing on a socioecological model, empowerment theory, and self-efficacy
3. The ability to build and maintain relationships, form partnerships, and collaborate in meaningful ways

This model of community organizing through public health focuses public attention where needed in a way that builds resiliency in the affected community. This solid framework, built on guiding values of health equity and environmental justice, empowerment, and popular education, led to four distinct outcomes:

1. Increased understanding of the multiple ways that housing influences health outcomes
2. Greater asthma control and reduced emergency utilization and hospitalization visits for clients using Multnomah County Health Homes Services, as well as improved coordination and relationships with providers

3. Housing protection for low-income renters
4. Health education opportunities to residents of affordable housing

Health as a Human Right: The Health Equity Approach

All communities want and need to shape their own environment. No group should be predictably and disproportionately affected by negative health outcomes. Fair and just outcomes are the result of fair and just opportunity. A health equity approach ensures that no one is systemically excluded from the right to health. To have a health equity approach to waste, we also need to be addressing social, environmental, and institutional factors.

Although public health on its own cannot reasonably tackle all the root issues associated with health rights violations and negative health outcomes, there are ways to address these issues that incorporate the public health perspective. Public health needs to build relationships with other specialized workforces to address concerns together and help them view their objectives through a public health lens. For many issues of waste, public health does not have jurisdictional authority, nor the responsibility to construct the systems of control for waste, but what public health does is serve as an important voice for strategies, and lends credibility to the science around intersection. We must step outside of public health in order to address the public's health. For instance, poor health outcomes associated with low-income/no-income families are readily seen statistically but are difficult to rectify without first addressing employment and wealth. Knowing that the exposure and burden of waste generation and disposal is disproportionately borne by the poor and by communities of color, the importance of aligning the practice of public health with a humans rights approach to health becomes clear.

Health equity obligates public health to address systems of injustice that lead to negative health outcomes. Public health's "core value" of justice can only be achieved by advocating just approaches within the profession and in partnership with non–health-oriented agencies. As it stands, justice as a core value has questionable validity. The sheer amount of health disparities, combined with the abundance of literature advocating social and environmental justice, discredits justice's status as a prioritized core value. Many health disparities are unjust, and as a profession, we seem to recognize these disparities as important with the intent to attenuate them. Recognizing health as a human right is essential for making good on the notion that aiding the most disadvantaged is the heart of a successful and just public health system and that this will take addressing related health indicators together, not as discrete variables.

Waste in its myriad forms is both an unavoidable reality, and a complex interaction of social, institutional, and environmental factors. The collective wisdom of communities in identifying and organizing to address issues of waste is necessary to know true environmental impact and need. Using community voices—the stories and experiences of those negatively affected—with scientific analysis and policy advocacy, communities all over the world continue to fight for health as a human right.

Further Reading

Department of Commerce and Labor, Bureau of the Census. 1906. *Mortality Statistics, 1900 to 1904*. Washington, DC: US Department of Commerce and Labor.

Marshall, J., et al. 2014. "Prioritizing Environmental Justice and Equality: Diesel Emissions in Southern California." *Environmental Science and Technology* 48: 4063–4068.

Meier, B., et al. 2014. "Translating the Human Right to Water and Sanitation into Public Policy Reform." *Science and Engineering Ethics* 20: 833–848.

Ngure, F., et al. 2014. "Water Sanitation, and Hygiene (WASH), Environmental Enteropathy, Nutrition and Early Child Development: Making the Links." *Annals of the New York Academy of Sciences* 1308: 118–128.

Pellow, D. N., et al. 2004. *Garbage Wars: The Struggle for Environmental Justice in Chicago.* Cambridge, MA: MIT Press.

Caste, Class, and Gender Issues in India: Street Sweepers and Waste Pickers

Michael Lytton

Municipal solid waste management in India involves both the formal and informal sectors. The formal economy comprises city and contract employees doing street sweeping, household garbage collection, and emptying of roadside bins. The informal economy is made up of waste pickers, itinerant recyclers, and middlemen (kabariwalas) who buy recyclable material. In both the formal and informal economies, much of this essential work is done by women, the working poor, and people of the lowest caste.

The caste system in India is a system of social stratification that historically separated communities into endogamous groups. Marriage within a specific group is required by custom or law. These groups are called jatis translated into English as castes. In India, caste is inherited. Your caste determines land rights, employment access, social class mobility, and access to health care.

Certain groups, known as Dalits (literally "broken people"), were the historically ostracized "out-caste" communities. Because the communities from which they were cast out are diverse, so are Dalits. They are at the bottom of the caste hierarchy. Dalits consist of social groups from throughout the country.

Between 1860 and 1920, the British, gave the best jobs only to the upper castes. The colonial administration adopted a policy of reserving a percentage of government jobs for the lower castes. This continued and expanded following independence in 1947. Formal lists of scheduled castes (Dalit) and scheduled tribes (Adivasi) were developed.

In traditional Hindu society, Dalit status was associated with jobs regarded as ritually impure, the impure, or lowly. Such humans were untouchable, a designation used to justify discriminatory practices.

Dalits were excluded from full participation in Indian social and economic life. They were forbidden to go to many areas. Other castes would go to great lengths to avoid any type of physical contact.

Street Sweepers

Indian municipal corporations are responsible for provision and maintenance of essential services, including solid waste management, sewer line management and road sweeping. The supreme court of India has issued guidelines for Solid Waste

Management (MSW-2000), and the central government works through the Ministry of Urban Development, urban local bodies, and municipal authorities for their implementation. The guidelines were prepared in consultation with the Central Pollution Control Board and include provisions for collection of garbage and street sweeping.

Chennai, the capital of the state of Tamil Nadu, is the largest commercial and industrial city of south India. In 2014, it had an estimated population of 4.9 million, making it the sixth-largest city in India. The urban metropolitan area population includes an estimated 9 million.

The Corporation of Chennai collects an estimated 4,500 metric tons of municipal solid waste per day. Street sweeping, collection, and transportation of waste are currently outsourced to contractors in three zones, with corporation staff responsible for the remaining seven. There are over 11,000 permanent sanitary workers and over 500 daily wageworkers.

Door to door collection of garbage has been implemented in all zones. It involves the use of 2,800 tricycles, which are unloaded into roadside dustbins. Manual road and street sweeping is done in day and night shifts. All commercial areas, particularly main roads, are swept at night (10:00 p.m. to 6:00 a.m.), because traffic makes it impossible to sweep them during the day.

Each 16 km of road is a designated unit, and mobile teams of sixteen workers sweep each unit. Each sweeper is provided with a 120 L wheeled bin and uses brooms and brushes to collect litter—officially and perhaps euphemistically referred to as "road dust" and "silt deposited during de-silting of storm water drains." The sweeper then unloads the wheeled bin into a 1100 L community bin located on the roadside. Brooms with long handles remain a primary request, because short-handled brooms have caused disc problems and long-term back pain for many sweepers.

Health issues are a major concern. Street sweepers continue to work in harsh conditions, including monsoon rains. They are prone to respiratory and skin diseases and lack the protective gear necessary to prevent injury and discomfort. Uniforms, gloves, masks, and boots for both municipal employees and contract sweepers are appropriate minimum requirements for occupational health and safety.

Sewer Workers and Manual Scavengers

On the lowest rung of the formal waste management ladder are manual sewerage workers and manual scavengers. In cities across the country, men clean septic tanks and unclog sewers under buildings and streets, and on a daily basis in rural India, low-caste women known as manual scavengers collect human excrement.

Clearing blockages mostly with bare hands, sewerage workers go unprotected into underground pipes and must rely on crude ways of keeping themselves safe. They contract gruesome skin and respiratory diseases. On their deaths, their families receive no compensation or social welfare.

Like sewerage workers, scavengers face health hazards. Repeatedly handling human excrement without skin, eye, or breathing protection has health consequences of persistent nausea and headaches, respiratory and skin diseases, anemia, diarrhea, cholera, trachoma, and carbon monoxide poisoning. Because of their place in the caste system, these workers have less access to health services.

Manual cleaning persists in India, despite long and costly efforts to improve public sanitation and despite laws and policies against caste-designated labor. Indians by the hundreds of millions continue to defecate in the open and rely on insanitary latrines. At the same time there has been a widespread failure to implement measures designed to end caste discrimination or to address entrenched caste-based views on who should be doing jobs such as manual cleaning. To many observers, manual scavenging is the worst surviving symbol of ancient caste-based customs.

Waste Pickers

Chennai, like most cities in India, has long had an informal waste management system operating in parallel with a municipal system. This informal system consists of waste pickers who perform the unofficial recycling function within the city.

The occupation is hazardous. Forced to use bare hands to rummage through garbage that includes food waste, dead animals, and excrement, waste pickers collect bits of reusable, repairable, and marketable materials. Tuberculosis, scabies, asthma, respiratory infections, cuts, and other injuries are common. Although called the informal recycling sector, it is one of survival in which food, shelter, clothing, and trash—anything with value—are the main priorities.

Further Reading

Waste Pickers Statistics. www.weigo.org.

Life in a Refugee Camp

Faduma Ali

When I lived in a refugee camp, I remember watching waste being dumped in front of my eyes. I can still hear the buzzing sounds of flies and feel the tickles of stench of all manner of wastes in my nostrils. I remember watching young children being buried next to where I lived in such degrading environments. There are many times I sit and ponder the struggles that my family back in Somali is going through. The lack of clean water and waste management, the ever prevalent reality of food shortages, the lack of nutrition, the health issues, and the overall low living conditions drive me to be a part of the new generation of change that has not forgotten. In the community I come from, many of my family were farmers and fisherman who relied heavily on food obtained from the ocean. However, for many years, members of organized crime syndicates and other western companies have been freely dumping massive amounts of radioactive nuclear waste into the unregulated shores off Somalia's coastline, poisoning the seas and devastating the local population. The illegal dumping of chemical waste into the Indian Ocean has serious effects on health, livelihoods, prospects for development, and overall human security for the Somali population. As a result of this dumping, many people have died in Somalia, including my uncle, a fisherman. My uncle, like many others, was exposed to the chemical toxicity of the drinking water and died in 2002 of kidney failure. This type of unequal human rights inspires me and motivates me every day to help change our current society. The inequality has caused so many to suffer among the population of Somalia, including through the death of many young children.

My literal experiences of basic survival, along having to adapt to new systems and learn new languages, has encouraged me to believe in myself no matter what life puts me through. More specifically, the collectivity of my experiences has been a major instigator motivating me to pursue a career in environmental health.

Living in a Refugee Camp

Inhaling fresh air free from pollution, toxic, and human waste was one thing I always desired as a child growing up in a Kenyan refugee camp, where fresh air was something that every young boy and girl dreamed about at night. I always dreamed of one day living undistracted by the sounds of the buzzing flies that fed on garbage dumped all around the camp by others because of lack of a proper garbage and waste disposal system. The smell of the burning garbage, trees, and waste were among those that surrounded me growing up in Dadaab refugee camp in Kenya. Remembering these images and smells has driven me to cultivate an interest in environmental issues. Since realizing my interest in environmental issues, I have come to the conclusion that the future of this earth rests in our ability to address the roots of the problem.

Dadaab refugee camp is home to many dislocated families who fled war and famine to find a better life. Conditions inside the camp, though, are not the better life many refugees had hoped for. The camp is currently home to more than 350,000 people, according to the World Health Organization (WHO). Because the camp accommodates only half of the current population, the camp is overcrowded. And many people reside in the outlying areas in poor, makeshift shelters and away from camp services and security. Sanitation, water, and food are limited, putting a big of burden on many refugees. Kenya as a nation is also facing environmental degradation thanks to population pressure in addition to its increasing refugee population. Excessive damage to the environment, competition with local populations over scarce resources, and depletion of natural resources can all adversely affect a country's decision to provide asylum to refugees. As I recall growing up, trees were felled to provide support for shelters and branches collected for firewood and charcoal; foliage was cut to feed livestock and tree roots dug up in extreme situations for firewood. The effect of refugees on delicate land is of particular concern, as this can have lasting effects on human welfare.

Furthermore, degradation of natural resources, particularly through deforestation, can have long-lasting environmental consequences. Land around refugee camps has been stripped clean of trees and vegetation. Many refugees cook their meals over wood fires, and shortage of burnable timber is becoming commonplace. The result has been widespread deforestation, soil erosion, loss of arable lands, and famine. Deforestation is life-threatening to populations dependent on firewood for their energy needs.

The Skull Valley Band of the Goshute Reservation and Nuclear Waste as Economic Development

Brent Merrill

One of the most controversial, yet at the same time overlooked, issues in Indian Country in recent years has been the decision by the people of the Skull Valley Band of the Goshute reservation to try to accept nuclear waste on their very rural homelands: reservation lands as a form of much-needed economic development. The decision has divided many people and been a source of ongoing attention for the tribe, which was recognized by executive order in 1917 and 1918. It is also an international dynamic between rich and poor countries.

Before recognition, the same executive order created two separate reservations and two separate governments for the Goshute people. Today there are the Confederated Tribes of the Goshute reservation and the Skull Valley Band of the Goshute reservation. The Skull Valley Band is governed by a nearly sixty-member general council made up of adult members and a three-member executive committee led by the tribal chairman. At its peak, the Goshute tribal population would have numbered 20,000. Today, there are about 500 members between the two modern-day incarnations of the tribe. The Skull Valley Band of the Goshutes includes around 120 members.

The effort by tribal leadership to find some sort of economic development endeavor to bring to the 17,248-acre reservation in east central Tooele County has been discussed and debated for generations, but the desolate and barren location is a true barrier to the tribe's goal to be self-sufficient. Nuclear waste found its way to the leadership table for discussion in the 1990s when repeated delays at the planned Yucca Mountain Site in Nevada led to the investigation of other viable tribal lands to create a place for spent nuclear fuel. Yucca Mountain was designed to be a permanent site for nuclear waste storage, but a place to keep the waste until it was ready to go became a priority and led to a look at the Skull Valley site. (The Yucca Mountain facility could be opened as soon as 2017.)

The project began with the tribe seeking to accept a proposal for a temporary facility to store nuclear waste on the land controlled by the Goshutes' executive council as a means of economic development. The tribe's reservation land is located forty-five miles southwest of Salt Lake City and is home to just thirty-one members of the tribe, as of the 2000 census. The remaining 100 or so members of the tribe live in towns nearby in Tooele County. The tribe is headquartered in Grantsville, Utah, and the area consists mainly of one commercial building, a store, and some scattered trailers on the lone highway running through the area.

Beyond the issue of how this endeavor affects the environment is the issue of the tribe's right to make decisions as a sovereign nation, whether the decision is popular or not. The desire to use their status as a sovereign nation in some way to benefit the tribal population economically is at the core of the decision to pursue the nuclear waste products for disposal. Tribal economic independence appears to have driven the tribe's efforts to this point.

The limited liability corporation known as Private Fuel Storage, LLC, proposed bringing 40,000 tons of high-level nuclear waste categorized as commercial irradiated nuclear fuel to the Goshute reservation on a temporary basis in 2004 and had the idea greenlit by the tribe in 2005, pending approval of an operating license from the U.S. Nuclear Regulatory Commission. The waste that was to be stored aboveground was in reality spent nuclear fuel rods contained in 4,000 steel canisters encased in concrete that needed to be placed above a concrete slab, in exchange for forty years' rent money that would have added up to, potentially, hundreds of millions of dollars.

On September 9, 2005, the Nuclear Regulatory Commission voted 4–1 to approve a construction and operating license. Private Fuel Storage (PRS) of Wisconsin represented a consortium of eight different nuclear utilities that systematically targeted tribes across the nation, and the Goshutes in particular, because of their desolate locations, were considered ideal for the enterprise.

Tribal lands were the preferred target of nuclear companies for waste storage activities for decades, leading Congress to create the Office of the Nuclear Waste Negotiator in 1987. The negotiator sent propaganda correspondence to every tribe in the nation, offering, in some cases, millions of dollars to accept or "host" high-level nuclear waste by creating and operating federally monitored retrievable storage sites on their lands. According to information published by the Radioactive Waste Project, of the initial sixty native communities targeted by PFS and like-minded companies looking to dump their high-level nuclear waste with the least regulatory oversight possible, fifty-nine were successful in keeping those companies off of their lands. The Skull Valley proposal was the only one to ultimately gain even preliminary approval.

The strategy involved sending letters en masse to tribal governments throughout the country before ultimately settling on about two dozen tribes for intense recruitment efforts. Before going after the folks in Skull Valley, the negotiator's office targeted the Mescalero Apache tribe in New Mexico. Tribal members rallied and successfully fought off the efforts of the negotiator's office to put nuclear waste products on their land, and the leaders of those successful efforts became advisors to other targeted tribes. Because tribal members rallied in such numbers and with such passion, the Office of the Nuclear Waste Negotiator was closed by Congress in 1994.

After the negotiator's office was shut down, the nuclear power industry replaced the efforts of the negotiator's office with their own efforts to lure tribes into a deal. The industry combined the resources of eight nuclear utility companies into a consortium and approached the Mescalero tribal council again. The coalition's proposal was denied by tribal referendum, and a full-court press approach began with the next tribe on the list—Skull Valley. Before approaching Skull Valley, the coalition reformed once again as PRS.

Protestors began to rally against the idea of having irradiated trains rolling through their backyards almost immediately. The protests drew high-profile native activists such as John Trudell, who held benefits titled "No Nukes on Native Lands" and also led to several high-profile arrests during those protest actions.

The protests were joined in spirit and effort by Goshute tribal members who formed a group they called Ohngo Gaudadeh Devia, or OGD. The name in the traditional language stands for "Mountain Community," and the group is a gathering of concerned members who plan activities that keep their issue in the news, such as their filing of an environmental justice contention with the Nuclear Regulatory Commission's Atomic Safety Licensing Board.

To counter the efforts of the successful tribal member protest groups, PRS began to systematically put their money where their mouth was by contributing to the fundraising efforts of the favorite projects of presidential and congressional campaigns and lobbied everyone they could to get the "temporary" sites established as soon as possible.

The toxic record of the land around the Goshute reservation in Utah reads like a disaster movie film festival billboard: nearby Magnesium Corporation (MagCorp) is a world-class air polluter that has been ranked the number-one polluter by the Environmental Protection Agency. MagCorp earned this distinction because of the high levels of chlorine gas and hydrochloric acid clouds the company produces. There are numerous hazardous waste pits and incinerators nearby, and a company called Envirocare has been creating a low-level nuclear waste situation like the one in Skull Valley just a few miles away. Envirocare has had ongoing hopes of taking in toxic waste several times more potent than its license currently allows and has applied for the right to do so.

Skull Valley has also been the site of a more public, more dramatic example of the toxic history of the area, being where 6,400 sheep were killed as a result of a XV nerve gas test on the Dugway Proving Ground in 1968. The bodies of the toxic sheep were then buried on the reservation lands without the knowledge or approval of the tribal government, as agreement requires. The tribal land is also near where Tooele's U.S. Army stores and stockpiles of chemical weapons are being systematically burned at the Deseret Chemicals Weapons Incinerator, which has a documented history of leaking material into the nearby environment.

If those nearby practices aren't dramatic enough examples of the toxic record of the tribe's land, then add to the potentially deadly equation the repeated and ongoing dropping of bombs on the Wendover Bombing Range, and you get an above average chance for the people of the area to be exposed to a toxic soup of potentially nasty substances. This history of the land and the land nearby has left the tribal leadership with very few options for viability as a government intent on providing for its membership.

The relationship between the Goshute tribe and PFS began in earnest when according to news reports at the time, then Tribal Chairman Leon Bear signed a lease agreement with the company on December 27, 1996. According to tribal bylaws, the decision to go into business with PFS was to be made by the tribe's general council—which at the time consisted of the sixty or so adult members of the tribe. Bear apparently made the decision to accept an undisclosed amount of money in exchange for accepting nuclear waste on to the tribe's land without the knowledge of its general membership. Bear had stated publicly that he saw his reservation lands as "wastelands" already.

The Nuclear Regulatory Commission issued its approval of the project in June 2000 when it decided that the amount of the tribe's compensation for receiving the hazardous materials onto the reservation offset any concern about a lack of environmental justice. The payments were estimated to be in the $60 million to $200 million range. It took them three years, but in 1999, PFS won over the local cattle ranchers who had been in opposition of their efforts with a monetary figure that gained their support and Tooele County officials followed suit and settled as well. Tooele County officials then supported the dump in their county.

Compensation in the form of enormous payouts were supposed to make everybody look the other way and in essence entice and encourage the Goshute tribal members to go and "buy a life" somewhere else. Those folks were targeted because of their location and courted in a manner afforded only top athletes and potential business prospects, without regard to their connection to the land and their ongoing desire to live on their land for time immemorial.

Even though it seemed as if events were leading up to the eventual storage of nuclear waste of the tribe's land, two distinct rulings changed everything in 2006. The Bureau of Indian Affairs (BIA) under the Department of the Interior and the Bureau of Land Management (BLM) voided the NRC agreement with the Goshute Band of the Skull Valley. The BLM denied a right of way to transfer and transport nuclear waste to the Skull Valley Goshute reservation, and the BIA issued a decision that disapproved of the proposed lease agreement between PFS and the Goshute tribe of the Skull Valley reservation. Both the tribe and PFS fought against the ruling, and the tribe filed a law suit against the Department of the Interior in July 2007. The suit sought a reversal of the 2006 ruling that voided the project.

Currently, the only viable economic enterprise on the Goshute reservation is the local landfill on the southwest corner of the reservation. Proponents of the storing of nuclear waste on reservation lands will say that safe storage of spent rods is possible and that science backs that claim. Those same proponents say that taking advantage of a unique and viable business opportunity such as storing nuclear waste in exchange for big money compensation is not only their sovereign right, but a smart business to get into for the tribe. Those folks will say that then Tribal Chairman Leon Bear was just doing his job and trying to find a way for the people of the tribe to have a viable future. Bear will say that he wanted new homes for his membership and new jobs and better health care for the people. He will say that he hoped the new jobs would bring more people back to the reservation to live.

Proponents will say that being in the nuclear waste storage business is not a political endorsement of the nuclear power industry as a whole. They will say that it seems hypocritical for Utah to fight their efforts for economic development when the state has studied and drawn plans to possibly create as many as seven nuclear power plants in Utah.

Opponents of the type of projects that bring potentially dangerous materials to rural areas just because they're rural will say that the connection to the land is not only culturally important, but also significant to their way of life and their traditions. Those opponents will also say that their good health and the good health of future generations should be the most important factor when making decisions about economic development on the tribe's traditional lands, especially if those economic development projects will bring known cancer-causing agents directly to sacred homelands.

Opponents of the project will say that one of the main concerns with allowing a project like the one that had been proposed is that if given a "temporary" license to store high-level nuclear waste products, the nuclear power industry would have likely settled in to the area for good. Planned temporary sites for storage of nuclear waste products might have become the permanent home for materials that can last on the Earth for eons. For example, one of the elements found in spent nuclear waste is Iodine-129, known to have a half-life of 16 million years.

Ironically, folks on both sides of the nuclear waste on reservation lands debate can adamantly agree that Utah is hypocritical in denying the tribe the right to entertain the idea of creating a nuclear waste repository on its lands, especially because the state is pursuing, at least to the point of studying the feasibility, several new nuclear power reactors. Each side of the issue argues that if the state is against nuclear waste in Utah, then why would the state be in the business of creating more waste?

Climate Justice

Robert William Collin

The effects of global warming on climate are and will be most severely felt along the tropics in Africa, Asia, and South America. Increased temperatures increase droughts and push countries over the tipping point into famine and persistent civil unrest. The western countries such as the United States and Germany are seen as the highest historical generators of greenhouse gas emissions. These countries received all the advantages of the energy that produced these high and persistent levels of greenhouse gas. The countries that receive the burden of green house gas emissions are not the ones who caused it and received energy benefits from doing so. Now large developing countries want the same energy benefits from the same sources. The benefits of greenhouse gas emissions went to developed countries that now want undeveloped countries to use nonpolluting energy sources, even if they have them. This is perceived as an unfair burden on developing countries. The issues of energy and pollution benefits and burdens are further heightened by many countries' producing petrochemicals for developed countries. Some African countries produce large amounts of oil for developed countries and receive few of the benefits. When some African countries are asked to reduce greenhouse emissions, it increases their environmental burden by lowering energy benefits and increasing costs. They do receive the burdens of climate change effects. Most current international postures involve developed and developing countries waiting for others to do more before they commit to action. A new greenhouse gas agreement will raise this issue and potentially move the dialogue forward.

China and U.S. Greenhouse Gas Agreement

If the greenhouse gases were proportional to past Western nation populations and incorporated petrochemical cars, trucks, and airplanes, then effects on global warming would be greater. On November 11, 2014, President Obama of the United States and President Xi Jinping of China signed a historic agreement on greenhouse gas emissions. Both leaders head the two largest greenhouse gas generators, and both came to power at a time when air pollution began to affect public health, especially in their countries' urban areas. They have both heavily invested in measures to protect the environment. President Xi Jinping is familiar with alternative energy sources and related production technologies. They decreased the initial cost of solar panels by 90 percent. In 2009, China provided $30 billion dollars to the solar panel industry. China relies heavily on different types of coal for energy and was rapidly constructing coal-fired power plants. Under President Jinping, the rate of construction has decreased. Under President Obama, coal-fired power production decreased 20 percent from 2005. President Obama is a prominent advocate for environmental justice and for sustainability. In 2007, then Senator Obama supported a reduction of 80 percent of U.S. greenhouse gas emissions.

Critics observe that the agreement is voluntary, primarily because the current U.S. Senate opposes greenhouse gas reform at costs to industry and would not ratify a treaty with these agreements. The target levels of emissions for the United States are a 26–28 percent reduction of 2005 emissions by 2025. China agreed to aim for a transition to a fifth more non-fossil energy. By contrast, the European Union committed to a 40 percent reduction of emissions from 1990 levels by 2030. Germany committed to a transition to 60 percent of its energy from cleaner sources by 2024–2027.

The agreement occurs as the level of carbon dioxide reaches figures not seen for 3 million years—in 2014, 400 parts per million. The last time the Earth was that high in carbon dioxide, global temperatures were 5–8 °F warmer. Carbon dioxide levels are expected to continue to increase to historic proportions because of green house emissions. China is just beginning to rein in massive emissions, and only 3 of 74 cities monitored meet air quality standards.

The political context began greenhouse gas negotiations meetings beginning in Lima, Peru, at the end of November 2014 and concluding in Paris, France, in one year. The agreement signals recognition by the largest polluters that climate change effects can and should be avoided.

Menstruation and Wastes

Susan Lea Collin

Menstruation is a natural occurrence that is taken for granted by many cultures globally, whether positively or negatively. Some regard this process as a precious event and hold females in high regard, whereas others shun females during this time. One of the effects on females is lower school attendance and higher school dropout rates. Some studies show a 33–61 percent increase in absences due to lack of menstrual hygiene provisions, such as private latrines, water, and sanitation. Some societies use this natural event as a means to keep females out of governing bodies. Many cultures have men running the community rules and laws, and females are left out because they do not have the education that the males have received. Why? Because they miss school, having limited to no resources for managing their periods hygienically. Those who have the power to allocate resources choose to not increase resources in this area, controlling the ability of females to participate in education and potentially affect the laws of the community in positions of power.

The effect of menstruation globally is quite profound. When the cumulative effects of menstrual fluids are included, their significance as part of the modern, overcrowded international city increases. The country with the most women in its population is China. As of 2014, China's population of women is around 657 million, with India running a close second at around 600 million women. Most women will have approximately 350 menses in their lifetimes. (Female ancestors had around 100 because of constant pregnancy and breastfeeding.) This equates to approximately 3,000 days of menstruation in an average woman's lifetime. Menstrual fluid is the correct name for the flow, though many refer to it as menstrual blood. The average volume of menstrual fluids during a monthly event is 2.4 tablespoons, with 1–6 tablespoons of total menstrual fluid. Cultures vary in the management of disposing of menstrual waste. Tampons, pads, menstrual cup, and torn cloth are the top means for managing menstrual fluids, each having some serious concerns to consider from a personal level to global effect. Tampons are known to have trace amounts of dioxin, and these trace amounts are cumulative over the 350 menses a woman will have. Considering that a woman may use an average of fifteen tampons per menses, this translates into 5,250 dioxin exposures in a lifetime of menstruating. Dioxin is a highly toxic compound produced as a byproduct in different manufacturing processes, notably herbicide production and paper bleaching. Studies have found detectable levels of dioxin in a number of tampon brands. The FDA monitors this but depends on companies to provide data. According to Greeniacs.com, this data is not available to the public, and this lack of transparency is very much a concern. Tampons are hitting one of the most absorbent areas of a woman's tissues, and the exposure to dioxin is very direct. Menstrual pads have similar issues regarding pesticide residues and adhesive chemicals.

Moving away from the individual effect of menstrual waste disposal and toward the effect on the world globally, these items must be discarded. It is estimated that 7 billion tampons are disposed of annually just in the United States. Plastic applicators do not biodegrade, and cardboard applicators can take up to six months to biodegrade in landfills. There is data that shows that daughters typically purchase the same products their mothers did and that for the sake of women's health and environmental health, women need to be encouraged to use more sustainable means for managing menstrual wastes, such as the menstrual cup. A menstrual cup is a reusable cup inserted to internally collect menstrual blood. Though much healthier for feminine health, there are still concerns regarding disposal of menstrual fluids.

The fourth most common option for managing menstrual fluids is simply torn rags that are optimally washed out and dried for next use. Females' capacity to manage their periods is affected by cultural and environmental factors. These include limited access to affordable and hygienic sanitary materials of any kind and limited disposal options. This causes women to manage their periods in ineffective, uncomfortable, and unhealthful ways. Some of these choices can provide vectors for infectious diseases. Natural materials such as ashes, sand, mud, leaves, dung, and animal skins are used to manage menstrual fluids. Sometimes menstrual clothes are cleaned in rivers. Rags are typically not incinerated because of the lack of resources, and require water for washing. As global warming continues, this safe disposition of menstrual wastes will become more difficult to achieve. Climate change effects of increased temperatures and drought also decrease traditional venues for washing clothes.

Consider that menstrual fluids are the result of the lack of a pregnancy, which causes the nutrient-rich lining in the uterus to be excreted. This nutrient-rich lining is perfect for indirect transmission of diseases. Most vectors require a blood meal to sustain life and reproduce. Without the ability to thoroughly clean menstrual rags, women are exposed to vectors that are living in the limited water supply, eating the menstrual fluid, and then reused, providing a warm and moist entry into a woman's body.

All sexes desire safety, hygiene, and dignity in the private functions surrounding waste. Menstrual wastes are taboo in many cultures, a waste generator kept behind closed doors. Because menstrual fluid is a waste, can be an infectious vector, and it is different than many other wastes in now commanding a higher profile. Secret cultural waste practices and widely different conceptions of privacy will emerge in more public policy discussions. Equal rights and special considerations for women are necessary for accurate measures of environmental effects, the health of women, and containment of infectious disease vectors.

Further Reading

Chrisler, J., et al. 2015. "Body Appreciation and Attitudes toward Menstruation." *Body Image* 12: 78–81.

Grose, G. 2014. "Sociocultural Attitudes Surrounding Menstruation and Alternative Menstrual Products: The Explanatory Role of Self-Objectification." *Health Care for Women International* 35: 677–694.

Thakur, H., et al. 2014. "Knowledge, Practices, and Restrictions Related to Menstruation among Young Women from a Low Socioeconomic Community in Mumbai, India." *Frontiers in Public Health* 2: 72.

Environmental Justice and Waste

Robert William Collin

Environmental justice is the disproportionate effect of benefits and burdens of environmental decisions. Because implemented environmental decisions are almost always local in their effects, it is easier to notice whether a particular group of people does not receive the benefits other groups are getting. Over time, the cumulative effects of environmental burdens can become more severe and require public health attention. The groups not receiving environmental benefits and receiving environmental burdens tend to be ethnic or socioeconomic groups that are politically oppressed.

Human communities—cities, towns, and villages—and human bodies are where complex policy decisions and their environmental consequences accumulate. Communities generate, store, transfer, and accumulate wastes every day, year after year. These wastes range from early sewage wastes that accumulate with industrial wastes. Both these wastes have increased globally. Industrial wastes now include radioactive, pharmaceutical, and pesticide wastes. Population growth increases the amount, and generally the concentration, of human wastes. So does urbanization. Per-capita generation of municipal solid wastes goes up in cities. Issues of environmental disproportionality become self-evident in the current context of a rapidly urbanizing global population. Urban sanitation is beginning to improve globally. Most countries have increased coverage and decreased income-based disparities in urban sanitation. In rural areas, some countries have slightly increased their coverage and have increased income-based disparities.

Human bodies, especially those born into communities where wastes from humans and industry accumulate, also bioaccumulate wastes to which they are exposed through the land, air, and water where they live, work, play, learn, and worship. The recent advent of environmental law and regulation is not based on protecting the vulnerable, the young, the old, or women. Globally, the reach of the international and national government over behavior that affects the environment is weak, so environmental laws or policies are not fully implemented. Many international and national environmental agreements and environmental effect assessments are voluntary.

Human exposure to waste is still accumulating. The increasing effects of cumulative waste exposure affect those exposed first and longest—usually those closest living to trash and wastes. Such people can be waste pickers, garbage collectors,

---

Call to Action on Sanitation from the United Nations

In 2013, the UN secretary general issued a call to end open defecation by 2025 to help countries meet 2015 Millennium Development Goals (MDG) for sanitation.

Open defecation and poverty go hand in hand. From 1990 to 2012, the poorest countries generally made little progress. Approximately 1.1 billion people out of 7 billion people worldwide defecate in the open.

Open defecation is an indicator of poverty and lack of access to sanitary facilities. Along with other unsanitary practices, open defecation has directly effect infectious diseases, health, education, and gender equality. High open defecation rates are associated with high infant mortality rates, low nutrition, extreme poverty, and large wealth disparities. Women, children, and disabled people are vulnerable to violence if they must leave their homes to defecate. When given the choice to go somewhere without a bathroom or stay home, the choice is to stay home. It affects education, because parents do not want to send their children to school if the bathroom is not sanitary or safe. The lack of safe sanitation affects billions of people, along with their everyday movements. The Call to Action did precede a period of rapid sanitation improvement. Many countries met their MDG goals, and many other countries are proceeding in the direction of doing so.

---

urban residents, scavenger communities, schoolchildren, farm workers, and all those who work the waste stream of any given human settlement. In 1987, a study in the United States by the United Church of Christ concluded that the best way to predict where a controlled or uncontrolled hazardous waste facility is located is by the race of the surrounding community. The more African Americans in the community, the more likely there is to be a hazardous waste facility—to a 1 in 10,000 chance of being random. Many countries have similar ethnic or socioeconomic disparities.

Demographics are dynamic and hard to measure accurately in the United States and many countries, but waste always increases over time in every community on Earth.

Further Reading

Agyeman, J. 2013. *Introducing Just Sustainabilities: Policy, Planning and Practice*. London, UK: Zed Books.

Bullard, R. 2005. *The Quest for Environmental Justice: Human Rights and the Politics of Pollution*. Berkeley, CA: Counterpoint.

Pellow, D. 2007. *Resisting Global Toxics: Transnational Movements for Environmental Justice (Urban and Industrial Environments)*. Cambridge, MA: The MIT Press.

Roberts, J., and Parks, B. 2006. *A Climate of Injustice: Global Inequality, North–South Politics, and Climate Policy (Global Environmental Accord: Strategies for Sustainability and Institutional Innovation)*. Cambridge, MA: The MIT Press.

Walker, G. 2012. *Environmental Justice: Concepts, Evidence and Politics*. New York: Routledge.

Human Rights and Waste

Robin Morris Collin

The shape of the waste trade—its partners, its transit routes, and the content of the stream—forms a system that profound affects the ability of ecosystems to survive and support life within a bioregion. Many elements of this system remain opaque or impossible to see because of cultural resistance, because of difficulty perceiving effects at ecological levels, and because of their underlying unethical or illegal nature. Decisions about the risks created by this system remain often very unaccountable, in the hands of persons far removed from the risks they impose on others.

This trade links developed and less developed communities and nations in a system that moves resources from some of the poorest, often wartorn, communities to the wealthiest. It moves waste generated by production and consumption for wealthy communities and nations to destinations—sinks—in poor communities and less developed nations.

The routes these wastes follow to their ultimate destination trace a path of exposures through the production cycle, consumption cycle and post-consumer "grave." Tracing these routes shows a pattern of manufacture and use that exposes labor, the environment—especially the oceans—and communities along these transit routes to the dangers and health consequences of waste and pollution. Decisions about the acceptability of exposure and the ultimate decency of the system are rarely made by those most affected by the systematic exposures; instead they tend to be made by persons far removed from the risks of exposures. The content of the waste stream are all the end products that flow from household, residential, consumer, industrial processes. They are categorized by the nature of the content and its processing, and they can be mapped.

The nature of hazards posed to the environment by transit and dumping are visible to the extent that humans observe and consider them, but the observation and consideration has been influenced by cultural practices assigning waste streams and their management to reviled classes and communities, further limited by our abilities and willingness to collect data from the environmental systems affected by waste storage and transit. Political vulnerability, cultural revulsion, and economic manipulation collaborate to create levels of uncertainty and factual unknowns about waste and pollution that undermine the ability of science to effectively predict and manage. As wastes accumulate and interact in unpredictable ways in the environment and in human bodies, unanticipated consequences emerge in the context of climate change.

Waste and Pollution Threaten Sustainability: Depletion and Loss of Resilience

In development "sustainability" is often defined as providing for current needs without diminishing the ability of future generations to provide for their needs. This principle is summarized as "intergenerational equity" and also incorporates intragenerational equity in the provision of current needs.

Waste and pollution threaten sustainability in both the intergenerational and intragenerational senses of the term. Waste of resources leads to depletion and loss of resilience in ecosystems and their services. Depletion deprives contemporaries and posterity access to resources and ecosystem services that are necessary for life and health.

Pollution poisons the ecosystems and their ability to generate services on which life depends. This is the consequence of pollution for contemporaries as well as future generations. Trashing the environment by adding pollutants to it clearly threatens contemporary and future supplies of clean air, clean water, and healthful soils, including by failure to use known and accessible methods of treating human waste and excretion.

The poorest populations are most dependent on ecosystem services and sanitation security. The lack of ecosystem services and basic sanitation compromises the health and economic development of the poorest communities and nations.

Sustainable Production and Consumption: Beyond Pollution and Toxicity: Toward Closed-Loop Systems

How that human societies manufacture what they need and want, and how they consume the products they create, is responsible for the creation of end products that create waste and toxify our ecosystems when these systems do not account for these end products.

The development conundrum is that even as the systems of production and consumption meet human needs and aspirations, they may pessimize the ecosystems on which all life depends. Ecosystem services are the benefits that humans derive from the way that natural system function. Our skill at exploiting these functions has elevated human survival but pessimized the system. Sustainability shifts focus onto the connections between the system parts or "stakeholders." That focus increasingly comes to rest on what humans have created as "waste" and "pollution."

One theory about nature holds that nature produces no waste. Thus in all natural systems, end products of natural processes are the start of a new natural process—so-called closed loops. Human production and consumption create open loops, by contrast, creating end products that don't clearly connect to the next cycle of production or producing end products that poison the well of natural resources.

The response of design and engineering professionals has been to create closed loops in the system of human production and consumption. In these closed loop designs, the end product of one process becomes the raw material for a new process. Design consciousness is also alert for the use and production of hazardous materials. This means a close look at the supply chain as well as the end products of manufactures and consumption. This response can focus attention on new systems and redesign of existing systems and can employ new technology or create new partners based on old technology. The science or art of replicating natural closed feedback loops is captured in the nascent study of biomimicry.

Carrying Capacity, Environmental Footprint, and Loss of Resilience: Use Toward Collapse

The idea that each bioregion and every biotone has a resilience quota—a knowable amount of ecosystem support for the life within it—is postulated as that of "carrying capacity." Waste and pollution challenge this capacity by overuse to depletion of ecosystems services. Various calculators of this carrying capacity look at individual behaviors to measure their effects on the ecosystem. Much of the management value of such a concept and measure lies in its power of self-efficacy: When we know better, we do better.

The tragedy of the commons describes what happens to shared goods when no one recognizes the power of the individual to affect the common good. The power of private property is precisely that it empowers and elevates the individual over the community from which that individual emerges. While protecting and dignifying the individual, this attribute of private property transfers the power to decimate others who depend on the functionality of the system to those who can pay the market price. This aspect of autonomy is incommensurable with a system whose connectivity is its only protection from overuse/abuse and collapse.

Inequality of Wealth Fuels Loss of Resilience and Collapse

Extraordinary wealth, and the sense of entitlement of intergenerational wealth creates a buffer around individuals, fostering an illusion of disassociation with the fundamentals of natural systems. In addition, the creation of an ultrawealthy class exponentially increases the likelihood of depletion and extinctions as individuals without conscience are empowered and enabled financially to imperil others without their consent. Inequality of income creates a class of people who can afford to eat the last fishes of a species. Wealth gives a few individuals the ability to make a choice with widespread consequences for communities and whole ecosystems— for example, a rock star who wants to kill a rare white buffalo. Other factors must constrain the behavior that propels the tragedy.

Wealthy people can buy water until there is no water left or oxygen until there is no oxygen left. Moderate and widespread prosperity would have sought ways to conserve the resource before its depletion. Wealth and depletion are joined in a system that allows the wealthiest to buy the last water and oxygen. Collapse will affect all alike; wealth may buy time but alone does not necessarily invest in solutions.

Feces as Medicine

The human gastrointestinal system is loaded with all types of gut flora in a state of dynamic balance. Some infections, medical conditions, and environmental exposures can alter that balance. *Clostridium difficile* is a common infection that is resistant to antibiotics. In the United States, about 300,000 hospital patients per year get *Clostridium difficile*, and 14,000 die annually from it. Symptoms are severe diarrhea, fever, and vomiting. It is a global problem of unknown proportions.

But it can be treated with feces with healthy gut flora. This is not a new process. It is used on farm animals and is found in ancient medical texts. The process involves collecting healthy stool samples, screening them for diseases, diluting the feces, and getting it into the digestive tract using enemas, colonoscopies, or a tube through the nose into the stomach. Indeed, concentrated fecal microbes are now available in pill form.

Affluence and Waste

In development literature, a formula for managing human generated environmental impacts is IPAT: Impact, Population, Affluence, and Technology. The formula is meant to capture the relationship between environmental effects and the factors of population, affluence, and technology.

Waste is the unacknowledged common denominator in this formula. Human-generated waste grows as population grows; it's a positive loop for which our best hope lies in slowing the growth of population. And the best technique is clearly education and employment opportunities for women. Affluent populations are exponentially the most wasteful populations. There is more platinum in the landfills of Japan than in the world's crust. E-waste is one of the fastest growing sources of waste, and it is generated as affluent populations discard their technology in favor of the latest, most powerful electronic device. The wasteful effects of affluence fueled by conspicuous consumerism may be mitigated by cultural adaptations—for example, if computers or cars are shared by units of the population such as family or community rather than individual ownership. Technology has come to rely increasingly on rare minerals or rare earths as fundamental constituents of their items. Miniaturization has lessened the effect of technology in traditional resource areas but has greatly increased the effect of technology on energy demands and on the demand for the rare constituent elements. For example, silicon is such a fundamental component of the computer sector that its cradle is called "Silicon Valley." Some of the world's poorest and most wartorn countries are incredibly rich in these rare minerals, also call "rare earths." Some have suggested that corporations who seize these assets while supporting domestic chaos ought to pay restitution to the victims of their technology-driven pillage.

Beyond manipulation of these basic terms, understanding the role that waste plays in sustainability is a sound premise. Challenging the consumeristic lifestyle that creates vast amounts of waste, challenging the conspicuous consumption marketing philosophy that fuels an ever-evolving list of material desires, and understanding the idea of closed loops from nature and biomimicry can transform the manufacturing and consuming of technology in fundamental way.

Many affluent communities have invested in approaches the preserve the value of resources in postconsumer waste products in programs that encourage and facilitate recycling and reuse of consumer articles rather than sending them to a landfill. These programs can generate waste of their own and contribute to greenhouse gases as they process materials for new uses. Other programs encourage manufacturers to internalize spent materials by requiring manufacturers to be responsible for the end-of-life-cycle product that they have created. These programs are called extended producer responsibility, or intelligent product, systems. They encourage the manufacturer to redesign the waste stream, eliminating waste and pollution in the production process.

Other factors greatly influence the environmental footprint and affect the carrying capacity of ecosystems. Certain industrial sectors have a much larger environment footprint and thus a greater effect on carrying capacity. Agriculture, transportation, construction, and other industry are the greater contributors to climate change, waste streams, and the creation of pollution in the environment. Globalization has vastly increased the demand for throughput of resources for consumer goods, as well as the generation of waste. And although population does increase effects, including waste, more population is not necessarily equivalent in effect on the environment. It is well documented that affluent populations generate far more waste and pollution per person than less developed populations do.

All Waste Is Local: Municipalities and Waste

The locus of waste and pollution is a matter of where that geographic space is. That place is always local in essential ways. The ecological and cultural characteristics of a place strongly influence whether it will become the recipient of waste, especially toxic waste. Communities of color and poor communities and nations are the sinks into which toxic and hazardous waste flow, as the environmental justice and climate justice movements have demonstrated over and over again. These communities are also the least benefited by the generation of these byproducts of development.

Cities, towns, counties, and other municipalities handle all the waste stream for the simple reason that the generation of waste and pollution is always local and place-based. They are the location for treatment from human wastes to industrial wastes. The powers of these units of government are often dwarfed by their responsibilities, especially when it comes to the funding of infrastructure. Many municipalities may raise taxes to support their responsibilities, but the nature of local elective politics makes raising taxes a losing strategy. Fees are a different path to funding mandates and a path that may embrace the "polluter pays" approach. Imposing fees on waste generators based on the amount of waste (particularly hazardous waste that must be treated and stored) may avoid the tough political issues of elective accountability. Yet it is these localities—cities, towns, counties, and municipalities all across the world—that are tasked with managing the variety of risks posed by waste, especially toxic and hazardous waste. These localities rarely possess independent funding for managing waste. They rely on local tax resources, supplemented by federal resources, to provide for their own needs. When those resources are insufficient, there is simply no provision made for sanitation, further weakening these communities. They are weakened environmentally as these wastes accumulate and spread throughout interconnected ecosystems, infiltrating water, soil, and air. They are weakened in terms of vulnerability to public health hazards and weakened in their ability to attract economic development opportunities other than waste.

Mayors and the leaders of other municipalities have also joined forces to address issues related to waste, sanitation, and ultimately climate change in the Compact of Mayors and similar agreements.

Agenda 21, the work plan for the Rio Declaration of principles of sustainable development, calls on local authorities to address the problems of sustainability. "Ultimately, decisions about waste are up to local government for implementation" (Agenda 21, Chapter 28). Far from the top-down modality of many "soft law" treaties involving national governments, Agenda 21 calls for action from the lowest level of government consistent with effective action. And despite their chronic underfunding, local governments have rallied, banding together in groups to share ideas and best practices for addressing sustainable development needs respecting waste and sanitation. Agenda 21 called on local governments to implement its principles through local leadership, community mobilization, and planning across social, economic, and environmental concerns. Local governments have joined to share ideas, skills, and replicate projects especially as regards local responsibilities for the management of waste and pollution at the local level.

The inescapable reality of local waste management comes to rest in the method of disposal of wastes in landfills. Landfills take land from other productive uses and make them unusable for many types of development and cultivation. The cost of landfills may not be adequately reflected in the market price, as the opportunity cost for land and the length of time required for remediation of wastes is uncertain. When productive land is used to warehouse waste or—worse—used to warehouse toxic and hazardous pollutants, the finite resource of land has been arrogated to unproductive use for some incalculable period of time.

Some waste-producing nations have taken increased responsibility for building capacity at local levels to manage waste streams of their own, as well as capacity to accept waste streams from outside as a form of economic development. Domestic public policies that require extended product responsibility encourage waste producers within nations to diminish their production of waste and toxic hazardous pollutants, and international policies that force repatriation of wastes under certain circumstances, also encourage greater responsibility of waste producers and waste-producing nations. These policies force producers of waste to internalize their own products, recognizing the true and full costs that those wastes impose on the environment and community. For example, extended product responsibility laws often require manufacturers to accept the end products of consumer waste at the end of the product's lifecycle. In addition, there are many tax and fee proposals that would force the cost of waste management onto the producer rather than socializing this cost through publicly funded waste management systems. These are so-called "polluter pays" funding strategies.

Illegal dumping of waste is a problem that affects developed and less developed nations alike. When discovered, the effects may overwhelm the ability of the involuntary host to manage. The concept of forced repatriation of illegally dumped waste shifts the burden of dealing with this legacy to the source. (See IMPEL European Union Network for the Implementation and Enforcement of Environmental Law at impel.eu/tag/illegal-waste-shipments/.)

The Right to Sanitation from "Soft Law" to "Hard Law"

The United Nations General Assembly recognized the human right to water and sanitation on July 28, 2010, in Resolution 64/292, which states that clean drinking water and sanitation are essential to the realization of all human rights. The resolution calls upon member states and international organizations to provide financial resources, capacity-building, and technology transfer to help countries, in particular developing countries, provide safe, clean, accessible and affordable drinking water and sanitation for all.

In his call to action on March 21, 2013, UN Deputy Secretary General Jan Eliasson stated that of the 7 billion people on earth, 6 billion have mobile phones, but only 4.5 billion have access to toilets or latrines. He states that "solutions exist, and affordable, safe, effective and sustainable approaches and technologies are available." This is not a question of technology or, in many instances, money. As Goal 7 of the UN Millennium Development Goals says: "The vast majority—82 percent—of people practicing open defecation now live in middle-income, populous countries."

This lack of access to sanitation undermines achievement of many of the Millennium Development Goals. Lack of access to sanitation can cause and worsen malnutrition. Lack of access to sanitation undermines access to education, especially for women. Lack of access to sanitation kills 1.4 million children younger than 5 from diarrhea each year, according to the World Health Organization. It exposes women to violence and predation. Specifically, Target 7.C commits members to the goal of reducing by half the proportion of the population without sustainable access to safe drinking water and basic sanitation.

Successful efforts have used strategic partnerships with community, religion, and culture to educate and enforce measures to increase safe access to sanitation. For example, in India, some communities have instituted the requirement of a toilet as a prerequisite for marriage.

Litigation in several countries has also established a duty to provide safe drinking water and access to private sanitation relying on international human rights commitments, as well as national constitutions guaranteeing the right to human life and health.

In *Civil Association for Equality and Justice vs. City of Buenos Aires, Chamber for Administrative Matters of the City of Buenos Aires* (July 18, 2007), an Argentinian court ordered the city to build infrastructure to provide water services to residents of four informal settlements within the city and, in the interim, to provide water by means of tanker trucks and cisterns until such infrastructure was built. The court relied on a close connection between the right to water and the right to life.

In *Perumatty Grama Panchayat vs. State of Kerala* (December 16, 2003), the state's high court recognized that water extracted by a Coca-Cola plant operating pursuant to a license was disrupting the local water cycle, endangering natural resource held in trust for the public. Regional courts later affirmed the license pending a scientific assessment.

In *Environment and Consumer Protection Foundation v. Delhi Administration* (October 3, 2012), the supreme court of India connected the rights to water and sanitation to the right to education and ordered that water and sanitation facilities be provided at all schools. As a result, the court issued several orders requiring all schools to provide toilet facilities. The court wrote,

> It is imperative that all the schools must provide toilet facilities. Empirical researches have indicated that wherever toilet facilities are not provided in the schools, parents do not send their children (particularly girls) to schools. It clearly violates the right to free and compulsory education of children guaranteed under Article 21-A of the Constitution.

In *Beja and Others vs. Premier of the Western Cape and Others* (April 29, 2011), the high court of South Africa enforced a right to privacy enclosures around communal toilets, holding that sanitation and minimal privacy of users are included in fundamental rights guaranteed by the Constitution.

Other courts in South Africa and Paraguay have upheld the rights of residents to water services despite loss of lands and lack of payment of fees, relying on constitutional right to life guarantees. However, residents of the city of Detroit whose water services have been terminated have met with no such success in the courts of the United States.

Risk Management and Perception: A Bridge to Sustainability

When risks are managed in ways that protect the most vulnerable populations who may be affected by them, the safest protocols are used. The costs of those safest protocols fall on the risk generator, not on potential victims. This is one version of the precautionary principle at work.

Most risk managers are well-educated, European or white males older than 30. That population is not only a minority, but it is a very privileged minority, thanks to wealth. Wealth and other social factors such as race and gender insulate individuals from experiences of vulnerability and risks experienced by others. The fact that exposure decisions are made by those least likely to experience the consequences runs counter to the precautionary principle and results in risk decisions that externalize the consequences onto others.

Insurers, underwriters, and development bankers typically make risk management decisions. The Equator principles are a risk management framework infusing social, economic and environmental factors into the risk decisions of financial institutions. The Equator principles require consideration of social and environmental risks—not merely compliance with local norms. In addition, these principles require stakeholder engagement and a method for redress of grievances.

To achieve Millennium Development Goals for sanitation, waste management and planning for human sanitation will require massive investments from international development organizations. Addressing cultural and social barriers and considerations in this mostly unheralded and unexamined area of development must transcend the frameworks for most risk management planning to include accountability to women and girls, disabled and vulnerable persons, and the poor, whose needs for water and sanitation are no less real for their poverty.

Waste and pollution are the single greatest contributors to the postindustrial problems of sustainability. Together these contributors change the landscape of human life and all life that depends on current ecosystem services. The management and resolution of these factors is often invisible until tragedy or collapse is threatened. Underfunded and unglamorized work of local governments and civil society activists is at the forefront of efforts to raise consciousness in multiple forums about how to address the creation, transit, and deposition of waste and pollution.

Further Reading

ICLEI, Local Governments for Sustainability ACCESSanitation, www.accessanitation.org.

Part II
Country Profiles

AFGHANISTAN

Afghanistan is an ancient landlocked country whose 31 million inhabitants reside on 652,864 km² of land in many small communities. Overall, 49 percent of the population is urbanized, and 16 percent lives in a city having more than 100,000 inhabitants. More than 500 million refugees are in exile.

Afghanistan is in southern Asia, east of Iran and north and west of Pakistan. It has no coastline. It is geologically active, having annual earthquakes, landslides, and avalanches. The climate is arid to semi-arid, with cold winters and hot summers. The terrain is mountainous, with plains in the north and southwest. There are limited freshwater resources, though there are many rivers and some reservoirs. Much of the snow from the mountains flows as water into the contiguous countries of Iran, Pakistan, and Turkmenistan. Afghanistan has a history of soil degradation, overgrazing, deforestation, and air and water pollution. Many years of war have created both damage and waste, including sewage, solids, biohazards, unexploded and exploded ordnance, abandoned bases and their attendant wastes, and human remains. What waste treatment exists is quick and dirty. One practice is to use fuel oil to burn abandoned equipment and sites. The dense smoke so created is laden with particulate matter, metals, and greenhouse gases, and all nearby people, including soldiers, are affected by toxic burning waste dumps. Such burning wastes can include animal and human wastes, medical wastes, oil, paint, fuel, metals, unexploded ordnance, and munitions.

Current Waste Practices

Many years of war have destroyed any existing waste infrastructure and created other considerable and long-lasting environmental effects. Fifty-nine percent of the population suffers malnutrition. The life expectancy is 42 years. It is estimated that 66,700 people die a year in Afghanistan from dirty drinking water. Water quality is very poor. Seventy-eight percent of the urban population has access to an improved source of drinking water, but only 42 percent has access to improved sanitation facilities. Forty-two percent of the rural populace has access to an improved drinking water source, and only 30 percent has access to improved sanitation facilities.

Afghanistan has the highest rate of respiratory infection in the world, as well as among the highest asthma and diarrhea rates. Data, however, is anecdotal as a result of past and present political strife.

The capital city of Kabul produces about 110,000 tons of solid waste annually, placed by residents in public pickup locations. More than 3 million people reside in Kabul, and there are about 2,000 sanitation workers and 110 garbage trucks. Some trash is dumped in the Dashte Chemtala plains 7 km north.

Decades of recent war and violent civil conflict have seriously degraded sewer and water infrastructure. Sanitation facilities are often deemed more acceptable targets for their decreased risk of civilian casualties. About a fifth of the population openly defecates in rivers also used for drinking. There is little recycling save for informal garbage picking. These waste practices provide primary disease vectors through direct exposure to wastes, as well as secondary disease vectors through indirect exposures from vermin and insects.

Emissions and Industry

In 2008, Afghanistan generated 814 metric tons of greenhouse gases. This does not include emissions from military conflict, which are substantial owing to waste burning practices.

Traditional agriculture occupies 82 percent of the population. The main crops are wheat, barley, rice, corn, cotton, and some vegetable and fruits. Grapes, raw fur skins, and cotton were Afghanistan's three chief exports in 2013. Agriculture accounted for 78 percent of all emissions. Within this sector, enteric fermentation accounted for 43 percent of emissions, agricultural soils 39 percent, and manure management almost 14 percent. This high amount of greenhouse gas emissions from manure indicates the presence of large amounts of untreated feces.

Afghanistan produces crude oil and maintains proved reserves. Energy emissions accounted for 20 percent of all emissions. Within this sector, transport accounted for 45 percent of emissions, and energy industries about 13 percent.

Industrial emissions accounted for 2 percent of all emissions, almost all of it having to do with mineral products. Afghanistan has large petrochemical and mineral deposits, with about 1,400 mineral sites known. The range of minerals excavated includes gemstones such emeralds, garnets, and rubies as well as copper, gold, zinc, salt, sulfur, chromite, and barite. The completion and operation of the Trans-Afghanistan pipeline will increase the incidence of industrial processes.

Major Waste Issues

The lack of waste infrastructure is a major issue. The risk of public health effects from wasteborne diseases will increases without a way to handle all the waste created by a large urbanizing population recovering from war. Waste becomes concentrated more quickly without water. Clean water, safe sanitation, and solid waste disposal are the major waste issues. As military forces leave Afghanistan, large amounts of trash remain, adding to these basic waste issues. The current practice of burning everything in open pits will increase greenhouse emissions. As international attention to rebuilding Afghanistan heightens, the waste infrastructure will be of top priority.

Decades of war have destroyed the most of Afghanistan's water infrastructure. Pump stations for freshwater have often been targets in military confrontations.

With little natural water save that provided by mountain runoff, the need for a reservoir system is paramount, but many of these have been destroyed, so only about a third of the mountain runoff stays in Afghanistan. Thanks to temperature increases resulting from global warming, the snow melts earlier each year. With little water available from the melting snow, it is feared that about half Afghanistan's wells may run dry. Agriculture uses almost 99 percent of the water for irrigation, and many community-based conflicts are over water rights. Only about 12 percent of the land is arable, and much less without water. Afghanistan currently has access to approximately 65 km^3 of renewable water resources, a low figure.

There is a great risk of infectious diseases' growing and developing, including cholera, hepatitis A, hepatitis B, malaria, and typhoid. Warm, highly polluted ecosystems combined with a demolished waste infrastructure provide a good environment for many infectious diseases. The lack of public health intervention in most human settlements adds to the problem. As militias and others move through Afghanistan, the vectors for national, regional, and international spread of disease increase.

There is a chance that infectious disease vectors will expand. Rapid population growth and urbanization, very poor sanitation practices and facility access, unaccountable greenhouse gas inventories, and lack of environmental or public health data put Afghanistan at risk for more infectious diseases. Long droughts and desertification have had substantial environmental and public health effects. With increasing temperatures, desertification will increase, heightening these effects. There are inadequate public resources in the country to handle internal, regional, and global health concerns. International intervention is already occurring, but more is needed.

Further Reading

Elyan, D., et al. 2014. "Non-Bacterial Etiologies of Diarrheal Diseases in Afghanistan." *Transactions of the Royal Society of Tropical Medicine and Hygiene* 108: 461–465.

Forouhar, A., and K. Hristovski. 2012. "Characterization of the Municipal Solid Waste Stream in Kabul, Afghanistan." *Habitat International* 36: 406–413.

Gon, G., et al. 2014. "The Contribution of Unimproved Water and Toilet Facilities to Pregnancy-Related Mortality in Afghanistan: Analysis of the Afghan Mortality Survey." *Tropical Medicine and International Health* 19: 1,488–1,499.

Office of the President of Afghanistan. www.presodent.gov.af.

ALBANIA

Approximately 3.2 million people live on 28,748 km^2 of land and 362 km of coastline in Albania, which is one of the least educated and poorest countries in Europe, with its economy primarily agricultural and self-sufficient. Albania, once part of the ancient Byzantine and Ottoman empires, gained independence from the Ottoman Province of Rumelia in 1912 under a communist government that isolated the country from the rest of the world until 1992, when it lost power. Transition to a democratic government has been challenged by corruption and degraded infrastructure. Albania is developing its waste infrastructure with help from the European Union (EU). In 2009 Albania joined NATO, seeking admission to the EU but needing help to meet EU standards. The "ascension" process is the long process of applying for membership to the EU. The EU offers an Instrument for Pre-Accession Assistance to candidate and potential candidate countries, including Albania.

Albania borders Greece, Macedonia, Serbia, and Montenegro. About a fifth of the land is arable—578,000 ha. Natural resources include water, oil, and gas. Just under a third of the land area is forested. The climate is mild, and the terrain is mountainous, with some plains along the coast.

Current Waste Practices

Most Albanians live in small communities. Forty-five percent of the people are urbanized, but only 9 percent live in a city having more than 100,000 inhabitants. Although access to water is good, access to food is not. About a quarter of the populace suffers malnutrition. Ninety-six percent of the urban population has access to an improved source of drinking water, and 95 percent has access to improved sanitation facilities. Ninety-four percent of the rural population has access to an improved drinking water source, and 93 percent access to improved sanitation facilities. Most of the water is used in agriculture. Sixty-two percent of freshwater goes to agricultural uses, 27 percent to domestic uses, and 11 percent to industrial uses. Much of the country has some form of waste collection—and 85 percent of the population municipal waste collection. Most of these wastes are left to rot in rough landfills or are covered by dirt or burned. In 2009, 1,313,000 tons of municipal wastes were collected. It is likely that even more was generated that was disposed of in open dumps.

Albania is a small European country with a good environmental record, in part because of its political isolation until the early 1990s. Because of the expense of disposing of hazardous wastes in surrounding affluent countries, such as Germany and Austria, as well as the low-cost disposal available in the past in Albania, illegal hazardous and other waste routes historically terminated in Albania. In light of issues of environmental accountability, it is suspected that illegal dumping of hazardous wastes from domestic and international sources still continues in Albania. The globalization of the legal and illegal waste trade may have expanded the historic range of international waste trade from regional sources in Western Europe to include other industrialized nations as sources of legal and illegal wastes.

Emissions and Industry

Albania generated 3,101.7 metric tons of greenhouse gas emissions in 1994, a 56.5 percent decrease from 1990. However, it is likely that these emissions have since increased.

There is substantial arable land in Albania. Agricultural products include wheat, corn, fruits, vegetables, and meat and dairy products. Agricultural emissions accounted for 34 percent of all emissions in 1990. In 1990, within this sector, enteric fermentation accounted for 85 percent of emissions, agricultural soils for 9 percent, and manure management for 6 percent.

Albania produces crude oil and maintains proven reserves. However, electricity availability can be intermittent. The power grid is down for at least 194 days a year, one of the highest rates in the world. Energy emissions accounted for 56 percent of all emissions. Within this sector, manufacturing industries and construction accounted for 32 percent, transportation for 27 percent, and energy industries for 19 percent. Industrial emissions accounted for 4 percent of all emissions, all classified as "other"—a sign of inadequate monitoring. Albanian industries include food processing, textile and chemical manufacturing, and metal processing, all of which can pollute air and water. Waste emissions accounted for 6 percent of all emissions. Within this sector, solid waste disposal on land accounted for 86 percent of emissions, and wastewater handling for 14 percent.

Major Waste Issues

Wastes are a major political issue in Albania now. In recent history, much toxic waste has been illegally transported and disposed in Albania—in one case distributed as "humanitarian aid" to poor farmers. This case is emblematic of the pre-1990 waste dynamic of shipping wastes to eastern European countries under the guise of "humanitarian aid" or "recycling."

Albanians face a likelihood of infectious diseases' growing and developing with global warming. Hepatitis A, hepatitis B, tetanus, tick-borne encephalitis, and typhoid fever are known or presumed to occur here. Two percent or more of the population is known to be infected—and presumed to be persistently infected—with hepatitis B.

Further Reading

Albanian Prime Minister's Office. www.kryeministria.al.

"Albania's New Government Bans Waste Imports." www.balkaninsight.com/en/article/albania-bans-waste-imports.

Dumi, Ali, and Gelina Maliqi Ramolli. 2012. "Optimal Management Helps Reducing Risks for Potable-Water Resources in Albania." *Chinese Business Review* 11: 460–466.

ALGERIA

Approximately 38 million people live in Algeria in a land area of 2,381,741 km^2. Sixty-three percent of Algerians are urbanized, and a quarter of Albanians live in a city having more than 100,000 inhabitants. The country is sparsely populated outside the cities. Only about 3.15 percent of the land is arable. Four percent of the land area supports more than 65 percent of the people, making the region very sensitive to climate changes. Algeria is divided into three regions: the Tell (4 percent of land), the Hauts Plateaux (9 percent of land), and the Sahara (87 percent of land). It shares borders with Libya, Mali, Mauritania, Morocco, Niger, Tunisia, and the western Sahara.

Algeria is the largest country in Africa. It has extensive mineral deposits, including iron ore, phosphates, uranium, lead, and zinc. Algeria exports large amounts of natural gas to Europe—about 1.1 million barrels a day, the thirteenth most of 182 exporting countries. The climate is arid to semi-arid, with very hot summers featuring occasional sandstorms.

Phosphorous and Waste: The New Recycling

Phosphorous is a highly used fertilizer. It requires large amounts of petrochemicals to process it so it can be part of fertilizers. Unprocessed phosphorus is not accessible to plants, because it binds to other chemicals in the soil. When oil prices rapidly increased in 2007, the price of processing also increased, which in turn dramatically increased the price of phosphorous. This caused large food decreases and famine in many countries.

The amount of phosphorus is limited, and the last proven big deposits are in Algeria, China, and Morocco. The United States, Russia, and South Africa still have substantial quantities. It takes millions of years for the environment to produce phosphorous.

World demand is large, and 80 percent of fertilizer leaves agricultural fields and ends up in manure and waterways, whence it reaches the ocean. Municipal waste-water treatment plants in the United States already pull out phosphorous, because it can cause algae blooms. It is processed into a slurry and brought to hazardous waste landfills. Processing would be required to make it accessible to current plants. Research into how to process phosphorous from sewage is continuing.

Plants have grown reliant on phosphorus-based fertilizers and lost their ability to pull it out of the soil. New research is developing plants that can get more phosphorous out of the soil. Experiments with rice has developed plants that grow more grain in phosphorous-low soil.

The Sahara Desert covers most of Algeria. The country has few forests but has 1,866,000 ha of wetlands of international importance. About 80 percent of the land has sustained very little direct human effect, increasing the area of wilderness. Wilderness areas are often necessary to protect ecosystems but are decreasing in area because of human impacts of development, noise, pollution, and climate changes. Delicate ecosystems, such as many desert ecosystems, may not have the resilience of other ecosystems and take longer to recover, if they recover at all.

Current Waste Practices

"Access" here is broadly defined to mean any access at all. Woman and small children often relieve themselves in the safer predawn hours at sanitation facilities and other places deemed safe for them. Nine hundred municipalities have waste management plans. About a quarter of the population suffers malnutrition. Sixty-five percent of freshwater is used for agriculture, 22 percent for domestic purposes, and 13 percent for industrial purposes. Water is often polluted with agricultural chemical runoff, raw sewage, and petrochemical refining and mineral mining wastes.

Algeria collects about 9,000 tons of waste a year, placing nearly all of it in landfills. However, few municipal wastes are collected. About 57 percent of municipal solid wastes are stored in open dumps, 30 percent burned in open areas, and 10 percent landfilled. There are ten operational sanitary landfills thirty-two built, forty-two under construction, and twenty-seven under study.

Hazardous Wastes

Algeria generated 325.1 kilotons of hazardous wastes in 2010. There are no treatment centers for hazardous or industrial wastes, though two were under construction and may be viable soon. A large accumulation of 4,483,500 tons of nonhazardous and inert wastes and 2,008,500 tons of hazardous wastes were awaiting disposal in 2010. There is little transparency in hazardous wastes accounting so it is unknown how much is there now, but it is suspected that it is higher.

37,000 tons per year of medical wastes having infectious potential were generated in 2010. There are about 178 incinerators installed to treat it, 131 of them operational. It is assumed that the majority of infectious medical wastes are disposed of in landfills.

There is very little recycling in Algeria. In 2010 about 4–5 percent of municipal solid waste was recycled. None was composted. Recycling is interpreted broadly to include any potential reuse.

Algeria collected 8,500,000 tons of municipal waste in 2003, almost all of it landfilled. Eighty percent of the population enjoyed municipal waste collection.

Emissions and Industry

In 2000, Algeria generated 111,022.6 metric tons of greenhouse gases.

Agricultural products include wheat, oats, olives, fruit, and livestock. Emissions from agricultural wastes accounted for 6 percent of all emissions in 2000. Within this sector, enteric fermentation accounted for 60 percent of emissions, and manure management for 30 percent. The presence of such a large effect on the part of manure is an indication of the volume and rate of decay of waste there. This unusually high amount of greenhouse gas emissions from manure indicates the presence of large amounts of untreated feces.

Algeria produces substantial amounts of crude oil and maintains large proven reserves. Oil production per capita is high. Emissions from energy wastes accounted for 79 percent of all emissions. Within this sector, energy industries accounted for 32 percent of emissions, transportation for 14.6 percent, and manufacturing and construction for 9 percent. Fugitive emissions and "other" accounted for about 44 percent of emissions within this sector. Fugitive emissions are essentially unregulated air pollution. The chemicals in fugitive emissions can pose significant risks for the environment and human health, especially when they are such a large part of overall emissions. Fugitive emissions can combine with dust storms to distribute the pollution over a large area of both land and water.

Algeria generated at least 2.5 million tons of nonhazardous and inert industrial wastes in 2010. In 2000, Algeria's industrial processes accounted for 5 percent of all gas emissions. Within this sector, mineral products accounted for 59 percent of emissions, metal production for 21 percent, and chemical industries for 20 percent.

Waste emissions accounted for 11 percent of all emissions, a very high figure. From 1994 to 2000, these emissions increased about 142 percent. It is likely that they have increased since then. Within this sector, solid waste disposal on land accounted for two-thirds of greenhouse gas emissions, waste incineration about a quarter, and wastewater handling 8 percent.

Major Waste Issues

In the early 1960s the French used parts of Algeria for nuclear testing, conducting thirteen underground tests near Reggane. There is controversy about the long-term effects of these tests. Italy and other countries ship their radioactive wastes illegally to Algeria. However, Algeria is a nuclear weapon–free zone. It does operate two research reactors and a number of nuclear research centers. Estimates put the amount of uranium in the southern Sahara Desert at 26,000 tons. Major waste issues continue unabated.

Today, Algeria suffers dumping of raw sewage, oil and gas refining wastes, mineral and mining wastes into waterways leading to the Mediterranean Sea. There is a possibility of infectious diseases' growing and developing in polluted water. Currently, hepatitis A, hepatitis B, and typhoid fever are significant risks. Two percent or more of the population is known to be infected or presumed to be persistently infected with hepatitis B. There is currently a low risk of malaria in the Illizi area. Schistosomiasis, which is transmitted via freshwater snails, did occur here but is currently not a risk. Exposures routes include swimming, bathing, and cleaning clothes or dishes in freshwater.

The major waste issue for Algeria is containing the public health threats posed by infectious diseases. As temperatures rise, violent weather increases, and ocean levels rise, the vectors for many diseases currently there will increase in prevalence, and new diseases may be introduced or reintroduced.

Further Reading

Abdelbaki, C., et al. 2014. "Efficiency and Performance of a Drinking Water Supply Network for An Urban Cluster at Tlemcen, Algeria." *Desalinization and Water Treatment* 52: 2,165–2,173.

Guermoud, N. 2009. "Municipal Solid Waste in Mostaganem City (Western Algeria)." *Waste Management* 29: 896–902.

Hamiche, A., et al. 2015. "A Review of the Water and Energy Sectors in Algeria: Current Forecasts, Scenario and Sustainability Issues." *Renewable and Sustainable Energy Reviews* 41: 261–276.

People's Democratic Republic of Algeria. www.el-mouradia.dz.

Zawahri, N., et al. 2011. "The Politics of Assessment: Water and Sanitation Millennium Development Goals in the Middle East." *Development and Change* 42: 1,154–1,178.

ANGOLA

Angola is home to 18.6 million people. Fifty-three percent of the populace lives in urbanized areas, and a fifth lives in a city having more than 100,000 inhabitants. Angola has among the fastest-growing population rates in the world. The capital and largest city is Luanda, with a population of 3.8 million. There are also many small communities throughout the country.

Angola become independent from Portugal in 1975 and has seen waves of violent civil unrest since then. Portuguese is still the official language, although there are many indigenous languages, such as Kimbundu and Bakongo. Religious and ethnic divisions dominate governmental decisions.

The coastline along the Atlantic Ocean is 1,650 km. It is the seventh-largest nation in Africa, having 1,246,699 km^2 of land. It has a tropical climate with a dry season. It relies on rigorous natural resource extraction of oil, natural gas, diamonds, gold, and iron ore for economic development. Almost half of Angola is made up of forests and woodlands. A plateau rises to 6,000 feet from coastal lowland. Most of the land on the plateau is desert or savannas. There are hardwood forests in the northeast. Overall forested areas cover about 48 percent of land area. Angola is rich in biodiversity and contains unknown species of plants and animals.

Mining, overfishing, deforestation, and decades of civil war exacted a significant environmental toll. Diamond mining significantly affected waterways and sometimes rerouted them to facilitate mining. Mosquitoes, which breed in old mining pits filled with water, spread malaria and other diseases.

Current Waste Practices

Current waste practices are basic. Pit toilets, latrines, drainage ditches, and cesspools are the alternatives to open defecation. There is a lack of access to clean drinking water despite large freshwater sources. Fifty-four percent of urban people and 78 percent of rural people do not have access to fresh drinking water. Rapid urban population growth will only make this worse. About half the population suffers from malnutrition. The death rate from intestinal infectious diseases in Angola is 36.43 per 100,000, among the highest rates in the world. Diarrhea, respiratory infection, malaria, and asthma rates are high. The life expectancy at birth was about 42 years in 1990, increasing to 50 years in 2010. The mortality rate for children younger than 5 years was about 160.5 per 1,000 as of 2010, one of the world's highest. The infant mortality at birth that year was 98 per 1,000, according to World Bank Indicators.

Cholera occurs in rural and urban areas in Angola. Although data is incomplete, Angola leads Africa in cholera outbreaks. At least 18,422 people got cholera and 513 died in 2007. Fifty-one percent of the population has access to an improved water source, separating drinking water from wastewater. Fifty-eight percent has access to proper sanitation facilities, which separate the wastes from the outside environment. Chronic malnutrition affects about 35 percent of people. Lack of basic water treatment generally indicates little to no waste treatment. Years of conflict destroyed what water and sanitation infrastructure existed, as well as public health services. The first national elections in sixteen years were held in September of 2008, and there is greater political stability than in the country's recent history.

Recycling

The government takes an active role in recycling efforts, though the influence of government varies. The Environment Ministry is considering a law that allows the recycling of tires. The purpose of the law is to increase the standard of living and discourage tire burning in public streets. The Department of Waste and Sanitation Management in the Ministry of the Environment promotes more recycling companies and is currently seeking more consistent recycling standards as part of a Strategic Plan on Waste Management. One goal is to value what may be "garbage" as a means for survival.

Hazardous Waste

Approximately 5,495 kg of medical waste is produced every year, and about 30 percent is considered contaminated and dangerous. Angola signed the Minamata Convention on Mercury in 2013 to reduce the production and use of mercury in product manufacturing and other industrial processes.

Emissions and Industry

In 2005 Angola generated 61,610.8 metric tons of greenhouse gases, a 33 percent increase from 2000. These emissions do not include emissions from military conflict, and it is likely that the amount is actually much higher.

Sixty percent of freshwater is used for agriculture. Emissions from agricultural wastes accounted for 36.6 percent of all emissions. Within this sector, agricultural soils accounted for 52 percent of emissions, enteric fermentation 46 percent, and manure management 1 percent.

Sixty-one percent of emissions came from the energy sector. Within this sector, 100 percent are fugitive emissions. There is little regulation of air emissions in the energy sector. In a wartorn country desperate for energy and energy-based economic development via oil and gas extraction, there is little incentive to regulate air emissions from energy sources. Fugitive emissions are essentially unaccounted waste streams into the air. Fugitive emissions can affect regional ecosystems and the public health because they can fall from the air to the land and water.

Emissions from solid wastes account for 1.5 percent of all emissions. Emissions from waste come from solid waste disposal on land (79 percent), and wastewater handling (21 percent). Greenhouse gas emissions from waste increased almost 50 percent from 2000 to 2005.

Major Waste Issues

Current waste issues are many. Population increases lead to the overuse of land for cattle grazing and land intensive agricultural practices. This leads to soil erosion and loss of woodlands. This in turn leads to desertification, a form of ecosystem breakdown. Deforestation issues are driven by local needs for wood for fuel as well as by international demand for tropical lumber. This leads to loss of biodiversity and water pollution. Fishing is a large industry affected by these environmental effects. Overfishing by local and international fishing fleets combined with the petrochemical pollution along the coast present significant environmental effects to the marine environment.

There is a risk of many infectious diseases, including yellow fever and cholera all over the country. Yellow fever is transmitted via mosquito bites. Cholera is transmitted via contaminated food and water. Diphtheria is also known to occur in Angola as well. Vectors include breathing, contact with infected objects, and infected skin lesions. Hepatitis A and hepatitis B also exist here. Two percent or more of the population is persistently infected with the hepatitis B virus. All these diseases are facilitated by poor sanitation, contaminated water, and polluted air. Public health aspects of waste are on the front line of waste issues.

More urban residents live their daily lives crossing garbage heaps, as here in the streets of Angola. Lack of waste collection results in garbage heaps in most cities. (Alan Gignoux/Dreamstime.com)

There is a chance that infectious disease vectors will expand. The tropical conditions, rapid population growth and urbanization, very poor sanitation practices and facility access, unaccountable greenhouse gas inventories, and a lack of environmental or public health data make Angola at risk for more infectious diseases. Long droughts and desertification have substantial environmental and public health effects. With increasing temperatures, desertification will increase and increase these effects. There are inadequate public resources in the country to handle internal, regional, and global health concerns. International intervention is already occurring, but more is needed.

Further Reading

Ferreira-Baptista, L., and E. De Miguel. 2005. "Geochemistry and Risk Assessment of Street Dust in Luanda, Angola: A Tropical Urban Environment." *Atmospheric Environment* 39: 4,501–4,512.

Foeken, D. W. J., et al. 2013. *Sanitation in Africa: Access to Improved Sanitation Facilities and Improvement Index.* Leiden, The Netherlands: African Studies Center.

Official Portal of the Angolan Government. www.governo.gov.ao.

Reed, Kristin. 2005. *Crude Existence: Environment and the Politics of Oil in Northern Angola.* Oakland: University of California Press.

ANTIGUA AND BARBUDA

The Caribbean nation of Antigua and Barbuda have a population of 90,156 people, living on 442.6 km² of land and 153 km of coastline. Thirty-nine percent of the population is urbanized, and 33 percent lives in a city having more than 100,000 inhabitants. The islands of Antigua, Barbuda, and Redonda form the country of Antigua and Barbuda. The tiny island of Redonda is now a nature preserve. The English formed a slave colony on Antigua in 1667 for sugar cane production. In 1981 Antigua and Barbuda became independent. The capital city is St. John's, located on Antigua.

Antigua and Barbuda are islands between the North Atlantic Ocean and the Caribbean Sea. They are essentially limestone and coral. The climate is a steady maritime climate, although hurricanes can occur from July to October. There are limited natural resources and occasional droughts.

Current Waste Practices

Most communities use basic sewer and water services, but little water is treated before being discharged into local water sources. Antigua and Barbuda collects about 136,000 tons of municipal waste a year, with it all landfilled. Not all waste is collected. It is likely that waste is illegally dumped in the surrounding ocean. The waste from the cruise liner tourist trade is a large and unaccounted part of waste practices. Often these vessels, as well as others, empty their bilges before they get to port. The bilges contain all kinds of solid, liquid, and hazardous wastes. They also contain diseases such as typhoid and cholera.

Emissions and Industry

In 2000, Antigua generated 597.8 metric tons of greenhouse gas emissions, a 53.8 percent increase from 1990. This does not include emissions from shipping, so overall emissions are likely to be higher.

Agricultural products include cotton, coconuts, livestock, fruits, vegetables, sugar cane, and mangos. Agricultural emissions accounted for 17.5 percent of all emissions. Within this sector, agricultural fields produced 53.5 percent of emissions, manure management 24 percent, and enteric fermentation 23 percent. This is an unusually high amount of greenhouse gas emissions from manure, indicating the presence of large amounts of untreated feces.

Oil and electricity production and consumption per capita are low. Energy emissions accounted for 62 percent of all emissions. Within this sector, transportation accounted for 49 percent of emissions and energy industries 47.5 percent.

Waste emissions accounted for 20 percent of all emissions. Almost all this comes from solid waste disposal on land. These emissions increased 56 percent from 1990 to 2000. This is an unusually high percentage of emissions from wastes. As e-waste and other wastes enter the island waste stream, it is likely that they are burned with the other garbage. The increase in greenhouse gas emissions from burning this wastes will increase the overall amount of emissions.

Major Waste Issues

Trash on land and in the water is a big problem. Emissions from manure management and from solid wastes are large and indicate large volumes of wastes. Waste issue may begin to threaten the tourist trade and the marine environment.

There are risks of infectious disease. Hepatitis A and B are present. Hepatitis B is present in 2 percent or more of the population. Dengue fever is present in Antigua and Barbuda and has potential to occur because the mosquito that carries it is found on the islands. With increases in temperature from global warming, it is likely that this disease will increasingly occur.

Further Reading

Antigua and Barbuda Government. www.ab.gov.ag.
United Nations Stock Taking Report. www.sustainabledevelopment.un.org.
Vigilance, C., and J. Roberts, eds. 2011. *Tools for Mainstreaming Sustainable Development in Small State*. London, UK: Commonwealth Secretariat.

ARGENTINA

Argentina borders the South Atlantic Ocean, between Chile and Uruguay. It is the eighth-largest country in the world, with 2,780,400 km² and 4,889 km of coastline. The climate is mainly temperate. It is dry in the southeast and sub-Antarctic in the southwest. Argentina's population is approximately 42.6 million, with 90 percent in urban areas and 74 percent living in a city having more than 100,000 inhabitants. About a fifth live in overcrowded conditions and 8 percent suffers malnutrition.

Argentina has environmental problems of deforestation, soil degradation, desertification, and air and water pollution. Argentina did lead the world in setting voluntary greenhouse gas targets. It is a party to many international environmental agreements, including ones controlling hazardous wastes, marine dumping, ship pollution, and climate change.

Current Waste Practices

Most communities use basic sewer and water services, but little water is treated before being discharged into local water sources. Eighty-eight percent of the population receives municipal waste collection. Waste practices vary greatly. What recycling activity there is occurs around Buenos Aires. Some cooperatives recycle solid inorganic wastes, such as glass. New landfills and local recycling programs are starting to grow. About half of the municipal solid waste is organic waste; 16 percent is plastic wastes.

Laws and regulations about waste are poorly implemented. As is the case in many nations, the municipality has the responsibility for waste management without much support from regional or national agencies. Ninety-eight percent of the urban population has access to an improved drinking water source, and 91 percent has access to an improved sanitation facility. Eighty percent of the rural population had access to an improved drinking water sources, and 77 percent had access to improved sanitation facilities. About 10 percent of urban sewage is treated before being discharged into water.

The new National Urban Waste Management Project encourages new landfills and recycling programs. Traditionally most urban solid waste management uses what landfills it can. Most of the trash that is picked up is left at waste transfer stations not far from the cities. As landfills close, waste transfer locations become filled to overcapacity. As in the United States, waste transfer sites are less regulated than landfills. The trash builds up and becomes a public and environmental health hazard. Sometimes the trash heaps are burned. Poor people scavenge the trash heaps for food and useable objects along with dogs, pigs, and rats. The pattern of trash removal is common in many cities. The National Urban Waste Management Project seeks to change this pattern. With the backing of this policy some communities are seeking environmentally sensitive and sustainable approaches. The city of Mar del Plata is one example. With 620,000 people and a collapsed old landfill, the community was ready for some new approaches. The local economy relied on 9 million tourists a year, and the presence of trash and vermin decreased tourist demand. With the help of the National Urban Waste Management Project, a landfill was built under very high environmental standards. It can handle 600 tons of waste a day. It was built with a waterproofing and drainage system, a way to treat landfill leachates, and catchment systems for incinerating greenhouse gases, reducing greenhouse gas emissions and odors. As part of Argentina's National Strategy for integrated municipal waste management, planning is under way for biogas-based energy technologies at the provincial and local level. They expect a design of business models for electricity and heat production based on biogas using digesters with methane recapture from trash. They also want these biogas systems to be adapted to local conditions.

Hazardous Wastes

Argentina is the first country in South America to use nuclear energy. Argentina has 3,234 heavy metal tons of spent nuclear fuel. It has two operating nuclear power reactors, three radioactive waste disposal facilities, eleven radioactive waste storage facilities, and six facilities that process nuclear wastes. Much of the wastes come from uranium mining of six uranium mines and the tailings left behind. Some of the mines are closed but not cleaned up. The Argentine government's strategic plan is planning to dispose of nuclear wastes in "engineered surface systems" for isolating wastes for up to fifty years, large near-surface repositories for isolating radioactive wastes up to 300 years, and deep geological repositories for any that take longer than 300 years to break down safely.

Other hazardous wastes are mixed in other waste streams. In the case of medical wastes, this makes it dangerous to separate and recycle wastes because of health risks of infectious diseases. Medical wastes are a challenge to many nations fighting infectious diseases. They are often incinerated at the medical facility.

Emissions and Industry

The deterioration of the Antarctic ozone layer created a hole in the atmosphere in southern Argentina. Ozone depletion is a climate change that affects people, plants, and livestock because it increases the amount of ultraviolet radiation exposure.

In 2000 Argentina generated 282,000.8 metric tons of greenhouse gases, a 22 percent increase from 1990. With the high rate of economic and industrial growth since then, it is likely that emissions have increased.

Argentina has 27.9 million ha of arable and permanent farmland, the tenth most of 148 nations. Permanent crops such as corn and oats occupy 2.2 million ha, fifteenth most out of 181 countries. Obtaining biogas from agricultural wastes such as manure is a goal. Use of biogas power generation decreases greenhouse gases such as methane. Small-scale biogas pilot projects are in effect, as are about ten large commercial sites, and are expected to move into municipal solid waste biogas technologies. Three current policies focus on implementation challenges for biogas energy from municipal solid waste. These systems require process operation and maintenance. Biogas systems require healthy microorganisms that require a stable control of feedstock and environmental parameters such as temperature and humidity. This is easier with agricultural biogas systems because of the consistency of the feedstock. The cost of biogas is more expensive than grid-based electricity, which is a challenge for implementation. The actual site selection process is also a challenge, as it is for most waste site selection. Chosen sites will have public health and environmental effects, such as of emissions, odors, and water quality. It can also affect the local ways of informally handling wastes, decrease demand for recycling, and affect the quality of life for nearby communities.

Agricultural emissions accounted for 44 percent of all emissions in 2000. Within this sector, expansion of agricultural fields accounted for 52 percent of emissions, enteric fermentation 46 percent, and manure management 1 percent. The livestock sector is a large part of agriculture. Manmade lagoons are often constructed near dairy farms, feed lots, and piggeries and the solid and liquid wastes moved there, where aerobic and anaerobic microbes break them down. From here, the wastes go directly in a nearby creek, stream, river, or lake. Many of the treatment lagoons are over capacity, and the waste does not break down before discharge. Some wastes are not treated by lagoons and go directly into nearby water bodies. There is no waste management planning for livestock wastes. These wastes can overwhelm lakes and rivers and cause ecological degradation.

Argentina relies almost exclusively on fossil fuels to met energy demands. Two-thirds of electricity production is based on fossil fuels. Hydroelectric power contributes a third of energy production. Energy emissions accounted for 47 percent of all emissions in 2000. Within this sector, transportation accounted for 30.4 percent of emissions, energy industries 27 percent, and manufacturing industries and construction 11.6 percent.

There are regulations of industrial wastes. Industrial emissions accounted for 4 percent of all emissions. Within this sector, metal production accounted for 52 percent of emissions, mineral products 29 percent, and chemical industries 9 percent.

Waste accounted for almost 5 percent of greenhouse gas emissions. These emissions increased by almost 50 percent from 1990 to 2000. Within the waste sector, emissions came from disposal of waste on land and wastewater management in equal parts. With the increase in population, rate of growth, and urbanization, it is likely that waste emissions have increased substantially.

Major Waste Issues

Buenos Aires, the capital, is awash with garbage. The Buenos Aires metropolitan area covers 248 km^2 and is home to about 11 million people. The amount of waste is increasing by a third from 2005 to 2009 to approximately 5,000 tons of municipal wastes per day. About a fifth of it goes to two dumps in Ensenada and Gonzalez Catan, which courts have ordered closed. Residents complain of pollution and of leachates' affecting water quality. Two more landfills are planned but are still in the planning stages. Site selection is political and difficult. All this is in the context of a 2006 law called the Zero Garbage Law, which established waste reduction goals of about a third reduction by 2010. So far, the United Nations Millennium Development goals for sanitation are not met and are not likely to meet 2015 deadlines.

There are infectious diseases in Argentina, including a risk of yellow fever, especially in Corrientes and Misiones provinces. Mosquitoes transmit yellow fever. With global warming, the environment suitable for the mosquito will expand. Hepatitis A, B, and malaria are all risks in all or part of the country. Two percent of the country is infected persistently with hepatitis B. Typhoid is transmitted through contaminated water and food. There is a risk of dengue fever in the province of Buenos Aires and northern provinces. Given the increase in waste and the old to non-existent sanitation infrastructure, it is likely that disease vectors will expand.

The urban waste problem is being addressed in some areas. The Buenos Aires urban area recently built twenty waste treatment plants and plans to build fifteen more. This would raise the treated urban sewage rate to 80 percent if the population remained stable. It is an open question whether this is enough to keep up with a rapidly urbanizing population with climate change effects.

Further Reading

Davis, F. 2014. "Review of *Enemy in the Blood: Malaria, Environment, and Development in Argentina.*" *Journal of History of Medicine and Allied Sciences* 69: 329–331.

Pablo Seco Pon, Juan, and Eugenia Becherucci. 2012. "Spatial and Temporal Variations of Urban Litter in Mar del Plata, the Major Coastal City of Argentina." *Waste Management* 32: 343–348.

President of Argentina. www.presidencia.gov.ar.

Sanchez-Triana, Ernesto, and Santiago Enriquez. 2012. Using Policy-based Strategic Environmental Assessments in Water Supply and Sanitation Sector Reforms: the Cases of Argentina and Colombia." *Impact Assessment and Project Appraisal* 25: 175–187.

ARMENIA

The Armenian Soviet Socialist Republic ended in 1990 when the Independent Republic of Armenia was formed. Currently, approximately 3 million people live on Armenia's 28,454 km² of land. Sixty-four percent of the population is urbanized, and 54 percent lives in a city having more than 100,000 inhabitants. Four percent live in overcrowded conditions. Eighteen percent suffers malnutrition.

Armenia's recent industrial and political history affects its current waste landscape. When it was a republic of the Soviet Union, industries such as the chemical industry, electroplating, metallurgy, and mining were dominant. There was little or no little environmental control. The demise of the Soviet Union led to sharp economic decline. Replacing state-run centralized waste management with private-sector waste firms is a challenge. Natural resources became overused as residents' use of firewood led to deforestation. Environmental regulation of waste sites did not exist in policy, planning, or practice. The waste sites of the past did not segregate wastes, so many hazardous wastes from industrial development still remain. In addition, many of these waste sites are still used, making their effect on the environment and on public health is cumulative. As waste continues to be generated, ravines, gorges, creeks, streams, and rivers are now becoming increasingly used as informal trash dumps. Although there are more than 300 streams, many are very small, and some are seasonal. Cleaning these waste sites to levels of public safety is a concern of present-day communities. Even the tourist industry is concerned, because trash is everywhere.

Armenia is landlocked, with Azerbaijan, Georgia, Iran, and Turkey as neighbors. About 15 percent of the land is arable. It is very mountainous, with valleys, plateaus, and plains between mountain ranges. The mountains help keep the climate dry in the winter and hot in the summer, although significant regional variations are partially dependent on altitude. The mountains also feature earthquakes in this region.

Current Waste Practices

Most communities use basic sewer and water services, but little water is treated before it is discharged into local water sources. Armenia collected 411,000 tons of municipal waste in 2009 and all of this waste is landfilled. Almost everyone has access to sanitation facilities. Seventy-two percent of the population receives municipal waste collection. There are about 45 urban landfills and 430 rural landfills. About 1.5 million ton of municipal waste is accumulated per year. There is little recycling. The largest landfill is the Nubarashen landfill, holding 7.5 million tons and receiving about 102,000 tons a year. These landfills are not built or maintained to international standards, including of environmental assessments. Many of these sites contain toxic chemicals that leach into nearby water sources. Armenia established a Waste Research Center in 2005 to research the adverse human health and environmental effects of landfills, classification of hazardous waste standards, and collection and analysis of research on best available pollution control and abatement practices and best environmental practices.

The Ministry of Nature Protection controls environmental policy. The Department of Hazardous Substances and Waste Management focuses on all kinds of waste. These government agencies help implement the National Law on Wastes, adopted in 2004. The goal of this law is to minimize waste generation and increase waste reuse. This law relies on economic incentive, but not all these economic incentives are offered—or large enough.

Nuclear Wastes

Armenia operates one nuclear power facility, which generates a third of the electricity for the country. Radioactive wastes are also generated by some industrial and medical activities. There is one decommissioned nuclear power reactor. There are no disposal, storage, or waste processing facilities. Government policy on spent fuel is still under development. There is controversy about the restart of the Metasmor nuclear power plant because of the seismic activity at the site.

Hazardous Wastes

In 2008, Armenia generated 431,000 tons of hazardous wastes. The import and export of nonhazardous wastes and transboundary transit through Armenia generally occurs without any notice. The import of all wastes for storage and burial is prohibited. The import of wastes and raw materials for reuse is allowed. This issue is compounded by the lack of landfills.

Persistent Organic Pollutants

Persistent organic pollutants (POPs) are powerful chemicals with adverse environmental and public health effects. A common and highly regulated POP are Polychlorinated Biphenyls or PCBs. Eleven other similar chemicals are designated for destruction, with more chemicals proposed. POPs environmental effects include species population decreases, lowered resistance to diseases, and congenital abnormalities. They are spread all around the planet by winds and water. POPs generated in one country can have effects in other countries far away. They also persist in the environment because they can pass from part of the food chain to another. The bioaccumulation of POPs weakens ecotones, such as the Arctic. Armenia's history of uncontained long-term industrial wastes, as well as of both burning them and burying them, raises national and global concern about POPs in Armenia.

Emissions and Industry

In 2006 Armenia generated 6,422.8 metric tons of greenhouse gases. This is a 74 percent decrease from 1990.

Agricultural emissions accounted for 18 percent of all emissions. Within this sector, enteric fermentation accounted for 74.6 percent of emissions, expansion of agricultural fields 20 percent, and manure management 5 percent.

Energy emissions accounted for 69 percent of all emissions. Within this sector, energy production accounts for 21.5 percent of emissions, transportation 21.3 percent, and manufacturing and construction 15.3 percent. Industrial emissions accounted for 5 percent of all emissions. Within this sector, mineral products accounted for all emissions.

Waste emissions accounted for 8 percent of all emissions. Within the waste sector, solid waste disposed on land accounted for 90 percent of emissions and wastewater management 10 percent. This decreased about 10 percent from 1990 to 2006.

Major Waste Issues

Armenia faces many challenges in handling trash. There is no integrated waste management policy. There is inconsistency in waste laws, which hampers enforcement efforts. A large challenge is the lack of information about the scale of the waste issue. Information about amount, content, reusability, and toxicity is not known. This is important for municipal solid waste, because these are goods consumed after a long production and distribution chain with environmental effects all along the way, from resource extraction and manufacturing to consumption and final disposal. Financial resources and technical expertise is a challenge in many communities.

Climate change could dramatically affect Armenia. Climate change observers there note rising temperatures, sea level rise, melting glaciers, and changes to water flow. There are concerns about fires, flooding, and landslides. There is a risk of infectious diseases. Hepatitis A, hepatitis B, and typhoid occur here. More than 2 percent of the Armenian population is persistently infected with hepatitis B. As temperatures increase, it is likely that some vectors will expand, especially mosquito-borne viruses.

Further Reading

Armenian Environmental Network. www.armenia-environment.org/integrated-waste-management-project-iwmp/.

Armenian Parliament. www.parliment.am.

Dvorska, A., et al. 2012. "Obsolete Pesticide Storage Sites and Their POP Release into the Environment-an Armenian Case Study." *Environmental Science and Pollution Research* 19: 1,944–1,952.

Watenpaugh, K. 2014. "Between Communal Survival and National Aspiration: Armenian Genocide Refugees, the League of Nations, and the Practices of Interwar Humanitarianism." *Humanity: An International Journal of Human Rights, Humanitarianism and Development* 5: 159–181.

Yu, Winston, et al. 2014. *Towards Integrated Water Resources in Armenia.* Washington, DC: World Bank Group.

AUSTRALIA

Australia is the smallest continent and the sixth-largest country in the world. Altogether, 20.2 million people reside on Australia's 7.62 million km² of land, with 58,920 km² of water. This includes the island of Tasmania, at 67,800 km². With more than 25,000 km of coastline, Australia ranks seventh among nations having the longest coastlines. Eighty-eight percent of the population is urbanized, and 72 percent lives in a city having more than 100,000 inhabitants. The largest cities are Sydney, Melbourne, Brisbane, Perth, Adelaide, and Canberra. One percent of the populace lives in overcrowded conditions. Life expectancy is 82 years. The death rate from intestinal infectious diseases is 0.62 per 100,000 people, which is very low. Almost everyone has access to sanitation facilities.

The climate varies regionally with temperate conditions in the southeast, tropical conditions in the north, and arid to semi-arid conditions elsewhere. Climate change is monitored because it alters weather patterns. The annual average daily mean temperatures have increased by 0.9 Celsius since 1910. Increased periods of extended drought, fires, and floods are linked to climate change. The average mean sea level increased 210 mm since 1880, and the sea surface temperatures increased by 0.8 degrees Celsius. About 6 percent of the land is arable, and 25,500 km² are irrigated. Australia has more coral reefs than anywhere else in the world—48,960 km².

Current Waste Practices and Recycling

Most communities use basic sewer and water services, but little water is treated before being discharged into local water sources. Australia collected 8,903,000 tons of municipal waste in 2009; almost 70 percent of this waste is landfilled, and 30 percent is recycled.

Australia is second out of seventeen countries in municipal waste generation per person per year. Municipal waste generation per capita is about 690 kg a year. In 2010, about 53.7 million tons of waste were generated and imported. Households generated 12.4 million tons of waste, about half organic and a quarter paper and cardboard. Construction generated about 16.5 million tons; services such as trade, transport, finance, education, and housing another 11.9 million tons; and manufacturing 8.5 million tons; 0.6 million tons of wastes were imported. Other waste sources generated 3.8 million tons. About 3.7 million tons of wastes are exported. These waste measures do not include liquid waste, radioactive waste, mineral wastes from the mining industry, wastewater (untreated effluent, sewage water, and trade waste) air emissions, fly ash (produced by burning wastes, sometimes by incinerators or field burning), and fishing wastes. These other categories of waste, though not counted, do affect the environment and public health.

The main government agency for waste policy is Hazardous Waste Section of the Department of Environment, Water, Heritage, and the Arts. State, territorial, and local governments manage municipal wastes. Eight Australian states and territories have economic incentives for waste management and reductions. In 2009, Australia set a National Waste Policy focusing on less waste and more resources.

The policy listed six areas of waste policy priority. The first is taking responsibility for wastes at every stage from production to consumption all the way to the end of the useful life of the goods. The second emphasizes market-based approaches for waste management, even suggesting the export of Australian waste treatment technologies as part of economic development. The third priority is to pursue sustainability, meaning less waste and more reuse of waste. Another priority is to reduce the hazardous content of wastes through transparent waste recovery, handling, and disposal. The fourth priority is to extend waste management capacity to remote regions and indigenous communities. The last priority is to develop accurate information on the amount, type, transit routes, and destinations of waste.

In terms of recycling early self-sufficiency made reuse of materials a necessity. In 1815, Australia's first paper mill used recycled rags to make paper. In the 1920s, waste paper was collected for reuse in Melbourne. This practice spread throughout Australia in the 1940s.

Recycling of clothes and household necessities by charitable organizations and church groups is a centuries-old tradition. Old clothes are given to organizations that give, or sell for low prices, these items to low-income people in need.

Steel recycling started in 1915. Recycling the metal in cars is a standard practice now, even batteries. Recycling aluminum cans is also a standard practice. In 1975 Australian municipalities began to use magnetic separation to recover steel waste.

There is strong government support for recycling. Curbside recycling began in the late 1980s and now includes metropolitan areas and regional centers. Households separate paper, glass, aluminum, plastics, paperboard milk and juice containers, and steel cans. Plastic bags are separately recycled and increasingly regulated. Organic wastes are increasingly being recycled using composting and mulching approaches. Large-scale worm farming is also used to reduce organic wastes including human and animal wastes. The result is used as organic fertilizer with the hope of replacing chemical fertilizers that form part of the chemical run off into the ocean that affects the viability of the Great Barrier Reefs.

In 1999 Australia agreed to the National Packaging Covenant. This agreement institutionalizes curbside recycling by decreasing the environmental effects of consumer packaging waste and develops policies of product stewardship by the manufacturer and lifecycle environmental management of the consumer good, from production to use to final disposal. The covenant is far-reaching, covering the supply chain for packaging. This includes producers, wholesalers, distributors, retailers, governments, and brand owners of packaging.

E-waste is a growing problem in Australia. E-waste is a broad category of wastes encompassing any used electronic equipment that requires electricity or electromagnetic fields to work and that has reached the end of its useful life—including computers, cell phones, televisions, and electric appliances. E-wastes contain hazardous materials as well as nonrenewable metals. Australia estimates that only 10 percent to 17 percent of these wastes are recycled. Much of this waste is recyclable, and doing so generally reduces its effects on people and the environment. Lead, mercury, phosphorus, and cadmium can leach from landfills and degrade the environment. Gold, silver, nickel, platinum, aluminum, zinc, and copper can also be reused, reducing their effect on the environment, including mining and processing costs of getting them from other sources. E-waste can be recycled efficiently, but efforts are just beginning.

Illegal waste dumping is a problem addressed by the government. Illegal dumping occurs worldwide and generally means dumping solid and hazardous wastes in public areas or remote areas of land, inland waterways, and oceans without approval of the government. Wastes are dumped illegally because of the costs of proper disposal of wastes. They are also illegally dumped to avoid knowledge of the type, source, and destination of wastes. Sometimes waste depots and transfer stations are filled to capacity and illegal dumping occurs because of the lack of an accessible waste depot or repository. Furniture, packaging, organic wastes, construction materials, old tires, abandoned cars, and hazardous wastes are the most frequently illegally dumped goods in Australia. Roadways, bush lands, and multiunit residential units, unsecured property, abandoned structures, and vacant industrial buildings are the locations for most illegal dumping. Dumping of hazardous waste materials is increasing and includes industrial waste, oil and other liquid wastes, asbestos, and medical wastes.

There are many environmental effects of illegal dumping of trash. It can leach contaminants into sensitive ecosystems, block water drainage, and provide exposure vectors of hazardous materials to communities. Illegal dumping is taken seriously in some areas. Some local governments are spending $400,000 annually removing and properly disposing of illegally dumped materials. Other communities are fighting illegal dumping with community education, cleanups, and regulatory enforcement. They provide ways residents can discard wastes, such as scheduled cleanups, on-call cleanups, and accessible waste disposal facilities. Enforcement measures include judicial sentences for illegal dumping convictions that can be as high as $250,000 and seven years in jail. In Western Sydney, a Regional Illegal Dumping Squad works continuously to stop illegal dumping using surveillance, covert operations, helicopters, and trail bikes.

Hazardous Wastes

Australia describes hazardous wastes as waste that poses substantial or potential threats to the public or environment. Following international norms, hazardous waste is characterized by ignitability, reactivity, corrosivity, and toxicity. Hazardous wastes in Australia have increased because of population growth and attendant use of consumer goods and services, increased business in chemical products, increased use of oils and pesticides, increasingly hazardous household waste (such as e-waste), and more medical and pharmaceutical wastes. In 2009, Australia exported 38,620 metric tons of hazardous wastes and imported 16,000 metric tons. It generated 14,470,065 metric tons of hazardous wastes.

Nuclear Wastes

There are no operating nuclear power facilities in Australia, but there is uranium mining. There are two disposal facilities, twelve storage facilities, and one processing facility. Australia does not have a working definition of waste and its categories.

Persistent Organic Pollutants (POPs)

Australia has a National Implementation Plan to fulfill its international treaty obligations to reduce the use, production, and stockpiles of POPs. The plan describes the roles and requirements of Australian government levels, the Environment Protection and Heritage Council, and other chemical management groups. Australia still uses some POPs to kill giant termites.

Emissions and Industry

In 2011 Australia generated 552,286 metric tons of greenhouse gases, a 32.2 percent increase from 1990.

Australia is a large producer and exporter of cotton. Other products include wheat, barley, sugar cane, rice, fruits, cattle, sheep, and poultry. The Australian government assists farm managers and owners in issues such as biodiversity, weed and pest management, soil management, water management, and waste management. In Victoria, owners and occupiers of land have legal responsibilities for farm wastes, though this is not the case everywhere. In order of preference, waste avoidance, reuse, and recycling are prioritized. The least preferable are land disposal, containment, and treatment. Agricultural emissions accounted for 15 percent of all emissions. Within this sector, enteric fermentation accounted for 65 percent of emissions, agricultural soils 17.8 percent, and prescribed burning of savannas 12.3 percent.

Australia is the fourth-largest producer of coal, behind China, the United States, and India. It also produce crude oil and maintains proven reserves. Electricity consumption per capita is high and electricity production per capita slightly less. Oil production per capita is high and oil consumption per capita slightly lower. About 90 percent of electricity is produced from fossil fuels. Australia has large natural gas reserves—an estimated 2.4 trillion ft^3. Energy emissions accounted for 76 percent of all emissions. Within this sector, energy industries accounted for 55 percent of emissions, transportation 21 percent, and fugitive emissions 10 percent. Fugitive emissions are essentially unaccounted waste streams into the air. Fugitive emissions can affect regional ecosystems and public health because they can fall from the air to the land and water. Industrial emissions accounted for 6 percent of all emissions. Within this sector, metal production accounted for 38 percent of emissions, mineral products 20 percent, and chemical industries 18 percent.

Waste emissions accounted for 2.3 percent of all emissions. Within this sector, solid waste disposal on land accounted for 78 percent of emissions, and waste-water handling accounted for 21 percent. Emissions from solid waste decreased by 26 percent from 1990. Although greenhouse gas emissions are generally high, communities in Australia try to decrease them. Because waste is a local service, communities can develop strategies to reduce greenhouse gas emissions by the way solid waste is treated. Some communities are experimenting with waste-to-energy conversion.

Major Waste Issues

Australia faces some major environmental issues that affect its waste policy. Years of illegal dumping will present major clean up challenges in the future as waste effects environmentally accumulate and move through water systems. Overgrazing by livestock and introduced species has created soil erosion. Soil salinity is rising because of the overuse of poor-quality water. The Great Barrier Reef is threatened by soil runoff, industrial wastes, pesticides, and other trash; increasing use in shipping; and increased tourism. Both shipping and tourism increase the waste generated in and around the Great Barrier Reef.

The geographic location of Australia makes it prone to ecological changes and rapid temperature increases due to global warming. As an island country, it will directly face many of the challenges of rising ocean levels. Climate change observations note increased temperatures, increases in the intensity and frequency of severe drought, and fluctuations in season lengths and intensity. The projected effects of climate change are continued increases in temperature, decreases in precipitation in some regions, increases in extreme rainfall events, and increases in drought. There is concern about the contamination of the water supply: Australia is vulnerable to freshwater limits. Another vulnerability is the extreme differences in annual rainfall from year to year. This affects ecosystems, agriculture, and public safety. Primary concerns are water quantity, water quality, water sanitation, extreme weather events, and ecosystems. Some of the water quality issues are increased salinity of freshwater and increases in toxic algae blooms. Australia is developing a water supply system using desalinization plants and pipelines. Drought is the main extreme weather event, especially in southwest Australia. Some parts of northern Australia may get more floods. The government of Australia is actively and dynamically developing new environmental and waste policy in response to climate changes.

There are some risks of infectious disease. Hepatitis A, hepatitis B, and Japanese encephalitis occur here. Two percent or more of the populace is persistently infected with hepatitis B. Japanese encephalitis is transmitted to humans from animals, such as pigs and birds, via mosquito. A vaccination is available. Dengue is a risk in the state of Queensland. Though it is likely that vectors will increase from some waste-based infectious diseases, Australian communities and all levels of government are focused on planning for this.

Further Reading

Australian Government Dept. of the Environment. www.environment.gov.au.

Christoff, Peter. 2013. *Four Degrees of Global Warming: Australia in a Hot World.* New York: Routledge.

Climate Change Impacts on Water Systems. www.oecd.org.

Dufty-Jones, Rae, and John Connell. 2014. *Rural Change in Australia: Population, Economy, Environment.* Burlington, VT: Ashgate Publishing Co.

Heijnen, Marieke, et al. 2014. "Shared Sanitation versus Individual Household Latrines: A Systematic Review of Outcomes." www.plosone.org.

Waste Management Association of Australia. www.askives.com/how-is-waste-management-done-in-australia.html.

AUSTRIA

Austria was a small nation after its defeat in World War I. It was occupied by Nazi Germany in 1938. With the defeat of Germany in World War II, Austria was occupied by the Allies. In 1955 Austria became independent nation. In 1995 it entered the European Union. It is now a democratic nation with substantial economic power. It often leads the world in its approaches to wastes. It is home to approximately 8.4 million people, who live on 83,871 km² of land. Two-thirds of the population is urbanized, and 37 percent lives in a city having more than 100,000 inhabitants. Two percent live in overcrowded conditions.

Almost everyone has access to sanitation facilities. The death rate from intestinal infectious diseases is 0.13 per 100,000 people, which is very low. Most of the population resides in the eastern lowlands. The mountains do have communities, and tourism inflates the population and the volume of trash during skiing and hiking seasons. However, the steep slopes and avalanche and landslide risks, poor growing soils, and long periods of cold weather make year-long residency low.

It has many neighboring countries, including the Czech Republic, Germany, Hungary, Italy, Liechtenstein, Slovakia, Slovenia, and Switzerland. The main river is the Danube. The climate is temperate, with cloudy and cold winters. The terrain is mountainous, with six peaks more than 3,500 m (11,483 ft). Mountain snow is possible year round. In the valleys, summers are cooler with passing showers. Global warming and other climate changes could change current climatic conditions in Austria.

Current Waste Practices and Recycling

There is universal access to sanitation. There are tours of its extensive sewer and tunnel system. There is about 100,000 km of public sewers in Austria. Sewer maintenance, including cleaning, is the responsibility of wastewater utilities. These utilities operate via municipalities. In sewer systems everywhere deposits build up and restrict the capacity of the sewer system. This can increase storm water overflow discharges into water. This overflow can be untreated wastes. As Austrians value their rivers and fish, they require that sewers be cleaned. Most sewer systems are designed to be self-cleaning using gravity and water flow. However, blockages, floods, and pipe corrosion require cleaning. Recently new applications to sewer cleaning are using a zoom camera to do sewer inspections, specifically assessing the degree of sediments. This helps focus cleaning efforts where they are needed the most. There is also experimentation with using different kinds of jet sprays to clean sewers.

Austria collects 4,941,000 tons of municipal wastes. Less than 1 percent is landfilled. About 30 percent is incinerated, 30 percent recycled, and 40 percent composted. Everyone has municipal waste collection services. Austria generates about 560 kg per capita per year. It spends about $10.80 per capita per year for municipal waste treatment.

Austria recycles about 63 percent of the municipal solid wastes, among the highest in Europe. Even though waste generation increased by 7 percent from 2001 to 2010, recycling rates remained stable. Austrian future predictions of recycling project rates as high as 70 percent. Beginning in 1991, all municipal waste incineration plants has energy recovery systems for heating the community. Austria was an early adopter of all policies to divert biodegradable municipal waste from landfills, and now puts very little biological municipal wastes into landfills. In 1992 Austria began a separate waste collection practice that included biogenic wastes. About 105 kg/capita was collected separately in 2008. One reason for separate collection of wastes is to improve the quality of the compost produced to decrease its environmental effects and increase its value. In 2004 Austria implemented a landfill ban that prohibited waste having a total organic carbon content more than 5 percent.

Austria uses seventeen mechanical biological treatment plants. This is part of the municipal solid waste stream that is not separated out, called "residual." The process begins with separating the wastes into three groups—metals, plastics, and biodegradable wastes. The amounts of hazardous materials in biologically treated output are often too high for use as compost. The waste output of this treatment process is about 57 percent biologically treated, 40 percent incinerated, and 2.2 percent recyclable metals. Austria uses forty-two operating waste incineration facilities.

Austrians have used large, slow-burning wood and coal stoves for heat for many years. The use of incinerators to treat wastes is embraced by the Austrian government. Incinerators are controversial, because even if heat is retained, there are environmental effects on surrounding land, air, and water. The incinerator or "thermal" waste treatment technology is dynamic, but essentially combustion is used to burn wastes—sometimes all kinds of waste and other times a specific type of waste. Heavy metals and chlorinated organic chemicals can enter the incinerator. Heavy metals are spread as emissions in incinerators through stack gases and tiny particulate matter. This includes lead, cadmium, and mercury. Chlorinated organic chemicals undergo changes that turn them into dioxins and are released in stack gases and residual ashes. In addition to dioxins, other chemicals, such as PCBs, PAH, and VOCs, are released into the atmosphere. These chemicals are particularly toxic and are the subject of international law. These chemicals tend to persist in the environment for a long time. They resist degradation as they move through ecosystems and cause harm to living organisms. They also tend to bioaccumulate in living organisms. Although the sheer bioaccumulation of a chemical could be considered safe, most people would avoid chemical bioaccumulation if given the choice. These particular groups of chemicals are not safe. They are toxic because of their adverse effects on people and on the environment.

The Austrian Federal Waste Management Plan outlines the national policy toward waste management. Each company having more than twenty employees submits a waste management concept to the government. The Austrian Waste Management plan of 2011 lists all recycling and waste treatment facilities, including other waste processing facilities. The capacity for single facilities, such as incinerators, is listed.

Government and educational institutions support community capacity building, higher education, and training on waste and water management issues. Training for water supply operators and sewer networks is well established. Courses in biological sewage treatment, safe drinking water, sanitation, ecosystems, recycling, and organic farming are offered frequently.

Austria exerts hazardous waste controls that go beyond many international requirements. They have no controls on the transit of hazardous wastes. In 2009, 1,809,000 metric tons of hazardous wastes were generated. 345,616 metric tons were exported along with 148,248 metric tons of other wastes. 213,493 metric tons of hazardous wastes were imported, along with nonhazardous wastes of 35,728 metric tons. Austria is at the forefront of international environmental policies on hazardous wastes.

Nuclear Wastes

The 1989 Chernobyl nuclear accident drifted into Austria, and it is still affected by the incident today. Cesium-137, a radioactive isotope, is still found in the soil. Its half-life is about thirty years. Although there is not much research, communities are concerned with higher rates of cancer in these areas. In 1978, Austria closed a new nuclear power plant.

Austrian federal constitutional law forbids the handling of any kind of nuclear weapons or nuclear power plants. In Austria, the producers of radioactive wastes are responsible for the safe storage and treatment of the wastes they generate. This includes the costs of storage, treatment, and long-term waste disposal costs. This is an application of the "polluter pays" principle. Sometimes they will return sealed containers to the manufacturer for disposal if it can be found. Because they have no nuclear reactors, they have no facilities for spent fuel and other high-level radioactive wastes. There are other mid- and low-level radioactive wastes, and Austria strictly regulates all aspects of their movement, storage, and treatment.

Austria has one nuclear waste storage facility and two processing facilities.

Emissions and Industry

Austria generated 80,059 tons of greenhouse gases in 2012, representing a 0.1 percent increase from 1990.

There is only 1.39 ha of arable land. The many farms that exist in Austria are small. About 80 percent of national food demand is met by farming. Cotton is exported. Other products are grains, potatoes, wine, fruit, dairy products, cattle, pigs, poultry, and lumber. Wheat and corn are imported. Fertilizer consumption was 208,300 metric tons in 2002. Agricultural emissions accounted for 9 percent of all emissions. Within this sector, enteric fermentation accounted for 43 percent of emissions, agricultural soils 41 percent, and manure management 16.5 percent. This is a high amount of greenhouse gas emissions from manure, indicating the presence of large amounts of untreated feces.

Austria produces a small amount of crude oil and maintains proven reserves. It does have proven natural gas reserves of about 10.82 billion m^3, but little natural gas production. Electricity consumption and production per capita is low. Oil consumption is slightly higher than oil production per capita. There are hydropower resources.

Energy emissions accounted for 75 percent of overall emissions. Within this sector, transportation accounted for 36 percent of greenhouse gas emissions, manufacturing industries and construction 26 percent, and energy industries 21 percent. Industrial emissions accounted for 14 percent of all emissions. Within this sector, metal production accounted for 50 percent of emissions, mineral products 27 percent, and chemical industries 6 percent.

Wastes accounted for 2 percent of all emissions. Within this sector, solid waste disposal on land accounts for 73 percent of emissions and wastewater handling 17 percent. Some wastes are incinerated. There are current waste treatment programs with waste-to-energy conversion.

Major Waste Issues

Austria is a model of effective waste policies in many areas, such as recycling. It is a party to most of the major international treaties and European Union agreements on waste reduction on all levels. The environmental cost of being a crossroads for Europe includes air pollution. Substantial air and soil pollution accumulations are degrading forests. In 1990, 37 percent of the forests suffered acid rain damage. Air pollution comes from coal and oil fueled power stations, industrial trucks, and the many trucks driving through Austria. Soil pollution is from agricultural chemicals used for fertilizer and pesticides.

Persistent organic pollutants (POPs) are powerful chemicals with adverse environmental and public health effects. Austria is a party to many international treaties, including the Stockholm Agreement to eliminate POPs. In the mountainous regions, there is concern that some POPs may accumulate in other nearby alpine areas.

There are some infectious disease risks. Hepatitis A and tick-borne encephalitis (TBE) occur here. TBE occurs mainly below 1,400 m and when the ticks are most active, generally March to November. With temperatures rising, the environment for ticks may expand to higher altitudes and have a longer season of potential exposure.

Austria is preparing for climate change. Climate change observations note increases in temperature, decreases in mountain snowfall, and glacial shrinking.

Projected effects include fluctuations in seasonal precipitation distribution, reduction in duration of mountain snow cover, glacier retreat, melting of mountain permafrost, and increased landslides, mudslides, and avalanches. Projected increases in hydropower are analyzed. The increased sedimentation in the water may overload current hydropower technology. Austria's key vulnerability is its mountainous terrain. Mountain ecosystems are very sensitive to climate changes. Primary concerns are around water quantity, supply, and sanitation. There is concern about extreme weather events and ecosystem damage in some mountainous regions. There is also concern about longer droughts in southeastern Austria.

Further Reading

Austrian Parliament. www.parlament.gv.at.

Climate Change Impacts on Water Systems. www.oecd.org.

Goetz, Jason N., et al. 2014. "Modeling Landslide Susceptibility for a large Geographical Area Using Weights of Evidence in Lower Austria, Austria." *Engineering Geology for Society and Territory* 2: 927–930.

Nowak, O., et al. 2015. "Ways to Optimize the Energy Balance of Municipal Wastewater Systems: Lessons Learned from Austrian Applications." *Journal of Cleaner Production* 88: 125–131.

AZERBAIJAN

Azerbaijan was annexed by the Soviet Union in 1922 but declared its independence in 1991. There is still conflict over the Nagorno–Karabakh enclave with Armenia. Corruption in government is a problem, and presidential term limits were eliminated in 2009. Petrochemical development has helped finance recent reductions in poverty and improvements in basic infrastructure. The capital city is Baku, which has one of the biggest and best harbors for petrochemicals in the Caspian Sea. Altogether, 9.6 million people live on Armenia's 86,000 km² of land. Fifty-two percent of the population is urbanized, and 23 percent lives in a city having more than 100,000 inhabitants. About a quarter suffers malnutrition. The life expectancy is 72 years. There are many small communities throughout the country.

Azerbaijan borders Armenia, Georgia, Iran, Russia, Turkey, and the Caspian Sea. The climate is warm and dry, with regional differences. In the northern mountainous region, it is colder. Along the Caspian Sea coast, the weather is moderate, with cooler temperatures and more rainfall. The terrain is varied, though much of the land is flat. About 7 percent to 10 percent of the land is arable. The Great Caucasus Mountains rise up to the north. Natural resources include oil, gas, bauxite, and iron ore.

Current Waste Practices

Waste practices can be basic, especially in rural areas. Pit toilets, latrines, cesspools, drainage ditches, and open defecation are the options. Large cities have more modern sewer and water facilities. Eighty-eight percent of the urban population has access to an improved drinking water source, and 71 percent has access to an improved sanitation facility. Seventy-one percent of the rural population had access to an improved drinking water sources, and 78 percent had access to improved sanitation facilities. Water quality is very poor. In 2009, 1,603,000 tons of municipal waste was collected, though the amount of waste generated is greater. It is estimated that 24,000 tons of hazardous wastes were generated in 2009.

Emissions and Industry

Azerbaijan generated 43,166 metric tons of greenhouse gases in 1994, a 29 percent decrease from 1990. The largest sector of all emissions is "other" at 77 percent of all emissions. This amount of unaccounted waste can affect the environment and public health. It is likely that emissions are greater than reported.

Agricultural products include tobacco, livestock, cotton, grain, tea, and fruit. Agricultural emissions accounted for 8 percent of all emissions of the reporting sectors. Enteric fermentation accounted for 7 percent of emissions within this sector and agricultural fields for 15 percent. This is a high amount of greenhouse gas emissions from manure, indicating the presence of large amounts of untreated feces.

Azerbaijan produces a substantial amount of crude oil with large proven reserves. Oil production per capita is among the highest in the world. Energy emissions accounted for 10 percent of all emissions. Within this sector, the largest was "fugitive emissions," at 93 percent of emissions. This indicates a lack of monitoring, environmental regulation, and enforcement of environmental laws. It can also indicate pollution at levels that affect the environment and public health. Fugitive emissions are essentially unaccounted waste streams into the air. Fugitive emissions can affect regional ecosystems and the public health, because they can fall from the air to the land and water. Industrial emissions are insufficiently reported.

Waste emissions accounted for 4 percent of all emissions. Within this sector, most of the 80 percent of emissions came from solid waste disposal on land. Waste policy is still developing, and environmental policy overall is still evolving.

Major Waste Issues

The Caspian Sea is one of the most ecologically degraded seas in the world. Highly industrialized pollutants dominate the land, air, and water around most large human settlements along its coast. Numerous oil spills have destroyed land and marine life. Strong agricultural pesticides and defoliants run off into the waterways and into the Caspian Sea.

Climate change observers note increased temperatures and sea level rise. According to the National Climate Change Center of Azerbaijan, water resources are projected to decrease by 15 percent to 20 percent from present-day levels. The Caspian Sea is projected to rise 120–250 cm by 2020–2040. Adaption measures include new dams and reservoirs, improvements to the waste management system, and a plan for reconstruction of existing water and irrigation systems. There is concern about drought and wildfires, as well as flooding along the coast. There is grave concern of the effects on agricultural productivity.

Infectious diseases, such as hepatitis A, hepatitis B, tuberculosis and typhoid, occur here. Two percent or more of the population is persistently infected with hepatitis B. There is some risk of malaria. This is a rapidly urbanizing population. With overcrowding and a weak waste infrastructure, Azerbaijan is likely to increases its infectious disease vectors as temperatures rise. There is little accountability for waste.

Further Reading

Ali, H., et al. 2011. "Study of Arsenic in Drinking Water: A Case Study in East Azerbaijan Province." *Medical Journal of Tabriz University of Medical Sciences* 33: 25–31.

Aliyeva, Gulchohra, et al. 2012. "The Legacy of Persistent Organic Pollutants in Azerbaijan: An Assessment of Past Use and Current Contamination." *Environmental Science and Pollution Research* 20: 1993–2008.

Ministry of Ecology and Natural Resources of Azerbaijan Republic. www.eco.az.

President of Azerbaijani. www.president.gov.az.

B

BAHRAIN

Bahrain means "two seas" in Arabic. Altogether, 1.2 million people live on 758 km^2 of an archipelago in the Persian Gulf; 0.97 percent of Bahrain's inhabitants are urbanized, and 26 percent live in a city having more than 100,000 inhabitants.

Bahrain is a group of islands in the Gulf of Bahrain. It is northwest of Qatar and east of Saudi Arabia. Bahrain is connected to Saudi Arabia via a causeway. The terrain is mostly flat, rising slightly higher toward the interior. It is a desert climate. Summers are very hot and humid. There are droughts and dust storms, with warm, dry winters. Natural resources include oil, gas, and fish.

Current Waste Practices

Everyone has municipal waste collection services and access to an improved drinking water sources and a sanitary facility. In 2009, Bahrain generated 35,000 tons of hazardous wastes.

Emissions and Industry

In 2000, Bahrain generated 22,372.8 metric tons of greenhouse gases, a 14 percent increase from 1994.

Agricultural emissions accounted for none of the greenhouse gas emissions. Within this sector, agricultural soils accounted for 60 percent of emissions, enteric fermentation 38 percent, and manure management 1 percent.

Bahraini crude oil production is high and their proven reserves are large. Electricity consumption per capita is among the highest in the world. Energy emissions accounted for 77 percent of all emissions. Within this sector, energy producing industries accounted for 41 percent of emissions. Manufacturing industries and construction accounted for 41 percent of the emissions. Industrial emissions accounted for 11 percent of all emissions. Within this sector, metal production accounted for 77 percent of emissions and the chemical industry another 25.4 percent. Petrochemical oil refineries produce large amounts of fugitive and "de minimis" emissions that are not included in international reports, so the figures listed here for greenhouse gases may actually be too small.

Waste emissions accounted for 11 percent of emissions in 2000. Emissions increased about to 12 percent from 1994 to 2000. All emissions within this sector come from solid waste disposal on land. It is likely that much of the waste stream is not accounted for in shipping, and because shipping is dominated by oil tankers, it is likely that actual greenhouse gases are higher.

Major Waste Issues

Serious environmental degradation is caused by pollution. Bahrain is a hub for the international transportation of Mideast petroleum products. There are frequent oil spills every year. Nearby coral reefs and plants have decreased. Freshwater is often polluted. Bahrain relies on desalinization plants for more and more of its potable water.

Bahrain is an urban nation likely to experience temperature increases from global warming. An increase in violent weather may increase drought and dust storms. Rising ocean levels will challenge pollution control and abatement efforts on these islands. There are infectious diseases there now. Hepatitis A and B occur here. Bahrain is an island nation with a functional sanitation system for now. It is unknown how much illegal ocean dumping occurs. Bahrain is both a destination and transfer point for international commercial and tourist travel, and this may expand infectious disease vectors. Bahrain is currently a wealthy country and could develop public health systems that mitigate the public health and ecological effects of pollution.

Further Reading

Al-Sayyad, A., and R. Hamadeh. 2014. "The Burden of Climate-Related Conditions Among Laborers at Al-Razi Health Center, Bahrain." *Journal of the Bahrain Medical Society* 25: in press.

El-Khoury, Gabi. 2014. "Water Indicators in Arab Countries: Selected Indicators." *Contemporary Arab Affairs* 7: 339–349.

Kingdom of Bahrain Portal. www.oservices.bahrain.bh.

Larson, Kurtis. 1983. *Life and Land Use on the Bahrain Islands: The Geoarchaeology of an Ancient Society*. Chicago: University of Chicago Press.

Musawi, M. 2013. "Rotavirus Gastroenteritis in Children Under 5 Years in the Kingdom of Bahrain: Hospital Based Surveillance." *Clinical Epidemiology* 5: 269–275.

Sabbagh, M., et al. 2012. "Resource Management Performance in Bahrain: A Systematic Analysis of Municipal Waste Management, Secondary Material Flows and Organizational Aspects." *Waste Management and Research* 30: 813–824.

BANGLADESH

Bangladesh is a tropical, weather-battered, and poverty-stricken nation in Asia. The 149 million people of Bangladesh live on 147,570 km^2 of land. A quarter of the people are urbanized, and only 9 percent live in a city having more than 100,000 inhabitants. There are many small communities in Bangladesh. Almost half the populace suffers malnutrition. A third lives below international poverty levels. The life expectancy is 63 years.

Bangladesh borders India, Myanmar, and the Bay of Bengal. The terrain is mainly flat. The many tributaries of the Ganges and Brahmaputra rivers transverse this low-lying nation. There are many small deltas inland and large delta and estuaries near the Bay of Bengal. There are rolling hills in the southeast. Floods and drought occur in low-lying areas. The water table fluctuates wildly. It receives some of the highest amounts of rain in the world. Just under half of the populace lives within 10 m of sea level. The climate is tropical, and the summers are very hot and humid. The winters are warm. The monsoon season is June to October. Natural resources include timber, gas, and coal.

Current Waste Practices

Waste practices are basic—drainage ditches, cesspools, latrines, pit toilets, and open defecation. Eighty-five percent of the urban population has access to an improved drinking water source, and 57 percent has access to an improved sanitary facility. Eighty percent of the rural population has access to an improved drinking water sources, and 55 percent has access to an improved sanitary facility. The death rate from intestinal infectious diseases is 25.2 per 100,000 people, which is high. The open defecation rate in 2012 was 40 percent, down from 86 percent in 1990.

76,000 tons of hazardous wastes were generated in 2005. Bangladesh recycles end-of-life ships for steel and other recyclable materials and shares 70 percent to 80 percent of the global market with Pakistan and India. This industry develops in countries with very low labor costs, little occupational safety, and little environmental law enforcement. Many ships contain wastes and hazardous materials and can pose threats to human health and the environment. Instead of properly disposing of hazardous and toxic wastes, many vessels at end of life load up with them and bring them into this type of recycling market.

Emissions and Industry

Bangladesh generated 99,442.2 metric tons of greenhouse gases in 2005, a 116 percent increase from 1994. Much of this increase is a function of the waste produced by a surging population growth rate and the need for food.

Almost 62 percent of the land is cultivable, one of the highest percentages in the world. Agricultural products include bananas, tea, tobacco, jute, wheat, spices, and fruit. Agricultural emissions accounted for 43 percent of all emissions. Within this sector, manure management accounted for 41 percent of emissions, enteric fermentation 24 percent, rice cultivation 18 percent, and agricultural soils 16 percent. This is an unusually high amount of greenhouse gas emissions from manure, indicating the presence of large amounts of untreated feces. Feces is often considered a fertilizer and when so used can emit greenhouse gases.

Electricity can intermittent. The power grid is down for most of the year. In 2002, the grid was down 249 days, among the least functioning in the world. Bangladesh is among the top producers of crude oil, with high proven reserves. It is among the lower end of oil consumption per capita. Energy emissions accounted for 39 percent of all emissions. Within this sector, energy industries accounted for 33 percent of emissions, manufacturing industries and construction 29 percent, and transportation 14 percent. It is likely that emissions from energy are higher than reported because of the lack of environmental monitoring of the petrochemical and recycling industries. Industrial emissions accounted for 3 percent of all emissions. Within this sector, the chemical industry accounted for 97 percent of emissions and mineral products for 3 percent.

Waste emissions accounted for 15 percent of all emissions. Within this sector, wastewater handling accounted for 98 percent of emissions and solid waste disposal on land 2 percent. It is likely that emissions are higher, because these figures do not include emissions from shipping.

Major Waste Issues

The main environmental issues in Bangladesh are pollution of the land and water. People farm flood-prone land that is saturated in polluted water. Agricultural pesticide runoff and naturally occurring arsenic have contaminated groundwater, found in almost 85 percent of the nation.

The major waste issue is the threat to the public health from pollution. The greenhouse gas emissions from manure management are among the highest in the world. There are numerous infectious diseases here. Cholera, diphtheria, hepatitis A, hepatitis B, dengue fever, Japanese encephalitis, malaria, and typhoid all occur. Two percent or more of the resident population is persistently infected with hepatitis B. Japanese encephalitis is not well documented but is presumed to be widespread in Bangladesh. Typhoid fever is highly endemic. There are areas of consistently high malaria risks.

With global warming, more violent weather, and rising ocean levels in the context of poor to non-existent sanitation, Bangladesh will experience growth of infectious disease vectors. The number of hospital beds and doctors per capita is among the lowest in the world. The rate of infant mortality is high. International engagement is necessary to prevent future outbreaks of infectious diseases from becoming epidemics.

Further Reading

Bangladesh Government. www.bangladesh.gov.

Huda, T., et al. 2012. "Interim Evaluation of a Large Scale Sanitation, Hygiene and Water Improvement Program on Childhood Diarrhea and Respiratory Disease in Rural Bangladesh." *Social Science and Medicine* 75: 604–611.

Lewis, David. 2011. *Bangladesh Politics, Economy, and Civil Society.* Cambridge, UK: Cambridge University Press.

Minamoto, K., et al. 2012. "Short and Long Term Impact of Health Education in Improving Water Supply, Sanitation and Knowledge about Intestinal Helminths in Rural Bangladesh." *Public Health* 126: 437–440.

Responding to the Impacts of Climate Change. www.christianaid.org.uk.

BARBADOS

Barbados is an island in the Caribbean Sea, with a population of 273,000 people and a total area of 430 km. The terrain is flat and rises to the interior, with 97 km of coastline. Fifty-three percent of the population is urbanized, and 4 percent lives in a city having more than 100,000 inhabitants. Three percent lives in overcrowded conditions.

A narrow coastal plain and many ocean beaches make this nation a popular tourist destination. The climate is tropical—hot and humid. The rainy season is from June to October. Natural resources include oil, gas, and fish.

Current Waste Practices and Recycling

Almost everyone on the island has access to sanitation facilities. The government agency responsible for waste policies and laws is the Ministry of the Environment, Water Resources, and Drainage in the Environmental Protection Department. Waste generators are responsible for the disposal of their own wastes prior before export in consultation with the Environmental Protection Department. There are no disposal or recovery/recycling facilities available.

Emissions and Industry

In 1997 Barbados generated 4,056.4 metric tons of greenhouse gases, a 24 percent increase from 1990. Because greenhouse gases from shipping are not included, this is likely to be higher now.

Agricultural products include sugar cane, vegetables and cotton. Agricultural emissions accounted for only 1.6 percent of all emissions. Within this sector, agricultural soils accounted for 60 percent of emissions, enteric fermentation 35 percent, and manure management 4.6 percent.

Energy emissions accounted for 50 percent of all emissions. Within this sector, energy industries account for 80 percent of emissions and transportation 12.4 percent. Much of these emissions are from diesel fuel imported to run generators for power. Industrial emissions accounted for 4 percent of all emissions. Within this sector, mineral products accounted for all emissions.

Waste emissions accounted for 44 percent of all emissions. Emissions from waste increased 1,025 percent from 1994 to 2005. Emissions from waste skyrocketed because of improved and inclusive environmental monitoring as well as population growth and very limited space for waste disposal. It is likely that significant illegal dumping of wastes occurs.

Major Waste Issues

With the rise in population and tourism, public health becomes a major waste issue. Trash heaps and ocean beaches with trash negatively affect the tourist trade. Tourists themselves come from all over the world. Hepatitis A, hepatitis B, and the Chikungunya virus occur here. The Chikungunya virus was thought to be limited to Africa, but there were four outbreaks as of September 2014.

Current environmental problems are also waste problems, such as wastes from shipping. Illegal solid waste disposal sites have leached into groundwater sources of freshwater. Climate changes and attendant rising ocean levels and violent weather will have significant effects on Barbados. Higher temperatures and flooding will expand some infectious disease vectors.

Further Reading

Barbados Government Portal. www.gov.bb.

Ministry of the Environment, Water Resources, and Drainage. October 2009. *National Report to the United Nations Commission for Sustainable Development: Chemicals, Mining, Transport, and Waste Management.* Barbados: Barbados Environment Division.

Nurse, L., et al. 2012. "Confronting the Challenges of Sewerage Management in the Caribbean: A Case Study from the Island of Barbados." *Environment: Science and Policy for Sustainable Development* 54: 30–43.

BELARUS

In 1988, almost three-quarters of the nuclear fallout from the Chernobyl nuclear disaster fell on the Belorussioan Soviet Socialist Republic, now Belarus. Many people, animals, and plants suffered radiation poisoning. Cancer rates and other health anomalies persist today. The 9.6 million people live on 207,600 km² of land. Seventy-two percent are urbanized, and half live in a city having more than 100,000 inhabitants. The capital and largest city is Mensk (Minsk), with 1,837,000 people.

Five percent of the population suffers malnutrition. The death rate from intestinal infectious diseases is 0.43 per 100,000 people, which is very low. The infant mortality is very low, at about 6 per 1000. Life expectancy is about 72 years. However, long-term health effects from the Chernobyl nuclear explosion include a 40 percent increase in congenital birth defects.

Belarus is landlocked and borders Russia, Latvia, Lithuania, Poland, and Ukraine. It is primarily flat, with historically good agricultural soils. Rolling forested lowlands mix with wetlands, forty-two rivers and streams, and 11,000 lakes. About a third of the country is forested. It has a temperate climate, with cool and wet winters and cool and humid summers. Natural resources include timber, dolomite, granite, peat, oil, natural gas, and chalk.

Belarus has a relationship with Russia based on energy and industrialization. In 2011, Russia loaned Belarus $3 billion in exchange for the sale of Belarus factories to Russian companies. That November, Russia loaned another $14 billion for control of the natural gas pipeline running to Europe. Due to human rights violations and other political issues, the European Union drew back from Belarus in 2012. The elections of 2012 were confrontational. The winning side claimed a 74 percent voter turn out and the losing side, which boycotted the election, 19 percent.

Current Waste Practices and Recycling

All of the urban population has access to an improved drinking water source, and 91 percent has access to an improved sanitary facility. Most of the larger communities have sewer systems and cisterns for sewage wastes, though very little is treated before being discharged into water.

Belarus collects about 3,347,000 metric tons of municipal waste in 2009. Everyone has municipal waste collection service. Almost all this waste is disposed of in landfills, which range from open trash heaps in the country to sanitary landfills to hazardous waste treatment facilities with landfills as part of the process.

Recycling is challenged by the possible radioactivity of recyclable materials, such as metal. If radioactive metals were recycled, the effects of radiations would spread into the recycled metals market. In March 2014, Belarus enacted a recycling tax on cars. With the rise of e-waste in waste streams, Belarus is facing a problem of landfill space and appropriate waste disposal.

There are no nuclear power plants, but Belarus has fourteen nuclear waste disposal, two storage, and zero processing facilities. Radioactive wastes are generated from medicine, industry, research, and remediation of the Chernobyl nuclear explosion.

Emissions and Industry

In 2011 Belarus generated 26,146.9 tons of greenhouse gases, a 66 percent decrease since 1990. The dramatic decline of population, commerce, and industry after the Chernobyl disaster contributed to the decline in greenhouse gas emissions. Agricultural emissions accounted for 27 percent of all emissions. Within this sector, agricultural soils accounted for 61 percent of emissions, enteric fermentation 27 percent, and manure management 11 percent.

Energy emissions accounted for 61 percent of all emissions. Belarus produces crude oil and maintains large proven reserves of both oil and natural gas. Within this sector, energy industries accounted for 55 percent of emissions, manufacturing industries and construction 15 percent, and transportation 12 percent. Industrial emissions accounted for 5 percent of all emissions. Within this sector, mineral processes accounted for 65 percent of emissions and the chemical industry 33 percent. Petrochemical mining, refining, and transit contribute to chemical industry emissions in their production processes.

Waste emissions accounted for about 8 percent of all emissions. Within this sector, solid waste disposal on land accounted for the majority of greenhouse gas emissions. The greenhouse gas emissions gas emissions from waste grew by 152 percent. This surge in the growth of greenhouse gas emissions from wastes even during industry decline indicates a history of illegal waste practices. Post-Chernobyl environmental monitoring increased dramatically, and so did wastes.

Major Waste Issues

The biggest environmental issue in Belarus is nuclear wastes. In 1986, the Chernobyl nuclear power plant in northern Ukraine exploded 16 km south of Belarus. Well over half of the high level radioactive fallout descended on Belarus, affecting 20 percent of the country and 2 million people. More than 160,000 citizens were permanently evacuated from highly contaminated areas. The radiation is now in the soils and underground water. There is a rise of radiation-associated diseases.

Cleanup after the disaster was slow, leaving radiation in water, animals, agricultural products, and wetlands.

Belarus is involved with a number of ongoing projects with the World Bank. The World Bank supports the post–Chernobyl Recovery Project to the tune of $80 million, the water supply and sanitation project for $60 million, an integrated solid waste management project for 42.5 million, and an energy efficiency project for $215 million, achieving the elimination of 1,800 tons of persistent organic pollutants, a policy of integrated environmental regulatory permitting, and eighty-five community projects. Currently, the construction of a waste separation plant in Grodno is expected to divert 20,000 tons of solid wastes from landfills, handling 120,000 tons of waste a year.

Belarus suffers from widespread chemical wastes in the soil, especially pesticides. Large amounts of industrial pollution are found in all major cities. Climate change effects are seen in increased temperatures, variations in rainfall, decreased wind speeds, and changes in snow cover.

Infectious diseases occur here. Diphtheria, hepatitis A, hepatitis B, tick-borne encephalitis, and typhoid all are risks. Two percent or more of the population has hepatitis B persistently. Tick-borne encephalitis currently occurs below 1,400 m and between March and November. Some of these infectious diseases will increase with higher temperatures. The vectors of tick-borne encephalitis may spread to higher altitude and greater distances, lasting for longer seasons. Enhanced public health measures may mitigate urbanization's effect on some disease vectors, such as typhoid.

Further Reading

Agyeman, Julian, and Yelena Ogneva-Himmelberger. 2009. *Environmental Justice and Sustainability in the Former Soviet Union*. Cambridge, MA: MIT Press.

Belarus Government Portal. www.president.gov.by.

Chernobyl Accident. www.world-nuclear.org.

Outon, D., and V. Kashparov, eds. 2009. *Radioactive Particles in the Environment*. Dordrecht, Netherlands: Springer Netherlands.

Wilson, Andrew. 2012. *Belarus: The Last European Dictatorship*. New Haven, CT: Yale University Press.

BELGIUM

Belgium is a small and highly developed western European country. The land area is 30,230 km², with 66.5 km of coast. Altogether, 10.7 million people live here. Ninety-seven percent are urbanized, and 34 percent live in a city having more than 100,000 inhabitants. The capital city is Brussels, which has a population of 1.9 million people.

Belgium borders France, Germany, Luxembourg, the Netherlands, and the North Sea. The terrain is varied. The Meuse and Schelde rivers are important for commercial shipping. There are mountains in Ardennes Forest, but the land is generally flat. The climate is humid, with cool and rainy winters. There are limited natural resources.

Current Waste Practices and Recycling

Everyone has access to improved sanitation and safe drinking water. The death rate from intestinal infectious diseases is 0.84 per 100,000 people, which is low. In Belgium, communities are responsible for collecting and treating household wastes. Sometimes several communities cooperate to do so. The collection and treatment of industrial and hazardous wastes is a legal responsibility of the private sector.

Belgium collects about 5,300,00 ton of municipal waste a year, and from this only about 5 percent was landfilled, about 35 percent incinerated, 35 percent recycled, and about 24 percent composted. The biggest city in Belgium has one municipal waste incinerator. The government charges fees to use it to encourage recycling. Recycling in Belgium is comprehensive. Recycling is assumed to include material recycling and biotreatments. Almost 60 percent of the municipal solid waste stream is recycled, with about a third of that composted. Parts of Belgium have banned new landfills and incineration or heavily taxed them. This increases recycling. There is mandatory waste separation by households, with minimum quality waste thresholds for separated and residual wastes. Beginning in 1995, the Flemish Public Waste Agency developed thirty-one reuse centers with 107 shops. Reuse centers take in a part of the waste stream that includes furniture, clothes, electrical equipment, and toys.

Nuclear Wastes

About 70 percent of the nuclear wastes produced are from the nuclear power industry. The rest comes from nuclear research, medical uses, and industrial uses. Almost half the energy produced in Belgium comes from nuclear power. Belgium was an early adopter of nuclear energy in the 1960s. In 2012, there were seven nuclear power reactors. In 2003, the Belgium government began a gradual phase-out of nuclear energy for commercial electricity production. No new nuclear plants will be built, and the rest will be gradually phased out or decommissioned. Furthermore, the government requires a complete listing of all Belgium nuclear liabilities in the Inventory of Nuclear Liabilities. There is one decommissioned nuclear power reactor, one disposal facility, thirteen storage facilities, and three processing facilities.

Hazardous Wastes

Belgium exerts stronger controls over hazardous wastes than required by international law. Belgium also restricts the transportation of hazardous wastes and other wastes. In 2008 Belgium generated 5,919,000 tons of hazardous wastes.

In 2009 Belgium exported 197,290 metric tons of wastes and 655,288 metric tons of hazardous wastes. 1,417,046 metrics tons of hazardous wastes and 34,370 metric tons of other wastes were imported.

Waste policy in Belgium prioritizes preventing and reducing waste production, preventing or reducing the damaging aspects of waste, recycling wastes, and organizing waste disposal for all wastes that cannot be prevented or recycled. The Flemish hold manufacturers liable for the real and full costs of wastes from their products. This application of the "polluter pays" principle also includes charging households for waste based on volume and weight and charging recycling fees paid at product purchase. Mixed or unseparated wastes are charged higher rates than separated wastes.

Belgium integrates design into waste management issues through a program called "Ecolizer." It is a tool provided by the government to teach designers and goods producing facilities ecodesign principles and application to lifecycle environmental effects.

Belgium also works with industry to reduce waste via environmental policy agreements. These agreements focus on the relationship of government to a particular company. They specify issues of waste prevention, selective waste collections, financing, monitoring, and reporting requirements and schedules. Environmental Policy Agreements are used as management tools to increase the accountability of waste producers and market direction toward recycling. This collaborative relationship allows the Belgian government to more fully understand the business world. It offers the businesses the opportunity to participate in relevant policy activities, giving some protection from legal liability.

The goal of reducing wastes and their hazards rests on basic principles with the goal of separating waste generation from economic growth. First is the "polluter pays" principle, whereby the producer of the waste is responsible for its safe disposal. Landfills are the lowest priorities for waste treatment, and there is a landfill tax. The highest level of waste treatment is recycling. The regional governments develop and assist private markets for recycling and higher levels of waste treatment.

Emissions and Industry

Belgium generated 120,172 tons of greenhouse gases in 2011, a 16 percent decrease from 1990.

Agricultural products include vegetables, meats, and dairy products. Agricultural emissions accounted for 8 percent of all emissions. Within this sector, agricultural soils accounted for 40 percent of emissions, enteric fermentation 37 percent, and manure management 23 percent. This is a high amount of greenhouse gas emissions from manure, indicating the presence of large amounts of untreated feces.

Belgium produces 10,530 bbl of crude oil a day, higher than many small nations. However, it has no proven reserves. Energy emissions accounted for 81 percent of all emissions. Within the energy sector, transportation accounted for 28 percent of all emissions, manufacturing industries and construction 24 percent, and energy industries 23 percent. Industrial emissions accounted for 10 percent of all emissions. Within this sector, 45 percent of emissions came from mineral products and 30 percent from chemical industries.

Waste emissions accounted for between 1 percent and 2 percent of all emissions. Solid waste disposal on land accounted for 41 percent of emissions, incineration

33 percent, wastewater handling 25 percent, and the rest other. Greenhouse gas emissions from waste grew 39 percent from 1990 to 2011 as incineration use grew.

Major Waste Issues

Belgium waste policy emphasizes the formation and development of private markets. Currently, the government is analyzing ways to reduce hazardous wastes using different economic approaches, focusing on positive economic return, private sector financing, and developing the ability to return hazardous wastes to their owners.

As recycling is prioritized, a system of plastic bags to segregate wastes has been implemented in Brussels. Bags of segregated waste are placed on the curbs for pickup. The streets are very narrow, and the use of many separate containers would clog the streets. However, the plastic bags of garbage also clog the streets, and are not as durable as containers.

Belgium has few infectious diseases compared to many other countries. A conscientious approach to waste planning and policy helps Belgium manage possible temperature increases. However, rising ocean levels in the North Sea may present greater challenges.

Belgium is preparing for global climate change. Climate observations note temperature increases, increases in flooding due to increases in ground surface permeability, and more intense droughts. Belgium is vulnerable to flooding and salinization of freshwater. Projected effects include more precipitation and heavy rainfall events. Primary concerns are water quality and quantity, sanitation, floods and droughts, and damage to ecosystems. Belgium is beginning a green spatial planning policy aimed at reducing groundwater fluctuations by reducing paved surfaces. Permeable surfaces allow water to slowly seep into the ground and replenish groundwater more slowly. Belgium is also engaging sustainable development incorporating issues of climate change.

Further Reading

Belgium Government Portal. www.belgium.be.

Climate Change Impacts on Water Systems. www.oecd.org.

Dujardin, J., et al. 2014. "Combining Flux Estimation Techniques to Improve Characterization of Groundwater–Surface Water Interaction in the Zenne River, Belgium." *Hydrogeology Journal* 22: 1,657–1,668.

BELIZE

Belize is a coastal Central American nation, with thick and diverse mangrove swamps and cays along the Atlantic Ocean. The interior is dense, with hardwood forests. Three hundred twelve thousand people live on 22,966 km^2 of land and 516 km of coastline. Belize is racially and ethnically one of the most diverse countries in the world. The Maya, Creoles, Garifuna, and mestizos are the main cultural groups, with Indians, Chinese, and other smaller groups making up the rest of the population. About half of the population is urbanized, and a quarter lives in a city having more than 100,000 inhabitants. Belize is the least densely populated country in South America. Twenty-two percent of the populace suffers malnutrition.

Guatemala, Mexico, and the Caribbean Sea share boundaries with Belize. The climate is tropical, hot, and humid, and with regional differences from the coast to the mountains. The rainy season is May to November, and the dry season is February to May. Belize occasionally gets hurricanes. Forty percent of the population lives within 10 m of sea level.

There are about 450 offshore islands. The third largest barrier reef in the world is off the coast of Belize. The Belize Barrier Reef is about 300 km long, part of a larger reef system called the Mesoamerican Barrier Reef. The Belize Barrier Reef is a very diverse ecosystem. Environmental effects of pollution from increased shipping, tourism, and fishing, along with polluted water runoff from land and increases in ocean temperatures all damage coral reefs.

Current Waste Practices and Recycling

Belize collected 163,000 tons of municipal waste in 2008, all landfilled. Only half of the population enjoys municipal waste collection. There is a substantial amount of illegal dumping, trash heaps, and burning garbage. Belize City and other major communities have basic modern sanitation. In rural areas, waste practices are more primitive. Pit toilets, latrines, drainage ditches, cesspools, and the ocean are used.

Ninety-eight percent of the urban population had access to an improved drinking water source, and 93 percent had access to an improved sanitary facility. Ninety-nine percent of the rural population has access to an improved drinking water source, and 87 percent has access to an improved sanitary facility. This is a big improvement. This World Bank definition means how many people have adequate access to excreta disposal sites. These sites must prevent human, animal, and insect contact with excreta for it to be an improved sanitation facility, so to protect people using these facilities from rats, snakes, spiders, scorpions, and other biting and venomous creatures. It is also to protect the public health from disease vectors such as cholera.

Recycling is just beginning, currently part of informal waste practices. About 75 percent of the waste going to the open dumps and future landfills is recyclable. The Belize Tourism Industry Association runs a project called the Recycling Network of Belize. It is the first of its kind in Belize. It arranges collection centers and waste transport, accepting all kinds of waste, some for free and some for a fees, such as in the case of e-wastes. Belize collects about 165,000 tons of municipal waste a year and disposes of it in landfills. Not all waste is collected, and informal dumps prevail. Belize is currently embarking on a large waste infrastructure project that includes construction of a new regional waste disposal facility, closure of at least four large open dumpsites, and construction of four waste transfer facilities to separate wastes and help recycling. This project commissioned a waste characterization analysis to assess current solid waste generation and create a cost recovery policy for solid waste collection and final disposal.

Emissions and Industry

In 1994, Belize generated 6,335 metric tons of greenhouse gases. This did not include wastes from shipping and tourism, so the actual amount a greenhouse gases today is higher.

There is only 3.3 percent arable land, or about 70,000 ha. Bananas, cacao, sugar, fish, and lumber products are exported. Agricultural emissions accounted for 4 percent of all emissions. Within this sector, agricultural soils accounted for 56 percent of all emissions, enteric fermentation 22 percent, prescribed burning of the savannas 14 percent, and manure management 2 percent.

Belize produces crude oil and maintains proven reserves. Belize also exports oil, about 4,345 barrels per day. Oil production is higher than oil consumption per capita. Electricity production and consumption are low. Recent discoveries of oil are increasing oil exploration efforts. There are now nine companies holding oil exploration licenses. They are doing land and seismic surveys and drilling exploration wells. There are no proven reserves of natural gas. Energy emissions accounted for 10 percent of all emissions. Within this sector, transportation accounted for 52 percent of emissions, energy industries 23 percent, and manufacturing industries and construction 6.6 percent. There were no emissions reported for industry.

Waste emissions accounted for 86 percent of all emissions, which is unusually high. Almost all the greenhouse gas emissions from this sector come from wastewater management.

The garbage disposal site at Dangriga in Belize. This is the main waste disposal site that serves the Garifuna city of Dangriga and the small towns of Silk Grass, Hopkins, and Sittee River. As more expatriots move to the tiny Central American country, cultural differences in waste management practices arise. (Roi Brooks/Dreamstime.com)

Major Waste Issues

Belize faces major waste issues. There is water pollution from sewage, industrial wastes, and pesticide and fertilizer runoff from agricultural processes. Solid waste and sewerage are a problem in many areas.

There is also concern that cruise ships and tourist excursions are dumping trash. There is an informal waste industry, and this influx of trash is an increase in their business. It is a difficult issue, because ecotourism is an important business, and tourists generally do not want to see trash, even though it may be theirs.

There are infectious diseases present in Belize. Hepatitis A, hepatitis B, dengue fever, and typhoid present risks. Two percent or more of the population is persistently infected with hepatitis B. There is currently a low risk of malaria in rural Belize. Climate change effects could be severe. Increased temperatures, rising sea levels in the Caribbean Sea, more violent weather, and international tourism, will increase the vectors of infectious diseases. International efforts to preserve the barrier reef may help focus attention to sanitation issues in nearby Belize City.

Further Reading

Belize Government Portal. www.belize.gov.bz.

Carruthers, David V. 2008. *Environmental Justice in Latin America: Problems, Promise, and Practice*. Cambridge, MA: MIT Press.

Kaminsky, R. et al. 2014. "High Prevalence of Soil-Transmitted Helminths in Southern Belize-Highlighting Opportunity for Control Interventions." *Asian Pacific Journal of Tropical Biomedicine*." 4: 345–353.

Wells, E., et al. 2014. "The Impacts of Tourism Development on Perceptions and Practices of Sustainable Wastewater Management on the Placencia Peninsula, Belize." *Journal of Cleaner Production*: in press.

BENIN

Benin is a west African nation on the Gulf of Guinea. Altogether, 9.9 million people live on 114,763 km^2 of land and 121 km of coastline. The population growth rate is high—almost 3 percent. There are many small communities throughout the nation. Forty percent of the population live in urban areas, and 19 percent live in a city having more than 100,000 inhabitants. Forty-five percent suffers malnutrition. Life expectancy is 60 years. Famine is a major concern; 12 percent of the population suffers from chronic malnutrition.

Benin borders the Bight of Benin, Burkina Faso, Niger, Nigeria, and Togo. The climate is tropical—hot and humid. There are weather extremes, such as floods and droughts. Water quality is decreasing and desertification is an ever-present dynamic. The terrain is flat along the Gulf, rising to a forested and wet plateau, and then to hills and small mountains. Natural resources include timber, oil, marble, and limestone.

Current Waste Practices

Waste practices are basic—latrines, pit toilets, drainage ditches, cesspools., and open defection. Eighty-four percent of the urban population had access to an improved drinking water source, and only 25 percent had access to an improved sanitary facility. Sixty-eight percent of the rural population has access to an improved drinking water source, and just 5 percent has access to an improved sanitary facility. The open defecation rate in 2012 was 54 percent, down from 80 percent in 1990.

Emissions and Industry

In 2000 Benin generated 6,251 metric tons of greenhouse gases, an 84 percent decrease from 1995. The end of oil mining in the 1980s caused a significant decrease in greenhouse gas emissions.

Agricultural products include corn, cotton, yams, cassava, nuts, beans, and livestock. Almost 24 percent of the land is arable, and there is heavy reliance on agriculture. Agricultural emissions accounted for 68 percent of all emissions. Within this sector, agricultural soils accounted for 53 percent of emissions, enteric fermentation 29 percent, prescribed burning of savannas 8 percent, field burning of agricultural residues 3 percent, and manure management 2 percent.

Benin has some proven crude oil reserves but low production. Oil consumption per capita is among the lowest in the world. Ninety-nine percent of installed energy capacity is from fossil fuels. Energy emissions accounted for 30 percent of all emissions. Within this sector, transportation accounted for 48 percent of emissions, and 8.4 percent come from energy industries. Industrial emissions accounted for no greenhouse gas emissions.

Wastes emissions accounted for 2 percent of all emissions. Greenhouse gas emissions from waste decreased by 55 percent from 1995 to 2000. Within this sector, 74 percent of emissions came from wastewater management and 21 percent from solid waste disposal on land.

Major Waste Issues

Public health is the major waste issue. Infectious diseases pose a significant risk here and include yellow fever, cholera, hepatitis A, hepatitis B, meningococcal meningitis, tuberculosis, typhoid, malaria, dengue fever, and schistosomiasis. Two percent or more of the population is persistently infected with hepatitis A. There is a high risk of malaria throughout the country. Benin is part of the Sub-Saharan Meningitis Belt. Public health data is scarce. Six hundred twenty-five cases of cholera and three deaths were reported in 2012. There are periodic outbreaks of meningococcal disease. The death rate from intestinal infectious diseases is 31.38 per 100,000 people, among the highest in the world. The number of hospital beds and doctors per capita is among the lowest in the world.

Benin will be severely affected by global warming. Rising temperatures will expand the vectors of many infectious diseases. Rising ocean levels and violent weather will disrupt a weak to non-existent sanitation system. The expanded and robust disease vectors will lead to increased outbreaks if infectious diseases. Without international engagement, it is likely that these outbreaks will become epidemics.

Further Reading

Benin Government Portal. www.gouv.bj.

Emergency Urban Environment Project. www.worldbank.org.

Jenkins, M., and S. Cairncross. 2010. "Modeling Latrine Diffusion in Benin: Towards a Community Typology of Demand for Improved Sanitation in Developing Countries." *Journal of Water and Health* 8: 166–183.

OECD. 2012. *Benin: Strategic Environmental Assessment in Development Practice*. Paris, France: OECD Publishing.

BHUTAN

Bhutan drapes over the southeast slope of the Himalayas, with large mountains and steep valleys. In 2008, the Bhutan Peace and Prosperity Party won the parliament and began the movement toward a democracy. 726,000 people live on Bhutan's 38,394 km^2 of land. There are mainly small communities throughout this mountain nation. Only 11 percent of inhabitants are urbanized, and just 3 percent live in a city having more than 100,000 inhabitants. Agriculture is the main occupation of about 90 percent of the people. Agriculture contributes about 36 percent of the gross domestic product. About half the population suffers malnutrition. Life expectancy is 63 years.

The climate is regionally different. It is tropical in the southern plains, the central valleys experience cool winters and hot summers, and the Himalayas experience severe winters and cool summers. Parts of Bhutan are very rainy, having among the highest average rainfall in the world. It is a landlocked mountainous country, with China and India as neighbors. Water availability is a problem for many areas, and the situation is getting worse. Natural resources include timber, hydropower, and gypsum.

Current Waste Practices and Recycling

Waste policy is controlled by the National Environment Commission Secretariat. Within these offices, the chief environment officer in charge handles waste issues. Bhutan is just beginning to regulate wastes. The death rate from intestinal infectious diseases is 6.16 per 100,000 people. As part of economic development, the Economic Development Policy included exemptions from sales tax, customs taxes, income tax, and business taxes for waste management in 2010.

Many of the landfills are filled and still accept trash. There are designated dumping sites where trash is occasionally burned. There is informal and sometimes illegal waste dumping. Many rivers are degraded by human waste and trash. One hundred percent of the urban population had access to an improved drinking water source, and 73 percent had access to an improved sanitary facility. Ninety-four percent of the rural population has access to an improved drinking water source, and just 29 percent has access to an improved sanitary facility. The population is growing rapidly and urbanizing quickly, generally without adequate waste infrastructure.

Bhutan's first waste management and recycling effort began in 2010. About 49 percent of solid wastes are organic materials, 25 percent paper, 14 percent plastics, and about 4 percent glass, with textiles, metals, and e-waste making up the rest of the known solid waste flow.

Hazardous Wastes

There is little infrastructure, technology, facilities, or private investment for managing hazardous wastes. There are few restrictions for the export of wastes. Imports of hazardous wastes and other wastes for final disposal are restricted. In 2009, Bhutan enacted the Waste Prevention and Management Act, restricting importation of wastes. The regulations necessary to enforce this law are still being developed.

Emissions and Industry

In 2000, Bhutan generated 1,555.9 metric tons of greenhouse gases, a 20 percent increase from 1994. Air pollution is a problem, with air emissions from India settling in Bhutan. Industrial operations in Bhutan operate without environmental constraint, including three of the four cement plants. Climate change is affecting the mountains by increasing temperature and melting glaciers. This increases landslides, avalanches, and glacial lake outburst floods. The actual amount of glacial loss is controversial in Bhutan. Most of the research indicates that most glaciers are receding, but some may be getting larger.

Only 2.5 percent of land is arable, and the soil quality low in plant nutrients. Agricultural products are rice, corn, citrus, some grains, dairy products, and eggs. Livestock are raised throughout Bhutan. Assessing market value is difficult because of the religious beliefs in Bhutan, which is about three-quarters Buddhist. Buddhism forbids the killing of animals. There are about 250,000 head of livestock. There are many types of rangeland in Bhutan, including alpine grasslands, temperate shrublands, and subtropical forests. Water buffaloes, yaks, cattle, sheep, and other animals are raised on rangelands and on fallow agricultural fields. Rangelands are forests or permanent grasslands owned by the government and provide about half the fodder for livestock. Livestock provide the basis for the rural economy and community, directly providing meat, milk, and clothing. Yak hair is used as a textile. An adult yak produces 1.2 kg of hair and 0.3 kg of wool per year. Some provide power to haul wagons and other farm equipment. In the harsh weather of the Himalayan Mountains, yaks are heavily relied on for the transportation of people and goods. Many farms rely on cattle to provide manure as fertilizer. Chemical fertilizers are used to a small degree, but manure is the primary source of plant nutrients. It is estimated that that the annual wastes of livestock produce 20,000 tons of nitrogen, 4,500 tons of phosphorus, and 33,000 tons of potassium. Manure production is a big factor in livestock management. Even the bedding used by animals is based on soaking up urine. It is then used as fertilizer. Sometimes it is hauled for long distances to cultivate crops and rice. Farmers without livestock will borrow cattle to manure their farms. Sometimes the manure is burned to an ash to make it easier to transport. This loses much of the nitrogen and carbon in the manure, but the phosphorus stays about the same.

Agricultural emissions accounted for 64.5 percent of all emissions. Within this sector, enteric fermentation accounted for 40 percent of emissions, agricultural soils 37 percent, and manure management 17 percent. Manure management, combined with poor to no sewer infrastructure in growing urban areas, may increase these emissions. This is an unusually high amount of greenhouse gas emissions from manure, indicating the presence of large amounts of untreated feces. Manure is a commonly used fertilizer and in the process of decomposition emits methane and other greenhouse gases.

Bhutan has no oil or natural gas reserves, so oil is imported. Energy emissions accounted for 17 percent of all emissions. Within this sector, transportation accounted for 44 percent of emissions and manufacturing and construction 40.3 percent. Industrial emissions accounted for 15 percent of all emissions. Within this sector, 64 percent of emissions were from mineral products, 28 percent from metal production, and 7.7 percent from chemical industries.

Waste emissions accounted for 3 percent of all emissions. Within this sector, 86 percent of emissions came from solid waste disposal on land and 14 percent from wastewater handling.

Major Waste Issues

Current environmental and waste challenges are soil erosion and the lack of safe drinking water. Soil erosion is partially caused by overgrazing and deforestation.

There is a substantial risk of infectious diseases. Cholera, dengue fever, diphtheria, hepatitis A, hepatitis B, Japanese encephalitis, malaria, tuberculosis, and typhoid occur. Two percent or more of the population is persistently infected with hepatitis B. Japanese encephalitis is currently a risk at the southern borders with India, its main transmission time from July to December. The main risk of malaria is along the border with India. With increased temperature, the range of many infectious diseases may grow to include higher altitudes over longer distances and during longer seasons. The number of hospital beds and doctors per capita is among the lowest in the world. The infant mortality is high, and the life expectancy is low. Robust infectious disease vectors will overwhelm a weak public health system and increase the chance that outbreaks of infectious diseases become epidemics. International engagement will be necessary to contain diseases enhanced by global warming.

Further Reading

Bhutan Government Portal. www.nab.gov.bt.

Dorji, D., et al. 2014. "Epidemiology of Helicobacter Pylori in Bhutan: The Role of Environment and Geographic Location." *Helicobacter* 19: 69–73.

Hakcrow, G., et al. 2013. "Developing Behavior Change Communication for Improving Fecal Sludge Management in Bhutan." *Journal of Water, Sanitation, and Hygiene for Development* 131: 2166. London: International Water Association.

Water Environment Federation. 2009. *Manure Pathogens: Manure Management, Regulations, and Water Quality Protection.* Alexandria, VA: WEF Press.

BOLIVIA

Most of Bolivia is at a high altitude, with the Altiplano plateau averaging almost about 3,750 m. Lake Titicaca is the highest commercially navigable lake in the world, with an altitude of 3,812 m. The capital city, La Paz, is the highest administrative capital city in the world at 3,630 m (11,910 ft). Altogether, 10.5 million people are land-locked on 1,098,581 km² of land. Sixty-four percent of Bolivians are urbanized, and 45 percent live in a city having more than 100,000 inhabitants. Forty percent live in overcrowded conditions, and a third suffers malnutrition. Twenty-three percent live under the international poverty rate. Life expectancy is 66 years.

Bolivia borders Argentina, Brazil, Chile, Paraguay, and Peru. The terrain is diverse. From the tall Andes Mountains, the land becomes a plateau, gradually reaching the flat lowlands of the Amazon Basin. The climate is equally diverse. The higher the altitude, the colder and drier the air becomes. In the Amazon Basin it is tropical—hot and humid. The northern and eastern regions comprise the Oriente, a vast lowland area covering two-thirds of the nation. Natural resources include natural gas, timber, gold, oil, silver, iron, tin, zinc, and hydropower.

In 2005 the first ethnically indigenous president, Evo Morales, asserted the rights of the indigenous population and eventually nationalized the energy industry. He also tried to legalize coca as a cultural practice and created an antagonistic relationship with U.S. drug trafficking agencies. In 2013, President Morales expelled the U.S. Agency for International Development. Coca is the source of cocaine, which is illegal in many nations, including the United States. The general reason it is illegal is because of the threat that addiction causes to the public health, safety, and welfare. However, in less developed nations, where everyday and medically necessary painkillers are scarce, use of native plants to relieve pain is traditional. Indigenous people in Bolivia chew the coca leaves. Some is transported to places where it is processed and then transported. Rural Bolivians are very poor and find the small income they receive from this commerce useful for their economic and community development.

Current Waste Practices

Most communities use basic sewer and water services, but little water is treated before being discharged into local water sources. In 2006, Bolivia collected 955,000 tons of municipal wastes. Only 49 percent of the population receives municipal waste collection services. Much of the garbage and trash is taken to open dumps outside human settlements. Ninety-six percent of the urban population had access to an improved drinking water source, but just 35 percent had access to an improved sanitary facility. Seventy-one percent of the rural populations has access to an improved drinking water source, but only 10 percent has access to an improved sanitary facility. Water quality is poor. The death rate from intestinal infectious diseases is 17.42 per 100,000 people, which is high. Little sewage is treated before being discharged into waterways . Seventy percent of urban sewage is not treated before being discharged into water.

Hazardous Wastes

947,334 metric tons of nonhazardous wastes were generated in 2009. There are no disposal facilities and only one or two recovery/recycling facilities. The amount of imported hazardous wastes is not known.

Emissions and Industry

In 2004, Bolivia 1,555.9 generated metric tons of greenhouse gases, a 20 percent increase from 1990.

Agricultural products include coffee, cocoa, cotton, soybeans, sugar cane, corn, rice, and timber. Agricultural emissions accounted for 26.7 percent of all emissions. Within this sector, enteric fermentation accounted for 77 percent of emissions, agricultural soils for 9.4 percent, prescribed burning of savannas 5.7 percent, and manure management 4 percent.

Crude oil production and proven reserves are among the top half of the world. Bolivia has high oil production and consumption per capita. Energy emissions accounted for 20.7 percent of all emissions. Within this sector, transportation accounted for 47 percent of emissions, energy industries 20.7 percent, and manufacturing industries and construction 18 percent. Industrial emissions accounted for 48.7 percent of all emissions. Within this sector, 96.4 percent comes from the consumption of halocarbons and SF6.

Waste emissions accounted for 4 percent of all emissions. Emissions increased 848 percent from 1990 to 2004. Within this sector, wastewater management accounted for 56.6 percent and solid waste disposal on land 47 percent. The sewer and water pollution, population increases, agricultural runoff of fertilizers and pesticides, and industrial pollution all contribute to this large increase in greenhouse gas emissions from wastes.

Major Waste Issues

One of the main environmental issues is also a waste issue. There is a significant amount of water pollution from industrial activities. Industrial emissions accounted for a very large amount of overall greenhouse gas emissions. When greenhouse gas emissions are industrial, the airborne industrial pollutants fall on to the land and into waterways, compounding the problem of industrial discharges directly into the water. So far the United Nations Millennium Development goals for sanitation are not met and are not likely to meet 2015 deadlines.

Infectious diseases are a current risk, including yellow fever, dengue fever, hepatitis A, hepatitis B, malaria, tuberculosis, and typhoid. Two percent or more of the population is persistently infected with hepatitis B. There is little risk of malaria above 2,500 m in the Andes Mountains, but there is a high risk of malaria in the Amazon River Basin. There is a moderate risk of malaria in rural areas under 2,500 m.

Many of these diseases travel along with other diseases. Bolivia is underserved with sanitation and safe drinking water and has a high rate of urbanization and overcrowding. There are few hospital beds and doctors. With rising temperatures, more violent weather, overcrowded urban areas, and poor sanitation the risk of infectious diseases grow. It is likely that many will expand into higher altitudes and for longer distances over Bolivia's varied terrain.

Further Reading

Bolivia Government Portal. www.boliviaweb.com.

Carruthers, David V. 2008. *Environmental Justice in Latin America: Problems, Promise, and Practice*. Cambridge, MA: MIT Press.

Environmental Dissonance: Global Warming and Bolivia's Kallawaya Healers. http://upsidedownworld.org.

Helgegren, I., et al. 2014. "Contextualizing Sustainable Development for Small Scale Water and Sanitation Systems in Cochabamba, Bolivia." *Urban Environment*, 217–225.

Responding to the Impacts of Climate Change. www.christianaid.org.uk.

Symonds, E., et al. 2014. "A Case Study of Enteric Virus Removal and Insights into the Associated Risk of Water Reuse for Two Wastewater Treatment Pond Systems in Bolivia." *Water Research* 65: 257–270.

BOSNIA AND HERZEGOVINA

2014 brought the worst flooding in at least 100 years to Bosnia and Herzegovina. Rivers surged with massive volume and washed out roads, waste infrastructure, and the power grid. The population is currently at 3.8 million people, with a land area of 51,209 km^2. The small 20 km coastline along the Adriatic Sea has no natural harbors. Forty-six percent of the populace is urbanized, and 37 percent lives in a city having more than 100,000 inhabitants. Twelve percent suffers malnutrition.

Bosnia and Herzegovina borders Croatia, Montenegro, Serbia, and the Adriatic Sea. The terrain is mainly mountainous. The northern region is Bosnian and is heavily forested mountains. The southern region is the Herzegovinian and is dominated by flat agricultural land. The climate varies with altitude. The higher mountains have longer, colder winters. The winters along the coast are warmer and rainier. Natural resources include iron ore, coal, lead, zinc, chromite, cobalt, nickel, timber, manganese, and hydropower.

Current Waste Practices and Recycling

Most communities use basic sewer and water services, but little water is treated before it is discharged into local water sources. Bosnia and Herzegovina collected 1,422,000 tons of municipal waste in 2009, all landfilled. Sixty-seven percent of the population receives municipal waste collection. All the population has access to an improved drinking water source, and 99 percent has access to an improved sanitation facility. Ninety-eight percent of the rural population has access to an improved drinking water sources, and 92 percent has access to an improved sanitation facility. Modern sewers are used in most places.

In 2008, 92,000 tons of hazardous wastes were generated. 2,000 metric tons of hazardous wastes for recovery/recycling were imported in 2009, and 4,870 metric tons were generated within the country. 4,870 metric tons of hazardous wastes were exported. There are no measures to control the movement of hazardous wastes—no legislation, regulations, or guidelines, and no private sector waste reduction or control initiatives. The importation of hazardous wastes for final disposal is generally prohibited, but enforcement is poor.

Bosnia and Herzegovina is developing its waste infrastructure with help from the European Union (EU). Bosnia and Herzegovina seeks admission to the EU but needs help to achieve EU standards. The "ascension" process is the long process of applying for membership to the EU. The EU offers an Instrument for Pre-Accession Assistance to candidate and potential candidate countries, such as Bosnia and Herzegovina.

Emissions and Industry

Bosnia and Herzegovina generated 16,118.5 metric tons of greenhouse gases in 2001, a 53 percent decrease from 1990.

Agricultural products include corn, wheat, vegetable, and livestock. Agricultural emissions accounted for 14 percent of all emissions. In 1990 within this sector, agricultural soils accounted for 51.6 percent of emissions, enteric fermentation 33.6 percent, and manure management 15 percent. This is a high amount of greenhouse gas emissions from manure, indicating the presence of large amounts of untreated feces. There are no data for 2001 reports.

Energy emissions accounted for 76.5 percent of all emissions. In 1990 within this sector, 66 percent of emissions were from the energy industries, and 9 percent were from transportation. In 2001 all the emissions were fugitive. Fugitive emissions are essentially unregulated air pollutants. They can threaten public health, agricultural products, ecosystems, and the atmosphere. Industrial emissions from industrial processes were 4 percent of all emissions. In 1990 within this sector, metal production accounted for 73 percent of emissions, and mineral products accounted for 21 percent of emissions. There are no data for 2001.

Waste emissions were 6 percent of all emissions. Within this sector, solid waste disposed on land accounted for all emissions in 1990. There are no data for 2001.

Major Waste Issues

Many of the environmental issues are also waste issues. Civil conflict from 1992 to 1995 eliminated sewer and water infrastructure. Raw sewage is discharged into to waterways without treatment. Industrial processes, such as metal production, regularly pollute the water and air.

Infectious diseases, such as hepatitis A, hepatitis B, tuberculosis, and tick-borne encephalitis (TBE) exist here. Two percent or more of the population is persistently infected with hepatitis B. There is a risk of TBE in areas below 1,400 m. Usually the ticks are most active from March to November.

Rising temperatures and violent weather may expand some infectious disease vectors. The range for TBE could expand to higher altitudes, longer distances, and longer active seasons.

Further Reading

Government of Federation of Bosnia and Herzegovina Ministry of Environment and Tourism. www.fbihvlada.gov.ba.

Hillerbrand, Rafaela C., and Rasmus Karlsson, eds. 2008. *Environmental Policy in Bosnia and Herzegovina: Post Socialism Development and Local Governance.* Oxford, UK: Inter-Disciplinary Press.

State of Environment Report of Bosnia and Herzegovina for the United Nations Development Program. www.undp.or.

BOTSWANA

The Kalahari Desert dominates the western region of Botswana, an African nation. Two million people live on Botswana's 585,370 km^2 of land, though some boundaries remain disputed. Most of the population is in the eastern part of the country. There are many small communities throughout the nation. Fifty-seven percent of the population is urbanized, and 13 percent lives in a city having more than 100,000 inhabitants. Twenty-seven percent live in overcrowded conditions, and a third suffers malnutrition. About a quarter live under international poverty levels. Life expectancy is 56 years. Diarrhea and respiratory infections are elevated.

The climate is semi-arid with warm winters and very hot summers. Rain usually falls between October and March. Droughts occur in many areas. Even in the rainy season stream flow is not reliable. Internal rivers have water flow for ten to seventy-five days per year. About two-thirds of freshwater comes from groundwater. Groundwater mining is practiced, as evidenced by the more than 21,000 boreholes in the country. Currently water comes from old wells. Salinity intrusion on freshwater sources is a problem, and freshwater sources are drying up. There are several salt lakes in the north. Irrigation and livestock accounted for about 41 percent of water consumed, municipalities 41 percent, and mining and energy industries 18 percent.

Botswana is landlocked, sharing borders with Namibia, South Africa, and Zimbabwe. There are natural resources in diamonds, copper, nickel, salt, soda ash, potash, coal, iron ore, and silver.

Current Waste Practices and Recycling

Waste practices are basic—pit toilets, latrines, drainage ditches, and cesspools. Ninety-nine percent of the population has access to an improved drinking water source, and only 75 percent has access to an improved sanitation facility. Ninety-two percent of the rural population has access to an improved drinking water sources, and only 41 percent has access to an improved sanitation facility.

In the growing capital city of Gaborone, the pit toilet handles sewage waste in many areas. Trash covers streets, and dirty streams of water and waste line them. The waste treatment plant is over capacity. There are plans and policies to extend sewer coverage in the city.

Hazardous Wastes

The Department of Waste Management and Pollution Control is responsible for waste management. There are no restrictions on the export of hazardous and other wastes for final disposal or recovery. There are also no prohibitions on the importation of hazardous and other wastes for disposal or recovery. There are no waste disposal sites or waste recycling or recovery industries. Botswana does restrict the transportation of hazardous wastes and other wastes from any departure. Requests must be made in advance. Forms and permits are required. Dates of transit are required to help arrange for police escorts at borders.

The Waste Management Act was passed in 1998. Regular inspections of industries and other waste producers are used to help enforcement. Industries are required to have waste management plans for the wastes they produce. One of the main policy goals is developing and maintaining a registry of all industries that import and export hazardous wastes. Botswana is developing guidelines on managing hazardous wastes.

Emissions and Industry

In 2000 Botswana generated 6,139.5 metric tons of greenhouse gases, a 34 percent decrease from 1994.

Only 0.45 percent of the land is arable, and many of the soils are low in nutrients and water retentiveness. Agricultural products include corn, millet, beans, sorghum, sunflowers, and livestock. Emissions from agricultural wastes accounted for 30 percent of all emissions in 2000. In 2000 within this sector, enteric fermentation accounted for 96 percent of gas emissions and manure management 4 percent. This is in stark contrast to 1994, when prescribed burning of the savannas accounted for 60 percent of emissions within the agricultural sector and enteric fermentation accounted for only 38 percent of emissions.

Electricity can be intermittent. The power grid is down for at least twenty-two days a year. Energy emissions accounted for 69 percent of all emissions. Within this sector, manufacturing industries and construction accounted for 34.5 percent of emissions. Transportation accounted for 11.5 percent. Forty-six percent of emissions in this sector are "other." It is likely that these are energy industries, because in 1994 energy industries accounted for 45.5 percent of emissions in the energy sector. There is no mention of energy industry emissions in the 2000 reports. Industrial emissions in 2000 were not reported. In 1994, industrial process accounted for 2 percent of all emissions and was 100 percent the chemical industries.

Many landfills are not covered or secured. Greenhouse gas emissions from solid wastes accounted for 2 percent of all emissions in 2000. Within this sector, solid waste disposal on land accounted for 87 percent of emissions and wastewater management 4 percent.

Major Waste Issues

The lack of waste infrastructure and growing population will increase water pollution, trash, and disease. Groundwater supplies are not being recharged to meet increasing demands from agriculture, cities, and industry. Currently there is a risk of infectious diseases, especially cholera, dengue fever, hepatitis A, hepatitis B, malaria, schistosomiasis, tuberculosis, and typhoid. Two percent or more of the population is persistently infected with hepatitis B. There are areas and times of high risk for malaria. From November to June, there is a high risk of malaria in northern Botswana.

There is grave concern about the effects of climate change on food production, access, and distribution and the risks of famine. Climate change observers in the country note more extreme weather events and floods, as well as increased incidence and geographical spread of diarrhea and malaria. Increases in temperature and violent weather in the context of water deprivation and poor sanitation will expand vectors of most infectious diseases. The lack of medical care interferes with controlling outbreaks and increases the risk of epidemics.

The major waste issue is to protect the public health. The steps necessary for this to develop to the point of effectiveness are very challenging. It is not currently possible for Botswana to meet these challenges, and it is likely that international assistance will increase. Epidemics can pose public health threats to the country, the region, and the world population.

Further Reading

Alexander, K., et al. 2013. "Climate Change is Likely to Worsen the Public Health Threat of Diarrheal Disease in Botswana." *International Journal of Environmental Research and Public Health* 10: 1,202–1,230.

Bolaane, B., and H. Ikgopoleng. 2011. "Towards Improved Sanitation: Constraints and Opportunities in Accessing Waterborne Sewerage in Major Villages of Botswana." *Habitat International* 35: 486–493.

Foeken, D. W. J., et al. 2013. *Sanitation in Africa: Access to Improved Sanitation Facilities and Improvement Index*. Leiden, The Netherlands: African Studies Center.

Republic of Botswana Government Portal. www.gov.bw.

BRAZIL

The mighty Amazon River and its more than 200 tributaries drain about a third of the massive nation that is Brazil, where more than 201 million people live on 8,511,965 km^2 of land. There is 7,491 km of coastline. Eighty-four percent of the population is urbanized, and 45 percent lives in a city having more than 100,000 inhabitants. Brazil is predominantly urban. About 7 percent of inhabitants suffers malnutrition. 25,100 deaths a year are attributed to unsafe water.

Brazil is the fifth-largest country in the world and the largest country in South America. As a large country, it borders on many countries, including Argentina, Bolivia, Colombia, French Guiana, Guyana, Paraguay, Peru, Suriname, Uruguay, and Venezuela. Brazil has many natural resources, such as bauxite, gold, iron ore, nickel, manganese, phosphates, tin, platinum, uranium, petroleum, hydropower, and timber. The climate is tropical—hot and humid. It is more temperate in the southern regions. There are reoccurring droughts in the northeast. In the south, there are floods. Water is generally plentiful. Total renewable water resources are 8,233 km^3, among the most in the world. About 7 percent of the land is arable, about 19 percent is meadows and forests, and 67 percent is woodlands and forests.

Current Waste Practices and Recycling

Most major cities have basic modern sewers. In rural areas, the waste practices are basic—pit toilets, latrines, drainage ditches, cesspools, and the bush.

In 2007, Brazil collected 51,432,000 tons of municipal wastes. Eighty-seven percent of the population receives municipal waste collection services. About 70 percent is sent to landfills and 30 percent dumped outside the city limits. About a fifth of the mostly urban population does not have regular waste pickups or cleaning. Only 20 percent of wastewater is treated and discharged appropriately. Less than a third of the sewage from the largest cities is treated. One hundred percent of the urban population has access to an improved drinking water source, and 85 percent has access to an improved sanitation facility. Eighty-five percent of the rural population has access to an improved drinking water sources, and 44 percent has access to an improved sanitation facility. The death rate from intestinal infectious diseases is 14.43 per 100,000 people, which is high.

Waste pickers and scavengers are part of the strong informal waste economy in Brazil. It is estimated that there are 800,000 scavengers and that 35,000 are affiliated with loosely organized waste scavenging cooperatives. About a third of scavengers live in extreme poverty. Some cities seek to incorporate scavengers into waste segregation programs as an opportunity to include and appreciate them. A social goal of some emerging recycling policies is to decrease the vulnerability of waste pickers and increase their dignity, safety, and citizenship.

The Art of Waste Pickers: In Praise of Invisible Superheroes

Waste pickers collect trash from urban areas and dumpsites in many developing nations. In many countries, the major recycling is done by waste pickers eking out a living without the support or protection of the government.

In Brazil it is estimated that about a third of the waste is recycled, primarily by about 1 million waste pickers known as *catadores*. In São Paulo, some waste pickers collect trash in carts called *carrocas*. These carts are not uniform, and many are pulled or pushed by the *catadores*.

Since 2007, an artist named Mundano has painted bright and beautiful art on the trash carts. His art is described as funky, featuring bright cartoon faces. His purpose is to show thanks to the *catadores*. Mundano started a street movement in São Paulo that spread through out Brazil and reached international audiences in October of 2014 at the TEDGlobal Conference. In his talk there, he described waste pickers as "invisible superheroes."

Although the waste pickers and informal waste economy recycle an unknown amount of solid wastes, officially very little of the solid waste stream is separated, and many parts of major urban areas, such as Rio de Janeiro, do not reach the whole city. Cities are working to improve that by including the informal waste economy, incorporating the 2010 National Solid Waste Policy, and prioritizing recycling in trash pickups and developing separation centers. About thirty aluminum manufacturing companies have one of the highest rates of reclamation and recycling in the world. Other methods of increasing recycling are public information campaigns, incubation and training of waste collectors cooperatives, and environmental education.

Persistent Organic Pollutants (POPs)

Persistent organic pollutants (POPs) are powerful chemicals with adverse environmental and public health effects. A common and highly regulated POP is polychlorinated biphenyls, or PCBs. There are other similar chemicals designated for destruction, with more chemicals proposed. POPs' environmental effects include species population decreases, lowered resistance to diseases, and congenital abnormalities. They are spread all around the planet by winds and water. POPs generated in one country can have far-reaching effects in distant countries and oceans. POPs have been found in remote areas of Brazil. They persist in the environment because they can pass from part of the food chain to another. The bioaccumulation of POPs weakens ecotones and threatens sustainability.

Brazil signed the Stockholm Convention on POPs in 2004. Part of its obligation under this convention is to develop a National Implementation Plan to reduce and eliminate POPs. This plan is to establish inventories of the production, use, stockpiles, wastes, and waste sites. DDT, one of the POPs, was produced and used in Brazil from 1962 to 1982. Another POP is PCBs, present in Brazil. Brazil now has three companies licensed to incinerate PCB liquids and one to dispose of PCB-contaminated solid wastes. Most of the chemicals forbidden by the Stockholm Convention were produced, imported, or used in Brazil in the recent past.

About 1,500 contaminated sites are listed on Brazil's inventory. About 510 are targeted for cleanup and site remediation. About twenty-five sites have already been cleaned up. Another approximately 830 sites are proposed for listing. Several areas are now testing mother's milk for the presence of POPs. The World Bank is funding a project called "National Program for the Integrated Management of Contaminated Sites." The goal of this project is to establish a sustainable funding mechanism for remediation of contaminated sites. Most trash is transported to landfills when done officially, but the informal waste economy dumps trash illegally on land and in water. Cities are working to improve their landfill capacity and decrease environmental effects. Rio de Janeiro, Sao Paulo, and Curitiba increased recycling rates through increasing recycling practices. The Gramacho landfill outside of Rio de Janeiro is planned to recapture methane for energy conversion.

Hazardous Wastes

There are no restrictions on the exportation of hazardous wastes and other wastes for final disposal or recovery, but this is not usual practice. Generally hazardous wastes are shipped to developed countries for waste treatment and to developing countries for waste recovery. Brazil does limit imports of hazardous wastes pursuant to the 2010 National Policy on Solid Waste but has no limits on exported wastes.

Nuclear Wastes

Brazil has two nuclear power plants and a large uranium mine and processing industrial facility. The uranium mining and milling wastes are kept in a 29 ha dam system in Minas Gerais. Brazil also has two nuclear waste disposal, five storage, and four processing facilities.

Emissions and Industry

Brazil generated 862,808.9 metric tons of greenhouse gases in 2005, almost a 50 percent increase from 1990.

Agricultural products make up about 11 percent of the gross domestic product. If a broad definition of "agribusiness" is used that includes raw materials, processing, sales, and machinery and tools supply, the contribution is about 27 percent. Fertilizer consumption was fourth out of 166 countries in 2002, at 7.68 million metric tons. Agricultural products include coffee, soybeans, wheat, rice, corn sugar cane, cocoa, and beef. About a third of exports are from the agribusiness sector. 54,000 km^2 of land is irrigated, among the highest proportions in the world.

Agricultural emissions accounted for 48 percent of all emissions. Within this sector, enteric fermentation accounted for 58 percent, agricultural soils 34 percent, manure management 4.6 percent, and field burning of agricultural residues 1 percent.

Brazil produces a substantial amount of crude oil and maintains large proven reserves. Oil and electricity production and consumption per capita are high. There are 395.5 billion m^3 of proven natural gas reserves. There is about 2,000 km of pipelines for crude oil, 3,800 km for petroleum products, and 1,095 km for natural gas. Energy emissions accounted for 38 percent of all emissions. Within this sector, 41 percent came from transportation, 24 percent from manufacturing and construction, and 16 percent from energy industries.

Industrial products compose 38 percent of the gross domestic product. Industrial emissions accounted for 9 percent of all emissions. Industrial wastes tend to be incinerated. About eight commercial industrial waste sites that take mixed industrial wastes including organochlorides, exclusively for industrial chemical manufacturing wastes, nine for airport wastes and biomedical wastes, and eleven

Exploding Manhole Covers

Manhole covers are heavy metal covers for sewer and other infrastructure entrances. They can weigh from 35 to 140 kg and can explode several hundred feet into the air.

These explosions can be deadly and can happen throughout a sewage system. Sewage systems share infrastructure with electrical power systems, so generally the cause is a slow burning electrical fire under the manhole cover. This creates flammable gases that can ignite when the electrical connection degrades. Other sewer gases include hydrogen sulfide, carbon dioxide, methane, and ammonia. Methane is highly flammable. Cables become frayed from lack of maintenance, vermin chewing the wires, and ground movement. Some industrial and commercial discharges into sewer systems can introduce corrosive chemicals.

Other inflammable gases can accumulate in sewer systems; especially slow or backed-up systems. Measuring gases around them and examining electrical wiring can usually prevent exploding manholes. Some new manhole covers are being produced that have slots in them through which gases can be detected.

just for hospital wastes. Within this sector, metal production accounted for 54 percent of emissions, mineral products 25 percent, and the chemical industries 12 percent.

Waste emissions accounted for 5 percent of all emissions. These emissions increased 43.5 percent from 1990 to 2005. Within this sector, solid waste disposal on land accounted for 56.5 percent of emissions, with 43 percent from wastewater management.

Major Waste Issues

Water pollution caused by oil spills, mining, and urban wastes is a major issue. The waste infrastructure is old and increasingly challenged by increasing population and industrialization. Deforestation of the Amazon is an international environmental issue. Logging and timber production, along with savanna burning, both affect the Amazon watershed and add to air and water pollution.

Diphtheria, hepatitis A, dengue fever, tuberculosis, typhoid, yellow fever, and the wild polio virus occur. There is a risk of malaria in the Amazon River basin, but low risk elsewhere in Brazil. The wild polio virus was detected in sewage sample from the International Airport of Viracopos in Campinas, São Paolo. The airport's waste is monitored for environmental conditions and infectious disease. Brazil is at low risk from this virus now.

Climate change effects include rising temperatures and ocean levels. As temperatures and violent weather increase and ocean levels rise, Brazil will see the expansion of current infectious disease vectors. International travel routes go through Brazil with increasing frequency. Internal travel routes into the Amazon River Basin are also increasing, providing a vector for some infectious diseases. To fight the spread of dengue fever, Brazil released large groups of mosquitoes with bacteria that disable dengue fever. Urban overcrowding, inadequate sanitation services, and poor rural health services provide a risk that outbreaks of disease may become epidemics.

Further Reading

Amazon River in Brazil. www.mdweil.com/amazon-river-pg.

Brazil Government Portal. www.brasil.gov.br.

Duarte, H., et al. 2014. "An Ecological Model for Quantitative Risk Assessment for Schistosomiasis: The Case of a Patchy Environment in the Coastal Tropical Area of Northeastern Brazil." *Risk Analysis* 34: 831–846.

Ferro, G., et al. 2014. "Efficiency in Brazil's Water and Sanitation Sector and its Relationship with Regional Provision, Property and the Independence of Operators." *Utilities Policy* 28: 42–51.

Responding to the Impacts of Climate Change. www.christianaid.org.uk.

BULGARIA

The rapid and recent transition of power characterizes current leadership in Bulgaria, an eastern European nation. The prime minister resigned after one year of rule in July 2014. Professor of Law Geori Bliznashki was appointed interim president until the next election. This region has seen many changes since its Thracian origins in 3500 BC.

Today, 7.7 million people live on 110,879 km^2 of land with 2,390 km^2 of freshwater. Bulgaria is an urbanized nation, with 70 percent of the population living in urban areas and 37 percent living in a city having more than 100,000 inhabitants. The capital and largest city is Sofia, with a population of 1.2 million. Nine percent of Bulgaria's population suffers malnutrition.

The climate is hot and dry in the summer, with cold, damp winters. It shares boundaries with Greece, Macedonia, Romania, Serbia, and Turkey. Bulgaria historically controlled land routes between Europe and the Middle East and Asia. Natural resources include bauxite, copper, lead, zinc, coal, and timber.

Current Waste Practices

Most communities use basic sewer and water services, but little water is treated before being discharged into local water sources. About all of the population has access to improved sanitation facilities. The death rate from intestinal infectious diseases is 0.56 per 100,000 people, which is very low. There are modern sewer systems in most major communities.

Nuclear Wastes

Bulgaria has two nuclear power reactors and four decommissioned reactors. It also has three nuclear waste disposal, nine storage, and four waste processing facilities.

Hazardous Wastes

In 2008, Bulgaria generated 13,053,000 tons of hazardous wastes. Decisions about wastes are made in the Industrial and Hazardous Waste Management Department at the Waste Management and Soil Protection Directorate. The 2009 Waste Management Act, along with the National Waste Management Program, is the major government waste policy. The main focus of this policy is to minimize waste as much as possible. To this end it encourages a variety of things, such as tax breaks, increased disposal costs, and emphasis on recycling. It plans to construct new waste treatment facilities as funds become available. Large generators of hazardous wastes will be expected to handle their own wastes in accordance with law. Bulgaria restricts the export of hazardous waste for final disposal but does not restrict imports of hazardous wastes for recovery. The transit of hazardous wastes through the country is controlled. In 2009, Bulgaria exported 362 metric tons of hazardous wastes and imported 28,500 metric tons, along with thirty-three metric tons of other wastes. Bulgaria generated 792,636 metric tons of hazardous wastes in 2009. Landfills range from controlled sanitary landfills to uncontrolled open dumps. They can emit greenhouse gases such as methane, depending on type of landfill, type of wastes, and age of the landfill. Many landfills reach capacity as they age and the population increases. In an older industrial and urbanized country such as Bulgaria, many landfills and many illegal dumps are old and leach chemicals into the soil and water. The potential for environmental effects increases as wastes accumulate over time without cleanup or remediation.

Bulgaria collects about 3,600,000 tons of municipal waste a year, disposing of it mostly in landfills. Most of the population enjoys municipal waste collection.

Emissions and Industry

Bulgaria generated 66,133 metric tons of greenhouse gases in 2011, representing a 46 percent decrease from 1990.

3.17 million ha are arable. Products include vegetables, fruits, tobacco, wheat, barley, sunflowers, sugar beets, and livestock. Agricultural emissions accounted for 9 percent of all emissions in 2011. Within this sector, agricultural soils and enteric fermentation accounted for the majority of emissions, 70 percent. Manure management accounted for 19 percent of emissions. This is an unusually high amount of greenhouse gas emissions from manure, indicating the presence of large amounts of untreated feces.

Manufacturing has decreased significantly. Industrial emissions accounted for 6 percent of all emissions. Within this sector, the chemical industry accounted for 20 percent of emissions. Mineral products accounted for 68 percent of emissions and metal production 2 percent.

Industrial waste producers are pursuing measures to reduce the amount and hazards of wastes. They are seeking cleaner technologies as funds become available. Industries are pursuing certification under international environmental management systems, such as the International Standards Organization (ISO). Product manufacturers are learning life cycle analysis for the design phases.

Bulgaria has oil production and reserves, as well as natural gas reserves. About 3,384 bbl per day of crude oil is produced, and 73,740 bbl per day of refined petroleum are exported. There is about 5.66 billion m^3 of proven natural gas reserves. Energy emissions create the most emissions. Energy emissions accounted for 80 percent of all emissions. Within this sector, energy industries accounted for 70 percent of emissions, and transportation accounted for 16 percent.

Waste emissions accounted for 5 percent of all emissions in 1988 and increased to 6 percent in 2011. Solid waste disposal on land accounted for 77 percent of emissions, and wastewater handling accounted for 22 percent of emissions. In 2011, waste incineration began.

Major Waste Issues

Past and present air and water pollution pose great challenges. Rivers are polluted with raw sewage, heavy metals from metallurgical plants, and industrial wastes. The large number of polluted industrial waste sites, combined with increasing energy emissions, combine to make a toxic mix that can present risks to public health and the environment.

There are infectious diseases, such as hepatitis A, hepatitis B, and tick-borne encephalitis. Two percent or more of the population is persistently infected with Hepatitis B. Ticks are most active in vegetation under altitudes of 1,400 m and between March to November. Global warming could expand the tick environment to higher altitudes at farther distances and during longer seasons.

Further Reading

Bellinger, Ed, ed. 2000. *Environmental Assessment in Countries in Transition.* Portland, OR: Books International.

Bulgarian Government Portal. www.government.bg.

FitzSimons, D., et al. 2011. "Burden and Prevention of Viral Hepatitis in Bulgaria." *Vaccine* 29: 8,471–8,476.

Scheinbrg, A., and P. Mol. 2010. "Multiple Modernities: Transitional Bulgaria and the Ecological Modernization of Solid Waste Management." *Environment and Planning: Government and Policy* 28: 18–36.

BURKINA FASO

Burkina Faso was once closely associated with France, under the name of Upper Volta. The country became independent in 1960, and the name was changed in 1984 to Burkina Faso, which means "land of upright men." Altogether, 17.8 million people live on 272,967 km^2 of land. It is the third poorest country in the world. Its population is growing, and urbanization is increasing. Urban populations represent 26.5 percent of the total population with an estimated annual growth rate of 6 percent. Between 1975 and 2000, there was a 200 percent increase in urban populations. Around 16 percent live in overcrowded conditions. Eight percent do not have durable housing.

The terrain consists of flat plains, high savannas, and low hills in the west and southeast. There is a desert region in the north. The warm season is from March to May. There is a 20 percent chance that it will rain every day and a 90 percent chance that it will be in the form of thunderstorms. From February to June, the temperatures are hot. The cold season is from July to September. There is a 63 percent chance that it will rain every day, and an 85 percent of that being thunderstorms. The humidity ranges from a low of 4 percent, around early March, to 97 percent and more around the end of August.

Current Waste Practices

Waste practices are basic, including latrines, pit toilets, cesspools, drainage ditches, and open defecation. Ninety-five percent of the urban population has access to an improved drinking water source, and half has access to an improved sanitation facility. Ninety-five percent of the urban population has access to an improved drinking water source, and half had access to an improved sanitary facility. Seventy-three percent of the rural population has access to an improved drinking water source, but only 6 percent has access to an improved sanitation facility.

Most waste is not landfilled. 666,000 tons of municipal waste were collected in 2009, most of it landfilled. However, only 6 percent of the population has access to an improved sanitation facility. The open defecation rate in 2012 was 65 percent. Hazardous wastes are found here from many unknown sources. There are few technical or financial resources to handle most kinds of waste.

Emissions and Industry

Burkina Faso generated 5,968 metric tons of greenhouse gas emissions in 1994, the last available data. Civil unrest and lack of political stability has hampered or destroyed environmental monitoring, assessment, or the ability to develop a regulatory framework for integrated waste management or environmental regulation. Greenhouse gas emissions are likely to be higher now because of increased population and sustenance reliance on agriculture.

Agricultural products include cotton, peanuts, shea nuts, millet, corn, rice, and livestock. Agricultural emissions accounted for 79 percent of all emissions. Within this sector, enteric fermentation accounted for 88 percent of emissions, manure management 4 percent, agricultural soils 3.6 percent, and prescribed burning of the savannas 3 percent.

Oil and electricity production and consumption per capita are low. Energy emissions accounted for 15 percent of all emissions. Within this sector, transportation accounted for 36 percent of emissions and energy industries 0.5 percent. "Other" was the largest category, generating 55 percent of emissions in this sector. Industrial emissions accounted for none of the overall emissions according to reports from the government there now.

Waste emissions accounted for 6 percent of all emissions. Within this sector, solid waste disposal on land accounted for 56 percent of emissions and "other" for 44 percent. The amount of greenhouse gas emissions from wastes is not known.

Major Waste Issues

One of the most challenging waste issues in Burkina Faso is the lack of information. The major waste issue is the protection of public health both in the country and the region. Yellow fever, cholera, hepatitis A, hepatitis B, meningococcal meningitis, typhoid, malaria, dengue fever, and schistosomiasis exist in the region. Two percent or more of the population is persistently infected with hepatitis B. There is a high risk of malaria. There is a risk of yellow fever in all parts of the country.

There is a chance that infectious disease vectors will expand from outbreaks to epidemics. Tropical conditions, rapid population growth and urbanization, very poor sanitation practices and facility access, unaccountable greenhouse gas inventories, and a lack of environmental or public health data put this country at risk for more infectious diseases. There are long droughts and desertification that have substantial environmental and public health effects. With increasing temperatures, desertification will increase and increase these effects. There are grave concerns about climate change effects and food security. This has prompted stronger efforts of waste management, and waste management policies are increasing their efforts in the following areas (in order of priority): recycling plastics, setting up collection for municipal wastes, privatizing health care wastes, and understanding e-wastes, industrial wastes, and hazardous wastes. There are inadequate public resources in the country to handle internal, regional, and global health concerns. International intervention is already occurring, but more is needed.

Further Reading

Burkina Faso Global Partnership on Waste Management. www.unep.org.

Burkina Faso President. www.presidence.bf.

Burkina Faso, Waste Status. United Nations Environment Programme. www.unep.org.

Central Africa Regional Program for the Environment, Regional Development Strategy 2012–2020, US Agency for International Development. www.usaid.gov.

Foeken, D. W. J., et al. 2013. *Sanitation in Africa: Access to Improved Sanitation Facilities and Improvement Index*. Leiden, The Netherlands: African Studies Center.

McConville, J., et al. 2011. "Bridging Sanitation Engineering and Planning: Theory and Practice in Burkina Faso." *Journal of Water, Sanitation and Hygiene for Development*. 1: 205–212.

BURUNDI

Burundi's recent history is one of violent civil unrest, quelled for now. After separating from Rwanda in 1959, Burundi officially gained independence in 1962. In 1972, one outbreak of violence resulted in about a quarter-million dead, and 300,000 refugees escaped to Tanzania. In the next ten years of fighting, about another 300,000 people died. It is not known how many have died in or fled from these conflicts since then.

Altogether, 10.9 million people live on Burundi's 27,830 km² of land. It is a nation of small communities. About 10 percent of the population is urban. Burundi population density is among the highest in Africa. Its population is growing rapidly—about 3.3 percent a year. Its per capita income is among the lowest in the world.

The Democratic Republic of the Congo, Rwanda, and Tanzania border land-locked Burundi. Much of the terrain is mountainous. Most of this nation rests on a high plateau separated by deep valleys. The land drops in altitude and flattens in the east. Lake Tanganyika forms part of the eastern boundary. The climate is varied depending on altitude but generally is tropical. There are two rainy seasons, one from February to May and the other from September to November. Natural resources include uranium, peat, copper, gold, tin, limestone, and hydropower.

Current Waste Practices

Waste practices in Burundi are basic—latrines, pit toilets, drainage ditches, cess-pools, and open defecation. Fifty percent of the rural population and only 44 percent of the urban population has access to a sanitation facility. Seventy-three percent of the rural population and 82 percent of the urban population uses safe drinking water. People now get their water from contaminated sources. In 2004, more than 22 percent of children younger than age 5 died from diarrheal diseases. Burundi's recent history is of violent armed conflict. There have been four wars since the early 1960s, in which millions of people died or were displaced. Water supplies and waste infrastructure were targeted and destroyed in all these conflicts. There are no functional railway lines and about 1,300 km of paved roads. Very little sewage is treated. Wastewater flows untreated into Lake Tanganyika.

Emissions and Industry

In 2005, Burundi generated 26,474 metric tons of greenhouse gases, a large increase of 1,226.7 percent from 1990. Part of this increase is the large increase in population and the reliance on agriculture. Agricultural products include coffee, bananas, tea, cotton, corn, sorghum, manioc, and livestock. Agricultural emissions accounted for 98 percent of all emissions. Within this sector, agricultural soils accounted for 98 percent of emissions and enteric fermentation almost 2 percent.

The electrical grid is out for almost 136 days a year. Energy emissions accounted for 1 percent of all emissions. Within this sector, "other sectors" accounted for 60 percent of emissions and transportation 30 percent. Industrial emissions accounted for no greenhouse gas emissions.

Waste emissions accounted for almost 1 percent of all emissions. Within this sector, wastewater handling accounted for 95 percent of emissions, and solid waste disposal on land almost 5 percent.

Major Waste Issues

There is a chance that infectious disease vectors will expand from outbreaks to epidemics. The tropical conditions, rapid population growth and urbanization, very poor sanitation practices and facility access, unaccountable greenhouse gas inventories, and a lack of environmental or public health data put this country at risk for more infectious diseases. There are long droughts and desertification that have substantial environmental and public health effects. Famine is common. Burundi is enhancing communication and monitoring systems to develop more information on local climate change effects. The capital city of Bujumbura is heavily polluted and enjoys little to no waste collection. There is still a need for a sanitary landfill and a system. There are inadequate public resources in the country to handle internal, regional, and global health concerns. Women from vulnerable populations are taking the lead in waste management. Currently there are four waste management projects that employ ex-combatants and returnees to collect wastes. Eighty percent of these are female. International intervention is already occurring, but more is needed. Burundi is increasing sanitation coverage, and international assistance is increasing since conflicts have ceased.

Further Reading

Burundi Government Portal. www.burundi-gov.bi.

Ekane, Nelson, et al. 2014. "Multi-Level Sanitation Governance: Understanding and Overcoming Challenges in the Sanitation Sector in Sub-Saharan Africa." *Waterlines* 33: 242–256.

Foeken, D. W. J., et al. 2013. *Sanitation in Africa: Access to Improved Sanitation Facilities and Improvement Index*. Leiden, The Netherlands: African Studies Center.

Women Bring Solutions to Waste Management in Burundi. www.undep.org.

C

CAMBODIA

The magnificent Hindu temple of Angkor was built long before Cambodia was a country. Cambodia began to emerge as a nation after struggling to break free of French colonial rule in 1949. Border disputes, internal political instability and conflict still haunt this nation. Today, 14 million people live on Cambodia's 181,035 km² of land and 443 km of coastline. Twenty percent of inhabitants are urbanized, and only 8 percent live in a city having more than 100,000 inhabitants. Forty-four percent suffers malnutrition. Life expectancy is 62 years. About a third live below international poverty levels.

The Gulf of Thailand, Vietnam, Laos, and Thailand border Cambodia. The climate is tropical—hot and humid. The rainy season is May to November, and the dry season is December to April. The Mekong River is a prominent feature as is Tonie Sap, the largest freshwater lake in Southeast Asia. Natural resources include oil, timber, gemstones, iron ore, phosphates, and manganese.

Current Waste Practices

Waste practices are basic in most areas—latrines, pit toilets, cesspools, drainage ditches and open defecation. Eighty-seven percent of the urban population has access to an improved drinking water source, and 73 percent has access to an improved sanitary facility. Fifty-eight percent of the rural population has access to an improved drinking water source, and only 20 percent has access to a sanitary facility. The open defecation rate in 2012 was 54 percent, down from 88 percent in 1990.

The death rate from intestinal infectious diseases is 32.31 per 100,000 people, among the highest in the world. Trash is essentially moved to the edge of town. Waste pickers are part of the informal waste economy and perform some recycling functions. Animals such as rats, snakes, birds, dogs, and pigs rummage through it. Occasionally the trash is burned. The Phnom Penh municipality does have one project on recycling using waste pickers who go from house to house collecting solid wastes, which are separated for recyclables. These are sold to waste haulers for transport to Vietnam and Thailand. Biodegradable wastes are composted and sold. One of the largest obstacles is educating communities. Many people are only now learning that recycling can be good for the environment. There is community and government interest in biogas power generation.

Emissions and Industry

In 1994, the last year for which data is available, Cambodia generated 12,762.6 metric tons of greenhouse gases. It is estimated that more than 80 percent of the people use hardwood charcoal, although it is technically illegal to produce. This type of charcoal production leaves about a quarter of the wood as dust and generates large amounts of greenhouse gases. With population increases and dependence on agriculture, it is likely that these emissions have increased substantially.

Agricultural products include rice, rubber, corn, vegetables, cashews, tapioca, and silk. Practice in Cambodia is to use manure as fertilizer for crops. Agricultural emissions accounted for 83 percent of all emissions. Within this sector, enteric fermentation accounted for 32 percent of emissions, rice cultivation 30 percent, agricultural fields 21 percent, and manure management 15.7 percent. This is a high amount of greenhouse gas emissions from manure, indicating the presence of large amounts of untreated feces. Manure is frequently used in many crops, including rice. Many wastes are in watery environments, which can facilitate the spread of infectious diseases.

Some oil is produced, and there are no proven natural gas reserves. Energy emissions accounted for 15 percent of all emissions. Within this sector, transportation accounted for 44 percent of emissions, "other" for 32 percent, and energy industries for 17.6 percent. Industrial emissions accounted for 0.4 percent of all from mineral products.

Waste emissions accounted for 2 percent of all emissions. Within this sector, wastewater management accounted for 54.5 percent of emissions and solid waste disposal on land 45 percent.

Major Waste Issues

Illegal logging, fishing, and trash disposal have caused habitat loss, biodiversity decline, and public health concerns. In most rural areas, there is no access to safe drinking water. Cambodia has some of the dirtiest water in the world as measured by BOD (biological oxygen demand). There are infectious diseases here. Climate change observers in Cambodia note increased temperatures, some extreme weather events, and rising sea levels. There is concern about flooding and infectious diseases.

Cholera, diphtheria, hepatitis A, hepatitis B, Japanese encephalitis, tuberculosis, typhoid, malaria, dengue fever, and schistosomiasis occur in Cambodia. There is a high risk of malaria. Japanese encephalitis is widespread and is a particularly great risk from May to October. Two percent or more of the population is persistently infected with hepatitis B.

There is a strong possibility that infectious disease vectors will expand beyond the ability of Cambodia to control them. Lack of sanitary facilities, polluted water, and high manure greenhouse gas emissions will combine with increases in temperature and violent weather, and with rising ocean levels, to increase infectious disease vectors.

Further Reading

Cambodian Council of Ministers. www.presscocm.gov.kh.

Coates, Karen J. 2005. *Cambodia Now: Life in the Wake of War.* Jefferson, NC: McFarland & Co.

Karagiannis-Voules, D., et al. 2015. "Geostatistical Modeling of Soil-Transmitted Helminth Infection in Cambodia: Do Socioeconomic Factors Improve Predictions?" *Acta Tropica* 141: 204–212.

Shaheed, A., et al. 2014. "Water Quality Risks of 'Improved' Water Sources: Evidence from Cambodia." *Tropical Medicine and International Health* 19: 186–194.

2006 Status of Waste Management in Cambodia. http://www.env.go.jp/recycle/3r/en/asia/02_03-1/09.pdf.

CAMEROON

Cameroon is a Central African nation formed in 1960, after control by the French and British. Economic development has steadily increased, especially after annexing the Bakassi Peninsula from Nigeria in 2006. This peninsula contains large proven oil reserves. 19,522,000 people reside on 475,650 km² of land and 402 km of coastline. Fifty-five percent of the population is urbanized, and 27 percent lives in a city having more than 100,000 inhabitants. Two-thirds lives in overcrowded conditions, and a third suffers malnutrition. Malaria, diarrhea, and asthma rates are high.

Cameroon borders Central African Republic, Chad, Republic of the Congo, Equatorial Guinea, Gabon, Nigeria and the Bight of Biafra. The terrain is varied, with mountains in the west. The coast and interior regions are flat. The climate is tropical along the coastline, and ranges to semi-arid and hot inland. Natural resources include oil, bauxite, timber, iron ore, bauxite, and hydropower.

Current Waste Practices

Most waste practices are basic, and people use pit toilets, latrines, cesspools, drainage ditches, and open defecation. Ninety-five percent of the urban population has access to an improved drinking water source, and 58 percent has access to an improved sanitary facility. Fifty-two percent of the rural population has access to an improved drinking water sources, and only 36 percent has access to an improved sanitation facility.

Cameroon collects about 7,300,000 tons of municipal waste a year, disposing of most of this in landfills. Illegal dumping and trash heaps occur in many areas. Only 62 percent of the population has municipal waste collection. In 2008, nine tons of hazardous wastes were generated.

Between 2009 and 2011, Cameroon had its worst cholera outbreak since the 1970s. In 2011, 786 cholera deaths were reported. The areas having lower access to clean water and sanitation had the highest cholera rates. Neighboring nations affected by the epidemic were Niger, Nigeria, and Chad. All four nations met to coordinate transboundary issues having to do with cholera.

Emissions and Industry

In 1994, the latest year for which United Nations data is available, Cameroon generated 165,725 metric tons of greenhouse gases. With population increases and a dependence on agriculture, it is likely that actual greenhouse gases are now much higher. Agricultural practices related to manure management that creates greenhouse gases have increased substantially since 1994.

Agricultural products include coffee, cocoa, cotton, rubber, grains, bananas, livestock, and timber. About 425,000 bales of cotton are exported yearly. Agricultural emissions accounted for 62 percent of all emissions. Within this sector, manure management accounted for 79 percent of emissions. This is an unusually high amount of greenhouse gas emissions from manure, indicating the presence of large amounts of untreated feces. Prescribed burning of the savannas account for 14.6 percent of emissions.

Cameroon produces crude oil and has substantial proven oil reserves. Oil consumption per capita is low. Energy emissions accounted for 2 percent of all emissions. Within this sector, other is the largest category, with 44 percent of emissions, followed by transportation at 42 percent. Manufacturing and construction accounted for 7 percent and energy industries 6 percent. Industrial emissions accounted for 35 percent of all emissions. Within this sector, metal production accounted for 99 percent of emissions. Metal production is often associated with chemical industry emissions, but none were reported.

Waste emissions accounted for 1 percent of all emissions. Within this sector, solid waste disposal on land accounted for 61 percent and wastewater management 38.5 percent.

Major Waste Issues

Corruption and lack of environmental monitoring create the foundation for most environmental and trash problems. Desertification and deforestation are major environmental problems. The amount of trash and pollution makes controlling waterborne diseases a national and international issue. There is a high risk of major infectious diseases. Bacterial and protozoal diarrhea, hepatitis A, hepatitis E, dengue fever, malaria, meningococcal meningitis, schistosomiasis, typhoid fever, and yellow fever—among other diseases—occur here.

There is a chance that infectious disease vectors will expand in Cameroon thanks to urbanizing in already overcrowded conditions that are not served by sanitation facilities. There is a lack of information on public health or environmental conditions. The greenhouse gas emissions from manure management are among the highest in the world. Increased temperature, more violent weather, and rising ocean levels will increase desertification. Some of diseases may increase in outbreaks that can become epidemics overwhelming Cameroon public health. More international engagement is needed to prevent global vectors from expanding. Even without the exacerbating influence of climate change, Cameroon's disease vectors will expand. Public health of the nation and region is the largest waste issue.

Further Reading

Blakeney, Michael, Thierry Coulet, Getachew Mengiste, and Marcelin Tonye Mahop, eds. 2012. *Extending the Protection of Geographical Indications: Case Studies of Agricultural Products in Africa*. New York: Earthscan Publishing.

Central Africa Regional Program for the Environment, Regional Development Strategy 2012-2020, US Agency for International Development. www.usaid.gov.

Ekane, Nelson, et al. 2014. "Multi-Level Sanitation Governance: Understanding and Overcoming Challenges in the Sanitation Sector in Sub Saharan Africa." *Waterlines* 33: 242–256.

Foeken, D. W. J., et al. 2013. *Sanitation in Africa: Access to Improved Sanitation Facilities and Improvement Index*. Leiden, The Netherlands: African Studies Center.

Profitos, J., et al. 2014. "Muddying the Water: A New Area of Concern for Drinking Water Contamination in Cameroon." *International Journal of Environmental Research and Public Health* 11: 12,454–12,472.

Republic of Cameroon Presidential Portal. www.prc.cm.

CANADA

Canada is a nation of vast open spaces and abundant wildlife. Canada's population is more than 34 million people. Eighty percent are urbanized, and 79 percent live in a city having more than 100,000 inhabitants. The vast majority of Canadians—90 percent—live within 100 miles of the U.S. border.

Canada is large country. Its land mass is about 9,984,670 km^2, and water coverage is 891,163 km^2. The Great Lakes is one of biggest areas of freshwater on the planet. Canada's total coastline is 202,080 km long, the longest of any nation. After Russia, it is the second-largest country in the world. About a third of its land mass is forested. About 80 percent of the land mass has sustained low human impact, ranking it among the nations with the most wilderness. Canada borders the United States, the North Atlantic Ocean, the North Pacific Ocean, and the Arctic Ocean. The terrain is varied. There are large mountain ranges, such as the Canadian Rockies. The interior has vast plains as well as extensive wetlands. The climate is also varied. Ninety-eight percent of the country is snow-covered in winter. At higher altitudes, the weather is cold and windy. Northern Canada has a very cold arctic climate. Natural resources are numerous and include timber, hydropower, fish, oil, coal, diamonds, iron ore, gold, copper, nickel, potash, silver, and zinc.

Current Waste Practices and Recycling

Almost everyone has access to sanitation facilities. Canada's large size and relatively low population have historically mitigated environmental and public health effects of garbage. Canada collects about 13,500,000 tons of municipal waste a year. About 68 percent of Canada's solid wastes are disposed of in landfills. Canada generates about 31 million tons of solid wastes a year and has more than 10,000 landfill sites. These landfills account for 38 percent of the country's total methane emissions. Total garbage disposal costs in Canada are estimated at $1.5 billion per year.

Landfills range from controlled sanitary landfills to uncontrolled open dumps. They can emit greenhouse gases such as methane, depending on the type of landfill, the type of wastes, and the age of the landfill. Many landfills reach capacity as they age and the population increases.

Municipal waste is a major component of many landfills. It covers a broad array of materials. It includes waste generated by households and collected by local services. It also includes light commercial waste such as store and office wastes, restaurant wastes, cleaning wastes from large cleaning projects, and wastes from parks.

Canada spent $11.50 per capita on municipal waste treatment and generated 640 kg per capita per year. This is the fifth highest in the world. Municipal sewage is the largest source of water pollution in Canada. Two hundred billion liters of raw sewage is discharged in water per year. Canada is held to stringent sewage treatment standards, with three basic levels of waste treatment pursued. The first level, the primary level, reduces part of the solids. The secondary level further reduces solids and removes some pollutants. The tertiary level removes remaining solids and reduces most pollutants to safer levels. Canada's goal was to have all urban centers served by secondary levels of sewage treatment. The U.S. Environmental Protection Agency requires coastal cities to have secondary treatment, but such a goal is aspirational, and many communities cannot afford any level of waste treatment. Calgary, Edmonton and Whistler, British Columbia operate tertiary sewage systems. This sewage becomes clear effluent and dried waste usable for fertilizer.

Canada manages hazardous wastes and hazardous recyclable materials. Local governments establish collection, recycling, and disposal programs. Measures, metrics, and criteria for the licensing of hazardous waste creators, carriers, and waste treatment facilities is the role of provincial and territorial governments. The role of the federal government is to regulate transboundary movements of hazardous wastes and recyclable materials.

Canada recycles about 25 percent to 30 percent of its waste. The number of Canadians recycling increases every year, and in some areas, the number of recycling programs is much higher than the national average. The availability of recycling programs at the local level increases the level of recycling by engaging citizens and providing them access to recycling efforts. About 22 percent of the recycled garbage is organic household wastes, newsprint and cardboard make up about 17 percent each. As the number and types of recycling facilities and recycling programs increase, the recycling effort will increase the amount of garbage recycled, and decrease pressure on landfills.

Canada receives imported hazardous waste from the United States. The United States and Canada share a 5,500-mile border that has a heavy concentration of waste management facilities. In tracking the movement of hazardous materials in North America, Canada was found to be a "Pollution Haven." About thirty states send their hazardous wastes to Canada, much of it to Quebec. Of Mexico, the United States, and Canada, Canada has the weakest rules. Because of this, companies in the United States can ship it to Canada with less regulation than the United States or Mexico. Canada allowed open-pit treatment of raw hazardous wastes. When the United States enacts stronger hazardous waste disposals laws that require treatment, companies ship this type of waste to Canada. Also, in the United States the creator of the hazardous waste remains liable for those wastes, whereas in Canada it does not. Another reason for the transboundary shipment of hazardous recycle wastes is that Canada may have waste treatment that can recycle the hazardous wastes. It could also be that this type of facility is closer, decreasing risks of environmental effects from transportation.

Canada and the United States are currently cooperating in the transboundary ship of all wastes including hazardous wastes. Canada exports about 4 million tons of municipal solid waste to the United States a year. The United States exports about 455,000 tons of hazardous wastes to Canada a year. Because of the controversies surrounding hazardous wastes, accurate measures of the true volume of transboundary hazardous materials and waste transit are estimates.

Air Pollution

Air pollution is as complex as water pollution in the number and variety of chemicals that comprise air pollution. Air pollution has different emission sources, chemical characteristics, ecological persistence, and environmental and human health effects. Canada regulates four general categories of air pollutants. Criteria air contaminants, such as sulfur dioxide, are a major category. Heavy metal, toxic chemicals and substances, and persistent organic pollutants are the three remaining categories.

The Canadian Council of Ministers of the Environment sets air quality standards that apply to areas whose population totals more than 100,000 inhabitants, but there are few consequences for failure to achieve the required air quality standard. Provinces and territories are able to develop stricter air quality standards. Canada also employs an Air Quality Health Index designed to help people makes choices about exposure to polluted air. It measures the air quality in terms of public health risks, describes the level of health risks of different air quality, and notes any special risks that could affect vulnerable people, giving hourly readings and forecasts. The Air Quality Health Index measures ground-level ozone, particulate matter, and nitrogen dioxide.

Acid rain is an issue in Canada, though stricter air quality controls and better enforcement of them in both the United States and Canada have led to air pollution decreases. However, though some Canadian lakes have been saved from the environmental effects of acid deposition, many more continue to be affected. Eastern Canada is especially affected, because the soils lack natural alkalinity to counteract the acids. Acid rain is the deposition of sulfur dioxide and nitrogen oxides, which in the environment change into sulphuric acid, ammonium nitrate, and nitric acid. The damage cause by acid deposition is significant. It can affect insects, fish, animals, and people and pose public health threats. Sulphur dioxide reacts with water vapor and other airborne chemicals to create fine particles of sulphate. Sulphates are associated with heart and respiratory problems and with increased asthma issues. Approximately half of wet sulphate deposition in parts of eastern Canada comes from the United States. About 10 percent of this type of acid deposition in the northeast United States comes from Canada. Air pollution in Canada can increase acid deposition. Up to half of Canada has low-alkalinity soils. Some lakes have borderline levels of pH imbalances that could get worse in terms of environmental effects depending on the proximity, type, and volume of the air pollution. Waste incineration also emits chemicals and particulate matter into the air. Heavier pollutants, such as many metals, fall to the ground closer to the source than lighter-weight gases and chemicals.

Water Pollution

Water pollution in Canada is any release of any material, energy, or organism that could cause immediate or long-term harmful effects to the natural environment. Drinking water, wastewater, and uses of water are regulated by a federal agency, with provinces given substantial freedom to have higher standards. Developing and enforcing water quality standards is a continuing process.

Canada has as much as a fifth of the freshwater on Earth. In some areas of Canada, water can be scarce at times, but generally, water is plentiful. The Canadian Water Quality Index alerts water managers and the public to water quality issues.

Another area of waste focus is the arctic water of Canada. Arctic coastal communities do not have waste treatment facilities. Wastes from other parts of the world have doubled in these waters over the last decade, mostly plastics. Canada implemented the Arctic Waters Pollution Prevention Act in 1970.

Nuclear Wastes

In terms of nuclear energy Canada operates twenty-two nuclear power reactors in five locations. The nuclear waste is stored either on site or at temporary facilities. Few communities want to host a permanent waste site that could be active for 10,000 years or more. The nuclear waste is stored in copper and steel cases designed to last 100,000 years. Currently there are plans to develop a large central storage facility underground by 2035.

Canada's nineteen nuclear power reactors contribute about 15 percent of Canada's produced electricity. Six reactors are decommissioned. There are no disposal facilities, but there are twenty-two storage sites and two processing facilities.

Some of the issues affecting wastes are air pollution and resulting acid rain. Acid rain contains chemicals that interfere with the ecosystems of lakes, rivers, and forests. Air pollution from coal-burning energy sources, metal smelting, and vehicle emissions are also a persistent issue. In places, coastal oceans are becoming saturated with agricultural, industrial, mining, logging and wood production, and untreated municipal wastes. This can create dead zones in ocean estuaries.

Emissions and Industry

In 2008 Canada accounted for 2 percent of global carbon dioxide emissions. It includes emissions from sources like fossil fuel combustion, cement manufacturing, and gas flaring.

In 2011, Canada generated 702,000 metric tons of greenhouse gases, 79 percent of all of Canada's emissions. From 1990 to 2005, emissions steadily increased primarily due to increased emissions from petrochemical and transportation industries. They declined in 2009, primarily because of reduced emissions from coal-fired power plants and manufacturing. The industrial focus went more into service sectors than in manufacturing, decreasing emissions.

Canada's primary agricultural products are wheat, barley, oilseed, tobacco, fruits, vegetables, dairy products, forestry products, and fish. Canada consumes 2.61 million metric tons of fertilizer, the eighth-most in the world. Agricultural emissions account for 8 percent of all emissions. Within this sector, agricultural soils accounted for 55 percent of greenhouse gas emissions, enteric fermentation 33 percent, and manure management 12 percent.

The generation of electricity can create large amounts of wastes, as in the case of traditional coal-fired generators. Petrochemical sources of energy for transportation and heating also create wastes. Canada's main source of electricity is hydropower. Sixty percent of their energy is based on hydropower. Twenty-eight percent of electricity production comes from petrochemical products, and about 13 percent comes from nuclear energy.

The energy sector accounted for 81 percent of all emissions. Within that sector, transportation accounted for 35 percent of emissions, energy industries 27 percent, manufacturing and construction 14 percent, and fugitive emissions 11 percent. Fugitive emissions are essentially unaccounted waste streams into the air. Fugitive emissions can affect regional ecosystems and the public health, because they can fall from the air to the land and water.

Biomass generation accounted for about 1.4 percent of total electricity generation, with more than sixty bioenergy plants generating 1,700 megawatts. Biofuels and renewable wastes together account for 4.8 percent of total primary energy. Biomass energy production can have environmental effects in the land and water depending on the biomass feedstock and the efficiency of the production processes.

Their primary industrial products are transportation equipment, chemical manufacturing, processed and unprocessed mineral production, food products, wood and paper products, fish products, and petroleum and natural gas. Their primary exports are motor vehicles and parts, industrial machinery, aircraft, telecommunications equipment, chemicals, plastics, fertilizers, wood pulp, timer, crude petroleum, natural gas, electricity, and aluminum. Canada produced 3.12 million tons of aluminum in 2009, ranking it the fourth-highest producer in the world.

Industrial processes accounted for 8 percent of all emissions. Within this sector, metal production accounted for 31 percent of emissions, mineral products 15 percent, and chemical industries 13 percent.

Waste emissions accounted for 3 percent of all greenhouse gas emissions. Emissions from waste increased about 14 percent from 1990 to 2011. Within this sector, solid waste disposal on land accounted for 92 percent of greenhouse gas emissions, wastewater handling about 4.6 percent, and incineration 3 percent.

A major part of this is raw sewage. Feces contain pathogens, toxic chemicals, metals, and pharmaceutical wastes. This waste is in addition to other wastes from primary and secondary sewage treatment plants as well as from agriculture, logging, and manufacturing. It is a controversial issue in parts of Canada, such as Victoria, British Columbia. Overall there is uncertainty about the cumulative effects of sewage buildup in places such as the Juan De Fuego straits, where effluent plumes rise to the ocean's surface eight months of the year. Many feel that environmental waste management relies overmuch on the principle of dilution over time to reduce environmental effects. This is particularly troublesome for heavy metals, which are slow to dilute and can persist in food chains in ecosystems.

There have been large and long sewage spills in Ottawa and Winnipeg. This further challenges the principle of dilution, because a spill can overwhelm and degrade an ecosystem before it can recover. The sewage issue continues to grow, but so does the resolve of the government to facilitate waste treatment.

Major Waste Issues

Canada is a large nation with a relatively small but growing population. As Canada becomes more industrialized, environmental and public health effects will increase without regulation. There are few infectious wasteborne diseases in Canada now. Some wastes in some locations are showing signs of accumulation and ecosystem saturation, such as acid deposition in eastern Canada and sewage in southwestern Canada. Canada usually pursues active public notice and participation, prioritizes economic development over environment, and collaborates with other nations to control waste at its borders.

The United States and Canada formed the Great Lakes Water Quality Agreement to increase water quality and decrease ecological damage in 1972. The agreement was revised on September 7, 2012. The revisions increase the measures to decrease ecological harm from shipping wastes, municipal sewage, and toxic chemicals. The revisions broadened the scope of the agreement to include nearshore environments, invasive species, habitat destruction, more new toxic discharges, coastal community education and involvement, and the effects of climate change.

Canada is prepared for climate change effects on water systems. Climate observations have noted consistent glacial retreat, seasonally lower lake and river levels, and lower water levels in the Great Lakes. They anticipate an increase in precipitation, though summer precipitation in the south-central prairies is expected to decline. Primary concerns are water quality and quantity on a seasonal and regional basis, as well as extreme weather events. The key vulnerability is the Arctic, a fragile ecosystem where environmental effects of global warming include melting permafrost and tundra. A large amount of methane is contained in these areas and with warming could be released into the atmosphere. Canada is changing engineering practices, climatic design information, and building codes in preparation and reaction to climate changes.

Further Reading

Canadian Government Portal. www.canada.ca.

Climate Change Impacts on Water Systems. www.oecd.org.

Durant, Darrin, and Genevieve Fuji Johnson, eds. 2010. *Nuclear Waste Management in Canada: Critical Issues, Critical Perspectives,* Vancouver, Canada: University of British Columbia Press.

Great Lakes Water Quality Agreement. www.epa.gov/glnpo/glwqa/.

Jimenez, A., et al. 2014. "Water, Sanitation, and Hygiene and Indigenous Peoples: A Review of the Literature." *Water International* 39: 277–293.

Oberg, G., et al. 2014. "The Notion of Sewage as Waste: A Study of Infrastructure Change and Institutional Inertia in Buenos Aires, Argentina and Vancouver, Canada." *Ecology and Society* 19:19.

Real Time Water Quality Monitoring Program. www.env.gov.nl.ca.

Thomas, Katie. 2014. *Linkages between Arctic Warming and Mid-latitude Weather Patterns.* Washington, DC: National Academies Press.

CENTRAL AFRICAN REPUBLIC

Slave traders ravaged the landscape of this sub-Saharan nation from the sixteenth century to the nineteenth century. After a conflict-ridden period of French rule, the Central African Republic was born in 1960. Today, 4.4 million people live on 622,984 km^2 of land. It is a nation of small communities. A third of the population is urbanized, and a fifth lives in a city having more than 100,000 inhabitants. A third lives in overcrowded conditions, and 45 percent suffers malnutrition. Two-thirds lives under international poverty levels.

The Central African Republic borders Cameroon, Chad, the Democratic Republic of the Congo, and the Republic of the Congo, South Sudan, and Sudan. The terrain is flat, with hills in the southwest and northeast. There are many rivers, with the Ubangi and the Shari being the two largest. The climate is tropical. The winters are hot and dry, and the summers are warm to hot and wet. In the north, very hot, dry, dusty winds, called harmattan winds, occur.

Current Waste Practices

Waste practices are basic, with pit toilets, latrines, drainage ditches, cesspools, and open defecation. Ninety-two percent of the urban population has access to an improved drinking water source, and only 43 percent has access to an improved sanitation facility. Half the rural population has access to an improved drinking water source. Diarrhea, respiratory infections, malaria, and asthma rates are high. The death rate from intestinal infectious diseases is 36.19 per 100,000 people, among the highest in the world. The average life expectancy is 51 years.

This is little municipal collection of trash. When there is, the trash is often taken to the edge of town and dumped. Sometimes it is burned.

Emissions and Industry

The Central African Republic generated 37,737 tons of greenhouse gas emissions in 1994. Since then, the population has increased. In light of the country's reliance on agriculture, it is likely that actual current greenhouse gases are much higher.

There are about 700 km of paved road and few air flights for the whole country. Small agrarian communities dominate the nation. Cotton, timber, coffee, tobacco, bananas, and palm oil are primary agricultural products. Agriculture accounted for 43 percent of all emissions. Within this sector, agricultural soils emit 62 percent of greenhouse gas emissions, prescribed burning of savannas 25 percent, enteric fermentation 13 percent, and manure management 1 percent.

Energy accounted for 50 percent of all emissions. Within this sector, the largest category is "other" at 99 percent. There is limited electricity, some of that produced by hydropower. Most locations use diesel-powered generators. Fuel supply lines are intermittent.

According to old records, there were no greenhouse gas emissions from industrial processes. Most manufacturing is unregulated and serves local markets. The Central African Republic is a large producer of diamonds, with seven major diamond-exporting corporations. Gold mining can also have significant environmental effects. Diamonds, uranium, timber, and gold are all natural resources in the country.

Almost 7 percent of emissions come from wastes. Within this sector, 97 percent is other, and 3 percent is solid waste disposal on land. There is no public accountability for greenhouse gas emissions from wastes.

Major Waste Issues

The lack of information and monitoring pose large obstacles for control of trash and sewage. The major waste issue is the protection of the public health nationally and regionally. Infectious diseases are a major concern. Currently infectious diseases include cholera, dengue fever, hepatitis A, hepatitis B, malaria, polio, schistosomiasis, typhoid, and yellow fever. Two percent or more of the population is persistently infected with hepatitis B.

The lack of public health and sanitation facilities combined with urban growth and overcrowding provide environments for infectious diseases now. The infant mortality rate is among the highest in the world, and the number of hospital beds per person is among the lowest. The chance of a male reaching 65 is about 25 percent. The number of doctors per person is among the lowest in the world.

Climate change observers in the Central African Republic note decreased rain and higher temperatures. There is grave concern about food security and famine. With increased temperatures and violent weather, it is very likely that these diseases will develop outbreaks that reach epidemic proportion. With increases in violent weather, the hot, dry, dusty winds could increase, which in turn will increase current environmental issues of desertification and deforestation.

Further Reading

Central Africa Regional Program for the Environment, Regional Development Strategy 2012–2020, US Agency for International Development. www.usaid.gov.

Foeken, D. W. J., et al. 2013. *Sanitation in Africa: Access to Improved Sanitation Facilities and Improvement Index*. Leiden, The Netherlands: African Studies Center.

Gire, S., et al. 2014. "Genomic Surveillance Elucidates Ebola Virus Origin and Transmission during the 2014 Outbreak." *Science* 12: 1,369–1,372.

Zinga, I., et al. 2013. "Epidemiological Assessment of Cassava Mosaic Disease in Central African Republic Reveals Importance of Mixed Viral Infection and Poor Health of Plant Cuttings." *Crop Protection* 44: 6–12.

CHAD

The separation between petroleum wealth and energy poverty defines the landscape of Chad. In 2000, the World Bank loaned $200 million to help build an oil pipeline to Cameroon on the condition that 80 percent of the revenues go to health, education, and social welfare programs. After the pipeline was completed, the national leader redirected the revenue to the military and to finance government. A large simmering controversy evolved between the World Bank and Chad that included frozen bank accounts, renegotiated agreements, and intense political maneuvering. Chad is rated as one of the most corrupt nations in the world. This prevents its meaningful engagement in powerful international venues. In response to climate change measures, Chad does not have reliable institutional resources to use the financing available from the United Nations to implement climate change adaptation and mitigation regulations, policies, or programs. As contentious as some of these controversies are, Chad is nonetheless an environmental partner in the global community because of its environmental and public health risks.

Today, 11.2 million people live on Chad's 1,284,000 km^2 of land. The climate is tropical in the south and touches the Sahara Desert in the north. Chad shares borders with Cameroon, Central African Republic, Libya, Niger, Nigeria, and Sudan. Chad is politically unstable and engaged in armed border disputes with Sudan. The terrain is varied. There are mountains in the northwest, desert in the north, and lowlands in the south. In the center, the terrain is flat. Lake Chad is drying up quickly. It borders western Chad, as well as Cameroon, Nigeria, and Niger. The lake is now 20 percent or less of its original 26,000 km^2. The UN cited poor water maintenance and overirrigation by shoreline nations as reasons for lake shrinkage. The loss of freshwater has had devastating effects on both people and landscape. Food and water have decreased, and tensions between the neighboring nations have increased.

Natural resources include petroleum, uranium, and gold. Much of the petroleum is in proven reserves. More oil fields are currently under exploration.

Current Waste Practices

Waste practices are basic, including pit toilets, latrines, drainage ditches, cesspools, and open defecation. Seventy percent of the urban population has access to an improved drinking water source, but just 30 percent has access to an improved sanitation facility. Forty-four percent of the rural population has access to an improved source of drinking water, and only 6 percent has access to an improved sanitation facility. The open defecation rate in 2012 was 65 percent.

Emissions and Industry

Chad generated 8,021.1 metric tons of greenhouse gas emissions in 1993, the latest year for which data is available. Since then, population has increased, and in light of the reliance on agriculture, it is likely that greenhouse gases have increased.

Agricultural emissions accounted for 91 percent of all emissions. Within this sector, manure management accounted for 68 percent of emissions, rice cultivation 23 percent, and prescribed burning of the savannas 9 percent. This is an unusually high amount of greenhouse gas emissions from manure, indicating the presence of large amounts of untreated feces. Manure is often used as fertilizer. For some crops, such as rice, the manure is in water and provides both a source of greenhouse gas emissions and an infectious disease vector. Agricultural products include cotton, sorghum, millet, rice, potatoes, and livestock. The range of livestock includes camels, goats, cattle, and sheep.

Energy emissions accounted for 4 percent of all emissions. Within this sector, other accounted for all emissions. Chad is among the top oil producers in the world. Chad produced 104,500 bbl/day of crude oil in 2012 and in 2013 had 1.5 billion bbl of proven reserves of crude oil. Chad has the lowest per-capita energy consumption in the world. There is little electricity production or electrical energy available for most of the population. Industrial emissions accounted for no emissions according to government reports, but this is unlikely considering the amount of petrochemical processing and transit. It is likely that energy and industrial greenhouse gas emissions are much higher now.

Waste emissions accounted for 5 percent of all emissions. Within this sector, solid waste disposal on land accounted for 71 percent of emissions and other 29 percent. There is little public waste accountability.

Major Waste Issues

All major issues are challenged by the lack of information and monitoring in this nation. The major waste issue is the protection of the public health nationally and regionally. Infectious diseases are a major concern. Currently infectious diseases include cholera, dengue fever, hepatitis A, hepatitis B, meningitis, polio, schistosomiasis, typhoid, and yellow fever. There is a high risk of malaria. Two percent or more of the population is persistently infected with hepatitis B. There is a risk of yellow fever in areas south of the Sahara Desert. Recent research on meningitis demonstrates that high levels of wind-driven dust increase meningitis rates. A possible reason is that tiny abrasions in the throat caused by dust increase vulnerability. If the wind is a good indicator of potential meningitis outbreaks, then public health officials may be able to distribute vaccines more effectively. Climate change effects that increase the severity and duration of windstorms and lengthen their seasons of occurrence may spread meningitis to other parts of Africa. Other climate change effects include temperature increases and the droughts and floods that follow. There is grave concern about food security and the risk of famine.

A lack of public health and sanitation facilities, combined with urban growth and overcrowding, provides environment for infectious diseases. The infant mortality rate is among the highest in the world, whereas the number of hospital beds per person is among the lowest. The chance of a male reaching 65 is about 33 percent. The number of doctors per person is among the lowest in the world. With increased temperatures and violent weather it is very likely that these diseases will develop into outbreaks that reach epidemic proportion. Increases in violent weather will increase current environmental issues of desertification and deforestation.

Further Reading

Central Africa Regional Program for the Environment, Regional Development Strategy 2012–2020, US Agency for International Development. www.usaid.gov.

Ekane, Nelson, et al. 2014. "Multi-Level Sanitation Governance: Understanding and Overcoming Challenges in the Sanitation Sector in Sub-Saharan Africa." *Waterlines* 33: 242–256.

Environmental Justice Case Study: The Chad/Cameroon Oil and Pipeline Project. www.umich.edu.

Foeken, D. W. J., et al. 2013. *Sanitation in Africa: Access to Improved Sanitation Facilities and Improvement Index.* Leiden, The Netherlands: African Studies Center.

President of Chad. www.presidcetchad.org.

CHILE

Chile dominates the western coast of South America. Punta Arenas is the southernmost city in Chile as well as in the world. The southernmost point in South America and Chile is Cape Horn, is a 424 m rock on Horn Island. Altogether, 17.1 million people reside on Chile's 756,102 km² of land, which includes 12,290 km² of water. There is 6,435 km of coastline. Eighty-eight percent of Chileans are urbanized, and 57 percent live in a city having more than 100,000 inhabitants. Most of the population lives along the coast, in cities.

The climate is temperate with regional variation. Chile is cool and humid in the south and arid in the north. The driest desert in the world, the Atacama Desert, is in the north. Some areas have never had recorded rainfall. Water is so scarce that some communities use mesh nets to capture moisture from the fog, piping it into storage areas. This is also Chile's primary mining area. Chile's natural resources include copper, timber, iron ore, molybdenum, nitrates, and rare metals. It is the largest producer of copper, holding about 28 percent of the world's reserves. A third of the nation is covered by the Andes Mountains. Earthquakes occur in Chile more than in many other countries. It shares borders with Peru, Bolivia, the Pacific Ocean, and Argentina. Chile also claims 1.2 million km² of Antarctica, as well as Easter Island (3,219 km west) and the Juan Fernandez Islands (644 km west).

Current Waste Practices and Recycling

Chile collects about 6,160,000 tons of municipal wastes each year. Ninety-nine percent of the urban population has access to an improved drinking water source, and 98 percent has access to an improved sanitation facility. Seventy-five percent of the rural population has access to an improved drinking water source, and 83 percent has access to an improved sanitation source. The death rate from intestinal infectious diseases is 3.21 per 100,000 people, which is low.

Most communities use basic sewer and water services, but little water is treated before being discharged into local water sources. Chilean sewer and sanitation systems were maintained and developed by municipalities in the 1970s and 1980s. Gradually, control was turned over to the private sector. The cities are served by about fifty-three businesses. Two large companies serve half the urban population, about six medium-sized businesses serve about a third, and about fifty small businesses serve 15 percent. There are four state-owned water utilities that may privatize some of these services to attract capital to improve efficiencies in an aging water system in areas of drinking water safety, sewers, and sewage treatment.

Urban solid waste is composed of 50 percent organic matter, 19 percent cardboard and paper, 10 percent plastics, 4 percent textiles, 2 percent metals, and 2 percent glass. Less than 15 percent of solid wastes are recovered or recycled. Ninety-seven percent of wastewater is dumped in waterways without treatment. Places such as Vitacura and Easter Island are developing recycling programs and practices. Generally, recycling programs are increasing in use.

In 2009 Chile began to organize and focus its environmental regulation and law. As a general policy, Chile privatizes many governmental functions. In 2010, Chile became the first South American country to join the Organization for the Economic Cooperation and Development. This organization requires high environmental standards and is also pushing Chile to develop and implement stricter environmental regulations that increase public participation and recognize the rights of indigenous peoples.

Hazardous Wastes

E-waste is a growing hazardous waste issue, along with other mining wastes. It is estimated that 2,600 tons of e-wastes from mobile phones and 10,500 tons of computer wastes enter the waste stream annually. About 5 percent of hazardous waste is made into fuels. The rest is buried underground in metal containers. Officially, the government tracks waste, but it relies on self-reporting. Some businesses avoid the cost of regulation by dumping hazardous wastes in waterways or unpopulated regions.

Nuclear Wastes

Chile has no nuclear power plants, disposal sites, or processing facilities. It does, however, have three storage sites for radioactive wastes. This suggests that it is on the receiving end of nuclear wastes from other nations.

Emissions and Industry

In 2006 Chile generated 78,955.2 metric tons of greenhouse gases, a 55 percent increase from 1993.

Agricultural products make up about 6 percent of the gross domestic product. Emissions from agricultural wastes accounted for 17 percent of all emissions. Within this sector, agricultural soils accounted for 51 percent of emissions, enteric fermentation 34 percent, and manure management 14 percent.

In 2012, 17,340 bpd of crude oil was produced, meeting about half to a third of domestic demand. There are proven natural gas reserves of 97.97 billion m^3. Most of the energy comes from hydropower, so water shortages have a direct effect on energy production and availability. Energy shortages cause brownouts and blackouts throughout Chile. Mining requires large amounts of power, and when energy is scarce because of water, mining operations may take water or energy from communities. Mining operations also create large amounts of particulate matter. This dust is blown onto the nearby glaciers in the Andes Mountains, causing them to melt more quickly.

Energy emissions accounted for 73 percent of all emissions. Within this sector, energy industries accounted for 36 percent of emissions, transportation 29.5 percent, and manufacturing and construction 23 percent.

Chile is dominated by mining. Copper comprises about half of all exports, which total approximately $60 billion a year. Gold, silver, coal, and iron ore are all also mined and processed. The government gets mineral revenues from mining of royalty taxes between 4 percent and 9 percent. This money is important for many local governments whose community members are employed by the mining sector. This affects other areas of industrial production and pollution. Steel production increased 95 percent from 1980 to 2003—from 704,000 tons to 1,374,000 tons.

Emissions from within this sector accounted for 7 percent of all emissions. Within this sector, mineral products accounted for 57 percent of emissions, metal production 36 percent, and chemical industries 6.5 percent. Metal manufacturing comprises about 6 percent of the gross national product.

Waste emissions accounted for 3 percent of all emissions. These emissions increased 867.5 percent from 1993 to 2006. Within this sector, solid waste disposal on land accounted for 91 percent of emissions, wastewater management 4 percent, and incineration 1 percent.

Major Waste Issues

Raw sewage is a major form of water pollution in urban areas. Only 3 percent of wastewater is treated before being discharged into water. With temperature increases and more violent weather in the context of rapid urbanization, it is likely that infectious disease vectors will expand. Currently hepatitis A, hepatitis B, and typhoid occur here. Two percent or more of the population is persistently infected with hepatitis B. On Easter Island, there is a risk of dengue fever. It is possible that without increased public health measures, new diseases could arise.

In the Atacama Desert, where much mining occurs, water availability for mining is clashing with the water needs of traditional communities and creating substantial environmental effects. As mining expands, the groundwater in the aquifers shrink. As the quantity of groundwater declines, so does its suitability as drinking water because of the increased concentration of salt and other chemicals. Indigenous people are also exerting their rights to water and mining revenues in tribal lands.

Chile is preparing for more climate changes. Climate change observers note temperature increases in the Central Valley and in the Andes Mountains. Most of the freshwater comes from the melting snow in the mountains. As more snow melts, overall freshwater resources decrease. Lack of freshwater sources is a vulnerability in several regions. The glaciers are retreating because of the higher temperatures. There are 1,835 glaciers. The Patagonian ice fields contain a large volume of ice— 15,000 km^2. However, ice decreases in ocean and on the Pacific Ocean coast are also noted. Projected effects are increased temperatures, changes in precipitation patterns, a higher snowline in the mountains, decreasing available water, decrease in water system function of diluting and regulating liquid waste emissions, and increases in droughts. Primary concerns include water quality, quality, sanitation, extreme weather events, and ecosystem damages. Decreased freshwater, increased salinization of freshwater sources, decreased surface water quality resulting from increased severe weather events, more drought, and decreased biodiversity are part of these primary concerns. Chile is preparing more the creation of new sources of freshwater. They plan to build more reservoirs and groundwater infiltration facilities. In 2008, the Glaciology and Snow Unit was created within the Ministry of Public Works. Its mission is to inventory and monitor the glaciers, and its goal is to develop an adaption process for climate change effects and vulnerability in water management systems.

Further Reading

Carruthers, David V. 2008. *Environmental Justice in Latin America: Problems, Promise, and Practice*. Cambridge, MA: MIT Press.

Chilean Government Portal. www.gob.cl.

Climate Change Impacts on Water Systems. www.oecd.org.

Hill, Margot. 2013. *Climate Change and Water Governance: Adaptive Capacity in Chile and Switzerland*. Heidelberg, Germany: Springer E-books.

CHINA

Since 5000 B.C., humans have inhabited what is now China, roughly bordered by the Gobi Desert in the north and laced with three large river systems. The Pearl River is 2,197 km long, the Yangtze River is 6,300 km long—the third longest river in the world—and the Yellow River is 5,464 km long. These river systems have nourished human civilization for centuries.

Today, 1,315.8 billion people live on 9.6 million km^2 of land. China is the third-largest country in the world and has 27,060 km^2 of water. However, water quality is poor. China has more than 18,000 km of mainland coastline. Although the urban centers are large, there are also many small communities scattered throughout the country. Forty percent of the population is urbanized, and 37 percent lives in a city having more than 100,000 inhabitants. Twenty-two percent suffers malnutrition.

The climate differs regionally, being subarctic in the north and tropical in the south. China shares borders with fifteen countries along a land boundary of 22,800 km. It claims the tallest mountain the world, Mt. Everest. There are three basic geological levels in China. The first level is the Qinghi–Tibet Plateau, with a median altitude of 4 km, encompassing part of the Himalayan Range. The second level is about 1 km to 2 km in altitude. There are three large plateaus there—the inner Mongolian, Loess, and Yunnan–Guizhou. The third level is regions less than 500 m in altitude. Included in this region are north and northeast China, and it also includes the lower Yangtze valley plains and the Great Plains of China. About 5,400 islands are part of China's territorial waters, which comprise China's total maritime area of 4.73 million km². China has an exclusive economic zone of twelve nautical miles, a contiguous zone of twenty-four nautical miles, and a continental shelf of 200 nautical miles. China has many natural resources, including coal, iron ore, oil, gas, tin, mercury, rare metals, and uranium.

Current Waste Practices and Recycling

Waste practices vary widely. Generally, in rural areas, there is a greater chance that sanitation will be more basic, with use of pit toilets, latrines, drainage ditches, and cesspools. There are sewer systems in most urban centers.

China collected 157,340,000 tons of municipal waste in 2009, 56 percent of it landfilled, 13 percent incinerated, and 1 percent composted. Ninety-eight percent of the urban population has access to an improved drinking source, and 74 percent has access to an improved sanitation facility. Eighty-five percent of the rural population has access to improved drinking water sources, and 56 percent has access to an improved sanitation facility.

Some cities in China have had sewers for as long as 900 years, such as Guangzhou. Today in China, 83 percent of the people have access to sanitation. The intestinal disease death rate is about 5 percent. Accurate waste management data is not available for most of China. It is difficult to know how much and where most waste generated by activities having large environmental effects, such as mining, damming rivers, burning coal, and city growth, is sent. Because of rapid industrialization and rapid rise of a large consumer class, even more trash is on the way. The cumulative effects of unchecked environmental damage are merging with trash from the cities.

One of the problems of rapidly urbanizing cities is rapid trash generation. China is among the highest generators of municipal solid wastes (msw) in the world at about 210 million tons per year in the major cities. In all China in 2008, 155 million tons of msw were collected and transferred. Only 100 million tons were disposed—82 percent in landfills, 15 percent incinerated, and about 3 percent in other ways. This is predicted to reach 480 million tons per year by 2030. It is estimated that current landfills will reach capacity by 2020 and that another 1,400 new landfills will be needed for municipal solid wastes. Most landfills are not strictly regulated, with no collection of methane, very little waste compaction or covering, and little treatment of landfill leachates—being part of the informal waste economy. There are basically three kinds of landfills in China: The first, the dump, is used mostly in small cities and some villages. There is no waste treatment or consideration of environmental protection. It is unknown how many of these exist, but as population increases these are likely to increase. About a third of land-fills are controlled landfills.

Antibiotic-Resistant Genes: A Limitation on Wastewater Reuse

Wastewater can contain many chemicals and sometimes include controversial biosol-ids. Seven Chinese cities use wastewater contaminated with drug-resistant microbes. Chinese parks using recycled water have about 8,600 times more microbial antibi-otic resistant genes than parks using freshwater. Because countries have different standards for water quality in the reuse of wastewater for irrigation, it is difficult to evaluate the extent of worldwide recontamination with dirty wastewater. China also uses antibiotics heavily, which may explain some of the microbial resistance to antibiotics.

There is some waste treatment, along with pollution control measures. This is limited by the lack of adequate site selection and the lack of protection of soil and groundwater from landfill leachates. Sanitary landfills constitute about half of the landfill inventory. They provide the greatest pollution protection and waste treat-ment but are insufficient to keep up with waste generation. There are some pilot programs recapturing landfill gases for energy, with plans to expand to 300 such recovery systems in 2015.

The informal waste economy is a large part of waste treatment; waste pick-ers reclaim almost a fifth of China's waste. Waste pickers gather recyclable goods for payment and for food. Children are frequently used as waste pickers but are banned from government collection bins. They go through all kinds of landfills, including hazardous waste landfills. Former landfills or dumps containing chem-icals are called brownfields, and China has an estimated 5,000. Another factor is China's rising middle class. Many will want cars and the same things as people in other countries. This rush to buy consumer goods brings an increased trash load because of the lack of recycling and diminishing landfill space.

China's loose waste regulations attract other wastes from other countries that have strict regulations and higher fees. China imports about 40 percent of the world's plastic scrap, reprocessing it to make clothing and many goods. As a result, China's landfills are reaching capacity faster than planned. The United States once sent much of its recycling to China, but that is changing. China now only accepts plastic that has been cleaned and sorted, because otherwise it must be landfilled. In 2013, China rejected 68,000 tons of U.S. recyclable plastic for failing to meet these standards. There is a 10 percent to 20 percent decline in U.S. plastic scrap entering China.

First Chinese American Female Billionaire: Recycling

Zhang Yin is the world richest self-made woman in the world, worth an estimated $3.4 billion. Years of hard work as an accountant and business advisor in Hong Kong helped her make contacts with large investment firms. Before she left Hong Kong for the United States, she formed a company that bought scrap paper from the United States for disposal or recycling in China. When she moved to Pomona, California, in 1990, she started a waste collection company from her modest apartment. She was able to secure low shipping rates for vessels going from the United States to China because of the low rate of return cargo. China is generally in need of paper to recycle, because paper from wood is scarce. Eighteen percent of world demand for recycling paper is from China

The company, Chung Nam Inc., became the biggest exporter of waste paper from the United States anywhere, and especially to China. In 1998 she expanded the business into cardboard manufacturing and has continued to diversify.

There is little waste separation at home, and trash collection varies widely across the country. In some municipalities, residents take their trash to the outlying edges of suburbs. Part of the trash is often coal residues and plastics. Smaller cities and villages use open-air dumps in the edge of town. More and more municipalities are starting recycling programs and building landfills that capture released methane.

Hazardous Wastes

China generated 13.57 million tons of hazardous wastes. The export of hazardous wastes for final disposal is allowed when there is no capacity in China to handle them. The export of hazardous wastes for recovery is allowed. China does regulate the movement of hazardous wastes moving through its borders. The Solid Waste Law and the Ocean Environmental Protection Law forbid the transit of hazardous waste over land or water in China. The state regulates the disposal of hazardous wastes using permits. Different levels of government can issue hazardous waste permits for landfill disposal. There are about 400 permits for different types of hazardous wastes.

14,298,000 metric tons of hazardous wastes were generated in China in 2009. Nine hundred fifty-eight metric tons of hazardous wastes were exported, 395 metric tons of other wastes were exported, and 6 metric tons of other wastes were generated.

Nuclear Wastes

China's twenty-one operating nuclear power reactors contribute 2 percent to 3 percent of the total produced electricity. There are no disposal facilities. There are seven storage and seven processing facilities.

Persistent Organic Pollutants

Persistent organic pollutants (POPs) are powerful chemicals with long-lasting destructive environmental effects on all animals and can spread throughout the world. POPs contamination is found in farm produce, water, soil, mother's milk, and sediments. China signed the Stockholm Convention on POPs in 2001 and ratified it in 2004, when it entered into force. As part of its responsibility, China needs to develop a National Implementation Plan detailing POP inventories and final disposition. China's plan is to eliminate production, use, import, and export of some POPs chemicals. It plans to investigate and update inventories of POP release from unintentional production and make inventories of electrical equipment containing POP wastes, establishing best available technology and best environmental practices to control dioxin waste in primary industries.

Hong Kong is often under a separate environmental policy.

Emissions and Industry

In 2008 China generated 23 percent of global carbon dioxide emissions, the highest of any single nation. In 2005 China generated 7,465,861.7 metric tons of greenhouse gases, an 84 percent increase from 1994. (Air pollution contributes to respiratory and heart disease, the leading cause of death in China.)

Smoke pollution from the Hangzhou steelworks industrial buildings in China. Urban air pollution is severe in many Chinese cities. Heavy industrialization without environmental controls has degraded public health and spurred several recent national clean air initiatives in China. (Zhaojiankang/Dreamstime.com)

Agricultural products include rice, wheat, potatoes, corn, peanuts, millet, teas, apples, barley, cotton, pork, and fish. China has 135.56 million ha of arable and permanent cropland, among the most in the world. 5,641,410 km^2 are irrigated, the second most in the world.

The Chinese demand for meat has increased rapidly in the last few years. From 2004 to 2008, total meat production increased 10 percent. In 2008, animal wastes in China represented about 2.7 billion tons of manure a year. Agricultural wastes are a bigger part of water pollution than industry is. In 2010, farming was responsible for 44 percent of chemical oxygen demand (organic compounds), 67 percent of phosphorus discharges, and nitrogen discharges. This comes from manure from all livestock as well as poultry. There are about 4.2 million large-scale pig, cattle, and poultry farms, as well as countless small farms. Manure in the water causes blue-green algae blooms because the nitrogen and phosphorus deplete oxygen necessary for aquatic life. To partially address this problem, the Chinese Ministry of Agriculture is promoting biogas digesters. Eighty million residential methane digesters and 10,000 large biogas plants are planned by 2020. Biogas generators degrade waste into usable cooking gas and fertilizer and may decrease greenhouse gas emissions from manure.

Agricultural emissions accounted for 11 percent of all emissions. Within this sector, enteric fermentation accounted for 37 percent of emissions, agricultural soils 25 percent, rice cultivation 20 percent, and manure management 17 percent. This is a high amount of greenhouse gas emissions from manure, indicating the presence of large amounts of untreated feces.

China produced 4.42 bbl of crude oil per day in 2012, exporting 50,650 bbl per day. It consumes about 8.2 million bbl per day, the third highest in the world. It exports 623,000 bbl of refined petroleum per day, among the most in the world. It has 3.52 trillion m^3 of natural gas. China consumed 4.43 trillion kWh in 2011, the highest in the world. It has installed electrical generation capacity of 1.15 kW, the highest in the world in 2012. Oil and electricity consumption and production per capita are among the highest rates in the world. Much of this energy is generated using coal-fired power plants, the source of much air pollution. It is estimated that about 28 million tons of coal ash a year enters the general waste stream as solid wastes or as particulate matter in air.

Energy emissions accounted for 77 percent of all emissions. Within this sector, energy industries accounted for 42 percent of emissions, manufacturing and construction 36.6 percent, and transportation 7.4 percent.

China produces the most aluminum, buses, and cars in the world. China uses about half of the world's nickel and supplies 5 percent of the global supply. China supplies about 57 percent of world pig iron and 45 percent of global crude steel production. Copper production is expanding smelter and refinery operations. Many mines are illegal and illegally dump wastes into rivers. For example, the Hejiang River was found contaminated with cadmium and thallium. One hundred twelve illegal mines were required to stop production to reduce pollution that affected about 30,000 people downstream.

Industrial emissions accounted for 10 percent of all emissions. Within this sector, mineral products accounted for 67 percent of emissions, metal production 7 percent, and chemical industries 6 percent. There is a high consumption of halocarbons, much of it from the use of brown coal, accounting for about 21 percent of emissions in this sector.

About a third of municipal solid waste (msw) is not properly disposed. Cities are rapidly growing and so is trash. Municipal solid waste in Beijing is estimated to grow 8 percent a year. Waste emissions accounted for 1.5 percent of all emissions. It is estimated that about 40 percent of the rivers in China are very polluted. About 20 percent of the rivers are too toxic for any contact. Some rivers are so polluted that there is concern that they may start burning.

The use of manure and human wastes is a widespread practice in agricultures, with a four-century tradition. However, some crops such as rice are emerged in water, which acts as a source for greenhouse gases and as an infectious disease vector. Biogas is being explored as waste reduction off grid energy source.

Within this sector, wastewater management accounted for 56 percent of emissions, solid waste disposal on land 41 percent, and incineration 2 percent. This is a substantial increase in incineration waste treatment. Incineration in China is expanding, because incinerators take less land than landfills. During incineration, waste volume decreases 90 percent and waste weight is reduced by 75 percent. Incineration residues are reused even though they can contain toxic materials. Incinerators are major sources of dioxin. Advanced filter technology promises to reduce this by supercooling the gases before they are filtered. Heavy metals are not destroyed and escape into the air, nearby soils, and waterways. Fly ash is sent to the landfill, and bottom residual ash is reused in construction. Heavy metals in these ashes can leach into surrounding soils. The dioxin is attached to the surface of the ashes and is not as soluble as heavy metals are.

Major Waste Issues

The main waste issue for most of urban China is air and water pollution. Parts of China now suffer acid rain because of the use of brown coal. Water shortages occur in the north, and water pollution occurs in many regions, caused by discharging untreated sewage and other wastes directly into waterways. China places low priority on pollution control, and enforcement of the weak laws that exist is poor. China's polluted air and water are on such a large scale that it is an international concern. China does have technical assistance and training on waste management at the National Center of Solid Waste Management, Nanjing Institute of Environmental Science, and Chinese Research Academy of Environmental Science.

Public health is emerging as a major waste issue. Currently, dengue fever, hepatitis A, hepatitis B, Japanese encephalitis, malaria, schistosomiasis, tick-borne encephalitis (TBE), and typhoid occur. Two percent or more of the population is persistently infected with hepatitis B. There is a high risk of malaria in Yunnan and Hainan provinces. TBE is a high risk in Heilongjiang, Jilin, and Mongolia provinces below 1,400 m altitude between March and November. Climate change effects are varied over such a large and diverse region. With increases in temperature, more violent weather and rising ocean levels in the context of large-scale urbanization, overcrowding, and poor sanitation, it is likely that infectious disease vectors will expand to higher altitudes, longer distances, and longer seasons.

Further Reading

Marks, Robert B. 2011. *China: Its Environment and History*. Lanham, MD: Rowman and Littlefield Publishers.

Mertha, Andrew C. 2010. *China's Water Warriors: Citizen Action and Policy Change*. Ithaca, NY: Cornell University Press.

Shapiro, Judith. 2012. *China's Environmental Challenges*. Cambridge, UK: Polity Press.

Tibetan Government in Exile. www.tibet.net.

Ying, L., et al. 2014. "Use of Human Excreta as Manure in Rural China." *Journal of Integrative Agriculture* 13: 434–442.

COLOMBIA

Colombia is a multi-ethnic nation, the populace being 58 percent mestizo, 20 percent white, 14 percent mulatto, 4 percent black, 3 percent mixed black–Amerindian, and 1 percent indigenous peoples. Together, 46 million people live on 1.1 million km^2 of land and 100,210 km^2 of freshwater. Colombia has a 3,208 km coastline, with 1,760 km along the Caribbean Sea and 1,448 km along the North Pacific Ocean. Seventy-three percent of the population is urbanized, and 41 percent lives in a city having more than 100,000 inhabitants. Bogota is the largest city in Colombia as well as in South America. Twenty-seven percent live in overcrowded conditions, and 16 percent suffers malnutrition. Colombia has one of the largest populations of internally displaced persons.

The climate is tropical along the coast and eastern plains. It gets some of the highest amounts of rain in the world. It is cooler in the highlands. Columbia shares its borders with Brazil, Ecuador, Panama, Peru, and Venezuela. Natural resources include petroleum, natural gas, coal, iron ore, nickel, copper, gold, and emeralds. It has the largest coal reserves in South America.

Current Waste Practices

Many of the waste practices in rural areas are basic—pit toilets, latrines, cesspools, and drainage ditches. In 2008, 7,437,000 tons of municipal wastes were generated. 79,000 tons of hazardous wastes were generated in 2008. It is estimated that trash is increasing from 4 percent to 8 percent a year. Private trash haulers provide hauling services for about 60 percent of the people. When solid wastes from waste pickers and industries are included, about three-quarters of the trash goes to landfills, about 20 percent is informally and formally recycled, 4 percent is illegally dumped, and 1 percent goes to recycling facilities.

Most communities use basic sewer and water services, but little water is treated before being discharged into local water sources. Ninety-nine percent of the urban population has access to an improved drinking water source, and 82 percent has access to an improved sanitary facility. Seventy-two percent of the rural population has access to an improved drinking water source, and 63 percent has access to improved sanitation facilities.. About 95 percent of urban sewage is not treated before being discharged into water. Approximately 154 of 1,068 municipalities treat sewage.

There is a prominent informal economy of waste pickers who rummage through waste for recyclables and food. Waste pickers are now being paid as recyclers in some places. It is estimated that Bogota has 15,000 waste pickers. About 5,000 are organized as the Bogota Recyclers Association. The country's highest court recognized the waste pickers' rights in solid waste management and ordered affirmative actions for their protection.

Emissions and Industry

In 2004 Colombia emitted 153,884.8 metric tons of greenhouse gases, a 30 percent increase from 1990.

Agricultural products include coffee, bananas, rice, tobacco, sugar cane, cocoa, vegetables, and forest products. Just less than 2 percent of the land is arable. 10,870 km^2 of land is irrigated, among the highest amounts in the world. Pesticide use is high—16.7 kg per person per year. Agricultural emissions accounted for 44.5 percent of all emissions. Within this sector, enteric fermentation accounts for 48 percent of emissions, agricultural soils 47 percent, rice cultivation 2 percent, and manure management 2 percent.

Colombia produces substantial amounts of crude oil and maintains large proven reserves . There are 169.9 billion m^3 of proven natural gas reserves, but little production. Oil and electricity consumption and electricity production per capita are low. There is civil unrest, with Brazil's energy network a target. Four hundred electric towers were bombed in one rebel attack. Gas and oil pipelines are also targets. Seventy percent of electricity comes from hydroelectric power. Droughts have caused power shortages as energy demand increased. Coal- and gas-fired power plants are planned to produce 20 percent of the country's electricity, which will increase greenhouse gas emissions. Carbon dioxide emission from coal increased from 1.75 million metric tons in 1990 to 2.88 in 2000. Carbon dioxide from petroleum increased from 7.39 million metric tons to 10.22 in the same time period.

Energy emissions accounted for 43 percent of all emissions. Within this sector, transportation accounted for 33 percent of emissions, energy industries 23 percent, and manufacturing and construction 20 percent. "Other" sectors and fugitive emissions accounted for 23 percent of emissions in this sector. Energy emissions are a large part of all emissions. Such a high proportion of unaccounted emissions can affect the environment and public health. Fugitive emissions are essentially unaccounted waste streams into the air. Fugitive emissions can affect regional ecosystems and the public health because they can fall from the air to the land and water. Industrial emissions accounted for 6 percent of all emissions. Within this sector, metal production accounted for 42 percent of all emissions, mineral products 37 percent, and chemical industries 6 percent.

Waste emissions accounted for 6.6 percent of all emissions. Within this sector, the disposal of solid wastes on land accounted for 88 percent of emissions and wastewater handling 12 percent.

Major Waste Issues

Water pollution is a major waste issue. There is soil and water quality damage from pesticide and fertilizer runoff. About 75 percent of publicly provided water is not potable. Only about a quarter of wastewater received any kind of treatment. Many current sewage systems do not have the size or water to handle modern waste flows. Access to safe water is very limited in rural areas. the United Nations Millennium Development goals for sanitation are not met and are not likely to meet 2015 deadlines.

Currently, dengue fever, hepatitis A, malaria, typhoid, and yellow fever occur here. The risk of yellow fever centers on Barranquilla, Cali, Cartagena, and Medellin. There is a high risk of malaria in rural areas below 1,600 m altitude. Enteritis, hepatitis, and typhoid are endemic. With climate change–increased temperature, more violent weather and rising ocean levels in the context of large-scale urbanization, overcrowding, and poor sanitation, it is likely that infectious disease vectors will expand to higher altitudes, longer distances, and longer seasons.

Further Reading

Chammartin, F., et al. 2013. "Soil-Transmitted Helminth Infection in South America: A Systematic Review and Geostatistical Meta-Analysis." *The Lancet* 13: 507–518.

Colombia Environmental Assessment. www.eia.nl/en/countries/sa/colombia/.

Sanchez-Triana, Ernesto, and Santiago Enriquez. 2012. "Using Policy-Based Strategic Environmental Assessments in Water Supply and Sanitation Sector Reforms: The Cases of Argentina and Colombia." *Impact Assessment and Project Appraisal* 25: 175–187.

Van Drunen, Michiel A., B. Lasage, and C. Dorland. 2006. *Climate Change in Developing Countries.* Oxfordshire, UK: CAB International North America.

CONGO REPUBLIC

The Congo River dominates the equatorial African nation of the Congo Republic. It forms part of the southern border with the Democratic Republic of the Congo before it enters the Congo Republic and goes into the Atlantic Ocean. The river system provides transportation, commerce, and power to millions of people for more than 9,000 miles. There are approximately forty hydropower plants along the river. Most of the contiguous nations do not have extensive roads or railways and rely on the river exclusively for goods and services. Although relied upon, there are many parts of the river that have risks of waterfalls and surging rapids.

Today, 4.5 million people live in the Congo Republic on 2.27 million km^2 of land. Sixty percent are urbanized and just over half live in a city having more than 100,000 inhabitants. There are many small communities throughout the nation.

The capital and largest city is Brazzaville, which has 1.3 million people. About a third suffers malnutrition. Life expectancy is 56 years. Malaria rates are high. Diarrhea and some cancer rates are elevated.

The Congo Republic borders Angola, Burundi, Central African Republic, and the Democratic Republic of the Congo, Rwanda, South Sudan, Tanzania, Uganda, and Zambia. The terrain is flat, with mountains in the east. There are abundant natural resources. The Congo has the most renewable water sources in the world. Other natural resources include cobalt, copper, petroleum, tantalum, diamonds, zinc, gold, silver, uranium, coal and timber. The climate is regional. It is hot and humid in the equatorial river basin, generally drier and cooler in the southern highlands and cooler and wetter in the eastern highlands.

Current Waste Practices

Waste practices are basic—pit toilets, latrines, cesspools, drainage ditches, and open defecation. Ninety-five percent of the urban population has access to an improved drinking water source, and only 20 percent has access to improved sanitation. Only 32 percent of the rural population has access to an improved drinking water source, and just 15 percent has access to improved sanitation facilities. The open defecation rate in 2012 was 24 percent, down from 57 percent in 1990.

Emissions and Industry

The Congo Republic, also known as Brazzaville, produces large amounts of oil. The economy is heavily dependent on the petrochemical industry. Oil and electricity production are high and consumption per capita low. Some natural gas is consumed and there are massive proven reserves. Petrochemical production is declining, and very little post-petrochemical production cleanup or environmental mitigation occurs. Accurate greenhouse gas emissions monitoring and reporting is not available. Because of the reliance on petrochemical production it is likely that greenhouse gas emissions are high.

Only 1 percent of the land is arable. Agricultural products include sugar, rice, cassava, coffee, cocoa, corn, and livestock. There are grave concerns about food security and climate change–increased temperatures and oceans level rise.

Major Waste Issues

Most sewage and water is not treated before being discharged into freshwater. Potable water and water pollution are a major waste problem. Public health and environmental monitoring is poor. The major waste issue is the protection of the public health nationally and regionally. Infectious diseases are a major concern. Currently infectious diseases include cholera, dengue fever, hepatitis A, hepatitis B, malaria, polio, schistosomiasis, typhoid, and yellow fever. Two percent or more of the population s persistently infected with hepatitis B. There is a risk of yellow fever in all areas of the country.

Conflict and Climate Change Effects: Near Real-Time Mapping of Climate Change, Conflict, and Aid in Africa

The measurement of the environmental effects of conflicts is important in monitoring global climate change. The weapons and wastes of war are not accounted for and are becoming larger and more hazardous.

The University of Texas program in Climate Change and African Political Stability now provides near real-time mapping of climate change vulnerability, conflict, and foreign aid for Africa (www.ccaps.aiddata.org). Climate change model parameters are population density, political violence, physical exposure to actual climate hazards, household and community resilience, and governance. Each of these categories has sets of indicators and can overlap indicators and parameter categories to show relationships between them. This program also tracks foreign aid projects, ranking them according to climate change relevance and generating a new map layer, for example. Evaluating projects that reduce climate change vulnerability are done the same way. Another data set scrutinizes conflicts in Africa based on intensity, issues, type of event, and actors (www.ccaps.aiddata.org/conflict). Combining climate change vulnerability and conflict maps shows the effect of conflict on climate change. The map format allows readers not literate in the language to see climate change, aid, and conflict relationships visually. These datasets are user friendly and are designed for a large range of preferences and filters (www.struasscenter.org/ccaps/data).

The lack of public health and sanitation facilities combined with urban growth and overcrowding provide environments for infectious diseases now. The infant mortality rate is high while the number of hospital beds per person is low. The chance of a male reaching 65 is about a third. The number of doctors per person is low. Climate change–increased temperatures and violent weather could facilitate these diseases to epidemic proportion. These outbreaks may become nationally uncontrollable and reach epidemic proportion, potentially affecting the region and planet. Substantial international assistance is necessary to develop locally and globally effective public health systems.

Further Reading

Central Africa Regional Program for the Environment, Regional Development Strategy 2012–2020, U.S. Agency for International Development. www.usaid.gov.

Mbete, R., et al. 2013. "Household Bushmeat Consumption in Brazzaville, the Republic of the Congo." *Tropical Conservation Science* 4: 187–202.

Mombouli, J. 2013. "Chikungunya Virus Infection, Brazzaville, Republic of Congo, 2011." *Emerging Infectious Diseases* 19: 1,542–1,543.

Mosnier, A., et al. 2014. "Modeling Impact of Development Trajectories and a Global Agreement on Reducing Emissions from Deforestation on Congo Basin Forests by 2030." *Environmental and Resource Economics* 57: 505–525.

COSTA RICA

Costa Rica is one of the few nations that does not have a military. In 1948 President Jose Figueres Ferrer abolished it. In 1949 the constitution was amended to forbid a standing army. Costa Rica has used the so called "peace dividend" to invest in the economic and ecological development of the nation.

Today, 4.7 million people live on Costa Rica's 51,100 km^2 of land, which has 40 km^2 of water. Costa Rica's coastline is 1,290 km long, with 212 km on the Caribbean coast and 1,016 km on the Pacific coast. Sixty-two percent are urbanized, and 46 percent live in a city having more than 100,000 inhabitants. Twenty-two percent live in overcrowded conditions.

Costa Rica is in Central America and borders Nicaragua, Panama, the Caribbean Sea, and the North Pacific Ocean. The climate is subtropical. The rainy season is May to November and the dry season December to April. Hydropower is one Costa Rica's primary natural resources. The country gets some of the highest amounts of rain in the world. The terrain is mountainous, with numerous volcano cones and several major volcanoes. There are small coastal plains on the west side of the country.

Current Waste Practices and Recycling

All the urban centers have basic sewer systems. In rural areas, waste practices can become more basic, including pit toilets, latrines, cesspools, and drainage ditches. Slightly over half of the towns deposit solid waste in their own outdoor dumps and about 15 percent share dumps, with the remaining waste in "partially controlled" dumps. Many landfills are near or over capacity. About 1.3 million tons per year is disposed of in four large landfills. Landfills are slowly developing, and a private waste haul industry is growing. There is some interest in developing waste treatment plants, which the government is encouraging. About 1.28 million tons of municipal waste is collected a year. About 73 percent of the population receives municipal waste collection. About 60 percent of this waste is in open dumps, 15 percent is in landfills, and about 250 tons is illegally dumped. There are strong local recycling efforts, and the national government has developed e-waste laws that are starting to be implemented.

Hazardous Wastes

There are no restrictions against the export of hazardous wastes and other wastes for final disposal or recovery. The import of hazardous wastes and other wastes for final disposal is prohibited. Importation for recycling or material recovery is allowed.

The dependence on the tourism industry encourages the development and growth of recycling practices. Some municipalities have trash pickups, and some have recycling.

All the urban population has access to an improved water drinking water source, and 95 percent has access to improved sanitation. Ninety-one percent of the rural population has access to an improved drinking water source, and 96 percent has access to an improved sanitation facility. Three percent of urban sewage is treated before being discharged into water. Of this, 33 percent receives primary waste treatment and 67 percent receives secondary waste treatment.

Emissions and Industry

Costa Rica generated 12,114 metric tons of greenhouse gas emissions in 2005, a 99 percent increase from 1990.

Almost 5 percent of the land is arable. 1,080 km² of land is irrigated. Fertilizer use is 385 kg per person per year, which is high. Pesticide use is 51.2 kg per person per year, also very high. Bananas are a leading export. Other agricultural products include pineapples, melons, coffee, sugar, corn, rice, beans, potatoes, beef, poultry, timber, and dairy products. Agriculture accounted for 38 percent of all emissions. Within this sector, agricultural soils accounted for 54 percent of emissions, enteric fermentation 40 percent, and rice cultivation 5 percent.

Costa Rica produces some crude oil and maintains proven reserves. Oil and electricity consumption and production per capita are low. Costa Rica relies on hydropower for almost 85 percent of its power needs. Energy emissions accounted for 47 percent of all emissions. Within this sector, transportation accounted for 68 percent of emissions, manufacturing and construction 18 percent, and energy industries 4 percent. Industrial emissions account for 4 percent of all emissions. Within this sector, mineral products account for 100 percent of greenhouse gas emissions.

Wastes emissions account for 11 percent of all emissions. Within this sector, solid waste disposal on land accounts for 50 percent of emissions and wastewater management 50 percent.

Major Waste Issues

Costa Rica applies international principles of environmental waste management, such as the precautionary principle and sustainable development. However, many cities have grown quickly and increased municipal solid waste generation faster than waste systems can accommodate. There are currently infectious diseases such as dengue fever, malaria, hepatitis A, and typhoid. There is a moderate risk of malaria in Limon Province and a low risk in low-lying rural areas. Costa Rica is economically dependent on ecotourism, and the environmental and health issues attendant on uncontrolled garbage could affect tourism. Costa Rica is also an international tourist destination and global crossroads. It is the destination of many cruise ships. A common environmental controversy with shipping of all types is where the sewage and all the other wastes are dumped. It is a common practice to dump them in port. The waste of increased shipping and tourism can be the carrier of infectious diseases. Increased temperatures, rising ocean levels, and increases in violent weather combined with increased global travel will increase infectious disease vectors. Public health is the major waste issue in urban areas.

Costa Rica is often used as a model of sustainable development and humanitarian principles. Like many countries, it is facing waste issues in the context of other environmental issues. Costa Rica faces other environmental issues, such as deforestation for expansion of agriculture, soil erosion, coastal water pollution, and air pollution. As a world leader in sustainable development, Costa Rica will develop policies on waste.

Further Reading

Bower, K. 2014. "Water Supply and Sanitation of Costa Rica." *Environmental Earth Sciences* 71: 107–123.

Costa Rican Government. www.costaricaweb.com.

Dallas, Stewart, Brian Scheffe, and Goen Ho. 2004. "Reedbeds for Greywater Treatment-Case Study in Santa Elena-Montverde, Costa Rica." *Ecological Engineering* 23: 55–61.

Evans, Sterling. 1999. *The Green Republic: A Conservation History of Costa Rica.* Austin: University of Texas Press.

COTE D'IVOIRE

Originally known as the Ivory Coast, Cote d'Ivoire began as many small tribal communities. There are at least sixty tribes present in the country today. These tribal affiliations have created tension and civil unrest and pose a continuing challenge to the nation.

Today, 22.4 million people live on Cote d'Ivoire's 322,463 km² of land. Fifty-one percent of the population is urbanized, and the population is rapidly urbanizing, at about 3 percent per year. There is pervasive overcrowding in the cities.

The climate differs regionally. Generally it is hot and humid along the coast and drier north. There are three seasons. In March, the weather is warm and dry. From March to May, it is hot and dry. From June to October, it is hot and wet. Cote d'Ivoire borders Burkina Faso, Ghana, Guinea, Liberia, Mali, and the North Atlantic Ocean. The terrain is flat, with mountains in the northwest. There is an abundance of natural resources. These include petroleum, natural gas, diamonds, manganese, cobalt, copper, iron ore, gold, nickel, and hydropower.

Current Waste Practices

Waste practices are basic—pit toilets, latrines, drainage ditches, cesspools, and open defecation. Ninety-one percent of the urban population has access to an improved drinking water source, and just 36 percent has access to improved sanitation facilities. Sixty-eight percent of the rural population has access to an improved drinking water source, and just 11 percent has access to improved sanitation facilities. Currently there are efforts to create productive sanitation by promoting ecological sanitation. This means separating wastewater from drinking water. It often includes natural degradation of wastes when possible. Developing policies also include municipal wastewater and sludge management, and facilitating household water connection to public water supply systems in urban areas. Currently, the Ministry of Sanitation, along with the Ministry of Planning and the Ministry of

Health, will include the elimination of open defecation in the 2014–2016 Poverty Reduction Strategy and in the national health and nutrition plan.

Emissions and Industry

Cote d'Ivoire generated 271,197.5 metric tons of green house gas in 2000, a 49 percent increase from 1994. It is likely that greenhouse gas emissions are higher because of increased population and heavy dependence on agriculture.

Agricultural emissions accounted for 72 percent of all emissions. Within this sector, agricultural soils accounted for 91 percent of emissions, manure management 3 percent, and enteric fermentation 3 percent. Agricultural products include coffee, cocoa beans, bananas, palm kernels, sugar, corn, rice, timber, cotton, and rubber. Cote d'Ivoire is one of the largest producers of both cocoa and coffee.

Cote d'Ivoire produces some crude oil and maintains proven reserves. Energy emissions accounted for 26 percent of all emissions. Within this sector, energy industries accounted for 87 percent of emissions, fugitive emissions 9 percent, and transportation 3 percent. Fugitive emissions are essentially unaccounted waste streams into the air. Fugitive emissions can affect regional ecosystems and the public health, because they can fall from the air to the land and water. Petrochemical and natural gas production is high and per-capita oil consumption low. Industrial emissions accounted for none of the emissions. This is unlikely, because petroleum processing and transit alone generate demand for chemical manufacturing and create industrial emissions.

Waste emissions accounted for 4 percent of all emissions. Within this sector, solid waste disposal on land accounted for 98 percent of emissions and wastewater handling 2 percent.

Major Waste Issues

The major waste issue is the protection of the public health nationally and regionally. Water pollution from raw sewage, industrial pollutants, and agricultural practices poses a major challenge. Infectious diseases are a major concern. Currently infectious diseases include cholera, dengue fever, hepatitis A, hepatitis B, schistosomiasis, typhoid, and yellow fever. There is a high risk of malaria. Two percent or more of the population is persistently infected with hepatitis B. There is a risk of yellow fever in all areas of the country.

The lack of public health and sanitation facilities combined with urban growth and overcrowding provide environments for infectious diseases now. The infant mortality rate is high but the number of hospital beds per person low. The chance of a male's reaching age 65 is about a third. The number of doctors per person is low. Climate change effects create grave concern for food security and risk of famine. They include increased temperatures and violent weather, which can lead to droughts and floods. It is very likely that disease outbreaks will develop. These outbreaks may become nationally uncontrollable and reach epidemic proportion, potentially affecting the region and planet. Substantial international assistance is necessary to develop locally and globally effective public health systems. Increases in violent weather will increase current environmental issues of desertification and deforestation.

Further Reading

Central Africa Regional Program for the Environment, Regional Development Strategy 2012–2020, U.S. Agency for International Development. www.usaid.gov.
Cote d'Ivoire Government. www.gouv.ci.
Hurlimann, E., et al. 2014. "The Epidemiology of Polyparasitism and Implications for Morbidity in Two Rural Communities of Cote d'Ivoire." *Parasites and Vectors* 7: 81–95.
Kone, S., et al. 2014. "Health and Demographic Surveillance System Profile: The Taabo Health and Demographic Surveillance System, Cote d'Ivoire." *International Journal of Epidemiology* 43: in press.
Matthys, Barbara, et al. 2006. "Urban Farming and Malaria Risk Factors in a Medium-Sized Town in Cote D'Ivoire." *American Journal of Tropical Medicine and Hygiene* 75: 1223–1231.
Obrist, Brigit, et al. 2007. "Interconnected Slums: Water, Sanitation and Health in Abidjan, Cote d'Ivoire." *The European Journal of Development Research* 18: 319–336.

CROATIA

Croatia emerged as an independent nation from conflict with a Serbian-dominated Yugoslavian Army after passing a declaration of independence in 1991. UN peace-keeping forces were deployed, but fighting continued for a decade. Croatia is still recovering from this conflict but is moving forward. In 2003, Croatia began its application to the European Union. In July 2013, Croatia joined the European Union.

Today, 4.5 million people live on 56,594 km^2 of land with 620 km^2 of water. Croatia has 1,777.3 km of coastline, along the Adriatic Sea. Fifty-six percent of Croatians live in urban areas, and 32 percent live in a city having more than 100,000 inhabitants.

The climate has hot summers and cold winters. Along the coast, the summer is dry and winters are not as cold. Croatia borders Bosnia and Herzegovina, Hungary, Serbia, Montenegro, and Slovenia. The terrain consists of low mountains near the coastline and flat land along the Hungarian border. Natural resources include oil, coal, iron ore, bauxite, calcium, gypsum, silica, and salt.

Current Waste Practices and Recycling

About half of the population is served by municipal sewers. Water quality is poor. The plan is to move away from untreated wastes in dumps to a waste infrastructure that can manage and dispose of wastes more efficiently. Some wastes are exported for proper treatment and disposal. Municipal wastes constituted about half the wastes. 3,157,963 tons of wastes were generated in 2010. Croatia collected 1,788,000 tons of municipal waste in 2009, almost all of it landfilled, with about 2 percent incinerated. Ninety-three percent of the population receives municipal waste collection.

Croatia experienced armed civil conflict in 1992–1995, and waste practices are in the context of war reconstruction. Information is difficult to find, and sanitation practices range from rudimentary to well-planned. Removal of military waste is necessary and dangerous. Unexploded landmines can detonate years after deployment.

In 2007 the Croatian Parliament adopted the National Plan on Waste. One of the goals of the plan is to avoid and reduce waste generation and the hazards of waste. One of the strategies for doing this is to develop more education around waste issues. Another strategy for this goal is to separate waste at the point of production. Waste producers who produce more than 150 tons of nonhazardous wastes or more than 200 kg of hazardous wastes are required to plan waste management for four years. Remediation of the polluted environment is a policy consideration. Another goal of the plan is to recover wastes for energy development. In 2005–2009, laws were enacted that focused on packaging and packaging wastes.

Hazardous Wastes

Altogether, 58,000 tons of hazardous wastes were generated 2008. Transportation of nonhazardous wastes for disposal and recovery is allowed, as is the transportation of hazardous wastes if the person moving it is registered with the government. Croatia controls the export of hazardous wastes and other wastes for final disposal or recovery. The import of hazardous wastes and other wastes are controlled and is not permitted unless it is recoverable, to create a new product or raw material. There are no hazardous waste landfills in Croatia, but 213,000 metric tons of hazardous wastes were generated in 2009. Altogether, 17,510 metric tons of hazardous wastes was exported. Croatia has no nuclear power reactors, disposal facilities, or processing facilities, but it does have one storage facility for nuclear wastes. There are plans to build a hazardous wastes incinerator.

Recycling

The recycling rate is 4 percent. Recycling was first reported in 2007. There are ambitious plans to increase the amount of municipal solid waste that is recycled. Croatia is developing its waste infrastructure with help from the European Union.

Emissions and Industry

Croatia generated 28,256 tons of greenhouse gases in 2011, an 11 percent decrease from 1990.

Almost 16 percent of the land is arable. Agricultural products include wheat, corn, fruits, vegetables, livestock, and dairy products. About 37 km^2 of land is irrigated. Agricultural emissions accounted for 12 percent of all emissions. Within this sector, agricultural soils accounted for 66 percent of greenhouse gas emissions, enteric fermentation 24 percent, and manure management 11 percent.

Croatia produces crude oil and maintains proven reserves. In 2013, there was 24.92 billion m^3 of proven natural gas reserves. Energy emissions accounted for

74 percent of all emissions. Within this sector, energy industries accounted for 31 percent of emissions, transportation 28 percent, manufacturing and construction 15 percent, and fugitive emissions 10 percent. Fugitive emissions are essentially unaccounted waste streams into the air. Fugitive emissions can affect regional ecosystems and the public health, because they can fall from the air to the land and water. Industrial emissions accounted for about 11 percent of all emissions. Within this sector, chemical industries accounted for 43 percent of emissions, mineral products 40 percent, and metal production 1 percent.

Waste emissions accounted for 4 percent of all emissions, increasing 91 percent from 1990 to 2011. Within this sector, solid waste disposal on land accounted for 71 percent of emissions and wastewater handling 28.5 percent.

Major Waste Issues

Croatia is pursuing international environmental management policies such as those of the International Organization for Standardization (ISO). Croatia is identifying which industrial sectors create the most wastes and is targeting technological developments in cleaner production to these industries. The environmental situation is challenging. Air pollution from metallurgical plants and increased acid rain is affecting forests, crops, and communities. Coastal pollution from industrial and municipal wastes remains a large issue. Wastes are increasing, but there are few municipal waste recovery and treatment plants. Wastes from past, present, and near future activities are likely to have significant effects on public health and the environment. Croatia has started a cleanup program of the most high-risk areas. The infectious diseases currently here are hepatitis A, hepatitis B, and tick-borne encephalitis (TBE). Two percent or more of the population is persistently infected with hepatitis B. TBE is a risk below 1,400 m between the Sava and Drava rivers from March to November.

Climate change–increased temperatures, ocean levels, and more violent weather will challenge reconstruction efforts and affect agriculture. It will also increase the range of hospitable environments for infectious diseases.

Further Reading

Bellinger, Ed, ed. 2000. *Environmental Assessment in Countries in Transition.* Portland, OR: LLC. Books International.

Croatia Environmental Profile. www.eea.europa.eu/soer/countries/hr.

Croatian Presidents Office. www.predsjednik.hr.

Richardson, Mervyn. 2002. *Effects of War on the Environment: Croatia.* Danvers, MA: CRC Press.

CUBA

In December 2014, President Obama reopened diplomatic relations with Cuba, ending a historic embargo of trade and travel between Cuba and the United States. Cuba is a large island nation off the tip of Florida. Altogether, 11.3 million people live on its 109,884 km^2 of land and use its 1,040 km^2 of freshwater.

Cuba has 5,700 km of coastline and also includes many small nearby islands. Seventy-six percent of the population is urbanized, and 39 percent lives in a city having more than 100,000 inhabitants. Information about the large U.S. military base, Guantanamo Bay, is difficult to obtain because of U.S. national security concerns.

The climate is tropical—hot and humid. The terrain is mountainous in the southeast and south central area, known as Sierra Maestra. The dry season is November to April, and the rainy season is May to October. Natural resources include cobalt, iron ore, nickel, copper, salt, and oil.

Current Waste Practices and Recycling

Ninety-six percent of the urban population has access to an improved drinking water source, and 94 percent has access to an improved sanitation facility. Eighty-nine percent of the rural population has access to an improved drinking water source, and 81 percent has access to an improved sanitation facility.

Cuba collected 4,263,000 tons of municipal solid waste in 2009. About 75 percent of the population receives municipal waste services. Eighty-seven percent is landfilled, 5 percent recycled, and 8 percent composted. Some wastes may be illegally dumped in the surrounding Atlantic Ocean.

The Center for Environmental Inspection and Control in the Ministry of Science, Technology, and Environment sets environmental policy. In 2008, a seven-year plan focusing on the environment was approved. This is called the National Program of Fighting Against the Pollution of the Environment. Part of this program is to consider hazardous wastes management plans and their relationship to industry and other parts of society.

Industry and other waste generators are required to conform to the requirements and policies of the National Program of Fight Against the Pollution of the Environment. Some of the requirements segregate and direct waste to areas where they can be treated. Waste of galvanic sludge, used oils, old pesticides, and biomedical wastes are part of the new requirements. Cuba does operate a specifically engineered landfill for lead acid batteries, a specifically engineered landfill for asbestos waste, and an incinerator for pharmaceutical wastes, among other waste disposal sites. About twenty other sites recover, reuse, or recycle wastes.

There are informal communities of waste pickers who sort through trash for recyclable or otherwise usable materials.

Hazardous Wastes

1,417,000 tons of hazardous wastes were generated in 2007. Cuba does not have a large industry in the transboundary movement of hazardous wastes and other wastes. Cuba restricts the export of hazardous wastes and other wastes for final disposition or recovery. Hazardous wastes for final disposal are restricted as imports, but hazardous wastes for recovery or recycling are not restricted. Altogether, 1,535 metric tons of hazardous waste was exported in 2009.

Nuclear Wastes

Cuba has no nuclear power reactors, disposal facilities, or processing facilities. It does have one storage facility.

Recycling

Recycling is a way of life for Cubans. As an island nation embargoed by the United States, Cuba had to reuse and recycle a significant portion of the municipal solid waste stream. There are few formal policies on recycling. The United Nations operates a recycling center in Pinar del Rio province.

Emissions and Industry

In 1996, Cuba generated 40,194.9 metric tons of greenhouse gases, a 36 percent decrease from 1990. Cuba is currently building a gas incineration facility to dispose of Freon and comply with the UN elimination of CFCs.

Agricultural products include sugar, tobacco, citrus, coffee, rice, potatoes, beans, and livestock. Cuba focuses on biological methods instead of pesticides. For, example Cuba uses ants to keep sweet potato weevils out of crops. Sugar cane is a traditional crop.

Agricultural emissions account for 26 percent of all emissions. Within this sector, agricultural soils accounted for 66 percent of emissions, enteric fermentation 32 percent, manure management 1 percent, and rice cultivation 1 percent.

Cuba produces crude oil and maintains proven reserves. There are 70.79 billion m^3 of proven natural gas reserves. Energy emissions accounted for 66 percent of all emissions. Within this sector, energy industries accounted for 44 percent of emissions and manufacturing and construction 29 percent. Fugitive emissions, other emissions, and other sectors accounted for 25 percent of greenhouse gas emissions in this sector, whereas transportation is reported to create none. Fugitive emissions are essentially unaccounted waste streams into the air. Fugitive emissions can affect regional ecosystems and the public health, because they can fall from the air to the land and water. The high amount of fugitive emissions indicates potentially higher emissions than reported. Industrial emissions accounted for 3 percent of all emissions. Within this sector, mineral products account for 67 percent of emissions, metal production 31 percent, and chemical industries 2 percent.

Emissions from solid wastes account for 5 percent of all emissions. Within this sector, solid waste disposal on land accounted for 57 percent of emissions and wastewater management 43 percent.

Major Waste Issues

The lack of water is affecting water quality and sanitation. As population and economic development increases demands for water will increase. Currently some villages are filtering wastewater through slow sand based filtering processes.

Infectious diseases include cholera, dengue fever, hepatitis A, hepatitis B, and typhoid. In the first nine months of 2014, there were four outbreaks of Chikungunya virus, usually found in Africa. Climate changes of rising ocean levels, more violent weather, and increased temperatures could cause some infectious disease vectors to expand.

Further Reading

Cuban Government. www.cubagob.cu.

Guantanamo Bay. www.usmilitary.about.com/od/navybasesunits/ss/GuantanamoBay.htm.

Tobias, Robert, et al. 2009. "Developing Strategies for Waste Reduction by Means of Tailored Inventions in Santiago de Cuba." *Environment and Behavior* 41: 836–865.

CZECH REPUBLIC

A poet, playwright, and jailed dissident of the Communist party led the Czech Republic to independence. Vaclav Havel was elected president of Czechoslovakia in 1989, and after years of intense negotiations and conflict, the Czech Republic became an independent nation in 1993. In January 2013, this nation held its first direct popular vote for president.

Today, 10,516,000 people live on 78,865 km² of land with 1,620 km² of water. Seventy-four percent are urbanized, and 24 percent live in a city having more than 100,000 inhabitants. In 2005, the population density was 133 people per km², the highest among eighteen eastern European countries. Three percent of the population suffers malnutrition. There are about 335 deaths from cancer per 100,000 people, among the highest in the world. Heart disease rates are 149 per 100,000 people, about the fourth highest in the world. Chronic respiratory illnesses like asthma, emphysema, and bronchitis are epidemic in children younger than 14.

The climate is temperate, with cool summers and cold, humid winters. Natural resources include hard and soft coal, kaolin, clay, graphite, and timber. The Czech Republic is landlocked and shares borders with Austria, Germany, Poland, and Slovakia. The terrain varies. In the east, Moravia is hilly. In the west, Bohemia is flat, with rolling hills and low mountains.

Current Waste Practices and Recycling

In 2009, 3,310,000 tons of municipal waste was collected, a 4.2 percent increase from the year before. Everyone receives municipal waste collection services, and most people have access to an improved drinking water source, and improved sanitation facility. Almost 73 percent of municipal waste was landfilled, 10 percent incinerated, 2 percent recycled, and 2 percent composted.

Most communities use basic sewer and water services, but little water is treated before being discharged into local water sources. Almost 90 percent of the population gets drinking water from public systems. About 75 percent is attached to public sewer systems. Water quality is poor.

There are many landfills and otherwise contaminated areas from many years of industrialization and municipal trash generation. About 80 percent of all municipal solid waste is disposed in landfills. There are about 199 new landfills, eighteen composting facilities, fifty-two facilities for biological decontamination, fifty-three incinerators for hazardous wastes, three municipal waste incinerators, twenty-nine hazardous wastes incinerators, and sixty-four recycling and waste sorting facilities.

There are regional waste management plans in all fourteen regions of the Czech Republic. The government pledges financial support from federal and European Union funds, charges fees for landfill waste, and has started a financial reserve for reclamation of landfills.

About two-thirds of the population separates recyclable waste at home. There are collecting bins for recyclable materials in many communities. The hierarchy of waste management is to first reclaim raw materials and those used in primary resource consumption, then to try to reclaim energy from them. About two-thirds of wastes are recycled, and 10 percent are used as fuel.

Nuclear Wastes

The Czech Republic operates six nuclear power reactors that contribute about a third of the electricity. There are four nuclear waste disposal, eight storage, and six processing facilities. Many of the facilities are located in Dukovany. Radioactive wastes with low, intermediate, or short-lived radiation are separated out for disposal in a facility designed for that waste. The remaining radioactive wastes are disposed in a "planned deep geological repository." There are sites of radioactive wastes. Uranium mining and milling left radioactive land and tailing ponds. The remediation of the sites in Straz pod Ralskem and Dolni Rozinka is under way; there may be many other sites. Some sites take all wastes, from trash and chemical to biological and radioactive. Some nuclear facilities are being decommissioned, and new hazardous wastes landfills designed for radioactive wastes must be sited, built, and used. Finding new sites for new and recovered nuclear waste faces community resistance because of fear of public health and environmental effects. Municipalities selected for sites at the preliminary stage of planning reject many geological surveys.

Hazardous Wastes

The State Environmental Policy of 2004–2010 sought to reduce specific generation of hazardous wastes by a fifth in 2010, and its own evaluation concluded that these goals were met.

Almost 9 percent of all wastes generated are hazardous. In 2008, the Czech Republic generated 1,510,000 tons of hazardous wastes, but 5,324,244 metric tons of hazardous wastes were generated in 2009. That same year, 7,263 metric tons of hazardous wastes were exported, along with twenty-four metric tons of other wastes. Moreover, 10,465 metric tons of hazardous wastes were imported with 313 metric tons of other wastes. All waste exports for final disposal are prohibited except those to other European Union or Basel Convention members. They are taking an inventory of hazardous waste dumps site, establishing environmental effect processes, beginning environmental audits and training, and choosing target industries for environmental compliance.

Emissions and Industry

The Czech Republic is in an area subject to many environmental effects from decades of barely enforced industrial and waste practices. It is characterized by air and water pollution, degraded soil quality, and deforestation. Recent conflicts have caused economic decline that has exacerbated ecological decline. The Czech Republic generated 134,345 tons of greenhouse gases in 2011, a 32 percent decrease from 1990.

About 40 percent of the land is arable. Only 390 km^2 of land is irrigated. Agricultural products include wheat, potatoes, sugar beets, hops, fruit, pigs, and poultry. Agricultural emissions accounted for 6 percent of overall greenhouse gas emissions. About 62 percent came from agricultural soils, 25 percent from enteric fermentation, and 13 percent from manure management.

The Czech Republic produces crude oil and maintains proven reserves. There are 3.96 billion m^3 of proven natural gas reserves. Energy emissions accounted for 82 percent of all emissions. Within this sector, energy industries accounted for 53 percent of emissions, transportation 16 percent, manufacturing industries and construction 16 percent, and other 10 percent. Industrial emissions accounted for 10 percent of all emissions. Within this sector, metal production accounted for 45 percent of emissions, mineral products 30 percent, and the chemical industry 9 percent.

Waste emissions accounted for 3 percent of all emissions. Within this sector, solid waste disposal on land accounted for 74 percent of emissions, wastewater handling 21 percent, and waste incineration 5 percent.

Major Waste Issues

The Czech Republic is developing environmental management programs that include waste and landfill reclamation. Years of untreated waste generation have developed toxic hot spots that present risks to the public and environment. Years of environmental remediation will be necessary to reclaim former and present waste sites. Developing a safe and functional waste treatment infrastructure is a preliminary challenge. The current infectious diseases of hepatitis A, hepatitis B, and tick-borne encephalitis could expand some vectors with temperature increases.

The Czech Republic is preparing for climate change. Climate change observers noted increased rain and more extreme weather events. Projected effects include decreases in water and overall hydrology, higher winter temperatures, less snowpack, and severe weather events. The key vulnerability lies in water flow decreases and increased eutrophication. Primary concerns are loss of water quantity, decrease in water quality because of the increase in the concentration of pollutants, and extreme weather events. The Czech Republic has developed policies in response to concerns about projected effects. One is the program of renewal of the natural functions of the landscape. The goals of this policy are to improve natural functions of watercourses and their flows as well as the natural water retention of the land—and also establishing and restoring ecosystems. This policy also seeks to enforce responsibility and obligations of local and regional nature protection authorities, prepare and implement plans and programs for protected plants and animals, and develop more adaption measures to mitigate climate change effects on aquatic, forest, and nonforest ecosystems.

Further Reading

Auer, Matthew R., ed. 2005. *Restoring Cursed Earth: Appraising Environmental Policy Reforms in Eastern Europe and Russia.* New York: The Rowman & Littlefield Publishing Group.

Climate Change Impacts on Water Systems. www.oecd.org.

Ministry of the Environment of the Czech Republic. www.mzp.cz/en/state_environmental_policy.

Polak, M., and L. Drapalova. 2012. "Estimation of End of Life Mobile Phones Generation: The Case Study of the Czech Republic." *Waste Management* 32: 1,583–1,591.

DEMOCRATIC PEOPLE'S REPUBLIC OF KOREA (NORTH KOREA)

North Korea, a Communist nation, rests on a 966 km peninsula with the Sea of Japan in the east and the Yellow Sea in the west. It borders China, Japan, South Korea, and Russia. The climate is temperate. Most rain occurs in summer. The terrain is varied, with mountains and many hills. There are flat plains in the west, along the coast. Natural resources include hydropower, coal, lead, zinc, graphite, iron ore, gold, and magnetite. Today, about 22.5 million people live in North Korea, with access to 2,495 km of coastline. Sixty-two percent of the population is urbanized. Twenty-three percent lives in overcrowded conditions.

Current Waste Practices and Recycling

Waste management policies with guidelines are recent. In 2009, the Rural Sanitation and the Water Quality Monitoring and Surveillance guidelines were issued to address some of the major waste issues. A pilot water sector assessment surveyed was recently completed and will be the basis for a national waste plan. International assistance has helped build gravity-fed, electric, and solar water pumping stations; household latrine construction; medical waste management systems; and solid waste management and organic composting.

Most cities have sewer and water services but discharge untreated wastes into freshwater. Waste practices are basic in many places. Pit toilets, latrines, drainage ditches, and cesspools are sometimes used. Forty-two percent of households use shallow pit latrines, which require frequent cleaning. About 17 percent use pit latrines without a traditional squatting slab. About a third of mothers practice good hygiene when disposing of baby feces. Human wastes are used as fertilizer in agricultural areas, increasing risks from pathogens and helminthes.

Roughly 60 percent of the rural population and 58 percent of the urban population has access to sanitation facilities. One hundred percent of rural and urban populations use improved water sources.

Emissions and Industry

North Korea generated 87,330 metric tons of greenhouse gas emissions in 2002, a 58 percent decrease from 1990.

Agricultural products include rice, corn, soybeans, potatoes, and livestock. Agricultural emissions accounted for 3 percent of all emissions. Within this sector, rice cultivation accounted for 59 percent of emissions, enteric fermentation 34 percent, and manure management 7 percent.

Petrochemical production and use is low. Coal is production and use is high. Energy emissions accounted for 89 percent of all emissions. Within this sector, energy industries accounted for 34 percent of emissions, manufacturing and construction industries 25.5 percent, and transportation 2 percent. Fugitive emissions were 5 percent, other 6 percent, and other sectors 21 percent.

Industrial emissions accounted for 6 percent of all emissions. Within this sector, mineral products accounted for 45 percent of emissions, metal production 34 percent, and chemical industries 22 percent.

Waste emissions accounted for 1 percent of all emissions. Within this sector, wastewater handling accounted for 83 percent of emissions, solid waste disposal on land 12 percent, and incineration 5 percent.

Major Waste Issues

Waste issues are some of the major environmental issues here. Water and air pollution continue to increase leading to unsafe drinking water, deforestation, soil erosion, and risks of infectious diseases. Poor waste practices have degraded groundwater and decreased potable water.

There is a risk of major infectious diseases—hepatitis A, hepatitis B, malaria, Japanese encephalitis, and typhoid fever. Two percent or more of the population is persistently infected with hepatitis B. There is currently a low risk of malaria in southern areas. There is a good chance that infectious disease vectors will expand. North Korea is urbanizing into already overcrowded conditions. Climate change effects of rising temperatures, rising ocean levels, and increases in violent weather could facilitate the growth of infectious disease vectors with current waste management practices.

Further Reading

International Health: North Korean Catastrophe. www.nci.nlm.nih.gov.

Kim, S., et al. 2013. "Impact of Polycyclic Aromatic Hydrocarbon (PAH) Emissions from North Korea to the Air Quality in the Seoul Metropolitan Area, South Korea." *Atmospheric Science* 70: 159–165.

"North Korea Offers Cooperation with China on Cross Border River Pollution." www.koreaherald.com.

DEMOCRATIC REPUBLIC OF THE CONGO (ZAIRE)

About 75 million people live in the Democratic Republic of the Congo on 2,344,858 km² of land and a coastline of 169 km. It controls the lower Congo River and access to the South Atlantic Ocean. It is a nation of small communities. About 35 percent of the population lives in urban areas. More than half the people there live in overcrowded conditions. The northern areas are mainly tropical forests having fewer inhabitants.

Kinshasa is the state capital and the largest city, with population of about 8.8 million. The Democratic Republic of the Congo has had years of civil violence and political unrest that have destroyed what waste and sanitation systems existed. Refugee camps and boundary disputes still exist. Currently, the Democratic Republic of the Congo borders Angola, Burundi, Central African Republic, the Republic of the Congo, Rwanda, South Sudan, Tanzania, Uganda, and Zambia.

The terrain is flat, with eastern mountains. The climate is tropical, with a four-month rainy season. In the equatorial river basin, it is hot and humid. The Congo equatorial basin discharges water via the Congo River, the deepest river in the world. The water discharge of the Congo River into the Atlantic Ocean is second only to the Amazon River in South America. It is cooler and drier in the south. Lake Tananyika shares the eastern border with Tanzania and Burundi. There is an abundance of natural resources, including petroleum, diamonds, gold, copper, cobalt, uranium, timber, coal, and hydropower.

The Mount Nyiragongo volcano is active and affects much of the landscape. A 1977 eruption raced down the mountain at about 100 km/hr. Another major eruption in 2002 decimated the city of Goma. Since 2002, the population of Goma has increased to 1.1 million, from 400,000 in 2002—the city is growing rapidly in the shadow of an active volcano.

Civil unrest quickly followed independence, and political tension continues to this day that prevents any accurate monitoring of volcanic activity. There is concern about another eruption, as well as about radioactive elements found in the lava flows.

Current Waste Practices

Waste practices are basic—pit toilets, latrines, drainage ditches, cesspools, and open defecation. It is one of the poorest nations in the world and has one of the lowest access rates to drinking water in Africa despite having large amounts of freshwater in rivers and groundwater. Only about a quarter of the population is covered by government sanitation systems. Urban sanitation coverage is still recovering from war. Most of the rural water and sanitation systems are not functional. Wastewater and raw sewage is dumped untreated into the Congo River. The death rate from intestinal infectious diseases is 8.34 per 100,000 people. Seventy-nine percent of the urban population has access to an improved drinking water source, and just 24 percent has access to an improved sanitary facility. Only 27 percent of the rural population has access to an improved drinking water source, and 24 percent has access to improved sanitation facilities. About 1,000 tons of hazardous wastes are generated a year, and it is unclear how much other hazardous wastes are imported, or where they go.

The lack of solid waste management is so severe that in some urban areas, a number of people drown because rainwater drainage canals are blocked by trash. Most of the trash collected is brought to open landfills and dumps outside the city. Sometimes trash heaps are burned to make room for more trash. Communities of waste pickers scavenge the heaps for recyclables and sustenance. Because the open dumps are not compacted or covered, there were rejected as a source of biofuels. The methane emitted is sufficiently contained for most methane recovery programs. Air emissions from landfills and burning trash are probably higher than reported because of the scale of illegal dumping and burning of trash. In studies of ways to reduce greenhouse gas emissions, recycling municipal solid wastes and banning the burning of waste is are considered among the most effective.

Emissions and Industry

In 2003, the Democratic Republic of the Congo generated 45,999 metric tons of greenhouse gases, a 3 percent increase from 1994. These emissions are likely to be higher now because of the increased population and the reliance on agriculture.

Agricultural products include coffee, sugar, palm oil, rubber, tea, bananas, and wood products. Emissions from agricultural wastes accounted for 75 percent of all emissions. Within this sector, prescribed burning of savannas accounted for 85 percent of emissions, field burning of agricultural residues 11 percent, and manure management 0.19 percent.

Electricity can intermittent. The power grid was down at least 184 days a year in 2006, among the highest rates in the world. Crude oil production in 2012 was at the high end, with 20,000 bbl/day and 180 million bbl in proven reserves. Oil consumption per capita was among the lowest in the world. Energy emissions accounted for 8 percent of all emissions. Within this sector, transportation accounted for 23 percent of emissions and energy industries 16 percent. The sources for about 47 percent of emissions in this sector are reported as other. Industrial emissions accounted for 0.34 percent of all emissions. Within this sector, mineral products accounted for all emissions.

Waste emissions accounted for 1 percent of all emissions. Within this sector, solid waste disposal on land accounted for all emissions.

Major Waste Issues

Seasonal flooding, desertification, and deforestation are environmental issues that form the context for waste issues. Climate change effects of rising temperatures and more violent weather cause grave concerns about food security and famines. The lack of food and water weakens people and makes them less disease-resistant. In December 2006, there were 7,098 reported cases of cholera, including 101 deaths. From March 2010 to March 2011, more than 22,000 cases were reported. There are periodic outbreaks, but data about them is scarce. The worst cholera outbreaks occurred where water quality and sanitary conditions were very poor. Deadly Ebola hemorrhagic fever outbreaks occurred in 2003, 2004, and 2005.

The lack of waste treatment creates conditions for the increase in diseases. This is an international concern. An international product called WASH (water, sanitation, and hygiene) assisted fifty-seven water and sanitation projects from 2007 to 2008. These projects helped truck clean water, protect drinking water from springs, develop local responses to cholera, and increase public health education. Many more such projects, as well as an environmental remediation program, are necessary. The amount of trash and pollution makes controlling waterborne diseases a national and international issue. There is a high risk of major infectious diseases. Bacterial and protozoal diarrhea, hepatitis A, hepatitis B, dengue fever, malaria, meningococcal meningitis, schistosomiasis, typhoid fever, and yellow fever, among others occur here. There is a high risk of malaria.

There is a chance that infectious disease vectors will expand. The country is urbanizing into already overcrowded conditions that are not served by sanitation facilities. Large numbers of refugees are increasing the strain on public health and sanitation. In 2011, it was estimated that there were 1.5 million internally displaced persons (IDP) and 153,180 refugees from neighboring countries. There is a lack of information on public health or environmental conditions. The number of doctors is low, and infant mortality is high. Life expectancy for women is 51 years; for men, it is 47 years. Some of the diseases may increase in outbreaks that can become epidemics that overwhelm public health systems. More international engagement is needed to prevent global vectors from expanding. Even without the exacerbating influence of climate change disease vectors will expand. Public health is the largest waste issue.

Further Reading

Banza, Celestin Lubaba Nkulu, et al. 2009. "High Human Exposure to Cobalt and Other Metals in Katanga, a Mining Area." *Environmental Research* 109: 745–752.

Bompangue, Didier, et al. 2008. "Lakes as a Source of Cholera Outbreaks, Democratic Republic of Congo." *Emerging Infectious Diseases* 14: 798–800.

Burt, Murray, and Bilha Joy Keiru. 2011. "Strengthening Post-Conflict Peacebuilding through Community Water Resource Management: Case Studies from Democratic Republic of Congo, Afghanistan, and Liberia." *Water International* 33: 232–241.

Central Africa Regional Program for the Environment, Regional Development Strategy 2012–2020, U.S. Agency for International Development. www.usaid.gov.

Democratic Republic of the Congo President's Office. www.presidentrdc.cd.

Piarroux, R., et al. 2009. "From Research to Field Action: Example of the Fight against Cholera in the Democratic Republic of Congo." *Field Actions Sci. Rep.* 2: 69–77.

DENMARK

Denmark straddles the Jutland peninsula into the North and Baltic Seas. Denmark includes many islands nearby; the two largest are Sjaelland and Fyn. The capital and largest city is Copenhagen on the island of Sjaelland, having 1.3 million people. Altogether 5.5 million people live on 43,094 km² of land and 7,314 km of coastline, including 406 islands. Eighty-seven percent of the inhabitants are urbanized, and 38 percent live in a city having more than 100,000 inhabitants.

The climate is temperate, characterized by mild, windy winters and cool, humid summers. It shares a border with Germany and the North and Baltic seas. Its natural resources include petroleum, natural gas, fish, salt, chalk, stone, limestone, and gravel.

Current Waste Practices and Recycling

Denmark generated about 660 kg per person per year of waste, among the highest in the world. Denmark collected 4,530,000 tons of municipal waste in 2009, about 3 percent of it landfilled, 51 percent incinerated, 34 percent recycled, and about 16 percent composted. Landfilling waste that can be incinerated was banned in 1997. Everyone enjoys municipal waste collection. Landfill need was diminished by the environmental policies of the 1990s reducing the creation of wastes before most other countries. For example, almost all drink bottles are recycled. Sixty-four percent of wastes are recycled.

Paper and cardboard are baled for recycling in Jutland, Denmark. Recycling can reduce the pressure on landfill storage capacity, but still requires space for storage and processing. (Asist/Dreamstime.com)

All urban sewage is treated today. The Copenhagen sewer system was constructed in 1857 and was expanded from 1860 to 1910. Until the 1890s, toilets wastes were collected in latrines and transported to the country as fertilizer, as is the practice in many parts of the world today. Several visionary waste plans were proposed, but none was implemented at the time. Before and after construction of the sewers, runoff discharged directly into waterways, especially the harbor, leading to bad odors and sedimentation. The declining water quality directly affected public baths, a part of Danish culture. Many public baths closed, and others moved. Sedimentation decreases the clearance necessary for larger ocean vessels, especially oil tankers and cruise ships. Both petroleum and tourism are significant industries.

Sewer treatment plants and reservoirs to hold waste were built in the 1990s. There was also concern about sewage leaking into the groundwater and into lakes and streams. Today, the Copenhagen sewer covers 6,800 ha and includes 1,100 km of main sewer and 300 km of service piping. Modern waste technology is used to inspect the sewers. The public baths are now reopened, large oil tankers and cruise ships can move in the harbor, and the overall water quality standards tightened.

Hazardous Wastes

In 2008, Denmark generated 420,000 tons of hazardous wastes. Denmark restricts the transit, import, and export of hazardous and other wastes for final disposal or recovery. The reduction of hazardous wastes is implemented by the phasing out and outright banning of certain chemicals. Altogether, 14,882 metric tons of other wastes were imported in 2009. Additionally, 76,311 metric tons of hazardous wastes were imported. Moreover, 135,734 metric tons of other wastes were exported, and so were 84,746 metric tons of hazardous waste. Pharmaceutical wastes are returned to the dispensing chemist.

Disease and Injury Risks for Solid Waste Workers

Just as there are wastes everyday and everywhere, so, too, there are waste workers. They are exposed to all the public health dangers that exist with waste handling, storage, and treatment. These include many infectious diseases, allergic pulmonary disease, chronic bronchitis, hepatitis, parasites, and acute diarrhea, as well as on-the-job injury, accidents, and musculoskeletal problems. Waste pickers and scavenging communities often experience tuberculosis, bronchitis, asthma, pneumonia, dysentery, parasites, and severe malnutrition. Rat feces and urine spread hantavirus, the plague, and leptospirosis. Many rats excrete as they travel, expanding the disease vector to all parts of the waste stream and the surrounding communities.

The act of collecting waste is dangerous because of the dangerous chemicals in the wastes that can cut, combust, or chemically burn. Picking up and transferring municipal solid wastes involves physically moving it. Waste collectors can be killed in traffic accidents at the point of collection. In Denmark, waste collectors risk six times more infectious diseases, almost six times more work-related accidents, and almost three times more heart disease than the population. In the United States, waste collection is the seventh most hazardous job. The status of some waste workers is increasing. An elementary school in Seattle, Washington, sent waste collectors a Valentines Day card to express appreciation for their work.

The Soil and Waste Division of the Danish Environmental Protection Agency regulates wastes. The National Waste Plan of 2009–2012 outlines the waste policy priorities. A new plan on waste is currently being developed. Denmark is a world leader in sustainability and places waste in that context.

Emissions and Industry

Denmark generated 57,748 tons of greenhouse gases in 2011, an 18 percent decrease from 1990. Agricultural products include barley, wheat, potatoes, sugar beets, pork, dairy products, and fish. Agricultural wastes accounted for about 17 percent of overall greenhouse gas emissions in 2011, a slight decrease. Within this sector, agricultural soils accounted for about 53 percent of greenhouse gas emissions, enteric fermentation about 30 percent, and manure management almost 18 percent. This is a high amount of greenhouse gas emissions from manure, indicating the presence of large amounts of untreated feces.

Denmark produces crude oil and maintains proven reserves. Electricity consumption per capita is high, and production is moderate. Oil production and consumption per capita are slightly high. There are 42.98 billion m^3 of proven natural gas reserves. Hydrofracturing, a process for drilling and mining natural gas, is being explored. Energy emissions accounted for about 78 percent of overall greenhouse gas emissions in 2011, a slight decrease. Within this sector, energy industries accounted for about 45 percent of greenhouse gas emissions, transportation almost 30 percent, manufacturing industries and construction about 10 percent, and fugitive emissions and other almost 16 percent. Fugitive emissions are essentially unaccounted waste streams into the air. Fugitive emissions can affect regional ecosystems and the public health, because they can fall from the air to the land and water. Industrial processes accounted for 3 percent of overall greenhouse gas emissions in 2011. Within this sector, mineral products accounted for 52 percent of greenhouse gas emissions and the consumption of halocarbons and other long lasting gases, such as sulfur hexafluoride (SF_6), for 46 percent.

Solid wastes accounted for about 2 percent of overall greenhouse gas emissions in 2011, a slight decrease. Within this sector, solid waste disposal on land accounted for almost 67 percent of greenhouse gas emissions, down from 85 percent in 1990. Wastewater handling was about 16 percent of emissions and incineration almost 1 percent.

Major Waste Issues

Almost all the drinking water comes from the groundwater. Leaching from old waste dumps and industrial facilities could reach groundwater supplies. Hydraulic fracturing risks water quality if the natural gas leaks into the groundwater. Denmark uses advanced environmental management systems throughout government and industry. Technical assistance and training is available to industries and municipalities on an ad hoc basis.

Rising ocean levels may challenge current waste treatment and remediation efforts. Hepatitis A is the primary infectious disease present. The many isolated islands of Denmark may remain free of many infectious disease vectors because of the lack of exposure to them.

Denmark is preparing for climate change effects on water. Climate change observers note increased temperatures, increased precipitation, less snow cover, an earlier pollen season, and a longer growing season. Residents have observed a decreased need for ice breaking, a shorter sledging season, and a longer swimming season. Projected effects include increased temperatures, less snow cover, very heavy precipitation in fall and longer dry periods in summer, saltwater intrusion and loss of freshwater drinking sources, increased flooding owing to rising sea levels and increased precipitation, and downpours of rain 20 percent to 30 percent bigger. Vulnerabilities include fresh groundwater sources and the need for more irrigation. The primary concerns are about water supply, sanitation, and extreme weather events. Denmark has developed many policies and programs in response to these concerns and projected effects. They are rapidly upgrading their sewer and water capacity specifically to accommodate climate change. They are also developing and restoring wetlands to reduce flooding, such as Hede Enge wetland to reduce flooding in Aarhus. The goal is to increase the possibilities for Danish sewer and water companies to finance more intelligent and socioeconomically optimal climate change measures.

Further Reading

Cashmore, M. 2014. "Constructing Legitimacy for Climate Change Planning: A Study of Local Government in Denmark." *Global Environmental Change* 24: 203–212.

Climate Change Impacts on Water Systems. www.oecd.org.

Denmark Parliament. www.thedanishparliment.dk.

Niiranen, S., et al. 2013. "Combined Effects of Global Climate Change and Regional Ecosystem Drivers on an Exploited Marine Food Web." *Global Change Biology* 19: 3327–3342.

DJIBOUTI

Eritrea, Ethiopia, Somalia, and the Red Sea border Djibouti. Altogether, 792,198 people live on 23,200 km^2 of land and 314 km of coastline. About 80 percent of the population lives in urban areas, and two-thirds of those in Djibouti. There are influxes of refugees from other countries in the region. Forty-five percent of the settled population is poor, and 10 percent is destitute. Life expectancy is about 50 years.

Djibouti's terrain is flat, with mountains separating a plateau from the coast. The landscape is dominated by volcanic formations. The climate is a hot desert, though it can also be humid. The average annual rainfall is 150 mm. There are fluctuations in weather patterns, from drought to heavy rain that can result in floods. Forty percent of the population lives within 10 m of sea level. Natural resources include gold, marble, geothermal power, and salt.

Current Waste Practices

The capital city of Djibouti has an old sewer system that is in disrepair. Sewer backups cause overflows of sewer sludge on the surface, where they dry out. Waste practices are basic—latrines, pit toilets, drainage ditches, cesspools, and open defecation. Many urban residents live in shacks without sanitation or drinking water.

Fifty percent of rural populations and 99 percent of urban populations use adequate sanitation facilities. Half the rural population does not have access to safe drinking water. Many people must walk many kilometers daily for water and defecation. Many urban water sources are polluted. There is no waste treatment before waste is discharged into water.

There is some trash collection. Most of this trash ends up in open dumps landfills and dumps. Trash that is left is sometimes burned to clear streets. Trash as the dumpsite is burned to make room for more trash. There are many illegal dumps. Many of the existing landfills are over capacity and unwanted by neighboring communities, such as the Douda dump.

Emissions and Industry

Because of the low population, low level of industry, and sparse vegetation, overall emissions are low. Djibouti is a considered a carbon sink, because it can absorb more carbon than it creates. In 2000, Djibouti generated 1,071.8 metric tons of greenhouse gases, a 110 percent increase from 1990. It is likely that greenhouse gases emissions are higher because of the increased and rapidly growing population and dependence on agriculture.

Agricultural emissions accounted for 62 percent of all emissions. There are inadequate water supplies for Djibouti to produce enough food to meet basic food needs. Only 80 percent of current water demand can be met. There is little arable land. Agricultural products include cereal, fruits, vegetables, goats, camels, sheep, and animal hides. Many rural and nomadic communities engage in agriculture for sustenance.

Oil and electricity consumption and production per capita are low. Energy emissions accounted for 33 percent of all emissions. Within this sector, energy industries accounted for 48 percent of emissions, transportation 30 percent, manufacturing and construction industries 6 percent, and other sectors 16 percent. Agricultural soils accounted for 68 percent of emissions, enteric fermentation 31 percent, and manure management 1 percent. Industrial emissions were not reported.

Waste emissions accounted for 5 percent of all emissions. All emissions in this sector were from solid waste disposal on land.

Current Waste Issues

Many of the environmental issues are also waste issues. Most of the issues are around the lack of freshwater and increasing desertification. In this context, untreated wastewater can contaminate groundwater.

Climate change observers note rising sea levels, increases in temperature, and changes in precipitation. Increases in salinity and mineralization of freshwater sources, influx of sea water into coastal areas, and decreases in freshwater sources are primary concerns. The primary city of Djibouti is on the coast, and it is projected that between 26 percent and 45 percent of that population could be affected by floods. This would inundate current sanitation and drinking water resources.

Part of the climate change adaptation strategy is increasing coastal protection by increased use of rip-rap rock along the coast, strengthening of current breakwaters, installing a drainage system for rainwater, examining and monitoring the vulnerability of ecosystems, and development of appropriate regulations and institutional measures.

There is an inadequate public health infrastructure and shortages of medical personnel. The warm climate, rapid urbanization, and lack of data increase the risk of infectious disease outbreaks, and potential for epidemics. There are infectious diseases—cholera, hepatitis A, hepatitis B, malaria, schistosomiasis, and typhoid. There is a high risk of malaria. Public health of the country and the region is the searing waste issue. International aid is needed to mitigate the effects of climate change as well as to assist in the development of an integrated waste management system.

Further Reading

Djibouti Government. www.presidence.dj.

El-Khoury, Gabi. 2014. "Water Indicators in Arab Countries: Selected Indicators." *Contemporary Arab Affairs* 7: 339–349.

Foeken, D. W. J., et al. 2013. *Sanitation in Africa: Access to Improved Sanitation Facilities and Improvement Index*. Leiden, The Netherlands: African Studies Center.

Zawahri, N., et al. 2011. "The Politics of Assessment: Water and Sanitation Millennium Development Goals in the Middle East." *Development and Change* 42: 1154–1178.

DOMINICA

Dominica is an island of the Lesser Antilles island chain with the Caribbean Sea on the east side and the North Atlantic on the west side. The terrain is mountainous and volcanic. Seismic activity is common. There are 365 rivers on the island, and rainfall is plentiful. It is home to the second largest thermally active lake in the world, Boiling Lake. The climate is tropical—hot and humid. Natural resources include fish, timber, and hydropower.

More than 73 million people live on 754 km of land and 148 km of coastline. Almost three-quarters of the population is urban.

Current Waste Practices

Ninety percent of the population receives municipal waste collection. Most of this waste goes to one of the more than 340 open dumps. Some of the coastal villages dump trash over the side of cliffs into the ocean, where currents move it away. There are expanding opportunities to recycle discarded items, and community awareness is increasing. Most cities have sewer and water services but discharge untreated wastes into freshwater. Seventy-five percent of the rural population and 86 percent of the urban population has access to a sanitation facility. Ninety percent of the rural population and all the urban population uses safe drinking water. Most of the sanitary facilities are pit latrines and septic systems. Raw sewage is often discharged into rivers, into the ocean, or on land.

Emissions and Industry

In 2005, Dominica generated 181.9 metric tons of greenhouse gases, a 19.5 percent increase from 1990.

There is little arable land, but what there is is fertile thanks to the volcanic soil. Agricultural products include bananas, mangos, cocoa, and coconuts. Agricultural emissions accounted for 23 percent of all emissions. Within this sector, agricultural soils accounted for 60 percent of emissions, enteric fermentation 38 percent, and manure management 2 percent.

Oil and electricity consumption are low. Hydropower is the second most used energy after small diesel generators. Energy emissions accounted for 67 percent of all emissions. Within this sector, transportation accounted for 39 percent of emissions, energy industries 35 percent, manufacturing and construction 9 percent, and other 16 percent. Industrial emissions accounted for no emissions.

Waste emissions accounted for 10 percent of all emissions. Within this sector, solid waste disposal on land accounted for 52 percent of emissions and wastewater handling 48 percent.

Major Waste Issues

Water pollution continues to be a problem. Chemical effluents from hospitals and industries are discharged into the Belfast River. This is combined with untreated sewer discharges. The scale of unregulated dumpsites is also a challenge. Waste issues are often in the realm of Public Health. There are infectious diseases—dengue fever, hepatitis A, and hepatitis B. In 2014, there were Chikungunya virus outbreaks in the Caribbean. Climate change effects of sea level rise and more extreme weather events cause concern about flooding, landslides, health threats from emerging diseases, and emergency response capacity. Solid waste management is now a national priority because of the large dimensions of the waste issue. There is limited landfill space and no recycling system.

Dominica is aiming to become the "Organic Island," partially motivated by tourism. This includes accelerated and sustainable use of all natural resources including indigenous knowledge, forest products, nontimber forest products, food, water, renewable energy, and enhanced protection of biodiversity. Part of this strategy is to develop more recycling waste to energy plants and increase monitoring of diseases in liquid wastes. An integrated waste management system is necessary for this goal to be reached.

Further Reading

Government of Commonwealth of Dominica. www.dominica.gov.dm.

Management of Wastes in Small Island Developing States. www.islands.unep.ch.

Weiler, L., and O. DeHoorne. 2014. "Ecotourism as an Alternative to Sun, Sand, and Sea Tourism Development in the Caribbean: A Comparison of Martinique and Dominica." *Ecosystem Assessment and Fuzzy Systems Management Advances in Intelligent Systems and Computing* 254: 461–469.

DOMINICAN REPUBLIC

The Dominican Republic covers two-thirds of the Caribbean island of Hispaniola, shared with its neighbor Haiti. Ten million people live on 48,671 km² of land, with 350 km² of water. The Dominican coastline is 1,633 km long, with the Atlantic Ocean in the North and the Caribbean Sea in the south. Sixty-seven percent of the population is urbanized, and 43 percent lives in a city having more than 100,000 inhabitants.

The climate is tropical, generally warm and humid. There is little seasonal variation. Its natural resources include nickel, bauxite, gold, and silver. A mountain range runs through the middle of the country and has the highest mountain in the Caribbean, at 3,087 m.

Current Waste Practices

Most cities have sewer and water services but discharge untreated wastes into freshwater. Eighty-seven percent of the urban population has access to an improved drinking water source, and 87 percent has access to an improved sanitary facility. Eighty-four percent of the rural population has access to an improved drinking water source, and 87 percent has access to improved sanitation facilities. About 1,300 deaths a year are attributed to unsafe water.

Dominica collected 21,000 tons of municipal waste in 2005. Most of this goes to landfills. There are more than 340 open-air landfills without waste treatment or management. There is also trash burning in and outside the urban areas. There is an informal waste economy of waste pickers, who do some of the recycling.

There has been international assistance to increase sewer and water infrastructure. The Inter-American Development Bank loaned $25 million for waste and water management in Santiago de los Caballeros in 2012. The goal of this project is to provide water service for over 200,000 people for at least twelve hours a day. It also includes basic water and sewer infrastructure, such as pumping stations and pipes. The Water and Sewerage Corporation of Santiago is a project leader.

Emissions and Industry

In 2000, the Dominican Republic generated 26,433.2 metric tons of greenhouse gas emissions, an increase of 109.1 percent from 1990. It is likely that greenhouse gases are higher now because of increased population and reliance on agriculture.

Agricultural products include sugar cane, coffee, cotton, cocoa, tobacco, rice, beans, potatoes, corn, pigs, livestock, bananas, dairy products, and chicken eggs. Altogether, 3,065 km of land is irrigated. Agricultural emissions accounted for 22 percent of all emissions. Within this sector, agricultural soils accounted for 48 percent of emissions, enteric fermentation 42 percent, rice cultivation 6 percent, and manure management 4 percent.

A small of crude oil was produced in 2010, and there are no proven reserves. Electricity production and consumption per capita are low. Energy emissions accounted for 69 percent of all emissions. Within this sector, energy industries accounted for 51 percent of emissions, transportation 34 percent, and manufacturing and construction 6 percent. Industrial emissions accounted for 3 percent of all emissions. Within this sector, metal production accounted for 65 percent of emissions and mineral products 35 percent.

Waste emissions accounted for 6 percent of all emissions. Within this sector, wastewater management accounted for 58 percent of emissions, solid waste disposal on land 42 percent, and incineration 0.12 percent.

Major Waste Issues

Many of the current waste issues are related to water shortages and substandard infrastructure. Mining is a large industry that uses much water and creates water pollution in the remaining water. Increasing populations also put more stress on an already insufficient waste system. Groundwater contamination because of the lack of waste treatment is a concern.

Since the cholera outbreak in 2010, the Dominican Republic has upgraded its public health response policy to include clean water, sanitation, and the promotion of hygiene. The Ministry of Public Health developed a Plan of Action of Environmental Health and the Prevention of Cholera. Although far from implemented, the goal of the plan is to improve drinking water and sanitation in the most vulnerable areas, develop capacity at the local level, assess options for treatment of human wastes, epidemiologically survey cases of cholera and diarrhea, and monitor water sources. There is still a risk of major infectious diseases. Hepatitis A, hepatitis B, cholera, dengue fever, malaria, schistosomiasis, and typhoid fever occur here. Two percent or more of the population is persistently infected with hepatitis B. Climate change effects of rising ocean levels, more violent weather, and higher temperatures will create even more conducive environments for already present infectious diseases. There is a good chance that infectious disease vectors will expand.

Further Reading

Baum, Rachel, et al. 2014. "Assessing the Microbial Quality of Improved Drinking Water Sources: Results from the Dominican Republic." *American Journal of Tropical Medicine and Hygiene* 90: 121–123.

Dominican President. www.presidencia.gov.do.

Pichler, A., and E. Stiessnig. 2013. "Differential Vulnerability to Hurricanes in Cuba, Haiti, and Dominican Republic: The Contribution of Education." *Ecology and Society* 18: 31.

ECUADOR

Perched on northwest corner of the South America, Ecuador is traversed by two large mountain ranges of the Andes Mountains. The tallest mountain is Chimborazo, at 6,272 m. The Galapagos Islands are part of this nation. They are famous for rare ecological diversity and are 966 km west of Ecuador.

Altogether, 14.4 million people live on Ecuador's 256,369 km² of land, with 6,720 km² of water. Sixty-three percent of the population is urbanized, and 48 percent lives in a city having more than 100,000 inhabitants. About a third lives in overcrowded conditions. About 1,100 deaths a year are attributed to unsafe water.

The climate varies regionally but is generally tropical. It is tropical along the coast, much cooler in the mountains, and tropical in jungle lowlands. It shares borders with the equatorial Pacific Ocean, Peru, and Colombia. Natural resources include hydropower, oil, timber, and fish. The terrain is varied. Along the coast the land is a coastal plain. From the coast, the terrain rises to the central highlands and becomes rolling land in the east, eventually rising to mountains.

Current Waste Practices and Recycling

Most cities have sewer and water services but discharge untreated wastes into freshwater. Nationally slightly more than half the population is connected to a sewer. Rural waste practices can be basic, with pit toilets, latrines, drainage ditches, and cesspools. Active efforts are being made to develop the sewer system in some cities. Ninety-six percent of the urban population has access to an improved drinking water sources, and 96 percent has access to an improved sanitation facility. Eighty-nine percent of the rural population has access to an improved source of drinking water, and 84 percent has access to an improved sanitation facility.

The Subsecretaria de Calidad Ambiental Ministerio del Ambiente develops policies around waste. This agency is developing an action plan to implement the National Regimen for Hazardous Chemical Products. Ecuador is developing a national policy on solid wastes and for cleaner production processes. Some chemicals are banned or severely restricted in Ecuador by the Environmental Ministry, though actual enforcement is a challenge.

Forty-nine percent of the population receives municipal waste collection services. There are some landfills, and there are few recovery or recycling facilities. Most trash is burned either in piles in town or in open dumps outside communities. Waste pickers often work in the streets and dumpsites scavenging for recyclable materials and sustenance. Nationally, about 28 percent of solid wastes make it to landfills. The rest ends up in open dumpsites or waterways or is burned.

Hazardous Wastes

In 2008, Ecuador generated 194,000 tons of hazardous wastes. Any transboundary movement of hazardous wastes is highly restricted. Forty-three metric tons of hazardous wastes were exported in 2009. Because wastes are not segregated, they become part the municipal wastes that go to stay in the street or go to the landfill or open dump.

Emissions and Industry

In 2006, Ecuador generated 247,989.7 metric tons of greenhouse gas emissions, a 39 percent increase from 1990. Greenhouse gas emissions are higher today because of increased population and reliance on agriculture.

Altogether, 4.5 percent of the land is arable. About 8,650 km^2 is irrigated. There is heavy dependence on agriculture. Agricultural products include bananas, coffee, cocoa, sugar cane, livestock, rice, potatoes, fish, and manioc. Agricultural emissions accounted for 85 percent of all emissions. Within this sector, agricultural soils accounted for 94 percent of emissions, enteric fermentation 3 percent, and manure management 1.86 percent.

Crude oil production is high, at 504,500 bbl/day produced, and consumption was moderate. There are almost 7 billion m^3 of proven natural gas reserves. Energy emissions accounted for 11 percent of all emissions. Within this sector, transportation accounted for 48 percent of emissions, energy industries 31 percent, and manufacturing and construction 9 percent. Industrial emissions accounted for 1 percent of all emissions. Within this sector, mineral products accounted for all emissions.

Waste emissions accounted for 3 percent of all emissions. Within this sector, wastewater management accounted for 72 percent of emissions and solid waste disposal on land 26 percent.

Major Waste Issues

Many environmental issues are also waste issues. Water pollution from oil production and untreated wastewater negatively affect fragile ecological areas in the Galapagos Islands and the Amazon Basin.

There has been international assistance to help develop the wastes infrastructure. In 2014, the Inter-American Bank loaned $120 million to improve water and sanitation. The goal of the project is to give 21,000 households water connections and 35,000 households new sanitation connections and to treat and dispose of 165 tons of waste a day.

There is a risk of major infectious diseases. Hepatitis A, hepatitis B, dengue fever, malaria, and typhoid fever occur here. Two percent or more of the population is persistently infected with hepatitis B. The risk of malaria is great below 1,500 m. Currently there is no risk in the Galapagos Islands or the city of Guayaquil. Climate changes of rising ocean levels, more violent weather, and higher temperatures will create more hospitable environments for already present infectious diseases. The large volume of commercial and tourist traffic may increase the range of environments and introduce new infectious diseases as well as spread current ones. The main waste issue will become focused on public health measures to prevent outbreaks and, after outbreaks grow, prevent epidemics. International assistance building basic waste infrastructure and a National Program for Investment in Water, Sanitation, and Solid Wastes are both indications that waste management is a high-priority issue.

Further Reading

Armijos, M. 2013. "Indigenous Autonomy and Resource Control through Collective Water Management in Highland, Ecuador." *Radical History Review* 116: 86–103.

Bhavnani, D., et al. 2014. "Impact of Rainfall on Diarrheal Disease Risk Associated with Unimproved Water and Sanitation." *American Journal of Tropical Medicine and Hygiene* 90: 705–711.

Ecuador Office of the President. www.presidencia.gob.ec.

Van Drunen, Michiel A., B. Lasage, and C. Dorland. 2006. *Climate Change in Developing Countries.* Oxfordshire, UK: CAB International North America.

EGYPT

The mighty Nile River has defined Egypt, its basin nourishing human civilization since recorded history. The Nile floods leave rich alluvial soil behind that is relied on for food. The nutrient rich soil spreads out in an alluvial fan that is about 160 miles wide when it discharges in to the Mediterranean Sea, from Alexandria to Port Said.

Today 85.3 million people live on 1,002,000 km² of land, with 6,000 km² of water, and 2,450 km of coastline. Forty percent of the population lives within 10 m of sea level. Water quality is poor. About 10,000 deaths a year are attributed to unsafe water. Twenty-four percent of the population suffers malnutrition.

The climate is arid, with very hot, dry summers and moderate winters. Weather differs regionally. The Nile River valley and delta extend to the Mediterranean Sea. The western desert is east from the Nile Valley to the Libyan border. The eastern desert is west from the Nile River to the Red Sea. The Sinai Peninsula is surrounded by the Gulf of Aqaba, the Gulf of Suez, the Suez Canal, the Mediterranean Sea, and the Sudan. Egypt's natural resources are petroleum, natural gas, iron ore, phosphates, manganese, talc, asbestos, lead zinc, and rare elements.

Current Waste Practices and Recycling

Altogether, 2,930,610,000 tons of municipal wastes were collected in 2008. Most cities have sewer and water services but discharge untreated wastes into freshwater. About 92 percent of urban residents have direct access to water in their home and to basic sanitation. About 90 percent of households in urban areas have public sewer systems. In rural areas waste practices are more basic—pit toilets, latrines, cesspools, and drainage ditches, and open defecation.

Water is not consistently available on a daily basis. About 40 percent of the population does not have access to water for more than three hours a day. Only 37 percent of rural areas have public sewer systems. There some water and wastewater treatment plants, but recent civil strife led to their lack of operation. Latrines often leak, because a generally high groundwater and lacks of maintenance cause leaks into the streets and groundwater contamination. Latrine trucks tend to dump that waste illegally and not in waste treatment plants. There are 372 municipal waste-water plants, and they treat about 10 million m^3 per day. Cultural practice is that women use household toilets, men use facilities at mosques, and children use the streets. Open defecation has decreased dramatically.

Egypt operates a number of landfills, including specialized landfills for industrial, inorganic wastes, contaminated soils, and biomedical wastes. There are some recovery and recycling facilities, including recycling lead from lead-acid batteries and incineration of organic solvent in a cement kiln as an alternative fuel. There is a large informal waste control sector of waste pickers, who do recycling and food foraging in all types of landfills and on city streets.

The Ministry of State for Environmental Affairs develops environmental policy, and within this agency, the Hazardous Chemicals and Waste Department focuses on waste. Egypt has a National Strategy for Waste Management, a National Strategy for Cleaner Production, and a National Environmental Action Plan for 2002–2017.

Hazardous Wastes

Although there are restrictions on the export of hazardous wastes and other wastes, it is allowed to Basel Convention countries that have the capacity to manage hazardous waste. No specific rule prohibits export of hazardous wastes and other wastes to other Basel Convention countries. Export of hazardous and other wastes can go to Basel Convention countries that have the capacity to manage hazardous wastes. Imports of hazardous and other wastes for final disposal or recovery are highly regulated. The presence of the Suez Canal and Egypt's maritime jurisdiction strictly control transit over land and water. New policies regarding hazardous waste transit cover modes of transportation, on-site interim storage rules, identification of wastes, permitting requirements, and recycling and final disposal plans.

A number of policies are aimed at hazardous wastes producers. These policies try to reduce hazardous wastes at their source, identify the specific waste, create safe on-site storage of wastes, label hazardous wastes, increase reporting on the generation of hazardous wastes, and develop inventories of old chemicals and pesticides. The government charges fees for landfill use and gives some tax exemptions to provide economic incentives to meet these objectives. Egypt also plans to involve Nongovernmental Organizations (NGOs) in hazardous waste management.

Emissions and Industry

In 2000, Egypt generated 193, 327.6 metric tons of greenhouse gas, a 65.5 percent increase from 1990. It is likely that actual greenhouse gas generation is now much higher because of population growth and dependence on agriculture.

Egyptians drive under a polluted sky in Cairo, Egypt on December 6, 2008. Many Middle Eastern voices are missing in the global dialogue on global warming, though these countries are severely affected by climate change. (AP Photo/Nasser Nasser)

Egyptian agricultural products include cotton, rice, wheat, corn, beats, fruit, vegetables, and livestock. About 35,300 km^2 of land is irrigated. Agricultural emissions accounted for 16 percent of all emissions. Within this sector, expanding agricultural fields accounted for 32 percent of emissions, manure management 29 percent, and enteric fermentation 25 percent. This is an unusually high amount of greenhouse gas emissions from manure, indicating the presence of large amounts of untreated feces.

Egypt produces substantial amounts of crude oil and maintains large proven reserves. There are 2.19 trillion in^3 of proven natural gas reserves, but little production. Energy industries accounted for 60 percent of all emissions. Energy production accounted for 36 percent of emissions, manufacturing industries and construction 23 percent, and transportation 23 percent. Industrial emissions accounted for 14 percent of all emissions. Within this sector, mineral products accounted for 62 percent of emissions, and chemical manufacturing accounted for 28 percent.

Waste emissions accounted for 9 percent of all emissions. Within this sector, solid waste disposal on land accounted for 67 percent of emissions, and wastewater management 33 percent.

Major Waste Issues

Egypt faces growing pollution problems, many around water and wastes. The Nile is the only consistent source of freshwater. Agricultural pesticide runoff, industrial wastes and raw sewage discharges directly in it. The rapid population growth further increases demands on the Nile for freshwater while increasing the amount of pollution in it. Piles of trash are commonly burned in the streets.

Without adequate treatment of wastewater there is a risk of major infectious diseases. Hepatitis A, hepatitis B, dengue fever, cholera, malaria, schistosomiasis, and typhoid fever occur here. Two percent or more of the population is persistently infected with hepatitis B. Climate change effects of rising ocean levels, more violent weather, and higher temperatures will create better environments for already present infectious diseases. The large volume of commercial and tourist traffic may increase the range of environments and introduce new infectious diseases as well as spread current ones.

Further Reading

El-Katsha, S., and S. Watts. 2007. "A Multifaceted Approach to Health Education: A Case Study from Rural Egypt." *International Quarterly of Community Health Education* 26: 189–210.

El-Khoury, Gabi. 2014. "Water Indicators in Arab Countries: Selected Indicators." *Contemporary Arab Affairs* 7: 339–349.

Ministry of State for Environmental Affairs Egyptian Environmental Affairs Agency. www. eeaa.gov.eg.

Van Drunen, Michiel A., B. Lasage, and C. Dorland. 2006. *Climate Change in Developing Countries.* Oxfordshire, UK: CAB International North America.

EL SALVADOR

Situated atop a volcanic plateau of 607 m, El Salvador is the smallest Central American nation. Altogether, 6.2 million people live on 21,041 km^2 of land, with 320 km^2 of water. There is a coastline on the Pacific Ocean of 307 km. It is the only Central American nation without a coastline on the Atlantic Ocean. Sixty percent of the population is urbanized, and 27 percent lives in a city having more than 100,000 inhabitants. Sixty-three percent lives in overcrowded conditions, and about a quarter suffers malnutrition. About a fifth lives below the international poverty level. Seven hundred deaths a year are attributed to unsafe water.

The climate is tropical. The rainy season is from May to October and the dry season from November to April. El Salvador shares boundaries with Guatemala and Honduras. Natural resources include hydropower and geothermal energy.

Current Waste Practices and Recycling

Most cities have sewer and water services but discharge untreated wastes into freshwater. In rural areas and some urban areas, waste practices are basic—pit toilets, latrines, drainage ditches, and cesspools. Ninety-four percent of the urban population has access to an improved drinking water sources, and 89 percent has access to an improved sanitation facility. Seventy-six percent of the rural population has access to an improved source of drinking water, and 83 percent has access to an improved sanitation facility. Total waste generation was about 113,000 tons, and municipal waste generation was 57,000 tons. Fifty-three percent of the population receives waste collection services. One percent of urban sewage receives primary waste treatment.

In 2006, the government began a strong effort to close down illegal wastes sites. Policies that required local governments to do an environmental assessment that includes a contract with one of the eleven designated sanitary landfill sites. These policies also require the creation of local environmental boards and carried stiff fines for noncompliance. Many local governments objected because they lacked financing to meet these requirements, noting that the policy did not include other aspects of waste management such as waste separation, transfer, and storage. There was also concern about the lack of community participation. Much waste is still illegally dumped. Trash is burned when more room is needed.

Emissions and Industry

In 1994, El Salvador generated 11,716.7 metric tons of greenhouse gases. Greenhouse emissions today are probably much higher because of population growth and reliance on agriculture.

Agricultural products include coffee, sugar, corn, rice, beans, cotton, and beef. About 450 km^2 of land is irrigated. Agricultural emissions accounted for 49 percent of all emissions. Within this sector, agricultural soils account for 68 percent of emissions and enteric fermentation 30 percent.

No oil is produced, and 16,160 bbl/day of crude oil is imported. Altogether, 44,040 bbl/day of refined petrochemical products are consumed domestically and 2,425 bbl/day exported. Energy emissions accounted for 39 percent all emissions. Within this sector, transportation accounted for 40 percent of emissions, energy industries 29 percent, and manufacturing and construction 15 percent. Industrial emissions accounted for 4 percent of all emissions. Within this sector, mineral products accounted for all emissions.

Waste emissions accounted for 7 percent of all emissions. Within this sector, solid waste disposal on land accounted for 61 percent of emissions and wastewater management 39 percent.

Major Waste Issues

Violent civil wars, devastating droughts and very powerful hurricanes have destroyed any waste infrastructure that may have existed. Between 1970 and 1992, it is estimated, 75,000 people were killed. In 1998, Hurricane Mitch laid waste to this nation. In 2001, major earthquakes rolled through the country, and that summer, a drought ruined four-fifths of food crops. Reconstruction of the entire waste system is a major waste issue.

Many of the environmental problems have waste issues. Mining operations are discharging toxic wastes into rivers. Agricultural uses of banned chemicals were a common practice until recently. Agricultural runoff of these chemicals and others are degrading water quality. Deforestation leads to soil erosion that pollutes the waterways. The illegal dumping of toxic wastes is affecting soils and will leach into groundwater sources. There is inadequate industrial and solid waste management, as well as many untreated discharges of pollution in waterways. Some of the waste issues are also public health concerns. There are infectious diseases—dengue fever, hepatitis A, and malaria. Chikungunya virus cases started in 2014.

Climate change effects of extreme weather events, increased rains and rising sea levels raise concerns about emergency preparedness. Environmental effects are already observed in the mangroves. The rising sea destroyed mangrove forests in western El Salvador in the Bajo Lempa area. The Ministry of Environment estimates that between 10 percent and 28 percent of its coasts will disappear in 100 years. Extreme weather events in 2009 and 2010 caused significant flooding and loss of life. There were climate refugees for months after these events. In 2010, the National Strategy on Climate Change was formed but is struggling against lack of resources.

Further Reading

Office of the President. www.presencia.gob.sv.

Perez-Pineda, F. 2013. "Estimating Willingness to Pay and Financial Feasibility in Small Water Projects in El Salvador." *Journal of Business Research* 66: 1750–1758.

Responding to the Impacts of Climate Change. www.christianaid.org.uk.

ERITREA

One of the hottest and driest places in Africa is the Red Sea coastal plain, which makes up about a third of Eritrea. Inland from the coast, the land rises to one of the highest landmasses in Africa. The capital city of Asmara is at about 2,440 m in elevation.

Today 6.23 million people live on Eritrea's 117,600 km^2 of land. It is a nation of small communities. Nineteen percent of Eritreans are urbanized, and 16 percent live in a city having more than 100,000 inhabitants. Eritrea has among the fastest-growing population rates in the world, though 44 percent suffer from malnutrition.

Eritrea borders on the Red Sea, Djibouti, Ethiopia, and Sudan. It includes many islands along the Red Sea coast as well as the Dankalia archipelago. The terrain is varied, with plains dominating the southwest and highlands descending east to a coastal plan. The climate is very hot and dry along the Red Sea. The highlands are wetter and cooler, but there are no year-round rivers. Natural resources include gold, zinc, potash, salt, and fish.

Current Waste Practices

Current waste practices are very basic—latrines, drainage ditches, pit toilets, cesspools, and open defecation. Seventy-four percent of the urban population has access to an improved drinking water sources, and 52 percent has access to an improved sanitation facility. Fifty-seven percent of the rural population has access to an improved source of drinking water, and just 4 percent has access to an improved sanitation facility—among the lowest access to sanitation facilities in the world. It is estimated that for Eritrea to have meet the UN's Millennium Development Goals for Sanitation by 2015, about 450,000 rural households would have needed to stop open defecation and use their own latrines.

In 2007, UNICEF and the government initiated the Community Led Total Sanitation program. Part of the program involves creating defecation-free zones, usually near a drinking water source. After several years of educational programs and pilot testing, the program was expanded. In 2014, almost half the 2,644 communities are receiving some type of education. Many villages are now 100 percent defecation-free, and many are developing more advanced waste management approaches. It is estimated that about 733,000 people from 2007 to 2014 have stopped open defecation. The National Rural Sanitation Policy and Strategy Direction of 2009 also collaborates with the Community Led Sanitation Program.

There is little waste collection. What waste is collected is taken to open landfill and dumps outside the settlement. Waste is not separated, so hazardous and toxic wastes end up in the landfill with other wastes. It is burned occasionally to make more room. Trash also accumulates in urban areas. Waste pickers scavenge streets and dumpsites for recyclable materials and sustenance.

Emissions and Industry

Eritrea generated 3,934 metric tons of greenhouse gases in 2000, a 6 percent decrease from 1994.

Agricultural products include sorghum, corn, cotton, tobacco, livestock and fish. Agricultural emissions accounted for 79 percent of all emissions. Within this sector, enteric fermentation accounted for 87 percent of emissions, agricultural soils 10 percent, and manure management 3 percent.

Electricity can be intermittent. The power grid is down for at least ninety-three days a year, among the highest rates in the world. Energy emissions accounted for 19 percent of all emissions. Within this sector, energy industries accounted for 19.5 percent of emissions and manufacturing and construction industries 9 percent. The other sources are nonspecific. Industrial emissions accounted for 1 percent of all emissions. Within this sector, mineral products accounted for all emissions

Waste emissions accounted for 2 percent of all emissions. Within this sector, solid waste disposal on land accounted all emissions.

Major Waste Issues

Protection of the public health is the main waste issue. Water and waste management is complicated by the presence of thousands of live landmines in a challenging environment. The environment is very dry and covered with steep slopes, lacks vegetative cover, and receives intense rainstorms occasionally. Even without human effects, the landscape does not hold soil well. Because of past conflicts, there are still live landmines that may detonate. This, combined with poor agricultural practices, dramatically increases sedimentation and water pollution.

There is a risk of major infectious diseases. Hepatitis A, hepatitis B, dengue fever, cholera, malaria, schistosomiasis, and typhoid fever occur here. Two percent or more of the population is persistently infected with hepatitis B. The risk of malaria is high throughout the country. Climate change effects of higher temperatures and drought raise grave concerns about food security and the risks of famine. Eritrea can also see swarms of locusts during very long periods. The locusts destroy food sources and increase further the risks of famine. These climate change effects may create more hospitable environments for already present infectious diseases. Unsafe sanitation practices in rural areas in this agrarian country may facilitate the spread of disease through waste. The main waste issue on public health measures to prevent outbreaks and, after outbreaks grow, to prevent epidemics.

Further Reading

Ekane, Nelson, et al. 2014. "Multi-Level Sanitation Governance: Understanding and Overcoming Challenges in the Sanitation Sector in Sub Saharan Africa." *Waterlines* 33: 242–256.
Eritrean Ministry of Information. www.shabait.com.
Foeken, D. W. J., et al. 2013. *Sanitation in Africa: Access to Improved Sanitation Facilities and Improvement Index*. Leiden, The Netherlands: African Studies Center.

ESTONIA

Altogether, 1.3 million people live on Estonia's 45,227 km^2 of land, with 2,840 km^2 of water. Sixty-nine percent of Estonians are urbanized, and 37 percent live in a city having more than 100,000 inhabitants. Three percent live in overcrowded conditions.

The climate is maritime, with wet, mild winters and cool summers. There are more than 1,400 manmade and natural lakes. Off its coast are over 1,500 islands. Estonia borders Latvia and Russia. Natural resources include oil shale, peat, and phosphorite.

Current Waste Practices and Recycling

There are modern sanitation facilities and sewer systems. Ninety-nine percent of the urban population has access to an improved drinking water sources, and 96 percent has access to an improved sanitation facility. Ninety-seven percent of the rural population has access to an improved source of drinking water, and 94 percent has access to an improved sanitation facility.

Seventy-nine percent receives municipal waste collection services. Municipal wastes constitute about 3 percent of the waste stream. There are five landfills for nonhazardous wastes and four for hazardous wastes. Many landfills have been closed, many of them industrial dumps or closed industrial facilities. About thirteen landfills for municipal solid wastes remain. Approximately 60 percent of the trash is biodegradable. About 19 percent is plastic, and 17 percent is paper and cardboard wastes. Municipal waste generation increased from 1993 to 1997 from 337,000 tons to 593,000 tons. Estonians average about 350 k of municipal waste a year. Estonia collected 464,000 tons of municipal waste in 2009, almost 62 percent of it landfilled, 11 percent recycled, and about 9 percent composted.

Hazardous Wastes

In 2008, Estonia generated 7,538,000 tons of hazardous wastes. The generation of hazardous wastes has increased and represents almost 40 percent of all wastes. These wastes are primarily from the oil shale industry, which generates about three-quarters of all wastes. Estonia operates one nuclear waste disposal facility and one storage facility. There are no nuclear power plants or processing facilities.

Emissions and Industry

Estonia generated 20,956 tons of greenhouse gases in 2011, a 48 percent decrease from 1990.

Almost 14 percent of the land is arable. Agricultural products include vegetables, potatoes, livestock, dairy products, and fish. Agricultural emissions accounted for 6 percent of all emissions. Within the sector, agricultural soils accounted for almost 56 percent of emissions, enteric fermentation 32 percent, and manure management almost 12 percent.

In 2010, crude oil production was small—11,000 bbl/day—and exports were 7,624 bbl/day, with none imported. Refined petroleum products are consumed at the rate of 26,340 bbl/day. Oil shale is mined and made into crude oil. This process requires more processing and creates pollution. This process is currently being used in the United States with an Estonian mining business. Hydrofracturing of this shale for natural gas is being explored and is a controversial issue in the United States because of underground seepage into freshwater.

Energy emissions accounted for 89 percent of all emissions. Within the sector, energy industries accounted for almost 80 percent of emissions, transport 12 percent, manufacturing and construction about 4 percent, and fugitive and other 4 percent. Industrial emissions accounted for almost 3 percent of overall emissions. Within this sector, minerals production accounted for almost three-quarters of emissions, an increase of about 15 percent from 1990. The chemical industry went from 40 percent of emissions in this sector in 1990 to 0 percent in 2011. The civil violence and war targeted these facilities. The consumption of halocarbons and SF_6 went from 0 percent to about 26 percent in the same period.

Waste emissions accounted for almost 2 percent of all emissions, one of the few areas to increase greenhouse gas emissions. Within the sector, solid waste disposal on land increased from 52 percent in 1990 to 65 percent in 2011. Wastewater handling decreased from 47 percent to 10 percent emissions.

Major Waste Issues

Estonia has made significant advances in decreasing pollution. Oil shale production processes can emit substantial greenhouse gases. Waste from past and present industries and war present formidable clean up challenges. As these sites remain unclean, with no environmental mitigation, they will leach into waterways. The coast is polluted in some areas now.

Infectious diseases include hepatitis A, hepatitis B, and tick-borne encephalitis. Rising ocean levels and more violent weather will challenge current rebuilding efforts. Waste issues evolve in this context and will also be a challenge. However, rebuilding efforts are persistent, and restoration and improvement of sewer and water treatment services is likely.

Estonia is preparing for climate change effects on water. Climate change observers note increased temperatures, increased precipitation, decrease in snow cover and sea ice, increase in range of seasonal weather extremes, and increase in extreme weather events. Projected effects include increases in groundwater recharge, earlier snowmelts, less moisture in the soil, increased risk of drought, increased temperatures, and increases in extreme weather events. Key vulnerabilities are drinking water quality, coastal erosion from sea level rise, and flooding. Their concerns are water quality, quantity, and sanitation. There is also concern about extreme weather events and ecosystem damages. Ecosystem damages are based on increased sensitivity of ecosystems to human and climate pressures. There is some concern about heavy rains' leaching pollutants into drinking water sources, as well as about algae blooms in warmer water temperatures. Estonia developed climate change adaption strategies to respond to these concerns and projections. In 2009, they created the Emergency Law, which requires environmental risk assessments and extreme weather crisis management plans every two years, the first being completed in 2011. Local plans must take account of flood risks. The law also created Rescues Centers designed to improve communication in extreme weather events, such as flooding.

Overall, Estonia is emerging from the ecological damages of recent war to reenter the European stage of global environmental engagement.

Further Reading

Agyeman, Julian, and Yelena Ogneva-Himmelberger. 2009. *Environmental Justice and Sustainability in the Former Soviet Union.* Cambridge, MA: MIT Press.

Auer, Matthew R., ed. 2005. *Restoring Cursed Earth: Appraising Environmental Policy Reforms in Eastern Europe and Russia.* New York: The Rowman & Littlefield Publishing Group.

Climate Change Impacts on Water Systems. www.oecd.org.

Estonia. www.politicresources.net.

Trotti, F., et al. 2013. "Estonian Waterworks Treatment Plants: Clearance of Residues, Discharge of Effluents and Efficiency of Removal of Radium from Drinking Water." *Journal of Radiological Protection* 33: 809.

ETHIOPIA

Ethiopia is the place of our first ancestors. Skeletons of *Aridipithecus ramidus kadabba,* between 5.8 million and 5.2 million years old, and *Australopithecus anamensis*, at about 4.2 million years old, were found here. It was one of the first sub-Saharan nations in Africa, once known as Abyssinia. Since then its boundaries have shifted, especially in the last century.

Today an estimated 93.9 million people live on 1.1 million km^2 of land, with 104,300 km^2 of water. It is a nation of small communities. Only 16 percent of Ethiopians are urbanized, and just 7 percent live in a city having more than 100,000 inhabitants. About half suffers malnutrition. The life expectancy is 56 years.

The climate is tropical, with significant regional variation. It is a landlocked country, and shares borders with Djibouti, Eritrea, Kenya, Somalia, South Sudan, and Sudan. The terrain is largely flat, with a central mountain range. Natural resources include natural gas, copper, gold, potash, and platinum. There is some hydropower in the central mountains.

Current Waste Practices

Waste practices are very basic—pit toilets, latrines, cesspools, drainage ditches, and open defecation. Ninety-seven percent of the urban population has access to an improved drinking water sources, and just 29 percent has access to an improved sanitation facility. Thirty-four percent of the rural population has access to an improved source of drinking water, and only 19 percent has access to an improved sanitation facility. Thirty-seven percent of the people openly defecate, a decrease from 92 percent in 1990. The urban sewer systems are old and need maintenance, with many areas lacking safe and clean sanitation facilities. Water quality is poor. Altogether, 112,100 deaths a year are attributed to unsafe water.

The local government, via private collection companies, collects trash from about four-fifths of the capital city of Addis Ababa. There is one open dump 13 km from the city center, with a 25 ha land area. Solid wastes are trucked in; bulldozers move it around and compact it. About three-quarters of solid waste is generated from households, 18 percent from commercial institutions, and 6 percent from street sweeping. About 60 percent is organic, and 15 percent is recyclable. The informal waste economy of waste pickers does the majority of recycling.

Emissions and Industry

Ethiopia generated 47,745 metric tons of greenhouse gas emissions in 1995, an 11 percent increase from 1990. Detailed emissions data is scant. It is likely that greenhouse gas emissions are higher because of population growth and reliance on agriculture.

Agricultural products include coffee, grains, oilseed, cotton, potatoes, animal hides, qat, and livestock. Qat is a shrub grown and used here, its leaves ingested for their stimulating effects. About 13 percent of the land is arable. About 2,900 km^2 of land is irrigated. Pesticide use is among the lowest in the world. There are about

30.6 million farm workers and agricultural is the predominant industry and culture. It contributes almost half the gross domestic product and is also the biggest source of greenhouse gas emissions. Most of the waste practices relate to an agrarian lifestyle. An informal network of small farmers diverts wastewater for crops such as lettuce, carrots, kale, beans, tomatoes, peppers, and onions. No is little environmental enforcement or public education around the use of wastewater and sewage for human food crops.

Agricultural emissions accounted for 81 percent of emissions. Within this sector, other accounted for 100 percent of emissions.

There is almost 25 billion m^3 of proven natural gas reserves. Oil consumption per capita is among the lowest in the world. Energy emissions accounted for 16 percent of emissions. Within this sector, other accounted for all emissions. Emissions from industrial processes account for less than 1 percent of emissions. Within this sector, other accounted for 100 percent of greenhouse gas emissions.

Emissions from solid wastes accounted for 3 percent of all emissions. Within this sector, other accounted for 100 percent emissions.

Major Waste Issues

Ethiopia is a rapidly growing, impoverished population with significant challenges to measure and plan around wastes. Access to safe and clean water and sanitation is one of the largest waste issues.

A group of women collecting water from a river near Konso in Southern Ethiopia. Fresh water is a scarce necessity in many places. Women are frequently responsible for getting water, and must travel greater and greater distances for it. (Edwardje/Dreamstime.com)

The lack of waste infrastructure and growing overcrowded urban population will increase water pollution, trash, and disease. Groundwater supplies are not being recharged to meet increasing demands from agriculture, cities, and industry. Currently there is a risk of infectious diseases—cholera, dengue fever, hepatitis A, hepatitis B, malaria, meningococcal meningitis, schistosomiasis, tuberculosis, and typhoid. Two percent or more of the population is persistently infected with hepatitis B. Areas below 1,400 m are at high risk for malaria.

Climate change effects cause grave concern about food security and famine. Increases in temperature and violent weather in the context of water deprivation and poor sanitation will expand vectors of most infectious diseases. Ethiopia has the lowest number of doctors and hospital beds per capita any other country. The lack of medical care interferes with controlling outbreaks, and increases the risk of epidemics.

The major waste issue is to protect the public health. The steps necessary for this to develop to the point of effectiveness are very challenging. It is not currently possible for Ethiopia to meet these challenges without international assistance. Epidemics can pose public health threats to the country, region, and to the world population.

Further Reading

Cochrane, L., and P. Costolanski. 2013. "Climate Change Vulnerability and Adaptability in an Urban Context: A Case Study of Addis, Ababa, Ethiopia." *International Journal of Sociology and Anthropology* 5: 192–204.

Dsikowitzy, L. 2013. "Assessment of Heavy Metals in Water Samples and Tissues of Edible Fish Species from Awassa and Koka Rift Valley Lakes, Ethiopia." *Environmental Monitoring and Assessment* 185: 3117–3131.

Ethiopian Parliament Information. www.ethiopar.net.

Kass, Gebrie. 2009. *Management of Domestic Solid Waste in Ethiopia*. Saarbrucken, Germany: VDM Verlag.

Mekonnen, K., et al. 2015. "Occurrence, Distribution, and Ecological Risk Assessment of Potentially Toxic Elements in Surface Sediments of Lake Awassa and Lake Ziway, Ethiopia." *Journal of Environmental Science and Health* 50: 90–99.

F

FRENCH GUIANA

French Guiana is a dependency of France. It is heavily subsidized by France and has among the highest standards of living in South America. The European Space Agency operations center launches communications satellites here.

Today, 232,000 people live on of 90,000 km² of land and 378 km of coastline. Forty percent of the population lives in the capital city of Cayenne. There are many small rural communities away from the coast.

Brazil, Suriname, and the North Atlantic Ocean border French Guiana. The land rises from coastal wetlands along the ocean to hills. There are low mountains in the west called the Tumac–Humac Mountains. More than twenty rivers flow to the ocean. The Maroni River forms the border with Suriname and the Oyapock river forms the border with Suriname. The climate is tropical—hot and humid. Natural resources include oil, bauxite, gold, timber, and clay. Agricultural products include sugar, rice, cocoa, maniac, fruits, vegetables, and livestock.

Current Waste Practices

There is little municipal waste collection. Ninety percent of the population use improved drinking water sources and have improved sanitation. It is slighter higher in urban areas and slightly lower in rural areas. Hazardous wastes are disposed of in incinerators at hospitals. Most trash is dumped on the edge of town. There are two official dumps for the twenty-two municipalities.

Emissions and Industry

There is little data about greenhouse gases. Because French Guiana is a dependency of France, these emissions are part of France's emissions. There is international focus on a manmade reservoir as a case study on the effect of climate change on gases in freshwater.

Major Waste Issues

Major waste issues are picking up trash and reporting all wastes. E-waste is a major issue. French Guiana generates and receives substantial amounts of e-waste, most dumped outside town or in the ocean along with other trash.

There are infectious diseases, including dengue fever, hepatitis A, hepatitis B, malaria, and typhoid. There is a high risk of malaria in some areas, as well as a risk that infectious disease vectors will grow as climate change effects intensify.

Climate change effects of increased temperature, hotter summers and wetter rainy seasons, and rising sea levels cause concerns about drought, floods, fires, and landslides. The coastline is unstable, being essentially an estuary of the Amazon River basin, its sedimentation and currents are controlled by changeable and dynamic characteristics. The prospect of more intense and extreme weather-related events increases concern about coastal flooding. The vast majority of the population lives along the coast.

Further Reading

Europe's Spaceport. www.esa.int.

French Guinean Prefecture. www.guyane.pref.gouv.fr.

Njoh, A. 2013. "Colonialization and Sanitation in Urban Africa: A Logistics Analysis of the Availability of Central Sewerage Systems as a Function of Colonialism." *Habitat International* 38: 207–213.

FRENCH POLYNESIA

French Polynesia comprises islands and archipelagoes in the South Pacific far from other major countries. The terrain is mixed. There are some islands that have mountains, the tallest being Mont Orohena, at 2,240 m. Other islands are low and surrounded by coral reefs. The climate is tropical. Hot temperatures are moderated by wind from the east-southeast. The hurricane season is from the end of January to mid-March. Natural resources include fish, cobalt, timber, and hydropower. There is little arable land. Agricultural products include coconuts, fish, coffee, vegetables, meat, and dairy products. About 277,250 people live on 3,660 km² of land and 2,500 km of coastline.

French Polynesia has a history of radioactive and hazardous wastes from the years of nuclear research in the area. The French established a nuclear testing base here in 1963 and performed nuclear testing in the region. Before that, the United States operated a nuclear testing program, detonating twenty-three atmospheric nuclear bombs between 1946 and 1958. The first hydrogen bomb was tested here, it alone contaminating a 100 mi circle of ocean. France denoted 193 bombs in the air and water between 1966 and 1996. Most of this dangerous waste was never cleaned up or remediated. Nuclear wastes can last thousands of years, having devastating effects on life and the regional ecology.

Current Waste Practices

Everyone has access to improved drinking water. Ninety-seven percent has access to improved sanitation facilities. Most of the collected and uncollected waste is dumped in lagoons. Often, when the lagoons become too full of waste, it is packed down with heavy equipment. Local communities are warned to not plant vegetables near these sites. A few new dumpsites are being planned and developed. There are some local recycling activities. The government is proposing taxes on imported goods that have heavy packaging, so to reduce wastes going into the dumps.

Emissions and Industry

French Polynesia is a dependency of France. As such greenhouse gas emissions reporting is under the control of France. French Polynesia was not mentioned in French National Communications under the United Nations Framework Convention on Climate Change agreement pursuant to the Kyoto Treaty, and French Polynesia does not report it.

Major Waste Issues

Climate change effects of rising sea levels, more intense weather events, and increased temperature cause concern about floods, drought, and emergency planning. Infectious diseases include hepatitis A, hepatitis B, dengue fever, malaria, typhoid, and yellow fever. There is a high risk of malaria and chikungunya virus outbreaks in the region.

The major waste issue is to clean up nuclear wastes and remediate their effects on the people and the environment, establishing environmental monitoring systems and reports.

Further Reading

Blakeney, Michael, Thierry Coulet, Getachew Mengiste, and Marcelin Tonye Mahop, eds. 2012. *Extending the Protection of Geographical Indications: Case Studies of Agricultural Products in Africa.* New York: Earthscan Publishing.

Caron, David D., and Harry N. Scheiber. 2014. *The Oceans in the Nuclear Age: Legacies and Risks.* Boston: Martinus Nijhoff.

La Presidence de la Polynesie francaise. www.presidence.pf.

FINLAND

Finland's landscape is one of forests, lakes, rivers, wetlands, and coastlines. Altogether, 5.4 million people live on 336,851 km² of land, with 34,330 km² of water. Sixty-one percent of Finnish are urbanized, and 42 percent live in a city having more than 100,000 inhabitants. Life expectancy is almost 80 years. Excluding islands, the coastline is 1,126 km long. Finland is an environmental world leader in several areas including sustainability. It is a party to all major international environmental agreements.

The climate is cold temperate, with occasional subarctic conditions, moderated by ocean currents and more than 60,000 lakes. There are 179,584 islands, some very small. Many are part of the archipelagoes of Finland. The terrain is low, with rolling hills. Most of the country is less than 180 m above sea level. It shares borders with Norway, Sweden, and Russia. Natural resources include timber, iron ore, lead, copper, zinc, gold, silver, and chromites. About a quarter of land is above the Arctic Circle, where the sun does not set for seventy-three days in the summer and does not rise for about fifty days in winter.

Current Waste Practices and Recycling

Finland collected 2,562,000 tons of municipal waste in 2009, a 7.4 percent decrease from 2008. Forty-six percent of the waste is landfilled, 18 percent incinerated, 24 percent recycled, and about 12 percent composted. Everyone in the country receives municipal waste collections services and has access to an improved drinking water source and sanitation facility.

At first wastewater was discharged directly into waterways. The first wastewater plants were built in 1910, in Lahti and Helsinki. Everyone now has access to a safe and sanitary facility, though about 1 million residents and 1 million tourists live in areas without municipal sewers. There are now about 550 wastewater purification facilities. In 2003, there were about fifteen hazardous wastes landfills, 162 nonhazardous waste landfills (down from 351 in 1998), and seventy-one inert landfills. There are robust policies and practices around recycling. Ninety-eight percent of glass bottles are recycled, and about 70 percent of paper is recycled. Waste collection and recycling is more difficult in the rural areas because of the costs of transport. Households are accepting of recycling and will separate recyclables, a key part of a successful recycling program.

The amount of municipal wastes going to landfills has declined as recovery and recycling increase. There is an active program to close old landfills and perform environmental remediation. The goal is to make them recreational areas with biodiverse landscapes, including rare species. New waste regulations are household-specific, requiring a waste plan that is filed with house documents if there is a toilet in the house. These regulations do not include households without toilets if the amount of wastewater is low and no risks of pollution exist.

The Ministry of the Environment within the Finnish Environmental Institute controls waste policy. The 1993 Finnish Waste Act defines waste as "any substance or object that the holder discards, intends, or is required to discard." The 2008 National Waste Plan sets targets for the reduction of the amount and hazardousness of wastes. In 2008, Finland generated 2,163,000 tons of hazardous wastes. This plan is changing its measures as environmental conditions change and monitoring improves.

Regional waste plans are done by the Centers for Economic Development, Transport, and the Environment. Five regional waste plans specify the measures necessary for implementation of the Waste Plan.

The strategic plan for implanting waste policy goals develops objectives, policy instruments, and designates the responsible entity for implementation. The objective of the waste management plan is to improve the material efficiency of production and consumption. Promoting recycling is a major objective. Developing a safe, streamlined system of waste management is another major objective.

The plan also encourages agreements between government and industrial sectors for promoting materials efficiency. Finland has an extensive program of education, community outreach, and advisory services aimed at preventive measures minimizing waste and the dangers of waste to the public health and environment. Government and industry share this policy. For example, Ekokem, Ltd., is the major hazardous waste disposal facility in Finland. It has two high-temperature incineration plants, a physical chemical plant, and a special landfill. Because this facility is one of the largest, it has valuable expertise that it shares with others in the waste industrial sector.

Finland segregates exported waste into different categories. Iron oxides, rubber waste, and wastewater treatment sludge are separated. Imported waste is also segregated. Wastewater treatment of sludge and treated wood wastes are separated from general group of other wastes.

Nuclear Wastes

In 1977, Finland began the commercial use of nuclear power. Finland now operates four nuclear power reactors that produce about a third of the country's electricity. There are three disposal, ten storage, and four processing facilities. There is controversy around site selection for the disposal of spent nuclear fuel underground in Olkiluoto, which is near an existing nuclear power plant.

Hazardous Wastes

Finland goes beyond the requirements of the Basel Convention in defining hazardous wastes. Wastes that contain metal compounds, alkaline metals, and aromatic compounds (such as creosote, perchlorate, and peroxides) are hazardous by Finnish standards. Altogether, 25,346 metric tons of hazardous wastes were imported and 1,647 metric tons of other wastes imported in 2009. Altogether, 24,437 metric tons of other wastes and 86,365 metric tons of hazardous wastes were exported. There are no restrictions for the import of hazardous wastes and other wastes for recovery. There are also no restrictions on the transit of hazardous or other wastes.

Emissions and Industry

Finland generated 67,033 tons of greenhouse gases in 2011, a 4.9 percent decrease from 1990.

There are 2.23 million ha of arable land. Additionally, 685.8 km^2 of land is irrigated. Because of its northerly latitude and short growing season, most agricultural production is in the south. Agricultural products include barley, wheat, sugar beets, dairy products, and fish. There is high use of fertilizers in some places. To reduce their use, Finland now has protective zones, introduced taxes on fertilizers, limited fertilizer usage-to-yield expectations, and improved fertile storage and use of manure.

Agricultural emissions accounted for 9 percent of all emissions. Within this sector, agricultural soils accounted for 60 percent of greenhouse gas emissions, enteric fermentation about 27 percent, and manure management about 12 percent.

Oil production is the major source of greenhouse gas emissions. Finland produced 13,530 bbl/day of crude oil in 2012. A total of 204,800 bbl/day of refined petroleum products were consumed in 2011, along with 144,400 bbl/day in exports. Electricity consumption per capita was among the highest in the world, at 16,420.75 kW.

Energy emissions accounted for almost 80 percent of all emissions. Within this sector, energy industries accounted for 46 percent of emissions, transportation almost 25 percent, manufacturing and construction 18 percent, and fugitive and other sources about 10 percent.

Some of the primary industries in Finland are metals and metal products, electronics, machinery and scientific instruments, shipbuilding, pulp and paper, chemicals, and clothing. Finland is very industrialized and has a free market economy having strict government protection of the environment and the public health, safety, and welfare. Twenty-two percent of the labor force works in this sector. Thirty-two percent of the labor force works in public services. Industrial emissions accounted for 8 percent of all green house gas emissions. Within this sector, metal production accounted for 42 percent of emissions, metal production 42 percent, and mineral products 24 percent.

Waste emissions accounted for 3 percent of all emissions. Within this sector, solid waste disposal on land accounted for almost 84 percent of all greenhouse gas emissions and wastewater handling 10 percent.

Major Waste Issues

Finland's waste management policy is organized, goal-driven, and highly collaborative. The major focus of policy is implementation with meaningful environmental outcomes. However, there are challenges: Mining wastes and old industrial sites pose a threat to waterways. There are many paper and pulp mills producing paper and pulp products. Many are along rivers and the ocean coasts and discharge wastes in to these water bodies. Infectious diseases include hepatitis A and tick-borne encephalitis.

Finland is preparing for climate change effects on water systems. Climate change observers note increases in the temperature, especially in the winter. Projected effects include temperatures increases, substantial increases in precipitation, greater intensity and frequency of heavy rainfall, risk of drought, shorter and discontinuous snow season, hydrological shifts in seasonal mountain water runoff, and species extinction in marine ecosystems. Like many countries, Finland's key vulnerability is its small water utilities and wastewater systems with combined sewers. Housing and infrastructure may weaken with increases in extreme weather and seasonal changes. Finland is actively developing policies and programs to adapt to climate change. There is a large ongoing research focus and study on climate change nationally and regionally. Part of their approach includes national land use guidelines, better climate change communications, water resource management and flood risk plans, flood forecasting and monitoring, and developing instructions for preparing water treatment plants for extreme weather events.

Finland is a global leader in environmental protection and sustainability. Its waste management approaches, policies, and programs serve as models for many nations.

Further Reading

Climate Change Impacts on Water Systems. www.oecd.org.

Lehtoranta, S., et al. 2014. "Comparison of Carbon Footprints and Eutrophication Impacts of Rural On-Site Wastewater Treatment Plants in Finland." *Journal of Cleaner Production* 65: 439–446.

Present Status of Environmental Sanitation in Finland. www.ncbi.nlm.nih.gov/pmc/articles/PMC2542071/.

FRANCE

France is bordered by both the Atlantic Ocean and the Mediterranean Sea. It is an historic crossroads for Europe, the Middle East, and Africa. French colonies and other land acquisitions historically have spanned the planet. French was the international language of diplomacy, and many nations still speak French.

Today, 63 million people live on France's 551,500 km^2 of land, with 3,374 km^2 of water. There are 3,427 km of coastline. Seventy-seven percent of the French population is urbanized, and 42 percent lives in a city having more than 100,000 inhabitants. Life expectancy is 81 years.

The climate differs regionally, reflecting the range of topography. Generally there are mild winters and cool summers. The southern coast can be hot in the summer. Higher altitudes in the mountains have harsher winters. France is one of the largest countries in Europe. It shares borders with Andorra, Belgium, Germany, Italy, Luxembourg, Monaco, Spain, and Switzerland. Natural resources found in France include coal, iron ore, zinc, bauxite, uranium, arsenic, potash, timber, fish, gold, and oil.

Current Waste Practices and Recycling

In 2010, France generated 355 million tons of municipal solid wastes. Six million tons were recycled, and almost six tons were incinerated. In 2005, France had thirteen hazardous waste sites. In 2008, France generated 10,893,000 tons of hazardous wastes.

Almost all households have access to public drinking water. There are two primary water treatment facilities. The government runs one and the other is private.

Animals and Trash Homes

Many animals use the trash around them for food and shelter. Birds, squirrels, and many other animals use trash for shelter. Now bees do, too, including caulking instead of their usual resin. The bee species *Megachile campanulae* does not build hives but does build little nests in holes in trees and plants. It now uses caulking to seal it instead of its self-produced resin. Another bee species, *Megachile rotundata*, now uses plastic shopping bags instead of leaves for its nests.

Scientists are studying these bees to examine their adaptability to urban and to degraded areas.

By law, a township having more than 2,000 people is required to have a municipal waste plant. Private wastes from homes and hotels usually use septic tanks or a private waste treatment plant. The owner is required to have a waste system and can choose between a septic tank with pipes and filters or can sign onto the township system. The septic system has to meet water purifications standards and is inspected. Two basic septic tanks are allowed. Some older ones take bathroom waste only and work by allowing waste to soak into the ground. New tanks take all the water wastes and treat it with filters before it is discharged. There are other requirements regarding distance from the house and from freshwater and amount of land. If the owners choose a septic system that uses no electricity, they can receive a no-interest loan from the government for the private waste facility. About 5 million households use septic tanks, more commonly in rural areas. Cesspools, where water wastes drain from the house to a hole, are forbidden. Some townships cannot afford a large municipal waste treatment plant, so they build a small one, and some also people have to get private waste treatment. The European Union required that all cities having more than 15,000 people have secondary water treatment in 2000. The goal was to have all urban centers served by secondary levels of sewage treatment.

Recycling of municipal solid waste increased from 26 percent to 35 percent of this waste stream from 2001 to 2010. They now extend manufacturer responsibility for wastes, increasing recycling. Landfill and incinerator taxes are used

A recycling bin on a public parking lot near a highway in France helps keep trash off the road. Making it easy for people to recycle is part of a community recycling program. (Kartouchken/ Dreamstime.com)

to suppress their use. Biodegradable municipal wastes decreased as part of the municipal waste flow, from about 22 percent in 2006 to about 20 percent in 2010, or about 7 million tons of biodegradable municipal wastes. At the same time, organic recycling increased, from about 14 percent of municipal solid wastes up to about 17 percent.

Nuclear Wastes

Commercial use of nuclear power in France started in 1959. There are fifty-eight operating nuclear reactors in France, supplying almost three-quarters of electrical needs. Twelve nuclear power plants are decommissioned. There are three nuclear waste disposal, four storage, and two processing facilities. In the 1970s, France shipped the most waste to Africa of any western European country. Many European countries shipped their wastes legally and illegally to Africa. Many European countries had colonies there with established commercial routes.

In 2010, 1,320,000 cm equivalents of nuclear wastes were produced, among the highest amounts in the world and an almost 13 percent increase from 2007. This is predicted to increase. Because siting these kinds of waste sites is politically difficult, the wastes are often stored at the production or energy facility. High-level nuclear wastes are 0.2 percent of the overall volume of nuclear wastes but carry 96 percent of the radioactivity. Intermediate-level long-lived nuclear wastes are 3 percent of the volume and carry 4 percent of the radioactivity. Low- and intermediate-level short-lived wastes are 63 percent of the volume and carry 0.02 percent of the radioactivity. Twenty-seven percent of the volume is very low-level radioactive waste and carries 0.01 percent of the radioactivity. Finding sites for radioactive wastes is controversial. The national government asked for volunteers from municipalities on a list of 3,000 geologically evaluated sites. Forty responded at first, but many withdrew in the face of community resistance. The 2006 Planning Act on sustainable management of radioactive materials and wastes created the National Assessment Board, an advisory board that annually assesses the state of research on the management of radioactive wastes in the context of incorporating the latest developments into policy and practice.

Emissions and Industry

In 2012, France emitted 496,221 tons of greenhouse gases, an 11 percent decrease from 1990.

About 26,000 km² of land is irrigated. Agricultural products include wheat, cereals, potatoes, sugar beets, beef, dairy products, and fish. Agricultural emissions accounted for 18 percent of all emissions. Within this sector, agricultural soils accounted for 51 percent of emissions, enteric fermentation almost 32 percent, and manure management almost 17 percent. This is a high amount of greenhouse gas emissions from manure, indicating the presence of large amounts of untreated feces.

Oil is one of the biggest sources of greenhouse gas emissions. In 2012, France produced 72,300 bbl/day of crude oil, importing 1.3 million bbl/day with no exports. Refined petroleum consumption is 1.79 million bbl/day, and exports are 464,300 bbl/day. In 2013, there was 10.7 billion m^3 of proven natural gas reserves, but little in production. Electricity consumption was 471 billion kWh in 2010, the fifth-highest in the world. Electricity production was also high, at 530.6 billion kWh.

Energy emissions accounted for almost 72 percent of all greenhouse gases. Within this sector, transport accounted for 38 percent of emissions, manufacturing and construction almost a fifth, and energy industries 15 percent. Other sectors accounted for almost 26 percent and fugitive emissions for just over 1 percent. Industrial emissions accounted for 7 percent of all greenhouse gases. Within this sector, consumptions of halocarbons account for 49 percent of greenhouse gases, mineral products 32 percent, metal production about 10 percent, and the chemical industry 8 percent.

Waste emissions accounted for almost 3 percent of all greenhouse gases. Within this sector, solid waste disposal on land accounted for 69 percent of emissions, wastewater handling 15 percent, and waste incineration 10 percent. Waste incineration decreased slightly from 1990.

Major Waste Issues

France is a large and historically industrialized nation. It faces challenges in overall waste management in several areas. There is air pollution from industry and processes and vehicles that contribute to the formation of acid rain. Agricultural pesticide and fertilizer runoff contribute to the water pollution from municipal wastes. The final disposition of nuclear wastes is a difficult issue as more is created and fewer wastes sites developed. In French Polynesia, the French and the United States conducted nuclear testing. French Guyana and French Polynesia are dependencies of France, but their wastes are not included in French reporting.

Currently there is not a major risk of infectious disease outbreaks. Rising ocean levels, more violent weather, and temperature increases may change that. France is an historic international destination and crossroads. Global commerce runs through France and could expand disease vectors.

France is preparing for climate change effects on water systems. Climate change observers note increased temperatures, melting glaciers in the French Alps and Pyrenees, and variation in the growth cycle of fruit and trees. Projections include increases in days with low water, reduction in soil humidity, decrease in snow, and increases in duration and intensity of summer droughts. A key vulnerability is the loss of freshwater in the southwest of France. In response to these concerns and projections, France developed new policies. The Reform of the Insurance Scheme for Natural Disasters, promotion of water use efficiency, and planning to prevent flood risks are recent examples of the new policies. Activities include flood risk mapping, mapping of climate change vulnerability of ground water, and providing information about these risks to the nation.

Further Reading

Barnes, D. 2006. *The Great Stink of Paris and the Nineteenth-Century Struggle against Filth and Germs.* Baltimore, MD: Johns Hopkins University Press.

Climate Change Impacts on Water Systems. www.oecd.org.

French Prime Minister. www.gouvernement.fr.

Troesch, S., et al. 2014. "Constructed Wetlands for the Treatment of Raw Wastewater: The French Experience." *Water Practice and Technology* 9: 430–439.

GABON

Dense tropical forests cover most of this sub-Saharan country. Despite tremendous oil wealth, Gabon still lacks, roads, health care, and sanitation. Most of the income from oil profits does not return to the country.

Today, 1.64 million people live on Gabon's 267,668 km² of land and 885 km of coastline. Eighty-four percent of the population is urbanized, and 45 percent lives in a city having more than 100,000 inhabitants. Twenty-six percent suffers malnutrition. Four hundred deaths a year are attributed to unsafe water.

Gabon borders Cameroon, the Republic of Congo, and Equatorial Guinea. It has savanna in the east and south. There is a narrow plain along the coast, with a hilly interior. Only 1.21 percent of the land is arable, among the lowest figures in the world. The climate is tropical—always hot and humid. Among the many natural resources are timber, petroleum, natural gas, hydropower, uranium, gold, and diamonds.

Current Waste Practices

In rural areas and in many parts of urban areas, waste practices are basic—latrines, pit toilets, drainage ditches, cesspools, and open defecation. Ninety-five percent of the urban population has access to an improved drinking water sources, and just 33 percent has access to an improved sanitation facility. Only 41 percent of the rural population has access to an improved source of drinking water, and 30 percent has access to an improved sanitation facility.

About 38 percent of households have waste collection in the capital city of Libreville, but there are broad disparities. Eighty percent of the trash is collected in the wealthier city center but only 6 percent in poor areas of the city. In 2009, the United Nations Development Program, local governments, and the Public Health Ministries Hygiene Department collaborated on the Shared Urban Solid Waste Management Project. The goals of this project were to eradicate poverty, improve public and primary health care conditions through better hygiene, and clean up the environment. Two hundred young people in eleven project teams cleaned up waste for 300,000 residents.

Emissions and Industry

In 2000, Gabon generated 6,159.6 metric tons of greenhouse gas emissions, a figure 5 percent lower than in 1994. It is likely that greenhouse gas emissions are higher now because of higher population and reliance on agriculture.

Gabon produces agricultural products of cocoa, coffee, sugar, palm oil, cattle, and fish. Agricultural emissions accounted for 6 percent of all emissions. Within this sector, agricultural soils accounted for 58.5 percent of emissions, prescribed burning of the savannas 28 percent, and manure management 5 percent.

The energy sector accounted for 86 percent of all emissions. Seventy-three percent of the emissions within this sector were fugitive emissions. Generally this indicates a lack of environmental regulation. Fugitive emissions are essentially unaccounted waste streams into the air. Fugitive emissions can affect regional ecosystems and the public health, because they can fall from the air to the land and water. Of known emitters, energy production accounted for 10 percent of emissions and transportation 8 percent. Crude oil production and proven oil reserves are high. Oil consumption per capita is low. Uranium production per capita is among the highest in the world. Emissions from industrial processes accounted for almost 2 percent of all emissions. Within this sector, all emissions came from mineral production.

Waste emissions accounted for 7 percent of all emissions. Within this sector, solid waste disposal on land accounted for 52 percent of emissions and wastewater handling 47 percent.

Major Waste Issues

Environmental issues frame waste issues here. The petrochemical industry has polluted vast amounts of freshwater. Less than half the rural population and about 97 percent of the urban population has freshwater.

Although documentation is difficult to find, it is suspected that Gabon could be a dumping ground for international hazardous wastes. Gabon is at the receiving end of electronic wastes. There are radioactive mining wastes left from over forty years of mining in southern Gabon.

The lack of waste infrastructure and growing heavily urbanized population will increase water pollution, trash, and disease. Currently there is a risk of infectious diseases—cholera, dengue fever, hepatitis A, hepatitis B, malaria, schistosomiasis, tuberculosis, and typhoid. Two percent or more of the population is persistently infected with hepatitis B. There is a high risk for malaria.

Climate change effects of increases in temperature, rising ocean levels and violent weather creates grave concerns for agricultural food security and risk of famines. These climate changes in the context of poor sanitation will expand vectors of most infectious diseases. The lack of medical care interferes with controlling outbreaks and increases the risk of epidemics.

Further Reading

Blakeney, Michael, Thierry Coulet, Getachew Mengiste, and Marcelin Tonye Mahop, eds. 2012. *Extending the Protection of Geographical Indications: Case Studies of Agricultural Products in Africa*. New York: Earthscan Publishing.

Foeken, D. W. J., et al. 2013. *Sanitation in Africa: Access to Improved Sanitation Facilities and Improvement Index*. Leiden, The Netherlands: African Studies Center.

Gabon. www.en.legabon.org.

Zabbey, N., and H. Uyi. 2014. "Community Responses of Intertidal Soft—Bottom Macrozoobenthos to Oil Pollution in a Tropical Mangrove Ecosystem, Niger Delta, Nigeria." *Marine Pollution Bulletin* 82: 167–174.

THE GAMBIA

The Gambia is among the smallest nations of Africa, with an average width of 32 km (20 mi). It follows the Gambia River, an important transit route for the region.

The Gambia is a long, narrow country going from the North Atlantic Ocean following a large river inland. It is bordered by Senegal. The climate is tropical—hot and humid. It is a small country having a stable history. Environmental challenges are coastal erosion, pollution, waste management, and rapid population growth. Almost 40 percent of the population lives within 10 m of sea level.

Today, 1.7 million people live on 11,295 km² of land. Fifty-four percent live in urban areas, and 19 percent live in a city having more than 100,000 inhabitants. Gambia has among the fastest-growing population rates in the world. It is also one of the most impoverished countries in the world. Fifty-nine percent of the population lives below the international poverty level. Twenty-eight percent suffers malnutrition. Life expectancy is 59 years.

Current Waste Practices

Waste practices are basic in rural areas and in many parts of urban areas, where Gambians use latrines, pit toilets, cesspools, drainage ditches, and open defecation. Ninety-two percent of the urban population has access to an improved drinking water source, and 70 percent has access to an improved sanitation facility. Eighty-five percent of the rural population has access to an improved source of drinking water, and 65 percent has access to an improved sanitation facility. Some municipal wastes are collected by local government and tracked to open landfills and dumpsites. The legal landfills have been at overcapacity for many years, such as the Mile 2 and Bakateh Dumpsites. There are few disposal facilities for solid wastes. Waste pickers scavenge the dumps and street for recyclable materials and sustenance.

In 2011, the Gambian Ministry of Health and Social Welfare developed the Gambia National Strategy for Sanitation and Hygiene for 211–2016. The Gambia has reached the UN Millennium Development Goal of clean water for half the population by 2015. However, it has not met the UN Millennium Development Goal 7 for sanitation.

Emissions and Industry

In 2000, Gambia generated 19,383 tons of greenhouse gases, an increase of 355 percent from 1993. It is likely that greenhouse gas emissions are much higher today because of rapid population growth and unrestrained petrochemical development.

Agricultural emissions accounted for 8 percent of all emissions. Within this sector, agricultural soils accounted for 69 percent of emissions, enteric fermentation

19 percent, rice cultivation 10 percent, burning of savannas and agricultural residues 1 percent and manure management less than 1 percent.

Energy emissions accounted for 2 percent of overall emissions. Within this sector, transportation accounted for 29 percent of emissions, energy industries 24 percent, manufacturing and construction almost 2 percent, and a large group of other sectors 45 percent. Industrial emissions accounted for 89 percent of overall emissions. Within this sector, consumption of halocarbons accounted for 94 percent of emissions and metal production 6 percent. Many of these emissions are generated in petrochemical production processes.

Waste emissions accounted for 1 percent of overall emissions. Within this sector, solid waste disposal on land accounted for 79 percent of emissions and wastewater handling 21 percent.

Major Waste Issues

The Gambia has a well-planned approach to many environmental and sanitation issues, but there are large gaps. There are many state agencies having overlapping jurisdictions, causing interagency conflict and confusion in service delivery. Urban waste management is challenged by trash from households and small industries that clogs city streets, waterways, and sewers. The lack of hygienic disposal of fecal wastes, sanitary landfill management, and monitoring surface and groundwater are moving environmental issues into the public health arena. The protection of the public health is the major waste issue. Infectious diseases are a major concern. Currently infectious diseases include cholera, dengue fever, hepatitis A, hepatitis B, malaria, meningococcal meningitis, schistosomiasis, typhoid, and yellow fever. There is a high risk of malaria. Two percent or more of the population is persistently infected with hepatitis B. There is a risk of yellow fever in all areas of the country.

Climate change effects of increased temperatures and violent weather may facilitate these diseases. These outbreaks may become nationally uncontrollable and reach epidemic proportion, potentially affecting the region. Substantial international assistance is necessary to develop locally and globally effective public health systems. The Gambia is highly dependent on development aid for sanitation programs and is challenged to coordinate aid programs.

Further Reading

Central Africa Regional Program for the Environment, Regional Development Strategy 2012–2020, U.S. Agency for International Development. www.usaid.gov.

Foeken, D. W. J., et al. 2013. *Sanitation in Africa: Access to Improved Sanitation Facilities and Improvement Index*. Leiden, The Netherlands: African Studies Center.

Jacob, N. 2013. "A Feasibility Study on Recycling of Plastic Wastes into Useful Energy and Its Management System in the Gambia." *Current Research in Microbiology and Biotechnology* 1: 29–45.

National Environment Agency—the Gambia. www.nea.gm.

Republic of the Gambia. www.statehouse.gm.

GEORGIA

Georgia is an industrial urban nation. Years of Soviet-controlled industrialization have left behind a toxic legacy. Now Georgia is struggling to clean up the environment. Altogether, 4.3 million people live on Georgia's 69,700 km² of land. Fifty-two percent of Georgians are urbanized, and 40 percent live in cities having more than 100,000 inhabitants. Fifteen percent suffers malnutrition.

Georgia borders the Black Sea, Turkey, Russia, Armenia, and Azerbaijan. It also includes the Abkhazia and Ajara autonomous republics, but there are continuing disputes surrounding these areas. In May 2014 the presidential offices of Abkhazia were taken over by protestors and formed a Provisional National Council. Generally the climate is temperate. The terrain is mountainous, with valleys that open up into flood plains. Natural resources include oil, coal, timber, hydropower, copper, manganese, and iron ore.

Current Waste Practices

Although current waste practices include modern sanitation facilities, the sewer and water infrastructure is in need of repair and upgrading. One hundred percent of the urban population has access to an improved drinking water sources, and 96 percent has access to an improved sanitation facility. Ninety-six percent of the rural population has access to an improved source of drinking water, and 93 percent has access to an improved sanitation facility. Sixty percent of the population receives municipal waste collection services. In 2009, 880,000 tons of municipal wastes were collected. Most of this trash, or municipal solid wastes, is hauled to landfills of all types, many illegal. Some of these landfills are the sites of industrial wastes from earlier periods.

The Waste and Chemical Substances Management Department in the Ministry of Environmental Protection and Natural Resources regulates waste practices and develops waste policy. The official definition of waste in the context of transboundary movement is in development. There are no economic incentives for waste reduction or control. Illegal waste disposal in waterways has caused flooding in urban areas. There is water pollution in Mtkvari River and Black Sea. Most of the sewage discharges into rivers untreated. The ecosystem of the Black Sea is substantially degraded by untreated sewage, agricultural runoff of pesticides and fertilizers, and petrochemicals. There is significant air pollution in Tbilisi, Kutaisi, and Rustavi.

Hazardous Wastes

There are no restrictions on the export of hazardous or other wastes from Georgia. The import of hazardous and other wastes for import is restricted. Georgia does exert control of transit of any wastes in its territorial water, air space, and continental shelves. The Law of Georgia on Transit and Import of Waste (1997) controls the terms and conditions for any waste transportation. The actual amount of hazardous wastes and other wastes generated is unknown.

Emissions and Industry

In 2006, Georgia generated 12,218.7 metric tons of greenhouse gases, a 73 percent decrease from 1990.

Agricultural products include livestock, grapes, tea, vegetables, and citrus. Agricultural emissions accounted for 27 percent of all emissions. Within this sector, agricultural soils accounted for 47 percent of emissions, enteric fermentation 44 percent, and manure management 9 percent.

Energy emissions accounted for 49 percent of all emissions. Within this sector, energy industries account for 25 percent of emissions, transportation 21.5 percent, and manufacturing and construction 11 percent. Fugitive emissions and other sources were reported to be about 42 percent. Fugitive emissions are essentially unaccounted waste streams into the air. Fugitive emissions can affect regional ecosystems and the public health, because they can fall from the air to the land and water. Georgia produces some oil and has some oil reserves. Oil consumption is low. About thirty-nine days a year are without any electrical power. Industrial emissions account for 15 percent of the overall emissions. Within this sector, chemical industries account for 50 percent of emissions, mineral products 38 percent, and metal production 12 percent.

Waste emissions account for 9 percent of the overall emissions. Within this sector, solid waste disposal on land accounted for 80 percent of greenhouse gas emissions, and wastewater management 20 percent.

Major Waste Issues

Georgia experienced environmental degradation under Soviet Union control and has not recovered. The decommissioning of Russian nuclear power plants is an ongoing controversy. There are many contaminated industrial sites. Georgia's state of waste policy is in the early stages of development and is moving slowly. Sewage is inadequately treated and emptied into the Black Sea. Climate change effects of rising temperature, and violent weather will challenge current waste cleanup and remediation efforts.

Further Reading

Government of Georgia. www.government.gov.ge.

Kordzaia, Dimitri. 2011. "Making the Case for Palliative Care in Developing Countries: The Republic of Georgia." *Journal of Palliative Medicine* 14: 539–541.

Ministry of Environment and Natural Resource Protection in Georgia. www.moe.gov.ge.

GERMANY

Germany today is a modern industrialized nation that embraces environmental protection and sustainability. In Europe, Germany is the largest economy and second largest population, after Russia. Germany was divided into East and West Germany for many years. In 1990, East and West Germany reunified. It is centrally located in Europe, with excellent ocean access. Germany's population was 82 million people in 2013. About three-quarters are urbanized, and 32 percent live in a city having more than 100,000 inhabitants.

Germany borders on two seas, the Baltic Sea and the North Sea. It has 2,389 km of coastline. Germany has a strong maritime presence. Seas within its jurisdiction extend twelve nautical miles from land, and an exclusive economic zone extends 200 nautical miles from land. Its total land area is 357,121 km^2, and freshwater area is 8,350 km^2. Total renewable water resources in 2011 were 154 km^3. Germany has many neighbors in its 3,790 km land boundary, including Austria, Belgium, Denmark, France, Netherlands, Poland, and Switzerland. The climate is cool, cloudy, and rainy. The terrain is hilly with lowlands in the north and mountains in the south.

Germany has natural resources of coal, lignite, natural gas, iron ore, copper, nickel, uranium, potash, and arable land. Agriculture is less than 1 percent of Germany's economy. Industry is 28 percent of the economy and services are 71.2 percent. Germany produces and processes iron, coal, and chemicals. They also manufacture machinery, vehicles, electronic equipment, ships, and textiles.

Current Waste Practices and Recycling

One hundred percent of the population has improved drinking water sources and waste facility access. Germany places importance on waste recovery and treatment. Everyone receives municipal waste collection services and has access to an improved drinking water source and sanitation facility. Landfilling organic waste was banned in 2004. About 75 percent of municipal wastes are sent for recovery, greatly decreasing the need for landfill space. In 1991, Germany passed a law requiring manufacturers to minimize waste in processing and packaging to decrease the flow of solid waste into landfills. Siting nontreated municipal wastes in landfills has been illegal since 2005. In the 1980s, Germany hosted about 2,000 landfills and in the year 2000 hosted about 160 facilities. It plans to reduce this number. This resulted in nearly no emissions of landfill gases, such as methane. The gross generated quantity of waste in 2007 was 386.9 million tons, with 35.8 million tons from waste treatment plants. Altogether, 41.8 million tons of waste was household wastes.

Local authorities in Germany are generally responsible for waste disposal. There are thirty-two "Competent Authorities" who handle regional waste issues. With reunification in 1990, heavily polluted parts of East Germany joined West Germany. The federal government enacts laws and regulations on waste treatment, providing both guidelines and means of enforcement.

There is a long history of sewage treatment in Germany. Nineteenth-century Germany experienced rapid industrialization and urban population increases. Diseases such as typhoid remained constant until adequate sewage removal systems protected the public health. The treatment of sewage is the process of removing physical, biological, or chemical pollution. The goal is to produce treated effluent and a reusable solid waste that is contamination-free. Biological oxygen demand (BOD) measures this in waste regulations in Germany.

BOD defines wastewater, measuring the amount of putrescible organic matter in water. When large amounts of sewage enter the water dissolved bacteria consume oxygen. A high BOD indicates high levels of sewage. High levels of sewage foster algae blooms and other oxygen-depleting factors. Remaining low levels of dissolved oxygen stress aquatic life. BOD evaluates the oxygen needs of the bacteria as they decompose organic material. BOD is a measure of the strength of the environmental effects of sewage on aquatic ecosystems. BOD measurements must be constant and accurate. This type of sewer waste monitoring is one of the more advanced methods used by governments and could be a part of evaluating environmental effects for sustainability issues.

The three basic levels of waste treatment are applied in Germany. The first level, called the primary level, reduces part of the solids. The secondary level further reduces solids and removes some pollutants. The tertiary level removes remaining solids and reduces most pollutants to safer levels. This effluent can be discharged into freshwater or reused as gray water for other purposes. The European Union required all cities having more than 15,000 people to have secondary treatment in 2000, with a goal of having all urban centers served by secondary levels of sewage treatment. This is a common goal in many waste regulatory schemes but is seldom sufficiently financed for implementation. Tertiary waste treatment systems are costly and require maintenance and monitoring. Even with advanced waste treatment regulations, thirty-two different kinds of pharmaceutical drug residue are found in German sewers.

The treatment of the leftovers from the biological treatment of wastes is called sewer sludge. This disposal of untreated sewage sludge was discontinued in 2005. About 2.1 million tons of sewer sludge was produced in 2008. Sewage sludge from German sewage treatment facilities contains high levels of phosphorus. It is recycled as fertilizer because of the phosphorus. Almost a third of the sewage sludge is recycled in agriculture, though this is a small part of the economy. About half of sewer sludge is incinerated. Germany has the operating capacity for about 19 millions of residual municipal wastes, though they often operate below this level.

Nuclear Wastes

Finding a final site for nuclear waste is controversial. In some sites, such as the Asse nuclear waste site, 14,000 barrels of waste have unknown contents. Currently, Germany operates nine nuclear power plants generating about 15 percent of the country's electricity. Twenty-seven have been decommissioned. Germany has one disposal facility, sixteen storage facilities, and no processing facilities. In 2011, Germany decided to reduce its nuclear power reliance and develop more renewable sources. However, electricity generation from coal increased almost 17 percent from 2011 to 2012 as the nuclear power plants were being phased out. It is estimated that this phaseout of nuclear power increased carbon dioxide emissions by about 22 million tons per year. Currently Germany is developing a site selection procedure for a final repository for nuclear wastes. This is the same controversy many nations face. In the meantime, nuclear wastes keep increasing. They either stay on site or at transfer sites or are exported to nations willing to take them.

Pharmaceutical Wastes

Pharmaceutical wastes are often hazardous wastes and regulated by law. Enforcement is generally limited to large industries and large hospitals. Regulated medical wastes is usually infected or otherwise biohazardous wastes. As concern about infectious diseases increases, new policies are developing around pharmaceutical wastes. The U.S. Environmental Protection Agency is developing a new rule specifically for hazardous wastes pharmaceuticals.

There are many different kinds of chemicals in the pharmaceutical waste stream. Personal use of chemicals can lead to direct and indirect effects on the environment, and is pollution. Some of them are removed by primary waste treatment. Others are not and remain in the wastes. If the water is for discharge into water, it is supposed undergo secondary and tertiary waste treatment. This removes even more chemicals, but not all of them. If the water is reused for agricultural irrigation, the chemicals come with it. If it is discharged into waterways, then marine life is severely affected. Fish exposed to chemicals can become androgynous, changing gender from male to female, as in the case of salmon in the Columbia River, Washington. Eating those fish exposes people to these chemicals. Moreover, many U.S. tribes consider fish an important cultural icon.

Many of these drugs are prescription or illegal drugs. Steroids, birth control pills, methamphetamines, cocaine, OxyContin, and other drugs are found in sewage. High blood pressure medications, neurological drugs, over-the-counter anti-inflammatory drugs, reproductive hormones, and antibiotics can end up in sewers in detectable amounts. Illegal drugs can be detected in sewage.

A world leader in the recycling of packaging wastes, Germany recycled about 78.8 percent of the 16 million tons of packaging wastes in 2006. In 2007, the amount of waste paper in Germany was estimated to be 15.4 million tons. They measure the ration of waste paper in the regular production of paper to determine the waste paper utilization rate. In Germany, this was 68 percent. The waste glass recycling rate was about 84 percent in 2006. Around 98 percent of the 12.5 million tons of plastic wastes was recycled. Both industry and community try to reduce packaging waste. The availability of recycling programs increases the level of recycling by engaging citizens and industry and providing them access to recycling efforts of government.

Hazardous waste disposal is another issue in Germany. Hazardous wastes are defined by the European Union to include sludge from water purification plants, among a long list of materials and chemicals. Imports of hazardous wastes and other wastes are highly restricted. In 2006, Germany exported 263,176 metric tons of hazardous wastes, along with 254,837 metric tons of other waste exports. That same year, it imported 2,418,156 metric tons of hazardous wastes and 371,034 metric tons of other wastes. Generally, the importation of wastes for final disposal in Germany from nonparties to the Basel Convention is prohibited. There are no restrictions on the movement of hazardous wastes within Germany. Fifty-six landfills are used for hazardous wastes, with four permanent underground storage facilities. Thirty-five facilities incinerate hazardous waste, and 650 facilities use chemicals to treat hazardous wastes. There are 125 facilities that treat soils with hazardous materials and eight facilities that treat waste oil. The distinction between facilities is difficult, because many facilities can handle more than one waste stream. Many of these waste treatment facilities try to generate electricity. In 2008, Germany generated 22,323,000 tons of hazardous wastes.

Germany is a major stakeholder in international waste trade and environmental policy. As such, it is a signatory to major waste treaties, such as the Rotterdam Convention on the Prior Informed Consent (PIC) Procedure for Certain Hazardous Chemicals and Pesticides in International Trade, the Convention on Access to Information, Public Participation in Decision-Making, and Access to Justice in Environmental Matters (Aarhus Convention), among many others. Pursuant to these agreements, Germany is to establish a Pollution Release and Transfer Register publicly accessible through the Internet, free of charge, and searchable, presenting standardized, timely data on a structured, computerized database, covering releases and transfers of at least eighty-six pollutants—such as greenhouse gases, acid rain pollutants, ozone-depleting substances, heavy metals, and certain carcinogens, such as dioxins—and covering releases and transfers from certain types of major point sources, such as thermal power stations, mining and metallurgical industries, chemical plants, waste and wastewater treatment plants, paper, and timber. Germany is required to work collaboratively with other countries developing these waste management systems.

Emissions and Industry

Germany generated 939,083 tons of greenhouse gases in 2012, a 25 percent decrease from 1990. As one of the world leaders in energy efficiency, Germany decreased emissions while maintaining steady economic growth. An advanced environmental regulatory system and strong enforcement at the local level helped it achieve this reduction.

Agricultural products include fruit, cabbages, potatoes, pigs, cattle, poultry, and wheat. Agricultural emissions accounted for 7 percent of overall emissions. Within this sector, agricultural soils accounted for 59 percent of emissions, enteric fermentation 30 percent, and manure management 11 percent. Pesticide and fertilizer use is high.

Crude oil production and proven reserves are high along with high consumption. Natural gas production and consumption are high. Energy emissions accounted for 84 percent of overall emissions. Within this sector, energy industries accounted for 46 percent of emissions, transportation 20 percent, manufacturing and construction industry 15 percent, fugitive emissions 1 percent, and other 18 percent. Germany is ninth globally in the production of electricity, with about 560 billion kWh.

Fifty-five percent of the electricity is from fossil fuels, 23 percent nuclear sources, and 3 percent hydroelectric plants. All these sources can produce pollution. Because of the volume of energy used and the types of energy in Germany's energy mix, emissions into the air and surrounding ecosystems are large. The carbon dioxide emissions from the consumption of energy are estimated at 794 million in 2010, the seventh-highest in the world. In 2010, Germany used incineration for waste treatment of residual municipal waste. Approximately seventy incineration plants operated, all used to also generate electricity.

Thirteen percent of installed electrical capacity is from renewable sources such emissions by 40 percent in 2020 and 80 percent by 2050, and replace waste-producing energy sources with renewable sources. In 2010, about 50 percent of the renewable energy individuals or agricultural interests owned capacity. These sources include wind farms, solar power, biogas generation, and increased efficiencies in energy usage.

Industrial emissions accounted for 7 percent of overall emissions. Within this sector, the chemical industry accounted for 29 percent of emissions, mineral products 28 percent, and metal production 24 percent.

Waste emissions accounted for 1 percent of overall emissions. Within this sector, solid waste disposal on land accounted for 75 percent of emissions, wastewater handling 18 percent, and other 7 percent.

Major Waste Issues

Issues of waste from energy production via coal-burning electricity generation and industry are drivers of environmental policy now. The sulphur dioxide emissions can cause acid deposition. This, in turn, affects the health of the forests. It can also degrade historical structures.

Another issue in Germany around waste is the dumping of raw sewage and industrial discharges. Feces contain pathogens, toxic chemicals, metals, and pharmaceutical wastes. This waste is in addition to other waste from primary and secondary sewage treatment plants, as well as agriculture, logging, and manufacturing.

Germany is an international leader in environmental protection and industrial expansion. Currently there are few infectious diseases. Tick-borne encephalitis is a risk below 14,000 feet between March and November. Germany's excellent public health policies include sanitation, and it is prepared for increasing temperatures, rising ocean levels, and more violent weather.

Germany is preparing for climate change effects on water systems. Climate change observers note increases in precipitation and rainfall distribution. Projected effects include increases in flooding, heavier and more frequent rainfall, more frequent low water, and increases in soil and water temperatures. Another effect from intense rainfall events is overwhelming drainage infrastructure and entering the water without waste treatment. Population increases in urban areas that do not maintain or expand sewer and water systems has the same effect in many countries. The capacity of sewer and water systems is not enough to handle heavier rains and population increases without system maintenance and expansion. A public health projection is that there may be extremely frequent and localized pathogens. Germany is vulnerable to seasonal drought risks and some flooding. There is concern about water quantity and extreme weather events, but there is no projection of drinking water supply problems, even under changed climatic conditions. Germany has a number of responses to climate change. There are many national climate change information sources, many with real time data. KomPass focuses on climate effects and adaptation in water management. Deutscher Wetterdienst focuses on current weather, public alerts for severe weather events, and the current and future climate. Germany supports a major contingent of climate change research areas—meteorological, hydrological, and transit effects. In 2011, the urban development processes were required to include climate protection and climate adaptation as a guiding principle in planning processes. Regulatory control of environmental effects at the local level is how Germany reduced its greenhouse gas emissions.

Further Reading

Climate Change Impacts on Water Systems. www.oecd.org.

Dimitriou, K., and P. Kassomenos. 2014. "Decomposing the Profile of Particulate Matter in Two Low Polluted German Cities—Mapping of Air Mass, Residence Time, Focusing on Long term Potential Impacts." *Environmental Pollution* 190: 91–100.

German Federal Government. www.bundesregierung.de.

Kruger, O., et al. 2014. "Complete Survey of German Sewage Sludge Ash." *Environmental Science and Technology* 48: 11811–11818.

Uekotter, Frank. 2014. *The Greenest Nation? A New History of German Environmentalism.* Cambridge, MA: Massachusetts Institute of Technology Press.

GHANA

Ghana was the first sub-Saharan nation to gain independence. In 1957, Ghana shed British colonial governance and helped usher in a new era of decolonialization and national independence in Africa. It is a multi-ethnic nation having at least 100 ethnic groups, each with its own language. Altogether, 24.3 million people live on Ghana's 238,533 km² of land. It is becoming more urbanized, but there are still many small communities. Forty-eight percent of Ghanaians are urbanized, and 20 percent live in a city having more than 100,000 inhabitants; 28 percent suffers malnutrition. Ghana borders Burkina Faso, Cote d'Ivoire, and Togo. Natural resources include timber, hydropower, diamonds, petroleum, silver, and fish. The terrain is flat. The climate is tropical, with humidity in the southwest and dryness in north and along the coast.

Current Waste Practices

In urban areas such as Accra, about a fifth of households have indoor plumbing. There are broad sanitation disparities, and generally only the wealthy have indoor plumbing. Waste practices in rural areas and many parts of urban areas are basic— latrines, pit toilets, drainage ditches, cesspools, and open defecation. About 20,300 deaths a year are attributed to unsafe water. Ninety-one percent of the urban population has access to an improved drinking water sources, and just 19 percent has access to an improved sanitation facility. Eighty percent of the rural population has access to an improved source of drinking water, and a mere 8 percent has access to an improved sanitation facility. There are no wastes defined or considered hazardous within Ghana. When they are exported, goods such as engines and used clothing are monitored. A few facilities reclaim lead from used vehicle batteries. There is no data about the import or export of hazardous wastes and other wastes for either final disposal or recovery. Ghana is preparing its waste policy for wastes that are transported within its boundaries and for the wave of e-wastes.

About a fifth of the population of Accra receive weekly house-to-house solid waste collection services. Most of this population is wealthy. Many other communities use centralized communal trash bins that are collected. Together, these two methods move a little more than half the solid waste to landfills. This waste is trucked to open landfills and dumpsites. Communities of waste pickers scavenge streets and dumpsites for recyclable materials and sustenance. The Ghanaian Environmental Protection Agency plans to replace or upgrade all landfills around Accra by 2020.

Ghana has no nuclear power reactors, disposal facilities, or processing facilities. It does have one storage facility. This may attract interest from countries seeking to export their nuclear wastes.

Emissions and Industry

Ghana generated 18,227 metric tons of greenhouse gas emissions 2006, a 97.5 percent increase from 1990. It is likely that greenhouse gases are higher now because of population growth and the reliance on agriculture.

Ghana is a major producer of cocoa. Other agricultural products include coffee, rice, cassava, corn, bananas, and timber. Agricultural emissions accounted for 35.5 percent of overall emissions. Within this sector, agricultural soils accounted for 54 percent of emissions, enteric fermentation 26.5 percent, and rice cultivation 16 percent, and manure management almost 3 percent.

Crude oil production and consumption is moderate, but there is persistent petrochemical exploration, especially in the contiguous Gulf of Guinea. Energy emissions accounted for 51 percent of overall emissions. Within this sector, transportation accounted for 34 percent of emissions, energy industries 26 percent, and manufacturing and construction 10 percent. Emissions from industrial processes accounted for 1 percent of all emissions. Within this sector, mineral products accounted for 53 percent of emissions and metal production 47 percent.

Ghana generates at least 3 million tons of solid waste a year. Emissions from wastes account for 12 percent of emissions. Within this sector, solid waste disposal on land accounted for 72 percent of emissions and wastewater management 28 percent.

Major Waste Issues

Ghana faces significant waste issues. Old practices of taking trash to the edge of town and burning it persist in urban and rural communities. The government privatized waste management at many levels but many cannot afford it.

The lack of waste infrastructure and growing population will increase water pollution, trash, and disease. Groundwater supplies are not being recharged to meet increasing demands from agriculture, cities, and industry. Waste management issues are becoming matters of public health. Currently there is a risk of infectious diseases. Cholera, dengue fever, hepatitis A, hepatitis B, malaria, meningococcal meningitis, schistosomiasis, and typhoid. Two percent or more of the population is persistently infected with hepatitis B. There is high risk for malaria.

Climate change effects cause concern about food security and famines. Increases in temperature and violent weather in the context of water deprivation and poor sanitation could expand vectors of many infectious diseases. The lack of medical care interferes with controlling outbreaks, and increases the risk of epidemics.

Further Reading

Arku, R., et al. 2014. "Personal Particulate Matter Exposures and Locations of Students in Four Neighborhoods in Accra, Ghana." *Journal of Exposure Science and Environmental Epidemiology*: forthcoming.

Blakeney, Michael, Thierry Coulet, Getachew Mengiste, and Marcelin Tonye Mahop, eds. 2012. *Extending the Protection of Geographical Indications: Case Studies of Agricultural Products in Africa*. New York: Earthscan Publishing.

Foeken, D. W. J., et al. 2013. *Sanitation in Africa: Access to Improved Sanitation Facilities and Improvement Index*. Leiden, The Netherlands: African Studies Center.

Government of Ghana. www.ghana.gov.gh.

Kpan, J., et al. 2014. "Heavy Metal Pollution in Soil and Water in Some Selected Towns in Dunkwa-on-Offin District in the Central Region of Ghana as a Result of Small Scale Gold Mining." *Journal of Agricultural Chemistry and Environment* 3: in press.

GREECE

This ancient nation covers three large peninsulas in the Mediterranean Sea, and many of the numerous surrounding islands. Long renowned as a historical site and popular tourist destination, Greece faces significant environmental issues. The cumulative wastes of thousands of years of waste with the present-day effects of tourism.

Today, 11.1 million people live on Greece's 130,800 km² of land and 13,676 km of coastline. Fifty-nine percent of Greeks are urbanized, and 46 percent live in a city having more than 100,000 inhabitants.

Greece is between Albania and Turkey. The Aegean Sea, the Ionian Sea, and the Mediterranean Sea all border Greece. The climate is mild and characterized by wet winters and dry summers. The land is mountainous. There are natural resources of lignite, oil, iron ore, heavy metals, marble, and salt.

Current Waste Practices

Greece collected 5,386,000 tons of municipal waste in 2009, 81 percent of it land-filled, 17 percent recycled, and about 1 percent composted. Many landfills are over or near capacity. The Ministry of Environment, Physical Planning, and Public Works controls waste policy. There are a few disposal facilities for hazardous wastes, such as asbestos. There are about thirteen recovery and recycling facilities. A few mix liquid and solid wastes to produce fuel. A few other facilities recycle lead batteries. The rest focus on recycling and reusing lubricant wastes. As a general national strategy, recycling and reuse are promoted. If possible, wastes that can be used for energy production are segregated from the waste stream before exportation.

Greece has modern sanitation facilities. One hundred percent of the urban population has access to an improved drinking water sources, and 99 percent has access to an improved sanitation facility. Ninety-nine percent of the rural population has access to an improved source of drinking water, and 97 percent has access to an improved sanitation facility. Water quality is poor.

Hazardous Wastes

Altogether, 333,155 metric tons of hazardous wastes were generated in 2009. Altogether, 4,927,137 metric tons of other wastes were generated. Moreover, 1,247 metric tons of hazardous wastes were imported and 4,442 metric tons exported in 2009. They report that no other wastes were exported or imported. Hazardous wastes and other wastes are restricted for import and export for both final disposal and recovery. Transportation of all wastes through Greece must carry insurance in case of an accident in Greece.

Emissions and Industry

Greece generated 87,500 metric tons of greenhouse gases in 2012, an 8.4 percent increase from 1990.

Agricultural products include cereals, beets, olives, beef, and dairy products. About 2.8 kg of pesticides per ha were used in 2000, seventh-highest of forty-five countries. Agricultural emissions accounted for 8 percent of all emissions. Within this sector, agricultural soils accounted for 53 percent of emissions, enteric fermentation 34 percent, and manure management 11 percent, and rice cultivation 1 percent.

Energy emissions accounted for 79 percent of all emissions. Within this sector, energy industries accounted for 63 percent of emissions, transportation 18 percent, manufacturing and construction industries 6 percent, and fugitive emissions almost 2 percent. Industrial emissions accounted for 9 percent of all emissions.

Within this sector, consumption of halocarbons accounted for 41 percent of emissions, mineral products 39 percent, metal production 11 percent, and chemical industries 9 percent.

Waste emissions accounted for 4 percent of all emissions. Within this sector, solid waste disposal on land accounted for 68 percent of emissions, wastewater handling 31.5 percent, and incineration 1 percent. About 80 percent of solid wastes are buried in landfills. This is double the average landfill rate fore the European Union.

Major Waste Issues

Solid waste disposal via illegal and unsanitary landfills is a significant issue. Landfills range from controlled sanitary landfills to uncontrolled open dumps. They can emit greenhouse gases such as methane depending on the type of landfill, the type of wastes, and the age of the landfill. Many landfills reach capacity as they age and the population increases.

The European Commission sued Greece to close 1,100 illegal landfills in 2005. In 2013, seventy illegal landfills remained, and the European Commission threatened to file suit. Strong local opposition to regional waste treatment plants and local governance issues make it difficult to enforce waste policy. More than half of illegal waste sites are on islands that are cut off from the mainland, complicating enforcement.

Greece is preparing for climate change effects on water systems. Climate change observers note increased temperatures, loss of precipitation, and increased frequency of extreme weather events. Projected effects include increases in temperature, decreases in precipitation, salinization of freshwater sources, and major droughts. A primary concern is that the Mornos River Basin water supply pressure is decreasing, affecting water quantity, quality, and sanitation. In response to these concerns and projections, the Greek government undertook several activities. One is to build more water infrastructure. For example, the Acheloos water transfer project includes four major dams and reservoirs, a 17.4 km water channel, and two tunnels.

Further Reading

Barcelo, Damia, and Mira Petrovic, eds. 2012. *Waste Water Treatment and Reuse in the Mediterranean Region*. Heidelberg, Germany: Springer Press.

Climate Change Impacts on Water Systems. www.oecd.org.

Guerineau, H., et al. 2014. "Source Tracking of Leaky Sewers: A Novel Approach Combining Fecal Indicators in Water and Sediments." *Water Research* 58: 50–61.

Hellenic Republic, Prime Minister's Office. www.primeminister.gov.gr.

GREENLAND

Greenland is essentially the largest island in the world. Greenland's ice sheet is 30 million km^3 of ice and is up to 5 km thick. It is one of the least densely populated countries in the world. Fifteen thousand people live in the largest city, the capital, Nuuk. The population of 57,714 people lives on 2.17 million km^2 of land and 44,087 km of coastline, the third longest coastline of any nation. It is located between the Arctic and Atlantic Oceans.

The climate is arctic to subarctic, with very cold winters and short cool summers. There is no arable land. A flat and sometimes gradually sloping icecap covers about three-quarters of Greenland. The coast is rocky with some mountains.

Current Waste Practices

The entire population has access to sanitation facilities. Only about 25 percent of solid wastes are recycled. Most of the waste is disposed of in open dumps or small-scale incinerators. The annual amount of solid wastes generated is about 50,000 tons but records are scarce. The dumps have no collection or treatment of gases like methane or of landfill leachates. There are efforts to increase recycling.

Emissions and Industry

Overall Greenland emitted about 763.83 metric tons of greenhouse gas emissions in 2011. Most of the reporting on greenhouse gas emissions comes via Denmark. As worldwide interest in the carbon dioxide atmospheric history frozen in Greenland's ice fields increases, the focus on specific greenhouse gas emissions from Greenland also increases.

Emissions from energy accounted for the majority Greenhouse gas emissions. Emissions from industrial processes accounted for 7 metric tons greenhouse gas emissions. There is little heavy industry. Forty-seven metric tons of greenhouse gases were generated by manufacturing industries and construction, 116 metric tons from transportation, and 22 metric tons from wastes. Fishing, sealing, and whaling are historic and modern commercial enterprises.

Nuclear Wastes

There is an agreement between Denmark and Greenland to mine uranium in the arctic. Predrilling estimates are for 575 million pounds of uranium. With this mining, rare earth metals such as yttrium found on the site are also mined. Nuclear waste can be very harmful if it comes in contact with environment.

Major Waste Issues

The human population of Greenland is so small in the vastness of the arctic ecology that effects have thus far been small. Localized effects do accumulate and affect sensitive arctic ecologies, but global warming is having a dramatic effect in Greenland. One way global air pollution is affecting Greenland is a species is a microbe called cryoconite. This comes from a mixture of windblown soot and dust that contributes to glacial melting. It covers parts of Greenland and decreases the reflectivity of the snow, absorbing rather than reflecting energy. Glacial melting contributes to rising ocean levels. Warming air and water further contribute to rapid glacial melting. Glaciers are losing mass faster than any recent time.

Climate change effects on Greenland could be rapid. They also could be drastic if nearby ocean currents are altered by the decrease in salinity because of the freshwater runoff from the glaciers.

Further Reading

Bory, A., et al. 2014. "A Chinese Imprint in Insoluble Pollutants Recently Deposited in Central Greenland as Indicated by Lead Isotopes." *Environmental Science and Technology* 48: 1451–1457.

Government of Greenland. www.dk.nanoq.gl.

Greenland Ice Sheet, National Snow and Ice Data Center. www.nsidc.org/greenland-today/.

Thomas, Katie. 2014. *Linkages between Arctic Warming and Mid-Latitude Weather Patterns.* Washington, DC: National Academies Press.

GUATEMALA

Guatemala, a country in Central America, was once the domain of the mighty Mayan Empire. The Maya reached the peak of their power in AD 600. In AD 900, they left their massive stone cities for an unknown reason. The Mayans were an advanced nation with significant achievements in mathematics, astronomy, architecture, and calendars.

Today Guatemalan Mayans comprises about 9 percent of the population. It is a diverse nation having over 100 recognized languages and many ethnicities from European, Spanish, and indigenous heritages. The 14.3 million inhabitants live on 108,889 km² of land and 400 km of coastline. There are many small communities. Forty-seven percent of the population is urbanized, and 23 percent lives in a city having more than 100,000 inhabitants. It is one of the most populated countries of Central America. From 1960 to 1996, armed conflicts dominated the country.

Guatemala is bordered by the Pacific Ocean, the Caribbean Sea, Belize, El Salvador, Honduras, and Mexico. The range of current extreme weather related events include hurricanes, volcanic eruptions, earthquakes, and tsunamis. The climate is tropical—hot and humid. It is cooler and less humid in the highlands. The terrain is primarily mountainous. There are narrow coastal plains and a limestone plateau.

Current Waste Practices

Most cities have sewer and water services but discharge untreated wastes into freshwater. Waste services are basic, especially in rural areas. Pit toilets, ditches, latrines, and cesspools are used. About a third of the people have municipal waste collection. About 800,000 tons of municipal waste is collected. In 2006, Guatemala generated 822,000 tons of hazardous wastes Guatemala maintains one of the largest and most toxic landfills in Central America in Guatemala City. The landfill is about forty acres and straddles a deep ravine. All wastes are placed in it, from dead bodies to hazardous industrial wastes and everything in between. The practice of siting landfills and waste generally in the ravines of mountainous areas is continued in many communities around the world. Unfortunately, water is at the base of the ravines and can become polluted. Nine percent of urban sewage is treated before discharge in to water. Of this, 46 percent receives primary treatment and 54 percent secondary treatment. The urban area has about sixteen wastewater treatment plants, but most of them are not operational owing to poor design, lack of spare parts, and lack of qualified operators. About 3,900 deaths a year are attributed to unsafe water.

More than half the population suffers malnutrition. Most urban populations have access to water sources, and about 94 percent of rural populations have water access. About 90 percent of the urban population and 80 percent of the rural population has access to improved sanitation.

Recycling

In 2007, Guatemala approached Mexico and Germany for help developing integrated solid waste expertise and capacity. Integrated solid waste practices would separate out recyclable and hazardous materials. More than 2,000 environmental inspectors, municipal employees, and community residents were trained in integrated solid waste principles. These individuals have gone on to train others in Guatemala in integrated solid waste management.

Emissions and Industry

In 1990, Guatemala generated 14,742.2 metric tons of greenhouse gases. It is likely that current emissions are much higher because of population growth, reliance on agriculture, and subsequent industrialization in some areas.

Sugar cane, bananas, coffee, corn, beans, livestock, and cardamom are some of Guatemala's agricultural products. Thirty-five percent of the land is arable, and about 20 percent supports permanent crops. Agricultural emissions accounted for 60 percent of all emissions. Within this sector, agricultural soils accounted for 46 percent of emissions, enteric fermentation 28 percent, manure management 24 percent, field burning of agricultural residues 1 percent, and prescribed burning of savannas 1 percent. This is an unusually high amount of greenhouse gas emissions from manure, indicating the presence of large amounts of untreated feces.

Crude oil production is strong but declining. Oil and natural gas exploration is currently searching for more oil. In July 2013, Guatemala awarded six oil concessions for oil exploration. As of July 2014, only one of these has been followed by a contract to drill. There is also similar research and exploration with natural gas. There is natural gas, buts the size of gas fields and their economic viability depends on ease of access to it and the quality of the gas. In February 2014, a large company invested $15 million in drilling a large second well to determine this. One way access to natural gas underground is improved by a developing process of hydrofracking. This process forces water and solvents into the gas layers to squeeze the gas from the rocks beneath. It is controversial, because the gas can leak into nearby water tables. Technology is moving very rapidly with hydrofracking, and many nations are experimenting with it. Emissions from energy accounted for 31 percent of all emissions. Within this sector, transportation accounted for 46.5 percent of emissions, manufacturing and construction 18 percent, and energy industries 4 percent. Fifty-one percent of power is generated by hydropower, decreasing the greenhouse gas emissions in the industry sector. Emissions from industrial processes accounted for 4 percent of all emissions. Within this sector, mineral products accounted for emissions.

Waste emissions accounted for 5 percent of all emissions. Within this sector, solid waste disposal on land accounted for 78 percent of emissions and wastewater management 4 percent.

Major Waste Issues

Finding sanitary landfill space is a pressing need. The landfill in Guatemala City is a continuing issue. It is estimated that about 30,000 people live around the landfill, essentially scavenging food, clothing, shelter, and recyclable items. In 2005, there was at least one reported methane fire. Nearby communities are now restricted from direct access to the open garbage, in theory, but they are not protected from landslides that occur there during the rainy season. Because of the accumulating weight and volume of the trash, the effects of leachate on soil stability, and regional seismic activity, landslides can affect nearby and downstream communities.

The lack of waste infrastructure and growing population will increase water pollution, trash, and disease. Currently there is a risk of cholera, dengue fever, hepatitis A, malaria, and typhoid. There is low risk for malaria. Climate change effects of rising temperatures, rising sea levels, and violent weather in the context of poor sanitation could expand vectors of most wasteborne infectious diseases.

Further Reading

Divelbiis, W., et al. 2013. "Environmental Health and Household Demographics Impacting Biosand Filter Maintenance and Diarrhea in Guatemala: An Application of Structural Equation Modeling." *Environmental Science and Technology* 47: 1638–1645.

Lindquist, E. 2014. "A Cluster Randomized Controlled Trial to Reduce Childhood Diarrhea Using Hollow Fiber Water Filter and/or Hygiene-Sanitation Educational Interventions." *American Journal of Tropical Medicine and Hygiene* 13: forthcoming.

Ministry of Environment and Natural Resources, Government of Guatemala. www.undp-alm.org.

Ortuste, F. 2012. *Living without Sanitary Sewers in Latin America: The Business of Collecting Fecal Sludge in Four Latin America Cities*. Washington, DC: The World Bank.

GUINEA

In March 2014, the deadly Ebola virus developed into an epidemic in Guinea in the worst outbreak ever. It spread to Sierra Leone and Liberia and continues to spread. The death toll is currently in the thousands and mounting. Health care workers have fled the country because of hostile communities and unsafe working conditions.

Many nations have set up special screening protocols for Ebola in airports. Some nations are considering prohibiting travel from nations with Ebola. Ebola is now beginning to be contained in some urban areas. This epidemic has changed the role of the international community in public health and infectious diseases.

Guinea borders Sierra Leone, Liberia, Cote d'Ivoire, Mali, Senegal, and Guinea-Bissau. The terrain is flat along the coast and mountainous in the interior. The climate is tropical—hot and humid. The rainy season is from June to November, with harmattan winds possible from December to May. Natural resources include diamonds, gold, uranium, iron ore, hydropower bauxite, and fish. Altogether, 11.2 million people live on 245,857 km of land and 320 km of coastline. It is nation of many small communities. Thirty-nine percent of the population lives in urban areas.

Current Waste Practices

Waste practices are basic—pit toilets, latrines, drainage ditches, and open defecation. Only 11 percent of the rural population and 31 percent of the urban population has access to improved sanitation facilities, among the lowest rates of access in the world. Only 35 percent of the rural population and 78 percent of the urban population has access to an improved water source.

Guinea has been the place of final disposition of international hazardous wastes both illegally and legally. In the 1980s, Guinea was offered $600 million to take U.S. hazardous wastes via a multinational corporation. This was four times more than the country's annual budget at the time. Guinea refused that specific offer, but others were accepted, and there is little enforcement against the illegal hazardous waste trade.

Recycling

There is a number of private recycling companies but not enough to meet the volume of trash produced. Trash is disposed of in bins. Sometimes it is taken to the dump. These dumps support communities who scavenge the trash for items of value, including recyclable items like paper, plastics, and metals. Sometimes trash is burned in the dumps to make room for more trash. Many dumpsites have waste picker communities scavenging the site for recyclables and sustenance.

Emissions and Industry

Guinea generated 5,057.6 tons of greenhouse gases in 1994. It is likely that greenhouse gas emissions are higher because of population increases and reliance on agriculture.

Agricultural products include coffee, rice, cassava, bananas, sweet potatoes, pineapples, and livestock. Agricultural emissions accounted for 50 percent of all emissions. Within this sector, enteric fermentation accounted for 56 percent of emissions, prescribed burning of the savannas 31 percent, and rice cultivation 12 percent.

Energy emissions accounted for 40 percent of all emissions. Within this sector, energy industries accounted for 35 percent of emissions, transport 31 percent, and other 34 percent. Industrial emissions accounted for no emissions. There are emissions from mineral products and metal production.

Waste emissions accounted for 7 percent of all emissions. Within this sector, solid waste disposal on land accounted for all emissions.

Major Waste Issues

Guinea faces waste issues in a broad context of other large environmental challenges. There are inadequate amounts of safe water, high amounts of soil contamination, and mining practices having large environmental effects. Trash is rapidly accumulating in the capital city, and there are concerns about public health.

Trash cascades down a cliffside near homes in Equatorial Guinea's capital, Malabo, in 2002. Population growth and rapid urbanization increase the daily volume of trash, which accumulates in surrounding ecosystems. (AP Photo/Christine Nesbitt)

The major waste issue is the protection of the public health nationally and regionally. Infectious diseases are a major concern. Currently infectious diseases include cholera, dengue fever, hepatitis A, hepatitis B, malaria, meningococcal meningitis, schistosomiasis, typhoid, and yellow fever. There is a high risk of malaria. Two percent or more of the population s persistently infected with hepatitis B. There is a risk of yellow fever in all areas of the country. About 5,500 people have died from cholera in the last forty-two years. There is current concern that the current outbreak of the dreaded Ebola virus could spread rapidly. Bodily fluids transmit it. In a country with poor sanitation, these bodily fluids are exposed to a larger population. To stop this, the Ministry of Health forbids the sale of and consumption of bats, because they are carriers of Ebola. Recently, large sections have been quarantined from the rest of the country, as is the current case in Liberia.

The lack of public health and sanitation facilities combined with urban growth and overcrowding provide environments for infectious diseases now. Guinea is deficient in basic water and sanitation services. About 60 percent of the residents in the capital city are connected to water, 80 percent are connected to any electricity, and 60 percent live in squatter communities. There is civil strife and institutional instability. In the last five years, about 80 percent of the trash has been collected. The infant mortality rate is among the highest in the world and the number of hospital beds per person among the lowest. The chance of a male's reaching 65 is about 1 in 3. The number of doctors per person is low and infant mortality high. Climate change effects of increased temperatures and violent weather will facilitate these diseases. With rises in sea level and increases in violent weather, the hot dry and dusty winds could increase and spread meningitis.

Further Reading

Foeken, D. W. J., et al. 2013. *Sanitation in Africa: Access to Improved Sanitation Facilities and Improvement Index*. Leiden, The Netherlands: African Studies Center.

McGovern, Mike. 2012. *Unmasking the State: Making Guinea Modern*. Chicago, IL: University of Chicago Press.

Official Web Page of the Republic of Equatorial Guinea. www.equatorialguieaecuatorialpress.com.

Roka, M., et al. 2012. "Prevalence of Intestinal Parasites in HIV—Positive Patients on the Island of Bioko, Equatorial Guinea: Its Relation to Sanitary Conditions and Socioeconomic Factors." *Science of the Total Environment* 15: 404–411.

GUINEA-BISSAU

Guinea-Bissau borders Senegal and Guinea. This is a low-lying, wet nation that includes more than twenty-five islands in the Atlantic. The highest point is only 984 ft, or 3,000 m. There are no railroads and only 965 km of paved roads. Most travel is done by waterways on six large rivers and their tributaries. There are vast wetlands, mangrove forests, and rain forests. The climate is tropical—hot and humid. The rainy season is from June to November. Harmattan winds can occur from December to May. Natural resources include timber, bauxite, granite, fish, and phosphates. Another natural resource is the range of biodiversity. More than

70 percent of the country is covered in forests, and 45 percent of these are primary forests. There are 2,243 species of trees, representing a high degree of biodiversity. About 1.7 million people live on 28,000 km² of land and 350 km of coastline. Thirty percent of the population is urbanized. The coast is dominated by coral reefs and is very irregular. There are many estuaries leading to the interior, and the capital city of Bissau is on the largest estuary.

Current Waste Practices

Waste regulations are very old and do not address modern waste streams. Municipal solid wastes, health care wastes, and waste plastics are the highest priorities. There are many state agencies to handle environmental issues generally, and these have overlapping jurisdictions that impair regulatory growth and implementation.

Waste practices are basic—pit toilets, latrines, drainage ditches, cesspools, and open defecation. Only 54 percent of the rural population and 94 percent of the urban population has access to improved drinking water sources. Although freshwater is abundant, it is not available because of a lack of infrastructure, and during the dry season it is difficult to meets the needs of the population. Only 57 percent of the urban population and just 23 percent of the rural population has access to minimally safe sanitation facilities. Some trash is collected in urban areas and trucked to open landfills and dumps. All legal landfills have been over capacity for years. Trash is burned occasionally to make room for more trash. Waste pickers scavenge city streets and dumps for recyclable materials and sustenance.

Emissions and Industry

Guinea-Bissau generated 1,694 metric tons of greenhouse gases in 1994. It is likely that greenhouse gas emissions are higher because of population increases and the reliance on agriculture.

Agricultural products include corn, rice, beans, cassava, cotton, timber, fish, cashews, and palm kernels. Agricultural emissions accounted for 86 percent of all emissions. Within this sector, agricultural soils accounted for 55 percent of emissions, enteric fermentation 24 percent, rice cultivation 12 percent, field burning of agricultural residues 7 percent, and prescribed burning of the savannas 2 percent.

Electricity can be intermittent. The power grid is down for at least 110 days a year, among the highest rates in the world. Energy emissions accounted for 11 percent of all emissions. Within this sector, other accounted for 99 percent of emissions and energy industries 1 percent. Industrial emissions accounted for no emissions. There are emissions from the chemical industry.

Waste emissions accounted for 3 percent of all emissions. Within this sector, solid waste disposal on land accounted for 98 percent of emissions and wastewater handling 1 percent.

Major Waste Issues

The waste management structure is old, and what is modern is not enforced. Basic waste practices of collection, waste separation, transportation, storage and disposal are inadequate to meet current demands. Although there are some sanitation regulations, they are not enforced, and many health care institutions are not aware of waste management practices. Plastic wastes are a large part of the waste stream, and much of it could be recycled. There is little legislation and regulation concerning this waste stream, hazardous wastes, and industrial wastes. Because of the weak regulatory landscape, waste issues are in the realm of public health. The major waste issue is the protection of the public health nationally and regionally. Infectious diseases are a major concern. Currently infectious diseases include cholera, dengue fever, hepatitis A, hepatitis B, malaria, meningococcal meningitis, schistosomiasis, typhoid, and yellow fever. There is a high risk of malaria. Two percent or more of the population is persistently infected with hepatitis B. There is a risk of yellow fever in all areas of the country.

The lack of public health and sanitation facilities combined with urban growth and overcrowding provide environments for infectious diseases now. The infant mortality rate is among the highest in the world and the number of hospital beds per person among the lowest. The chance of a male's reaching 65 is about 1 in 3. The number of doctors per person is low and infant mortality high. With increased temperatures and violent weather, it is very likely that diseases will develop outbreaks reaching epidemic proportion. With increases in violent weather, the hot dry and dusty winds could increase, which, in turn, will increase current environmental issues of desertification and deforestation.

As one of the poorest and least developed nations in the world, Guinea-Bissau has also been a target for legal and illegal hazardous waste dumping. Some of the legal offers to transport and dispose of hazardous wastes would have substantially increased much-needed revenue, but other African nations strongly objected, and the deal was terminated. Because of the lack of effective monitoring and regulation, it is likely that the illegal waste trade, inclusive of e-wastes, has continued. Guinea-Bissau also relies on international assistance for waste management and is challenged to coordinate aid efforts effectively.

Further Reading

Foeken, D. W. J., et al. 2013. *Sanitation in Africa: Access to Improved Sanitation Facilities and Improvement Index*. Leiden, The Netherlands: African Studies Center.

Guinea-Bissau. www.republica-da-guine-bissau.org.

Machado, A., and A. Bordalo. 2014. "Prevalence of Antibiotic Resistance in Bacteria Isolated from Drinking Well Water Available in Guinea-Bissau (West Africa)." *Ecotoxicology and Environmental Safety* 106: 188–194.

GUYANA

Guyana is a South American country with the North Atlantic Ocean, Brazil, Suriname, and Venezuela at its borders. Most of the country is rolling highlands. There is a low coastal plain and a savanna in the south. Tropical forests dominate more than four-fifths of this country. The climate is tropical—hot and humid. There are two rainy seasons: May to August and November to January. Altogether, 751,000 people live on 214,969 km² of land and 459 km of coastline. It is a nation of small communities. Twenty-eight percent of the population of Guyana is urbanized, and 28 percent lives in a city having more than 100,000 inhabitants. Eighteen percent suffers malnutrition. More than half the population lives within 10 m of sea level.

Current Waste Practices

Most cities have sewer and water services but discharge untreated wastes into freshwater. Waste in rural areas and some urban areas are basic—pit toilets, latrines, drainage ditches, and cesspools. About 200 deaths a year are attributed to unsafe water. Much of the water and sewer system is very old in the urban centers. Flooding during the rainy seasons often clogs drains with waste. Septic tanks and pit toilets are not maintained and are leaking into nearby canals, ditches, and streams. Broken water and sewerage pumps, cracked and open sewers, and clogged pipes can quickly create unhealthy conditions in densely populated urban areas. Most solid waste is trucked outside of urban areas and left as dumps. The only city, Georgetown, does incinerate some wastes but cannot keep up with the volume. Georgetown is the only area served by a communal sewer service, and it discharges to the Dimerara River.

Under the Caribbean Planning for Adaption to Climate Change Guyana is beginning to create climate change inventories and evaluate coastal and marine management. Often this investigation leads to the discovery of old and current illegal waste sites.

Some wastes are collected by local government and hauled to open landfills and dumps site. Occasionally the garbage is burned. There is no separation of wastes, so hazardous, medical, and radioactive wastes are mixed with municipal wastes. Guyana is developing regulations about the use, possession, and importation of radioactive materials. Radioactive materials are used in health care and in mining. Some radioactive materials have been imported but are not accounted for anyplace.

Recycling

Recycling is just beginning as a policy. There is an informal community of waste pickers that sell what they can scavenge from open pit landfills and illegal dumps sites. Some industries recycle paper, asserting that paper recycling will save energy and landfill space and reduce water pollution by a third and air pollution by three-quarters. Plastic recycling is a big part of recycling in Guyana because of the large amount of plastic trash. In 2003, there was 7,811,214 lbs of legally imported plastics. The number is probably higher because of the amount of illegally imported plastics, which is unknown. It is also larger because containers of petrochemical by products, pharmaceuticals, and beauty products are counted by content only, not the plastics used in their marketing and storage. Also the materials in e-waste are both metals and plastics. E-waste is observably increasing, but the dimensions of its growth are unknown.

Emissions and Industry

In 2004, Guyana generated 3,071.7 metric tons of greenhouse gas emissions, a 13 percent increase from 1990. Current greenhouse gases are likely to be higher because of population increases and reliance on agriculture.

Agriculture is the biggest part of the economy. Guyana produces sugar cane, rice, shrimp, beef, pork, and poultry. About 2 percent of the land is arable. Agricultural emissions accounted for 44 percent of all emissions. Within this sector, rice cultivation accounted for 44 percent of emissions, enteric fermentation 30 percent, agricultural soils about 13 percent, field burning of agricultural residues 11 percent, and prescribed burning of the savannas and manure management 1 percent.

Guyana has renewable energy resources in hydropower, biomass, biogas, solar, and wind power. It also produces some crude oil and wants to drill for more. There is a continuing dispute with Suriname over the coastal borders and claim to the oil fields. Neighboring Venezuela claims major portion of maritime oil claims. Emissions from energy accounted for about 54 percent of all emissions. Within this sector, energy industries accounted for 45 percent of emissions, transportation 19 percent, manufacturing and construction 12 percent, and other energy sectors 25 percent.

Emissions from wastes accounted for 3 percent of all emissions. This increased from 0 percent to 3 percent from 1990 to 2004. Within this sector, solid waste disposal on land accounted for 82 percent of emissions and wastewater handling 18 percent.

Major Waste Issues

The lack of regulation, infrastructure, and public awareness of waste pose major challenges. The increasing population and increasing volume of trash is increasing awareness. Guyana is beginning to develop policies about the movement of hazardous wastes in and out of its boundaries. Its lack of policy, law, and enforcement makes it a country likely to be on the receiving end of the illegal waste trade. The lack of waste infrastructure and growing population will increase water pollution, trash, and disease. Currently there is a risk of infectious diseases such as dengue fever, hepatitis A, hepatitis B, malaria, and typhoid. There is high risk for malaria. Climate change effects create grave concern because of risks to food security. Increases in temperature, ocean levels and violent weather in the context of poor sanitation could expand vectors of most infectious diseases. Epidemics can pose public health threats to the country, region, and to the world population. Both waste infrastructure and climate change adaption may require international assistance.

Further Reading

Guyana Office of the President. www.op.gov.gy.

Mielet, M., and C. Claeys. 2014. "The Implementation and Reception of Policies for Preventing Dengue Fever Epidemics: A Comparative Study of Martinique and French Guyana." *Health, Risk, and Society* 16: 581–599.

Smith, N., A. Halton, and J. Strachan, eds. 2014. *Transitioning to a Green Economy: Political Approaches in Small States.* London, UK: Commonwealth Secretariat.

HAITI

The climate is mainly tropical and semi-arid in the mountains. Haiti is subject to powerful storms from June to October. There is desertification because of extensive deforestation, soil erosion, and flooding. Occasionally there are earthquakes, which, combined with heavy rain, can cause landslides.

Altogether, 9.9 million Haitians reside on 27,750 km² of land and 1,771 km of coastline. Thirty-nine percent of the population is urbanized, and 31 percent lives in a city having more than 100,000 inhabitants. Twenty-six percent live in overcrowded conditions. It shares the island of Hispaniola with the Dominican Republic to he east.

Current Waste Practices

Eighty-five percent of the urban population has access to an improved drinking water source and just 24 percent has access to an improved sanitation facility. Half the rural population has access to an improved drinking water sources, and just 10 percent has access to an improved sanitation facility. There were 179,379 cholera cases, including 3,990 deaths in 2010 and 2011. This outbreak spread rapidly because of the limited access to safe water and basic sanitation. Much of the limited access was the result of internal population movements of displaced people from the January 2010 earthquake, which was a magnitude 7.0 on the Richter scale, with an epicenter 15 km southwest of major population centers. At least 220,000 people were killed.

Even before the last earthquake, residents of Haiti did not have much access to any health care and were at high risk of many diseases caused by wastes. The open defecation rate in 2012 was 21 percent, down from 48 percent in 1990. Trash is trucked to dumps. People scavenge through the trash, along with pigs and goats. Current waste practices are hindered by natural disasters, such as earthquakes and hurricanes. After natural disasters, the volume of medical wastes increases, lessening the ability of the country to treat any waste. The volume of human excrement piles up, creating vectors for public health threats. Post–natural disaster living arrangements are overcrowded and lend themselves to rapid transmission of disease. Only about 20 percent of the trash is collected, a figure that drops to almost nothing after a natural disaster. Drainage canals often become clogged with all sorts of waste. Garbage trucks are often broken. At one point, trash trucks illegally dumped their solid waste at the end of the road to the dump, forcing subsequent trucks to do the same.

Recycling

There is little official recycling except for the groups of people who pick over the trash for metals, plastics, glass, and paper of value. There is no segregation of waste streams in the dumps, so all hazardous, industrial, medical, and biochemical wastes exist together.

Emissions and Industry

In 2000, Haiti generated 6,683.1 metric tons of greenhouse gases. It is likely that greenhouse gas emissions are now much higher because of increased population and dependence on agriculture.

Agricultural emissions accounted for 71 percent of the overall greenhouse gas emissions. Within this sector, agricultural soils accounted for 29 percent of emissions, enteric fermentation 60 percent, rice cultivation 10 percent, manure management about 1 percent, and field burning of agricultural residues about 1 percent.

Haiti ranks last in the world for per-capita energy consumption. Commercial energy use is second-least in the world. Emissions from energy accounted for 23 percent of the overall emissions. The main source of emissions in this sector is transportation, with 8 percent. Manufacturing and construction industries accounted for 18 percent and energy industries accounted for 12 percent. Emissions from industrial processes accounted for no emissions.

Emissions from wastes accounted for 3 percent of all emissions. Within this sector, waste water management accounted for 26 percent of emissions and solid waste disposal on land 74 percent.

A tent city in Port-au-Prince, Haiti, on August 28, 2010. Natural disasters like hurricanes and cyclones can devastate countries. Tent cities and other recovery efforts always face sewage disposal challenges. Proper sewage disposal is especially necessary to avoid diseases such as cholera. (Arindam Banerjee/Dreamstime.com)

Major Waste Issues

Haiti faces serious issues of environmental degradation, which provides a landscape for waste issues and public health degradation. There is unconstrained deforestation, subsequent soil erosion, and lack of clean water. The United Nations Millennium

Development goals for sanitation are not met and are not likely to meet 2015 deadlines.

There are plans to reestablish the incinerators to more efficiently burn all wastes. Removing human wastes from settlements is increasing, and two more lagoons are planned, having 25,000 m³ capacity each.

The lack of waste infrastructure and growing population will increase water pollution, trash, and disease. Currently there is a risk of infectious diseases such as cholera, dengue fever, hepatitis A, hepatitis B, malaria, and typhoid. Two percent or more of the population is persistently infected with hepatitis B. There were cases of chikungunya virus in 2014. Climate change effects of increases in temperature, rising ocean levels, and violent weather in the context of poor sanitation could expand vectors of most infectious diseases. Haiti is fragile and vulnerable to more natural disasters. Epidemics can pose public health threats to the country, the region, and the world population.

Further Reading

Fung, I., et al. 2013. "Modeling the Effect of Water, Sanitation and Hygiene and Oral Cholera Vaccine Implementation in Haiti." *American Journal of Tropical Medicine and Hygiene* 89: 633–640.

Gelting, R., et al. 2013. "Water, Sanitation and Hygiene in Haiti: Past, Present, and Future." *American Journal of Tropical Medicine and Hygiene* 89: 665–670.

Haitian Government. www.haiti.org.

Hubbard, B., et al. 2014. "Development of Haiti's Rural Water, Sanitation and Hygiene Workforce." *Journal of Water, Sanitation and Hygiene for Development* 4: 159–163.

HONDURAS

Honduras borders the Caribbean Sea, the North Pacific Ocean, Guatemala, El Salvador and Nicaragua. The interior is mountainous. There are narrow coastal plains near the ocean and sea. The climate is generally subtropical and slightly cooler in the mountains. Natural resources include timber, gold, silver, copper, lead, zinc, iron ore, antimony, and coal. It is one of the three most vulnerable countries in the world to climate change. Earthquakes, landslides, regional volcanic eruptions, and floods provide an unstable context for rapid climate change.

Altogether, 7.6 million people live on Honduras's 112,492 km² of land and 832 km of coastline. It is a nation of small communities. Forty-six percent of Hondurans are urbanized, and 61 percent live in a city having more than 100,000 inhabitants. There is civil conflict, which resulted in a coup d'état in 2009.

Current Waste Practices

Most cities have sewer and water services but discharge untreated wastes into freshwater. About 1,200 deaths a year are attributed to unsafe water. Thirty percent of the population suffers from malnutrition. Ninety-five percent of the urban population has access to an improved drinking water source, and 85 percent has access to an improved sanitation facility. Waste practices in rural areas are basic—pit toilets, latrines, drainage ditches, and cesspools. Seventy-nine percent of the rural population has access to an improved drinking water sources, and 69 percent has access to an improved sanitation facility. Only 10 percent of the wastewater receives any treatment before going into the water. About a fifth of the major sewerage systems have wastewater treatment facilities. Water is available from government water systems for limited periods each day in many places. There are about 4,300 rural water supply systems that get their water from different local sources. About 57 percent get their water from springs, 34 percent from brooks, 5 percent from rivers, and 4 percent from groundwater. Rural communities rely heavily on about 15,000 dug wells for freshwater.

Honduras developed a National Implementation Plan for Persistent Organic Pollutants in 2008. Part of this plan is to develop an inventory of pesticides. Regulations for this plan are being developed. In 2005, a national inventory of pesticides uncovered 14.7 metric tons of DDT, which was exported in 2008.

Nongovernmental organizations provide environmental education, develop projects at the community level, and work for clean, safe water. They often implement types of recycling programs. There are few disposal or recycling facilities available.

Emissions and Industry

In 2000, Honduras generated 10,298.1 metric tons of greenhouse gas emissions, a 5 percent decrease from 1995. Greenhouse gas emissions are likely higher now because of increased population and dependence on agriculture.

Nine percent of the land is arable. Agricultural products include bananas, coffee, citrus, corn, beef, fish, and timber. Emissions from agricultural wastes account for 43 percent of the overall emissions. Within this sector, enteric fermentation accounted for 46 percent of emissions, agricultural soils 28 percent, and manure management 25 percent. This is an unusually high amount of greenhouse gas emissions from manure, indicating the presence of large amounts of untreated feces.

Honduras has low petrochemical production, consumption and proven reserves. Hydropower and other alternative energy sources are used for energy. Emissions from energy accounted for 33 percent of the overall emissions. Within this sector, transportation accounted for 66 percent of emissions, energy industries 20 percent, and manufacturing and construction industries 3 percent. Emissions from industrial processes accounted for 7 percent of the overall emissions. Within this sector, mineral products accounted for 100 percent of emissions.

Emissions from wastes accounted for 17 percent of the overall emissions, which is high. Within this sector, wastewater management accounted for 51 percent of emissions, solid waste disposal on land 32 percent, and waste incineration 17 percent.

Major Waste Issues

The wastes issues are embedded in current environmental issues and controversies. The urban population is growing, taxing an already overwhelmed sanitation system. Deforestation, soil erosion, and mining have significant environmental effects on water. The largest source of freshwater, Lago de Yojoa, is polluted from metals mining. Other rivers have heavy metals in them. The ocean waste is a substantial problem. About 12 million people live in the drainage area that goes into the nearby ocean.

The lack of waste infrastructure and growing population will increase water pollution, trash, and disease. Currently there is a risk of infectious diseases such as cholera, dengue fever, hepatitis A, malaria, and typhoid. Increases in temperature, rising ocean levels, and violent weather in the context of poor sanitation could expand vectors of most infectious diseases.

Further Reading

Deal, J. 2011. "Health Impact of Community-Based Treatment Systems in Honduras." *Journal of Anthropology* 2011: 1–6.

Honduras. www.in-honduras.com.

Smith, W. 2013. "Hurricane Mitch and Honduras: An Illustration of Population Vulnerability." *International Journal of Health System and Disaster Management* 1: 54–58.

HUNGARY

Hungary is a landlocked nation in central Europe. It is bordered by Austria, Croatia, Romania, Serbia, Slovakia, Slovenia, and Ukraine. The landscape comprises gently rolling hills. Cold and humid winters and warm summers characterize the climate. Ten million people live on Hungary's 93,028 km² of land. Most people live in a city. Sixty-six percent are urbanized, and 32 percent live in a city having more than 100,000 inhabitants.

Current Waste Practices and Recycling

All of the population has access to an improved drinking water source and to a modern sanitation facility.

Hungary collected 4,312,000 tons of municipal waste in 2009; 74 percent was landfilled, 9 percent was incinerated, 13 percent recycled, and 2 percent composted. Ninety-two percent of the population receives municipal waste collection services. In 2008, Hungary generated 671,000 tons of hazardous wastes. Landfill space is an issue, as is raising the landfills to a sanitary level.

Nuclear Wastes

Hungary operates four nuclear power plants that supply more than half of the country's electricity. There are also two nuclear waste disposal, two storage, and four processing facilities. Much of the radioactive wastes are placed in sealed steel drums, then cemented in en masse and placed in a shallow ground disposal site designed for 600 years. There is public resistance to the expansion of this site, so the new nuclear waste is stored on site. The government is focused on the selection of a site for final disposition of radioactive wastes.

Emissions and Industry

Hungary generated 41,589 metric tons of green house gas emissions in 2012, a 46 percent decrease from 1990.

About 47 percent of the land is arable, a high proportion. Agricultural products include wheat, sunflower seeds, corn, potatoes, livestock, poultry, and dairy products. Agricultural emissions accounted for 14 percent of overall emissions. Within this sector, agricultural soils accounted for 58 percent of emissions, enteric fermentation 17 percent, and manure management 24 percent. This is an unusually high amount of greenhouse gas emissions from manure, indicating the presence of large amounts of untreated feces.

Emissions from energy accounted for 73 percent of the overall emissions. Within this sector, energy industries accounted for 36 percent of emissions, manufacturing and construction 9 percent, and transportation 24 percent. Industrial emissions accounted for 7 percent of overall greenhouse gas emissions. Within this sector, mineral products accounted for 30 percent of emissions, chemical industries 13 percent, and metal production 5 percent.

Waste emissions account 5 percent of overall greenhouse gas emissions. Within this sector, solid waste disposal on land accounted for 78 percent of emissions, wastewater handling 18 percent, and incineration 3 percent.

Major Waste Issues

Hungary must improve waste management and act to prevent more water pollution, though it is a member of the European Union. Hazardous waste management and radioactive waste management are ongoing waste problems. In the 1980s, a plan to build regional hazardous waste final disposition sites failed to be implemented. There is one modern incinerator for these wastes, one chemically secure landfill, and an unknown number of waste storage and transfer stations.

The sewer infrastructure is currently a high environmental priority for Hungary. In 1991, public sewer connections reached areas populated by half the people, but only 42 percent were connected to it. Little of the waste collected by public systems was treated before reintroduction into water. Since then large investments by the European Union and new laws and policies improved the sewer and waste treatment process. The progress is slow but moving in the direction of a better sanitation system.

Hungary is preparing for climate change effects on water systems. Climate change observers note increases in flooding and drought. Projected effects include increases in temperatures, frequency of and intensity of heavy precipitation, floods in inhabited areas, decreases in annual renewable water reserves, loss of some lakes, and increased drought. There are key vulnerabilities in increased floods because of a limited potential to heighten dams. Already a third of the lowlands are easily inundated by water. In the Great Plain area, there is a limited amount of freshwater. Hungary is also vulnerable because the quality and quality of water flows are affected by the water use and pollution of other countries in the region.

In response to these concerns and projection the Hungarian government is just beginning to develop policies, regulatory instruments, and economic instruments to address climate change adaption. There is an initiative called Hungarian Alliance of Climate-Friendly Cities. This includes local government and nongovernmental organizations that provide technical advice to help cities include climate change adaptation strategies in their planning and development.

Further Reading

Auer, Matthew R., ed. 2005. *Restoring Cursed Earth: Appraising Environmental Policy Reforms in Eastern Europe and Russia.* New York: The Rowman & Littlefield Publishing Group.

Climate Change Impacts on Water Systems. www.oecd.org.

Hungarian. www.kormany.hu.

Lakatos, G., et al. 2014. "The Management and Development of Constructed Wetlands for Treatment of Petrochemical Waste Waters in Hungary: 35 Years of Experience." *Ecohydrology and Hydrobiology* 14: 83–88.

ICELAND

Iceland is a large island dividing the Greenland Sea and the North Atlantic Ocean. The terrain is varied. There are large flat ice fields, and deep fjords mark the coast. There are mountainous glaciers in the interior. The highest point is Hvannadalshnukur, which is 2,110 m at the Vatnajokull glacier. The climate is temperate. The winters are mild and the summers cool. Natural resources include fish, geothermal power, and hydropower. Iceland is subject to volcanic eruptions, which significantly affect the ice and air. In 2010, the Eyjafjallajokult volcano erupted, creating rapid ice melt that led to floods and covered western Europe in ash. Since August 2014, the Baroarbunga volcano has been erupting large amounts of magma at the rate of thousands of cubic meters per hour. The Baroarbunga iceshed is the largest by volume in Europe. There is grave concern about a vent opening up under the ice and repeating the floods and ash of earlier volcanic eruptions on a larger scale. Many of the gases generated by volcanic eruptions have significant climate effects. Altogether, 321,0000 people live on Iceland's 103,000 km² of land and 4,970 km of coastline. Most people live in a few urban communities. Ninety-three percent are urbanized, and 59 percent live in a city having more than 100,000 inhabitants.

Current Waste Practices

All populations have complete access to improved drinking water sources and improved sanitation facilities.

Iceland collected 177,000 tons of municipal waste in 2009, and almost 68 percent of the waste is landfilled, 10 percent incinerated, 13 percent recycled, and about 2 percent composted. Everyone has waste collection service. In 2004, 9,000 tons of hazardous wastes were generated in Iceland. Ninety-five percent of Iceland's total waste was household and industrial waste. Reykjavik is the primary waste collection and treatment location.

Iceland is developing its waste infrastructure with help from the European Union (EU). Iceland seeks admission to the EU but needs help to meet EU standards. The "ascension" process is the long process of applying for membership to the EU. The EU offers an Instrument for Pre-Accession Assistance to candidate and potential candidate countries, such as Iceland.

Emissions and Industry

Iceland generated 4,467 metric tons of greenhouse gas emission in 2012, representing a 26 percent increase from 1990.

Agricultural products include fish, potatoes, sheep, pork, and vegetables. Agricultural emissions accounted for 15 percent of all emissions. Within this sector, agricultural soils accounted for 52 percent of emissions, enteric fermentation 36 percent, and manure management 12 percent.

Electrical energy consumption per capita is among the highest in the world. Oil production per capita is low and consumption per capita is high. Energy emissions accounted for 38 percent of all emissions. Within this sector, transportation accounted for 50 percent of emissions, manufacturing and construction industries 11 percent, and fugitive emissions 10 percent. Fugitive emissions are pollutants that go uncounted. They can spread from the air into the ecosystem through the land and water. They can affect the environment and public health. Industrial emissions accounted for 42 percent of all emissions. Within this sector, metal production accounted for 92 percent of emissions.

Waste emissions accounted for 4 percent of all emissions. Within this sector, solid waste disposal on land accounted for 89 percent of emissions, wastewater handling 6 percent, and incineration 4 percent.

Major Waste Issues

Major waste issues are the inadequate treatment of wastewater and water pollution from agricultural fertilizer runoff. One possible effect of global climate change is the change in ocean currents.

Iceland is preparing for climate change effects on water systems. Climate change observers note increased temperatures, more precipitation in warmer periods, and receding glaciers. Projected effects include temperatures increases, precipitation increases, increased water runoff from melting glaciers, changes in the courses of glacier rivers thanks to glacier melting, and more frequent heat waves. A key vulnerability is the loss of glaciers, which currently cover 10 percent of the landmass. With rising temperatures and ocean levels Iceland faces increasing environmental challenges. Large portions of the ice mass are melting above and, along the coast, below the ice sheet. The Icelandic government began a national climate change strategy in 2007 in the Ministry of Environment. The Icelandic Meteorological Office forecasts weather, monitors geohazards, and conducts scientific studies on climate change. It measures glaciers and the water in them, known as glaciohydrology.

Further Reading

Climate Change Impacts on Water Systems. www.oecd.org.

Government Offices in Iceland. www.government.is.

Maizels, Judith, and Chris Caseldine, eds. 2013. *Environmental Change in Iceland: Past and Present*. Heidelberg, Germany: Springer Publishing.

Thomas, Katie. 2014. *Linkages between Arctic Warming and Mid-latitude Weather Patterns.* Washington, DC: National Academies Press

INDIA

India is a large, growing nation steeped in cultural traditions. India occupies 2.4 percent of the total landmass of the world (3,287,263 km^2) but supports 17.3 percent of the world population (1.27 billion). It is the eighth-largest country in the world (in area) and the second most populous. The growth rate is 1.58 percent. Because the population is so large, the rate of growth results in a large population increase.

India has the largest rural population globally, with 890 million, followed by China, at 645 million. Currently 30.1 percent of the population, approximately 381 million, lives in urban areas, a number projected to increase to about 600 million by 2030. Four cities—Delhi, Mumbai, Kolkata, and Bengaluru—are megacities (urban agglomerations having more than 10 million inhabitants), and Ahmedabad, Hyderabad, and Chennai are projected to be megacities by 2030. India is expected to add 404 million urban dwellers by 2050. Declining rural opportunities and low wages in the agricultural sector contribute to the pace of urbanization.

In 2011, more than 68 million people lived in slums in India, up from 52 million in 2001. Some 17.4 percent of households in urban areas were living in slums, and in the nineteen cities having million-plus population, 25 percent of households lived in slums.

India is a large country having varied terrain and climate. It borders Bangladesh, Bhutan, Burma, China, Nepal, Pakistan, the Bay of Bengal, and the Arabian Sea. Some of the highest mountains in the world are in the Himalayas, to the north. The Deccan Plateau lies in the south. In the west are deserts. The climate is equally varied. Generally, the climate ranges from temperate in the north to tropical in the south. At the high altitudes of the Himalayas, it is much colder. Natural resources include petrochemicals, diamonds, coal, natural gas, iron ore, chromite, and limestone. India has 7,000 km of coastline and approximately 14,500 km of inland navigable waterways. The polluted Ganges River is 2,525 km (1,569 mi) long.

Waste generation in India could be as high as 1.3 lbs. per person per day, which is comparatively low. (The United States averaged 4.6 pounds per person per day in 2009.) The population in India is much larger and rapidly urbanizing. Urbanization is usually accompanied by even greater increases in per-capita waste. The lack of adequate landfill space turns waste transfer stations into the equivalent of landfills.

Nuclear Wastes

India operates twenty-one nuclear power reactors that supply about 4 percent of its electricity. There is no nuclear waste disposal, storage, or processing facility. There is also uranium mining and processing. Currently the emphasis is on research and

Waste to Energy in India

Of the estimated 62 million tons of municipal solid waste (MSW) generated annually by 377 million urban Indians, more than 80 percent is disposed of indiscriminately at dumps by municipal authorities. The untapped resource has a potential to generate 439 megawatts (MW) of power from combustible wastes and 72 MW of electricity from biogas. Waste conversion technologies include a wide array of thermal, biochemical and chemical technologies capable of converting MSW into useable heat, electricity or fuel.

According to the Ministry of New and Renewable Energy (MNRE) estimates, there is a potential of about 1,460 MW of power from MSW and 226 MW from sewage. There is also potential to recover 1,300 MW of power from industrial wastes—from distilleries, pulp and paper mills, food processing, and starch industries.

Although the MNRE has encouraged pilot projects for promoting WtE projects in the country, few commercial-scale plants are successfully operating. In 2012, the Central Pollution Control Board reported that municipal authorities had set up 172 biomethanation plants, twenty-nine refuse-derived fuel plants, and eight waste-to-energy (WtE) plants, but by mid-2014, many of these plants were not operational. The reasons for the failure or underperformance of the plants were many, including low calorie value of waste, poor segregation, nonsupply of committed quantity, inappropriate choice of technology, poor financial and logistical planning, and opposition from people in the neighborhood. At the same time, municipal policies, programs, and management structures do not adequately address the challenge of managing municipal solid waste. There is an absence of a strong policy framework, inadequate infrastructure, poor governance capacity, and a lack of dependable and sustainable government support.

The benefits of waste-to-energy as an alternative to disposing of waste in landfills or burning it in the open are clear and compelling. But citizens and municipal authorities must first change their attitude toward waste and acknowledge their shared responsibilities to keep cities clean, protect public health and safeguard the environment. This requires serious efforts to reduce waste, recover recyclable materials, and generate energy, which also means recognizing waste as a valuable resource—for revenue, nutrients, new products, and energy. Such changes are required urgently.

development into the final disposition of radioactive wastes. In 2005, India produced 22,300 metric tons of uranium, with continued reserves.

Emissions and Industry

In 2008, India accounted for 6 percent of global carbon dioxide emissions, tying Russia as the third largest global emitter. This does not include changes in land use, such as deforestation. This type of land use change is a substantial contributor to carbon dioxide. It does include emissions from sources such as fossil fuel combustion, cement manufacturing, and gas flaring. In 2000, India generated 1,523,766.6

metric tons of greenhouse gases, a 25.5 percent increase from 1994. It likely that the current greenhouse gas emissions are much higher because of population growth, reliance on agriculture, and rapid industrialization.

India has low per-capita emissions of greenhouse gases but is the world's fourth-biggest generator of them because of its sheer size. In 2013, its emissions rose more than 5 percent.

Landfills are significant sources of greenhouse gases (GHGs), such as methane, that can be up to twenty-six times more powerful than carbon dioxide (CO_2) as a greenhouse gas. India is one of the world's largest methane emitters from solid waste disposal. India also has many cows, whose wastes emit methane. There are more than 280 million cows in India—more than a quarter (28.3 percent) of the entire world population of cows.

Agricultural products include bananas, coffee, wheat, rice, jute, tea, sugar cane, onions, lentils, fish, poultry, sheep, and goats. Agricultural emissions accounted for 23 percent of all emissions. Within this sector, enteric fermentation accounted for 59 percent of emissions, rice cultivation 20 percent, agricultural soils 16 percent, and manure management 1 percent.

India produces some crude oil and has substantial proven crude oil reserves. Per-capita oil consumption is low, but national consumption was high. It is the second-largest consumer of electricity in the world, but per capita usage is low. There are about sixty-seven days without electricity every year. Many locations do not have electricity or have limited use per day. Emissions from energy accounted for 67 percent of the overall emissions. Within this sector, energy industries accounted for 53 percent of emissions, manufacturing and construction 22 percent, and transportation 10 percent.

Industrial emissions accounted for 6 percent of the overall emissions. Within this sector, mineral products accounted for 60 percent of emissions, chemical industries 22 percent, and metal production 10 percent.

Emissions from wastes accounted for 3.5 percent of all emissions. Within this sector, wastewater management accounted for 80.5 percent of emissions and solid waste disposal on land 19.5 percent. Today, India is one of the world's largest methane emitters from solid waste disposal. Because methane is an aggressive greenhouse gas, it will affect global warming on a large scale.

Critical Challenges

India is the largest and fastest-growing consumer of groundwater in the world. That groundwater is combined with a big growing population and a challenged sewer and water system.

Urbanization in developing countries often occurs near rivers and ports. Freshwater is a necessity for growing cities, wildlife, and agriculture. However, the location and population growth over time near these water systems enhances the effects of pollution. The groundwater and forest fuels eventually become affected by the pollution. Most of the large volume of wastes is discharged untreated into rivers, lakes, and streams.

Each day, thousands of gallons of raw sewage flow into the sacred Ganges River in Varanasi, India. In some locations along the river, the pollution dramatically exceeds all public and environmental safety levels. Many people use this water for drinking and bathing. (AP Photo/ John McConnico)

According to the World Health Organization (WHO), each year 344,000 children under the age of five die as a result of diarrhea. Altogether, 454,400 deaths a year are attributed to unsafe water.

In India, indoor air pollution associated with cooking and heating is a very serious threat to the health of children under five years. Since 2000, 14 percent of Indians gained access to sanitation facilities, but the country is not on track to meet its Millennium Development Goals.

There are major disparities in access to improved services between urban and rural areas. There is better access to water and sanitation services in urban areas. According to reports by UNICEF, only 48 percent of the Indian rural population has good toilet and sanitation facilities. A 2014 survey revealed that 90.7 million rural households do not have toilets at all and that another 10.4 million households in the country do not have functional toilets, taking the total number of households needing toilets in India to 110.1 million.

Globally, India has the 597 million people practicing open defecation. The challenge is to build and maintain sanitation facilities and sewage management systems. India is not reducing open defecation as quickly as other nations are. The proportion of open defecators to the total population has declined slightly in the past decade, but rapid population growth has meant just that more exposure to more human waste.

Open defecation remains a predominantly rural phenomenon—65 percent of rural Indians relieve themselves behind bushes, in fields, or by roadsides—yet the

Indian Census 2011 shows that 12.6 percent, or roughly 48 million urban Indians, still defecate in the open. Slums typically lack adequate water and sanitation services, and 18.9 percent of Indian slum householders defecate in the open.

No city has a complete sewage treatment system, and drainage ditches and informal canals that contain wastes feed most rivers. Urban services are poor and rural services often non-existent. Sanitation, solid waste removal, water, roads and public transportation are often listed as high priorities but still remain under-financed. The problem of sanitation in urban areas is very serious, because almost all cities have a large part of their population not connected to a sewer system. The 2011 census showed that only 32.7 percent of urban people were connected to a piped sewer system. In many rapidly growing urban areas in developing nations, the provision of water is controversial and difficult. Although local government can control water supply, the creation of wastes from illegal settlements cannot be controlled. As potable water decreases in India, there is a renewed emphasis on sanitation. However, large parts of some cities remain unconnected to the sewage system, because they are illegal.

Inadequate infrastructure and management systems are at the heart of the waste-water crisis. Solid waste management is one of the most essential functions of local authorities in India. Nevertheless, it has also been one of the least prioritized services for decades. Managing solid waste well and affordably is one of the key challenges of the 21st century and is a critical responsibility of each city government. Effective municipal solid waste (MSW) management systems are largely absent, and current services are inefficient and incur high costs. The implementation and enforcement of basic regulations is often disappointing, with some decrees issued in 2000 not yet fully implemented. The current status of solid waste management accounts for the 25–50 percent of ULB total expenditures. Metros and big cities collect between 70–90 percent of MSW, whereas smaller cities and towns collect 40–50 percent. About 15 percent is processed through informal and unsafe recycling.

The most common ways to treat waste in India are uncontrolled landfilling and burning. More than 91 percent of the MSW collected is landfilled or dumped on open land on the edge of a community or city. Of this, an estimated 10 percent is openly burned in landfills, and of the uncollected MSW, 2 percent is burned on the streets. Dumping and burning are causing severe environmental pollution and health problems, first by spreading toxic compounds from uncontrolled combustion and second by leakage of sewage from unsanitary landfills and dumping grounds into the groundwater.

A study found that informal recyclers handle 27 percent of the waste generated in Delhi, and if they were to disappear, the city would have to pay its contractors to collect and dispose of an additional 1,800 tons of waste every day.

Major Waste Issues

The waste issues are intertwined with a myriad of environmental challenges in such a large and varied country. There is significant air and water pollution in many urban locations. This will get worse as India rapidly industrializes. A high rate of overcrowding and urbanization is accompanied increases in the already large amount of raw swage and industrial wastes that pollute most waterways.

The lack of waste infrastructure and growing population will increase water pollution, trash, and disease. This, in turn, will place greater pressure on an already over taxed public health system. The number of hospital beds and doctors is low, and infant mortality is higher than in most countries. With rising ocean levels, increasing temperatures, and more violent weather, many infectious disease vectors could expand within and outside of India. India is an international destination and global crossroads. It is rapidly growing, urbanizing, and industrializing. However, it is also an ancient home for strongly held beliefs and practices regarding wastes. For example, the caste system places one class of people in the role of waste cleaners. When the great Indian independence leader Mahatma Gandhi said sanitation is more important than independence, he was addressing the role of waste in the lives of all castes.

Currently there is a risk of infectious diseases such as cholera, dengue fever, hepatitis A, hepatitis B, Japanese encephalitis, malaria, schistosomiasis, and typhoid. Typhoid fever is endemic and is a risk. Japanese encephalitis is transmitted seasonally, varying from region to region. Two percent or more of the population is persistently infected with hepatitis B. Climate change effects of temperature increases, rising ocean levels, and violent weather in the context of poor sanitation could expand vectors of most infectious diseases. The Bay of Bengal is currently under examination for cholera growing there.

Many efforts are being made to reduce environmental effects and protect public health from the dangers of waste. Currently India is developing waste to energy conversion technologies to reduce the strain on landfills. India was the first country to place legal liability on producers of electronic goods for recycling and reducing electronic or e-wastes. Communities are also taking the initiative and building capacity for the development of access to sanitary, safe, water, and waste facilities.

Michael Lytton

Further Reading

India Ministry of Drinking Water and Sanitation. www.india.gov.in.

Hirve, S., et al. 2014. "Psychosocial Stress Associated with Sanitation Practices: Experiences of Women in a Rural Community in India." *Journal of Water, Sanitation and Hygiene for Development*: in press.

Hueso, A., and B. Brian. 2013. "An Untold Story of Policy Failure: The Total Sanitation Campaign in India." *Water Policy* 15: 1001–1017.

Patil, Sumeet R., et al. 2014. "The Effect of India's Total Sanitation Campaign on Defecation Behaviors and Child Health in Rural Madhya Pradesh." *PLOS Medicine* www.plosmedicine.org.

INDONESIA

Indonesia is spread across southeast Asia between the Pacific and Indian Oceans. It is an archipelago with coastal lowlands and mountains in the interior of larger islands. It borders Timor-Leste, Malaysia, and Papua New Guinea. The climate is tropical—hot and humid. It gets some of the highest amounts of rain in the world.

E-wastes and Biologically Soluble Circuits

The rise of electronic and computer technology creates generations of wastes, some containing hazardous materials. It is the fastest-growing waste stream. E-waste dumps and landfills can cause cancer to those who live close by. The United Nations predicts that e-waste will increase by almost a third by 2017.

One way to reduce waste is in materials design. Combining very thin lines of silicon, magnesium, and silk makes an electrical circuit that can dissolve harmlessly inside the body. The applications of soluble circuits are just beginning. Currently there is a dissolvable circuit board printable on a 3D printer. By making electronic products with easily degradable materials, the amount of e-waste can be reduced.

It is slightly cooler in the highlands. Natural resources include fish, petroleum, tin, natural gas, nickel, timber, bauxite, copper, and coal. It is endowed with a deep biodiversity. However, Indonesia has the highest number of threatened mammalian species in the world—185.

Altogether, 252 million people are spread out on Indonesia's 1.83 million km^2 of land, with 93,000 km^2 of water. It is ranked fourth highest in population. Its coastline is the second longest in the world, at 54,716 km.

Current Waste Practices and Recycling

About 9,601,000 tons of municipal waste was collected in 2008, though much more was generated. Illegal ocean dumping of wastes in the region is endemic from local and international waste sources. Ninety-two percent of the urban population has access to improved drinking water sources, and 73 percent has access to improved sanitation facilities. Most cities have sewer and water services but discharge untreated wastes into freshwater. Rural waste practices are more basic in rural areas—pit toilets, latrines, drainage ditches, and cesspools. Seventy-four percent of the rural population has access to improved drinking water sources, and 73 percent has access to improved sanitation facilities. About 31,700 deaths a year are attributed to unsafe water.

Collected waste is taken to open landfills and trash dumps, where it is occasionally burned to make room for more trash. Waste pickers scavenge these sites and city streets for recyclable materials and sustenance. It is a common practice, although technically illegal, to dump trash into the ocean. There are many illegal dumpsites.

One dumpsite is on the island of Untung Jawa. The island is about 3 km long, with 2,000 residents. It is essentially a trash dump for the massive city of Jakarta. Wastes from surrounding ocean wastes form its coastline. Residents have observed that ocean wastes were separate and affected the coast as little pieces of floating debris. They became alarmed when little islands of wastes began to wash up. As a waste site, the island has been over capacity for years. Local residents are making significant waste management efforts. They hired about fifteen waste collectors with garbage collecting motorcycles and a garbage boat in an effort to keep the wastes at the specific waste site. Streets now have communal waste collection sites that segregate wastes as wet, dry, or hazardous. They began five garbage banks that pay residents for recyclable materials from the coastline. Trash that can't be reused or recycled is burned. The ash is used to make bricks.

Indonesia does not operate any nuclear power reactors but does operate several research nuclear reactors. The research reactors dispose of spent fuel to the United States. There is no disposal or processing facility. There are two nuclear waste storage facilities. There is one research reactor examining the production of reactor fuel elements. Some European nations are pairing with Indonesia so that it does not become a dumping ground for international wastes, especially rapidly increasing volumes of e-waste. The intent is to prevent Indonesia and similarly situated countries from receiving toxic and hazardous wastes beyond the capacity to handle it. Improving recycling facilities, training waste personnel, and building waste treatment facilities are some of the goals in Indonesia. The Swiss started the Mobile Phone Partnership and the Partnership on Action on Computing Equipment. Among other actions, they partnered with Indonesia to work on the problem of e-waste disposal in countries that cannot handle it in an environmentally sound manner.

Emissions and Industry

In 2000, Indonesia generated 554,333.5 metric tons of greenhouse gases, a 108 percent increase from 1994. It is likely that current greenhouse emissions are higher because of population increase, rapid petrochemical industrialization, and reliance on local agriculture.

About 12 percent of the land is arable. Agricultural products include rice, cassava, peanuts, rubber, cocoa, coffee, palm oil, and bananas. Agricultural emissions accounted for 13 percent of all emissions. Within this sector, rice cultivation accounted for 47.5 percent of emissions, agricultural soils 29 percent, enteric fermentation 17 percent, and manure management 2.5 percent.

Energy is a large industry. Crude oil production was 974,300 bbl/day in 2012. There is about 4 billion bbl in proven reserves. About a million bbl/day of refined petrochemical products were produced in 2009. Emissions from energy accounted for 51 percent of all emissions. Within this sector, energy industries accounted for 30 percent of emissions, manufacturing and construction 23 percent, and transport 20 percent. Fugitive emissions accounted almost 10 percent of emissions in this sector. Emissions from industrial processes accounted for almost 8 percent of all emissions. Within this sector, mineral processes accounted for 68 percent of emissions, chemical industries 24 percent, and metal production 7 percent.

Emissions from wastes accounted for 28 percent of all emissions. Within this sector, "other" accounted for 85 percent of emissions, solid waste disposal on land 12 percent, and waste incineration 2 percent. Such a large amount of unaccounted waste emissions indicates air and water pollution.

Major Waste Issues

Water and air pollution from industrial wastes, sewerage, and deforestation continue to significantly affect the environment. Water pollution is threatening groundwater sources. Heavy winds can push as much as 100 tons of trash a day on some of the coasts. The coastal waste blown in is primarily the waste that floats.

There is a large amount of emissions from wastes, and most of the information is not specific. Currently there is a risk of infectious diseases such as cholera, dengue fever, hepatitis A, hepatitis B, Japanese encephalitis, malaria, schistosomiasis, and typhoid. Typhoid fever is endemic and a risk. Japanese encephalitis is transmitted seasonally but these can vary from region to region. Two percent or more of the population is persistently infected with hepatitis B. There is a high risk of malaria, though varying with time and place. Climate change effects of increases in temperature, rising ocean levels, and violent weather in the context of poor sanitation will expand vectors of most infectious diseases.

Further Reading

Engel, S., and A. Suslio. 2014. "Shaming and Sanitation in Indonesia: A Return to Colonial Health Practices?" *Development and Change* 45: 157–178.

Indonesia Government. www.indonesia.go.id.

White, W. 2011. "Confronting Culture to Overcome Sector Failure: Sanitation in Indonesia." *Journal of Water, Sanitation and Hygiene for Development* 1: 269–278.

IRAN

Afghanistan, Armenia, Azerbaijan Iraq, Pakistan, Turkey, Turkmenistan, the Persian Gulf and Caspian Sea border Iran. The terrain is mountainous with a high desert in the interior. The climate is dry except for the Caspian coast, where it is cooler and less arid. There are droughts, floods, sandstorms and earthquakes. Much of the country is a desert. Natural resources include oil, gas, coal, iron ore, lead, manganese, and zinc.

About 74 million people live on Iran's 1,628,750 km^2 of land and a 2,440 km coastline. Sixty-seven percent of Iranians are urbanized, and 42 percent live in a city having more than 100,000 inhabitants. A third of the population lives in overcrowded conditions. Its recent history includes war and violence in a politically unstable part of the Mideast.

Current Waste Practices

It is estimated that at least 40,000 tons of waste is generated per day. About 90 percent of these wastes are taken to landfills, and 10 percent recycled. Most of the recycled wastes are organic materials that are used as compost. In rural areas and in parts of some urban areas waste practices are basic, including pit toilets, latrines, cesspools, and drainage ditches. Iran has the eighth-dirtiest water in the world as measured by BOD (biological oxygen demand). Years of war have destroyed many sewer and water facilities and records. Approximately 92 percent of rural, and 97 percent of the urban populations have access to an improved water sources. Both urban and rural populations have access improved sanitation facilities.

The Ministry of Health and Medical Education supervises water quality control of all drinking water from source to consumption. Water management is a deep-rooted cultural practice. Ancient water infrastructure is still used., such as over 30,000 Qanats (water retention areas) Ancient water guidelines were written over the portals of the grand mosques and public gathering places. Water supply and quality are closely monitored. However, little wastewater is treated before discharge into the water system.

General guidance is being developed to separate, collect and dispose of hazardous wastes. Iran does restrict the export and import of hazardous wastes and other wastes. Iran studied all 30 provinces for potential hazardous waste disposal sites. The import and export of hazardous wastes and other wastes is not reported. Iran has one operating nuclear power reactor supplying less than 1 percent of the country's electricity. There is one disposal facility. There are two storage facilities and no processing facilities. Iran is building a second nuclear power plant.

Emissions and Industry

In 2000, Iran generated 483,669.2 metric tons of greenhouse gas emissions carbon dioxide equivalents, a 25.5 percent increase from 1994.

Agricultural emissions accounted for 9 percent of all emissions. Within this sector, agricultural soils accounted for 55 percent of emissions, enteric fermentation 39.5 percent, and rice cultivation 3 percent, and manure management 2 percent.

Emissions from energy accounted for 78 percent of all emissions. Within this sector, energy industries accounted for 24 percent of emissions, transportation 20 percent, and manufacturing and construction 12 percent. Fugitive emissions and "other" accounted for about 44 percent of emissions in this sector. Fugitive emissions are essentially unaccounted waste streams into the air. Fugitive emissions can affect regional ecosystems and the public health, because they can fall from the air to the land and water. Emissions from industrial processes accounted for 6 percent of all emissions. Within this sector, metal production accounted for 48 percent of emissions, mineral products 43 percent, and chemical industries 8 percent.

Emissions from solid wastes accounted for 7 percent of all emissions. Within this sector, wastewater management accounted for 67 percent emissions, and solid waste disposal on land 33 percent.

Major Waste Issues

Many of the major environmental problems are waste issues. The air is polluted from oil refineries. Industrial wastes and untreated sewage pollute the water. One of the major waste issues is the protection of drinking water supplies from water pollution. The major waste issue is the protection of public health both in the country and the region from polluted water. Infectious diseases found in

Iran include cholera, hepatitis A, hepatitis B, meningococcal meningitis, typhoid, malaria, dengue fever, and schistosomiasis. Two percent or more of the population is persistently infected with hepatitis B. Climate change concerns are about increasing droughts, extreme weather events, rising sea levels, and floods.

Further Reading

Amouei, A., et al. 2012. "Quantity and Quality of Solid Wastes Generated by Health Centers in North Iran." *Journal of Applied Technology in Environmental Sanitation* 2: 159–164.

Hoseinzadeh, E., et al. 2014. "Evaluation of Aydughmush River Water Quality Using the National Sanitation Foundation Water Quality Index, River Pollution Index, and the Forestry Water Quality Index." *Desalination and Water Treatment*: forthcoming.

Iran-Northern Cities Water Supply and Sanitation Project. www.documents.worldbank. org. (Site assessed 10.4.14.).

Iran President's Office. www.president.ir.

IRAQ

Iraq is both an ancient birthplace of civilization and current battleground. Currently, 28,807,000 people reside on Iraq's 438,317 km² of land and 58 km of coastline. Roughly 67 percent of the population is urbanized, and 58 percent lives in a city having more than 100,000 inhabitants. It is a nation with much human conflict. Iraq and Iran engaged in war from 1980 to 1988. In 1990, Iraq invaded Kuwait, leading directly to UN sanctions. Iraq became a sovereign independent state with occupied forces in 2003. Iraq has one of the largest populations of internally displaced persons. It is a country devastated by war and deeply rooted civil conflicts. Almost 2 million people are displaced, in addition to the 2 million refugees in neighboring countries. The health of the population suffered. Infant mortality went from 50 per 1,000 in 1990 to 125 in 2004. About a third of the population suffers malnutrition. The life expectancy is 56 years.

The climate is mainly desert, with mild to cool winters and hot, dry summers. There is occasional flooding in the northern mountainous regions. One of the primary environmental issues is desertification and the loss of potable water.

Current Waste Practices

Waste practices are very basic, including pit toilets, latrines, cesspools, drainage ditches, and open defecation. Sixty-one percent of the people have a drinking water supply. Many locations have no water or have water available for only a small part of the day. Only about half the inhabitants have adequate excreta disposal. About 23,400 deaths a year are attributed to unsafe water. Cholera was detected in parts of Iraq in 1966 and since then has moved in waves from north, spreading to the center and then to the south. In December 2007, it was estimated that more than 30,000 people had acute watery diarrhea, and 4,467 tested positive for cholera, including twenty-four deaths. These are laboratory-confirmed cases, and in the context of war and civil strife, most cases are never reported. Several strains of cholera have been reported all through Iraq, with the highest-risk areas in densely populated, low-income communities in Baghdad—Sadr City, Me'dain, Baladiat, Al Resafa, and Al Karach. There is little health data now, and the need for a coordinated cholera outbreak response effort is unaddressed. Iraq collected 5,446,000 tons of municipal waste in 2005, about 12 percent being incinerated. This does not meet need or demand for waste treatment and disposal.

There is now international assistance for waste management. The UN Development Program, in collaboration with the European Commission, UNICEF, UN-Habitat, and the World Health Organization, is developing the Water and Sanitation Master Planning and Capacity Building Program. Water quality and level of sanitation are being analyzed in six governorates with the goal of using the information to develop sewer and water priorities. In addition to support for developing master plans, the governorates of Al—Anbar, Sulaymaniyah, and Thi-Qar are getting specialized waste equipment such as large garbage compacters and collection containers.

Emissions and Industry

The state of war in Iraq is overwhelming to data gathering systems, so data on emissions and industry is not available.

Major Waste Issues

The major waste challenge is to rebuild waste infrastructure. Waste collection, transfer, storage, treatment, and disposal all need basic infrastructure and more resources to meet the demands of the population. The major waste issue is the protection of public health in both the country and the region. There are many infectious diseases here, in particular yellow fever, cholera, hepatitis A, hepatitis B, meningococcal meningitis, typhoid, malaria, and schistosomiasis. Two percent or more of the population is persistently infected with hepatitis B.

Climate change effects include increased temperatures and more drought and fires. There is a good chance that infectious disease vectors will expand from outbreaks to epidemics. The rapid population growth and urbanization, poor sanitation practices and facility access, and a lack of environmental or public health data put this country at risk for more infectious diseases. With rising temperatures, desertification will occur more often and increase these effects. There are inadequate public resources in the country to handle internal, regional, and global health concerns. The challenge for the waste management system is how to integrate these dynamics in an integrated waste management policy and practice.

Further Reading

Aanab, A., and S. Singh. 2012. "Critical Assessment of Environmental Quality of Baghdad, Iraq." *Journal of Environmental Engineering* 138: 601–606.

Alanbari, M., et al. 2014. "Application of Simapro& on Karbala Wastewater Treatment Plant, Iraq." *Journal of Earth Sciences and Geotechnical Engineering* 4: 55–68.

Republic of Iraq General Secretariat. www.cabinet.iq.

Zolnikov, Tara Rava. 2013. "The Maladies of Water and War: Addressing Poor Water Quality in Iraq." *American Journal of Public Health* 103: 980–987.

IRELAND

Ireland is a large island off the coast of western Europe. Ireland shares a border with the United Kingdom and the Atlantic Ocean. Northern Ireland is part of the United Kingdom and covers six counties. The terrain is mainly rolling hills in the interior and small mountains near the coasts. The North Atlantic current moderates the climate. The climate is mild, with humid summers and cool winters. Natural resources include peat, natural gas, limestone, dolomite, silver, zinc, lead, and copper. Altogether, 4.5 million people live on 68,890 km² of land and 1,448 km of coastline. Sixty percent of the population is urbanized, and 32 percent lives in a city having more than 100,000 inhabitants.

Current Waste Practices and Recycling

Access to improved drinking water sources and sanitation facilities is very good. Ireland collected 3,300,000 tons of municipal waste in 2009, almost 61 percent of it landfilled, about 3 percent incinerated, almost 32 percent recycled, and about 3.5 percent composted. However, landfill space is running out, causing waste issues in many places.

In 2009, Ireland exported 172,882 metric tons of hazardous wastes and imported 2,891 metric tons of hazardous wastes. Ireland restricts the import and export of hazardous and other wastes for disposal and for recovery or reuse. Hazardous wastes and other wastes are also restricted while transported in Ireland.

There are a small number of disposal and recycling facilities, but the overall waste policy goal now is to become self-sufficient in terms of waste management.

The Waste Management Act of 1996 requires the Environment Agency to prepare a national Hazardous Waste Management Plan. The 2008 plan focuses on waste prevention and on reducing the hazards from waste. The 2004 National Waste Prevention Programme develops information and data on all waste. The 2009–2012 Prevention Plan is now in place. Under the Waste Management Act, local government authorities, or municipalities, are required to develop and implement a Waste Management Plan intended to prevent, reduce, and recover or recycle wastes.

An Economic Study of Solvent Recycling and Treatment was performed in 2009. A project developed from this study to develop the treatment and re use of waste solvents nationally, and not export them. In 2010, another study, the Technical and Economic Aspects of Developing a National Difficult Waste Facility, focused on wastes not able to be incinerated. Parts of this study include factors of site selection requirements, all-island perspectives, economic appraisals, and socioeconomic assessment.

Emissions and Industry

Ireland generated 58,531 metric tons of greenhouse gas emissions in 2012, a 6 percent increase from 1990.

Agricultural products include potatoes, wheat, beef, and dairy products. Agricultural emissions accounted for 31 percent of all emissions. Within this sector, enteric fermentation accounted for 49 percent of emissions, agricultural soils 36 percent, and manure management 15 percent.

Ireland produces a small amount of crude oil and has few proven reserves. Peat is used for fuel for heat in many households. Consumption of peat per capita is among the highest in the world. Any burning of peat creates greenhouse gas emissions, especially inefficient combustion. Inefficient combustion not only loses energy but generates more particulate mater into the air. Energy emissions accounted for 63 percent of all emissions. Within this sector, energy industries accounted for 35 percent of emissions, transportation 29 percent, and manufacturing and construction industries 35 percent.

Ireland is engaged in a sustainability study that will set environmental benchmarks for all major industrial sectors. Industrial emissions accounted for 4 percent of all emissions. Within this sector, mineral products accounted for 57 percent of emissions and consumption of halocarbons 43 percent.

Waste emissions accounted for almost 2 percent of all emissions. Within this sector, solid waste disposal on land accounted for 80 percent of emissions, wastewater handling 16 percent, and waste incineration 4 percent.

Major Waste Issues

The major waste issue is pesticide and fertilizer runoff into water systems. About a third of the rivers are unsafe for swimming or fishing because of sewage and agricultural runoff.

Climate change effects of rising ocean levels, temperature changes, and more violent weather could affect public health. Public health systems are poor compared with other western Europe countries. One possible effect of global climate change is the change in ocean currents. If the North Atlantic Current moved away from Ireland, temperatures could get much colder.

Ireland is preparing for climate change effects on water systems. Climate change observers note increased temperature, seasonal and spatial variance of precipitation, and increased extreme weather events on the west coast. Projected effects include temperature increases, wetter winters in the west, drier summers in the southeast, and less snow. Another projected effect is on water services and increased risk of pollution and contamination from wastes. A primary concern is about water supply and sanitation. In response to these concerns and projections, Ireland is developing regulatory instruments to control floods. The National Catchment-Based Flood Risk Assessment and Management Program considers future climate change scenarios. The National Climate Change Adaptation Framework requires an adaptation plan for climate change effects on water.

Further Reading

Climate Change Impacts on Water Systems. www.oecd.org.

Guinan, B., et al. 2005. *The Nature and Extent of Unauthorized Waste Activity in Ireland.* Washington, DC: Environmental Protection Agency.

Horrigan, M., et al. 2014. "The Use of Energy Analysis to Benchmark the Resource Efficiency of Municipal Waste Treatment Plants in Ireland." *South East European Conference on Sustainable Development of Energy, Water and Environment Systems*. Ohrid, Macedonia. Irish State. www.gov.ie.

ISRAEL

Israel is the ancient center of many of the world's dominant religions. Individuals having strongly held religious beliefs live and converge here. There is political tension in the Mideast generally, and Israel is involved in conflict with Palestine. Israel borders Egypt, the Gaza Strip, Jordan, Lebanon, Syria, the West Bank, and the Mediterranean Sea. The coast is a fertile, maritime plain, and the interior is slightly mountainous. Almost half the nation is a desert, primarily in the southern Negev region. Altogether, 7.71 million people live on Israel's 22,072 km² of land and 273 km of coastline. It is very urbanized, with 92 percent of the population living in an urban area and 80 percent living in a city having more than 100,000 inhabitants. The capital city of Jerusalem has major sacred sites for several religions. Its population is about 800,000 people.

Current Waste Practices and Recycling

Access to improved drinking water sources and sanitation facilities is very good. Israel collected about 4,556,000 tons of municipal wastes in 2009. Most of this waste is landfilled or, as much as possible, recycled. The annual municipal waste production is approximately 5,232,000 metric tons per year. By weight, about 40 percent of this is organic wastes, 25 percent paper products, and 15 percent plastic.

Hazardous Wastes

The Hazardous Substances Division of the Ministry of the Environment makes waste policy in Israel. Israel has a small number of hazardous waste disposal facilities that use deep well injection, incineration, landfills, and chemical treatments to handle hazardous wastes disposal. The Ministry of the Environment promises to fund up to 40 percent of the capital costs for industries that invest in hazardous waste reduction to the levels specified by the Ministry. There are a few recovery and recycling facilities. They focus on fertilizer production, solvent reclamation, and used solvents incineration. There is a general policy toward waste reduction, recycling, and reuse of hazardous wastes. To meet this aspiration, more environmental permits were issued for recycling and reuse of hazardous wastes.

Altogether, 321,000 tons of hazardous wastes were generated in 2008. Israel restricts the movement of hazardous wastes, but does allow it by special permit in some cases. The import of hazardous wastes for final disposal is prohibited. The import of hazardous wastes for recovery or recycling is allowed if the facility operates in an environmentally sound way. The individual permits may specify terms and conditions unique to that facility. The transit of hazardous and other wastes are strictly controlled. It must be loaded and unloaded in the same port and cannot be transported by land. Israel does control exports of hazardous or other wastes for final disposal or recovery and recycling. In light of this heightened environmental enforcement of waste regulations, it is unlikely that Israel will be the recipient of toxic wastes from other nations.

Recycling

Recycling rates in Israel are about 14 percent for municipal wastes and 23 percent for all wastes. These rates have remained steady for more than a decade. Many trash dumps were closed and more recycling centers opened. About 58 percent of industrial wastes are recycled and 42 percent landfilled. Policy preparations are in place for the handling electronic wastes. The Sustainable Integrated Water management Policy covers source reduction, recyclables recovery, and disposal. Their goal is zero wastes in landfills.

Emissions and Industry

In 2010, Israel generated 75,415.5 metric tons of greenhouse gases, a 20 percent increase from 1996.

Agricultural products include cotton, citrus, vegetables, and poultry. Agricultural emissions accounted for 3 percent of all emissions. Within this sector, agricultural soils accounted for 47 percent emissions, enteric fermentation 31 percent, and manure management 22 percent. This is an unusually high amount of greenhouse gas emissions from manure, indicating the presence of large amounts of untreated feces.

Israel produces a small amount of crude oil and has moderate proven crude oil reserves. Oil consumption per capita is higher than most countries. Energy emissions accounted for 85 percent of all emissions. Within this sector, energy industries accounted for 66 percent of emissions, transportation 26 percent, and manufacturing and construction 7.5 percent. Industrial emissions accounted for 4 percent of all emissions. Within this sector, mineral products accounted for 74 percent of emissions and the chemical industry 26 percent.

Israel is at the cutting edge of increasing the efficient reuse of wastewater. Some of the high manure emissions could be from processes that reclaim wastewater through evaporation. Other wastewater recovery efforts examine systems like sand filtration. Waste emissions accounted for 8 percent of all emissions. Within this sector, solid waste disposal on land accounted for 84 percent of emissions, and wastewater management 16 percent.

Major Waste Issues

The major waste issue is the protection of scarce water sources. Israel's growing population and strong international tourism constrains an already scarce resource. The quality of water is impaired by agricultural pesticide and fertilizer runoff and industrial and municipal wastes. Higher-efficiency waste management and large water desalination plants are two ways that water quality problems are addressed.

With increasing temperatures, desertification will increase and heighten these effects. Israel's proximity to regional infectious disease risks and role as an international transportation hub may open up new infectious diseases vectors. Israel has an excellent public health system that is knowledgeable about these diseases.

Israel is preparing for climate change effects on water. Climate change observers note decreased rainfall and more extreme weather events, such as drought and flooding. Projected effects include temperature increases, decreases in precipitation, reduced water availability, reduced recharge of underground water aquifers, increases in desertification, increases in extreme weather events, sea level rise in the Mediterranean Sea, and salinity changes in the Sea of Galilee. The key vulnerabilities are around water scarcity. Israel consumes more water than its natural supply now. Primary concerns are about water quality, water quantity, and extreme weather event. In response to these concerns and projects, the Israeli government is developing a national adaptation strategy. In 2011, the Israel Climate Change Knowledge Center was established. The purpose is to develop materials and analyses for the national adaptation policy. Israel is also changing its infrastructure around water. There is intensive reuse of treated domestic wastewater. Effluent is discharged in sand filtration fields, where physical, biological, and chemical processes treat it before reaching underground water aquifers. There is a large program of building desalination plants, which convert seawater into potable water. Currently three facilities produce 320 million m^3 of potable water. Plans are under way to line the coast with desalinization plants to meet 100 percent of domestic water demand by 2050. Desalinization requires large amounts of energy and, depending on the source of energy, may generate greenhouse gases. The Israeli government encourages low-emission energy sources and efficient energy recovery systems in its desalinization plants. Israel's desalinization plants are some of the most energy- and cost-efficient.

Further Reading

Climate Change Impacts on Water Systems. www.oecd.org.

Israel Ministry of National Infrastructures, Energy and Water Resources. www.energy.gov.il.

Katz, D. 2013. "Policies for Water Demand Management in Israel." *Global Issues in Water Policy* 4: 147–163.

Orenstein, D., et al. 2013. *Between Ruin and Restoration: An Environmental History of Israel.* Pittsburgh, PA: Pittsburgh University Press.

Oron, G., et al. 2014. "Greywater Use in Israel and Worldwide: Standards and Prospects." *Water Research* 58: 92–101.

ITALY

Italy is a peninsula defined by mountains and seas. The Apennines run through the center of the country, and the Alps form the northern border. The Tyrrhenian Sea is on the west side and the Adriatic Sea on the east. Many surrounding islands are also Italian. The two largest islands are Sicily and Sardinia. Italy borders

Austria, France, the Holy See, San Marino, Slovenia, Switzerland, and the Mediterranean Sea. The climate is Mediterranean, though it can vary. The surrounding seas moderate the coastal weather. In the higher altitudes of the mountains, it is much cooler. Natural resources include oil, gas, coal, potash, zinc, marble, barite, feldspar, and sulfur.

Italy is the one of the historical centers of western European art and science. The Vatican City, the center of the Catholic Church, is situated in Italy. Today, 61.4 million people live on Italy's 294,020 km² with 7,600 km of coastline. Italy is a modern urban nation, with 68 percent living in cities, and 27 percent living in a city having more than 100,000 inhabitants.

Current Waste Practices and Recycling

The entire population is covered by municipal waste collection. Italy collected 32,500,000 tons of municipal waste in 2009. Almost 49 percent of the waste landfilled, 13 percent incinerated, 12 percent recycled, and about 35 percent composted. Landfill space is decreasing as waste is increasing. Large amounts of toxic and other wastes are found in the seas off both coasts.

Hazardous Wastes

Italy generated 6,655,000 tons of hazardous wastes in 2008. There are no hazardous waste facilities for disposal or for recovery and recycling available. There are no restrictions on the transit of hazardous wastes and other wastes. Italy restricts the export of hazardous wastes for disposal and for recovery or recycling. Hazardous waste for import for final disposal or recovery and recycling are also restricted.

In 2009, Italy imported 3,682 metric tons of hazardous wastes and 697,312 metric tons of other wastes. Altogether, 351,815 metric tons of other wastes were exported along with 1,216,223 metric tons of hazardous waste.

Emissions and Industry

Italy generated 460,083.5 metric tons of greenhouse gas in 2012, an 11 percent decrease from 1990.

Agricultural products include olives, fruit, vegetables, grapes, potatoes, dairy products, fish, and dairy products. Agricultural emissions accounted for 7 percent of all emissions. Within this sector, agricultural soils accounted for 48 percent of emissions, enteric fermentation 31 percent, and manure management 16 percent, and rice cultivation 4.5 percent. This is a high amount of greenhouse gas emissions from manure, indicating the presence of large amounts of untreated feces.

As an industrialized nation Italy uses a great deal of energy. Energy emissions accounted for 83 percent of all emissions. Within this sector, energy industries accounted for 33 percent of emissions, transportation 28 percent, manufacturing and construction industries 14.5 percent, and fugitive emissions of almost 2 percent. Industrial emissions accounted for 6 percent of all emissions. Within this sector, mineral products accounted for 49.5 percent of emissions, consumption of halocarbons 34 percent, chemical industries 6 percent, and metal production 6 percent.

Waste emissions accounted for almost 4 percent of all emissions. Within this sector, solid waste disposal on land accounted for 70 percent of emissions, wastewater handling 29 percent, and incineration 1.5 percent.

Major Waste Issues

The major waste issue is water pollution of inland waterways and the ocean coasts. The industrial waste treatment facilities are inadequate and let more pollution into the inland waterways where it flows into the ocean. Agricultural pesticide and fertilizer runoff follow the same hydrologic pathway to the sea. Air pollution is another waste issue. It is forming acid rain and defacing historic structures as well as affecting the environment.

Rising ocean levels, increasing temperature, and more violent weather will challenge waste control, abatement, and remediation efforts. Italy is preparing for climate change effects on water systems. Climate change observers note increased temperatures and regional changes in rainfall. Projected effects include degradation and decreases in water sources, increases in floods and landslides, glacier lake outburst flooding, more droughts, and fluctuation in mountain water runoff. Key vulnerabilities are the alpine mountains, widespread stress on water systems, and loss of alpine and glacial biodiversity. Primary concerns are about water quantity, extreme weather events, and ecosystem damage. In response to these concerns and projections, the Italian government developed policies and regulatory instruments, including climate change effects on water and sanitation. There is a National Committee to mitigate drought and desertification. There is also a National Plan for Biodiversity that includes ecosystem protection.

Further Reading

Cipolla, S., et al. 2014. "Heat Recovery from Urban Wastewater: Analysis of the Variability of Flow Rate and Temperature in the Sewer of Bologna, Italy." *Energy Procedia* 45: 288–297.

Climate Change Impacts on Water Systems. www.oecd.org.

Italian Prime Minister. www.palazzochigi.it.

Scalia, B., et al. 2014. "Sanitation Ability of Anaerobic Digestion Performed at Different Temperature on Sewage Sludge." *Science of the Total Environment* 467: 888–897.

J

JAMAICA

Jamaica is a mountainous island in the Caribbean Sea. There is a history of earthquakes in the region. The climate is tropical—hot and humid. It is cooler in the mountains. Natural resources include gypsum, limestone, bauxite, and hydropower. Altogether, 2.9 million people live on 10,990 km² of land and 1,022 km of coastline. Fifty-three percent are urbanized, and 27 percent live in a city having more than 100,000 inhabitants.

Current Waste Practices

Most cities have sewer and water services but discharge untreated wastes into freshwater. About 200 deaths a year are attributed to unsafe water. Ninety-eight percent of the urban population has access to an improved drinking water source, and 78 percent has access to improved sanitation facilities. Eighty-eight percent of the rural population has access to improved drinking water sources, and 82 percent has access to improved sanitation facilities. Jamaica collected 1,464,000 tons of municipal waste in 2009, 100 percent of it landfilled. Wastes are increasing, and landfill space on the island is decreasing. It is likely that significant amount of wastes are illegally dumped in the ocean by residents and tourists in large ships. Municipalities served about three-quarters of the population. Ten thousand metric tons of hazardous wastes were generated in 2006, and records are poor concerning the amount of hazardous wastes imported. The National Solid Waste Management Policy Act of 2000 established the National Solid Waste Authority. This authority simply works with private sector waste haulers. Because poverty is extensive, many people and communities cannot afford comprehensive waste management services.

Emissions and Industry

In 1994, Jamaica generated 8,394.2 metric tons of greenhouse gases. It is likely that greenhouse gas emissions are higher because of population increases and reliance on agriculture

Agricultural products include coffee, bananas, fruits, vegetables, poultry, goats, and milk. Agricultural emissions accounted for 92 percent of all emissions. Within this sector, agricultural soils accounted for 98 percent of emissions.

Jamaica produces a small amount of crude oil and has no proven reserves. Energy emissions accounted for 7 percent of all emissions. Within this sector, manufacturing and construction accounted for 50 percent of emissions, energy industries 27 percent, and transportation 15 percent. Industrial emissions accounted for 0.33 percent of all emissions. Within this sector, mineral products accounted for 100 percent of emissions.

Waste emissions accounted for 0.33 percent of all emissions. Within this sector, solid waste disposal on land accounted for 80 percent of emissions and wastewater management 20 percent.

Major Waste Issues

Some of the environmental problems are waste issues. Untreated sewage, oil, and industrial wastes are discharged into nearby water causing degradation of the coral reefs and other environmental and public health effects. Many people live in areas having a low water table. The major waste issue is the protection of public health both in the country and the region. There are infectious diseases in Jamaica, such as hepatitis A, hepatitis B, and dengue fever. Two percent or more of the population is persistently infected with hepatitis B.

Climate change effects of rising sea levels, more extreme weather events, increases in temperature, and seasonal variability all have a significant effect in this island country. There is a good chance that infectious disease vectors will expand from outbreaks to epidemics. The tropical conditions, rapid population growth and urbanization, poor sanitation practices and facility access, and a lack of environmental or public health data make this country at risk for more infectious diseases. There are inadequate public resources in the country to handle internal, regional, and global health concerns. So far the United Nations Millennium Development goals for sanitation are not met and are not likely to meet 2015 deadlines. There are few doctors and hospital beds and high infant mortality rate.

Further Reading

Allwood, P., et al. 2014. "Knowledge, Perceptions, and Environmental Risk Factors Among Jamaican Households with a History of Leptospirosis." *Journal of Infection and Public Health* 7: 314–322.

Heijnen, Marieke, et al. 2014. "Shared Sanitation versus Individual Household Latrines: A Systematic Review of Outcomes." www.plosone.org.

Jamaica Information Service. www.jis.gov.jm.

Smith, Nadine, Anna Halton, and Janet Strachan, eds. 2014. *Transitioning to a Green Economy: Political Approaches in Small States.* London, UK: Commonwealth Secretariat.

JAPAN

Japan is an archipelago of volcanic islands surrounded by the Sea of Japan and the North Pacific Ocean. The four main islands are Honshu, Hokkaido, Kyushu, and Shikoku. The terrain is mountainous. The climate is tropical in the south and cooler in the north. Natural resources include fish and hydropower. Japan is a modern industrialized nation. Most people live in cities. The capital and largest city is Tokyo, having over 37 million people. Overall, 127.3 million people live on Japan's 377,930 km² of land. The 29,750 km of coastline is the sixth longest coastline in the world. Sixty-six percent of the population is urbanized, and 64 percent lives in a city having more than 100,000 inhabitants. The live expectancy is 83 years.

Current Waste Practices

Japan collected 54,367,000 tons of municipal waste in 2003. Only 3 percent of the waste is landfilled, 74 percent incinerated, and 17 percent recycled. The entire population has access to improved drinking water sources and sanitation facilities. There are approximately 2,300 hazardous wastes final disposal sites and 19,500 waste recovery and recycling facilities. Japan does restrict the import and export of hazardous wastes and other wastes when imported for final disposal or recovery and recycling. The Ministry of the Environment must examine the application to review the environmental protection measures. The result is reported to the Ministry of the Environment and the Ministry of Economy, Trade, and Industry, which cannot issue an import permit until the Ministry of the Environment certifies that sufficient environmental measures are in place. The Office of Waste Disposal Management within the Ministry of the Environment controls and develops waste

Workers monitor video screens at a control room at one of Tokyo's 17 factory-sized incinerators, which burn garbage collected from the Tokyo metropolitan area around the clock. With the ever-increasing volume of trash and rapidly vanishing space to dispose of it, Japanese sanitation officials predicted the country would drown in its own waste if nothing were done. Some localities in Japan now have the highest recycling rates in the world. (AP Photo/Katsumi Kasahara)

policies. It is national policy to reduce the generation of hazardous wastes and maximize reuse and disposal within the country.

The 2000, the Basic Environmental Plan and the Basic Law for Establishing a Sound Material-Cycle Society were implemented. The principle behind these laws is the cyclical use and disposal of wastes. The policies in order of priority are restricting waste generation, encouraging reuse, recycling, heat recovery, and sound waste disposal. There is a substantial body of law and legislation on waste. These laws include the Waste Management and Public Cleansing Law, Law for Promotion of Effective Utilization of Resources, the Container and Packaging Recycling Law, and the Electric Household Appliance Recycling Law.

Recycling

Municipal waste generation per capita is very low for a developed country largely thanks to a strong recycling ethic and law. The recycling rate is about 21 percent and is designed to decrease wastes to landfills and incinerators. Municipal recycling programs are designed to fit the community to encourage participation. Cities such as Yokohama have ten or more categories of trash and require the residents to separate recyclables for curbside collection. Other cities have refined recycling into more comprehensive programs. Kamikatsu has forty-four or more categories of trash. Enforcement is strict, with community members patrolling the curbside bags for wrongly separated trash. Clear plastic bags with proper numbers on each bag are required.

Emissions and Industry

In 2012, Japan generated 1,200,539 metric tons of greenhouse gas.

There is limited arable land, but productivity is high. Japan grows enough food for about 60 percent of its population. Agricultural products include rice, fruit, vegetable, pork, dairy products, poultry and eggs, and fish. Agricultural emissions accounted for 2 percent of all emissions. Within this sector, enteric fermentation accounted for 27 percent of emissions, agricultural soils 26 percent, and manure management 24 percent, and rice cultivation 23 percent.

There are few energy resources, such as oil, gas, or coal. In 2010, Japan relied on foreign oil imports for almost half its needs. Hydropower is a major source of energy.

In the past two years, the Japanese have made use of a new source of energy called methyl hydrate. While originally tracking earthquake potential under sea they found methyl hydrate, or ice that burns. So far this ice is found along the continental shelves at about 200 feet deep and in the Alaskan tundra. It is more powerful than any other petrochemical energy source but has the potential to increase greenhouse gas emissions.

Energy emissions accounted for 92 percent of all emissions. Within this sector, energy industries accounted for 42 percent of emissions, manufacturing and construction industries 27 percent, and transportation 18 percent. Industrial emissions accounted for 5 percent of all emissions. Within this sector, mineral products accounted for 56 percent of emissions, consumption of halocarbons 38 percent, chemical industries 5 percent, and metal production 0.5 percent.

Waste emissions accounted for 1.5 percent of all emissions. Within this sector, waste incineration accounted for 68 percent of emissions, solid waste disposal on land 15 percent, and wastewater handling 13 percent. The reliance on waste incineration is very high.

Major Waste Issues

Some of the main environmental issues are also waste issues. Air pollution from fossil fueled power plants is causing acid rain that degrades fresh drinking water supplies and the environment. The major waste issue is the protection of public health. There are infectious diseases here, including Japanese encephalitis, hepatitis A, hepatitis B, tick-borne encephalitis, typhoid, dengue fever, and schistosomiasis. Two percent or more of the population is persistently infected with hepatitis B. Global warming, rising ocean levels, and more violent storms will challenge currently strong public health systems. The occurrence of natural disasters such as earthquakes, volcanic eruptions, tsunamis, landslides, and floods can create large environmental effects because of the current reliance on nuclear energy.

Japan is preparing for climate change effects on water systems. Climate change observers note less precipitation, more blue-green algae in lakes, increased flooding, heavy rainfall, more landslides, sinkholes from increased use of groundwater, and less water for freshwater cold weather fish. Projected effects include increases in temperatures, changes in daily temperature extremes, fluctuation in precipitation, increases in heavy rainfall, decreases in snowfall, groundwater contamination because of sea level rise, increases in drought, more blue-green algae in warmer lakes, decreases in flood safety control levels, and changes of species distribution in freshwater areas. In response to these concerns and projections, the Japanese government is enhancing land use regulations in flood prone areas. Local planning is based in part on the watershed and the watershed water supply plan. In 2010, the Approaches to Climate Change Adaption was developed to assist decision makers in designing and evaluating adaptation responses to climate risks.

In many areas of waste management, Japan is a regional and emerging world leader. It will face challenges of energy deficits and climate change effects. It has relied on nuclear energy, but there are international concerns about safety as well as nuclear waste final disposition.

Further Reading

Climate Change Impacts on Water Systems. www.oecd.org.

Pratama, M., et al. 2014. "Modeling Migration of Cs-137 in Sewer System of Fukushima City Using Model for Radionuclide Migration in Urban Environment and Drainage System." *International Journal of Engineering and Technology* 6: forthcoming.

Prime Minister of Japan and Cabinet. www.kantei.go.jp.

Tokuda, K., et al. 2014. "A Survey Conducted Immediately after the 2011 Great East Japan Earthquake: Evaluation of Infectious Risks Associated with Sanitary Conditions in Evacuation Centers." *Journal of Infection and Chemotherapy* 20: 498–501.

JORDAN

Israel, the West Bank, Saudi Arabia, Iraq, and Syria border the Middle Eastern country of Jordan. The Great Rift Valley separates the Jordan River. Mostly it is on flat terrain. The climate is desert, hot and semi-arid, though there is a rainy season from November to April. Natural resources include oil, potash, and phosphates. Altogether, 6.5 million people live on 89,328 km² of land and 26 km of coastline. Eighty-two percent are urbanized, and 49 percent live in a city having more than 100,000 inhabitants people. Jordan has among the fastest-growing population rates in the world.

Current Waste Practices

Water quality is very poor. Most cities have sewer and water services but discharge untreated wastes into freshwater. Eighty-seven percent of the rural population and 94 percent of the urban population has access to improved sanitation. Ninety-seven percent of the rural population and almost all the urban population has access to an improved water source. Much of this was assisted by international aid. In 2012, USAID spent $5.5 million in Jordan for reduction of public health threats. Another $19.3 million was allocated to improving water supply and sanitation. This resulted in 1.7 million people's getting improved service quality from existing improved water sources. Improved water service quality requires that the time to get water from an improved source be less than 30 minutes. It also resulted in 4,820 people gaining access to an improved sanitation facility. This requires either a new site or a rehabilitated site. An improved sanitation facility is one that separates the waste from anything else.

Altogether, 3,864,000 tons of municipal waste was collected in 2008. This waste is trucked to open landfills and dumpsites on the edge of town. It is occasionally burned to make room for more trash. Waste pickers scavenge these sites and the streets for recyclable materials and sustenance.

Emissions and Industry

In 2000, Jordan generated 19,401.9 metric tons of greenhouse gas, a 12 percent decrease from 1994.

Emissions from agricultural wastes accounted for 0.94 percent of all emissions. Within this sector, agricultural soils accounted for 99 percent of emissions, and manure management 0.36 percent.

Jordan produces a small amount of crude oil and maintains proven reserves. Natural gas production and consumption are high, with large proven reserves of natural gas. Energy emissions accounted for 77 percent of all emissions. Within this sector, energy industries accounted for 37 percent of emissions, transportation 24 percent, and manufacturing and construction 12.5 percent. Industrial emissions accounted for 8 percent of all emissions. Within this sector, mineral products accounted for all emissions.

Waste emissions accounted for 14 percent of all emissions. Within this sector, solid waste disposal on land accounted for 92 percent of emissions, and wastewater management 7 percent.

Major Waste Issues

Water scarcity is the all-encompassing issue. Because untreated wastewater can affect groundwater waste management is a big issue. The protection of public health both in the country and the region are high priorities. There are many infectious diseases here, in particular hepatitis A, hepatitis B, typhoid, dengue fever, and schistosomiasis. Two percent or more of the population is persistently infected with hepatitis B.

There is a chance that infectious disease vectors will expand from outbreaks to epidemics. Rapid population growth and urbanization, poor sanitation practices and facility access all facilitate infectious diseases. Long droughts and desertification have had substantial environmental and public health effects. With increasing temperatures, desertification will increase and heighten these effects.

Further Reading

Fraiwan, L., et al. 2013. "Medical Waste Management Practices in Southern Jordan." *Environment and Waste Management* 11: 255–266.

Government of Jordan. www.kinghussein.gov.jo.

Haddadin, M., ed. 2006. *Water Resources in Jordan: Evolving Policies for Development, the Environment, and Conflict Resolution.* Washington, DC: Resources for the Future.

Jaber, S., et al. 2014. "An Exploratory Comparative Study of Recent Spatial and Removal Characteristics of Cutaneous Leishmaniasis in the Hashemite Kingdom of Jordan and Syrian Arab Republic pre–Arab Spring and Their Health Policy Implications." *Journal of Applied Spatial Analysis* 7: 337–360.

KAZAKHSTAN

Kazakhstanis are making the slow transition to membership in the global community after years of rule by the Soviet Union. China, Kyrgyzstan, Russia, Turkmenistan, and Uzbekistan currently border Kazakhstan. The terrain is varied, with mountains in the west. The tallest mountain is Pik Khan-Tengri, at almost 7,000 m. There are deserts in the south. Most of the vast interior is flat. The climate is also varied. Overall, the winters are cold and the summers hot and dry.

Altogether, 17.7 million people live on Kazakhstan's 2,724,900 km² of land. There are many small communities. Fifty-seven percent of the population is urbanized, and 43 percent lives in a city having more than 100,000 inhabitants. Eighteen percent suffers malnutrition. Life expectancy is 64 years.

Current Waste Practices

Most cities have basic, old sewer systems. In rural areas, waste practices can be basic, with pit toilets, latrines, drainage ditches, and cesspools. Water quality is very poor. Kazakhstan is slowly developing enforcement of environmental laws and gaining appreciation for an integrated waste management. In November 2014, Kazakhstan began to plan for integrated waste management in eight cities and plans to increase waste management planning to include forty-one cities by 2020. Almost all this waste is disposed in illegal landfills around cities now, where it is occasionally burned. Any recycling done is performed by waste pickers.

Water is very scarce, limited to about 6,000 m³ per person per year. Available water sources that can be economically accessed are about 43 km³ a year. Groundwater provides drinking water for about 65 percent of the population. Poor irrigation practices along with high levels of water pollution are considered to be a direct cause of an increase in morbidity. Seventy-nine percent of the urban population and 36 percent of the rural population has access to water supply sources that do not require urgent repair. Sixty-three percent of the urban population has access to sewage connections that are not in need of urgent repair. There are about 23,500 km of water pipes and 11,200 km of sewage systems in urban areas. The Ministry of Public Health, through the Committee for Sanitary and Epidemiological Supervision, monitors drinking water quality and supply.

Emissions and Industry

Kazakhstan generated 283,550 metric tons of greenhouse gases in 2012, a 21 percent decrease from 1990.

There is a substantial amount of arable land. Agricultural products include cotton, wheat and other grains, and livestock. Agricultural emissions accounted for 8 percent of all emissions. Within this sector, enteric fermentation accounted for 57 percent of emissions, agricultural soils 23 percent, and manure management 19 percent. This is a high amount of greenhouse gas emissions from manure, indicating the presence of large amounts of untreated feces.

Kazakhstan produced substantial amounts of crude oil and maintains massive proven reserves. Energy emissions accounted for 85 percent of all emissions. Within this sector, energy industries accounted for 44 percent of emissions, manufacturing and construction industries 12 percent, and transportation 10 percent. Fourteen percent of energy emissions were fugitive emissions. Considering the overall size of this sector, the high amount of fugitive emissions will have a greater effect on the environment and public health. Industrial emissions accounted for 6 percent of all emissions. Within this sector, metal production accounted for 60 percent of emissions, mineral products 30 percent, and chemical industries 1.5 percent.

Waste emissions accounted for 1 percent of all emissions. Within this sector, solid waste disposal on land accounted for 86 percent of emissions and wastewater handling 14 percent.

Major Waste Issues

The main environmental issues are waste issues. Water quality dominates pollution and waste issues in this dry and arid climate. There are radioactive and otherwise toxic waste sites in many areas. The two biggest rivers are now diverted for irrigation, leaving behind sediment saturated with waste and agricultural runoff of pesticides and fertilizers. The major waste issue is the protection of public health both in the country and the region, primarily through groundwater protection.

Climate changes of increased temperatures and extreme weather events are creating concerns about droughts and fires. Water scarcity is emerging as a major concern. There is a chance that infectious disease vectors will expand from outbreaks to epidemics. Urban waste management is a growing challenge.

Further Reading

Climate Change and Its Impact on Kazakhstan's Human Development. www.hdr.undp.org. Government of the Republic of Kazakhstan. www.government.kz.

Khan, W., et al. 2014. "Refinery Wastewater Degradation with Titanium Dioxide, Zinc Oxide and Hydrogen Peroxide in a Photocatalytic Reactor." *Process Safety and Environmental Protection:* in press.

Roelen, K. 2014. "Beyond Averages: Child Well-Being in Kazakhstan." *Journal of Children and Poverty* 20: 91–110.

KENYA

Kenya is bordered by Tanzania, Uganda, South Sudan, Ethiopia, Somalia, Lake Victoria, and the Indian Ocean. The Great Rift Valley cuts through flat land that rises to a plateau in the interior. The highest mountain is Mount Kenya, at almost 6,000

Children play near waste in Kibera, Kenya, Africa's largest poor urban neighborhood, on December 6, 2010. Children in poor urban areas are often exposed to waste and suffer health consequences. (John Wollwerth/Dreamstime.com)

m. Western Kenya is hot and humid, whereas northern and eastern Kenya is hot and dry. The climate is tropical, with regional variations. The coast is hot and humid. The interior rises to over 5,000 m and moderates the heat and humidity. The dry season is from June to October. Natural resources include zinc, limestone, gypsum, and hydropower. More than 45 million people live on Kenya's 580,367 km² of land and a 536 km coastline. It is a nation dominated by small communities. Twenty-one percent of Kenyans are urbanized, and 16 percent live in a city having more than 100,000 inhabitants. Kenya gained nation status in 1963. There has been civil unrest and environmental destruction since 2007. The life expectancy is 53 years.

Current Waste Practices

Waste practices are basic, including pit toilets, latrines, drainage ditches, cesspools, and open defecation. Eighty-five percent of the urban population and 49 percent of the rural population has access to an improved water source, which involves separating drinking water from wastewater. Only 19 percent of the urban population and 48 percent of the rural population has access to proper sanitation facilities. The open defecation rate in 2012 was 13 percent. Thirty-one percent suffer chronic malnutrition. The primary cause of death is malaria, the child mortality rate is 120 per 1,000, and HIV prevalence is 6.1 percent. About 23,700 deaths a year are attributed to unsafe water. Diarrhea, malaria, and asthma rates are elevated.

Cholera was detected in 1971 and occurred in waves. In 2009, there were 11,769 cases of cholera, including 274 deaths confirmed in laboratories. Many areas do not report health information, so the numbers could be higher, especially in areas with civil strife and environmental destruction.

International assistance helped alleviate sanitation issues. In 2012, the World Bank International Development Association extended $300 million in credit to increase water and sanitation services in the fastest growing areas. This program sought to narrow the gap in services between rich and poor by developing a social connections program that tried to reach the poorest people.

Emissions and Industry

In 1994, Kenya generated 21,466.2 metric tons of greenhouse gases. It is likely that greenhouse gas emissions are higher because of population increases and the reliance on agriculture

There is a significant amount of arable land. Agricultural products include coffee, tea, wheat, corn, sugar cane, fruits, vegetables, livestock, dairy products, and poultry. Agricultural emissions accounted for 56 percent of all emissions. Within this sector, enteric fermentation accounted for 95 percent of emissions and manure management 4 percent.

The electrical grid is out for almost eighty-four days a year. Oil and electricity per capita production and consumption are low. Energy emissions accounted for 37.5 percent of all emissions. Within this sector, other accounted for 99 percent. Industrial emissions accounted for 5 percent of all emissions. Within this sector, mineral products accounted for 100 percent of emissions.

Emissions from wastes accounted for 1.5 percent of all emissions. Within this sector, wastewater management accounted for 55.5 percent of emissions, and disposal on solid land 44 percent.

Major Waste Issues

The lack of integrated waste management is a large challenge. Waste collection, transfer, storage, treatment, and final disposition are all without basic infrastructure and resources. There is water pollution from untreated sewage and industrial discharges, as well as degraded water quality from agricultural runoff of chemical fertilizers and pesticides.

Climate change observers note increased temperatures and sea level rise. There are concerns about droughts, fires, and floods. There are also concerns about widespread epidemics because of drought-induced food and water shortages. Kenya's agriculture is rainfed, making it vulnerable to climate change effects. Agriculture accounts for more than a quarter of the gross domestic product. In 2013, Kenya developed the National Climate Change Action Plan. Part of this effort was a massive forest restoration plan to combat green house gases. The Office of the Prime Minister also incorporates a Climate Change Unit for technical issues. The government is encouraging farmers to grow crops and raise livestock that are drought resistant. Kenya is developing climate change effect mitigation strategies for each sector and disaster preparedness for each urban area. Nairobi, the capital and largest city, has about 3.4 million people. The other large city is Mombasa, which has almost 1 million people.

A waste issue is the protection of public health both in the country and the region. Yellow fever, cholera, hepatitis A, hepatitis B, typhoid, malaria, dengue fever, and schistosomiasis occur in Kenya. Two percent or more of the population is persistently infected with hepatitis B. There is a chance that infectious disease vectors will expand from outbreaks to epidemics. With increasing temperatures, desertification will increase and heighten these effects. There are inadequate public resources in the country to handle internal, regional, and global health concerns. International intervention is already occurring, but more is needed.

Further Reading

Blakeney, Michael, Thierry Coulet, Getachew Mengiste, and Marcelin Tonye Mahop, eds. 2012. *Extending the Protection of Geographical Indications: Case Studies of Agricultural Products in Africa.* New York: Earthscan Publishing.

Dreilbelbis, R., et al. 2014. "The Impact of School Water, Sanitation and Hygiene Interventions on the Health of Younger Siblings of Pupils: A Cluster-Randomized Trial in Kenya." *American Journal of Public Health* 104: 91–97.

Lagerhvist, C., et al. 2014. "Health in Perspective: Framing Motivational Factors for Personal Sanitation in Urban Slums in Nairobi, Kenya Using Anchored Best–Worst Scaling." *Journal of Water, Sanitation and Hygiene for Development* 4: 108–119.

President of Kenya. www.president.go.ke.

KIRIBATI

Tropical islands characterize the tiny nation of Kiribati, a group of thirty-three coral atolls on the Pacific Ocean far from the main continents. It is situated directly on the Equator and is surrounded by a large natural system of coral reefs. The climate is tropical—hot and humid. Natural resources include fish. More than 103,000 people live on 811 km^2 of land and 1,143 km of coastline. Forty-seven percent are urbanized, and no city has more than 100,000 inhabitants.

Current Waste Practices

Sanitation is an issue of international concern and local quality of life. Freshwater is scarce, mostly from rainwater. There are inadequate sanitation and drinking water facilities. In 2014, there was freshwater for two hours every two days here.

It is estimated that about 35,000 people get sick from diarrhea, dysentery, acute diarrhea, and related diseases each year. Open defecation is traditionally practiced, which leaves wastes in bushes and by the ocean. In 2012, the capital city of South Tarawa's lack of water management for existing toilets, lack of hand washing, and open defecation in overcrowded conditions led to outbreaks of death in children from preventable infectious diseases.

Emissions and Industry

Kiribati emitted 18.6 metric tons of greenhouse gas in 1994. It is likely that greenhouse gas emissions are higher because of population increases and reliance on agriculture

There is little arable land. Agricultural crops include taro, breadfruit, sweet potatoes, vegetables, and fish. Agricultural emissions accounted for 2 percent of all emissions. Within this sector, enteric fermentation accounted for 99 percent of emissions and manure management 1 percent.

Energy emissions accounted for 66 percent of all emissions. Within this sector, other accounted for all emissions. Considering the overall size of this sector, the high amount of fugitive emissions will have a greater effect on the environment and public health. Fugitive emissions are essentially unaccounted waste streams into the air. Fugitive emissions can affect regional ecosystems and the public health, because they can fall from the air to the land and water. Industrial emissions accounted for none of the emissions.

Waste emissions accounted for 32 percent of all emissions. This is an unusually high percentage of overall greenhouse gas emissions. Within this sector, solid waste disposal on land accounted for 100 percent of emissions.

Major Waste Issues

The major waste issue is the protection of public health both in the country and the region. Rising ocean levels, more severe storms, and increased temperatures will have significant environmental effects. Infectious diseases include hepatitis A, hepatitis B, dengue fever, and typhoid. Two percent or more of the population is persistently infected with hepatitis B. There is a chance that infectious disease vectors will expand. There are inadequate public resources in the country to handle internal, regional, and global health concerns. There is international assistance. In 2014, the Asian Development Bank and Australia began a $22.5 million sewage project in South Tarawa. This project will upgrade existing sewer systems for improved access to low-income households and to begin education programs on sanitation behavior and hygiene.

Further Reading

Clarke, J. 2014. "Island Ways." *Engineering Insight* 15, iss. 4.
McIver, L., et al. 2014. "Assessment of the Health Impacts of Climate Change in Kiribati." *International Journal of Environmental Research and Public Health* 11: 5224–5240.

National Sanitation Policy 2010. www.climate.gov.ki.

Parliament of Kiribati. www.parliament.gov.ki.

Storey, Donovan, and Shawn Hunter. 2010. "Kiribati: An Environmental Perfect Storm." *Australian Geographer* 41: 167–181.

KOSOVO

Kosovo is one of the newest nations on Earth. In 2008, Kosovo declared independence from Serbia after bitter conflicts in the region. Albania, Macedonia, Montenegro, and Serbia border Kosovo. The terrain has a flat interior surrounded by mountains. Winters are cold with snow, and summers are hot and dry, although there are regional differences. Natural resources include lead, zinc, nickel, chrome, and hydropower.

Altogether, 1.8 million people live on Kosovo's 10,908 km² of land. Cities are rapidly increasing in population. Currently the capital and largest city of Pristina is home to about 400,000 people, Prizren 110,000, Peja 70,000, and Mitrovica 70,000.

Current Waste Practices

Most cities have sewer and water services but discharge untreated wastes into freshwater. Waste practices in rural areas can be basic—pit toilets, latrines, drainage ditches, and cesspools. Ninety percent of the urban population and only 10 percent of the rural population has waste collection services. Most of this waste is brought to dumps, and attempts are being made to increase sanitary landfills. It is estimated that almost 400,000 tons of solid wastes are produced per year, mostly from unsanitary landfills and untreated sewage. There is little official incineration. Like many nations, Kosovo is limited to medical wastes near hospitals. The Hydro-meteorological Institute monitors surface water quality at more than twenty hydrometric stations, but there is no monitoring of urban wastewater or groundwater. There are few water resources in Kosovo. All rivers are polluted with high levels of biological oxygen demand. There is also a lack of dissolved oxygen because of the lack of waste and water treatment. Emissions from manure management are high. Much waste is burned in homes and businesses. Waste generation per capita is low. Informal systems of recycling are culturally institutionalized. Waste separation and recycling systems are not in place.

Kosovo is developing its waste infrastructure with help from the European Union (EU). Kosovo seeks admission to the EU but needs help to raise them to EU standards. The "ascension" process is the long process of applying for membership to the EU. The EU offers an Instrument for Pre-Accession Assistance to candidate and potential candidate countries, such as Kosovo. In order to meet UN Millennium Development goals for sanitation, Kosovo would need to connect about 1 million more households to sewer systems, and the wastewater from 1.6 million more people would need to be treated.

Emissions and Industry

Kosovo generated 10.5 metric tons of greenhouse gases in 2009, an 11 percent increase from 2008. It is pursuing low emission economic development plan with help from the EU.

There is a substantial amount of arable land. More than half the country's land is agricultural. Agricultural emissions accounted for 13 percent of all emissions. Energy industries are the source of 82 percent of all emissions. Waste emissions accounted for 3 percent of all emissions.

Major Waste Issues

The major waste issues in Kosovo are reconstructing and constructing a waste infrastructure. Damages from civil conflict destroyed what waste infrastructure existed. The high levels of water pollution partially result from untreated wastewater. A major waste management challenge is to begin monitoring groundwater, developing a waste treatment infrastructure, and increasing decision-making capacity at the local level. Some of the waste clean up is also necessary because of radioactivity.

Further Reading

Ashford, Mary-Wynne, and Ulrich Gottstein. 2000. "The Impact on Civilians of the Bombing of Kosovo and Serbia." *Medicine, Conflict, and Survival* 16: 267–280.
Outon, D., and V. Kashparov, eds. 2009. *Radioactive Particles in the Environment.* Dordrecht, Netherlands: Springer Netherlands.
The Republic of Kosovo Prime Minister. www.kryeministri-ks.net.

KUWAIT

Kuwait is a low-lying nation in the Middle East, covered with a sandy desert. Altogether, 2.7 million people live on 17,818 km^2 of land and almost 500 km of coastline. Most people live in Kuwait City, which has a population of 2.4 million. Ninety-eight percent of the population is urbanized. In 2014, it had the fifth-fastest-growing population rate in the world.

Current Waste Practices

Kuwait collected 1,723,000 tons of municipal waste in 2009, 100 percent of it landfilled. Everyone has access to an improved water source and sanitation facilities. Almost all wastewater is treated. Kuwait provides sanitation assistance to countries in the region. In 2013, Kuwait gave $53 million to UNICEF for children's sanitation needs in Syria. The goal is to prevent the spread of disease from lack of adequate sanitation facilities.

Emissions and Industry

In 1994, Kuwait generated 32,373.4 metric tons of greenhouse gases. It is likely that greenhouse gas emissions are higher because of population increases and rapid urbanization.

Agricultural emissions accounted for 0.2 percent of all emissions. Within this sector, enteric fermentation accounted for 79.5 percent of emissions, agricultural soils 14 percent, and manure management 6 percent.

Kuwait produces large amounts of crude oil and maintains massive proven reserves. Electricity consumption is high and is higher than production. Oil consumption and production per capita are high. Energy emissions accounted for 95 percent of all emissions. Within this sector, energy industries accounted for 75 percent of emissions, and transportation 17 percent.

Industrial emissions accounted for 2 percent of all emissions. Within this sector, mineral products accounted for all emissions.

Emissions from wastes accounted for 2.4 percent of all emissions. Within this sector, solid waste disposal on land accounted for 90.5 percent of greenhouse gas emissions, and wastewater management 9.5 percent.

Major Waste Issues

The major environmental issue is freshwater. There are concerns about desertification and air and water pollution. Large desalinization facilities produce freshwater from saltwater. They are usually powered by fossil fuel and produce greenhouse gases. The biggest challenge in waste management is the harsh, dry desert environment.

Further Reading

Amiri Diwan of the State of Kuwait. www.da.gov.kw.

Hamoda, M., et al. 2012. "Artificial Ground Water Recharge Using Treated Wastewater Effluents." *Qatar Foundation Annual Research Forum Proceedings.*

Umar, M., et al. 2015. "Recent Advancements in the Treatment of Municipal Wastewater Reverse Osmosis Concentrate—An Overview." *Critical Reviews in Environmental Science and Technology* 45: 193–248.

KYRGYZSTAN

The large Tien Shan mountains dominate the Central Asian nation of Kyrgyzstan, covering 95 percent of the land. The highest mountain is Pik Pobedy, at 7,439 m. There are large valleys and basins before the foothills. China, Kazakhstan, Tajikistan, and Uzbekistan border Kyrgyzstan. The climate is varied. It is cold and dry in the mountains. As the altitude decreases, the climate becomes more temperate, with less severe winters and warmer summers. Some of the large valleys in the southwest are much warmer and wetter. Natural resources include oil, coal, gas, gold, lead, zinc, mercury and hydropower.

Kyrgyzstan is a nation of small communities. Altogether, 5.5 million people live on 199,951 km² of land. Thirty-six percent are urbanized, and 16 percent live in a city having more than 100,000 inhabitants. Life expectancy is 66 years.

Current Waste Practices

Kyrgyzstan collected 6,642,000 tons of municipal waste in 2009, but more is generated. All of the waste was landfilled or put in dumps on the edge of town.

Altogether, 5,581,000 tons of hazardous wastes were generated in 2008. Occasionally trash is burned to make room for more waste. Waste picker communities scavenge these site for recyclable materials and sustenance.

Most cities have sewer and water services but discharge untreated wastes into freshwater. Kyrgyzstan has the fifth-dirtiest water in the world as measured by BOD (biological oxygen demand). Fifteen percent of the rural population does not have access to an improved drinking water source. Six percent of the urban population does not have access to improved sanitation facilities.

The capital city of Bishkek is improving its waste system with loan of $11 million from the European Bank for Reconstruction and Development and a grant of $3 million. This project is to establish new solid waste collection points throughout the city, upgrade the collection vehicles, build the first European Union–compliant sanitary landfill in the region, and close the current open landfill and surrounding dumps. The existing landfill was built for about 3 million m^3 of trash and now contains more than 24 million m^3 of trash. Most of the project is through Tazalyk, which is a municipal solid waste business. They will also manage and operate the new landfill. The project will also resettle the community of waste pickers now living near the existing dumpsite. This includes livelihood restoration assistance for waste pickers.

Emissions and Industry

In 2005, Kyrgyzstan generated 22,329 metric tons of greenhouse gases, a 60 percent decrease from 1990.

Agricultural products include tobacco, cotton, fruits, vegetables, potatoes, and livestock. Agricultural emissions accounted for 16 percent of all emissions. Within this sector, enteric fermentation accounted for 87 percent of emissions, manure management 9 percent, and field burning of agricultural residues 2.5 percent.

Kyrgyzstan produces some crude oil and maintains proven reserves. Hydropower is a major source of energy. Energy emissions accounted for 74 percent of all emissions. Within this sector, transportation accounted for 28 percent of emissions, energy industries 25 percent, manufacturing and construction 7 percent, and fugitive emissions 4 percent. Industrial emissions accounted for 4 percent of all emissions. Within this sector, mineral products accounted for 95 percent of emissions and metal products 1 percent.

Waste emissions accounted for 5.5 percent of all emissions. Within this sector, solid waste disposal on land accounted for 78 percent of emissions and wastewater handling 22 percent.

Major Waste Issues

Water availability is limited and is based on agreements with five neighboring nations. Kyrgyzstan can keep a quarter of the water that originates from it, and several other countries can keep whatever comes into their country. A controversial issue is whether any compensation for water is required. All the quarter allocation is used. Almost 90 percent of it is used in irrigation and only 4 percent in municipal water systems.

Water pollution is a major problem that affects public health. Mining operations discharge significant amounts of industrial wastes into rivers. Inefficient irrigation methods have resulted in increasing salinization of the soil and surrounding water. Almost a quarter of households get water from nearby groundwater sources. There is extensive water pollution in all human settlements and no waste treatment before discharge into water. It is estimated that water pollution causes a quarter of the health problems. Infectious diseases in Kyrgyzstan include hepatitis A, hepatitis B, typhoid, and malaria. Two percent or more of the population is persistently infected with hepatitis B. Most wasteborne infectious diseases from water is in the south.

Another waste management challenge is the environment. It is seismically unstable in many areas, making the landscape prone to natural disasters such as avalanches, rockslides, mudslides, landslides, earthquakes, and flooding. This is a challenge to water management and waste treatment facilities in mountainous areas. Climate change will increase the range of hospitable environments for some infectious diseases. There is a chance that infectious disease vectors will expand. Population growth, urbanization, and poor sanitation practices and facility access put this country at risk for more infectious diseases.

Further Reading

Kyrgyz Republic Rural Water Supply and Sanitation Project. www.worldbank.org.

Sim, N., et al. 2013. "Waste Management and Recycling in the Former Soviet Union: The City of Bishkek, Kyrgyz Republic (Kyrgyzstan)." *Waste Management and Research* 31: 106–125.

Women in Europe for a Common Future. 2014. *Improving Water and Sanitation through Decentralized Cooperation in the Republic of Kyrgyzstan: A Feasibility Study Carried Out in the Frame of the United Nations Development Program Global Water Solidarity Platform.* Utrecht, Netherlands: Women in Europe for a Common Future.

LAOS

Cambodia, China, Myanmar, Thailand, and Vietnam border landlocked Laos. The terrain is mountainous. The Mekong River forms the boundary with Myanmar and Thailand. The climate is tropical, with a monsoon season from May to November. Natural resources include gold, tin, timber, and hydropower. Overall, 6.8 million people live on Laos's 236,800 km^2 of land. About a third of the population is urban, and the nation is urbanizing at a rapid rate. There are also many small rural communities.

Current Waste Practices

The majority of the population of Laos does not have access to potable water. Seventy percent of the rural population and 40 percent of the urban population does use an improved drinking water source. Sixty-two percent of the rural population and 13 percent of the urban population does not have access to improved sanitation. Waste practices are very basic—pit toilets, latrines, drainage ditches, cesspools, and open defecation.

There is governmental waste collection. Most but not all urban municipal wastes are trucked to open or uncontrolled landfills.

Emissions and Industry

In 2000, Laos generated 8,898.2 metric tons of greenhouse gases, a 30 percent increase from 1990. It is likely that greenhouse gas emissions are higher now because of population increases, urbanization and industrialization, and reliance on agriculture.

There is a substantial amount of arable land. Agricultural products include rice, coffee, tea, tobacco, sugar cane, cotton, corn, vegetables, poultry, and livestock. Agricultural emissions accounted for 86 percent of all emissions. Within this sector, rice cultivation accounted for 38 percent of emissions, agricultural soils 31 percent, enteric fermentation 27 percent, and manure management almost 4 percent.

Oil and electrical per capita production and consumption are low. Energy emissions accounted for 12 percent of all emissions. Within this sector, manufacturing industries and construction accounted for 44 percent of emissions, transportation 43 percent, and energy industries almost 2 percent. Industrial emissions accounted for less than 1 percent of all emissions. More than 98 percent of these were from mineral products.

Waste emissions accounted for almost 2 percent of all emissions. Within this sector, wastewater handling accounted for 83 percent of emissions and solid waste disposal on land 17 percent.

Major Waste Issues

Pollution in the air and water from waste is one of the main environmental problems. There is little municipal waste collection. Most trash is moved out to the edge of the village or city. Waste pickers peruse it and burn waste looking for recyclable materials, food, clothing, and shelter items.

Climate change effects create concerns of drought and flooding. Laos developed laws and regulation to increase climate resilience. They plan to increase irrigation, manage water flow during floods, and perform Climate Change Rapid Assessments.

There are infectious diseases in Laos, including cholera, dengue fever, hepatitis A, hepatitis B, Japanese encephalitis, and schistosomiasis. There is a high risk of malaria in many regions. Rapid urbanization in an inadequate waste infrastructure may increase disease vectors under current climate change scenarios.

Further Reading

Conlan, J. 2012. "Soil-Transmitted Helminthiasis in Laos." *American Journal of Tropical Medicine and Hygiene* 86: 624–634.

Crawshaw, L., et al. 2014. "Lessons from an Integrated Community Health Education Initiative in Rural Laos." *World Development* 64: 487–502.

Government of Laos. www.un.int/lao/government.php.

Snelder, D., and D. Lasco, eds. 2008. *Smallholder Tree Growing for Rural Development and Environmental Services: Lessons from Asia.* Heidelberg, Germany: Springer Press.

LATVIA

Belarus, Estonia, Lithuania, Russia, and the Baltic Sea border Latvia. The terrain is flat and low. The climate is temperate, with warm summers and wet winters. Natural resources include limestone, dolomite, peat, amber, timber and hydropower. Altogether, 2.8 million people live on 64,000 km^2 of land and 498 km of coastline. Sixty-eight percent are urbanized, and 42 percent live in a city having more than 100,000 inhabitants. Four percent live in overcrowded conditions.

Current Waste Practices

Most communities have modern sewer and water systems, but not all wastewater is fully treated before being discharged into freshwater. Eighteen percent of the urban population does not have access to improved sanitation facilities. Twenty-nine percent of the rural population does not have access to improved sanitation facilities.

About half the population has municipal waste collection. Latvia collected 4,312,000 tons of municipal waste in 2009. Almost 75 percent of the waste is landfilled, 9.4 percent incinerated, 13.4 percent recycled, and about 2 percent composted. About 82,130 metric tons of hazardous wastes was generated in 2001.

Emissions and Industry

Latvia generated 10,978.5 metric tons of greenhouse gases in 2012, a 58 percent decrease from 1990.

There is a substantial amount of arable land. Agricultural products include grains, potatoes, vegetables, pork, dairy products, fish, and eggs. Agricultural emissions accounted for 22 percent of all emissions. Within this sector, agricultural soils accounted for 62.5 percent of emissions, enteric fermentation 28 percent, and manure management 9 percent.

Latvia produces crude oil and maintains proven reserves. Large amounts of electricity are produced with hydropower. Energy emissions accounted for 66 percent of all emissions. Within this sector, transportation accounted for 39 percent of emissions, energy industries 26 percent, manufacturing and construction 13 percent, and fugitive emissions almost 1 percent. Industrial emissions accounted for 7 percent of all emissions. Within this sector, mineral products accounted for 85.5 percent of emissions.

Waste emissions accounted for 4.5 percent of all emissions. Within this sector, solid waste disposal on land accounted for 75 percent of emissions and wastewater handling 25 percent.

Major Waste Issues

The main environmental problems in Latvia are all waste issues. Water and sewer systems are a high priority. Air pollution and hazardous waste management are also priorities.

The major waste issue is the protection of public health. There are infectious diseases present in Latvia, including hepatitis A, hepatitis B, tick-borne encephalitis, and typhoid occur here. Two percent or more of the population is persistently infected with hepatitis B. Climate change observers note increased temperatures, more precipitation, and decreased snow coverage. The increase in temperatures could expand the range for ticks and the infectious diseases they can carry.

Further Reading

Agyeman, Julian, and Yelena Ogneva-Himmelberger. 2009. *Environmental Justice and Sustainability in the Former Soviet Union*. Cambridge, MA: MIT Press.

Bellinger, Ed, ed. 2000. *Environmental Assessment in Countries in Transition*. Portland, OR: LLC. Books International.

Latvian President's Office. www.president.lv.

LEBANON

Lebanon is bordered by Israel, Syria, and the Mediterranean Sea. The terrain is mainly a flat area along the coast, with a large valley inland called El Beqaa. There are mountains in the west. The climate is moderate and wetter than the surrounding countries. Summers are hot and dry, and winters are mild and wet. The Lebanon mountains receive heavy snow fall. Natural resources include iron ore, salt, limestone, and water. Altogether, 4.1 million people live on 10,400 km^2 of land and 225 km of coastline.

Eighty-seven percent of the population is urbanized, and 74 percent lives in a city having more than 100,000 inhabitants. The cities are densely populated. Ten percent live in overcrowded conditions. Forty-five percent suffers malnutrition.

Current Waste Practices

Waste practices are very basic, including pit toilets, latrines, drainage ditches, cesspools, and open defecation. Water quality is very poor.

Lebanon collected 1.72 million tons of municipal waste in 2009, almost 78 percent of it landfilled, 8 percent recycled, and about 14 percent composted. Altogether, 108,218 tons of hazardous wastes were generated in 2001.

Emissions and Industry

Lebanon generated 18,446.8 metric tons of greenhouse gases in 2000, a 17.5 percent increase from 1990.

Agricultural products include fruits, vegetables, tobacco, and livestock. Agricultural emissions accounted for 6 percent of all emissions. Within this sector, agricultural soils accounted for 77 percent of emissions, enteric fermentation 12 percent, and manure management 11 percent.

Electricity can be intermittent. The power grid is down for at least 188 days a year, among the most in the world. Energy emissions accounted for 75 percent of all emissions. Within this sector, energy industries accounted for 42 percent of emissions, transportation 28.5 percent, and manufacturing and construction industries 20.5 percent. Industrial emissions accounted for 10 percent of all emissions. Within this sector, mineral products accounted for 92 percent of emissions and metal production 7 percent.

Waste emissions accounted for 9.5 percent of all emissions. Within this sector, solid waste disposal on land accounted for 94.5 percent of emissions and wastewater handling 5 percent.

Major Waste Issues

Many environmental problems in Lebanon are also waste issues. Raw sewage and oil spills pollute the coast. There is air pollution, especially in the cities. The major waste issue is the protection of public health in both the country and the region. There are infectious diseases here, such as hepatitis A, hepatitis B, typhoid, and schistosomiasis. Two percent or more of the population is persistently infected with hepatitis B.

Further Reading

Haase, T. 2014. "Decentralization in Lebanon." *Public Administration, Governance, and Globalization* 9: 189–213.

Presidency of the Republic of Lebanon. www.presidency.gov.lb.

United Nations. 2007. *Lebanon: Post-conflict Environmental Assessment*. New York: United Nations Environment Programme.

LESOTHO

Lesotho is a highland African nation with its lowest point at 1,400 m and highest at 3,482 m. There are plateaus, rolling hills, and mountains. It is completely bordered by South Africa. The climate is temperate, with cool winters and rainy, hot summers. Diamonds are a natural resource.

Lesotho is a nation of small communities. Altogether, 2.2 million people live on 30,355 km² of land. Just 19 percent of the population is urbanized, and just 10 percent lives in a city having more than 100,000 inhabitants. Thirty-six percent lives below the international poverty level. Life expectancy is 42 years.

Current Waste Practices

Ninety-seven percent of the urban population has access to improved drinking water sources, but only 40 percent has access to an improved sanitary facility. Eighty-one percent of the rural population has access to improved drinking water sources, and just 25 percent has access to improved sanitation facilities. Waste practices can be very basic, including pit toilets, latrines, drainage ditches, cesspools, and open defecation.

There are also significant waste issues with e-wastes and hazardous medical wastes. Lesotho is grappling with these issues by developing plans and approaches. The goal for disposing hazardous medical waste is significant. Blood is a large component of this wastes and can be a vector for diseases if improperly disposed of. The recent Ebola outbreak has heightened sensitivities to this issue. Lesotho's lack of environmental enforcement may have attracted wastes from e-wastes internationally, thereby making it on the receiving end of a major new waste stream. There is both concern and hope around this issue, because some parts of this waste stream could be recycled or sold. It is still in the planning stages, and e-waste continues to come into the country.

Emissions and Industry

Lesotho generated 3,512.9 metric tons of greenhouse gases in 2000, a 93 percent increase from 1994. It is likely that greenhouse gases are higher now because of population increases and reliance on agriculture.

Agricultural products include wheat, corn, sorghum, barley, and livestock. Agricultural emissions accounted for 64 percent of all greenhouse gas emissions. Within this sector, enteric fermentation accounted for 72 percent of emissions. Energy and industrial emissions are unknown.

Waste emissions accounted for 3 percent of all greenhouse gas emissions. Within this sector, solid waste disposal on land accounted for 51 percent of emissions and wastewater handling 49 percent.

Major Waste Issues

The major waste issue is the protection of public health both in the country and the region. There are many infectious diseases here, with cholera, hepatitis A, hepatitis B, and typhoid present. Two percent or more of the population is persistently infected with hepatitis B.

There is a chance that infectious disease vectors from wastes will expand from outbreaks to epidemics. There are approximately 168 health centers and eight hospitals. There are historic issues of drug shortages and insufficient staff capacity. Climate change effects could increase infectious disease vectors that are created by wastes.

Further Reading

Africa Institute for the Environmentally Sound Management of Hazardous and Other Wastes. 2010. *Assessment of E-Waste Report: Kingdom of Lesotho.* www.africaninstitute .info.

Foeken, D. W. J., et al. 2013. *Sanitation in Africa: Access to Improved Sanitation Facilities and Improvement Index.* Leiden, The Netherlands: African Studies Center.

Lesotho Water and Sanitation Policy Support. www.eeas.europa.eu.

Showers, Kate B. 2005. *Imperial Gullies: Soil Erosion and Conservation in Lesotho.* Athens: Ohio University Press.

LIBERIA

Liberia is on the west coast of Africa and borders the North Atlantic Ocean, Guinea, Cote d'Ivoire, and Sierra Leone. The climate is tropical—hot and humid. The summers are rainy and hot, and the winters are dry and cooler. Natural resources include diamonds, iron ore, gold, timber, and hydropower. From the coast, the terrain becomes rolling hills with some mountains in the northeast. In 2014 and to the present Liberia had significant outbreaks of Ebola.

Four million Liberians live on 111,369 km² of land. There are many small communities. Fifty-eight percent of Liberians are urbanized, and 17 percent live in a city having more than 100,000 inhabitants. The life expectancy is 44 years. The infant mortality rate is high.

Current Waste Practices

Seventy-nine percent of the urban population has access to improved drinking water sources, and only 25 percent has access to an improved sanitary facility. Half of the rural population has access to improved drinking water sources, and only 4 percent has access to improved sanitary facilities. Waste practices can include pit toilets, latrines, drainage ditches, cesspools, and open defecation. Thirty-one percent of the people live in overcrowded conditions, and about 40 percent suffers malnutrition.

Very little waste is collected. Wastes include all kinds of hazardous and medical wastes. In the capital city of Monrovia, waste piles grow large enough to block city streets. Some wastes also taint public water sources. The governmental response has been to close wells that are too close to waste piles.

E-wastes are finding a place in Liberia. There are international efforts to enhance environmental governance and build capacity to monitor and control e-waste imports. Current efforts are to find out the volume and amount of e-wastes, as well as their sources and final disposition.

Emissions and Industry

Liberia generated 8,021.8 metric tons of greenhouse gases in 2000.

Agricultural products include coffee, rubber, cocoa, palm oil, cassava, sugar cane, bananas, goats, sheep, timber and hydropower. Agricultural emissions accounted for 32 percent of all emissions. Within this sector, enteric fermentation accounted for 96 percent of emissions, manure management 3 percent, and field burning of agricultural residues 1 percent.

Electrical energy production and consumption are low. There are frequent power outages in many places. Energy emissions accounted for 67.5 percent of all emissions. Within this sector, transportation accounted for 40 percent of emissions, energy industries 21 percent, and manufacturing and construction industries 2 percent.

Waste emissions accounted for 0.5 percent of all emissions. Within this sector, solid waste disposal on land accounted for 92 percent of emissions and wastewater handling 8 percent.

Major Waste Issues

The major waste issue is the protection of public health both in the country and the region. There is currently an outbreak of the deadly Ebola virus, which spreads through bodily fluids and by close contact. There are many other infectious diseases, such as yellow fever, cholera, hepatitis A, hepatitis B, typhoid, dengue fever, and schistosomiasis. Two percent or more of the population is persistently infected with hepatitis B. There is also a high risk of malaria.

There is a chance that infectious disease vectors will expand from outbreaks to epidemics. There are inadequate public resources in the country to handle internal, regional, and global health concerns.

Further Reading

Burt, Murray, and Bilha Joy Keiru. 2011. "Strengthening Post-Conflict Peacebuilding through Community Water Resource Management: Case Studies from Democratic Republic of Congo, Afghanistan, and Liberia." *Water International* 33: 232–241.

Electrical and Electronic Wastes. 2014. www.sustainabledevelopment.un.org.

Environmental Protection Agency of Liberia. 2013. *Liberia National Situation Report on the Sound Management of Chemicals*. New York: United Nations Development Program.

Executive Mansion. www.emansion.gov.lr.

LIBYA

Libya is a North African nation along the south coast of the Mediterranean Sea. The climate along the coast is cooler than the scorching flat desert of the interior. Algeria, Chad, Egypt, Niger, Sudan, and Tunisia border Libya. Natural resources include oil, gas, and gypsum.

Altogether, 5.9 million people live on Libya's 1,759,540 km² of land and 1,770 km of coastline. Eighty-five percent of Libyans are urbanized, and 85 percent live in a city having more than 100,000 inhabitants. About a fifth suffers malnutrition.

Current Waste Practices

Pit toilets, latrines, drainage ditches, cesspools, and open defecation are current waste practices. Urban areas do have modern sewage systems, but not everyone is connected to the system. Ninety-seven percent of the urban population has access to an improved sanitary facility. Ninety-six percent of the rural population has access to improved sanitary facilities. Waste collection practices are informal, and wastes often pile up in urban areas. What municipal solid wastes are collected are brought to open dumps outside of the community. Some of these wastes are occasionally burned.

Hospital wastes is a particular concern in Libya. Research from 114 health care facilities in Tripoli, Misurata, and Sirt indicates that there are no guidelines for collection, separation storage, or disposal of medical wastes. Close analysis of this particular waste stream found that 72 percent of hospital wastes are nonhazardous and 28 percent hazardous. The wastes from these hospitals were 38 percent organic, 24 percent plastics, and 20 percent paper. Medical instruments and tools were 26 percent of the hazardous waste.

Garbage bins stand full and uncollected in Tripoli, Libya, on March 24, 2011. The lack of waste collection can quickly turn waste collection points into trash heaps. (AP Photo/Jerome Delay)

Emissions and Industry

Libya generated about 366,000 metric tons of greenhouse gases in 2010. There is little emissions reporting.

Major Waste Issues

The major waste issue in Libya is the protection of public health both in the country and the region. Cholera, hepatitis A, hepatitis B, meningococcal meningitis, typhoid, and schistosomiasis are present in Libya. Two percent or more of the population is persistently infected with hepatitis B.

There is a chance that infectious disease vectors will expand from outbreaks to epidemics. Fresh drinking water is limited. Fresh piped water supplies are intermittent. Long droughts and desertification have had substantial environmental and public health effects. Climate change effects could expand waste-based disease vectors. There are inadequate public resources in the country to handle internal, regional, and global health concerns.

Further Reading

El-Khoury, Gabi. 2014. "Water Indicators in Arab Countries: Selected Indicators." *Contemporary Arab Affairs* 7: 339–349.

Environmental General Authority in Libya. www.ecomemaq.ntua.gr.

Sawalem, M., et al. 2009. "Hospital Waste Management in Libya: A Case Study." *Waste Management* 29: 1370–1375.

Strengthening Environment General Authority's Capacity for Sound Environmental Management in Libya. www.ly.undp.org.

LITHUANIA

Lithuania is bordered by the Baltic Sea, Latvia, Belarus, Poland, and Russia. Its terrain is flat, with extensive wetlands. The climate is temperate, with warm, wet summers and rainy winters. Natural resources include peat and amber. Altogether, 3.5 million people live on Lithuania's 65,300 km^2 of land and 90 km of coastline. Sixty-seven percent of Lithuanians are urbanized, and 42 percent live in a city having more than 100,000 inhabitants. Seven percent live in overcrowded conditions.

Current Waste Practices

Most cities in Lithuania have basic sewer and water services. Sixty-nine percent of the rural population and 95 percent of the urban population has improved sanitation access. Safe drinking water is generally available. Lithuania collected 1,206,000 tons of municipal waste in 2009. Ninety-one percent of the waste is landfilled, 3 percent recycled, and about 1.5 percent composted. In 2001, Lithuania generated 111,000 tons of hazardous wastes. Almost all municipalities have waste management plans, and almost 90 percent of the people receive waste management services.

As a member of the European Union, Lithuania is required to reduce the amount of municipal solid wastes sent to landfills by 65 percent from 1995 levels. The goal is to do this by 2016. There are more than 800 landfills, some illegal and most not up to sanitary levels. There are eleven large regional landfills. Forty-two percent of municipal wastes in 2008 were biodegradable, and 14 percent was paper and cardboard. Seventy-five percent of municipal wastes could be used for energy production, 35 percent was recyclable, and about 10 percent was "nonrecoverable."

Lithuania has prioritized closing illegal and unsanitary landfills and increasing waste to energy production, recycling, and universal waste management coverage.

Emissions and Industry

Lithuania generated 21,622.3 tons of greenhouse gas in 2012, a 55 percent decrease from 1990.

There is a substantial amount of arable land. Agricultural products include potatoes, grains, flax, vegetables, beef, eggs, dairy products, and sugar beets. Agricultural emissions accounted for 23 percent of all emissions. Within this sector, agricultural soils accounted for 61 percent of emissions, enteric fermentation 23 percent, and manure management 15 percent. This is a high amount of greenhouse gas emissions from manure, indicating the presence of large amounts of untreated feces.

Lithuania produces crude oil and maintains proven reserves. Oil production and consumption per capita are moderate. Electricity production and consumption per capita is high. Energy emissions accounted for 55 percent of all emissions. Within this sector, transportation accounted for 38 percent of emissions, energy industries 37 percent, manufacturing and construction 11 percent, and fugitive emissions 2 percent. Industrial emissions accounted for 17 percent of all emissions. Within this sector, chemical industries accounted for 51 percent of emissions and mineral products 48 percent.

Waste emissions accounted for 4.5 percent of all emissions. Within this sector, solid waste disposal on land accounted for 82 percent of emissions and wastewater handling 18 percent.

Major Waste Issues

The main environmental issues for Lithuania are waste issues. Contamination of groundwater is a large concern, and water quality is a major issue as well.

Climate change observers note increased temperatures and decreased snow cover. There are infectious diseases here, with hepatitis A, hepatitis B, and tick-borne encephalitis present. Two percent or more of the population is persistently infected with hepatitis B. There is a chance that infectious disease vectors will expand and that the range for ticks will expand with longer and warmer seasons.

Further Reading

Agyeman, Julian, and Yelena Ogneva-Himmelberger. 2009. *Environmental Justice and Sustainability in the Former Soviet Union.* Cambridge, MA: MIT Press.

Bellinger, Ed, ed. 2000. *Environmental Assessment in Countries in Transition*. Portland, OR: LLC. Books International.

Lane, Thomas. 2001. *Lithuania: Stepping Forward*. New York: Routledge.

Lithuania. www.lietuva.lt.

LUXEMBOURG

Luxembourg is a landlocked west European nation. The climate is temperate, with cool summers and mild winters. Belgium, France, and Germany border this small nation. The terrain is mainly rolling hills rising to low mountains in the north.

Luxembourg is an urbanized nation. Altogether, 507,000 people live on 2,586 km² of land. Eighty-three percent of the population is urbanized, and 19 percent lives in a city having more than 100,000 inhabitants.

Current Waste Practices

All the population has access to improved drinking water sources and access to an improved sanitary facility. There are modern sewer and water services. Luxemburg collected 349,000 tons of municipal waste in 2009, almost 17 percent of it landfilled, 36 percent incinerated, 27 percent recycled, and about 20 percent composted. The entire population has municipal waste services.

Luxembourg has had strong recycling policies since 1998. Manufacturers are required to set up an acceptable procedure to collect their packaging or register with a designated waste collector to do so. Products that contribute to national recycling policies have a green dot on them. Residents are required to separate their waste into recycling categories. Waste bins are encoded with a microchip or bar code that measures the weight of the bin and how times it's used to compute charges.

Emissions and Industry

Luxembourg generated 11,839.2 metric tons of greenhouse gases 2012, an 8 percent decrease from 1990.

Agricultural products include grapes, oats, potatoes, wheat, fruits and vegetables, livestock, and dairy products. Agricultural emissions accounted for 6 percent of all emissions. Within this sector, agricultural soils accounted for 46 percent of emissions, enteric fermentation 36 percent, and manure management 18 percent.

Oil and electricity consumption per capita is high, whereas oil and electrical energy production is low. Energy emissions accounted for 89 percent of all emissions. Within this sector, transportation accounted for 62 percent of emissions, manufacturing and construction industries 12 percent, and energy industries 10 percent. Industrial emissions accounted for 5 percent of all emissions. Within this sector, mineral products accounted for 71 percent of emissions and metal production 16 percent.

Waste emissions accounted for less than 1 percent of all emissions. Within this sector, solid waste disposal on land accounted for 52 percent of emissions, wastewater handling 21 percent, and other 28 percent.

Major Waste Issues

Luxembourg is preparing for climate change effects on its water systems. Climate change observers noted increased temperatures, variability in seasonal distribution of precipitation, increased flooding, and increased dry periods. Projected effects include increase in temperature, redistribution of seasonal rainfall, possible increase in public health risks related to water quality, and increased risk of floods and droughts. The key vulnerability is water quality deterioration resulting from heavier rainfalls, increasing erosion, and rapid infiltration of groundwater. Primary concerns are about water quality, quantity, and sanitation. There is also concern about extreme weather events. In response to these concerns and projections, Luxembourg developed policies and regulatory instruments to include climate change adaption. Most of these efforts focus on flood risk management. It participates in the regional Flood and Low Water Management Moselle–Sarre project to assess the effects of climate change in the Moselle and Saar catchments. Luxembourg supports research on climate changes related to vulnerability, mitigation, and emission projections. They are also increasing monitoring capacity to observe a long time series of surface and groundwater to separate natural variability, human influences, and climate change effects.

Further Reading

Climate Change Impacts on Water Systems. www.oecd.org.
Jury, C., et al. 2013. "Analysis of Complementary Methodologies to Assess the Environmental Impact of Luxembourg's Net Consumption." *Environmental Science and Policy* 27: 68–80.
Luxembourg Environmental Ministry. www.environment.public.lu.

MACEDONIA

Greece, Bulgaria, Serbia, Kosovo, and Albania border landlocked Macedonia. The terrain is mountainous, with deep valleys and large lakes. Summers are warm and dry, and winters are cold with high precipitation. Natural resources include iron ore, lead, zinc, copper, manganese, gold, silver, timber, and hydropower. Two million people live on Macedonia's 25,713 km² of land. Sixty-nine percent of Macedonians are urbanized, and 29 percent live in a city having more than 100,000 inhabitants. Eight percent live in overcrowded conditions. There are many small communities throughout this Balkan nation as well.

Current Waste Practices

Civil unrest and war in Macedonia destroyed important parts of the waste infra-structure. Macedonia is developing its waste infrastructure with help from the European Union (EU). Macedonia seeks admission to the EU but needs help to rise to EU standards.

Most of the waste is brought to dumps, uncontrolled rural sites, and a few sanitary landfills. Macedonia is developing laws and financing to increase the number of sanitary landfills and decrease uncontrolled sites. Most waste collection is in urban areas and collection rates vary from 40 percent to 70 percent of the urban population. Most of the population has access to improved drinking water sources and sanitation facilities. However, 18 percent of the rural population does not have access to improved sanitation facilities. In these areas, waste practices are basic, and people use pit toilets, latrines, drainage ditches, and cesspools.

Emissions and Industry

Macedonia generated 11,491.3 metric tons of greenhouse gases in 2009, a 13 percent decrease from 1990.

Agricultural emissions accounted for almost 12 percent of all emissions in 2010. Within this sector, agricultural soils accounted for 52 percent of emissions, enteric fermentation almost 35 percent, manure management more than 11 percent, field burning of agricultural residues and rice cultivation 1 percent.

Oil and electricity per capita production and consumption are low. Hydro-electric power production is high. Expanding oil and gas pipelines is considered necessary for economic recovery and development. Energy emissions accounted for 76 percent of all emissions in 2010. Within this sector, energy industries

Heavy snow and traffic congestion prevent waste collection in Skopje, Macedonia, forcing people to use garbage heaps on December 28, 2001. Weather, natural disasters, and lack of transportation routes can stop all waste collection. Trash continues to accumulate under all conditions. (AP Photo/Boris Grdanoski)

accounted for almost 68 percent of emissions, transportation almost 15 percent, manufacturing and construction 9 percent, and fugitive emissions 2 percent. Industrial emissions accounted for almost 4 percent of all emissions in 2010. Within this sector, mineral products accounted for 70 percent of emissions and metal production 30 percent.

Waste emissions accounted for 8 percent of all emissions. Within this sector, solid waste disposal on land accounted for 81 percent of emissions, wastewater handling 10 percent, and waste incineration almost 9 percent.

Major Waste Issues

Many of Macedonia's environmental problems are also waste issues. Air and water pollution are part of many waste practices. The air quality is poor around urban areas such as Skopje.

The major waste issue is the protection of public health both in the country and the region. Repairing a damaged waste infrastructure is a national priority. There are many infectious diseases in Macedonia, including hepatitis A, hepatitis B, and typhoid. Two percent or more of the population is persistently infected with hepatitis B.

There are political obstacles to regional approaches because of unresolved tension between neighboring countries, such as Greece.

Further Reading

Arben, Bakllamaja, and Hristov Georgi. 2013. *Macedonia Water and Wastewater Challenges.* Saarbrucken, Germany: AV Aksdemikerverlag GmbH & Co. KG.

Kendrovski, V., et al. 2014. "The Public Health Impacts of Climate Change in the Former Yugoslav Republic of Macedonia." *International Journal of Environmental Research and Public Health.* 11: 5975–5988.

Macedonia Government. www.vlada.mk.

MADAGASCAR

Madagascar is an island in the Indian Ocean off the coast of South Africa. It is known for its rare biodiversity in plants and animals. Lemurs, for example, thrive in all parts of the country. The coast rises quickly to a plateau and then mountains in the interior. The climate is tropical on the coast—hot and humid. The plateau climate is moderate with less heat and humidity. It is dry in the south. Natural resources include coal, chromite, bauxite, mica, fish, and hydropower.

Altogether, 22.6 million people live on Madagascar's 587,041 km^2 of land and 4,828 km of coastline. Twenty-seven percent of the population is urbanized, and 15 percent lives in a city having more than 100,000 inhabitants. There are many small communities on and around the island.

Overall, 64 percent of the population lives in overcrowded conditions. Fifty-three percent suffers malnutrition. Sixty-one percent lives beneath the international poverty level. Life expectancy is 59 years.

Current Waste Practices

Waste practices are basic, including pit toilets, latrines, drainage ditches, cesspools, and open defecation. About a fifth of the population has municipal collection services, but this is primarily an urban service. Seventy-seven percent of the urban population has access to improved drinking water sources, and only 48 percent has access to an improved sanitary facility. Thirty-five percent of the rural population has access to improved drinking water sources, and only 26 percent has access to improved sanitary facilities.

Madagascar collected 419,000 tons of municipal waste in 2007, almost 97 percent landfilled and the rest composted. In Seychelles, 44 percent of the waste was household waste, 19 percent industrial wastes, and almost 10 percent hospital and hazardous wastes. Madagascar generates among the lowest amounts of municipal per person in the world—about 9 kg per year. By comparison, the United States generates about 714 kg per year. Most of the landfills are basic dumps on the edge of the community. There is very little treatment of solid wastes or water. In 2002, Madagascar generated 1,905 tons of hazardous wastes. It is unknown how much was imported.

Emissions and Industry

Madagascar generated 29,343.9 metric tons of greenhouse gases in 2000.

There is little arable land on the island. Agricultural products include coffee, bananas, cocoa, cloves, peanuts, vanilla, livestock, and sugar cane. Agricultural emissions accounted for 89 percent of all emissions. Within this sector, agricultural soils accounted for 63 percent of emissions, enteric fermentation about 20 percent, and manure management about 15 percent. This is a high amount of greenhouse gas emissions from manure, indicating the presence of large amounts of untreated feces.

Electrical energy production and consumption are low. Almost eighty days a year have electrical outages. Energy emissions accounted for 8 percent of all emissions. Within this sector, transportation accounted for about 35 percent of emissions, energy industries about 23 percent, and manufacturing and construction about 13 percent.

Industrial emissions accounted for about 1 percent of all emissions. Within this sector, mineral products accounted for 100 percent of emissions.

Waste emissions accounted for about 1 percent of all emissions. Within this sector, wastewater handling accounted for 100 percent of emissions

Major Waste Issues

Madagascar faces many issues financing waste management. Only about a third of produced wastes are treated in disposal sites. Hazardous wastes are a big problem, there being no suitable disposal or recovery facilities. Madagascar is working with international groups to control the importation of hazardous waste by executing the hazardous wastes provisions of the Basel Convention. Hazardous waste management is ranked as the highest priority for capacity building.

E-wastes are also emerging as a high priority for capacity building. However, there is no legislation or money available to do so. Financing is needed to set up a basic e-waste infrastructure and policy. Currently there is confusion among state agencies about responsibilities for managing this waste stream.

Another motivating factor in waste management in Madagascar is the protection of public health in both the country and the region. Current infectious diseases are dengue fever, hepatitis A, hepatitis B, schistosomiasis, and typhoid. Two percent or more of the population is persistently infected with hepatitis B. There is a high risk of malaria. Health care wastes are regulated, but the regulations are not enforced. No money is allocated by the government for health care wastes, and public knowledge and professional expertise about the dangers of health care wastes is scant.

Further Reading

Government of Madagascar. www.wildmadagascar.org.

Njoh, A. 2013. "Colonization and Sanitation in Urban Africa: A Logistics Analyses of the Availability of Central Sewer Systems as a Function of Colonialism." *Habitat International* 38: 207–213.

Stringer, Lindsay C., et al. 2009. "Adaptations to Climate Change Drought and Desertification: Local Insights to Enhance Policy in Southern Africa." *Environmental Science and Policy* 7: 748–765.

MALAWI

The Great Rift Valley runs through the African nation of Malawi. From the Rift Valley, plateaus rise to about 1,000 m. Landlocked Malawi is bordered by Zambia, Mozambique, Tanzania, and Lake Malawi. The climate is subtropical—dry and seasonal. Ninety-five percent of the precipitation falls between November to April. Lake Malawi covers almost a fifth of Malawi. The north coast of Lake Malawi gets the heaviest rain. The climate is hotter in low-lying areas and more temperate in the northern plateaus. In the north the plateaus are higher—around 2,430 m. Natural resources include coal, bauxite, uranium, limestone, and hydropower. Altogether, 16.8 million people live on Malawi's 94,080 km² of land. There are also many small communities. Almost 16 percent of the population is urban. The rate of growth of urbanization is very high—slightly more than 4 percent.

Current Waste Practices

Waste practices are basic—pit toilets, latrines, drainage ditches, cesspools, and open defecation. About a fifth of the population has access to sewage systems or septic tanks. Fifty-three percent of the rural population and 50 percent of the urban population has access to a sanitation facility. Eighty-two percent of the rural population and 94 percent of the urban population has access to safe drinking water. Most waste is moved to open dumps, and some of it is burned. Waste picker communities do any recycling.

It is unlikely that Malawi will meet the Millennium Development goals in 2015. These goals require greater urban and rural access to safe water. Malawi has also attempted to finance waste management services with user fees. However, the money raised by these fees is not enough to run the system.

There are about five state agencies charged with waste management responsibilities. The Ministry of Energy and Mines develops national water policy and has six regional offices. The Directorate for Drinking Water and Sanitation implements national policies and maintains equipment and provides water services. The Water and Sanitation Regulatory Agency is charged with setting standards and rates for water and sanitation. The Jiro Sy Rano Malagasy is a water and waste management provider to fifty-nine urban centers and eight rural centers. Commune Service Providers cover those communities not covered by anyone else. The National Water and Sanitation Fund is charged with financing for water conservation and protection of water quality. These agencies are often in conflict as to jurisdiction and budget authority.

Emissions and Industry

In 1994, Malawi generated 7,070.3 metric tons of greenhouse gases. It is likely that greenhouse gases are much higher now because of population increases, the rate of population growth and urbanization, and reliance on agriculture.

There is a substantial amount of arable land. Agricultural products include coffee, tobacco, tea, sugar cane, bananas, cassava, sorghum and livestock. Agricultural emissions accounted for 45 percent of all emissions. Within this sector, agricultural soils accounted for 66 percent of emissions, enteric fermentation 20 percent, rice cultivation 10 percent, and burning savannas and agricultural residues 2 percent. The electrical grid is out for more than sixty-three days a year. Energy emissions accounted for 53 percent of all emissions. Within this sector, "other" accounted for virtually all emissions. Industrial emissions accounted for less than 1 percent of all emissions. Within this sector, mineral products accounted for all emissions.

Waste emissions accounted for slightly more than 1 percent of all emissions. Within this sector, solid waste disposal on land accounted for 91 percent of emissions and wastewater handling 10 percent.

Major Waste Issues

Many of the main environmental problems in Malawi are waste issues. Sewage, industrial discharges, and runoff of agricultural chemicals cause water pollution. However, waste management financing is an overshadowing issue. International assistance for waste management development is provided by a number of organizations. The World Bank helps efforts to rebuild waste infrastructure, create institutional capacity building, and extend services to rural areas. The African Development Bank supports institutional capacity building and rural waste management infrastructure.

Climate change effects of higher temperatures and precipitation changes cause concern about flooding, drought and fire. Much of the economy is based on agriculture. There is concern about diseases because of the endemicity of climate sensitive diseases such as malaria, cholera, and diarrhea. Malawi is prioritizing adaptation to climate change, because it affects those last able to handle them. Another goal is to reduce greenhouse gases to mitigate climate change effects.

A motivating factor in waste management is the protection of public health both in the country and the region. There are many infectious diseases here—cholera, hepatitis A, hepatitis B, typhoid, dengue fever, and schistosomiasis. Two percent or more of the population is persistently infected with hepatitis B. There is a high risk of malaria.

Further Reading

Cole, B., et al. 2014. "Exploring the Methodology of Participatory Design to Create Appropriate Sanitation Technologies in Rural Malawi." *Journal of Water, Sanitation and Hygiene for Development* 14: 51–61.

Foeken, D. W. J., et al. 2013. *Sanitation in Africa: Access to Improved Sanitation Facilities and Improvement Index*. Leiden, The Netherlands: African Studies Center.

Gutierrez, E. 2007. "Delivering Pro-poor Water and Sanitation Services: The Technical and Political Challenges in Malawi and Zambia." *Geoforum*: 5: 886–900.

Official Government Website. www.gov.mw.

MALAYSIA

Malaysia receives some of the highest amounts of rain fall in the world. The climate is tropical—hot and humid. There are two monsoon seasons. One season starts

April and ends in October, and the other starts October and ends in February. Malaysia is on the Malay Peninsula, bordered by Brunei, Indonesia, Thailand, and the South China Sea. The terrain is mountainous in the interior and flattens as it reaches the coast. Natural resources include oil, iron ore, gas, tin copper, baux-ite, timber, and hydropower. Altogether, 29.6 million people live on Malaysia's 330,803 km² of land and 4,675 km of coastline. Much of Malaysia is urbanized, although there are still small communities. Sixty-seven percent of Malaysians are urbanized, and 28 percent live in a city having more than 100,000 inhabitants.

Current Waste Practices

Before independence in 1957 local sanitary boards handled most wastes. After independence urban areas managed their own wastes, and the Ministry of Health managed rural areas. In 1994 a private corporation took over most waste manage-ment. In 2008, this business provided water and sewer services to eighty-eight of the 144 communities. In 2013, this business became a licensee for all communities.

All of the urban population has access to improved drinking water sources, and 96 percent have access to an improved sanitary facility. Ninety-nine percent of the rural population has access to improved drinking water sources, and 95 percent has access to improved sanitary facilities. In 2008, Malaysia generated 1,305 tons of hazardous wastes.

E-wastes have been regulated since 2005. This waste stream is of concern because it is so large and its volume is unknown, especially for imported e-wastes. Because of the high level of internally produced e-wastes, the waste management practices and policies were developed to limit the amount entering landfills. The policies for regulating e-wastes depend on the source of the e-wastes. For indus-tries that produce e-wastes it is required that the wastes go to a partial recovery facility or a full recovery facility, then to an integrated final treatment and disposal facility. For household e-wastes, it is required that they go to a nongovernmental sanitation organization or local waste authority or a private company, then to either a partial or a full recovery facility, and then to an integrated final treatment and disposal facility.

Emissions and Industry

In 2000 Malaysia generated 193,396.6 metric tons of greenhouse gases, a 41.5 percent increase from 1994. It is likely that greenhouse gas emissions today are much higher because of population increases, urbanization, and industrialization.

Agricultural products include bananas, rice rubber, palm oil, coconuts, cocoa, and pepper. Fertilizers are used heavily. Agricultural emissions accounted for 3 percent of all greenhouse gases. Within this sector, rice cultivation accounted for 76 percent of emissions and enteric fermentation 23 percent.

Malaysia produces crude oil and maintains massive proven reserves. Electricity production and consumption per capita are high. Energy emissions accounted for 76 percent of all emissions. Within this sector, "other" accounted for 87 percent of emissions and fugitive emissions 13 percent. A large amount of green house gases are not accounted for. This affects the land and water, causing significant environmental and public health effects. Fugitive emissions are essentially unaccounted waste streams into the air. Fugitive emissions can affect regional ecosystems and the public health, because they can fall from the air to the land and water. Industrial emissions accounted for 7 percent of all emissions. Within this sector, consumption of halocarbons accounted for all emissions.

Waste emissions accounted for 13.6 percent of all emissions. Within this sector, solid waste disposal on land accounted for 81 percent of emissions and wastewater management 17.5 percent.

Major Waste Issues

Along with air and water pollution, solid waste is a major environmental problem. more than half the 1,800 rivers are polluted, and waste is a major cause. Altogether, 23,000 tons of solid wastes are produced per day, a figure expected to rise to 30,000 tons per day by 2020. Less than 5 percent of solid wastes are recycled. Waste management is challenged by lack of data; lax storage and collection systems; mixing of solid, toxic and hazardous wastes; and poorly planned final disposition sites.

A motivating force in Malaysia's waste management is the protection of public health both in the country and the region. There are many infectious diseases here, including cholera, hepatitis A, hepatitis B, Japanese encephalitis, typhoid, malaria, dengue fever, and schistosomiasis. Two percent or more of the population is persistently infected with hepatitis B.

Further Reading

Manaf, L., et al. 2009. "Municipal Solid Waste Management in Malaysia: Practices and Challenges." *Waste Management* 29:2902–2906.
Official Portal for Malaysian Government. www.malaysia.
Saeed, M., et al. 2009. "Assessment of Municipal Solid Waste Generation and Recyclable Materials Potential in Kuala Lumpur, Malaysia." *Waste Management* 29: 2209–2213.
Teo, Y. 2014. "Water Services Industry Reforms in Malaysia." *International Journal of Water Resources Development.* 30: 37–46.

MALI

Algeria, Niger, Cote d'Ivoire, Burkina Faso, Guinea, Senegal and Mauritania surround landlocked Mali. The terrain is generally flat, with a grassy savanna in the south. The climate is regionally and seasonably varied. The general range is from subtropical in the south and dry in the north. There is a rainy season for some areas from June to November. Natural resources include uranium, gold, phosphates, granite salt, and hydropower. Sixteen million people live on Mali's 1,240,192 km^2 of land. There are many small communities throughout the country. Only 30 percent of the population is urbanized, and 11 percent lives in a city having more than 100,000 inhabitants. Thirty-nine percent suffers malnutrition.

Current Waste Practices

Eighty-one percent of the urban population has access to improved drinking water sources, and only 45 percent has access to an improved sanitary facility. Between 12 percent and 48 percent of households are connected to the public water supply, and only 1.5 percent of the population has a sewer connection. Waste practices are very basic—pit toilets, latrines, drainage ditches, cesspools, and open defecation. Forty-four percent of the rural population has access to improved drinking water sources, and only 32 percent has access to improved sanitary facilities. In Bamako, about half of the residents use groundwater wells. These are often near latrines and sewers, increasing disease vectors.

Municipal waste collection services are provided but they are spotty. There is a private sector waste collection market and a loose arrangement of government municipal waste collection. Many businesses complain about poor relationships with government, and many customers complain about poor services from both. Many poor people cannot afford private waste collection services. There is also a problem of using untreated wastes as fertilizer in agriculture. There is a national effort to include more poor people in the process of finding a solution to pollution via waste management improvements.

Emissions and Industry

Mali generated 12,298.7 metric tons of greenhouse gases in 2000, a 42 percent increase from 1995. It is likely that greenhouse gas emissions today are higher because of population increases and heavy reliance on agriculture.

There is a large amount of arable land. Agricultural products include rice, corn, millet, cotton, vegetables, and livestock. Agricultural emissions accounted for 71 percent of all emissions. Within this sector, enteric fermentation accounted for 55 percent of emissions, rice cultivation 21 percent, agricultural soils 15 percent, prescribed burning of the savannas about 6 percent, and manure management almost 3 percent.

The electrical grid fails almost eleven days a year. Oil and electricity production and consumption per capita are low. Energy emissions accounted for about 19 percent of all emissions. Within this sector, transportation accounted for about 28 percent of emissions, manufacturing industries and construction about 10 percent, and energy industries about 17 percent. Industrial emissions accounted for less than 1 percent of all emissions. Within this sector, mineral processes accounted for 100 percent of emissions

Waste emissions accounted for almost 3 percent of all emissions. Within this sector, solid waste disposal on land accounted for about 62 percent of emissions, wastewater handling about 24 percent, and incineration about 14 percent.

Major Waste Issues

The major waste issue in Mali is poor waste management that pollutes land and water environments. The cause of the pollution is inadequate or no sanitation in some areas, poor management of wastes as a whole, insecurity of land tenure, and excessive use of pesticides and fertilizers in agriculture.

The primary motivation for improving waste management is the protection of public health both in the country and the region. There are many infectious diseases here, such as yellow fever, cholera, hepatitis A, hepatitis B, meningococcal meningitis, typhoid, dengue fever, and schistosomiasis. Two percent or more of the population is persistently infected with hepatitis B. There is a high risk of malaria. If the wind is a good indicator of potential meningitis outbreaks, then public health officials may be able to distribute vaccines more effectively.

Further Reading

Cools, J., et al. 2013. "Integrating Human Health into Wetland Management for the Inner Niger Delta, Mali." *Environmental Science and Policy* 34: 34–43.

Fuller, J., et al. 2014. "Shared Sanitation and the Prevalence of Diarrhea in Young Children: Evidence from 51 Countries, 2001–2011. "*American Journal of Tropical Medicine and Hygiene* 13: 503.

Mali Official Government Site. www.primature.gov.ml.

Van Drunen, Michiel A., B. Lasage, and C. Dorland. 2006. *Climate Change in Developing Countries.* Oxfordshire, UK: CAB International North America.

MARSHALL ISLANDS

The Marshall Islands are a cluster of fragile islands spread across North Pacific Ocean. There are twenty-nine atolls and five islands in the country. It includes the islands of Bikini, Enewetak, and Majuro. The highest point of land is 10 m above sea level. The land is mainly flat and sandy, with coral limestone. The climate is tropical—hot and humid. The wetter season is from May to November. Extreme weather–related events such as hurricanes and tsunamis could have a severe effect on the islands and especially the atolls as oceans rise. Natural resources include coconuts, fish, and nearby minerals. Altogether, 70,000 people live of land and of coastline. Sixty-seven percent are urbanized. The rate of musculoskeletal diseases is among the highest in the world, which many conclude is the result of radiation from nuclear power and weapons testing in the area.

Current Waste Practices

Ninety-two percent of the urban population has access to improved drinking water sources, and 83 percent has access to an improved sanitary facility. Ninety-nine percent of the rural population has access to improved drinking water sources, and 53 percent has access to improved sanitary facilities.

The Marshall Islands collected 26,000 tons of municipal waste in 2007, almost 26 percent landfilled, 31 percent recycled, and about 6 percent composted. It is unknown how much waste is actually created because of the unknown amount of wastes dumped in the ocean. About 60 percent of the population has municipal waste services.

Agricultural products include coconuts, chickens, taro, fruit, vegetables, breadfruit, and fish. Most energy comes from fossil fuels. Diesel generators power many parts of the islands.

Major Waste Issues

Disposal of solid wastes is the most pressing waste issue. With small populations and primarily organic wastes, there was little concern about this. Populations have increased significantly, and imported items such as canned foods and cars accumulate with other wastes. Now the trash is collected in about sixty bins the size of a cargo container. From there it is taken to a landfill, where it is spread out and compacted to reclaim or make land. However, these landfills take all the wastes together. They are often placed in gabion baskets (a lagoon near the ocean separated by a sea wall). When high tides breach the wall, the waste simply floats out to sea. Other problems with landfill include lack of surface cover, little to no methane gas controls, poor facility access and security, and no record keeping.

Fresh drinking water is a major waste management issue because wastes can contaminate what little freshwater exists. To get more freshwater, the government distributed more than 3,000 water catchments to residents. About 70 percent of the population uses rainwater as the freshwater source.

The major motivation for waste management improvement is the protection of public health both in the country and the region. There are infectious diseases here. Hepatitis A, hepatitis B, typhoid, and dengue fever. Two percent or more of the population is persistently infected with hepatitis B.

Climate change effects of rising ocean levels and more severe weather could completely inundate the atolls and islands. Then most of the land mass could disappear under water. Can a country have no land and still be a country? Rising ocean levels and more severe weather will challenge public health systems and the current landfill practices.

Further Reading

Bikini Atoll. www.bikiniatoll.com.

Ichiho, H., et al. 2013. "An Assessment of Non-Communicable Diseases, Diabetes, and Related Risk Factors in the Republic of the Marshall Islands, Kwajelein Atoll, Ebeye Island: A Systems Perspective." *Hawaii Journal of Medicine and Public Health* 72: 77–86.

Office of the President of the Marshall Islands. www.rmi-op.net.

White, Ian, and Tony Falkland. 2010. "Management of Freshwater Lens on Small Pacific Islands." *Hydrogeology Journal* 18: 227–246.

MEXICO

Mexico borders Belize, Guatemala, the United States, the Caribbean Sea, and the North Pacific Ocean. The terrain is varied. Along the coasts it is flat, but the interior is mountainous. High desert plateaus cover much of the interior between the

Plants and Oil Pollution: A Cheaper, Cleaner, and Smarter Cleanup

Recent site analysis of the 5 million–barrel British Petroleum oil spill in the Gulf of Mexico shows that about 15 percent of the oil leak ended up on the bottom of the sea. Only 3 million barrels of the spill reached the surface of the sea. Locating the remaining 2 million barrels is a necessity for complete cleanup of the spill. History is replete with many petrochemical spills, leaks, discharges, explosions, fires, and emissions. Over time, the oil accumulates in the ecosystems of deserts, rivers, estuaries, ports, and depots.

Oil spills of all sizes leave behind a path of ecological destruction. One reason is that polycyclic aromatic hydrocarbons (PAHs) in oil do not degrade easily and persist in an ecosystem.

Current methods of cleaning up oil spills are expensive and ineffective. There is intensive research into plant-based cleanups of oil. Many plants can take the PAHs in oil but cannot break them down and then die. Some bacteria can break down the PAHs, but not in an outside environment. Researchers have injected plants with the bacteria in hopes that plants can take up the PAHs and also break them down. In 2014, researchers were successful in finding a basic bacteria–plant combination that could do both. Current experiments are under way to find the best combination of bacteria and plant combination for oil spills on land.

If these plants are successful in both cleaning up and breaking down some of the worst chemicals in petrochemicals, the rate of environmental restoration and remediation at spill sites will rapidly increase. Through the application of biotechnology, cleanups will cost less and create a cleaner environment.

mountains and the coasts. There are subtropical regions in the south. The climate is variable, from desert to tropical. Generally, the closer to the Equator, the more tropical the climate is in Mexico. Natural resources include oil, gas, gold, timber, silver, copper, and zinc.

Western Mexico is also known as Baja California. This is a 1,287 km peninsula that is surrounded by the Sea of Cortez on the East and the Pacific Ocean in the West. The Sea of Cortez is a deep sea and the birthing ground for several species of whales. The interior of Baja is a ridge of low mountains going from north to south. Although it is hot and very dry most of the year, severe tropical weather can affect Baja. Across the Sea of Cortez is the rest of Mexico.

116.2 million people live on Mexico's 1,964,375 km^2 of land and 9,330 km of coastline. Most people live in cities, although there many small communities spread across rural Mexico. Seventy-six percent of the population is urbanized, and 56 percent lives in a city having more than 100,000 inhabitants. Twenty-seven percent live in overcrowded conditions. Mexico City is the capital city and city with the largest metropolitan population—about 20 million people. Mexico City is slowly sinking from the weight of years of waste and development.

Current Waste Practices

Mexico collected 36,088,000 tons of municipal waste in 2006. Almost 96 percent of the waste is landfilled, and 3 percent is recycled. Most of the landfills are not sanitary landfills. Ninety percent of the population has municipal waste services. There is not enough landfill space, so there is illegal dumping. Much of this occurs outside of cities, but communities with moving water sometimes dump trash in the rivers.

Most communities have modern sewer and water systems, but not all wastewater is fully treated before discharge into freshwater. Ninety-six percent of the urban population has access to improved drinking water sources, and 90 percent has access to an improved sanitary facility. Eighty-seven percent of the rural population has access to improved drinking water sources, and 68 percent has access to improved sanitary facilities.

Most urban areas have sewer and water services. Thirteen percent of urban sewage is treated before being discharged into water. Of this, 14 percent receives primary treatment, 27 percent secondary treatment, and 59 percent tertiary treatment. In some rural communities, waste practices are basic—pit toilets, latrines, drainage ditches, and cesspools.

Emissions and Industry

Mexico generated 641,447.5 metric tons of greenhouse gases in 2006, a 51 percent increase from 1990. It is likely that greenhouse gas emissions are much higher now because of population increases, urbanization, and industrialization.

Agricultural products include bananas, vegetables, coffee, beans, rice, cotton, wood, livestock, and poultry. Agricultural emissions accounted for 7 percent of all emissions. Within this sector, enteric fermentation accounted for 82 percent of emissions, agricultural soils 15 percent, and manure management 2.5 percent.

Mexico produces a substantial amount of crude oil and maintains large proven reserves. Energy emissions accounted for 67 percent of all emissions. Within this sector, energy industries accounted for 35 percent of emissions, transportation 34 percent, manufacturing and construction industries 13 percent, and fugitive emissions 11 percent. Fugitive emissions are essentially unaccounted waste streams into the air. Fugitive emissions can affect regional ecosystems and the public health, because they can fall from the air to the land and water. Industrial emissions accounted for 10 percent of all emissions. Within this sector, mineral products accounted for 60 percent of emissions, metal production 19 percent, and chemical industries 5 percent.

Waste emissions accounted for 16 percent of all emissions. Within this sector, solid waste disposal on land accounted for 53 percent of emissions and wastewater handling 47 percent.

Major Waste Issues

Mexico's main environmental issues are also waste issues. Most urban areas discharge raw sewage into nearby waters. There are very few hazardous waste facilities, and illegal dumping of national and international hazardous wastes may occur here. Groundwater is becoming polluted and still being used, so quickly land subsidence is occurring on the Valley of Mexico. Public health is a major waste issue. Infectious diseases include cholera, dengue fever, hepatitis A, malaria, and typhoid.

Mexico is preparing for climate change effects on water. Climate change observers note temperature increases, intense rainfall, and intense drought. Projected effects include temperature increases, decline in annual rainfall with regional differences, decreased water quality, saltwater intrusion, increased severity of drought, and sea level rise. A key vulnerability is the threat to freshwater sources. Primary concerns are about water quantity and sanitation. There is also concern about extreme weather events, such as floods and droughts. In response to these

A line of trash covers the beach in Acapulco, Mexico, after a storm. The trash comes from the runoff from storm drains that empty into the bay and wash up on the beach. (Anthony Aneese Totah Jr./Dreamstime.com)

concerns and projections, Mexico is beginning climate change training for a few government agencies. Local basin councils are required to have drought guidelines and implement actions before, during, and after a drought.

Further Reading

Carruthers, D. 2008. *Environmental Justice in Latin America: Problems, Promise, and Practice*. Cambridge, MA: MIT Press.

Climate Change Impacts on Water Systems. www.oecd.org.

Collins-Dogrul, J. 2013. "Disease Knows No Borders: The Emergence and Institutionalization of Public Health Transnationalism on the U.S.–Mexico Border." *Journal of Borderlands Studies* 28: 61–73.

Herrera, V. 2014. "Does Commercialization Undermine the Benefits of Decentralization for Local Services Provision? Evidence from Mexico's Urban Water and Sanitation Sector." *World Development* 56: 16–31.

Mexican Presidency. www.presidencia.gob.mx.

Tiberghien, J. E., P. T. Robbins, and S. F. Tyrel. 2011. "Reflexive Assessment of Practical and Holistic Sanitation Development Tools Using the Rural and Peri-Urban Case of Mexico." *Journal of Environmental Management* 92: 457–471.

MOLDOVA

Moldova is a recently independent nation, having declared its independence from the Soviet Union in 1991. Romania and the Ukraine border Moldova. The terrain is generally flat with rolling hills. Almost two-thirds of the country is covered by very fertile soils. The land rises north from the Black Sea. The Dniester River runs along the eastern border with Ukraine. The climate is temperate, with warm summers and cool winters. Natural resources include lignite, limestone, and gypsum.

3.6 million people live on 33,371 km^2 of land in Moldova. There are many small communities throughout the country. Only 27 percent of the population is urbanized, and 27 percent lives in a city having more than 100,000 inhabitants. Twenty-two percent live below the international poverty line. Eleven percent suffers malnutrition.

Current Waste Practices

Most urban areas have basic sewer and water services. Virtually everyone has access to adequate sanitation facilities and potable water. Eighty-three percent of the rural population and 89 percent of the urban population has improved sanitation, but there is concern that the rural elderly may not be getting these services.

In 2009, 1,125 tons of hazardous wastes was generated and 2.27 million tons of local garbage was collected, most landfilled. Most landfills are not built to sanitary standards. They are not fenced, drained, or covered. Waste is dumped on the ground away from human settlements and cities. Total land space for landfills in 2012 was 1,304 ha, including unauthorized land. Unauthorized landfill land was more than half the total. It is likely that there are more illegal dumpsites.

Most municipal waste collection services are in urban areas and require citizens to pay for it. Only about 60 percent to 90 percent of municipal waste generated is collected. In rural areas, private waste collection services will transport the wastes, but most rural households cannot afford these services. The main method of household waste treatment is storing the waste on the ground, which causes soil and groundwater contamination, especially if these are pesticides or chemical fertilizers.

Emissions and Industry

Moldova generated 13,276.1 tons of greenhouse gases in 2010, a 69 percent decrease from 1990.

There is a substantial amount of arable land. Agricultural products include fruits, vegetables, grapes, grain, tobacco, beef, and milk. Agricultural emissions accounted for 16 percent of all gases in 2010. Within this sector, agricultural soils accounted for about 46 percent of emissions, enteric fermentation 28 percent, and manure management about 26 percent. This is an unusually high amount of greenhouse gas emissions from manure, indicating the presence of large amounts of untreated feces.

Coal is one of the main sources of energy. Energy emissions accounted for 67 percent of all emissions. Within this sector, energy industries accounted for almost 47 percent of emissions, transportation 21 percent, fugitive emissions 5.47 percent and the rest other. Fugitive emissions are essentially unaccounted waste streams into the air. Fugitive emissions can affect regional ecosystems and the public health, because they can fall from the air to the land and water. Industrial emissions accounted for 4 percent of all emissions in 2010. Within this sector, mineral products accounted for 81 percent of emissions and metal production almost 1 percent.

Waste emissions accounted for almost 12 percent of all emissions in 2010. Within this sector, solid waste disposal on land accounted for 88 percent of emissions and wastewater handling 12 percent.

Major Waste Issues

Runoff from the frequent use of strong pesticides and fertilizers pollutes the major rivers in Moldova. The primary challenge to an effective waste management system is an arcane and confusing legal context for waste. Most waste law here is governed by requirements from international treaties such as the Basel Convention and Stockholm Convention on Persistent Organic Pollutants. Environmental protection internally is covered by more than thirty-five pieces of legislation, and waste management is not specifically covered. The awkward juxtaposition of international laws on wastes and internal environmental laws that do not include all wastes creates confusion and conflict. Moldova is making the transition to a market economy and in doing so is introducing many new products to its populations. Many of these new products create wastes that were not regulated when the internal environmental laws were developed. E-waste is an example of this.

There are basic waste management challenges of proper landfill disposal. Waste in landfills is not covered or compacted, and there is little control over volume and type of wastes. The failure to separate out wastes prevents efficient methods of recycling.

The major motivation for improved waste management is the protection of public health. There are infectious diseases here—hepatitis A, hepatitis B, typhoid, and tick-borne encephalitis. Two percent or more of the population is persistently infected with hepatitis B. Climate change effects of increased temperature and rainfall variability could expand the range for tick-borne encephalitis.

Further Reading

Bellinger, Ed, ed. 2000. *Environmental Assessment in Countries in Transition.* Portland, OR: LLC. Books International.

Duca, Gheorghe. 2014. *Management of Water Quality in Moldova.* Heidelberg, Germany: Springer Press.

Government of the Republic of Moldova. www.molfova.md.

Sebastian, A., et al. 2013. "Menstrual Management in Low Income Countries: Needs and Trends." *Waterlines* 32: 135–153.

MONACO

Monaco, bordered by France and the Mediterranean Sea, is a modern and historic tourist location. The terrain is steep and rocky. The climate is Mediterranean, with rainy winters and dry, hot summers. There are few natural resources. There are many more tourists than residents, with around 1.5 million tourists each year. Monaco's 35,000 residents live on just 2 km^2 of land and 4.1 km of coastline. It is the second-smallest country in the world. Their life expectancy is 82 years.

Current Waste Practices

Monaco collected 37,000 tons of municipal waste in 2009, almost all incinerated, with some recycled. None goes to a landfill. About 9 percent is recycled. One hundred percent of the population enjoys improved drinking water sources and sanitation facilities. The entire country is covered by municipal waste services.

Emissions and Industry

Monaco generated 93.5 tons of greenhouse gas in 2012, a 15 percent decrease from 1990.

Agricultural emissions accounted for no emissions, one of the few countries for which this is true. Monaco uses seawater heat pumps for 17 percent of its electrical energy. Sixty-four facilities use exchangers take the heat from the ocean and convert it to energy. Heat pumps are used in cooler water, generally in the winter here. Globally, they are still in the experimental stage of application, being site-specific. Energy emissions accounted for 91.5 percent of all emissions. Within that sector, transportation accounted for 34 percent of emissions and energy industries 33 percent. Industrial emissions accounted for 7 percent of all emissions. Within that sector, consumption of halocarbons accounted for all emissions.

Waste emissions accounted for 1.3 percent of all emissions. Within that sector, wastewater handling accounted for 65.5 percent of emissions and waste incineration 34.5 percent

Major Waste Issues

Climate change effects of changing sea levels, increased temperatures, and more extreme weather events cause concern. The government of Monaco owns a fifth of the land and is committed to green spaces and best environmental practices. To address concerns, Monaco developed several policies to adapt to these changes. Increases in public transportation by bicycle, boat, and bus all help meet the goal of reducing greenhouse gas emissions by 20 percent of 1990 figures. They also want to change the infrastructure to use 20 percent of their energy from renewable sources, produced within Monegasque boundaries. The Bay of Monaco on the Mediterranean Sea is the main environmental concern. A major waste issue in the region is the pollution of the Mediterranean Sea.

Monaco is developing and maintaining marine preserves and waste diversion planning to protect the bay. They now use an electric boat to ferry people around the bay. Monaco is a wealthy country that attracts high-income residents and tourists. The government expressly seeks to become a model for environmental conservation and sustainability, in part motivated by economic development and tourism.

Further Reading

Meinesz, Alexandre, David Quammen, Daniel Simberloff, trans. 2002. *Killer Algae: The True Story of Biological Invasion.* Chicago: University of Chicago Press.
Monaco. www.gouv.mc.

MONGOLIA

Sweeping grassy steppes carve out the majority of the landscape in Mongolia. There are large mountains in the west, the tallest Hoh Nayramadlin Orgil, at 4,374 m. China and Russia are the two bordering nations. The climate is a dry and arid, with striking temperature extremes. The Gobi Desert dominates the interior. Natural resources include oil, coal, gold, silver, copper, tin, nickel, zinc, and phosphates.

Only 2.6 million people live on Mongolia's 1,564,116 km^2 of land. There many small communities throughout the country, some of these nomadic. Fifty-seven percent of the overall population is urbanized, and 29 percent lives in a city having more than 100,000 inhabitants. The capital city of Ulaanbaatar is also the largest, with a population of almost 1 million people. Twenty-seven percent of the country's population lives below the international poverty level. Twenty-eight percent suffers malnutrition. Life expectancy is 69 years.

Current Waste Practices

Water quality is very poor. Waste practices are very basic—pit toilets, latrines, drainage ditches, cesspools, and open defecation are especially used in rural areas. Eighty-seven percent of the urban population has access to improved drinking water sources, and 75 percent has access to an improved sanitary facility. Only 30 percent of the rural population has access to improved drinking water sources, and 75 percent has access to improved sanitary facilities. In the main city of Ulaanbaatar are about 103 wastewater treatment facilities. Forty-one are functional, and thirty-five are not operating. There are 877 km of underground pipes, and they are being repaired section by section. There are eight working biological water treatment facilities that treat about 200 million m^2 of wastewater annually. Although the overall volume of wastewater is unknown, it is much larger than what is treated.

In the 1990s, Mongolia signed onto the major international treaties—the Basel Convention, the Rotterdam Convention, and the Stockholm Convention. These treaties require substantial regulation of some kinds of wastes. In the early 2000s, Mongolia began to develop an internal waste management policy. In 2000, the

National Program on Waste Reduction was developed. In 2010, this plan began to develop revisions that include recycling principles of waste reduction, reuse, and recycling.

Most of the recycling efforts have focused on the few urban areas. Thousands of recycling bins have been distributed, and both user-pays programs and municipal efforts try to facilitate their use. About three-quarters of the waste is collected by the city, 15 percent by private organizations, and 5–10 percent uncollected.

Emissions and Industry

Mongolia generated 17,711 metric tons of green house gases in 2006, an 8 percent decrease from 1990.

Agricultural emissions accounted for 36 percent of all emissions in 2006. Within this sector, enteric fermentation accounted for 91 percent of emissions, agricultural soils 6 percent, and manure management almost 3 percent.

Energy emissions accounted for almost 58 percent of all emissions in 2010. Within this sector, energy industries accounted for 62 percent of emissions, transportation almost 19 percent, manufacturing and construction industries almost 4 percent, and fugitive emissions about 2 percent. Industrial emissions accounted for 5 percent of all emissions in 2010. Within this sector, consumption of halocarbons accounted for 86 percent of emissions and mineral production 14 percent

Waste emissions accounted for almost 1 percent of all emissions. Within this sector, wastewater handling accounted for 63 percent of emissions and solid waste disposal on land 37 percent.

Major Waste Issues

The major waste issue is to implement and enforce waste policies. International assistance for this process is provided by the World Bank for public services improvement of Ulaanbaatar. The World Health Organization financed a waste composition study of Ulaanbaatar. The Asian Productivity Organization supported a green productivity training that promotes waste management practices. There is also substantial assistance from private corporations such as Kokusai Kogyo, a Japanese company.

Further Reading

Jadambaa, A., et al. 2014. "The Impact of the Environment on Health in Mongolia: A Systematic Review." *Asia-Pacific Journal of Public Health*: in press.

Liu, X., et al. 2014. "Assessment of Metals in Dry Toilet Matters from Ulaanbaatar, Mongolia Using Biosolids Guidelines and Ecological Risk Index." *Frontiers of Environmental Science and Engineering* 8: 710–718.

Mongolian List of Government Websites. www.zasag.mn.

Shinee E., et al. 2008. "Healthcare Waste Management in the Capital City of Mongolia." *Waste Management* 28: 435–441.

MONTENEGRO

Montenegro is a new nation that emerged in 2006 from regional conflicts. It is bordered by Albania, Bosnia and Herzegovina, Croatia, Serbia, and the Adriatic Sea.. The terrain is mountainous, although there are many meadows and pastures. There are hot summers and cold winters. There are heavy snows in the mountains in the winter. Natural resources include bauxite and hydropower. Altogether, 653,500 people live on Montenegro's 13,812 km^2 of land and 293 km of coastline.

Montenegro's founders wrote that Montenegro is a civil, democratic, and ecological state. Today there are very few, if any, recycling facilities, and trash is a major problem. Iron and other metals are produced without environmental or public health attention. There are few filters on large smokestacks, and some steel producing plants do not have chimneys. For example, the Zeijezara iron factory in Niksic and the aluminum factory in Podgoricia polluted the air for years despite community protests.

Current Waste Practices

Most communities in Montenegro have modern sewer and water systems, but not all wastewater is fully treated before being discharged into freshwater. Eighty-eight percent of the rural population and 92 percent of the urban population has improved sanitation. Only about half the waste and trash produced is collected, so trash build-up is a major problem. Waste is dealt with locally, without national standards or enforcement of environmental law. This can create waste issues. For example, a local waste collection company dumped its collected waste in fifteen freshwater springs in the Vsove vode, which is in the north outside of Berane. Communities that rely on the springs have protested but with little result.

Emissions and Industry

Montenegro as a region generated 1,964.5 metric tons of greenhouse gases in 2003, a 5 percent increase since 1990.

Montenegro has substantial amount of arable land, about 37 percent. Permanent grassland occupies 87 percent of the country. Agricultural products include tobacco, fruits, vegetables, fish, and livestock. Agricultural emissions accounted for 12 percent of all emissions. There are no 2003 data, but there are 1990 data. Within this sector, enteric fermentation accounted for 54 percent of emissions and agricultural soils 46 percent.

Energy emissions accounted for 50 percent of all emissions. Within this sector, fugitive emissions accounted for all emissions. Fugitive emissions are essentially unaccounted waste streams into the air. Fugitive emissions can affect regional ecosystems and the public health because they can fall from the air to the land and water. Industrial emissions accounted for 35 percent of all emissions. Within this sector, metal production accounted for all emissions. Montenegro's industry produces steel, aluminum, timber, and textiles.

Waste emissions accounted for 2 percent of all emissions. There are no 2003 data, but there are 1990 data. Within this sector, solid waste disposal on land accounted for all emissions.

Major Waste Issues

Climate change effects and adaption are currently a high priority. There are concerns about flooding and drought. The economic, environmental, and human health climate change effects are the focus of government. They are seeking admission to several European regional organizations and are required to measure and monitoring certain environmental changes. They are currently developing and refining Montenegrin methodologies for observing waste effects to meet the European standards. Administrative and institutional structures are in place but lack financial resources to implement policy. There are plans for a new National Environmental Approximation Strategy, a National Investment Strategy, National Climate Strategy, and a National Waste Management Plan.

There is substantial international assistance to help Montenegro meet its waste management challenges and responsibilities. The World Bank has funded an industrial waste management and cleanup project designed to reduce contamination and public health risks from industrial areas. This project financed the design, construction, and remediation of selected industrial areas. This included slope stabilization in-site encapsulation, drainage, and revegetation. There is also a focus on managing current waste sites in a manner compliant with international treaties. This project also advances waste management practices by increasing capacity for planning at state agencies, project monitoring and evaluation, and environmental audits.

Further Reading

Bellinger, E., ed. 2000. *Environmental Assessment in Countries in Transition.* Portland, OR: LLC. Books International.
Climate Change in Montenegro. www.unfccc.me.
Draft National Strategy for Waste Management. www.uom.co.me.
Government of Montenegro. www.gov.me/en/homepage.

MOROCCO

Morocco borders Algeria, Western Sahara, Spain, the North Atlantic Ocean, and the Mediterranean Sea. The terrain is mountainous, surrounded by plateaus that fall into flat coastal areas. The north coast is mountainous. The climate is temperate, with cool summers and mild winters. It is hotter in the interior than the coasts. Natural resources include fish, forests, salt, iron ore, manganese, and phosphates. Altogether, 32.7 million people live on Morocco's 446,300 km² of land and 1,835 km of coastline. There are many small communities. Fifty-nine percent of Moroccans are urbanized, and 37 percent live in a city having more than 100,000 inhabitants. About a fifth suffers malnutrition.

Current Waste Practices

Waste practices are very basic—pit toilets, latrines, drainage ditches, cesspools, and open defecation. Burning trash is the prevailing method of waste treatment in many communities. Morocco places most of the collected municipal waste in a landfill. Morocco collected 6.5 million tons of municipal waste in 2000, 98 percent of it landfilled and 2 percent recycled. Most of the landfills are large open dumps in the edge of the community. There are roughly 300 large uncontrolled dumpsites, primarily outside of urban areas. It is estimated that 3,500 waste pickers live at these sites and that 10 percent are children of an indeterminate age. Although waste pickers do perform some recycling functions, they do so at great personal risk.

In 2008, the World Bank discovered that 70 percent of urban solid waste was collected. Less than 10 percent of this waste is disposed of properly.

Emissions and Industry

In 2000 Morocco generated 59,699.7 metric tons of greenhouse gases, a 34.5 percent increase from 1994.

Agricultural products include bananas, barley, fruits, vegetables, livestock, and wheat. Agricultural emissions accounted for 35 percent of all emissions. Within this sector, agricultural soils accounted for 72 percent of emissions, enteric fermentation 21 percent, and manure management 7 percent.

There is some crude oil production and proven reserves. Energy emissions accounted for 54 percent of all emissions. Within this sector, energy industries accounted for 35 percent of emissions, transportation 19 percent, and manufacturing and construction 15 percent. Industrial emissions accounted for 6 percent of all emissions. Within this sector, mineral products accounted for 100 percent of emissions.

Waste emissions accounted for 5 percent of all emissions. Within this sector, solid waste disposal on land accounted for 82 percent of emissions.

Major Waste Issues

In Morocco, solid waste management is the major environmental issues. About 5 million tons per years is generated, a volume increasing thanks to high and rapid population growth. Raw sewage and industrial effluents contaminate water supplies. Water quality is poor. Public health related to waste is a concern, for infectious diseases such as hepatitis A, hepatitis B, typhoid, and schistosomiasis exist here. Two percent or more of the population is persistently infected with hepatitis B.

The basic infrastructure for handling waste, as well as the technical expertise to build it and operate it, are lacking. Population and waste generation are increasing rapidly, with many landfill sites already overcapacity. Some of the landfill sites are ancient. Archeologists often dig old waste heaps for ancient relics of older civilizations. How this dynamic will affect Morocco is unknown, but it could also consume more landfill space. There is international assistance for Morocco from the World Bank. The bank allocated $271.3 million to Morocco for the development of a municipal solid waste plan with specific goals, giving a deadline of 2020. Part of this plan requires restoration of eighty large landfill sites that could include historic and cultural preservation issues. It also includes a goal of a large increase in the efficiency of municipal waste collection and raising recycling rates to 20 percent. This money is targeted to the urban centers, but a substantial part of the population resides in rural areas.

Further Reading

Abarghaz, Y., et al. 2013. "Lessons Learnt on Ecosan in Morocco: Case of Urine-Diversion Dehydration Toilets." *Journal of Water Reuse and Desalination* 3: 55–68.

Barcelo, Damia, and Mira Petrovic, eds. *Waste Water Treatment and Reuse in the Mediterranean Region.* Heidelberg, Germany: Springer Press.

El-Khoury, Gabi. 2014. "Water Indicators in Arab Countries: Selected Indicators." *Contemporary Arab Affairs* 7: 339–349.

Morocco Government. www.pm.gov.ma.

Zawahri, N., et al. 2011. "The Politics of Assessment: Water and Sanitation Millennium Development Goals in the Middle East." *Development and Change* 42: 1154–1178.

MOZAMBIQUE

Mozambique is low laying coastal nation in Africa with many large rivers. The biggest river is the Zambezi River, which serves as a primary transportation route to the interior. Zimbabwe, Tanzania, Malawi, Zambia South Africa, Swaziland, and the Indian Ocean border Mozambique. The climate is tropical to subtropical, with a rainy season from January to March. There is mainly dry, warm weather on the coast and slightly cooler weather in the western mountains. Periodically there are large floods. The country is also vulnerable to extreme weather events such as hurricanes. The terrain rises from coastal lowlands in the east eventually to the mountains in the far west. Natural resources include gas, coal, titanium, and hydropower.

Altogether, 24.1 million people reside on Mozambique's 801,590 km² of land and 2,470 km coastline. There are many small communities scattered throughout the country. About 35 percent of the population lives in urban areas, and 25 percent lives in a city having more than 100,000 inhabitants. The life expectancy is 50 years.

Current Waste Practices

Mozambique is the nation likely to receive illegal hazardous and e-wastes. Environmental enforcement is almost non-existent. In 2007, it was estimated that 222,000 tons of e-waste was illegally imported. By volume, 68 percent of this waste stream was computers, and 2 percent was mobile phones. It is suspected that televisions accounted for 30 percent of the flow. In terms of the number of any given device, 80 percent of the inventory was mobile phones. Because there are few recycling facilities, it is estimated that waste pickers "recycle" about 90 percent of the scrap metal.

Waste practices are basic, including pit toilets, latrines, drainage ditches, cesspools, and open defecation. Seventy-seven percent of the urban population and 29 percent of the rural population has access to an improved water source, which involves separating drinking water from wastewater. Thirty-eight percent of the urban population and 5 percent of the rural population has access to improved sanitation facilities. The open defecation rate in 2012 was 40 percent. Almost all the poorest 20 percent of the population of the practiced open defecation. Thirty-nine percent of the population is undernourished. The tuberculosis rate is 138 per 100,000, which is very high.

Cholera was identified in 1973. There have been waves of cholera outbreaks since then, generally occurring during the rainy season. In 2009, laboratory reports indicated 19,679 people who had cholera, including 155 deaths. The Gaza Province is an area where risk for cholera is high because of poor sanitary conditions, overcrowding, and major flooding. About 37 percent of Mozambique's population lives in overcrowded conditions, and almost 70 percent lives beneath the international poverty line.

Emissions and Industry

In 1994, Mozambique generated 8,223.9 metric tons of greenhouse gases, a 21.2 percent increase from 1990. It is likely that greenhouse gases are much higher now because of population increases, rates of population growth and urbanization, and reliance on agriculture.

There is a substantial amount of arable land. Agricultural products include cotton, tea, sugar cane, rice, cassava, coconuts, corn, fruits, and meat. Agricultural emissions accounted for 56 percent of all emissions. Within this sector, prescribed burning of the savannas accounted for 69 percent of emissions, rice cultivation 25 percent, and enteric fermentation 5 percent.

Energy emissions accounted for 22.5 percent of all emissions. Within this sector, transportation accounted for 45 percent of emissions, energy industries 18 percent, and manufacturing and construction 5 percent. Industrial emissions accounted for 0.6 percent of all emissions. Within this sector, mineral products accounted for 71 percent of emissions and metal production 29 percent.

Waste emissions accounted for 21 percent of all emissions. Within this sector, solid waste disposal on land accounted for 92 percent of emissions and wastewater management 8 percent.

Major Waste Issues

The major waste issue is the protection of public health both in the country and the region. There are many infectious diseases here, in particular cholera, hepatitis A, hepatitis B, meningococcal meningitis, typhoid, malaria, dengue fever, and schistosomiasis. More than 2 percent of the population is persistently infected with hepatitis B.

Further Reading

Foeken, D. W. J., et al. 2013. *Sanitation in Africa: Access to Improved Sanitation Facilities and Improvement Index*. Leiden, The Netherlands: African Studies Center.

Gonzalez-Gomez, F., et al. 2013. "Water Habits and Hygiene Education to Prevent Diarrheal Diseases: The Zambezi River in Mozambique." *African Development Review* 25: 563–572.

Government Ministries of Mozambique. www.commonwealthofnations.org.

Gujral, L., et al. 2013. "Cholera Epidemiology in Mozambique Using National Surveillance Data." *The Journal of Infectious Diseases* 208: 107–114.

MYANMAR

The Bay of Bengal, Bangladesh, India, Laos, China, and Thailand border Myanmar in southeast Asia. The interior has lowlands, surrounded by highlands. The climate is tropical—hot and humid. It is very rainy, and there are two monsoon seasons, one from June to September and the other from December to April. Natural resources include oil, gas, lead, zinc, copper, marble, tin, timber, and hydropower. Altogether, 55.2 million people live on 676,578 square acres of land and 1,930 km of coastline. There are many small communities throughout Myanmar. Only 31 percent of the population is urbanized, and 14 percent lives in a city having more than 100,000 inhabitants. Life expectancy is 60 years. Forty-one percent of the population suffers from malnutrition.

Current Waste Practices

Myanmar is engaged in waste management issues and emphasizes public engagement. Four regional waste management committees blanket the nation. The government explicitly recognizes communities, local governments, social organizations, waste pickers, businesses, and academics as stakeholders and generally seeks their inclusion in waste management decisions. The regional waste committees' goal is to develop a comprehensive waste disposal and collection system so cities will not have "repulsive" dumpsites. There is a strong recycling awareness, and public education about reducing use, reusing products, and recycling is part of waste management.

Most of the solid waste is organic. Most waste collection is informal. Some communities collect trash from block to block. Smaller communities may have a central waste collection point where residents bring their trash. Sometimes there is house-to-house collection, or other specialized collection services from businesses. Street sweeping is a traditional method for keeping dust and trash off the street and is part of waste management is most communities.

Seventy-five percent of the urban population has access to improved drinking water sources, and 86 percent has access to an improved sanitary facility. Sixty-nine percent of the rural population has access to improved drinking water sources, and 79 percent has access to improved sanitary facilities. In some areas waste practices are basic—pit toilets, latrines, drainage ditches, and cesspools.

Emissions and Industry

In 2005, Myanmar generated 38,374.9 metric tons of greenhouse gases, an increase of 12.9 percent from 2000. It is likely that greenhouse gas emissions are higher now because of population growth and reliance on agriculture.

There is a substantial amount of arable land. Agricultural products include rice, beans, sugar cane, fish, livestock, and pulses. Agricultural emissions accounted for 69 percent of all emissions. Within this sector, rice cultivation accounted for 46.5 percent of emissions, enteric fermentation 41 percent, agricultural soils 12 percent, and manure management 0.29 percent.

Myanmar produces crude oil and maintains proven reserves. Energy emissions accounted for 21.5 percent of all emissions. Within this sector, energy industries account for 37 percent of emissions, transportation 30 percent, and manufacturing and construction 9 percent. Industrial emissions accounted for 1 percent of all emissions. Within this sector, consumption of halocarbons accounts for 100 percent of emissions.

Waste emissions accounted for 8 percent of all emissions. Within this sector, wastewater management accounted for 99 percent of the emissions.

Major Waste Issues

The major waste issue is the lack of environmental regulation and enforcement. Myanmar intends to address these challenges directly. Its goals outline some of the challenges it faces. Myanmar wants to enact the Myanmar Environmental Protection Law, implement polluter-pays policy, strengthen the sewer system for domestic wastes in cities, and develop a framework for hazardous waste management. Eventually, it wants to design a solid waste master plan with guidelines for big cities, enact a hazardous waste law, and engage the international community more.

A major motivation for waste management is the protection of public health in both Myanmar and the region. Cholera, hepatitis A, hepatitis B, Japanese encephalitis, typhoid, dengue fever, and schistosomiasis occur here. Two percent or more of the population is persistently infected with hepatitis B. There is also a high risk of malaria.

Further Reading

Bajracharya, D. 2003. "Myanmar Experiences in Sanitation and Hygiene Promotion: Lessons Learned and Future Directions." *International Journal of Environmental Health Research* 13: 5141–5152.

James, Helen. 2009. *Security and Sustainable Development in Myanmar.* New York: Taylor and Francis.

Myanmar President's Office. www.president-office.gov.mm/en/.

Tun, A., et al. 2013. "Control of Soil—Transmitted Helminthiasis in Myanmar: Results of 7 Years of Deworming." *Tropical Medicine and International Health* 18: 1017–1020.

NAMIBIA

Namibia borders Angola, Botswana, South Africa, Zambia, and the South Atlantic Ocean. Its terrain is largely flat, with high desert plateaus. The climate is arid. There is little rain, and it is unpredictable. Natural resources include fish, salt, diamonds, gold, silver, zinc, cadmium, and hydropower. Altogether, 2.2 million people live on Namibia's 824,268 km^2 of land and 1,572 km of coast. There are many small communities, with only 35 percent of Namibians' living in urban areas. Only 2 percent live in a city having more than 100,000 inhabitants. Thirty percent suffers malnutrition. Life expectancy is 61 years.

Current Waste Practices

Namibia is sparsely populated and generates low amounts of solid wastes. However, it is very dry, and freshwater is scarce. Their goal is to avoid pollution of ground and surface water. There is very limited waste collection. There are 900 waste workers in the entire country, and about 500 of these are in Windhoek. Illegal dumping of trash is a common practice.

Waste collection practices differ. In very small communities, individuals handle their own wastes. In small communities, there may be a designated site for trash. It may or may not be fenced, covered, or compacted. In larger communities there may be a caretaker of the dumpsite, whose main responsibility is to burn the trash when the dump gets too full. The cities of Windhoek and Walvis Bay hire private contractors to take trash to the Kupferberg landfill. The trash may contain anything from e-wastes and medical wastes to hazardous wastes. This landfill hires trained "litter pickers" to sort out recyclable materials. Then the remaining wastes are compacted and covered with a layer of soil. Nothing is burned. Toxic and hazardous wastes remain. This landfill is designed for low environmental effect and eventual closure. It also has a special area for industrial hazardous wastes, lined to prevent leakage into groundwater.

Ninety-nine percent of the urban population has access to improved drinking water sources, and 60 percent has access to an improved sanitary facility. Eighty-eight percent of the rural population has access to improved drinking water sources, and only 17 percent has access to improved sanitary facilities. In rural areas, waste practices are very basic—pit toilets, latrines, drainage ditches, cesspools, and open defecation.

Emissions and Industry

Namibia generated 12,590 tons of greenhouse gases in 2000, an increase of more than 62 percent. Greenhouse gas emissions are likely higher now because of increased population and reliance on agriculture.

There is little arable land, and it is heavily used for agriculture. Agricultural products include fish, livestock, peanuts, millet, sorghum, and grapes. Agricultural emissions accounted for 74 percent of all emissions in 2000. Within this sector, enteric fermentation accounted for 97 percent of emissions and manure management 3 percent.

Namibia has no crude oil production or proven reserves. About eighteen days a year see electrical power outages, and when the system is operational, it is inconsistent. Energy emissions accounted for 24 percent of all emissions in 2000. Within this sector, transportation accounted for 47 percent of emissions, energy industries 11 percent, and manufacturing and construction industries almost 5 percent. Industrial growth is decreasing, and there is little data about it.

Waste emissions accounted for almost 2 percent of all emissions in 2000. Within this sector, solid waste disposal on land accounted for 65 percent of emissions and wastewater handling 35 percent.

Major Waste Issues

A basic, comprehensive waste management process is needed. Despite having at least eight state agencies responsible for wastes, waste management is lacking. Namibia's goals show their challenges. Their goals are to create an information system, create a tracking system for hazardous substances, improve pollution prevention and monitoring systems, increase recycling and increase public awareness to waste issues and to develop a national waste management plan. Without these basic protections, Namibia may become a dumping ground for illegal hazardous and e-wastes.

Mining wastes pose a significant challenge. Although the economic dependence on mining may have decreased, the environmental pollution continues to increase because of past and present practices. Public health, as related to waste management, is a major concern in Namibia. The natural freshwater sources are limited and desertification is increasing. Infectious diseases in the region include cholera, hepatitis A, hepatitis B, meningococcal meningitis, typhoid, malaria, dengue fever, and schistosomiasis. More than 2 percent of the population is persistently infected with hepatitis B.

Further Reading

Central Africa Regional Program for the Environment, Regional Development Strategy 2012–2020, U.S. Agency for International Development. www.usaid.gov.

Epfania, Lepaleni. 2013. *Encourage People's Participation in Waste Management, Eenhana-Namibia*. Saarbr, Germany: AV Akademikerverlag GmbH & Co. KG.

Republic of Namibia Office of the Prime Minister, www.opm.gov.na.

NEPAL

The highest mountain in the world, Mt. Everest, dominates the Himalaya Mountains, which tower over northern Nepal. China and India border Nepal. The terrain is varied. In the north, it is very mountainous, dominated by the Himalayas. Nepal's interior is hilly. In the south, a flat river plain dominates the terrain. The climate also varies. In the northern mountainous regions, the climate is very cold in the winter and cool in the summer. In the south, the winters are mild and the summers warmer. Natural resources include water, woodlands, quartz, copper, iron ore, and cobalt. Altogether, 30.4 million people live on Nepal's 147,181 km^2 of land. There are many small communities. Only 16 percent of the population is urbanized, and just 4 percent live in a city having more than 100,000 inhabitants. The capital and largest city is Kathmandu, with a regional population of more than 1.2 million people. About half the population suffers from malnutrition. The life expectancy is 62 years.

Current Waste Practices

About 524,000 tons per year of urban solid wastes from fifty-eight municipalities is generated. Most of these communities still use waste collection from open piles. The waste is then transported to an open dump. The waste infrastructure needs significant improvement. A framework on important waste issues such as e-wastes, organic composting, and landfill design and operation is needed. Public participation, recycling efforts, and technical capacities of local government need a much stronger effort.

Most cities have modern sewer and water systems but not all wastewater is fully treated before it is discharged into freshwater. Ninety-six percent of the urban population has access to improved drinking water sources, and 62 percent has access to an improved sanitary facility. Eighty-nine percent of the rural population has access to improved drinking water sources and only 30 percent has access to improved sanitary facilities. In rural areas waste practices are very basic—pit toilets, latrines, drainage ditches, cesspools, and open defecation. The open defecation rate in 2012 was 40 percent, down from 86 percent in 1990.

Emissions and Industry

In 1994, Nepal generated 31,188.9 metric tons of greenhouse gases. It is likely that greenhouse gases are higher now because of population increases and reliance on agriculture.

There is little arable land. Agricultural products include rice, corn, wheat, jute, pulses, and livestock. Agricultural emissions accounted for 87 percent of all emissions. Within this sector, enteric fermentation accounted for 40 percent of emissions, agricultural soils 31 percent, rice cultivation 23.5 percent, and manure management 5 percent.

Energy emissions accounted for 10.5 percent of all emissions. Nepal is experimenting with institutional and residential uses of biogas. Within this sector, "other sectors" accounted for 74 percent of emissions, transportation 14 percent, manufacturing and construction 10 percent, and energy industries 2 percent. Industrial emissions accounted for 0.5 percent of all emissions. Within this sector, mineral products account for 100 percent of greenhouse gas emissions.

Waste emissions from wastes accounted for 2 percent of all emissions. Within this sector, wastewater management accounted for 65 percent of emissions and solid waste disposal on land 35 percent.

Major Waste Issues

Water quality is a major issue. Nepal has the second-dirtiest water in the world as measured by BOD (biological oxygen demand). This is one indication that the wastewater treatment process is insufficient. The lack of a comprehensive framework and guidance on waste management poses the major challenge. It is a challenge that Nepal is facing directly. However, political instability may affect the development of a comprehensive framework. Currently Nepal is between moving away from monarchical leadership to a democratic form of government. There were open elections at one point, but the Communist party won, slowing down progress toward democratization. They are now in the process of writing a constitution, with the prospect of missing another deadline. A point of contention is that local regions want ethnic or religious identification and other groups want a federal approach. The latter approach would lend itself to developing a more comprehensive framework for waste management.

Most groups in Nepal recognize that wastes are a problem. Numerous studies are under way examining recycling potential wastes. Because most of the municipal wastes are organic, they could be composted. Nepalese agricultural traditions incorporate wastes as fertilizer. Nepal is also a destination point for many tourists traveling to see Mount Everest and the Himalayan mountain range. It is a crossroads for regional land travel. Most political groups recognize the economic value of tourism. Environmental tourists are sensitive to pollution issues and often possess technical expertise to perform environmental assessments.

Increased transportation can provide infectious disease corridors. Increased temperatures and more violent weather will challenge public health systems. There are infectious diseases, such as cholera, hepatitis A, hepatitis B, Japanese encephalitis, typhoid, malaria, and dengue fever. More than 2 percent of the population is persistently infected with hepatitis B. Protection of public health for residents and tourists is also a motivating force in developing a comprehensive framework for waste management.

Further Reading

Brief Appraisal of Existing Environmental Problems in Nepal. www.nepjol.info.
Government of Nepal—Office of the Prime Minister and Council of Ministers. www .opmcm.gov.np.

Lee, Norman, and Clive George. 2000. *Environmental Assessment in Developing and Transitional Countries: Principles, Methods and Practice*. New York: John Wiley and Sons, Ltd.

Lohani, S., et al. 2013. "Sustainable Biogas Production Potential from Urban Wastewater in Nepal." *International Journal of Environmental Science and Development* 4: 595–599.

NETHERLANDS

The Netherlands is one of the wealthiest nations in the world to face the direct threat of rising sea levels. About three-quarters of the population lives within 10 m of sea level. It is a nation that has evolved through massive ports. The Netherlands has successfully dealt with severe and long-lasting ocean flooding for centuries, but nothing on the scale it faces now. Many coastal cities in the United States, such as New Orleans, are monitoring Dutch approaches to the problem very closely.

Belgium, Germany, and the North Sea border the Netherlands. The terrain is flat, and much of it lies below sea level. The climate is temperate, with cool summers and wet winters. Natural resources include natural gas, oil, peat, limestone, and salt. Altogether, 16.8 million people live on the Netherland's 37,354 km² of land and 451 km of coastline. Eighty percent of the population is urbanized, and 52 percent lives in a city having more than 100,000 inhabitants.

Current Waste Practices

The Netherlands is one of the world's leaders of waste management. Its waste management infrastructure is one of the most efficient and comprehensive in the world. The regulatory structure includes numerous laws and regulations that are enforced. All aspects of waste are covered—financial, design, and even aesthetics. As residents of a small, wealthy urban nation mainly below sea level, the Dutch have had the ability and motivation to focus on effective waste management.

The Netherlands collected 10,159,000 tons of municipal waste in 2009, less than 1 percent of it landfilled, 33 percent incinerated, 28 percent recycled, and about 24 percent composted. In 1995, the Netherlands enacted one of the first landfill waste bans, covering more than thirty-five categories. Landfill fees were among the highest in the world until 2010, when they were abolished. So few people were using landfills, that it was not worth it to collect the fees: The cost of collection exceeded the revenue generated. The National Waste Plan set the recycling goal of the Netherlands at 60 percent of the waste stream by 2015.

The entire country is covered by municipal waste services, including access to improved drinking water sources and sanitation facilities. Only local government collects a small part of office and services waste. Most of it is collected by commercial waste collectors.

Emissions and Industry

The Netherlands generated 191,668.7 tons of greenhouse gases in 2012, a 9.5 percent decrease from 1990.

One-quarter of all land is arable. Agricultural products include dairy products, grain, fruits, vegetables, and livestock. Agricultural emissions accounted for 8 percent of all emissions. Within this sector, enteric fermentation accounted for 41 percent of emissions, agricultural soils 36 percent, and manure management 23 percent. This is an unusually high amount of greenhouse gas emissions from manure, indicating the presence of large amounts of untreated feces.

The Netherlands produces a substantial amount of crude oil and maintain robust proven reserves. Per-capita electricity and oil consumption is high. The Netherlands relies on natural gas for much of its energy needs, more than any other European nation. Energy emissions accounted for 84.5 percent of all emissions. Within this sector, energy industries accounted for 37 percent of emissions, transportation 21 percent, manufacturing and construction industries 16 percent, and fugitive emissions 1 percent. Industrial emissions accounted for 5 percent of all emissions. Within this sector, chemical industries accounted for 46 percent of emissions, metal production 15 percent, and mineral products 12 percent.

Waste emissions accounted for 2 percent of all emissions. Within this sector, solid waste disposal accounted for 81 percent of emissions and wastewater handling 18 percent.

Major Waste Issues

Some of the Netherlands' main environmental issues are also waste issues. Air pollution is causing acid rain. Water pollution is from runoff of agricultural pesticides and fertilizers. Heavy metals and other substances are found in the water.

The Netherlands is preparing for climate change effects on water systems. Climate change observers note increases in temperature and precipitation. The also note risks of flooding and water breaching water control infrastructure. Flooding is a danger both from the sea and from the rivers Rhine, Ijssel, and Meuse. The Netherlands is very vulnerable to rising sea levels. Twenty-four percent of the land is below sea level and has experienced major flooding events in the past. It is estimated that 60 percent of the country could be at risk of floods if there were no water defenses. Projected effects include increases in temperature, floods, sea level, salt intrusion, peak discharges from rivers in the winter, and drought. Sewer systems are projected to exceed their capacity during heavier summer rainstorms. Primary concerns are water quantity and extreme weather events. In response to these concerns and projection the Netherlands developed several new policies. One is the Delta Programme. The goal of this program is to keep future generations safe from flooding and ensure a safe drinking water supply. They are also reinforcing primary water defense structures along the coasts, rivers, and major deltas. The Dutch maintain an extensive research and monitoring operation of climate change effects. Their National Programme for Spatial Adaptation to Climate Change is designed to integrate spatial planning with climatic changes, a challenge for all countries.

The Dutch are international leaders in global water issues. They are working with the World Bank on clean drinking water and sanitation for 200 million

Sewage is treated at a wastewater treatment plant of Waternet, a regional water authority in Hilversum, Netherlands, on March 10, 2015. Harmful substances are removed, and then the water is released into a fresh water lake. Rising sea levels and salt water intrusion in its many low lying areas diminish fresh water resources in the Netherlands. (AP Photo/Peter Dejong)

people. Together they established a fund to loan money for water projects. The Dutch are contributing $50 million. So far, $21 billion has been loaned for these projects. The goal is to make $4–5 billion in loans annually for sanitation and water projects.

Further Reading

Climate Change Impacts on Water Systems. www.oecd.org.
Kirwan, M., et al. 2013. "Tidal Wetland Stability in the Face of Human Impacts and Sea-Level Rise." *Nature* 504: 53–60.
Netherland National Institute for Public Health and the Environment. www.riv.nl.
Netherlands Government. www.overheid.nl.

NEW ZEALAND

New Zealand comprises two islands—the North Island and the South Island. New Zealand lies in the South Pacific Ocean, bordering the Tasman Sea in the west and the South Pacific Ocean in the east. The terrain in the interior is mountainous, especially on the South Island. The tallest mountain is Mount Cook, at 3,754 m, in the heart of the Southern Alps. As the land reaches the coast, the terrain flattens. The climate is generally moderate, with mild, wet winters and warm summers. At higher altitudes, the weather is colder and windier. Extreme weather–related events such as earthquakes, volcanic eruptions, and tsunamis can occur here. Natural resources include gas, iron ore coal, gold, fish, timber, and hydropower. More than 4 million people live on the two islands on 37,354 km² of land. With 9,404 miles of coastline, it has the tenth most in the world. Eighty-six percent of the population is urbanized, and 70 percent lives in a city having more than 100,000 inhabitants.

Current Waste Practices

New Zealand approaches waste from a holistic environmental perspective that incorporates local, national, and global concerns. The 1991 Resource Management Act was among the first to incorporate sustainability and set up the framework for waste management. The purpose of the act was to achieve sustainable management of natural and physical resources. Under the act, the central government set national environmental standards with considerable deference to localities. The central government can issue policy statements and must issue a New Zealand Coastal Policy statement periodically. The central government is required to merge standards, polices, and coastal statements into regional policy statements. Regional councils cover soil, water, air, pollution, and coastal issues. They receive the regional policy statements from the central government and develop regional plans.

New Zealand collected 10,159,000 tons of municipal waste in 2009, and 85 percent of the waste was landfilled and 15 percent recycled. There is a general policy and ethic toward increasing recycling, reducing use, and reusing materials. The entire country is served by municipal waste services, including access to improved drinking water sources and sanitation facilities. In 2008, New Zealand generated 4,724 tons of hazardous wastes.

Emissions and Industry

New Zealand generated 76,048 tons of greenhouse gases in 2012, an increase of 25 percent from 1990.

Agricultural products include sheep, dairy products, fruits, vegetables, potatoes, wheat, meat, and fish. Agricultural emissions accounted for 46 percent of all emissions. Within this sector, enteric fermentation accounted for 68 percent of emissions, agricultural soils 30 percent, and manure management 2 percent.

New Zealand produces crude oil and maintains proven reserves. Electricity consumption per capita is high. Oil production and consumption per capita is moderately high. Energy emissions accounted for 42 percent of all emissions. Within this sector, transportation accounted for 43 percent of emissions, energy industries 24 percent, manufacturing and construction industries 16.5 percent, and fugitive emissions 7 percent. Industrial emissions accounted for 7 percent of all emissions. Within this sector, metal production accounted for 43 percent of emissions, mineral products 14 percent, and chemical industries 8 percent.

Waste emissions accounted for 5 percent of all emissions. Within this sector, solid waste disposal accounted for 87 percent of emissions and wastewater handling 13 percent.

Major Waste Issues

Climate change observers note increasing temperatures, fewer frost days, more droughts, more extreme rainfall events, and rises in sea level. Projected effects include lower river flows in summer and higher river flows in winter. There is concern about extreme weather events and the effect they have on agriculture and forestry. New Zealand is pursing climate change adaption policy on many fronts. Local councils are required to incorporate effects on climate change in their regional plans. The government freely distributes information to all who request it. This information often comes in the form of technical manuals on topics such as coastal hazards and climate change and tools for estimating effects of climate change on flood flow. It also comes in the form of maps of regional climate change effects freely available online. They maintain an ongoing research program. The National Institute of Water and Atmospheric Research researches climate-related effects on water.

Further Reading

Climate Change Impacts on Water Systems. www.oecd.org.
Dymond, J., et al. 2012. "Tradeoffs Between Soil, Water and Carbon—a National Scale Analysis from New Zealand." *Journal of Environmental Management* 95: 124–131.
Farrelly, T., and C. Tucker. 2014. "Action Research and Residential Waste Minimization in Palmerston North, New Zealand." *Resources, Conservation, and Recycling* 91: 11–26.
New Zealand Government Services and Information. www.govt.nz.

NICARAGUA

Nicaragua is the largest and most sparsely populated nation in Central America. Costa Rica, Honduras, the Caribbean Sea, and the North Pacific Ocean border Nicaragua. The terrain is mountainous and volcanic in the interior. There are coastal plains in the west and volcanoes near the east coast. The tropical climate is hot and humid. The temperature decreases with altitude. The rainy winter season on the west side of Nicaragua is from September to October. Rio San Juan receives large amounts of rain. Natural resources include lead, zinc, gold, silver, copper, fish, timber, and hydropower.

Altogether, 5.9 million Nicaraguans live on 130,373 km^2 of land and 910 km of coastline. Fifty-nine percent are urbanized, and 26 percent live in a city having more than 100,000 inhabitants. There are many small communities. About 19 percent of the population suffers malnutrition.

Current Waste Practices

Municipal waste collection services are generally available in urban areas. In Managua, only 19 percent of all recyclable wastes are recovered at all. The government recovers only 3 percent of recyclable waste, with 16 percent recovered by waste pickers. Most trash is simply collected, generally from a centralized location or collection box, and trucked to a landfill outside of town. Some trash is burned in town when the piles obstruct streets. Some of the streets are too narrow and curvy for sanitation vehicles to access. Some trash is burned at the landfill to make room for more trash. There is a significant community of waste pickers in Nicaragua. Some have organized into waste picker cooperatives. These communities occasionally resist dump closure, because waste picking is their livelihood. This can create resistance to using modern technologically based recycling approaches.

Ninety-eight percent of the urban population has access to improved drinking water sources, and 63 percent has access to an improved sanitary facility. Sixty-eight percent of the rural population has access to improved drinking water sources, and 37 percent has access to improved sanitary facilities. In rural areas waste practices are basic—pit toilets, latrines, drainage ditches, cesspools, and open defecation. Most of the urban areas have basic sewer and water, though not all are connected to the system. Twenty-one percent of urban sewage is treated before being discharged into water. Of this, 46 percent receives primary waste treatment, and 54 percent receives secondary levels of waste treatment before discharge.

Emissions and Industry

In 2000, Nicaragua generated 11,980.6 metric tons of greenhouse gases, a 57 percent increase from 1994.

There is a substantial amount of arable land. Agricultural products include coffee, bananas, cotton, rice, sugar cane, tobacco, beans, meat, dairy products and fish. Agricultural emissions accounted for 59 percent of all emissions. Within this sector, agricultural soils accounted for 48 percent of emissions, enteric fermentation 42 percent, manure management 5.5 percent, and rice cultivation 3 percent.

Oil and electricity production and consumption per capita are low. Energy emissions from energy wastes accounted for 33 percent of all emissions. Within this sector, energy industries account for 37 percent of emissions, transportation 31.5 percent, and manufacturing and construction 11.5 percent. Industrial emissions accounted for 3 percent of all emissions. Within this sector, mineral products accounted for all emissions.

Waste emissions accounted for 5.5 percent of all emissions. Within this sector, solid waste disposal on land accounted for 81 percent of emissions and wastewater management 19 percent.

Major Waste Issues

The major waste issues are in a pattern of overall environmental destruction. In 1981, 75 percent of the water sources were contaminated from agricultural pesticides runoff, half were polluted from raw sewage, and toxic industrial wastes polluted a quarter. Since then, population has increased, deforestation has decreased the ecological carrying capacity, and a war wreaked damage all across the country. The war included massive forest fires, with 250,000 farmers displaced. In the International Court of Justice, Nicaragua demanded $12 billion from the United States in direct and indirect environmental effects and for economic damages. Nicaragua is still recovering environmentally and economically, struggling to create a comprehensive waste management system but do not have one. Nicaragua has not met the United Nations Millennium Development goals for sanitation and is not likely to meet 2015 deadlines.

Further Reading

Flores, O., et al. 2013. "Monitoring Access to Water in Rural Areas Bases on the Human Right to Water Framework: A Local Case Study in Nicaragua." *International Journal of Water Resources Development* 29: 605–621.

Ministries of the Republic of Nicaragua. www.cancilleria.gob.ni.

Olley, J., et al. 2014. "Developing a Common Framework for Integrated Solid Waste Management Advances in Managua, Nicaragua." *Waste Management Research* 32: 822–833.

NIGER

Niger is bordered by Algeria, Benin, Burkina Faso, Chad, Libya, Mali, and Nigeria. The terrain is generally flat, with sand dunes. The climate is desert—hot and dry. In the farthest south, the climate is more tropical with higher humidity. Natural resources include oil, coal, uranium, iron, tin, gold, and salt. About 16.9 million people live on Niger's 1,267,000 km^2 of land. There are many small communities of people throughout the country. Only 17 percent of the inhabitants live in urban areas, and 10 percent live in a city having more than 100,000 inhabitants. In 2014 it had the fourth-fastest-growing population rate in the world. The population growth rate is around 3.5 percent, which is very high. Fifty-five percent of the population suffers malnutrition. Life expectancy is 42 years.

Current Waste Practices

Waste collection and treatment is inconsistent. Private sector collection and treatment of industrial wastes is available but very expensive. There are no guidelines or regulations on how to dispose of municipal solid wastes. There is little awareness of the benefits of waste segregation and recycling. There is some regulation of hazardous wastes, but enforcement is an issue. There are no policies or regulation on health care wastes or e-wastes. Niger collected 9.75 million tons of municipal waste in 2007. Almost 64 percent of the waste is landfilled, 12 percent incinerated, and 4 percent recycled. Niger generated 554,000 tons of hazardous wastes in 2005. It is not known how much hazardous wastes were imported. Most of these wastes end up in a landfill. There are communities of waste pickers around most large dumps who perform any recycling.

Pit toilets, latrines, drainage ditches, cesspools, and open defecation are typical waste practices. All the urban population has access to improved drinking water, but only 34 percent has access to improved sanitation. In rural populations, only 39 percent has access to improved drinking water, and only 4 percent has access to improved sanitation facilities. Each year, 40,300 deaths are attributed to unsafe water. Diarrhea, respiratory infections, and malaria rates are high.

Emissions and Industry

Niger generated 13,627 metric tons of greenhouse gases in 2000. It is likely that greenhouse gas emissions are higher now because of population increases, population and urbanization growth rates, and reliance on agriculture.

There is a substantial amount of arable land. Agricultural products include cotton, peanuts, cassava, rice, livestock, sorghum, and millet. Agricultural emissions accounted for 78 percent of emissions. Within this sector, enteric fermentation accounted for 54 percent of emissions, agricultural soils 43 percent, and manure management 2 percent.

Electricity and oil consumption and production are low. Annually there are more than eleven days without a working electrical grid. It can be difficult to get an electrical connection. Energy emissions accounted for 19 percent of all emissions. Within this sector, transportation accounted for 29 percent of emissions, energy industries almost 11 percent, and manufacturing and construction industries almost 4 percent. Industrial emissions accounted for less than 1 percent of all emissions. Within this sector, mineral products accounted for 100 percent of emissions.

Waste emissions accounted for almost 3 percent of all emissions in 2000. Within this sector, wastewater handling accounted for 100 percent of emissions.

Major Waste Issues

The main waste management issue is the lack of a regulatory structure. This lack of regulations allows Niger to be the final disposition site for illegal hazardous, medical, and toxic wastes. The primary motivation for waste management is the protection of public health both in the country and the region. There are many infectious diseases in Niger, including yellow fever, cholera, hepatitis A, hepatitis B, meningococcal meningitis, typhoid, dengue fever, and schistosomiasis. More than 2 percent of the population is persistently infected with hepatitis B. There is a high risk of malaria. There are few hospital beds and doctors, as well as low life expectancies and high infant mortality. There are inadequate public resources in the country to handle internal, regional, and global health concerns.

Further Reading

Central Africa Regional Program for the Environment, Regional Development Strategy 2012–2020, U.S. Agency for International Development. www.usaid.gov.

Ihayere, C., et al. 2014. "The Effects of the Niger Delta Oil Crisis on Women Folks." *Journal of African Studies and Development* 6: 14–21.

Niger Government. www.niger-gouv.org.

Omoweh, Daniel A. 2005. *Shell Petroleum Development Company, the State and Underdevelopment of Nigeria's Niger Delta: A Study of Environmental Degradation.* Trenton, NJ: Africa World Press.

NIGERIA

Benin, Cameroon, Chad, Niger, and the Gulf of Guinea border Nigeria. The terrain is varied. In the south it is flat and low, in the interior there are hills and plateaus,

---

Malaria Detectors from Magnets

Malaria infected about 207 million people in 2012. It is spread by mosquitoes that thrive in hot, wet weather. Climate change effects may increase their range, along with the potential for more people to get malaria, as discussed in many of the entries here.

There are two ways used now to diagnose malaria. The first is a blood prick on a paper that reacts in fifteen minutes. This method misses low less levels of the disease. The second is to look at the blood under a microscope. Though this method is more accurate, it takes days to weeks—if available at all in many countries. There are challenges in equipment, maintenance, and trained personnel.

A new method is being developed with faster response times and greater accuracy than microscope detection and greater accuracy than the blood tests. Sensitive magnets detect metallic attributes in the waste stream of malarial parasites. Malarial parasites go for hemoglobin and convert this to crystals of hemozoin, which increases the red cells' magnetism and can be detected easily by other magnets because of the attraction of metal to magnets. It is intended to increase response times and intervention, providing more early detection. With early detection, malaria can be arrested without a long-term hospital stay. A span of two to four days can make the the a big difference in the progression of the disease. The actual instrument uses advanced microelectronics and tracks actual nanoparticles. Prototypes are about 7 by 15 by 14 inches.

---

and in the north it is flat. There are mountains in the southeast. The climate is hot but varied—equatorial in the south, tropical in the center, and arid in the north. Natural resources include oil, gas, coal, iron, lead, and zinc. Altogether, 174.5 million people reside on Nigeria's 923,768 km^2 of land with an 853 km coastline. Forty-eight percent of the population is urbanized, and 27 percent lives in a city having more than 100,000 inhabitants. There are many small communities throughout all of Nigeria. The life expectancy is 48 years.

Current Waste Practices

Nigeria's waste practices are inconsistent and challenging by a dense, highly polluted urban landscape. There are five legal landfills and pervasive illegal dumping. Lagos has a population of about 21 million and generates 10,000 metric tons of trash a day. Most local governments collect 40 percent of the wastes. About 13 percent of recyclable materials are reclaimed from landfills, usually by waste pickers. There are efforts to improve waste management from the Lagos State Waste Management Authority. They are trying to burn the methane gas emitted from the massive Olushosun to create energy. The plan is to generate 25 megawatts a year in five years. National energy production is very low—about 3–4 MW a year.

Nigeria is also experimenting with user financing of trash pick ups in Kaduna. Waste collection is provided for free at first, and then the local government charges a small fee that can become mandatory. If the people are satisfied with the pickup service, they pay the fee. The fee charge is supposed to attract private sector businesses to bid on the waste collection.

Nigeria is one of the most rapidly growing nations in the world. Waste practices are very basic, with the use of pit toilets, latrines, drainage ditches, cesspools, and open defecation. Fifty-eight percent of the people have access to an improved drinking water source, which involves separating drinking water from wastewater. Thirty-two percent of the population has access to improved sanitation facilities. From 1990 to 2012, Nigeria's open defecation increased faster than anywhere else, from 23 million in 1990 to 39 million (23 percent) in 2012. Waste collection practices in small communities are informal.

Emissions and Industry

In 2000 Nigeria generated 212,444 metric tons of greenhouse gases, a 12 percent decrease from 1994. However, there are major gaps in reporting all emissions. It is likely that greenhouse gases are much higher now because of population increases and reliance on agriculture.

There is a substantial amount of arable land. Agricultural products include coffee, cocoa, peanuts, cotton, corn, rice, palm oil, cassava, rubber livestock, fish, and timber. Agricultural emissions were not reported for 2000, but in 1994, agricultural emissions accounted for 26 percent of all emissions. Within this sector, rice cultivation accounted for 45 percent of emissions, enteric fermentation 44 percent, prescribed burning of savannas 7 percent, and manure management 2 percent.

Nigeria produced a large amount of crude oil and maintains large proven gas and oil reserves. Oil and electricity consumption per capita is low. Energy emissions accounted for 72 percent of all emissions. There are all listed as "fugitive" emissions. Fugitive emissions are essentially air pollution. It is likely the source is from energy sector oil production and transit. Industrial emissions were not reported for 2000.

Emissions from wastes accounted for 1 percent of all emissions, down from 18 percent of overall greenhouse gas emissions in 1994. Within this sector, wastewater management accounted for all emissions.

Major Waste Issues

There is rapid deforestation, desertification, droughts and flooding affecting many parts of Nigeria, all of which can be related to waste management issues. Economic development is centered on the petroleum industry, and there is concern that environmental regulation could affect economic development.

The Niger River Delta is formed by the Niger River as it flows into the Gulf of Guinea. It is densely populated and covers 8 percent of Nigeria's landmass. Between 1976 and 2001, there were at the least 7,000 incidents of oil spills that saw no cleanup. In 2012, 2 million bbl of crude oil a day were extracted from this region. The Niger River Delta is one of the largest deltas in the world. It is heavily polluted by oil, as are the land and groundwater. Local scientists estimate that these spills could lead to a 60 percent reduction in food security and a 24 percent increase in childhood malnutrition.

There are many infectious diseases in Nigeria—most currently an outbreak of the deadly Ebola virus, but also yellow fever, cholera, hepatitis A, hepatitis B, meningococcal meningitis, typhoid, malaria, dengue fever, and schistosomiasis. Two percent or more of the population is persistently infected with hepatitis B. Public health concerns are a primary motivation for waste management. Famine is a real concern. Nine percent suffer chronic malnutrition, and 43 percent suffers malnutrition now.

The basic waste management issue is the insufficient regulatory structure and lack of any private sector investment. There are some recycling and composting microbusinesses emerging. E-waste recycling as a form of economic development is currently being studied.

Further Reading

Cross, P., and Y. Coombes, eds. 2014. *Sanitation and Hygiene in Africa: Where Do We Stand?* London, UK: IWA Publishing.
Government Ministries of Nigeria. www.odili.net.
Manton, J. 2013. "Environmental Akalism and the War on Filth: The Personification of Sanitation in Urban Nigeria." *Africa* 83: 606–622.

NORWAY

Norway clings to the west side of the Scandinavian Peninsula, from the North Sea to the Norwegian Sea. Sweden, Finland, and Russia also border Norway. The terrain is varied and in general is mountainous. The coastline is dotted with fjords, and there is arctic tundra in the north. Norway is the most northerly of all European nations. Warm ocean currents modify the climate. It is moderate along the coast, with warmer summers and cool, wet winters. The interior is much colder and wetter. It rains all year in the west. Natural resources include oil, gas, lead, iron ore, zinc, timber, fish, and hydropower. Altogether, 4.7 million people live on Norway's 323,781 km² of land. With 19,312 km of coastline, it has the eighth most in the world. Seventy-seven percent of Norwegians are urbanized, and 33 percent live in a city having more than 100,000 inhabitants.

Current Waste Practices

Norway is a world leader in waste management and environmental management generally. Norway collected 2,269,000 tons of municipal waste in 2009. Almost 14 percent of the waste was landfilled, 41 percent incinerated, 28 percent recycled, and about 16 percent composted. In 2013 only 6 percent of municipal solid waste was landfilled. Altogether, 2,269,000 tons of municipal waste was collected in 2009. A ban on landfill in 2009 has decreased municipal solid waste generation substantially. The next year only 6 percent of municipal solid waste was landfilled. Ninety-nine percent of the country is served by municipal waste services, including access to improved drinking water sources and sanitation facilities.

Recycling

Norway has a cultural ethic that embraces recycling and sustainability. It is a leading nation in the implementation and research of sustainable practices in many areas, including waste management. Municipal solid waste has decreased and greenhouse gas emissions have stabilized. Norway and Sweden are both in a trash deficit because they both incinerate garbage, often for energy.

Emissions and Industry

Norway generated 52,733 tons of greenhouse gases in 2012.

Agricultural products include wheat, barley, fish, meat, and milk. Agricultural emissions accounted for only 9 percent of all emissions. Within this sector, agricultural soils accounted for 47 percent of emissions, enteric fermentation 45 percent, and manure management 8 percent.

Crude oil production and consumption is high. Norway maintains massive proven oil reserves. Energy emissions accounted for 74 percent of all emissions. Within this sector, transport accounted for 39 percent of emissions, energy emissions 36 percent, fugitive emissions 8.5 percent, and manufacturing and construction industries 8 percent. Fugitive emissions are essentially unaccounted waste streams into the air. Fugitive emissions can affect regional ecosystems and the public health, because they can fall from the air to the land and water. Industrial emissions accounted for 15 percent of all emissions. Within this sector, metal production accounted for 56 percent of emissions, chemical industries 14 percent, and mineral products 13 percent.

Waste emissions accounted for 2 percent of all emissions. Within this sector, solid waste disposal on land accounted for 87 percent of emissions, and wastewater handling 13 percent.

Major Waste Issues

Norway's major waste issues are clustered around climate change adaptation measures. Norway is preparing for climate change effects on water systems. Climate change observers note increased temperatures, less precipitation, increased steam flow in spring and winter, earlier snowmelt, floods from heavy rainfall, shorter snow seasons, and rapid warming of the permafrost in the mountains. Projected effects include increases in temperatures, increases in precipitation, shorter snow season, challenges to the water supply and sewer system, more loose organic material in the water, and cyanabacterial blooms from warmer lakes. There is much vulnerability. Generally, the arctic has more increased temperatures than anywhere else. Many effects are noted. The ecosystem can be affected in many waters. The migratory patterns and pathways and plants and animals change, for example. The water temperature in many rivers and lakes may become too warm for native species of fish, such as salmon, trout, and char. Norway is also vulnerable to avalanches, landslides, and mudslides because of its alpine terrain. These increase with warming temperatures and more severe weather events. Primary concerns are about extreme weather events and ecosystem damages. The Norwegian government is developing many initiatives and programs to deal with climate change adaptation. There is an initiative to reduce greenhouse gas emissions and adapt to current and future climate change including the thirteen largest cities. Large infrastructure projects are under way. The Midgard Snake project aims to relieve sewer and water overflows during heavy rains and flooding, part of a new interruptive drain system that prevents polluted water from entering the fjord. It is basically a large tunnel (50,000 m^2 capacity) that can act as both a reservoir and overflow area. There are many sources of public information, including Climate Adaptation Norway.

Further Reading

Climate Adaptation Norway. www.KlimatilpasningNorge.

Climate Change Impacts on Water Systems. www.oecd.org.

Norwegian Government. www.regjeringen.no.

Venkatesh, G., et al. 2014. "Dynamic Metabolism Modelling of Urban Water Services: Demonstrating Effectiveness as A Decision—Support Tool for Oslo, Norway." *Water Research* 61: 19–33.

O

OMAN

Oman is essentially a vast coastal plain along the Arabian Sea. Saudi Arabia, United Arab Emirates, Yemen, the Arabian Sea, the Gulf of Oman, and the Persian Gulf border Oman. The terrain is generally flat desert, with mountains in the south and north. The highest mountain is Jabal Shams, at almost 3,000 m. The climate is desert—hot and dry—though less arid along the coast. In the far south, there is one monsoon season, from May to September. Natural resources include oil, gas, chromium, and copper. Altogether, 3.1 million people live on 309,500 km² of land and 2,092 km of coastline. In 2014, Oman had the fastest-growing population in the world. Seventy-one percent of the population is urbanized, and 36 percent lives in a city having more than 100,000 inhabitants.

Current Waste Practices

Most communities have modern sewer and water systems, but not all wastewater is fully treated before being discharged into freshwater. Sixty percent of rural populations and 98 percent of urban populations use adequate sanitation facilities. Thirty percent of the rural population and 40 percent of the urban population use improved drinking water sources. In rural areas, waste practices are basic—pit toilets, latrines, drainage ditches, cesspools, and open defecation.

Municipalities handle all nonhazardous wastes. Hazardous wastes were traditionally handled by the industries. Industries usually kept the hazardous wastes and material on the industrial site. Health care wastes are incinerated. In 2009, a royal decree was issued giving the government control over waste management. The purpose of the decree was to implement government policy on wastes, to integrate waste sector businesses with other sectors, and exert control over waste issues at all local levels including industry. One of the main goals is to elevate waste facilities to international and sustainable standards as soon as possible. However, there are many challenges. Waste management policy and planning are just beginning. Government unaccountability, lack of integrated waste management, and inadequate waste laws are also pervasive. There are plans to reduce the approximately 350 dumpsites into ten sanitary landfills. Setting up central treatment facilities, with transfer stations and collection vehicles and routes, is a new and ongoing challenge.

Emissions and Industry

Oman generated 20,878.7 tons of greenhouse gases in 1994. It is likely that greenhouse gases are higher now because of population increases and reliance on agriculture.

There is some arable land. Agricultural products include dates, camels, bananas, cattle and fish. Agricultural emissions accounted for 35 percent of all omissions. Within this sector, agricultural soils accounted for 95 percent of emissions and enteric fermentation 5 percent.

Crude oil production is high. Oman maintains massive proven oil reserves. Energy emissions accounted for 59 percent of all omissions. Within this sector, energy industries accounted for 60 percent of emissions, fugitive emissions 15 percent, and transportation 13 percent. Fugitive emissions are essentially unaccounted waste streams into the air. Fugitive emissions can affect regional ecosystems and the public health, because they can fall from the air to the land and water. Industrial emissions accounted for 3 percent of all omissions. Within this sector, mineral products accounted for 99 percent of emissions and chemical industries 1 percent.

Waste emissions accounted for 2 percent of all omissions. Within this sector, wastewater handling accounted for 69 percent of emissions and solid waste disposal on land 31 percent.

Major Waste Issues

Water quality is a major issue. Oman has the third-dirtiest water in the world as measured by BOD (biological oxygen demand). Ninety-seven percent of the urban population has access to an improved drinking water source, meaning that it is separate from sanitation facilities and other wastes. Current evidence suggests there is not enough water to meet growing needs for it. The quantities of consumed water exceed available water resources by about 378 million m^2 a year. Groundwater resources provide 94 percent of water needs, supplemented by desalinization plants, wastewater treatment and reuse, treatment and reuse of oil production water, and cloud seeding. There is some concern about wastewater's affecting groundwater sources.

Further Reading

Al-Kalbani, M. 2014. "Vulnerability Assessment of Environmental and Climate Change Impacts on Water Resources in Al Akhdar." *Water* 6: in press.

El-Khoury, Gabi. 2014. "Water Indicators in Arab Countries: Selected Indicators." *Contemporary Arab Affairs* 7: 339–349.

Oman Government. www.oman.om.

P

PAKISTAN

The south Asian country of Pakistan is bordered by Afghanistan, China, India, Iran, and the Arabian Sea. The terrain is varied—mainly plateaus and plains in the east and west. There are four geographic regions—the plateau of west Pakistan, the plains of the Indus and Punjab rivers, the hills of northwest Pakistan, and the mountains of north Pakistan. The climate is mainly hot and dry desert. There is some regional variation. There is a subtropical climate in the northeast in the mountain foothills. The mountain climates in the north vary widely with altitude. The second-highest mountain in the world, the K2, stands at 8,611 m. Natural resources includes gas, oil, coal, iron ore copper, salt, and hydropower. Altogether, 193.4 million people live on Pakistan's 796,095 km^2 of land and 1,046 km of coastline. There are many small communities and large cities. Thirty-five percent of Pakistanis are urbanized, and 27 percent live in a city having more than 100,000 inhabitants. The life expectancy is 63 years. Forty-two percent suffers malnutrition.

Current Waste Practices

Most communities have modern sewer and water systems, but not all wastewater is fully treated before discharge into freshwater. Ninety-five percent of the urban population has access to an improved source of drinking water, and 90 percent has access to improved sanitation facilities. In rural areas, waste practices are very basic and include pit toilets, latrines, drainage ditches, cesspools, and open defecation. Eighty-seven percent of rural populations have access to an improved drinking water source, and 40 percent have access to improved sanitation facilities. About 59,200 deaths per year are attributed to unsafe water. The open defecation rate in 2012 was 23 percent, down from 52 percent in 1990. There is little waste infrastructure in any urban area from waste collection to proper disposal. Less than half the solid wastes are collected. Most of these are transported to open landfills. Some basic recycling occurs from informal waste picker communities.

Recycling

Pakistan recycles end-of-life ships for steel and other recyclable materials and shares 70 percent to 80 percent of the global market with Bangladesh and India. This industry develops in countries with very low labor costs, little occupational safety, and little environmental enforcement. Many ships contain wastes and hazardous materials and can pose threats to human health and the environment.

There is an informal recycling groups of waste pickers, an estimated population of 90,000 people, many children. They are often focused on the materials in the increasing amounts of e-waste. There are recycling efforts with first-use paper products and some plastics.

Emissions and Industry

In 1994, Pakistan generated 160,589.2 metric tons of greenhouse gases. It is likely that greenhouse gases are much higher now because of large population increases, rapid urbanization and industrialization, and reliance on agriculture.

There is a substantial amount of arable land. Agricultural products include bananas, cotton, rice, wheat, fruit, vegetables, sugar cane, milk, meat, and eggs. Emissions from agricultural wastes accounted for 38.5 percent of all emissions. Within this sector, enteric fermentation accounted for 71 percent of emissions, agricultural soils 15 percent, rice cultivation 7 percent, and manure management 6.5 percent.

Pakistan produces crude oil and maintains proven oil reserves. Electricity production and consumption per capita is high. Oil consumption per capita is low. Energy emissions accounted for 52 percent of all emissions. Within this sector, manufacturing and construction accounted for 30 percent of emissions, energy industries 26 percent, transportation 22 percent, and fugitive emissions 26 percent. Fugitive emissions are essentially unaccounted waste streams into the air. Fugitive emissions can affect regional ecosystems and the public health, because they can fall from the air to the land and water. Industrial emissions accounted for 7 percent of all emissions. Within this sector, mineral products accounted for 38.5 percent of emissions, metal production 35 percent and chemical industries 26.5 percent.

Waste emissions accounted for 3 percent of all emissions. Within this sector, solid waste disposal on land accounted for 47 percent of emissions, other 48 percent, and wastewater handling 5 percent.

Major Waste Issues

Illegal dumping is a particular problem because of the volume and rate of growth of trash that is dumped in low-lying areas where toxic and hazardous materials leech into the water table. This, in turn, pollutes ground water. Groundwater pollution is a symptom of a lack of basic waste management infrastructure. There are no sanitary landfill sites. Waste collection is inconsistent. Trash is dumped in the streets and accumulates in piles that cause environmental and public health issues. What waste collection there is does not separate wastes, making recycling more difficult. Many citizens do not connect waste disposal with environmental and public health effects.

Pakistan has developed some environmental laws, established regulatory agencies, and accepted money, resources and technical assistance from the World Bank, but there are still significant regulatory gaps. There are still no national quality standards for solid waste management for example. Enforcement is poor.

The protection of public health both in the country and the region is another motivating factor driving development of a waste management approach. There are infectious diseases here. Cholera, hepatitis A, hepatitis B, dengue fever, Japanese encephalitis, malaria, and typhoid occur here. More than 2 percent of the population is persistently infected with hepatitis B.

Further Reading

Luby, Stephen, et al. 2011. "The Variability of Childhood Diarrhea in Karachi, Pakistan." *American Journal of Tropical Medicine and Hygiene* 84: 870–877.

Nabeela, F., et al. 2014. "Microbial Contamination of Drinking Water in Pakistan—A Review." *Environmental Science and Pollution Research* 21: 13929–13942.

Pakistan Government. www.pakistan.gov.pk.

Pakistan Shipbreaking Outlook. 2013. www.shipbreakingplatform.org.

PALESTINE

Palestine's borders tend to shift and have been disputed by neighboring countries, including Syria, Jordan, Israel, and Lebanon. The Dead Sea defines the western boundary, one of the saltiest large bodies of water in the world. The salt content increases as the Dead Sea shrinks. The terrain is flat along the coast, rising to hill and mountains toward the interior. It is desert in the south. The climate is Mediterranean—long, hot, and dry summers, and short cooler winters. Natural resources include gas. Agricultural products include olives, citrus fruits, vegetables, beef and dairy products.

About 4 million live on an indeterminate amount of land and 230 km of coastline. The region is about 225 km long and 50–115 km wide.

Current Waste Practices

The Palestinian state collected 1,350,000 tons of municipal waste in 2001, all of it landfilled. Seventy-five percent of the country is covered by municipal waste services. Eighty-six percent of the urban population has access to an improved source of drinking water, and 92 percent has access to improved sanitation facilities. Eighty-one percent of rural populations have access to an improved drinking water source, and 92 percent have access to improved sanitation facilities. Years of conflict have destroyed sewers, waste treatment facilities, sanitary facilities, and clean drinking water sources. It is likely that basic waste practices include pit toilets, cesspools, drainage ditches, latrines, and open defecation.

Emissions and Industry

There is some preliminary monitoring of greenhouse gas emissions. Intense and ongoing conflict impairs environmental and waste record keeping.

Major Waste Issues

Public health protection is a major issue related to waste management in Palestine. Much of the waste infrastructure was destroyed in the political conflict. Infectious diseases in the area include hepatitis A, hepatitis B, and typhoid. Two percent or more of the population is persistently infected with hepatitis B.

Further Reading

El-Khoury, Gabi. 2014. "Water Indicators in Arab Countries: Selected Indicators." *Contemporary Arab Affairs* 7: 339–349.

Geography of Palestine According to Palestinians. www.jewishvirtuallibrary.org.

Palestinian National Authority. www.minfo.gov.ps.

Zawahri, N., et al. 2011. "The Politics of Assessment: Water and Sanitation Millennium Development Goals in the Middle East." *Development and Change* 42: 1154–1178.

PANAMA

Panama receives some of the highest amounts of rain in the world. The Panama Canal connects the Caribbean Sea and Pacific Ocean. Colombia, Costa Rica, the Caribbean Sea, and the North Pacific Ocean border Panama. The terrain is mountainous in the interior and flattens out to coastal plains. The tropical climate is hot and humid. The rainy season is from May to January and the dry season from January to May. Natural resources include timber, copper, fish, and hydropower.

Altogether, 3.6 million people live on Panama's 75,417 km^2 of land and 2,490 km of coastline. Seventy-one percent of Panamanians are urbanized, and 29 percent live in a city having more than 100,000 inhabitants. Twenty-eight percent live in overcrowded conditions. Twenty-two percent suffers malnutrition.

Current Waste Practices

Most communities have modern sewer and water systems but not all wastewater is fully treated before being discharged into freshwater. Ninety-seven percent of the urban population has access to improved drinking water, and 75 percent has access to improved sanitation facilities. Thirty-five percent of the rural population has access to improved drinking water, and about half has access to improved sanitation facilities. In rural areas, waste practices include pit toilets, latrines, drainage ditches, cesspools, and open defecation. Six sewer systems serve 95 percent of the coastal population. Two systems that cover 85 percent of this population discharge raw sewage. So far, Panama has not met the United Nations Millennium Development goals for sanitation, and it likely will not meet 2015 deadlines.

Emissions and Industry

Panama generated 9,707.7 metric tons of greenhouse gases in 2000, a 9 percent decrease from 1994.

Agricultural products include bananas, coffee, rice, corn, vegetables, livestock, and fish. Agricultural emissions accounted for 33 percent of all emissions in 2000. Within this sector, enteric fermentation accounted for 53 percent of emissions, agricultural soils almost 40 percent, rice cultivation 4 percent, and manure management almost 3 percent.

Oil and electricity production and consumption per capita are low. Energy emissions accounted for 50 percent of all emissions in 2000. Within this sector, transportation accounted for 56 percent of emissions, manufacturing and construction industries almost 19 percent, and energy industries almost 19 percent. Industrial emissions accounted for 6 percent of all emissions in 2000. Within this sector, mineral products accounted for 100 percent of emissions.

Waste emissions accounted for more than 11 percent of all emissions in 2000. Within this sector, solid waste disposal on land accounted for 91 percent of emissions and wastewater handling 9 percent.

Major Waste Issues

Inadequate waste facilities have slowed attempts at economic development along the Panama Canal. Waste dumps and waste pickers create concern about public health threats in the whole region. Sometimes the amount of trash in rivers and streams that feed the Panama Canal actually obstructs the flow of ship traffic.

Massive construction projects in Cocoli, Panama, are expanding the Panama Canal to facilitate expanded energy transit, primarily for tankers with liquified natural gas or crude oil. Global reliance on petrochemicals continues to push maritime infrastructure development in the face of rising sea levels. (AP Photo/Arnulfo Franco)

Littering is a common practice. Investors are also concerned about the high level of corruption in waste management decisions around economic development.

Panama Canal is a large transit corridor for many ocean-going vessels from all over the world. As such, it is a transmission point for some infectious diseases. If the vessels dump their bilges and wastes in the water near the canal, whatever diseases are in the bodily fluids and organic wastes are discharged into the water. Cholera, hepatitis A, typhoid, malaria, and dengue fever do occur here.

Further Reading

Bayard, V., et al. 2012. "Impact of Rotavirus Vaccination on Childhood Gastroenteritis-related Mortality and Hospital Discharges in Panama." *International Journal of Infectious Diseases* 16: 94–98.

Carruthers, David V. 2008. *Environmental Justice in Latin America: Problems, Promise, and Practice*. Cambridge, MA: MIT Press.

Panama President. www.presidencia.gob.pa.

PARAGUAY

Argentina, Bolivia, and Brazil border the South American country of Paraguay, a landlocked nation. The terrain is divided by Rio Paraguay into east and west regions. The eastern region is called the Paranena, and the western region is called the Chaco region. In the eastern region the land moves from lowlands up to mountains. The vast majority of people live here. In the western region the land is a vast grassy plain. It experiences floods and droughts. The climate is subtropical. There is more rain in the east, and there are drier conditions in the west. Natural resources include iron ore, manganese, timber, and hydropower. Altogether, 6.2 million people live on Paraguay's 75,417 km^2 of land. There are many small communities, though 58 percent of the population is urbanized, and 25 percent lives in a city having more than 100,000 inhabitants. Thirty-eight percent of the population lives in overcrowded conditions.

Current Waste Practices

Most cities have modern sewer and water systems, but not all wastewater is fully treated before being discharged into freshwater. About 64 percent of the country is served by municipal waste services. Five hundred fifty-one tons of municipal waste was collected in 2009. Ninety-seven percent of the urban population has access to an improved source of drinking water, and 75 percent has access to improved sanitation facilities. Eighty-three percent of rural populations have access to an improved drinking water source, and half have access to improved sanitation facilities. In rural areas, waste practices are basic—pit toilets, latrines, drainage ditches, cesspools, and open defecation. Only 1 percent of urban sewage is treated before being discharged into water. All this receives secondary levels of waste treatment. In the capital city of Asunción, raw sewage is discharged into the Paraguay River from five outfalls. This and other waste issues are the subjects of planning for improvement.

However there are strong policies around recycling organic wastes. Organic waste treatment is profitable, employs many people, and includes waste-to-energy applications. In most communities it is an institutionalized waste management practice.

Emissions and Industry

In 2000, Paraguay generated 23,429.9 metric tons of greenhouse gases, a 58 percent decrease from 1990.

Agricultural products include coffee, cotton, corn, wheat, sugar cane, cassava, tobacco, fruits, vegetables, meat, eggs, and wood products. Agricultural emissions accounted for 79.5 percent of all emissions. Within this sector, enteric fermentation accounted for 56 percent of emissions, agricultural soils 41 percent, manure management 2 percent, and rice cultivation 1 percent.

There is modest production of crude oil and no proven reserves. Energy emissions accounted for 16 percent of all emissions. Within this sector, transportation accounted for 76 percent of emissions, manufacturing industries and construction 9.6 percent, and other sectors 15 percent. Industrial emissions accounted for 1.7 percent of emissions. Within this sector, mineral products accounted for 67 percent of emissions and metal production 33 percent.

Waste emissions accounted for 3 percent of all emissions. Within this sector, solid waste disposal on land accounted for 34 percent of emissions and other 66 percent. This is a big change from 1990, when solid waste disposal on land accounted for 1.5 percent of emissions and wastewater handling accounted for 98 percent.

Major Waste Issues

Some of Paraguay's major environmental issues are also waste issues. Urban water supplies are polluted, and there is not adequate waste disposal. Climate change observers note increased temperatures and changes in precipitation patterns. There are concerns about droughts and wildfires. The agricultural climate change strategy is both mitigation and adaptation. In this sparsely populated country, agriculture is the source of more than 95 percent of methane emissions and more than 70 percent of freshwater extractions. More than 60 percent of the country grazes livestock. Agricultural crops are vulnerable to weather extremes. Paraguay relies more on the weather, because it does not rely on irrigation. The policy goal is to mitigate climate change effects by decreasing greenhouse gas emissions per sector, especially the largest sector—agriculture. The policy goal for adaptation is to build resilience to effects by sustainable management of agricultural resources. A National Action Plan on Climate Change is being developed. The Ministry of Agriculture and Livestock is developing an internal capacity to make decisions about climate change.

Although laws, regulations, and state agencies exist, there are significant gaps in waste management. Regulations for industrial wastes, industrial plastics and e-wastes are not developed yet. There is inconsistency in how health wastes and municipal solid wastes are regulated.

In addition, Paraguay faces the issue of infectious diseases, including yellow fever, cholera, hepatitis A, hepatitis B, typhoid, malaria, and dengue fever. Two percent or more of the population is persistently infected with hepatitis B. The current risk of yellow fever is limited to the main city of Asunción.

Further Reading

Cunningham, Rad N., et al. 2012. "Hazards Faced by Informal Recyclers in the Squatter Communities of Asuncion, Paraguay." *International Journal of Occupational and Environmental Health* 18: 181–187.

Cuppens, Arnoud, et al. 2013. "Identifying Sustainable Rehabilitation Strategies for Urban Wastewater Systems: A Retrospective and Interdisciplinary Approach. Case Study of Coronel Oviedo, Paraguay." *Journal of Environmental Management* 114: 423–432.

Paraguay Water and Sanitation Sector Modernization. www.worldbank.org.

President of the Republic of Paraguay. www.presidencia.gov.py.

Swarts, Frederick A. 2000. *The Pantanal of Brazil, Bolivia, and Paraguay: Selected Discourses on the World's Largest Remaining Wetland System.* Salt Lake City, UT: The Wetland Institute and Paragon House Publishers.

PAPUA NEW GUINEA

Papua New Guinea is an island nation that borders Indonesia, the Coral Sea, and the South Pacific Ocean. The terrain is mountainous to coastal as the land nears the ocean. The climate receives some of the highest amounts of rain in the world. It is tropical, with two monsoonal seasons. The northwest monsoon is from December to March, and the southeast monsoon is from May to October. Natural resources include fish, timber, gas, gold, oil, copper, and silver.

Altogether, 6.43 million people live on Papua New Guinea's 462,840 km^2 on a group of islands having 5,152 km of coastline. There are many small communities, with only 13 percent of the population living in urban areas and just 6 percent living in a city having more than 100,000 inhabitants. Forty-four percent suffers malnutrition. Life expectancy is 62 years.

Current Waste Practices

Eighty-seven percent of the urban population has access to an improved source of drinking water, and 71 percent has access to improved sanitation facilities. In rural areas, waste practices are very basic—pit toilets, latrines, drainage ditches, cesspools, and open defecation. Just 33 percent of rural populations have access to an improved drinking water source, and 41 percent have access to improved sanitation facilities.

Most trash is collected and taken to a dumpsite. There is only one official landfill—the Baruni dumpsite—but there are many illegal ones. The government has started to remediate some of its significant environmental effects. Few recycling or waste reduction programs are offered by the government. Papua New Guinea did adopt the Solid Waste Management Strategy for the Pacific in 2009, but is still working out policies.

Emissions and Industry

In 1994, Papua New Guinea generated 727.6 tons of greenhouse gases. It is likely that greenhouse gases are higher now because of population increases and reliance on agriculture.

There is little arable land. Agricultural products include coffee, cocoa, tea, sugar, palm kernels, bananas, rubber, fruit, vegetables, pork, shellfish, and poultry. Agricultural emissions accounted for 77 percent of all emissions. Within this sector, other accounted for all emissions.

Papua New Guinea produces crude oil and maintains substantial proven reserves. Oil production per capita is high, and oil consumption per capita is low. Energy emissions accounted for 19 percent of all emissions. Within this sector, "other" accounted for all emissions. Industrial emissions accounted for almost 3 percent of all emissions. Within this sector, "other" accounted for all emissions.

Major Waste Issues

One of the waste issues in Papua New Guinea is the lack of information and monitoring of waste issues. Current environmental problems are industrial pollution from mining operations and rainforest deforestation from logging operations. The Ok Tedi copper and gold mine on Mt. Fubilan generates 80,000 tons of rocks and up to 120,000 tons of tailings a day. Today, only copper is mined. A landslide destroyed the original tailing pond. Landslides from tailing ponds are unique because of their extreme force. The tailings and sediment in the water have a substantial amount of weight that can cause the landslide to move faster and create more damage over a bigger area. After much controversy, the owners were not required to replace the tailing pond with anything. The environmental and community effects were significant. Rivers died for 70 km, and the fish stock decreased in all parts of the rivers. A community of 4,500 people, called the Yonggom, feel the direct effect of the mine pollution.

The lack of proper waste disposal is endemic. Public health concerns help drive the development of waste management policy. Cholera, hepatitis A, hepatitis B, meningococcal meningitis, typhoid, dengue fever, and schistosomiasis are just some of the infectious diseases present in Papua New Guinea. Two percent or more of the population is persistently infected with hepatitis B. Additionally, there is a high risk of malaria and yellow fever.

Further Reading

Au, N., et al. 2014. "Measuring the Efficiency of Health Services in Lower Income Countries: The Case of Papua New Guinea." *Development Policy Review* 32: 259–272.

Blakeney, Michael, Thierry Coulet, Getachew Mengiste, and Marcelin Tonye Mahop, eds. 2012. *Extending the Protection of Geographical Indications: Case Studies of Agricultural Products in Africa*. New York: Earthscan Publishing.

Management of Wastes in Small Island Developing States. www.islands.unep.ch.

Prime Minister of Papua New Guinea. www.pm.gov.pg.

PERU

Peru covers the west coast of South America for 2,414 km. Bolivia, Brazil, Chile, Colombia, Ecuador, and the South Pacific Ocean border Peru. The climate is variable, with a desert climate in the west. Along the ocean coast in the east the climate is tropical—hot and humid. The altitude of the high mountains affects climate conditions, but is generally much colder and windier. The tallest mountain is Nevada Huascaran, at 6,768 m. Natural resources include oil, gas, coal, silver, gold, copper, potash, and hydropower. Altogether, 29.8 million people live on Peru's 1,285,216 km² of land and 2,414 km of coastline. There are small communities in foothills of the mountains. Seventy-three percent of the population is urbanized, and 53 percent lives in a city having more than 100,000 inhabitants. Thirty-one percent of the population suffers malnutrition.

Current Waste Practices

Most Peruvian cities have modern sewer and water systems, but not all wastewater is fully treated before being discharged into freshwater. Peru collected 4,740,000 tons of municipal waste in 2001, almost 66 percent of the waste landfilled and 14 percent recycled. Seventy-five percent of the country is served by municipal waste collection. Peru generated 11,369 tons of hazardous wastes in 1994. Most landfills are open trash sites on the edge of the city.

Waste practices are basic in many rural areas, where people use pit toilets, latrines, drainage ditches cesspools and open defecation. Eighty-nine percent of the urban population has access to an improved source of drinking water, and 74 percent has access to improved sanitation facilities. Sixty-five percent of rural populations have access to an improved drinking water source, and 32 percent have access to improved sanitation facilities. Approximately 85 percent of urban raw sewage is discharged directly into water. The goal is to bring the national sewage discharge rate down to 40 percent. The open defecation rate in 2012 was 6 percent, down from 33 percent in 1990. Peru is unlikely to meet the 2015 deadlines for the United Nations Millennium Development goals for sanitation.

Peru does receive international assistance for waste management. The Inter-American Development Bank and the Japan International Cooperation Agency helped finance thirty-one sustainable waste management systems for solid wastes in 2012. The Inter-American Development Bank loaned $15 million for eight projects, and the Japan International Cooperation Agency is aiding the remaining twenty-three projects. The eight projects are designed to handle 23,000 tons per day. All the projects together are planned to handle 432 tons of municipal wastes a day and increase waste storage and transfer capacity from 22 percent of wastes to 90 percent of wastes. Peru's goal is to safely dispose or recycle 100 percent of municipal wastes by 2021.

Emissions and Industry

In 2000 Peru generated 63,197 metric tons of greenhouse gases, a 10 percent increase from 1994.

There is some arable land. Agricultural products include coffee, potatoes, beans, sugar cane, corn, fruits, vegetables, wheat, and livestock. Emissions from agricultural wastes accounted for 35.5 percent of all emissions. Within this sector, agricultural soils accounted for 43 percent of greenhouse gas emissions, enteric fermentation 46 percent, manure management 4 percent, rice cultivation 4 percent, and prescribed burning of savannas 2 percent.

Peru produces crude oil and maintains proven reserves. Energy emissions accounted for 40 percent of all emissions. Within this sector, transportation accounted for 39 percent of emissions, manufacturing and construction 13 percent, and energy industries 12 percent. Industrial emissions accounted for 12.5 percent of all emissions. Within this sector, metal production accounted for 73.5 percent of emissions, mineral products 25 percent, and chemical industries 1 percent.

Municipal waste workers in Lima, Peru, begin the day on August 30, 2008, by collecting trash. Municipal waste workers perform essential functions for many urban areas. Cities often have uneven municipal collection services, with poorer areas often overlooked. (Steve Estvanik/Dreamstime.com)

Waste emissions accounted for 11.5 percent of all emissions. Within this sector, solid waste disposal on land accounted for 84 percent of emissions and wastewater handling 16 percent. Waste is a major issue in air pollution.

Major Waste Issues

Peru faces challenges in key areas of waste management. There is a fundamental lack of data, as well as a lack of technical capacity to analyze it. Technical capacity is a challenge in financial, operational, and organizational waste management planning. There is little integration of local approaches with the national policy and little integration between international monitoring mechanisms and waste management. Environmental and public health issues include methane emissions from landfills and trash heaps, groundwater pollution, open burning, and surface water pollution.

Peru, like many nations, is faced with the challenge of protecting public health from infectious diseases such as yellow fever, hepatitis A, hepatitis B, typhoid, and dengue fever. Concerns about public health can drive the development of an integrated waste management policy, especially as population increases. More than 2 percent of the population is persistently infected with hepatitis B. There is also a high risk of malaria in the Amazon River basin.

Further Reading

Julian, T., et al. 2013. "Fecal Indicator Bacteria Contamination of Fomites and Household Demand for Surface Disinfection Products: A Case Study of Peru." *American Journal of Tropical Medicine and Hygiene* 89: 869–872.

Peru Government. www.peru.gob.pe.

Starn, Orin, Ivan Degregori, and Robin Kirk. 2005. *The Peru Reader: History, Culture, Politics*. Durham, NC: Duke University Press.

PHILIPPINES

The Philippines are an archipelago of more than 7,000 islands bordered by the South China Sea and the Philippine Sea, in east Asia. The terrain is mountainous, with some coastal lowlands. Mount Apo is the tallest mountain, at almost 3,000 m. The climate is tropical, with two monsoon seasons, one from November to April and the other from May to October. The range of current extreme weather–related events include hurricanes, volcanic eruption, earthquakes, and tsunamis. Natural resources include oil, silver, gold, nickel, cobalt, timber, salt, and hydropower.

Altogether, 105.7 million people live on the Philippines' 298,170 km^2 of land. There is a 36,289 km coastline, the fifth-longest in the world of any nation.

Current Waste Practices

Most cities have modern sewer and water systems, but not all wastewater is fully treated before being discharged into freshwater. Waste practices are basic in many rural areas, where people use pit toilets, latrines, drainage ditches cesspools, and open defecation. Eighty-nine percent of the urban population has access to an improved source of drinking water, and 74 percent has access to improved sanitation facilities. Sixty-five percent of rural populations have access to an improved drinking water source, and only 32 percent have access to improved sanitation facilities. About 5,000 tons of municipal waste was collected in 2001. Most such waste goes to open landfills. About three-quarters of the population is served by municipal waste collection.

The land Bank of the Philippines and the World Bank developed the Methane Recovery from Waste program in 2012. This program gives local governments, communities, and investors carbon credits for complying with the Ecological Solid Waste Management Act of 2000. The goal is to provide a financial incentive to convert dumps and trash heaps into sanitary landfills and decrease methane emissions at the same time. The first landfill gas recovery site was the first registered with United Nations Framework Convention on Climate Change.

Emissions and Industry

In 1994, the Philippines generated 100,866.6 metric tons of greenhouse gases. It is likely that greenhouse gases are higher now because of population increases and reliance on agriculture.

Agricultural products include coffee, coconuts, sugar cane, cassavas, rice, corn, bananas, mangoes, meat, eggs, and fish. Agricultural emissions accounted for 33 percent of all emissions. Within this sector, rice cultivation accounted for 40 percent of emissions, agricultural soils 26 percent, enteric fermentation 21 percent, manure management 11 percent, and field burning agricultural residues 2 percent.

The Philippines produce crude oil and maintain proven reserves. Oil production and consumption per capita is high. Energy emissions accounted for 49 percent of all emissions. Within this sector, transportation accounted for 33 percent of emissions, energy industries 31 percent, and manufacturing and construction industries 19 percent. Emissions from industrial processes accounted for 11 percent of all emissions. Within this sector, mineral products accounted for 45 percent of emissions and metal production 41 percent.

Waste emissions accounted for 7 percent of all emissions. Within this sector, solid waste disposal on land accounted for 60 percent of emissions and wastewater management 40 percent.

Major Waste Issues

The Philippines have a comprehensive waste management law. There is weak compliance with the law. The law forbade landfills after 2006, and there are still many legal and illegal landfills and dumpsites. Technical issues and the lack of capacity of local governments still are impediments to compliance. The lack of financing is another impediment. Although the national government may require certain types of landfill, the locality must pay for them.

Infectious diseases related to waste management issues are a major problem in the Philippines. Diseases such as cholera, hepatitis A, hepatitis B, Japanese encephalitis, meningitis, typhoid, malaria, and schistosomiasis occur here. Two percent or more of the population is persistently infected with hepatitis B. Concerns about public health push demand up for sanitary landfills.

Further Reading

Bennett, D. 2012. "Does Clean Water Make You Dirty? Water Supply and Sanitation in the Philippines." *Journal of Human Resources* 47: 146–173.

Philippines Government. www.gov.ph.

Responding to the Impacts of Climate Change. www.christianaid.org.uk.

POLAND

Poland is bordered by Belarus, the Czech Republic, Germany, Lithuania, Russia, Slovakia, and Ukraine. There are mountains in the south, but otherwise Poland is flat. The climate is temperate, with cold and sometimes severe winters and with mild summers featuring rain. Natural resources include natural gas, coal, sulfur, lead, silver, and amber. Altogether, 38.4 million people live on Poland's 311,888 km² of land and 440 km of coastline, along the Baltic Sea. Sixty-two percent of Poles are urbanized, and 32 percent live in a city having more than 100,000 inhabitants.

Current Waste Practices

When Poland ratified the Accession Treaty in 2003, it committed to achieving strategic targets in the reduction of municipal wastes in landfills, increased recycling levels, and developed materials for reuse. When Poland joined the European Union in 2004, it received significant funding from the Structural Funds and Cohesion Funds to achieve parity with other member nations. Subsequent EU directives required policies and goals on other waste issues, such as packaging wastes. Many of these targets set in 2003 and 2004, as well as subsequent EU directives, have not yet been met.

Most communities have modern sewer and water systems, but not all wastewater is fully treated before being discharged into freshwater. One hundred percent of the urban population has access to an improved source of drinking water, and 96 percent has access to improved sanitation facilities. One hundred percent of rural populations have access to an improved drinking water source, and 80 percent have access to improved sanitation facilities. Seventy-nine percent of the country enjoys municipal waste collection. Six percent of urban residents and 26 percent of rural do not have municipal waste collection. Poland collected 12,053,000 tons of municipal waste in 2009, with about 70 percent of the waste landfilled, 1 percent incinerated, 12 percent recycled, and about 6 percent composted. Many landfills are over capacity. Illegal trash dumping can be a problem, especially in rural areas.

Emissions and Industry

Poland generated 399,268 tons of greenhouse gases in 2012, a 30 percent decrease from 1990. Population is also decreasing.

A high proportion of the land is arable—about 35 percent. Agricultural products include cereal, fruits, vegetables, potatoes, wheat, dairy products, pork, poultry and eggs. Agricultural emissions accounted for 9 percent of all emissions. Within this sector, agricultural soils accounted for 55 percent of emissions, enteric fermentation 24.5 percent, and manure management 20 percent. This is an unusually high amount of greenhouse gas emissions from manure, indicating the presence of large amounts of untreated feces.

Poland produced a substantial amount of crude oil and has large proven reserves. Energy emissions accounted for 80 percent of all emissions. Within this sector, energy industries accounted for 53 percent of emissions, transportation 14.5 percent, manufacturing and construction industries 10 percent, and fugitive emissions 5 percent. Industrial emissions accounted for 7 percent of all emissions. Within this sector, mineral products accounted for 37 percent of emissions, chemical industries 21 percent, and metal production 9 percent.

Waste emissions accounted for 4 percent of all emissions. Within this sector, solid waste disposal on land accounted for 56 percent of emissions, wastewater handling 42 percent, and waste incineration 2 percent.

Major Waste Issues

The major environmental problems in Poland are also waste issues. Heavy industry has declined, but air- and water-polluting practices continue. Sulfur dioxide emissions generated by coal-fired power plants create acid rain. Industrial and municipal waste discharges into water are a major source of water pollution. Disposal of hazardous wastes poses substantial risk to people and the environment. When industry declined in the 1980s, many industrial plants and their wastes were never properly disposed of. Many old landfills and some current landfills need closing, because they do not meet sanitation standards. Some old landfills are closed before there are new waste treatment options available because of the volume of waste continuously produced. Old landfills that should be closed remain open as storage and transfer points until new facilities are built and operational. Poland does not separate wastes and includes hazardous wastes in the mix.

Poland is preparing for climate change effects on water systems. Climate change observers note increased temperatures, more precipitation, and increase in regional differences in precipitation. Projected effects include increases in temperature, longer summers, longer droughts, and worsened water quality. It is projected that heavily polluted lowland rivers will decrease substantially in water quality. Key vulnerabilities include water shortages and increased flood risks during extreme weather events. In response to these concerns and projections, the Polish government is beginning a National Adaptation Strategy.

There is concern that Poland lacks a strong modern infrastructure for the treatment of municipal wastes despite laws and financing. Recycling efforts and enforcement of pollution laws is also weak.

Further Reading

Andersson, Magnus. 1999. *Change and Continuity in Poland's Environmental Policy.* Alphen aan den Rijn, Netherlands: Kluwer Academic Press.

Auer, Matthew R., ed. 2005. *Restoring Cursed Earth: Appraising Environmental Policy Reforms in Eastern Europe and Russia.* New York: The Rowman & Littlefield Publishing Group.

Climate Change Impacts on Water Systems. www.oecd.org.

Polish Prime Minister. www.premier.gov.pl.

Ulfik, A., and S. Nowak. 2014. "Determinants of Municipal Waste Management in Sustainable Development of Regions in Poland." *Polish Journal of Environmental Studies* 23: 1039–1044.

PORTUGAL

Portugal borders Spain and the North Atlantic Ocean. Its terrain is mountainous in the north, with plains in the south. The climate is generally temperature with mild winters and warm summers. The north is usually colder and wetter than the south. Natural resources include fish, silver, gold, iron ore, uranium, cork, salt, marble, and hydropower. There are many small communities. Altogether, 10.8 million people live on Portugal's 92,207 mi^2 of land and 1,793 km of coastline. Fifty-eight percent of the Portuguese are urbanized, and 56 percent live in a city having more than 100,000 inhabitants.

Current Waste Practices

Though some wastewater is discharged into freshwater before being treated, most communities have modern sewer and water systems. Portugal collected 5,185,000 tons of municipal waste in 2009. Almost 62 percent of the waste is landfilled, 18 percent incinerated, 8 percent recycled, and about 12 percent composted. Everyone has municipal waste services and access to safe drinking water. Portugal generated 3,368 tons of hazardous wastes in 2008. Most landfills are sanitary landfills, but there are illegal landfills in some places. There may also be ocean dumping of some wastes.

Emissions and Industry

Portugal generated 69,752 tons of greenhouse gases in 2012, a 13 percent increase from 1990. It is likely that greenhouse gas emissions are higher now because of population growth and industrialization.

Agricultural products include grains, vegetables, livestock, fish, potatoes, and dairy products. Agricultural emissions accounted for almost 11 percent of all emissions. Within this sector, agricultural soils accounted for 40 percent of emissions, enteric fermentation 38 percent, manure management almost 19 percent, rice cultivation about 3 percent, and field burning of agricultural crop residues less than 1 percent. This is an unusually high amount of greenhouse gas emissions from manure, indicating the presence of large amounts of untreated feces.

Portugal produces a substantial amount of crude oil and maintains strong proven reserves. Energy emissions accounted for almost 70 percent of overall emissions. Within this, energy industries accounted for 36 percent of emissions, transportation 35 percent, manufacturing and construction industries 15 percent, and fugitive emissions almost 3 percent. Industrial processes emissions accounted for about 7 percent of overall emissions. Within this sector, mineral processes accounted for 63 percent of emissions, chemical industries 3 percent, and metal production about 2 percent.

Waste emissions accounted for almost 12 percent of overall emissions. Within this sector, solid waste disposal on land accounted for 62 percent of emissions, wastewater handling 38 percent, and waste incineration about 0.5 percent.

Major Waste Issues

One of the primary environmental issues is also a waste issue. There is substantial water pollution in coastal areas. Much of this is runoff from agricultural pesticide and chemical fertilizer use, sewage, and industrial pollution.

Portugal is preparing for climate change effects on water systems. Climate change observers note decreased annual water runoff, decreased surface and groundwater quality, saltwater intrusion into groundwater, and increased floods. Projected effects include temperature increases, reduced rainfall, less water, seawater intrusion into the groundwater, increased frequency and intensity of heat waves and heavy precipitation events, and loss of wetlands. Key vulnerabilities are lack of freshwater and increased flood risks. In response to these concerns and projections, Portugal is just beginning to develop policies, regulatory instruments, and economic instruments for climate change adaption. One initiative began in 1999. It is the Climate Change in Portugal: Scenarios, Impacts, and Adaptation Measures. In 2002, it focused on the Sado estuary, the Azores, and Madeira. There are new national laws to promote the efficient use of water in times of drought. They are also developing a strategic plan for water supply and wastewater treatment.

Further Reading

Climate Change Impacts on Water Systems. www.oecd.org.
OECD. 2011. *OECD Environmental Performance Reviews: Portugal 2011*. Paris, France: OECD.
Portugal Government. www.portugal.gov.pt.

Q

QATAR

Qatar is a wealthy oil-producing nation in the Middle East. Saudi Arabia and the Persian Gulf border Qatar. Its terrain is flat and mainly desert, with a very hot dry summer climate. Doha, the capital, has an average summer high temperature of 106 degrees. The spring comes with higher winds and dust storms. The winters are dry and cooler, with average highs of 80°F. Natural resources include oil, gas, and fish. Two million people live in Qatar's 11,586 km² of land and 563 km of coastline. Ninety-five percent of the population is urbanized, and 65 percent lives in a city having more than 100,000 inhabitants. In 2014, Qatar had the second fastest growing population rate in the world.

Current Waste Practices

In 2009 Qatar collected 789,000 metric tons of municipal wastes. Ninety-four percent went to a landfill, and 6 percent was composted.

Most cities have modern sewer and water systems, but not all wastewater is fully treated before being discharged into freshwater. Qatar has the fourth-dirtiest water in the world as measured by BOD (biological oxygen demand). There is little natural freshwater. There are no lakes or rivers. Everyone in the country has access to improved drinking water sources and sanitation facilities. Large amounts of water and electricity are free. Hazardous wastes are not allowed into the country.

Emissions and Industry

Agricultural emissions accounted for less than 1 percent of all emissions. Within this sector, enteric fermentation accounted for 95 percent of emissions, and manure management 5 percent.

Qatar produces large amount of crude oil, maintains massive oil proven reserves, and has 15 percent of global proven natural gas reserves. Oil and electricity production and consumption per capita is high. Energy emissions accounted for 91 percent of emissions. Within this sector, energy industries accounted for almost 71 percent of emissions, fugitive emissions more than 14 percent, transportation 10 percent, and manufacturing and construction 5 percent. The large emissions from this sector, particularly the fugitive emissions, indicate the potential for large environmental and public health effects. Fugitive emissions are essentially unaccounted waste streams into the air. Fugitive emissions can affect regional ecosystems and the public health because they can fall from the air to the land and water. Qatar emitted the most carbon dioxide per capita in the world.

Industrial emissions accounted for almost 8 percent of all emissions. Within this sector, the chemical industry accounted for more than 82 percent of emissions, mineral products almost 17 percent, and metal production just more than 1 percent.

Waste emissions accounted for less than 1 percent of emissions. Within this sector, solid waste disposal on land accounted for 81 percent of emissions, and wastewater handling almost 19 percent.

Major Waste Issues

Qatar is one of the wealthiest countries in the world. It is also a travel destination for wealthy people, often from areas having infectious diseases. There is a chance that infectious disease vectors will expand. There are long droughts and desertification that have substantial environmental and public health effects. With increasing temperatures, desertification will increase, in turn increasing these effects. Increasing dust storms bring their own health hazards, distributing waste and trash over long distances, scattering them over land and water. Rising ocean levels will have significant effects on coastal sanitation and desalinization systems. Qatar relies on desalinization plants for freshwater, often powered by fossil fuels and emitting greenhouse gases.

Qatar is responding to some environmental issues. Since 1995, the Qatar Foundation has advocated for less financial reliance on fossil fuels and more on knowledge-based economy. Large dust storms develop and impair solar panel efficiencies. Paper use reduction and recycling, sustainably harvested wood in places, and composting of some waste streams are policies. Qatar is very concerned with the effects of climate change and has hosted UN gatherings on the topic. In 2013, the Qatar foundation and the Potsdam Institute for Climate Impact Research founded the Climate Change Research Institute and Global Climate Change Forum, based in Qatar. Its goal is to build national capacity to adapt and mitigate environmental risks. It is researching extreme weather events, public health, water systems, ecosystems, food production, and sustainable urban development. Also in 2013, Qatar began a $2.7 billion program to improve sanitation, primarily to strengthen waste infrastructure, such as a large waste treatment plant south of Doha. Other projects include a large tunnel for wastewater and an irrigation system for wastewater reuse. To prepare for the World Cup in 2022, Qatar is budgeting $200 billion for infrastructure, including sanitation.

Further Reading

Althani, Mohamed A. 2013. *Jassim the Leader: Founder of Qatar.* London, UK: Profile Books Limited.

El-Khoury, Gabi. 2014. "Water Indicators in Arab Countries: Selected Indicators." *Contemporary Arab Affairs* 7: 339–349.

Qatar Government. www.mofa.gov.qa.

REPUBLIC OF KOREA (SOUTH KOREA)

North Korea, the Yellow Sea, and the Sea of Japan border South Korea. The terrain is generally low and mountainous, with coastal plains in the west and south. Forty-nine million people live on South Korea's 99,720 km² of land and 2,413 km of coastline. Eighty-one percent of the population is urbanized, and 74 percent lives in a city having more than 100,000 inhabitants. Population density in South Korea is among the highest in the world.

Current Waste Practices

Most wastes are classified as either municipal or industrial. From 1998 to 2009, municipal wastes increased by 14 percent—from 44,583 tons per day to 50,906. Industrial wastes increased substantially in the same time period—up 117 percent from 145,671 tons per day to 316,015 tons per day. Nineteen percent of municipal wastes are landfilled, 20 percent incinerated, and about 60 percent recycled. Eighty-five percent of industrial wastes are recycled, 10 percent landfilled, and 3 percent incinerated.

South Korea achieved the high rates of recycling through a series of long-term governmental programs. In 1995, South Korea applied the producer-pays principle to municipal wastes. People paid for waste disposal services based on the amount of waste produced. Citizens are required to buy plastic bags. The price of the bags is determined by the costs of waste management. The amount of waste produced per person declined from 1994 to 2007 by 26 percent, and the amount recycled increased by 213 percent. In 2000, South Korea implemented the Extended Producer Responsibility program requiring manufacturers to recycle packaging wastes. This program has broad coverage and includes a range of products such as electronics, batteries, metal cans, glass bottles, and some plastics. By requiring that manufacturers recycle packaging wastes, the overall amount of packaging decreases on all products. In 1998, South Korea implemented food waste reduction and recycling policies. In 2007, 92 percent of food wastes were recycled. In 2010, the Comprehensive Plan for Food Waste Reduction was implemented. This policy is very specific, issuing guidelines per sector. It also introduced a volume-based food waste fee system whereby the owner of the waste incurs expenses for it. Food waste is measured by measured rate plastic bags, bar code stickers, or RFID placement.

Most South Korean communities have modern sewer and water systems, but little wastewater is fully treated before it being discharged into freshwater. Waste practices can be basic in some rural areas, with pit toilets, latrines, drainage ditches cesspools, and open defecation.

Emissions and Industry

South Korea generated 542,893.9 tons of greenhouse gases in 2001, an 87.6 percent increase from 1990. It is likely that greenhouse gas emissions are much higher now because of population increases, population growth, and industrialization.

Agricultural products include rice, barley, fruits, vegetables, livestock, milk, chickens, eggs, and fish. Agricultural emissions accounted for 3 percent of all emissions. Within this sector, rice cultivation accounted for 45 percent of emissions, agricultural soils 21 percent, manure management 17 percent, and enteric fermentation 16 percent. This is an unusually high amount of greenhouse gas emissions from manure, indicating the presence of large amounts of untreated feces.

Large amounts of coal provide energy. Oil and electricity consumption per capita are slightly high. Energy emissions accounted for 83 percent of all emissions. Within this sector, manufacturing and construction industries accounted for 31 percent of emissions, energy industries 30 percent, transportation 20 percent, and fugitive emissions 1 percent. Industrial emissions accounted for 10.5 percent of all emissions. Within this sector, mineral products accounted for 50 percent of emissions, chemical industries 14 percent, and consumption of halocarbons 34 percent.

Waste emissions accounted for 3 percent of all emissions. Within this sector, solid waste disposal on land accounted for 61 percent of emissions, waste incineration 32 percent, and wastewater handling 6 percent. Gas emissions from incineration are high.

Major Waste Issues

Public health issues related to waste management is a major problem in South Korea. Infectious diseases in the area include yellow fever, cholera, hepatitis A, hepatitis B, meningococcal meningitis, typhoid, malaria, dengue fever, and schistosomiasis. More than 2 percent of the population is persistently infected with hepatitis B.

South Korea is extensively preparing for climate change effects on water systems. Climate change observers note increased temperatures, increased precipitation, increased runoff, more flooding, and winter droughts. Projected effects include increasing rain, a twofold increase in rainfall intensity, more algae outbreaks in public waters, and more droughts. Changes in aquatic ecosystems caused by higher temperatures and changes in water volume are also projected as climate change effects. Water quality is a key vulnerability. Because so many sources of drinking water are from lakes that are hypertrophic, the risk of algae in the water increases as temperatures increase and the water becomes warmer. The subtropical and maintains ecosystems are also vulnerable. Primary concerns are about water quantity, quality, and sanitation. Urban flooding, algae outbreaks, and a lack of potable water are the basis for these concerns. There are also concerns about extreme weather events and ecosystem damages. South Korea is focused on managing climate change effects in the context of rapid urbanization. One initiative is to address urban flooding. It increases sewer pipe facilities toleration for heavy rainfall events and durability. It also requires buildings over a certain size to have a rainwater reusing facility. The Korean Adaptation Center for Climate Change helps local governments develop climate change adaptation measures and runs the Climate Adaptation Information Delivery System. The Water Quality and Ecosystem Conservation Act includes climate change adaptation measures, such as requiring master plans on animal waste management and nonpoint source pollution. Currently research is under way in including climate change adaptation in environmental effect statements, algae reduction, better monitoring of aquatic ecosystem, and technology to reduce runoff and nonpoint source pollution. An aquatic ecosystem clinic program helps find causes of climate change effects on aquatic ecosystems and develop restoration solutions.

Further Reading

Climate Change Impacts on Water Systems. www.oecd.org.
Lee, S., et al. 2010. "Nationwide Groundwater Surveillance of Noroviruses in South Korea, 2008." *Applied and Environmental Microbiology* 77: 1466–1474.
South Korea Government. www.korea.net.

ROMANIA

Romania is in southeastern Europe. It borders the Black Sea, Bulgaria, Hungary, Moldova, Serbia, and Ukraine. Plains punctuated by the Transylvanian Alps and the Eastern Carpathian Mountains dominate the landscape. The climate is cold and cloudy in the winter, with sunny summers. Altogether, 21.7 million Romanians live on 238,391 km^2 of land and 225 kilometers of coastline. There are many small communities scattered throughout Romania. Fifty-four percent of the population is urbanized, and 33 percent lives in a city having more than 100,000 inhabitants.

Current Waste Practices

The National Waste Management Plan was developed in 2004. In 2006, Regional Waste Management Plans were developed. Romania collected 8,507,000 tons of municipal waste in 2009, almost 77 percent of it landfilled and 1 percent recycled. Fifty-four percent of the country is covered by municipal waste collection. In 2008, Romania generated 524,000 tons of hazardous wastes. Recycling is a low priority, and it is unlikely that Romania will meet the European Union goal of 50 percent recycling by 2020.

Most communities have modern sewer and water systems, but not all wastewater is fully treated before being discharged into freshwater. Ninety-nine percent of the urban population has access to an improved source of drinking water, and 88 percent has access to improved sanitation facilities. Seventy-six percent of rural populations have access to an improved drinking water source, and 54 percent have access to improved sanitation facilities.

Emissions and Industry

Romania generated 118,764.1 metric tons of greenhouse gases in 2012, a 58 percent decrease from 1990.

About 38 percent of the land is arable, which is high. Agricultural products include wheat, corn, barley, sugar beets, sunflower seeds, and sheep. Agricultural emissions accounted for 15 percent of all emissions. Within this sector, agricultural soils accounted for 45 percent of emissions, enteric fermentation 44 percent, and manure management 10 percent.

Crude oil production is about 101,600 bbl/day. There are 600 million bbl in proven reserves. Refined petrochemical production is about 117,000 bbl/day. Energy greenhouse gas emissions accounted for 69 percent of all emissions. Within this sector, energy industries accounted for 39.5 percent of emissions, manufacturing and construction industries 19 percent, transportation 18 percent, and fugitive emissions almost 10 percent. Fugitive emissions are essentially unaccounted waste streams into the air. Fugitive emissions can affect regional ecosystems and the public health, because they can fall from the air to the land and water. Industrial emissions accounted for 10.5 percent of all emissions. Within this sector, mineral products accounted for 40 percent of emissions, chemical industries 30 percent, and metal production 21 percent.

Waste emissions accounted for 5 percent of all emissions. Within this sector, accounted solid waste disposal on land for 51 percent of emissions and wastewater handling 49 percent.

Major Waste Issues

Romania's major waste issues are the lack of a comprehensive waste collection; and low priority placed on recycling and wastes clean up. Air and water pollution provide the context for most urban environments. Romania has received substantial assistance from the European Union to help them meet goals Romania committed to when they joined. About 300 million euros were given in support of municipal solid waste management to build ten waste management facilities in ten regions. Another 430 million euros were pledged for some of the remaining regions.

Further Reading

Auer, Matthew R., ed. 2005. *Restoring Cursed Earth: Appraising Environmental Policy Reforms in Eastern Europe and Russia*. New York: The Rowman & Littlefield Publishing Group.

Bellinger, Ed, ed. 2000. *Environmental Assessment in Countries in Transition*, Portland, OR: LLC. Books International.

Government of Romania. www.guv.ro.

Iancu, R., et al. 2013. "Environmental Indicators of Water Quality in the Cibin River (Transylvania, Romania)." *Transylvania Review of Systematical and Ecological Research* 15: 91–116.

RUSSIA

Russia borders many countries—Azerbaijan, Belarus, China, Estonia, Finland, Georgia, Kazakhstan, Mongolia, Norway, Poland, Ukraine, the Arctic Ocean, and the North Pacific Ocean. The terrain is varied, from sweeping plains to many hills and large mountains to vast tundra. The climate is also varied. It is very cold in Siberia, far north. In the south, it is much warmer, with warm summers. Annual precipitation is generally moderate, with most falling in the summer. Most winter precipitation is snow. The greatest amount of rain falls in the Caucasus Mountains, and the least in the Prikaspijskaya lowland. Natural resources include timber, oil, gas, coal, and minerals. Altogether, 143 million people live on Russia's 17,098,242 km² of land and 23,396 mi of coastline—the fourth-longest in the world. Seventy-three percent of Russians are urbanized, and 48 percent live in a city having more than 100,000 inhabitants although there are also many small and mid-size communities. Seven percent of the population lives in overcrowded conditions. The life expectancy is 66 years.

Current Waste Practices

Most communities have modern sewer and water systems, but not all wastewater is fully treated before it is discharged into freshwater. Ninety-nine percent of the urban population has access to an improved source of drinking water, and 74 percent has access to improved sanitation facilities. Ninety-two percent of rural populations have access to an improved drinking water source, and 59 percent have access to improved sanitation facilities. Water quality is poor. About 70 percent of water supply facilities are used to treat surface waters that run through polluted environments in urban areas. Thirty percent of water facilities treat groundwater sources. About 30 percent of wastewater is treated, and 70 percent is discharged into water bodies untreated. About 700 deaths per year are attributed to unsafe water.

Trash is a problem in Russia. In 2009, Russia collected 56,172,000 tons of municipal waste. Russia generated 122,883 tons of hazardous wastes in 2008. There is not a culture or policy of recycling, though there is adaptive reuse of some items and materials. To comply with obligations under the Basel Convention, Russia developed the Federal Law on Production and Consumption of Waste in the late 1990s. This began the national industrial waste management data system. Some regulatory measures to control waste generation and management are developed at the regional level. Some local and regional initiatives aim to reduce and recover wastes.

Emissions and Industry

In 2008, Russia accounted for 6 percent of global carbon dioxide emissions, equaling India as the world's third-largest global emitter of carbon dioxide. This does not include changes in land use, such as deforestation. It does include emissions from sources such as fossil fuel combustion, cement manufacturing, and gas flaring.

Trash cans overflow with trash in Kirov, Russia, in May 2010. Waste collection is a basic function of government. Without waste collection, trash heaps begin to form and the quality of life becomes degraded. (Smeshinka/Dreamstime.com)

Russia generated 2,295,045.4 metric tons of greenhouse gases in 2012, a 32 percent decrease from 1990.

Agricultural products include wheat, vegetables, fruit, livestock, dairy products, and poultry. Agricultural emissions accounted for 6 percent of all emissions. Within this sector, agricultural soils accounted for 55 percent of emissions, enteric fermentation 27 percent, and manure management 17 percent. This is an unusually high amount of greenhouse gas emissions from manure, indicating the presence of large amounts of untreated feces.

Russia produces among the highest amount of crude oil in the world, with large proven reserves. Electrical energy production from coal-fired power plants, per capita electricity production, and per capita electricity consumption are also among the highest in the world.

Energy emissions accounted for 82 percent of all emissions. Within this sector, energy industries accounted for 49 percent of emissions, transportation 13 percent, and manufacturing and construction industries 8.5 percent. Fugitive emissions accounted for 22 percent of emission in this sector. About a fifth of emissions in this sector are unaccounted for. Because of the size of this sector in overall greenhouse gas emissions, it is likely that this air pollution will affect the environment and public health, especially over time in urban areas. Fugitive emissions are essentially unaccounted waste streams into the air. Fugitive emissions can affect regional ecosystems and the public health, because they can fall from the air to the land and water. Industrial emissions accounted for 8 percent of all emissions. Within this sector, metal production accounted for 51 percent of emissions, mineral products 27 percent, and chemical industries 12 percent. The rate of industrial hazardous waste generation did not decrease proportionately to decreases in industrial production. Much of this waste remains where it is, and more is accumulating.

Waste emissions accounted for 4 percent of all emissions. Within this sector, solid waste disposal on land accounted for 64 percent of emissions and wastewater handling 36 percent.

Major Waste Issues

There is substantial water pollution from all sources in Russia. Soil pollution from agricultural chemicals seep into the groundwater with other toxic chemicals and wastes. The major waste issue is the protection of public health both in the country and the region. Infectious diseases include hepatitis A, hepatitis B, Japanese encephalitis, tick borne encephalitis, and typhoid. Two percent or more of the population is persistently infected with hepatitis B. There is a chance that infectious disease vectors will expand, but the cold northern climate may prevent many infectious diseases.

Climate change effects so far are increasing temperatures, more extreme weather events, thawing permafrost, decreasing snow, and decreasing ice. The thawing permafrost and tundra release large amounts of methane, with potential negative atmospheric consequences. In areas that are drying out, there is a dramatic increase in fires, such as in the Siberian peat lands. The tree lines are expanding to higher elevations as temperature rise in mountains, and animals such as the polar bear are decreasing rapidly. The arctic regions are warming faster than the global average. These climate changes will increase the bacteria in surface waters, challenge a weak sewer and water infrastructure, and provide more waterborne infectious disease vectors in some regions.

Russia's waste issues are rapidly evolving in some regions but are not developing in other regions. Generally, overall policy goals are to establish uniform land disposal facility standards for all types of waste, increase user-pays charges to waste generators, and upgrade municipal waste collection, transfer, and disposal facilities. The general process for achieving these goals is through the cooperative development of regulatory initiatives that tie local conditions to the federal government. One strategy to develop regional industrial waste management is to develop secure landfill and waste transfer facilities, support recycling and resource recovery initiatives, and prevent waste by using cleaner production methods.

Further Reading

Agyeman, Julian, and Yelena Ogneva-Himmelberger. 2009. *Environmental Justice and Sustainability in the Former Soviet Union.* Cambridge, MA: MIT Press.

Russian Government Homepage. www.gov.ru.

Spiridonov, S. I., et al. 2013. "Probabilistic Approach to Sanitation and Hygiene Standards for Content of Pollutants in Soil." *Russian Agricultural Sciences* 39: 447–450.

RWANDA

Rwanda is bordered by Burundi, the Democratic Republic of Congo, Tanzania, and Uganda. There is a chain of volcanoes in the northwest. From there, it is mountainous down to rolling hills and to plains and wetlands. The watershed divide between two large African drainage systems—the Congo and the Nile—goes through western Rwanda in a north–south direction. The western slope of this divide is steep—the eastern side much less so. The climate is temperate, though Rwanda is very close to the Equator. Its higher altitudes keep temperatures cooler. There are two rainy seasons: February to May and September to December. Rainfall is heavier in the mountains. Natural resources include gold, coffee, cassiterite, methane, hydropower, tea, and tungsten ore. Rwanda's population is rapidly growing. About 12.3 million people live on Rwanda's 26,340 km^2 of land. Ninety-nine percent of the population is urbanized, and only 6 percent lives in cites having more than 100,000 inhabitants. The largest and capital city is Kigali, with a population slightly greater than 1 million. The life expectancy is 60 years. More than half the population suffers malnutrition and falls beneath international poverty levels.

Current Waste Practices

Urban wastes are collected and taken to a landfill. The primary managed landfill is in Nyanza. Most of the many other landfill and dumping areas are unmanaged. Smaller communities often have litter bins. Some trash is burned, which is illegal. There is some recycling of organic materials and metals by nongovernment organizations. Medical wastes are often incinerated on site. The capital city of Kigali has a modern sewer system and is rapidly increasing the number of people served by it. In 2008, 80 percent of the cities population used pit latrines. Typically, public institutions are required to have their own waste system, but the new centralized sewer system will require them to connect to the main system. The city also implemented a law that requires real estate developers to install flush toilets connected to septic systems. Waste practices are basic in many rural areas—pit toilets, latrines, drainage ditches, cesspools, and open defecation. Seventy-six percent of the urban population has access to an improved source of drinking water, and just 52 percent has access to improved sanitation facilities. Sixty-three percent of rural populations have access to an improved drinking water source, and 56 percent have access to improved sanitation facilities.

Rwanda is studying e-wastes. There is concern about environmental effects and loss of the economic value of recycled materials, a growing waste stream within Rwanda. There is some concern about the illegal importation of e-wastes, along with other hazardous and toxic wastes. There is currently no legislation dealing with e-wastes. Waste pickers and landfills provide most materials recovery and recycling now.

Rwanda has increased household access to sanitation facilities more quickly than many other African nations, mainly by improving latrines. Open defecation was 8 percent in 1992, low compared to some countries from the same year.

Emissions and Industry

In 2005, Rwanda generated 6,180.1 metric tons of greenhouse gases, a 159.6 percent increase from 2002. It is likely greenhouse gas emissions are higher now because of population increases, population growth rate and urbanization, and reliance on agriculture.

Agricultural products include coffee, tea, bananas, beans, livestock, sorghum, and potatoes. Coffee and tea accounted for almost 40 percent of all exports. Agricultural emissions accounted for 83.5 percent of all emissions. Within this sector, agricultural fields accounted for 56 percent of emissions, manure management 25 percent of emissions, and enteric fermentation 18.5 percent. This is an unusually high amount of greenhouse gas emissions from manure, indicating the presence of large amounts of untreated feces.

Energy production and consumption per capita is low. Energy emissions accounted for 13 percent of all emissions. Within this sector, other emits 56.6 percent of emissions, transportation 34 percent, and energy industries 5.6 percent. Industrial emissions accounted for 2.4 percent of all emissions. Within this sector, mineral products were responsible for all emissions.

Waste wastewater management accounted for 1 percent of all emissions. Within this sector, solid waste disposal on land for 67 percent of the emissions wastewater handling accounts for 33 percent.

Major Waste Issues

The lack of a comprehensive waste management process is the main challenge. There is little waste separation, and most trash goes into unmanaged landfills and dumps. There is very little wastewater treatment. Public health is a major concern related to waste issues. Infectious diseases present in the region include yellow fever, cholera, hepatitis A, hepatitis B, meningococcal meningitis, typhoid, dengue fever, and schistosomiasis. Two percent or more of the population is persistently infected with hepatitis B. There is a high risk of malaria.

Climate change observers note increased temperature, heavier rainfalls, irregular and unpredictable rainfall. To prepare for climate change effects, Rwanda is establishing early warning and disaster preparedness systems, as well as beginning to policies for integrated watershed management in flood-prone areas.

Rwanda is striving to get everyone sanitation access. This requires that households work with them and agree to adopt basic sanitation principles. The government developed its Government-Based Environmental Health Promotion Program that uses a community hygiene club approach. There is no financial assistance for communities, and members must pass a hygiene course. Indicators measure hygienic performance in communities, including increased use of hygienic latrine in schools and homes, increased handwashing, safe drinking water access in schools and homes, zero open defecation, safe disposal of children's feces in every household, and increasing the number of households having bathing facilities, rubbish pits, pot drying racks, and clean yards.

Further Reading

Environmental Profile of Rwanda. www.vub.ac.be.

Republic of Rwanda. www.gov.rw.

Tsinda, A., et al. 2013. "Challenges to Achieving Sustainable Sanitation in Informal Settlements of Kigali, Rwanda." *International Journal of Environmental Research and Public Health* 10: 6939–6954.

Uwimpuhwe, M., et al. 2014. "The Impact of Hygiene and Localized Treatment on the Quality of Drinking Water in Masaka, Rwanda." *Journal of Environmental Science and Health* 49: 434–440.

SAMOA

Samoa is a group of two main islands, Saval'l and Upolu, in the South Pacific. The terrain is mountainous and volcanic. The tropical climate is hot and humid. The rainy season is from November to April and the dry season from May to October. Natural resources include fish, timber, and hydropower. Altogether, 195,500 people reside on Samoa's 2,842 km² of land and 403 km of coastline. There are many small communities throughout the islands. Only 22 percent of the population is urbanized, and no city has more than 100,000 inhabitants. The capital and largest city is Apia, with about 38,000 people.

Current Waste Practices

There is some municipal waste collection in urban areas. In the many small communities, trash is tossed into the rivers or ocean. Some of it is burned, some used as organic fill, and some composted. In many communities, there are no other options, because there is no landfill. A National Waste Management Policy now helps data collection, waste management planning, waste transfer and disposal, and public awareness. A Health Care Waste Management Strategy is in draft form. There is no central reticulated sewer system. Some businesses, the primary hospital, and hotels have on-site water treatment plants. Most people use septic tanks, pit latrines, or latrines over waterways. Ninety-six percent of the urban population has access to an improved source of drinking water, and 98 percent has access to improved sanitation facilities. Ninety-six percent of rural populations have access to an improved drinking water source, and 98 percent have access to improved sanitation facilities.

Emissions and Industry

In 1994, Samoa generated 560.8 metric tons of greenhouse gases. It is likely that greenhouse gases are higher now because of population increases and reliance on agriculture.

There is little arable land in Samoa. Agricultural products include coconuts, taro, coffee, bananas, cocoa, and yams. Agricultural emissions accounted for 77 percent of all emissions. Within this sector, agricultural soils accounted for 89 percent of emissions and prescribed burning of the savannas 5.5 percent.

Little electricity is generated or used. It takes about ten days to establish a connection to the electrical power system. Energy emissions accounted for 18 percent of all emissions. Within this sector, transportation accounted for 69 percent of emissions and energy industries 8.5 percent.

Emissions from wastes accounted for 5 percent of all emissions. Within this sector, other accounted for 100 percent of greenhouse gas emissions.

Major Waste Issues

The major waste issue is the lack of a sewer system. Vaiusu Bay is polluted by sewer wastes and chemicals. The microbial quality of the water and the high concentration of phosphorous in the bay and along the nearby coral reefs can create public health and environmental effects. The protection of public health is a concern, as hepatitis A, hepatitis B, typhoid, and dengue fever exist on the islands. More than 2 percent of the population is persistently infected with hepatitis B.

Climate change effects could be severe as sea levels rise. The city of Apia is flood-prone, and this may worsen. Climate change observers note increased temperatures, rising sea levels, and increased ocean acidification. About 25 percent of all carbon dioxide from human activities is absorbed in the oceans. As carbon dioxide increases, it heightens the acidification of the oceans. This, in turn, affects delicate balances in marine ecosystems, resulting in the decline of nearby coral reefs. More extreme weather events can raise the risks of tsunamis.

Further Reading

Lau, C. 2014. "Combatting Infectious Diseases in the Pacific Islands: Sentinel Surveillance, Environmental Health and Geospatial Tools." *Reviews on Environmental Health* 29: 1–142.
Samoan Government. www.samoagovt.ws.
Smith, N., A. Halton, J. Strachan, eds. 2014. *Transitioning to a Green Economy: Political Approaches in Small States.* London, UK: Commonwealth Secretariat.

SAUDI ARABIA

Saudi Arabia borders the Red Sea, Iraq, Jordan, Kuwait, Oman, Qatar, the United Arab Emigrates, and Yemen. The terrain is flat, with occasional sand dunes. The climate is desert—very hot and dry. It can be cold at night. Natural resources include oil, gas, gold, copper, and iron ore. Twenty-seven million people live on

---

Energy from Bodily Wastes

Researchers are using a tiny microbial fuel cell with energy generated from bacteria that eat bodily fluids. So far, experiments can generate one microwatt of power—enough to power implanted medical devices, such as diabetes trackers. One company wants to implant them in artificial kidneys and power them from the wastes there. One of the primary researchers, a professor of electrical engineering at King Abdullah University of Science and Technology in Saudi Arabia, has a goal of generating electricity from organic factory waste to power desalinization plants in poor coastal countries.

Saudi Arabia's 2,149,690 km² of land and 2,640 km of coastline. Eighty-one percent of Saudi Arabians are urbanized, and 40 percent live in a city having more than 100,000 inhabitants.

Current Waste Practices

In 2012, Saudi Arabia began an ambitious new regulatory regime to improve environmental and waste management. Part of the new regulations are the National Ambient Water Quality Standard, the Wastewater Discharge Standard, the technical guideline on the prevention of major chemical accidents, the Standard on Waste Transportation, environmental standards on material recovery and waste recycling, and guidance on the biological treatment of waste. These regulations are the foundation for a sustainable and comprehensive waste management strategy.

Most communities have modern sewer and water systems, but not all wastewater is fully treated before being discharged into freshwater. Water quality is very poor. Ninety-seven percent of the urban population has access to an improved source of drinking water, and 100 percent has access to improved sanitation facilities. Sixty-three percent of rural populations have access to an improved drinking water source, and it is not known whether they have access to improved sanitation facilities. An improved drinking water source is essentially a source of drinking water separated from all wastes.

Emissions and Industry

In 2000, Saudi Arabia generated 296,059.9 metric tons of greenhouse gases, a 79 percent increase from 1990.

Agricultural products include dates, citrus, wheat, barley, chickens, dairy products, and melons. Agricultural emissions accounted for 4 percent of all emissions. Within this sector, agricultural soils account for 61 percent of emissions, manure management 26 percent, and enteric fermentation 12 percent. The manure greenhouse gas emissions are high. This is an unusually high amount of greenhouse gas emissions from manure, indicating the presence of large amounts of untreated feces.

Saudi Arabia produces among the highest amounts of crude oil in the world, and has large proven reserves. Oil consumption per capita is also among the highest in the world. Energy emissions accounted for 82 percent of all emissions. Within this sector, energy industries accounted for 43 percent of emissions, transportation 23 percent, and manufacturing and construction industries 9 percent. Fugitive emissions made up 4 percent of emissions.

Emissions from industrial processes accounted for 6 percent of all emissions. Within this sector, mineral products accounted for 50 percent of emissions, metal production 30 percent, and chemical industries 19 percent.

Waste emissions accounted for 6 percent of all emissions. Within this sector, solid waste disposal on land accounted for 84 percent of emissions and wastewater handling 15 percent.

Major Waste Issues

The major waste issue in Saudi Arabia is the loss of water. Increasing desertification, decreasing groundwater, and lack of lakes and rivers are the consequences. Some of the cities are beginning to face unavoidable water shortage decisions. Cities such as Jeddah face challenges on how to plan for future development when there insufficient waste capacity and water supply for the present population. Raw sewage is dumped into treatment lagoons in some areas, but these are also over capacity—for example, in the Arbaeen lagoon. To get freshwater, Saudi Arabia developed a water desalinization network to remove salt and other impurities from seawater. There is substantial coastal oil pollution. These facilities require a large amount of energy, and petrochemical energy sources for their operation, such as gas and oil, can generate more greenhouse gases and pollution.

Climate change observers note increased temperatures and less water in Saudi Arabia. Researchers there are investigating bigger and stronger infrastructure, improved drainage, and water harvesting. With a new and comprehensive set of environmental laws and a powerful central government, Saudi Arabia can better plan for the future.

Further Reading

El-Khoury, Gabi. 2014. "Water Indicators in Arab Countries: Selected Indicators." *Contemporary Arab Affairs* 7: 339–349.

Kingdom of Saudi Arabia. www.shuri.gov.sa.

Saudi Arabia's Great Thirst. www.environment.nationalgeographic.com.

Tokui, Y., et al. 2014. "Comprehensive Environmental Assessment of Seawater Desalinization Plants: Multistage Flash Distillation and Reverse Osmosis Membrane Types in Saudi Arabia." *Desalination* 351: 145–150.

SENEGAL

Senegal became a nation in 1960. It is known as a stable country and participates in international peacekeeping. Worsening environmental conditions have hurt agricultural lifestyles, and there is large migration to urban areas. There is grave concern that climate change effects could affect agricultural production and cause famine. The capital and largest city is Dakar, with about 2.5 million people—the westernmost point in Africa.

The climate is tropical, hot, and humid. From December to April the dry season is dominated by hot, dry harmattan winds. The lowlands flood periodically and occasionally suffer drought. Altogether, 14.3 million people reside on Senegal's 196,712 km² of land. Forty-two percent of the population is urbanized, and 29 percent lives in a city having more than 100,000 inhabitants. There are many small communities.

Current Waste Practices

The capital city of Dakar is served by basic municipal waste and water services. About a third of the population has sewer connections, half has flush toilets that discharge into septic tanks, 15 percent has flush toilets discharging into cesspools, and 5 percent uses latrines. Dakar has among the best sewer systems in Africa. About 750 km of pipes and forty-five pumping stations discharge into a large sludge treatment plant. About 14 percent of the sewerage collected is treated before being discharged into waterways.

Waste practices are very basic—pit toilets, latrines, drainage ditches, cesspools, and open defecation. About a fifth of the population receives municipal waste services. Ninety-three percent of the urban population has access to an improved source of drinking water, and 70 percent has access to improved sanitation facilities. Fifty-six percent of rural populations have access to an improved drinking water source, and 39 percent have access to improved sanitation facilities. An improved water source is completely separate from waste. The quality of the water accessed is low. With so few people having access to water separated from waste, diseases occur.

The first outbreak of cholera was confirmed in 1971, and there have been five waves of outbreaks since then. In 2009, there were four reported cases and no deaths. A fifth of the population suffers malnutrition. The life expectancy is about 59 years.

Emissions and Industry

In 2000, Senegal generated 16,822.1 metric tons of greenhouse gases. It is likely greenhouse gas emissions are higher now because of increased population, rapid population and urbanization growth, and reliance on agriculture.

There is a substantial amount of arable land, though periodic droughts can decrease arability. Agricultural is dominated by small family farms, most less than ten acres and about 5 percent bigger than twenty-five acres. Agricultural products include peanuts, corn, millet rice, sorghum, cotton, vegetables poultry, fish, and livestock. Agricultural emissions accounted for 37 percent of all emissions. Within this sector, enteric fermentation accounted for 64 percent of emissions, agricultural soils 28 percent, rice cultivation 5 percent, and manure management 2.5 percent.

There is no crude oil production or proven reserves. Electricity production and consumption are low. Energy emissions accounted for 48 percent of all emissions. Within this sector, energy industries accounted for 27 percent emissions, transportation 23 percent, and other 41 percent.

Food processing is the largest manufacturing sector, and most of it is in or near Dakar. Industrial emissions accounted for 2 percent of all emissions. Within this sector, mineral products accounted for 85 percent emissions and other 15 percent.

Waste emissions accounted for 12 percent of all emissions. Within this sector, solid waste disposal on land accounted for 91 percent of emissions and wastewater management 9 percent.

Major Waste Issues

Chemical waste management issues are significant. About 9 percent of land in the Senegal River basin is chemically contaminated. This is in part a result of extensive dumping of toxic and hazardous wastes. Overall soil quality is very poor.

Trash is a significant problem in urban areas, piling up in the streets. Much trash is taken to unmanaged landfills. Flooding is another major urban waste problem. In the poor areas of Pikine and Rufisque, flooding causes frequent sanitation issues made worse when trash is not collected there and when dumps are located nearby.

Another major waste issue is the protection of public health in both the country and the region. There are many infectious diseases in Senegal, including yellow fever, cholera, hepatitis A, hepatitis B, meningococcal meningitis, typhoid, malaria, dengue fever, and schistosomiasis. More than 2 percent of the population is persistently infected with hepatitis B.

Further Reading

Blakeney, Michael, Thierry Coulet, Getachew Mengiste, and Marcelin Tonye Mahop, eds. 2012. *Extending the Protection of Geographical Indications: Case Studies of Agricultural Products in Africa*. New York: Earthscan Publishing.

Diener, S., et al. 2014. "A Value Proposition: Resource Recovery from Faecal Sludge—Can It Be the Driver for Improved Sanitation?" *Resources, Conservation, and Recycling* 88: 32–38.

Ekane, Nelson, et al. 2014. "Multi-Level Sanitation Governance: Understanding and Overcoming Challenges in the Sanitation Sector in Sub Saharan Africa." *Waterlines* 33: 242–256.

Foeken, D. W. J., et al. 2013. *Sanitation in Africa: Access to Improved Sanitation Facilities and Improvement Index*. Leiden, The Netherlands: African Studies Center.

Government of Senegal. www.gouv.sn.

SERBIA

Montenegro, Bosnia–Herzegovina, Croatia, Romania, Bulgaria, Hungary, Macedonia, and Kosovo border Serbia. The terrain is varied. It is mountainous in the southeast, while the interior is hilly, and the north is flat. There are cold winters and warm summers in the north and cold, snowy winters and dry summers in the south. Natural resources include oil, gas, copper, zinc, iron ore, chromite, antimony, silver, magnesium, limestone, pyrite, marble, and salt. Altogether, 7.2 million people live on Serbia's 88,361 km² of land. There are many small communities throughout Serbia. Fifty-two percent of the population is urbanized, and 20 percent lives in a city having more than 100,000 inhabitants.

Current Waste Practices

Most communities have modern sewer and water systems, but not all wastewater is fully treated before it being discharged into freshwater. Ninety-nine percent of the urban population has access to an improved source of drinking water, and 96 percent has access to improved sanitation facilities. Ninety-eight percent of rural populations have access to an improved drinking water source, and 88 percent have access to improved sanitation facilities. Serbia is dependent on outside water sources. About 25 percent of the population lives in communities of fewer than 2,000 inhabitants are not served by wastewater treatment plants. Serbia generated 8,228,000 tons of hazardous wastes in 2008.

Serbia is developing its waste infrastructure with help from the European Union (EU). Serbia seeks admission to the EU but is not quite up to EU standards. Only about a third of the population has organized sewage disposal. Less than 10 percent of communities have sewage treatment plants, many which are poorly functioning. Some urban area areas, tourist resorts, and public institutors have their own sewage system.

Emissions and Industry

In 1998, Serbia generated 66,342.4 metric tons of greenhouse gases, a 17.6 percent decrease from 1990.

There are large animal farms, and their waste is left in large, untreated lagoons. There is substantial arable land. Other agricultural products include wheat, maize, barley, sugar beets, onions, potatoes, and sunflowers. Agricultural emissions accounted for 14 percent of all emissions. Within this sector, agricultural soils account for 54 percent of emissions, enteric fermentation 30 percent, manure management 14 percent, and field burning of agricultural residues 2 percent.

About a third of the power comes from hydropower. There is crude oil production and substantial proven reserves. Energy emissions accounted for 76 percent of all emissions. Within this sector, energy industries account for 69 percent of emissions, transportation 7.6 percent, manufacturing and construction industries 7 percent, and fugitive emissions 5.5 percent.

Industrial emissions accounted for 5.5 percent of all emissions. Within this sector, mineral products account for 42 percent of emissions, metal production 39 percent, and chemical industries 19 percent.

Emissions from wastes accounted for 4 percent of all emissions. Within this sector, solid waste disposal on land accounted for 91 percent of emissions and wastewater management 9 percent.

Major Waste Issues

The main waste issue is water quality. Water pollution from all kinds of wastes has exceeded the capacity of the environment in many places. There is a stark need for financial investment in sewage collection, disposal, and treatment. The need now is to resume full operations in all existing sewage treatment and industrial wastewater treatment facilities. There is a related issue with growing accumulations of untreated sewage sludge that can overwhelm lagoon-based treatment processes. This is a risk when the oxygen level in the water becomes too low to support degradation processes. There is a need for a regulation framework that includes untreated sewage. Many traditional sludge treatment lagoons have been over capacity for decades.

Further Reading

Devic, G., et al. 2014. "Natural and Anthropogenic Factors Affecting the Groundwater Quality in Serbia." *Science of the Total Environment* 468: 933–942.

Government of the Republic of Serbia. www.srbija.

Vranes, A., et al. 2014. "Education on Human Rights and Healthcare: Evidence from Serbia." *Health Promotion International* 10: 1093.

SIERRA LEONE

The west African country of Sierra Leone is bordered by Guinea, Liberia, and North Atlantic Ocean. Its terrain begins with a belt of mangrove swamps in the west and slopes upward to mountains in the east. Sierra Leone's climate is tropical—hot and humid. The rainy season is from May to December, with strong storms at the beginning and end. Rapid deforestation is increasing desertification. Natural resources include diamonds, gold, iron ore, titanium, and chromite.

There have been years of civil strife and environmental devastation in Sierra Leone. About half the population suffers malnutrition. Health care systems and waste infrastructure are poor to non-existent. The average life expectancy was 40 years in 2006, and Sierra Leone has the among the highest infant mortality rates in the world. Most of these deaths are caused by malaria (14 percent), diarrhea (14 percent), and pneumonia (17 percent) and are related to water-based waste vectors. These three disease groups occur at some of the highest rates in the world, even with incomplete data. However, the under–5-year-old mortality rate has been steadily decreasing. More than 6 million people live on Sierra Leone's 71,740 kilometers of land and 402 km coastline. In 2010, 38 percent of the population was in urban areas, and 62 percent was in rural areas. There are many small communities. Forty percent of the urban population resides in the largest city, Freetown.

Current Waste Practices

Waste practices are basic, including pit toilets, latrines, drainage ditches cesspools, and open defecation. Eighty-seven percent of the urban population has access to an improved source of drinking water, and only 23 percent has access to improved sanitation facilities. Just 35 percent of rural populations have access to an improved drinking water source, and only 6 percent have access to improved sanitation facilities. The open defecation rate in 2012 was 28 percent.

About 20 percent of the population suffers chronic malnutrition. The first cholera outbreaks were reported in 1970. Outbreaks usually occur during the rainy season. The heavy rains cause flooding and contamination of water sources. Between January 2012 and December 25, 2012 there were 22,885 reported cases of cholera, including 298 deaths. About 16,200 deaths a year are attributed to unsafe water.

There is little enforcement of what sanitation or environmental laws exist. With international assistance, there have been efforts to protect natural resources. The European Union funded a community surveillance program to monitor illegal fishing on protected maritime areas. From 2010 to 2012, there were 252 reports of illegal trawler activity in one maritime area—near the Sherbo River. Communities documented these, and fines were levied, with the government collecting $100,000. This had a strong deterrent effect on illegal fishing, but there is nothing comparable in sanitation or public health.

Emissions and Industry

Sierra Leone generated 50.1 metric tons of greenhouse gases in 2010. Many emissions are not monitored and thus not included.

Agricultural products include coffee, rice, cocoa, palm kernels, palm oil, peanuts, fish, and livestock. Agricultural emissions accounted for 11 percent of all emissions. Forestry emissions from peat fires and wood decay accounted for 11 percent of all emissions.

Energy emissions accounted for 35 percent of all emissions. Industry emissions accounted for 18 percent of all emissions.

Waste emissions accounted for 4 percent of all emissions. Almost all waste is disposed of on land.

Major Waste Issues

The scale and range of waste issues have attracted international attention and assistance. One of the primary goals of the Millennium Development Goals is to halve the percentage of people who do not have sustainable access to water by 2015. Another goal is for 74 percent of people have basic access to safe drinking water and 65 percent to have sustainable access to basic sanitation. About 11 percent had access to basic sanitation in 1990. There has been little improvement. Persistent political strife prevents development and implementation of waste management systems.

The protection of public health is a major issue related to waste management in Sierra Leone and surrounding countries. Rapid population growth and urbanization put severe stress on health systems. There are many infectious diseases here. Currently, there is an outbreak of the deadly Ebola virus. Yellow fever, cholera, hepatitis A, hepatitis B, meningococcal meningitis, typhoid, malaria, dengue fever, and schistosomiasis are also present. Two percent or more of the population is persistently infected with hepatitis B. There is a high risk of malaria. International assistance may be required to begin a functional regulatory framework for waste management.

Further Reading

Ekane, N., et al. 2014. "Multi-Level Sanitation Governance: Understanding and Overcoming Challenges in the Sanitation Sector in Sub Saharan Africa." *Waterlines* 33: 242–256.

Environmental Justice Foundation. www.ejfoundation.org.

Nguyen, V., et al. 2014. "Cholera Epidemic Associated Consumption of Unsafe Drinking Water and Street Vended Water—Eastern Freetown, Sierra Leone, 2012." *American Journal of Tropical Medicine and Hygiene* 90: 518–523.

The Republic of Sierra Leone State House. www.statehouse.gov.sl.

SINGAPORE

Singapore is a small group of islands between Indonesia and Malaysia. The terrain is low, the highest point being Bukit Timah at 166 km. A small plateau in the interior catches rainwater. Its tropical climate is hot and humid. There are two monsoon seasons—December to March and June to September. In between monsoons there are also periods of heavy afternoon rains. Its natural resources include fish and deepwater ports. Altogether, 5.5 million people live on Singapore's 714 km^2 of land and 193 km of coastline. It is 100 percent urbanized.

Current Waste Practices

Most communities have modern sewer and water systems, but not all wastewater is fully treated before being discharged into freshwater. Singapore collected 6,114,000 tons of municipal waste in 2009, almost 2 percent of it landfilled, 41 percent incinerated, and 57 percent recycled. The whole country has access to an improved drinking water source and sanitation facilities. Everyone has municipal waste collection.

Singapore has a strong waste management system that quickly adopts new technology. Singapore is beginning to incorporate water recycling into its water management plan. In 2009, the community of Pulau Seringat on the nearby island of Sentosa installed a water-recycling program that converts 2,500 gallons wastewater a day into drinking water. Recycling systems that reuse gray water, or water that has been used, do not completely recycle the water. Singapore imports much of its water from Malaysia, and water recycling helps reduce this dependency.

Emissions and Industry

In 2000, Singapore generated 38,790 metric tons of greenhouse gases, a 44.4 percent increase from 1994.

Bottles of "Newater," or recycled wastewater, are stacked for visitors to the Newater education center in Singapore. Singapore, which has to buy a large percentage of its water from neighboring Malaysia, is promoting recycled wastewater as a means to increase the supply of fresh water in the country. Formally or informally recycled wastewater for drinking water is an emerging practice driven by drought and prolonged water scarcity. (AP Photo/Ed Wray)

Agricultural emissions accounted for none of the greenhouse gas emissions. Agricultural products include orchids, ornamental fish, fish, and chickens.

Singapore produces a small amount of crude oil and has no substantial reserves. Oil and electricity use per capita is among the highest in the world. Energy emissions accounted for 98 percent of all emissions. Within this sector, energy industries accounted for 55 percent of emissions, manufacturing and construction industries 28 percent, and transportation 15 percent. Industrial emissions accounted for 1.5 percent of all emissions. Within this sector, other accounted for all emissions.

Emissions from wastes accounted for 0.66 percent of all emissions. Within this sector, wastewater management accounted for 72 percent of emissions and waste incineration 28 percent.

Major Waste Issues

Many environmental problems are also waste problems. There is limited control of industrial pollution into the air and water. The small island nation has limited space for waste disposal. Growing demand for freshwater in the face of increased pollution has decreased the availability of freshwater.

Climate change effects will be increased flooding and stronger storms. Rising ocean levels will significantly affect this small island country. Climate change adaption to water systems is partially mitigated by Singapore's integrated water management policies. This approach reuses reclaimed water, protects urban rainwater catchments, uses estuaries to store freshwater, and desalinates seawater. The government supports research and technology into water issues. Water self-sufficiency is important to Singapore's sovereign status as a country. Land use and water management are controlled together.

Further Reading

Barnard, Timothy P., ed. 2014. *Nature Contained: Environmental Histories of Singapore.* Honolulu: University of Hawaii Press.

Chung, Lai Hong, and Lee D. Parker. 2010. "Managing Social and Environmental Action and Accountability in the Hospitality Industry: A Singapore Perspective." *Accounting Forum* 34: 46–53.

Singapore. www.gov.sg.

SLOVAKIA

The European nation of Slovakia is bordered by Austria, Czech Republic, Hungary, Poland and Ukraine. It has a varied terrain, with mountains in the interior and the north and lowlands in the southern region. Severe air pollution in the region creates acid rain that pollutes the lowlands. The terrain from the mountains to the lowlands comprises alluvial forests, plateaus, and foothills and sees intensive agricultural use. There are many wetlands in the lowlands, including peat bogs, salt marshes, and partially submerged meadows. The climate is moderate, with cool, dry summers and cold, humid winters. Natural resources include coal, copper, iron ore, salt, and manganese. Altogether, 5.5 million people live on Slovakia's

49,036 km² of land. There are many small communities. Fifty-six percent of the nation's population is urbanized, and 17 percent lives in a city having more than 100,000 inhabitants.

Current Waste Practices

Most communities have modern sewer and water systems, but not all wastewater is fully treated before being discharged into freshwater. About 65 percent of the population is connected to a public sewer system. Slovakia collected 1,837,000 tons of municipal waste in 2009. Almost 76 percent of the waste is landfilled, 9 percent incinerated, 2 percent recycled, and about 5 percent composted. Everyone in the country receives municipal waste collection. There are two incinerator plants for municipal solid wastes and eighteen incinerators for hazardous and other wastes. Ten percent of waste incineration is used to create energy. About 7 percent of municipal waste is collected to be recycled. Localities are required to separately collect paper, plastic, metallic, glass, and biodegradable wastes. Membership in the European Union requires a 50 percent recycling rate, a goal Slovakia hopes to reach by 2020. There are producer-responsibility policies for packaging, batteries, tires, and paper wastes.

Emissions and Industry

Slovakia generated 42,710.2 metric tons of greenhouse gases in 2012, a 42 percent decrease from 1990.

Agricultural products include wheat, corn, rye, potatoes, sugar beets, poultry, and livestock. Agricultural emissions accounted for 7 percent of all emissions. Within this sector, agricultural soils accounted for 56 percent of emissions, enteric fermentation 28 percent, and manure management 15 percent. This is an unusually high amount of greenhouse gas emissions from manure, indicating the presence of large amounts of untreated feces.

Slovakia produces substantial amounts of crude oil and maintains robust reserves. Energy emissions accounted for 68.5 percent of all emissions. Within this sector, energy industries accounted for 32 percent of emissions, manufacturing and construction industries 25 percent, transportation 22 percent, and 4 percent.

Industrial emissions accounted for 19 percent of all emissions. Within this sector, metal production accounted for 51 percent of emissions, mineral products 31 percent, and chemical industries 12 percent.

Waste emissions accounted for 5 percent of all emissions. Within this sector, solid waste disposal on land accounted for 75.5 percent of emissions and wastewater handling 17 percent.

Major Waste Issues

Slovakia's waste infrastructure is still in recovery from violent conflicts in the region. The waste issues now are to replace the destroyed sewage treatment plants.

There are currently a total of 400 plants still in operation. Most of these sewage treatment plants are obsolete and are often nonoperational. Currently some of the sewer sludge is used in agriculture as fertilizer. Some of Slovakia's major environmental issues are also waste issues, such as industrial discharges into waterways. Significant financial investment is needed to repair current waste infrastructure. Because water pollution is an important environmental issue, untreated sewage discharges into water receive priority in policy development.

Slovakia is preparing for climate change effects on water systems. Climate change observers note increased temperatures, decreased precipitation, and evidence of gradual desertification. Project effects include increases in temperature, increase in precipitation in the form of snow, increasing risks of avalanches, significant shifts in the temporal and spatial shifts of water runoff, more floods, longer droughts, cyclonal weather in summer, and effects on hydrological power sources. A primary concern is about floods and droughts. Floods can overwhelm sanitation systems. Droughts can affect safe drinking water availability. In response to these concerns and projections, the Slovak Republic developed policies and regulations. One initiative is the Landscape Revitalization and Integrated River Basin Management Program, whose goal is to prevent flooding in extreme weather events. Local government builds water-retaining landscapes, such as wetlands, to prevent floods and mitigate droughts. The National Plan of River Basin Management requires an assessment of dams and water infrastructure that includes consideration of climate change effects. Restored and new sewage treatment plants will need to consider climate change effects in their design and construction.

Further Reading

Climate Change Impacts on Water Systems. www.oecd.org.
Government Office of the Slovak Republic. www.government.gov.sk.
Myroshnychenko, V., et al. 2014. "Environmental Data Gaps in Black Sea Catchment Countries." *Environmental Science and Policy* (April): in press.
Slovakia Climate Stations. www.climate-zone.com.

SLOVENIA

Austria, Croatia, Hungary, and Italy border Slovenia. Its terrain is mountainous, with deep valleys. The climate is Mediterranean along the coast, with warm summers and cool winters. In the eastern valleys and plateaus, the summers are warm to hot and the winters cold. Natural resources include coal, lead, zinc, forests, and hydropower. Two million people live on Slovenia's 20,273 km² of land and 46.6 km of coastline. There are many small communities in Slovenia. Fifty-one percent of the national population is urbanized, and 21 percent lives in a city having more than 100,000 inhabitants.

Current Waste Practices

The Ministry of the Environment, Spatial Planning and Energy decides waste policy. Local government is responsible for many of the waste decisions but must hew to the regulatory framework. The regulatory framework is comprehensive, covering PCB removal, landfill wastes, waste management, and air emissions from hazardous waste incinerators, radioactive wastes, and medical wastes. Some NGOs are involved as representatives of the public. However, resources for effective environmental enforcement are scarce.

Most communities have modern sewer and water systems, but not all wastewater is fully treated before being discharged into freshwater. Everyone has access to improved drinking water sources and sanitation facilities.

Slovenia collected 913,000 tons of municipal waste in 2009, almost 69 percent of it landfilled, 9 percent incinerated, 2 percent recycled, and about 5 percent composted. Ninety-four percent of the population has municipal waste collection. Slovenia generated 153 tons of hazardous wastes 2008. Many landfills are open dumps outside cities. It is likely that there are many other illegal dumpsites.

Waste treatment is one of the biggest issues in environmental protection but also the area that has showed the greatest progress. Some rivers' water quality is improving.

Emissions and Industry

Slovenia generated 18,911 tons of greenhouse gases in 2012, a 6.4 percent decrease from 1990.

Agricultural products include hops, potatoes, wheat, corn, sugar beets, grapes, and livestock. Agricultural emissions accounted for 10 percent of all emissions. Within this sector, agricultural soils accounted for 37 percent of emissions, enteric fermentation 35 percent, and manure management 28 percent. This is an unusually high amount of greenhouse gas emissions from manure, indicating the presence of large amounts of untreated feces.

Slovenia produces some crude oil and does not maintain proven oil reserves. Energy emissions accounted for 82 percent of all emissions. Within this sector, energy industries accounted for 39 percent of emissions, transportation 37 percent, and fugitive emissions and other 13 percent. Industrial emissions accounted for 5 percent of all emissions. Within this sector, mineral products accounted for 57 percent of emissions and metal production 20 percent.

Waste emissions accounted for 3 percent of all emissions. Within this sector, solid waste disposal on land accounted for 74 percent of emissions, wastewater handling 25 percent, and incineration 1 percent.

Major Waste Issues

Air pollution in Slovenia is causing acid rain, rivers are polluted with municipal and industrial wastes, and coastal waters are laden with heavy metals, agricultural runoff and other toxic chemicals. The quality of freshwater in many small water supply systems is questionable.

Slovenia is preparing for climate change effects on water. Climate change observers note increased temperatures, variations in precipitation patterns, increased river temperatures, more frequent flash floods, less ice in Lake Bohinj, and more droughts. Projected effects include increases in temperature and changes in precipitation patterns regionally. A key vulnerability is the lack of available water. Primary concerns are about water quantity, quality, and sanitation. There is also concern about extreme weather events, such as floods and drought. Slovenia developed several economic instruments to address these concerns and projections. There is a tax for excessive drinking water consumption that is 50 percent higher than regular consumption. However, policies and regulatory instruments are just beginning to incorporate climate change issues. One regional initiative is the Drought Management Center for South-Eastern Europe, hosted by Slovenia. It focuses on develop monitoring and risk management systems for drought, but not especially on climate change.

Further Reading

Climate Change Impacts on Water Systems. www.oecd.org.
Krajnc, N., and J. Domac. 2007. "How to Model Different Socioeconomic and Environmental Aspects of Biomass Utilization: Case Study in Selected Regions of Slovenia and Croatia." *Energy Policy* 35: 6010–6020.
Republic of Slovenia. www.vlada.si.

SOMALIA

Somalia covers the east African coast along the Indian Ocean, making up part of the Horn of Africa. Djibouti, Ethiopia, and Kenya also border Somalia. About 10.4 million people live on Somalia's 637,657 km^2 of land. There are many small communities throughout the nation. Thirty-five percent of the national population is urbanized, and 20 percent lives in a city having more than 100,000 inhabitants. Forty-two percent suffers malnutrition. Life expectancy is 55 years.

Agricultural products include bananas, corn, sorghum, rice coconuts, sugar cane, beans, livestock, and fish. Oil and electrical energy production and consumption per capita are low. No natural gas is consumed, although there are massive proven reserves.

Current Waste Practices

Violent civil war has decimated waste infrastructures. There is little municipal collection of wastes. In urban areas, trash piles accumulate. The approximately 1.5 million people in the capital city of Mogadishu face conditions representative of the Somalia situation. It is a low-lying coastal city that experiences frequent and severe floods. There is no piped water supply, functional sewer system, or management of sewer sludge. Some local groups, such as NGOs, militia leaders, and small private businesses, provide some basic collection services, such as burning or removing old trash piles. The only financial aid reaching Mogadishu is emergency aid.

Waste practices are very basic, including pit toilets, latrines, drainage ditches, cesspools, and open defecation. Eighty-seven percent of the urban population has access to an improved source of drinking water, but only 23 percent has access to improved sanitation facilities. Just 35 percent of rural populations have access to an improved drinking water source, and only 6 percent have access to improved sanitation facilities. The open defecation rate in 2012 was 28 percent.

Emissions and Industry

There are no accurate measurements of greenhouse gas emissions in Somalia. The years of war and civil unrest degraded waste infrastructure and environmental rules and monitoring.

Major Waste Issues

The major wastes issue the absence of a waste infrastructure. Somalia is a country ravaged by war for years. Because wastes have been ignored for so long, the issues become public health issues. The major waste issue is the protection of public health in both the country and the region. There are many infectious diseases in Somalia, including yellow fever, cholera, hepatitis A, hepatitis B, meningococcal meningitis, typhoid, dengue fever, and schistosomiasis. Two percent or more of the population is persistently infected with hepatitis B. There is a high risk of malaria.

Without significant international intervention, Somalia will develop significant risks of rapidly eroding public health and ecological destruction. Some of these diseases may develop into regional outbreaks.

Further Reading

Somali Government. www.somaligovernment.org.
Vreede, E. 2012. "Children's Hygiene and Sanitation Training in Somalia." *Waterlines* 23: 12–13.
Zeid, A., et al. 2014. "Understanding the Crisis in Somalia." *Significance* 11: 4–9.

SOUTH AFRICA

Botswana, Lesotho, Mozambique, Namibia, Swaziland, Zimbabwe, and the Atlantic Ocean border South Africa. The terrain is high and flat in the large interior. Mountains in the west, south, and east define the interior. Njesuthi is the highest mountain, at 3,408 m. There are significant regional differences throughout South Africa. The northwest is dry in places. The Kalahari Desert is very dry and arid. The Eastern Transvaal contains broad and expansive savanna. The central plateau is dominated by rolling grassland. There are few lakes or rivers that can maintain the needs of population growth. Precipitation can vary regionally and annually. The climate is dry and sunny. It can snow in the mountains in the winter (from June to August). There is more rain from November to March. Natural resources include diamonds, gold, coal, iron ore, uranium, chromium, manganese, copper, salt, and gas. There are also many international, regional, national, and local game or wildlife preserves. The Kruger and the Kalahari Gemsbok National Parks are examples. The naturally diverse ecology attracts tourists.

Forty-nine million people live on South Africa's 1,221,037 km² of land and 4,620 km of coastline. Fifty-nine percent of South Africans live in urban areas, and

43 percent live in a city having more than 100,000 inhabitants. There are many small communities in addition to cities. The average life expectancy is 51 years.

Current Waste Practices

Ninety-nine percent of the urban population has access to an improved source of drinking water, and 86 percent has access to improved sanitation facilities. Waste practices are in rural areas can be very basic—pit toilets, latrines, drainage ditches, cesspools, and open defecation. Seventy-nine percent of rural populations have access to an improved drinking water source, and 67 percent have access to improved sanitation facilities. Altogether, 12,300 deaths a year are attributed to unsafe water.

Because of many years of racial segregation under apartheid, many people do not have a water supply. After apartheid, many black South Africans wanted the same water-based sewage as white South Africans. Many South Africans are too poor to afford this system, and South Africa's dry environment is water-deficient. A system of ventilated improved pit latrines is being implemented. These latrines prevent flies, which can carry diseases through feces on their feet. Sanitation and water in informal settlements and rural areas continue to be a challenge. There is inadequate reporting by local governments on many of these issues.

Recycling

There are substantial regional differences in approaches and ideas about recycling. Some is via municipal collection and some is via waste pickers. The recovery rates for some materials recycled both ways is estimated at 69 percent for metal cans, 59 percent for paper and paper products, 25 percent for glass, and 17 percent for plastic. Food containers lined with both paper and aluminum are difficult to recycle. This packaging is recycled into roof tiles and furniture at a recycling facility in Germiston, Gaiuteng.

Emissions and Industry

In 1994, South Africa generated 379,837.2 metric tons of greenhouse gases, a 9.4 percent increase from 1990. It is likely that greenhouse gases are higher now because of population increases, rapid urbanization and industrialization, and reliance on agriculture.

Agricultural products include bananas, wheat, corn, fruits, vegetables, meat, and dairy products. Agricultural emissions accounted for 9 percent of all emissions. Within this sector, enteric fermentation account for 50 percent of emissions, agricultural soils 44 percent, manure management 5 percent, and prescribed burning of the savannas 1 percent.

South Africa produces a substantial amount of crude oil and maintains robust proven reserves. Emissions from energy wastes accounted for 78 percent of all emissions. Within this sector, energy industries account for 56.67 percent of emissions, manufacturing and construction industries 18 percent, transportation 14.5 percent, and fugitive emissions 2 percent. Emissions from industrial processes accounted for 8 percent of all emissions. Within this sector, metal production accounted for 68.5 percent of emissions, mineral products 17.5 percent, and chemical industries 14 percent.

Emissions from wastes accounted for 4 percent of all emissions. Within this sector, solid waste disposal on land accounted for 93 percent of emissions and wastewater management 8 percent.

Major Waste Issues

The difference between white and black African service distribution is inequitable, and reconciling past inequities with today's infrastructure has only begun. Localities and residents are expected to pay for these services. Many of the historic inequities have created wealth disparities that prevent black Africans from affording theses services, and they go without them under most privatization and financing mechanisms. Policies are focusing on unaccounted for water, maintenance and rehabilitation of water assets, and full-cost pricing of water.

Other major issues related to waste management include water pollution from the runoff of agricultural pesticides and fertilizers, untreated sewer and wastewater discharge in urban areas, and significant air pollution that causes acid rain in some regions are some the main environmental issues.

Climate change effects include loss of biodiversity. Climate change observers in South Africa note significant declines in populations of indicator species, among other changes. One such species a large aloe tree called the flowering quiver tree. Many parts of the ecosystem rely on these flowers, as does the tourist industry. This plant and others are in decline. Research indicates significant population declines in penguins and other seabirds. There is concern that the increased temperatures and desertification will decrease animal populations in species such as the zebra and wildebeest. The decrease in available water is a major concern. Even without climate change, it is estimated that South Africa would lose surface water resources by 2050.

South Africa developed the National Climate Change Response Strategy to engage these observations and concerns. The South African Department of Environmental Affairs lists the top three climate change effects as infectious diseases and respiratory disease increase, extension of malaria prone areas, and the expansion of schistosomiasis. It is concerned about the likely epidemics of infectious diseases because of changes in the distribution of diseases carriers and the reduced cellular immunity resulting from ultraviolet light exposure. Longer and hotter summers expand the number of people exposed and time of exposure for malaria. Out of concern that malaria will be difficult to manage using current pesticides, an old, generally outlawed pesticide, DDT, was reintroduced.

Further Reading

McDonald, David A. 2002. *Environmental Justice in South Africa*. Athens: Ohio University Press.
Robins, S. 2014. "The 2011 Toilet Wars in South Africa: Justice and Transition between the Exceptional and Everyday after Apartheid." *Development and Change* 45: 479–501.
South Africa Government. www.gov.za.

SOUTH SUDAN

The Central African Republic, Democratic Republic of the Congo, Ethiopia, Kenya, Sudan, and Uganda border landlocked South Sudan. Several boundaries are in dispute. South Sudan was formed in 2011 after many years of civil war, splitting from Sudan. One of the world's largest wetlands covers more than 15 percent of the landmass. Called the Sudd, it is fed by the White Nile. The climate in South Sudan is primarily tropical—hot and humid. Natural resources include oil, iron ore, gold, diamonds, copper, zinc, silver, and hydropower.

Altogether, 8.3 million people live on South Sudan's 644,329 km² of land. There are many small communities throughout the country, with 83 percent of the population living in rural areas. Khartoum is by far the largest city, with almost 3 million people and 64 percent of the urban population. Life expectancy there is 54 years. There are unknown numbers of internationally displaced people and refugees. South Sudan has one of the largest populations of internally displaced persons.

Current Waste Practices

The waste infrastructure that did exist is now destroyed by years of civil conflict. There is little information on refugee camps, waste practices, environmental effects, or waste sites. Khartoum's experience is representative. The population growth rate is very high—about 4 percent. It is surrounded by about 100 shantytowns totaling 2–3 million inhabitants. Central Khartoum services about 70 percent of its population with a water network. Twenty-eight percent of central Khartoum is connected to a sewer system. Sixty-eight percent of this population use pit latrines and other basic methods.

Waste practices are very basic—pit toilets, latrines, drainage ditches, cesspools, and open defecation. The open defecation rate in 2012 was 77 percent. Overall, 32 percent of the population does not have access to potable water. Greenhouse gas emissions are unknown. There is little environmental or public health monitoring. More than half the population lives below international poverty lines.

Seventy-eight percent of the population depends on agriculture through crops or livestock. Very little of the arable land is cultivated. Agricultural products include cassava, groundnuts, rice, beans, and sorghum.

South Sudan produces crude oil and maintains massive proven reserves. Electricity production and consumption per capita are low. Oil is the primary export.

Major Waste Issues

War destroyed the waste infrastructure and public health system, and one major issue related to waste management is the spread of infectious disease, including cholera, hepatitis A, hepatitis E, meningococcal meningitis, typhoid, malaria, dengue fever, and schistosomiasis. Two percent or more of the population is persistently infected with hepatitis B. There is a risk of yellow fever in all parts of the country. International travel certificates—proof that the traveler does not have yellow fever—are not yet established.

Further Reading

Government of South Sudan. www.goss.org.

Hazra, Aniruddha. 2013. "Challenges in Setting Up a Potable Water Supply System in a United Nations Peacekeeping Missions: The South Sudan Experience." *International Journal of Hygiene and Environmental Health* 216: 88–90.

Johnson, Hilde F. 2011. *Waging Peace in Sudan: The Inside Story of the Negotiations That Ended Africa's Longest Civil War.* East Sussex, UK: Sussex Academic Press.

Karija, M., et al. 2013. "The Impact of Poor Municipal Solid Waste Management Practices and Sanitation Status on Water Quality and Public Health in Cities of the Least Developed Countries: The Case of Juba, South Sudan." *International Journal of Applied Science and Technology* 3:87–99.

SPAIN

Spain is bordered by Andorra, France, Gibraltar, Portugal, Morocco, the Mediterranean Sea, and the North Atlantic Ocean. The terrain is mountainous in many regions. The Pyrenees Mountains are found in the north. There are lowlands can be found in the Andalusia Plain in the southwest. There are many small rivers and few major ones. The coast is deeply indented with many coves, beaches, bays and estuaries. There are hot, dry summers and cold winters in the interior. Natural resources include coal, iron ore, copper, lead, uranium, zinc, potash, other metals, and hydropower.

Altogether, 47.4 million people live on Spain's 505,992 km² of land with a coastline of 4,964 km. Seventy-seven percent of the population is urbanized, and 42 percent lives in a city having more than 100,000 inhabitants.

Current Waste Practices

Although Spain still uses many landfills, it did meet the target set by European Union directives. Recycling rates showed continuous improvement—from 21 percent in 2001 to 33 percent in 2010. The EU Waste Framework Directive set the recycling rate at 50 percent recycling by 2020. Part of the reason for this success is the National Municipal Solid Waste Management Plan, which introduced several policies for municipal solid waste recycling that covered the range of recycling from collection to the latest recycling facilities. A landfill tax was introduced in urban centers. This decreased the amount of waste generated and helped increase material resource recovery.

Most communities in Spain have modern sewer and water systems, but not all wastewater is fully treated before being discharged into freshwater. Everyone in the country has access to an improved drinking water source and sanitation facilities.

Almost everyone in urban areas receives municipal waste collection, but not necessarily by household. Waste bins are placed in neighborhoods for residents collectively. Spanish residents pay an annual waste tax called *basura*. In rural areas, residents use septic systems or cesspools.

Emissions and Industry

Spain generated 340,808.6 metric tons of greenhouse gases in 2012, a 20 percent increase from 1990.

Almost a quarter of the land is arable. Agricultural products include bananas, grain, olives, wine, grapes, vegetables, sugar beets, fish, and dairy products. Agricultural emissions accounted for 11 percent of all emissions. Within this sector, agricultural soils accounted for 48 percent of emissions, enteric fermentation 27 percent, manure management 22 percent, and field burning of agricultural residues 1 percent. This is an unusually high amount of greenhouse gas emissions from manure, indicating the presence of large amounts of untreated feces.

Spain produces a moderate amount of crude oil with solid proven reserves. Electricity production and per capita consumption are also moderate. Energy emissions accounted for 78 percent of all emissions. Within this sector, energy industries accounted for 35 percent of emissions, transportation 30 percent, manufacturing and construction industries 17 percent, and fugitive emissions 1.6 percent. Industrial emissions accounted for 7 percent of all emissions. Within this sector, mineral products accounted for 50.6 percent of emissions, consumption of halocarbons 32 percent, metal production 12 percent, and chemical industries 4 percent.

Waste emissions accounted for 4 percent of all emissions. Within this sector, solid waste disposal on land accounted for 85 percent of emissions and wastewater handling 14.6 percent.

Major Waste Issues

Water quality is poor despite improved drinking water sources. To be a drinking water source, the water must be free from any wastes but not necessarily treated or purified. Spain is losing its water in many places and drying up. Climate change effects, pressure on agricultural to grow more profitable crops that tend to consume more water, and overdevelopment are contributing factors. Many of the environmental issues are waste issues. Raw sewage and industrial wastes from oil production and offshore oil rigs discharge directly into the Mediterranean Sea and waterways that drain into it. Air pollution and increasing desertification are primary concerns.

Spain is preparing for climate change effects on water systems. Climate change observers in Spain note increased temperatures, less rainfall, and increased drought. Projected effects include increases in temperature, decreases in precipitation, decreases in water resources, and increases in droughts. The key vulnerabilities are around water resource reduction. Primary concerns are water quality, quantity, and sanitation. There are also concerns about extreme weather events and ecosystem damage. In response to these concerns and projections, the Spanish government is engaged in several projects such as Climate Change in the Spanish Coastal Area and research into the vulnerability, effects, and adaptation to climate change in agriculture, water resources, and coasts. Spanish policy also includes climate change in its regulatory and economic agencies. The Spanish Network of Cities for Climate provides technical guidance to local government to identify effects and vulnerability to climate change.

Further Reading

Aragon, C.A., et al. 2013. "Current Situation of Sanitation and Wastewater Treatment in Small Spanish Agglomerations." *Desalinization and Water Treatment* 51: 2480–2487.

Avila, C., et al. 2013. "Integrated Treatment of Combined Sewer Wastewater and Stormwater in a Hybrid Constructed Wetland System in Southern Spain and Its Further Reuse." *Ecological Engineering* 50: 13–20.

Climate Change Impacts on Water Systems. www.oecd.org.

Government Offices of Spain. www.lamoncloa.gob.es.

SRI LANKA

Sri Lanka is an island in the Indian Ocean, south of India. The land is mainly a flat and sometimes rolling plain. There are mountains in the interior. Natural resources include limestone, graphite, gems, and phosphates. The climate is tropical, with two monsoon seasons—from December to March and June to October.

Twenty-two million people live on the island's 64,740 km^2 of land, including 980 km^2 of water. There are 1,340 km of coastline. Only 15 percent of Sri Lankans are urbanized, and just 8 percent live in a city having more than 100,000 inhabitants. There are many small communities.

Current Waste Practices

Water quality is poor. Waste practices can be basic in rural areas, including pit toilets, latrines, drainage ditches, cesspools, and open defecation. Ninety-nine percent of the urban population has access to an improved source of drinking water, and 88 percent has access to improved sanitation facilities. Ninety percent of rural populations have access to an improved drinking water source, and 93 percent have access to improved sanitation facilities. About 800 deaths a year are attributed to unsafe water. Eighteen percent of the population suffers malnutrition.

There are poor sanitary conditions in much of Sri Lanka. All wastes are brought together and burned, either in communities or on the edges towns. Open dumping sites in natural areas are causing water pollution. Waste is often dumped in drainage canals. This slows waste and water drainage, encouraging the proliferation of rats and mosquitoes. Waste pickup and transfer is handled by private businesses, some formally and some informally. Total municipal solid waste collection by government is about 2,900 tons per day. Most municipal sold waste in Sri Lanka is organic. About 63 percent of municipal wastes are biodegradable if recycled. The first sanitary landfill in Sri Lanka officially opened in 2014. The landfill was also the first built as part of a new effort at integrated solid waste management. This landfill is sited in Maligawatte, Dompe. Four more sanitary landfills are planned for Kalutara, Galle, Anduradhapura, and Kandy. About 40,000 tons of hazardous wastes are produced per year, but with no landfills designated for final disposition.

After the introduction of 3,000 small biogas generators from China, Sri Lanka established standards for biogas and that continue in use today. The Department of Animal Production and Health distributes 300–400 biogas plants annually. Biogas plants generally break down wastes and other feedstock materials to create methane, which can be used for heating, cooking, and light. In 2002, the Sri Lankan National Engineering Research Development Center started the Biogas and Biofertilizer Project at Muthurajawela. The goal of the project was to dispose of forty tons per week of vegetable wastes, help clean inland waterways, and produce 750 m^3 of biogas per day.

Recycling

There are twenty recycling plants for plastics, three for paper, one for glass, two for coconut shells, and two for PET bottles. Some of the plastics recycling plants are run by community based organizations. In 2000, Sri Lanka emitted 18,797.2 metric tons of greenhouse gas emissions carbon dioxide equivalents, a 5.7 percent decrease from 1993.

Emissions and Industry

Sri Lanka emitted 18,797.2 metric tons of greenhouse gases in 2000, a 30 percent decrease from 1993.

About 18 percent of the land is arable. Agricultural products include rice, sugar cane, grains, oilseed, tea, rubber, fish, and coconuts. Agricultural emissions accounted for 25 percent of all emissions. Within this sector, transportation accounted for 44 percent of emissions, energy industries 29 percent, and manufacturing and construction industries 8 percent.

Oil and electricity production and consumption are low. Energy emissions accounted for 61.5 percent of all emissions. Within this sector, transportation accounted for 44 percent of emissions, energy industries 29 percent, and manufacturing and construction industries 8 percent.

Emissions from industrial processes accounted for 2.62 percent of overall greenhouse gas emissions. Within this sector, mineral products accounted for 84.23 percent of greenhouse gas emissions and metal production 15.77 percent.

Waste emissions accounted for 11 percent of all emissions, which is high. Within this sector, rice cultivation accounted for 52 percent of emissions, enteric fermentation 26.5 percent, agricultural soils 16 percent, and manure management 4 percent.

Major Waste Issues

Freshwater resources are polluted by sewage and industrial wastes. There is very little sewage and waste infrastructure, which leads to rising concerns about the public health effects of the air pollution. Infectious diseases such as yellow fever, cholera, hepatitis A, hepatitis B, meningococcal meningitis, typhoid, malaria, dengue fever, and schistosomiasis occur in Sri Lanka. More than 2 percent of the population is persistently infected with hepatitis B.

Further Reading

De Silva, N., and H. Jayawickrama. 2012. "Can We Eliminate Soil-Transmitted Helminth Infections in Sri Lanka?" *The Ceylon Medical Journal* 57: 1–4.

Fernando, S., et al. "A Review—Septage Management Related Regulatory and Institutional Aspects and Needs in Sri Lanka." *Sabaragamuwa University Journal* 13: 1–15.

Government of Sri Lanka. www.gov.lk.

Gunawardana, I. P. P., et al. 2011. "Practical Issues of Partial Onsite Sanitation Systems: Two Cases Studies from Sri Lanka." *Tropical Agricultural Research* 22: 144–153.

SUDAN

The African nation of Sudan is bordered by the Central African Republic, Chad, Egypt, Eritrea, Ethiopia, Libya, South Sudan, and the Red Sea. Its terrain varies, though it is generally flat, with desert in the north. East of the Nile River is the Nubian Desert. The climate is generally desert—hot and dry. Almost no rain falls here, and there are no known oases. West of the Nile is the Libyan Desert. There are no consistent oases, but there are places where the water table occasionally rises to the surface. The annual floods from the Nile saturate parts of the south and provide water along the Nile valley for about a kilometer on each side as it flows to Egypt. The Blue Nile and the White Nile merge at Khartoum to form the Nile River. Many parts of the south are tropical. Some regions do have a rainy season around April to November. Natural resources include oil, chromium, iron, copper, silver, gold, and zinc.

Thirty-five million people live on Sudan's 1,086,788 km² of land and 850 km of coastline. Forty-one percent of the population is urbanized, and 17 percent lives in a city having more than 100,000 inhabitants. There are many small communities. In 2014, Sudan had the third fastest growing population rate in the world. About 18,000 deaths a year are attributed to unsafe water. Sudan has the seventh-dirtiest water in the world, as measured by BOD (biological oxygen demand). About half the population suffers from malnutrition.

Current Waste Practices

There is little waste infrastructure. Port Sudan is a city of about 500,000 people. It represents some of the waste issues in the nation. Water is scarce and the population growth rate very high. Trash is transported from city collections areas and trash heaps to three to five uncontrolled dumpsites having indeterminate boundaries. Communities of waste pickers live there, performing the bulk of any recycling activities. Medical, hazardous, and toxic wastes are mixed with trash. Liquid wastes include oil and other lubricants. Some parts of the dumps could be burning or smoldering at any time.

Waste practices are very basic in Sudan, where people use pit toilets, latrines, drainage ditches, cesspools, and open defecation. Sixty-seven percent of the urban population has access to an improved source of drinking water, and 44 percent has access to improved sanitation facilities. Just 52 percent of rural populations have access to an improved drinking water source, and only 14 percent have access to improved sanitation facilities. The open defecation rate in 2012 was 46 percent. In 2009, 175,000 tons of municipal wastes were collected. Sixty-seven percent of the population receives municipal waste collection.

Emissions and Industry

In 1995, Sudan emitted 54,194 metric tons of greenhouse gases. It is likely that greenhouse gas emissions are higher now because of increased population, population growth, and reliance on agriculture.

There is a large amount of arable land. Agricultural products include cotton, wheat, bananas, sorghum, cassava, mangos, papaya, and livestock. Agricultural accounted for 83.5 percent of all emissions. Within this sector, enteric fermentation accounted for 76 percent of emissions, agricultural soils 20.5 percent, manure management 3 percent, and field burning of agricultural residues 0.8 percent.

Sudan produces crude oil and maintains massive proven reserves. Electricity consumption per capita is low. Energy emissions accounted for 14 percent of all emissions. Within this sector, other accounted for 53 percent of emissions, transportation 25 percent, energy industries 7.5 percent, and manufacturing and construction industries 7.5 percent. Industrial emissions accounted for 0.32 percent of all emissions. Within this sector, mineral products accounted for all emissions.

Waste emissions accounted for 2 percent of all emissions. Within this sector, solid waste disposal on land accounted for 52 percent of greenhouse gas emissions and wastewater management 48 percent.

Major Waste Issues

Sudan's waste management infrastructure and regulatory processes are not developed. Current environmental policy is focused on reducing POPs in the Red Sea and the Gulf of Aden. Because of the lack of waste management, the risk of disease and ecological degradation is greater. Sudan faces the challenge of dealing with the spread of infectious disease, directly relating to poor waste management. As in other countries in the region, yellow fever, cholera, hepatitis A, hepatitis B, meningococcal meningitis, typhoid, malaria, dengue fever, and schistosomiasis. Two percent or more of the population is persistently infected with hepatitis B. Sudan experiences hot, dry, dusty winds. Recent research on meningitis demonstrates that high levels of wind driven dust increase meningitis rates. A possible reason is that tiny abrasions in the throat caused by dust increase vulnerability. If the wind is a good indicator of potential meningitis outbreaks, then public health officials may be able to distribute vaccines more effectively.

Further Reading

Foeken, D. W. J., et al. 2013. *Sanitation in Africa: Access to Improved Sanitation Facilities and Improvement Index*. Leiden, The Netherlands: African Studies Center.
Republic of Sudan General Secretariat of the Council of Ministers. www.sudan.gov.sd.

SURINAME

The South American nation of Suriname is bordered by Brazil, French Guiana, Guyana, and the North Atlantic Ocean. Its climate is tropical, generally hot and humid. The terrain is hilly in the interior and becomes coastal wetlands. Natural resources include fish, copper, iron ore bauxite, timber, and hydropower.

Altogether, 567,000 people live on Suriname's 163,820 km² of land and 385 km of coastline. Seventy-four percent of the population is urbanized, and 55 percent lives in a city having more than 100,000 inhabitants.

Current Waste Practices

Gold mining is a dominant industrial activity. Most mines are concentrated in the Greenstone Belt, in the eastern part of the island. Gold mining interests cover roughly 15 percent of the landmass but affect the environment and public health of the entire country. Controlling the environmental effects of the mines has been successful, and there is widespread contamination. Gold mines are small to mid-size and are many. Gold mining processes involve the uncontrolled use of mercury, open burning of gold amalgam, and discharge of untreated mining wastes into streams and rivers. The Greenstone Belt is in an area rich in biodiversity and sensitive ecosystems. It is also an area where indigenous people and maroons have land rights. There are controversial issues about the mining wastes but little action in the form of site remediation, cleanup, or waste treatment. Much of the population is economically dependent, directly or indirectly, on mining.

Although Suriname does have a general framework for waste management, it does have specific guidance or rules. There is little waste separation or recycling by the government. One private business, AmReCo, recovers some valuable materials from wastes, processing about two to three tons of plastic, paper, and cardboard. Some community organizations are also beginning basic recycling by residential waste separation. Waste collection and treatment is free for residents. Most of the urban waste comes from Paramaribo, Warnica, Para, and Commewijne by truck and is dumped in the only official landfill, the Ornamibo landfill. The Ministry of Public Works manages the landfill. The landfill was opened in 1999 as a temporary waste storage site and has been over capacity for years. Nearby residents are concerned about groundwater contamination.

Ninety-seven percent of the urban population has access to an improved source of drinking water, and 90 percent has access to improved sanitation facilities. Eighty-one percent of rural populations have access to an improved drinking water source, and 66 percent have access to improved sanitation facilities. Most urban areas have some type of sewage system. In rural areas, waste

A miner in Suriname shows his work conditions while mining at an open gold mine pit near the small town of Nieuw Koffiekamp on the edge of Suriname's rainforest, on August 13, 2010. As gold prices increased, hundreds of small mining operations began along the northeastern shoulder of South America, tearing up trees and discharging poisonous mercury into the water. Many people are faced with difficult choices between survival and environmental protection. (AP Photo/Andres Leighton)

practices can be basic—pit toilets, latrines, drainage ditches, cesspools, and open defecation. Only 1 percent of urban waste is treated before being discharged into water. All this waste receives secondary levels of waste treatment before discharge. In the capital city of Paramaribo, 15 percent use pit latrines, and many do not have access to any facilities. So far, Suriname has not met the United Nations Millennium Development goals for sanitation, and it is not likely to meet 2015 deadlines. Human health is currently affected by waste issues, and diseases such as yellow fever, cholera, hepatitis A, hepatitis B, typhoid, malaria, and dengue fever. More than 2 percent of the population is persistently infected with hepatitis B.

Emissions and Industry

In 2003, Suriname generated 3,338 metric tons of greenhouse gas emissions.

Agricultural products include rice, coconuts, palm kernels, plantains, meat, and fish. Agricultural emissions accounted for 25 percent of emissions. Within this sector, rice cultivation accounted for 92.5 percent of emissions and enteric fermentation 7.5 percent.

Suriname produces crude oil and maintains proven oil reserves. Energy emissions accounted for 72 percent of emissions. Within this sector, manufacturing and construction industries accounted for 57 percent of emissions, energy industries 22 percent, and transportation 15 percent. Industrial emissions accounted for 2 percent of emissions. Within this sector, mineral products account for all emissions.

Emissions from wastes accounted for 0.63 percent of emissions. Within this sector, solid waste disposal on land accounted for all emissions.

Major Waste Issues

The major waste challenge facing Suriname is the development and finance of a waste management system. There is a regulatory framework for waste management. However, there is little environmental enforcement or guidance. There is little data with which to make decisions and no consistent manner for getting data. There are needs for training and capacity development for state agencies and local government. Public awareness about waste management is low.

Suriname is a very low-lying country, vulnerable to climate change effects. Higher sea levels, increased intense weather events, and more precipitation cause concerns about flooding. Over three-quarters of the population live within ten meters of sea level. They fear that human health will be affected by climate change without UN assistance. Suriname was one of the first countries to create an agency to deal with climate changes—the Climate Compatible Development Agency. The goals of this agency are to coordinate climate change, seek international funding, and develop a Climate Compatible Knowledge Institute

Further Reading

Ouboter, P. E. *The Freshwater Ecosystems of Suriname*. Alphen aan den Rijn, Netherlands: Kluwer Academic Publishers.

Suriname National Assembly. www.dna.sr.

Van Drunen, Michiel, et al. 2006. *Climate Change in Developing Countries*. Oxfordshire, UK: CAB International North America.

SWAZILAND

Mozambique and South Africa border landlocked Swaziland. The topography ranges from low mountains to lowlands. There are mountains along the Mozambique border and rainforests in the northwest. Plateaus and rolling hills are located in eastern Swaziland. The climate is subtropical, with warm summers and mild winters. Rainfall varies but is generally greater at higher altitudes. Natural resources include diamonds, coal, talc, woodlands, and hydropower. Altogether, 1.4 million people live on Swaziland's 17,363 km^2 of land. Twenty-four percent of the population lives in urban areas, and just 7 percent lives in a city having more than 100,000 inhabitants. There are many small communities throughout the country. Thirty percent of the population is malnourished.

Current Waste Practices

Swaziland has a National Waste Management Strategy that consolidates and clarifies some of the waste management issues in prior legislation such as the National Environmental Management Act and the Waste Regulations. The Swaziland Environmental Authority operates a waste information system, monitors wastes, plans waste management, prepares waste reports for the State of the Environment Report, fulfills international obligations for monitoring and reporting wastes, and develops policies concerning waste. To accommodate differences in local capacity to report wastes, reporting mechanisms are designed to handle data in a way that allows for data improvement from local communities over time. Collection of data is limited to the most populated areas, but information from other areas can be added as local capacity and financing increases. Swaziland also runs pilot projects on waste management to observe the effectiveness of waste management techniques in the local environment. Past pilot projects include intermunicipal cooperation, health care wastes at Mbabane Hospital, recycling buyback centers, waste management systems in outlying urban areas of Kwaliseni, and commercial waste management systems in nonurban areas of Siphofaneni. The World Bank has supported programs to develop health care management programs. These programs implemented information and education campaigns for the public education about health care wastes, supported partnerships between the public and private sectors and civil society organizations, and helped develop a more comprehensive legal framework around health care waste management.

Most urban areas have some type of municipal and private waste collection. The trash is trucked to uncontrolled landfills and dumpsites. In rural areas, trash is burned on site or in communal dumpsites. Some trash is buried on site or off site, in communal dumpsites. About 80 percent of this waste is organic, 10 percent plastic, and 8 percent metal. With the rise of e-wastes, it is likely that the metal and plastic composition of the waste stream will increase. Much of the waste contains municipal solid wastes along with hazardous wastes. It is estimated that up to a fifth of the waste stream is hazardous.

In rural areas waste practices can be basic—pit toilets, latrines, drainage ditches, cesspools, and open defecation. Ninety-one percent of the urban population has access to an improved source of drinking water, and 64 percent has access to improved sanitation facilities. Sixty-five percent of rural populations have access to an improved drinking water source, and 55 percent have access to improved sanitation facilities.

Emissions and Industry

In 1994, Swaziland emitted 7,538.7 metric tons of greenhouse gases. It is likely that greenhouse gases are higher now because of population increases and reliance on agriculture.

Agricultural products include sugar cane, cotton, tobacco, corn, and livestock. Agricultural emissions accounted for 16 percent of all greenhouse gas emissions in

1994. Within this sector, enteric fermentation accounted for 41 percent of emissions, agricultural soils almost 23 percent, prescribed burning of the savannas almost 21 percent, and field burning of agricultural residues almost 16 percent.

The electrical grid is out almost twenty-nine days a year. Oil and electricity production and consumption are low. Energy emissions accounted for 14 percent of all emissions in 1994. Within this sector, transportation accounted for almost 42 percent of emissions, manufacturing and construction industries almost 29 percent, and fugitive emissions almost 8 percent. Fugitive emissions are essentially unaccounted waste streams into the air. Fugitive emissions can affect regional ecosystems and the public health, because they can fall from the air to the land and water. It was reported that there were no emissions from energy industries in this sector. This is very unusual, because currently used energy production almost always generates emissions. Industrial emissions accounted for 65 percent of all emissions in 1994. Within this sector, consumption of halocarbons accounted for all reported emissions. Primary industries are coal mining, wood pulp production, and sugar production.

Waste emissions accounted for almost 5 percent of all emissions in 1994. Within this sector, wastewater handling accounted for almost 94 percent of emissions and solid waste disposal on land about 6 percent.

Major Waste Issues

Although Swaziland has a strong regulatory framework for waste management, it still faces challenges of lack of capacity at the local level. Basic waste management practices are lacking. Most waste is not separated or treated. Landfills are not contained, and there are many illegal dumpsites. A major issue in Swaziland linked to poor waste management is the spread of infectious diseases, including cholera, hepatitis A, hepatitis B, typhoid, malaria, and schistosomiasis. Two percent or more of the population is persistently infected with hepatitis B. Concerns about the HIV virus brought international assistance to manage health care wastes. International assistance may assist the development of waste management practices in the future.

Further Reading

Government of the Kingdom of Swaziland. www.gov.sz.

Manyatsi, A., and M. Thwala. 2014. "Sanitation and Hygiene at Rural Schools in Swaziland: A Case Study of Ekhukhanyeni Constituency." *Research Journal of Environmental and Earth Sciences* 6: 278–283.

Proctor, J., et al. 2014. "Household-scale Environmental Health in the Ezulwini Valley, Swaziland." *African Journal of Environmental Science and Technology* 8: 219–233.

Stringer, Lindsay C., et al. 2009. "Adaptations to Climate Change Drought and Desertification: Local Insights to Enhance Policy in Southern Africa." *Environmental Science and Policy* 12: 748–765.

SWEDEN

Sweden, part of Scandinavia, shares its borders with Finland, Norway, and the Baltic Sea. Sweden's terrain is flat, with mountains in the west. The climate in the north is subarctic, with very cold winters and short, cool summers. In the south, the winters are cold and cloudy and the summers cool and less cloudy. Natural resources include iron ore, uranium, lead, copper, gold, zinc, silver, feldspar, timber, and hydropower.

Altogether, 9.1 million people live on Sweden's 450,295 km² of land and 3,218 km of coastline. Eighty-four percent of the population is urbanized, and 30 percent lives in a city having more than 100,000 inhabitants. No one lives below poverty levels. Everyone has access to an improved drinking water source and sanitation facilities.

Current Waste Practices

Swedish waste management is among the best in the world. Waste management is part of Swedish culture and today incorporates the most advanced methods in integrated waste management approaches. The first waste treatment plant began operations in the mid-1930s. Today tertiary waste treatment plants use chemical, physical, and biological methods to treat wastes. Much of the approach to waste is based on sustainability principles. Waste is conceptualized as resources not yet accessible. Local governments control their waste management systems, owning their businesses that manage sewage and solid wastes.

Sewer sludge is one of the largest and most pernicious waste problems the world over. It can be toxic and hazardous and is generally offensive. With poor waste management, it simply accumulates in lagoons, dumpsites, lakes, rivers, and coastlines. A very small amount is recycled as agricultural fertilizers. The problem with this approach is that untreated sewer sludge can be dangerous for the environment and public health. Testing and treating sewer sludge is expensive and time-consuming, increasing costs. Sweden has studied this issue for many years and wants to recycle phosphorus and other plant nutrients back into the soil. Sweden's goal is to recycle 60 percent of the phosphorus from sewer sludge back to arable land. Many developed nations are developing similar methods, but none as advanced as the Swedes'.

Most communities have modern sewer and water systems. Sweden generated 2,063,000 tons of hazardous wastes in 2008. Sweden collected 4,486,000 tons of municipal waste in 2009, almost 1 percent of it landfilled, 48 percent incinerated, 35 percent recycled, and about 14 percent composted. Everyone has municipal waste collection. Landfilling of sorted combustible waste was prohibited in 2002. The landfilling of organic wastes was prohibited in 2005. Sweden has a comprehensive recycling program, from collection to advanced recycling facilities.

Emissions and Industry

Sweden generated 57,604.2 metric tons of greenhouse gases in 2012, a 21 percent decrease from 1990.

Agricultural products include barley, wheat, sugar, beets, meat, and milk. Agricultural emissions accounted for 13 percent of all emissions. Within this sector, agricultural soils accounted for 57 percent of emissions, enteric fermentation 33 percent, and manure management almost 10 percent.

Sweden produces substantial amounts of crude oil and has no proven reserves. Oil and electricity production per capita is lower than oil and energy consumption. Energy emissions accounted for 73 percent of all emissions. Within this sector, transportation accounted for 45 percent of emissions, energy industries 24 percent, manufacturing and construction industries 20 percent, and fugitive emissions 2.2 percent. Industrial emissions accounted for 11 percent of all emissions. Within this sector, metal production accounted for 45 percent of emissions, mineral products 36 percent, and chemical industries 3.6 percent. Waste emissions accounted for 3 percent of all emissions. Within this sector, solid waste disposal on land accounted for 67.5 percent of emissions, wastewater handling 28 percent, and waste incineration 4 percent.

Major Waste Issues

The major environmental issues are also waste issues—acid rain from air pollution and water pollution of the North Sea and the Baltic Sea. The major waste issues are in the context of global warming.

Sweden is preparing for climate change effects on water systems. Climate observers note increased temperatures, differences in seasonal patterns, and floods. Projected effects include increases in temperature, increases in precipitation, increased risks of floods and landslides affecting hydropower network, decreases in snow, increases in water supply nationally but some decreases locally, extreme weather events that have potential consequences for urban storm drainage systems, sea level rise and saltwater intrusion along the coast, and damages to aquatic ecosystems. The primary concern is about extreme weather events, especially flooding. In response to these concerns and projections, the Swedish government developed initiatives, policies, and regulatory instruments. There is particular concern about the capacity of current dams. Dams are now assessed and built with express consideration of climate change effects. They are developing and implementing methods to prevent, avoid, and minimize climate change effects in development projects and processes. Accounting for flood risks in spatial planning is a basic component of this.

Sweden is an international leader in many aspects of waste management, environmental decision-making, and sustainability. Sweden also provides sanitation expertise in many parts of other countries.

Further Reading

Climate Change Impacts on Water Systems. www.oecd.org.

Government Offices of Sweden. www.government.se.

Lewis, L., et al. 2013. "The Swedish Model for Groundwater Policy: Legal Foundations, Decision-Making and Practical Application." *Hydrogeology Journal* 21: 751–760.

National Swedish Portal for Climate Change Adaption. www.klimatanpassning.se.

Schonning, C., and T. Stenstrom. 2004. *Guidelines on the Safe Use of Urine and Feces in Ecological Sanitation Systems*. Stockholm, Sweden: Stockholm Environment Institute.

SWITZERLAND

Austria, France, Italy, Liechtenstein, and Germany border Switzerland. The terrain is very mountainous, though there is a central plateau with rolling hills and lakes. Natural resources include timber, salt, and hydropower. Eight million people live on Switzerland's 41,285 km² of land. Three-quarters of the Swiss are urbanized, and 42 percent live in a city having more than 100,000 inhabitants. There are no populations below either the national or the international poverty level.

Current Waste Practices

Switzerland's waste management system is very comprehensive. All communities in Switzerland have modern sewer and water systems. The entire population has access to improved drinking water sources and improved sanitation facilities. Switzerland generated 1,112,000 tons of hazardous wastes in 2002. All polluted sites are registered and scheduled for remediation.

The total amount of municipal solid waste generated increased by 16 percent from 2001 to 2011. Everyone has municipal waste collection. About 34 percent of this waste is recycled. There is an integrated recycling system covering all aspects of recycling. There is very little use of landfills, but rather emphasis on a large incineration capacity. There are approximately thirty municipal waste incinerators. Imported municipal waste for incineration is deducted from internally generated

---

Space Waste

About 1,134 satellites operate in rotation around Earth. As technology continues to allow many countries to send satellites into space around Earth, the amount of space junk is expected to increase. Space junk travels at very high speeds and could cause significant damage on impact. The Joint Space Operations Center of the U.S. Strategic Command monitors about 15,000 pieces of space junk as well as all active satellites. Satellites operate at different altitudes for different reasons. Most satellites are in low earth obit, because it's cheaper to get them there and to get to them when needed. Low earth orbits are between 0 and 2,000 km above Earth. At this level, there are about 555 satellites and 11,500 pieces of space waste. Navigation satellites generally use medium earth orbit, 2,000 to 34,5000 km away from Earth. At this level, there are eighty-seven satellites and about 1,900 pieces of space waste. In high earth orbit, satellites observe the sun and Earth. High earth orbits are between 37,500 and 50,000 km above earth. There are twenty-three satellites and approximately 210 pieces of large pieces of space junk at this altitude. The three biggest generators of space waste are Russia (and formerly as the USSR), the United States, and China. France, Japan, and India also generate space waste.

There are two projects to reduce the increasing amount of space junk. One proposal is to attach incomplete nanosatellites that harvest, or recycle, space junk. Another project is called CleanSpace One, a satellite that would direct space junk into the atmosphere to burn it up.

and incinerated waste. Forty-eight percent of waste is incinerated. Seventeen percent of waste is composted. Switzerland gives broad discretion to the local governments—twenty-six cantons—to decide on waste issues but does review them for conformity to each other and to national policies.

Recycling

Switzerland's waste management policy is premised on reducing waste and recycling. Recycling rates for recyclable wastes that are collected separately are high and improving. Glass is the most recycled (95 percent), then aluminum (91 percent), tin (82 percent), paper and cardboard (78 percent), and batteries (71 percent).

Law requires recycling. In the area of electronic wastes, or e-wastes, the Swiss charge a disposal fee with electrical appliances. All manufacturers, retailers, and importers of electrical appliances are required to take back these appliances at the end of their life. The Swiss are international leaders in this area. They are leaders with the Basel Convention and started the Mobile Phone Partnership and the Partnership on Action on Computing Equipment. Among other actions, they partnered with Indonesia to work on the problem of e-waste disposal in countries that cannot handle it in an environmentally sound manner.

These approaches are based on an integrated approach to sustainable development. They consider the global flow of goods and conclude that end-of-life waste disposal is not enough for sustainability. To be sustainable, the approaches conclude that it is necessary to improve the social and environmental context of the good in its complete lifecycle—from production to final disposal.

Emissions and Industry

Switzerland generated 51,449 metric tons of greenhouse gases in 2012, a 2.7 percent decrease from 1990.

Agricultural products include fruits, vegetables, grains, meat, and eggs. Fertilizers are used frequently. Agricultural emissions accounted for 11 percent of all emissions. Within this sector, enteric fermentation accounted for 45 percent of emissions, agricultural soils 37 percent, and manure management 18 percent. This is a high amount of greenhouse gas emissions from manure, indicating the presence of large amounts of untreated feces.

Electricity and oil consumption per capita is moderate. Energy emissions accounted for 81 percent of all emissions. Within this sector, transportation accounted for 13 percent of emissions and energy industries 10 percent. Industrial emissions accounted for 7 percent of all emissions. Within this sector, mineral products accounted for 57 percent of emissions, consumption of halocarbons 41 percent, chemical industries 4.6 percent, and metal production 1 percent.

Wastes emissions accounted for 1 percent of all emissions. Within this sector, wastewater handling accounted for 42 percent of emissions, solid waste disposal on land 27 percent, and incineration 7.5 percent. Other accounted for 24 percent of emissions.

Major Waste Issues

Though it is a leader in waste management practices, Switzerland is not immune to environmental issues that stem from waste issues. Air pollution and acid rain, combined with water pollution from the runoff from agricultural pesticides and fertilizers, have significant environmental effects.

The major waste issue is the effect of climate change. Switzerland is preparing for climate change effects on water systems. Climate change observers in Switzerland note glacier recession, higher water temperatures, and greater flooding. Projected effects include ample precipitation, extremely dry periods lasting longer and occurring more frequently, habitats for cold-water fish decreasing and habitats for warm-water fish increasing, a higher snowline, and increased potential for landslides, loose rock fall, and avalanches. The intensity and frequency of heavy precipitation, floods, slope instabilities, landslides, rock falls, and droughts are projected to increase, but the Swiss note that in most cases of extreme weather events, the signals of the models are weak. The Swiss alpine regions are a key vulnerability. Primary concerns are about water quality, extreme weather events, and ecosystem management. In response to these concerns and projections, the Swiss government developed policies, regulatory instruments, and economic instruments. All real property owners are required to have natural disaster insurance.

The Swiss are reviewing all water laws, especially as they apply to alpine terrain. They are reviewing laws on sewage disposal to ensure potable water. At the same time, they are regionalizing their wastewater treatment plants. Some of the laws revised to accommodate climate change issues are designed to restore the natural flow of water. Local governments must allocate space for surface water and are required to plan and implement river flow restoration measures. Their national research program on sustainable water management examines the effects of climate change on the carrying capacity of the environment.

Further Reading

Climate Change Impacts on Water Systems. www.oecd.org.

Hill, Margot. 2013. *Climate Change and Water Governance: Adaptive Capacity in Chile and Switzerland*. Heidelberg, Germany: Springer E-books.

Mara, Duncan, et al. 2012. "Selection of Sustainable Sanitation Arrangements." *Water Policy* 9: 305–318.

Switzerland Federal Authorities. www.admin.ch.

SYRIA

Syria is bordered by Iraq, Israel, Jordan, Lebanon, Turkey, and the Mediterranean Sea. The terrain is mountainous in the west and desert plateau to the coast. It has a hot and dry desert climate, though it does rain along the coast. Natural resources include oil, gas, phosphates, manganese, iron ore, marble, and hydropower. Most of the oilfields are on the Euphrates Graben in the northeastern region.

Altogether, 20.5 million people live on Syria's 185,180 km² of land and 151 km of coastline. Fifty-one percent of the population is urbanized, and 38 percent lives in a city having more than 100,000 inhabitants. There are many small communities that live outside the cities.

Current Waste Practices

Syria is in the midst of violent civil and international conflict now. Water quality is very poor. Before the current conflict escalated into violent combat, 93 percent of the urban population had access to improved drinking water sources, and 96 percent had access to improved sanitation facilities. Eighty-six percent of the rural population had access to improved drinking water sources, and 93 percent had access to improved sanitation facilities. About 1,600 deaths a year are attributed to unsafe water. Twenty-nine percent suffers malnutrition. However, considering the recent civil unrest, it is likely that these numbers will increase. Sewer and water facilities are often military targets. They are considered more appropriate targets for advanced missile technology because of the lower risk of civilian casualties. Years of conflict have destroyed sewers, waste treatment facilities, sanitary facilities, and clean drinking water sources. It is likely that basic waste practices include pit toilets, cesspools, drainage ditches, latrines, and open defecation.

Syria collected 7.5 million tons of municipal waste in 2003; almost 94 percent landfilled, 5 percent incinerated, and 1 percent recycled. Seventy-four percent of the population receives municipal waste collection. Waste treatment is not a high priority in civil conflict except to destroy it. It is unlikely waste is treated now.

Emissions and Industry

It is difficult to know the status of greenhouse gas emissions because of the current violent civil and international conflict. Generally the use of petrochemicals, hazardous solvents, and increase in hazardous wastes create large increases in greenhouse gas emissions, depending on the intensity and duration of the conflict.

Agricultural products include wheat, cotton, olives, meat, dairy products, and milk. Agricultural emissions accounted for 5 percent of all emissions. Energy emissions accounted for 79 percent of all emissions. Syria produces large amounts of crude oil and maintains massive proven reserves. Oil and electricity production and consumption per capita are moderately high. Syria relies heavily on natural gas to decrease dependence on oil, so there is more for export. Natural gas proven reserves are large—8.5 trillion ft^3. In the late 1990s, Syria rapidly expanded infrastructure, exploration, and production of natural gas.

Industrial emissions accounted for 16 percent of all emissions. Most of this comes from oil operations and mining, which generate almost a third of the gross industrial output. Other industries include chemical manufacture, textiles, and clothing.

There is little, if any, data on waste emissions now in Syria. Waste and water infrastructure are often targeted in war. They are often considered safe targets for advanced missiles because of the decreased risk of loss of civilian life, sometimes referred to as collateral damage. As a result, the greenhouse gas emissions of wastes are not known.

Major Waste Issues

The waste infrastructure and policy is not functional. Some of the prewar environmental problems are also waste issues. There is little drinking water. Oil mining and refining wastes, chemical manufacturing waste, solid wastes, and raw sewage pollute many rivers, especially in urban areas. One major waste issue is the protection of public health, in both the country and the region, from infectious diseases such as hepatitis A, hepatitis B, typhoid, malaria, and schistosomiasis. Two percent or more of the population is persistently infected with hepatitis B.

Further Reading

El-Khoury, Gabi. 2014. "Water Indicators in Arab Countries: Selected Indicators." *Contemporary Arab Affairs* 7: 339–349.

Syria. www.syriaonline.com.

Verner, Dort, and Clemens Breisinger, eds. 2013. *Economics of Climate Change in the Arab World*. Washington, DC: The World Bank.

T

TAIWAN

Taiwan is an island off the coast of China, surrounded by the East China Sea, South China Sea, and Philippine Sea. The terrain is mountainous in the east and interior. The west is flatter. The climate is hot and humid, with monsoon season from June to August. Natural resources include gas, limestone, marble, coal, and asbestos.

Altogether, 23.3 million people live on Taiwan's 35,980 km² of land and 1,566 km of coastline. It is one of the most densely populated countries in the world. Taiwan lacks international recognition as a sovereign state and is actually considered by the United Nations to be part of China.

Current Waste Practices

In 2006, about a third of the population used wastewater treatment plants. Many places do not have sewers, and building them is a high priority. Solid wastes are incinerated, and some is disposed in landfills. There are twenty-four operating incinerators. All incinerators are waste-to-energy incinerators. Altogether, 2.9 million tons of waste produced about 295 megawatt-hours of electricity in 2008.

Recycling

Taiwan strongly supports recycling, and its programs have high community participation. Rates of recycling have recently increased and waste generation decreased. The per-capita amount of waste generated per day was 1.1 kg. In 2008, it was 0.5 kg per day. In 1989, about 60 percent of the population sorted their wastes; in 2008, almost everyone did. Separation of recyclable materials before municipal collection is required. Collections happen once or twice a week. Garbage trucks collect and separate more than thirty categories of waste.

One initiative aims to decrease and recycle food wastes. About three-quarters of food wastes is steam-disinfected and used as pig feed. Almost all the rest is composted to produce soil amendments. Taiwan also recycles some hazardous materials such as batteries and e-waste. Substantially more than half of all batteries and about half of all e-waste are recycled, despite the drastic increase of these wastes. The Waste Disposal Act requires manufacturers to assume responsibility for their wastes. The Taiwan Environmental Protection Administration also fights against illegal hazardous wastes by using a global positioning system to track hazardous wastes. However, there are concerns about low-level radioactive waste stored or disposed of in landfills.

A bicyclist in Taipei, Taiwan, covers her nose and mouth to protect herself from air pollution. Air pollution is known to have significant health impacts. In many polluted areas masks, scarves, and cloth are used to filter air. (Keith Levit/Shutterstock.com)

Emissions and Industry

In 2009, Taiwan generated 279.14 metric tons of greenhouse gases.

In 2010, agriculture emissions accounted for 1 percent of all emissions, energy emissions 11 percent, industry 46 percent, transportation 14 percent, services 14 percent, and residences 13 percent. Agricultural products include cotton, rice, tea, fruit, vegetables, flowers, fish, pigs, and poultry.

Taiwan produces a substantial amount of crude oil and maintains solid proven reserves. Oil and electricity production is high, but consumption per capita is higher. Natural gas is used for energy.

Major Waste Issues

Taiwan's excellent recycling program reduces stress on the waste infrastructure and helps integrated water management. There is concern about the pollution of groundwater, however. Many of the environmental issues are also waste issues, such as untreated sewage in waterways. As the population density increases, so, too, might pollution increase.

Climate change observers note increased temperatures, sea level rises, melting sea ice, wet areas getting more rain, and dry areas getting much less rain, leading to concerns about drought. There are infectious diseases in Taiwan, including hepatitis A, hepatitis B, dengue fever, Japanese encephalitis, and typhoid. To prevent infectious disease, the EPA developed programs, such as the Eradication of Dengue Fever Carrier Mosquitoes and Education Program.

Further Reading

Chou, R. 2013. "Addressing Watercourse Sanitation in Dense, Water Pollution-Affected Urban Areas in Taiwan." *Environment and Urbanization* 25: 523–540.

Taiwan Provincial Government. www.tpg.gov.tw.

Williams, Jack, and Ch'ang-yi David Chang. 2012. *Taiwan's Environmental Struggle: Toward a Green Silicon Island.* New York: Routledge.

TAJIKISTAN

More than 90 percent of the central Asian country of Tajikistan is mountainous and vulnerable to earthquakes. Glaciers in the mountains are the source for freshwater. The tallest point is Qullai Ismoili Somoni, at 7,495 meters. There are deep valleys in the north and southwest. Afghanistan, China, Kyrgyzstan, and Uzbekistan border Tajikistan. The summers are hot and winters mild. The weather at higher altitudes is much colder and windier. Natural resources include oil, uranium, coal, lead, zinc, silver, gold, and hydropower.

Altogether, 7.9 million people live on Tajikistan's 143,100 km^2 of land. Only a quarter of the population is urbanized, and 11 percent lives in a city having more than 100,000 inhabitants. The capital and largest city is Dushanbe, having a population of only about 800,000. Seven percent of the population lives under the international poverty level. A third suffers malnutrition. There are many small communities outside of the urban areas. Life expectancy is about 67 years.

Current Waste Practices

Water quality is very poor. Waste practices can be basic—pit toilets, latrines, drainage ditches, cesspools, and open defecation. Access to improved drinking water sources and sanitation facilities is generally good, but only 54 percent of the rural population has access to improved sanitation facilities. About a third have chlorinated piped water, and another third relies on springs, the rest relying on ditches and rivers. Five percent of the population is connected to public sewerage. Frequent power outages decrease water availability as water pumps stop functioning.

Only urban areas have waste services, and this is a small part of the population. The capital city of Dushanbe is the largest and has one unsanitary landfill. Outside the second largest city, Khujand, are about 54.8 million tons of radioactive uranium mining wastes in unsecured sites. Dumping hazardous and municipal solid wastes in open dumps on the edge of the community is the norm.

Emissions and Industry

Tajikistan generated 7,5000 metric tons of greenhouse gases in 2003, a 70 percent decrease from 1990.

Agricultural products include cotton, grain, fruits, vegetables, and livestock. There is heavy use of pesticides. Agricultural emissions accounted for 55 percent of all emissions in 2003. Within this sector, agricultural soils accounted for 53 percent of emissions, enteric fermentation 39 percent, manure management almost 6 percent, and rice cultivation 2.5 percent. Emissions from manure management increased substantially from 1990.

Tajikistan produces a substantial amount of crude oil and maintains moderate reserves. Oil consumption per capita is very low. Hydropower provides much of the electrical energy. Energy emissions accounted for almost 31 percent of all emissions in 2003. Within this sector, manufacturing and construction industries accounted for almost 29 percent of emissions, transportation more than 13 percent, energy industries almost 2 percent, and other about 50 percent.

Industrial emissions accounted for 8 percent of all emissions in 2003. Within this sector, metal production accounted for almost 79 percent of emissions, mineral products 15 percent, and the chemical industry more than 6 percent.

Waste emissions accounted for more than 6 percent of all emissions in 2003. Within this sector, solid waste disposal on land accounted for 95 percent of emissions and wastewater handling 5 percent.

Major Waste Issues

The sanitation infrastructure is inadequate in Tajikistan. Untreated wastewater, industrial discharges, and pesticide and fertilizer runoff from agricultural land use cause pollution in waterways. The major waste issue is the protection of public health both in the country and the region. Additionally, infectious diseases such as cholera, hepatitis A, hepatitis B, typhoid, and malaria can exist in Tajikistan. More than 2 percent of the population is persistently infected with hepatitis B.

There is a chance that infectious disease vectors will expand. Recent war and civil conflict have degraded water and waste infrastructure. There are long droughts and desertification that have substantial environmental and public health effects. With increasing temperatures, desertification will increase and heighten these environmental and public health risks, including by increasing groundwater contamination.

Further Reading

Information on Parliament. www.tajik-gateway.org.

Second Environmental Performance Review of Tajikistan Highlights Lack of Access to Clean Water and Sanitation and Need for Improved Waste Management. 2012. www .unece.org.

Sherkhonov, T., et al. 2013. "National Intestinal Helminth Study among Schoolchildren in Tajikistan: Prevalence's, Risk Factors and Perceptions." *Acta Tropica* 126: 93–98.

TANZANIA

The highest point in Africa, Mt. Kilimanjaro, is in Tanzania, standing at 5,895 meters. Mount Kilimanjaro is in the mountainous northeastern section of the country with other active volcanoes. Lake Victoria is in the west, the largest lake in Africa. The Indian Ocean borders Tanzania on the east. Burundi, Democratic Republic of the Congo, Kenya, Malawi, Mozambique, Rwanda, Uganda, and Zambia border Tanzania. The island of Zanzibar is separated from the mainland by a narrow channel about 50 km canal. There are two other Tanzanian islands—Pemba and Mafia. The terrain of the mainland varies, but most of it is at a high altitude, decreasing the effects of tropical heat and humidity. The climate is tropical along the coast, with more temperature highlands. There are both floods and drought in the central plateau. Deforestation and soil degradation occurs, leading to desertification in some parts. Some regions of Tanzania have two rainy seasons. One season is from March to May and the other from November to January. Natural resources include diamonds, gold, coal, tin, natural gas, and hydropower.

There are many small communities throughout Tanzania. Altogether, 48.3 million people reside on Tanzania's 945,087 km^2 of land and 1,424 km of coastline.

Current Waste Practices

There is little waste management. Zanzibar City, on the Tanzanian island of Zanzibar, has 25 km of sewer pipes that serve the historical center of Stone Town. Zanzibar City generates 200 tons of solid wastes a day. Less than half is collected. From there, it is brought to uncontrolled landfill or illegal sites. It is estimated that 9,000–12,000 m^3 of liquid wastes is disposed in the ocean per day. Sewer sludge is dumped in coastal mangrove forests. Maruhubi is one location where high tides and mangrove forests are used to discharge sewer sludge.

Only about 10 percent to 15 percent of the urban population has access to a sewerage system. Waste practices in Tanzania are very basic—pit toilets, latrines, drainage ditches, cesspools, and open defecation. Sixty-two percent of the people have access to improved drinking water sources, which involves separating drinking water from wastewater. Forty-seven percent of the population has access to improved sanitation facilities. Forty-four percent suffers chronic malnutrition. The first cholera outbreak was reported in 1974. There have been waves of outbreaks since then, with cases reported every year. In 2006, there were 14,297 reported cases, including 254 deaths.

Emissions and Industry

Tanzania generated 39,236.7 metric tons of greenhouse gases in 1994. It is likely that greenhouse gases are higher now because of population increases and reliance on agriculture.

There is a substantial amount of arable land in Tanzania. Agricultural products include coffee, tea, tobacco, cotton, corn, wheat, cassava, fruits, vegetables, and livestock. Agricultural emissions accounted for 76 percent of all emissions. Within this sector, enteric fermentation accounted for 40 percent of emissions, agricultural soils 38.6 percent, prescribed burning of the savannas 9.6 percent, rice cultivation 7 percent, field burning of agricultural residues 2.3 percent, and manure management 2 percent.

Oil and electricity production and consumption per capita are moderately low. Energy emissions accounted for 18 percent of all emissions. Within this sector, transport accounted for 24 percent of emissions, manufacturing and construction 6.5 percent, and energy industries 7 percent. Sixty-one percent of emissions in this sector were from other sources. Industrial emissions accounted for 1 percent of all emissions. Within this sector, mineral products accounted for 99 percent of emissions.

Waste emissions accounted for 6 percent of all emissions. Within this sector, wastewater handling accounted for 84.5 percent of emissions and solid waste disposal on land 16 percent.

Major Waste Issues

Waste management legal framework is basically in place, but practice does not follow the law. There is little separation of wastes, so toxic and hazardous wastes end up in dumpsites. All stages of waste management are insufficient—collection, storage, transportation, treatment, and final disposal. Waste management is particularly missing in the squatter communities around urban areas. It is estimated that 70 percent of the population of urban areas resides in squatter communities. Tanzanian health facilities deal with water- and sanitation-related cases an estimated 60 percent to 80 percent of the time. Tied to waste management issues, there is great concern over the spread of infectious diseases like yellow fever, cholera, hepatitis A, hepatitis B, typhoid, and malaria. Two percent or more of the population is persistently infected with hepatitis B.

There is a chance that infectious disease vectors will expand. Climate change effects of increasing temperatures will cause desertification to increase. There is grave concern about the effects on agricultural food security and the risk of famines.

Further Reading

Central Africa Regional Program for the Environment, Regional Development Strategy 2012–2020, U.S. Agency for International Development. www.usaid.gov.

Jenkins, M., et al. 2014. "Beyond 'Improved, Towards, Safe and Sustainable' Urban Sanitation: Assessing the Design, Management and Functionality of Sanitation in Poor Communities of Dar es Salaam, Tanzania." *Journal of Water, Sanitation and Hygiene for Development* 4: 131–141.

The United Republic of Tanzania. www.tanzania.go.tz.

THAILAND

Thailand's neighboring borders include Cambodia, Laos, Malaysia, Myanmar, the Andaman Sea, and the Gulf of Thailand. The terrain is mountainous with a central plateau. The Khorat Plateau covers a third of the land. The tropical climate is hot and humid. There are two monsoons seasons, one from mid-May to September and another from November to mid-March. Natural resources include gas, tin, rubber, lead, timber, fish, and gypsum.

Altogether, 67.4 million people live on Thailand's 513,000 km^2 of land and 3,219 km of coastline. Thirty-two percent of the population is urbanized, and 16 percent lives in a city having more than 100,000 inhabitants. There are many small communities. About 16 percent of the population suffers malnutrition.

UN Report: Thailand

In 2013, the UN special rapporteur on the human right to safe drinking water and sanitation went to Thailand. He reported that Thailand needs to establish an independent water and sanitation state agency. This regulating state agency would facilitate public participation and impose fines for non-compliance. Only one-fifth of community sewage is treated before being discharged into water.

Current Waste Practices

About a fifth of the wastewater is treated before being discharged into the water systems. Sewage, industrial wastes, and pesticide and fertilizer runoff from agricultural land uses are discharged directly into rivers. Waste practices are very basic—pit toilets, latrines, drainage ditches, cesspools, and open defecation. Seventy-five percent of rural populations and 60 percent of urban populations do not have access to safe drinking water. There is concern that the lack of water quality could be a human rights violation in migrant labor camps.

Thailand generated 41,410 tons of municipal solid waste a day in 2009. Most of this went a landfill. About two-thirds of municipal solid waste is organic waste, 17 percent plastic, 8 percent paper, 3 percent glass, and 2 percent metal. From the 1990s to 2014, there was a shift from dumping the wastes on the edge of town to disposal in a sanitary landfill. Most waste is still disposed of in open dumps. The metropolitan area of Bangkok generates between a quarter and a third of all municipal solid waste. About 40 percent of municipal solid waste is generated in rural areas. Many localities invested in large municipal solid waste anaerobic digestion plants. One was planned in Chonburi that could handle 320 tons of municipal solid waste a day. The plant investment was 26 million dollars. But this, like most others, failed. There is one anaerobic digestion plant in Rayong. Most sanitary landfills are outside of Bangkok, Chiang Mai, and Ubon Ratchathani.

Recycling

About 22 percent of waste is recycled. The government is encouraging waste reduction, material reuse, and recycling of goods and materials in the private and public sector, including by developing waste banks. Elementary and secondary students, teachers, parents, and administrators are encouraged to collect recyclable goods and materials for the waste bank. At the waste bank, the recyclable materials are removed. Sometimes the waste bank works with private sector recycling businesses.

Emissions and Industry

In 2000, Thailand generated 236,946.4 metric tons of greenhouse gases, a 5.8 percent increase from 1994.

Almost a third of the land is arable. Agricultural products include coffee, bananas, corn, rice, cassava, rubber, sugar cane, and coconuts. Agricultural emissions accounted for 22 percent of all emissions. Within this sector, rice cultivation accounted for 58 percent of emissions, enteric fermentation 16 percent, agricultural soils 15 percent, manure management 10 percent, and field burning of agricultural residues 1 percent.

Thailand produces a substantial amount of crude oil and maintains moderate proven reserves. Electricity and oil consumption per capita was lower than per-capita oil and electricity production. Energy emissions accounted for 67

A zero-waste village in Thailand separates its recycling for transport to a regional recycling facility in Ban Nam-Phu on March 14, 2014. Community-based efforts aimed at zero waste production can achieve high recycling rates. (Ttanothai/Dreamstime.com)

percent of all emissions. Within this sector, energy industries accounted for 41.6 percent of emissions, transportation 28 percent, manufacturing and construction industries 19 percent, and fugitive emissions 3 percent. Industrial emissions accounted for 7 percent of all emissions. Within this sector, mineral products accounted for 98 percent of emissions, and chemistry industries 2 percent.

Waste emissions accounted for 4 percent of all emissions. Within this sector, solid waste disposal on land accounted for 52 percent of emissions, wastewater management 47.5 percent, and incineration 0.25 percent.

Major Waste Issues

Waste treatment is a major concern in Thailand. Even King Bhumibol holds a patent for a wastewater aerator—the only monarch to hold a patent. Sixty-eight percent of municipal solid wastes are not treated properly. Municipal solid waste constitute between 60 percent and 70 percent of the overall waste stream. Many of the environmental issues are also waste issues, including air and water pollution. About 64 percent of municipal solid wastes are disposed in illegal dumps site or burned.

Infectious disease from improper waste management is a concern, with diseases such as cholera, hepatitis A, hepatitis B, Japanese encephalitis, typhoid, and dengue fever prevalent. More than 2 percent of the population is persistently infected with hepatitis B. There is a high risk of malaria in rural and forested areas.

Further Reading

Koottatep, T., et al. 2014. "Hydraulic Evaluation and Performance of On-Site Sanitation Systems in Central Thailand." *Environmental Engineering Research* 3: in press.

Leekoi, P., et al. "An Empirical Study on Risk Assessment and Household Characteristics in Thailand." *Middle-East Journal of Scientific Research* 21: 962–967.

Royal Thai Government. www.thaigov.go.th.

TIMOR-LESTE (EAST TIMOR)

Indonesia, the Banda Sea, and the Timor Sea border Timor-Leste. The climate is tropical, with hot and humid weather. The rainy season lasts from November to May and the dry season from June to October. The terrain is mountainous. There are floods, landslides, and hurricanes, though there is a risk of drought in the north. Natural resources include gold, oil, gas, manganese, marble, and fish.

Altogether, 1.1 million people reside on Timor-Leste's 14,874 km² of land and 706 km of coastline. Only 26 percent of the population is urbanized. There are many small communities outside the urban areas. Fifty-six percent of the population suffers malnutrition.

Current Waste Practices

The 2012 National Sanitation Policy addressed large gaps in the waste management policies. Waste practices are basic, especially in rural areas. Latrines, pit toilets, cesspools, drainage ditches, and open defecation are the options. Sixty-six percent of the urban population and 33 percent of the rural population has access to improved sanitation facilities. Only 77 percent of the urban population and 56 percent of the rural population has access to an improved water sources.

Waste collection involves residents placing their wastes into communal bins, where it is loaded on to trucks. It is dumped in a legal landfill of a dumpsite. Both occasionally burn the waste to make room. The Tibar dump collected waste from Dili and is managed by the sanitation department. A waste inspector determines the contents of the vehicle and directs it to the appropriate waste area. The categories are mixed rubbish, construction wastes, scrap metal, and expired goods. There is a community of waste pickers residing next to the dump.

Timor-Leste is aware of a growing influx of e-wastes from 1999 until the present. Although it is not regulated, some businesses are collecting it. It is unknown how much e-wastes and hazardous wastes are imported.

Emissions and Industry

Timor-Leste was formed in 2002 after years of violent conflicts that left waste infrastructure and emissions reporting processes destroyed. Years of conflict have destroyed sewers, waste treatment facilities, sanitary facilities, and clean drinking water sources.

Agricultural products include coffee, rice, sweet potatoes, cassava, soybeans, vanilla, and bananas. A common agricultural practice of cutting down forests and burning forests and fields has created problems of soil, fertilizer, and pesticide runoff into rivers. There is some crude oil production. Consumption of oil and electricity per capita is low. There are about 120 power outages a year. When this happens, diesel generators are used to create power. The generators emit significant amounts of greenhouse gases. There is little natural gas consumption, but there are large proven reserves.

Major Waste Issues

The 1999 civil war damaged the majority of waste infrastructure. Pumping stations, transmission pipes, tanks, and sanitary facilities were destroyed. Civil unrest in 2006 and 2008 prevented progress in reconstructing wartorn waste infrastructure. Climate change effects of rising sea levels and more extreme weather raise more concerns about flooding and landslides which further slow the recovery of waste infrastructure. There is specific concern about the capital city of Dili's flooding during storm surges.

A major concern is that the main cause of infant and newborn fatality, respiratory infections and diarrhea, a lack of water, poor sanitation, and hygiene. A major issue connected to waste management is the spread of infectious diseases, including hepatitis A, hepatitis B, Japanese encephalitis, meningococcal meningitis, typhoid, malaria, and dengue fever. Two percent or more of the population is persistently infected with hepatitis B.

Further Reading

Government of Timor-Leste. www.timor-leste.gov.

Joseph, A., and T. Iamaguchi. 2014. *Timor-Leste: The History and Development of Asia's Newest Nation.* Lanham, MD: Lexington Books.

Sarmento, D., and J. Cardoso. 2014. "Risk Assessment for Groundwater Resources in Dili, The Capital City of Timor-Leste." *International Journal of Interdisciplinary and Multidisciplinary Studies* 1: 180–191.

Shephard, Christopher J. 2013. *Development and Environmental Politics Unmasked: Participation and Equity in East Timor.* New York: Taylor & Francis.

TOGO

The west African nation of Togo is bordered by Benin, Burkina Faso, Ghana, and the Atlantic Ocean. The terrain rises from coastal wetlands to a plateau in the south and savanna in the north. The interior is dominated by rolling hills. The climate is tropical and hot.. Togo is semi-arid in the north and humid in the south. Natural resources include limestone, marble, phosphates, and fish.

Altogether, 7.3 million people live on Togo's 56,785 km² of land and 56 km of sandy coastline. The capital and largest city is Lome, having more than 1.5 million people. Overall, 40 percent are urbanized and 16 percent live in a city having more than 100,000 inhabitants. There are many small communities away from urban areas. Twenty-eight percent of the population suffers malnutrition. Life expectancy is 64 years.

Current Waste Practices

Only 37 percent of the residents of the capital city of Lome have municipal waste collection. Waste practices are very basic, with pit toilets, latrines, drainage ditches, cesspools, and open defecation. Eighty-nine percent of the urban population has access to improved drinking water sources, but just 26 percent has access to improved sanitation facilities. Only 40 percent of the rural population has access to improved drinking water sources, and just 3 percent has access to improved sanitation facilities. Diarrhea and respiratory infections rates are elevated.

E-wastes are a big and growing part of the waste stream. Although there is no clear policy on it, private businesses may begin to recycle it more. In the capital city of Lome, the WoeLab group created the first 3D printer made from e-wastes in 2014, using materials costing less then $100.

Emissions and Industry

In 2000, Togo generated 4,917.2 metric tons of greenhouse gases, a 15.5 percent increase from 1992. It is likely that greenhouse gas emissions are higher now because of population increases, rate of population growth, and reliance on agriculture.

There is a substantial amount of arable land. Agricultural products include coffee, cocoa, cotton, cassava, corn, beans, yams, rice, sorghum, livestock, and fish. Agricultural emissions accounted for 55 percent of all emissions in 2000. Within this sector, agricultural soils accounted for more than 77 percent of emissions, enteric fermentation almost 16 percent, manure management more than 3 percent, and prescribed burning of the savannas and field burning of agricultural residuals 3 percent.

Oil and electricity per capita production and consumption are low. Energy emissions accounted for almost 35 percent of all emissions. Within this sector, transportation accounted for more than 37 percent of emissions, manufacturing industries and construction more than 15 percent, and energy industries almost 6 percent. Industrial emissions accounted for more than 6 percent of all emissions. Within this sector, mineral products accounted for all emissions.

Waste emissions accounted for more than 3 percent of all emissions. Within this sector, solid waste disposal on land accounted for 54 percent of emissions and wastewater handling 46 percent.

Major Waste Issues

The lack of an adequate waste management policy is the main challenge. The treatment of waste is insufficient in collection, transportation, treatment, and disposal. The lack of water and waste treatment threatens groundwater purity. Contamination of the drinking water supply contributes to spread of disease. As in other countries, infectious diseases that are spread thanks to poor waste management include yellow fever, hepatitis A, hepatitis B, meningococcal meningitis, typhoid, dengue fever, and schistosomiasis. Two percent or more of the population is persistently infected with hepatitis B. There is also a high risk of malaria.

Climate change effects of increasing temperatures will increase desertification. The threat to agricultural food security and risk of famine create grave concerns. It will be difficult to develop an integrated waste management policy and practice in this context. There are inadequate public resources in the country to handle internal, regional, and global health threats should they arise.

Further Reading

Enyonam, T., et al. 2014. "Surveillance for Rotavirus Gastroenteritis in Children Less Than 5 Years of Age in Togo." *Pediatric Infectious Disease Journal* 33: 14–18.

Munang, M., et al. 2014. "Harnessing Ecosystem-based Adaptation to Address the Social Dimensions of Climate Change." *Environment: Science and Policy for Sustainable Development* 56: 18–24.

Republic of Togo. www.republicoftogo.com.

TONGA

Tonga is a group of 176 small islands in the South Pacific Ocean, about forty-one of them occupied. The climate is tropical. Islands having volcanic bases and those having limestone bases from years of coral accumulation divide the terrain. The climate is hot from December to May and cooler from May to December. Natural resources include fish and arable land.

Altogether, 106,000 people live on Tonga's 747 km^2 of land and 419 km of coastline. Twenty-four percent of the population is urbanized, though no city has more than 100,000 inhabitants. There are many small communities. The largest and capital city is Nuku'alofa, having a population of about 25,000 people.

Current Waste Practices

Almost everyone on the islands has access to an improved drinking water source and sanitation facilities. There is generally poor waste management. There is no centralized sewer system. About 75 percent of households use septic tanks, 10 percent flush pits, and 7 percent traditional pit toilets. Animal waste is significant. Tongatapu alone is estimated to have 90,000 pigs. A single full-grown hog create emit four times the waste of a person. These pigs roam freely around the island. Most of this waste is swept into a trash pile or moved into the bush. There is limited potable water and rapidly diminishing landfill space. About one-fifth of the population has municipal collection services. However, there are efforts to establish a functional Solid Waste Management Plan in Nuku'alofa on Tongatapu, the main island.

The Tapuhia Waste Management Facility was formed in 2000. Cultural practices of land ownership challenge many western approaches. The king owns all the land, and nobles manage the land for the king by allocating land to villagers. It is not bought or sold. The king does not like his land near a dump or a recycling facility, which complicates waste site selection processes. There are also efforts to compost more of the organic wastes. About 18 percent of Tongan households recycle metal and glass for cash.

Recycling

There are few recycling facilities and they are not near the waste facilities. Most waste is landfilled or illegally disposed in the ocean. Sanitary landfills are difficult to build here because of the lack of the right kind of clay necessary to line the land fill. Everything must be imported to the islands, including clay, heavy plastic landfill liners, pipes, batteries, pumps, and heavy equipment. E-waste is a major concern because of the high amount of electronics that comes onto the islands with no place to dispose of them. E-waste private and public responses are developing. The primary goals are to decrease public health risks, create employment, reduce greenhouse gas emissions, and recover valuable metals. Gold, silver, copper, palladium, and indium can be recovered from e-wastes. Several NGOs, such as the E-waste Tonga nonprofit group, develop collection and education programs on e-wastes. E-waste Tonga received $48,000 from the United Nations Global Environment Fund with assistance from the Civil Society Forum of Tonga.

Emissions and Industry

In 2000, Tonga generated 245.1 metric tons of greenhouse gases, a 6.9 percent increase from 1994.

Agricultural products include coconuts, cocoa, fruits, vegetables, ginger, bananas, and fish. Agricultural emissions accounted for 38 percent of all emissions. Within this sector, manure management accounted for 53 percent emissions, agricultural soils 30 percent, and enteric fermentation 16.5 percent and prescribed burning of the savannas 0.22 percent. This is an unusually high amount of greenhouse gas emissions from manure, indicating the presence of large amounts of untreated feces.

Oil and electricity per capita production and consumption are low. Energy emissions accounted for 40 percent of all emissions. Within this sector, transportation accounted for 57 percent of emissions, energy industries 28 percent, and manufacturing and construction 1.51 percent. Industrial emissions accounted for none of the emissions.

Waste emissions accounted for 22 percent of all emissions. Within this sector, wastewater management accounted for 54 percent of emissions and solid waste disposal on land 46 percent.

Major Waste Issues

Tonga faces a difficult waste management issue without an effective waste management strategy. Animal and human wastes now accumulate with other waste streams, such as e-wastes, medical wastes, and hazardous wastes. The fish population in nearby coastal waters has decreased substantially. Poor waste disposal practices have become breeding grounds for mosquitoes—borne diseases such as dengue. About half the households report waste-related illnesses such as diarrhea and gastrointestinal distress, dengue fever, and skin infections. Public health is at risk in Tonga thanks to poor waste infrastructure. Infectious diseases include hepatitis A, hepatitis B, typhoid, and dengue fever. Two percent or more of the population is persistently infected with hepatitis B.

Further Reading

Clarke, M., et al. 2014. "Water, Sanitation and Hygiene Interventions in the Pacific: Defining, Assessing and Improving 'Sustainability.'" *European Journal of Development Research* 26: 692–706.

Management of Wastes in Small Island Developing States. www.islands.unep.ch.
Tonga Government Ministries and Department. www.mic.gov.to.

TRINIDAD AND TOBAGO

Trinidad and Tobago form one country made of two islands in the Caribbean Sea
and the North Atlantic Ocean, off the coast of South America. The climate on the
islands is tropical. The rainy season is from June to December. Natural resources
include oil, gas, asphalt, and fish. Tobago is just 300 km^2. It is covered with forests
of hardwood trees.

Altogether, 1.2 million people live on the islands' 5,130 km^2 of land and 360 km
of coastline. Fourteen percent of the population is urban and 86 percent are rural.
There are many small communities away from urban centers.

Current Waste Practices

Water quality on the islands is poor. Ninety-eight percent of the urban population
has access to an improved source of drinking water, and 92 percent has access to
improved sanitation facilities. An improved drinking water source is one that is
separated from all wastes and not necessarily treated or purified. Ninety-three percent of rural populations have access to an improved drinking water source, and
92 percent have access to improved sanitation facilities. About 90 percent of the
population use pit latrines, septic tanks, and soakaways. Soakaways are essentially
waste pits in soil where water helps degrade the wastes. Many of the septic tanks
and soakaways are not cleaned and accumulate sewer sludge. Trinidad and Tobago
are expanding the central sewer. Many tourist facilities have their own sewer and
water treatment facilities.

Eleven thousand tons of hazardous wastes were generated in 2003. Because
of increased industrialization, these wastes are likely to be higher now. It is not
known how many tons of hazardous waste was imported. Because wastes are not
separated, hazardous waste is mixed with municipal waste. In 2002, 425,000
tons of municipal waste was collected. Ninety percent of the population receives
municipal waste collection. Most of this waste is brought to dumps on the edge of
cities. There is concern that some of this waste could be dumped into the ocean.
Very little waste is treated before it renters local waters. Concerns about sewerage
and water pollution are of long standing, going back to 1982, when the Institute of
Marine Affairs found high amounts of fecal coliform bacteria in the water.

Emissions and Industry

In 1990, Trinidad and Tobago generated 16,006.2 metric tons of greenhouse gases.
It is likely that greenhouse gas emissions are higher now because of increased population and industrialization.

Agricultural products include coffee, cocoa, rice, fruits, vegetables, and poultry.
Agricultural emissions accounted for 2 percent of all emissions. Within this sector,
agricultural soils accounted for 58 percent of emissions, enteric fermentation 27

percent, manure management 6 percent, rice cultivation 4 percent, and field burning of agricultural residue 3 percent.

Crude oil production is moderately high and proven oil reserves are substantial. Electricity consumption per capita is high. Energy emissions accounted for 62 percent of all emissions. Within this sector, energy industries account for 43 percent of emissions, manufacturing and construction industries 38 percent, and transportation 15 percent.

Industrial emissions accounted for 32 percent of all emissions. Within this sector, chemical industries accounted for 55 percent of emissions, metal production 40.5 percent, and mineral products 4.5 percent.

Waste emissions accounted for 4 percent of all emissions. Within this sector, solid waste disposal on land accounted for 53.6 percent of emissions and wastewater handling 46 percent.

Major Waste Issues

Waste management is challenged by a poorly regulated petrochemical industry and incomplete waste treatment infrastructure. Coastal water pollution has been an issue for decades. Animal wastes from pig farms and roving herds of pigs is another problem. Uncontrolled dump sites provide breeding grounds for mosquitoes that carry diseases. Infectious diseases are spread with poor waste management in Trinidad and Tobago, leading to instances of yellow fever, dengue fever, hepatitis A, hepatitis B, and typhoid. Two percent or more of the population is persistently infected with hepatitis B.

Rising ocean levels and more violent weather will significantly affect the environment on these two islands. Developing a waste management strategy is difficult, because many of the septic tanks and soakaways are over capacity. There are inadequate public resources in the country to handle internal, regional, and global health concerns.

Further Reading

Boopsingh, Trevor M., and Gregory McGuire, eds. 2014. *From Oil to Gas and Beyond: A Review of the Trinidad and Tobago Model and Analysis of Future Challenges.* Lanham, MD: University of America Press.

Middlelbeek, L., et al. 2014. "Built to Last? Local Climate Change Adaptation and Governance in the Caribbean—The Case of Informal Urban Settlement in Trinidad and Tobago." *Urban Climate* 8: 138–154.

Office of the Prime Minister. www.opm.gov.tt.

Teelucksingh, J. 2014. *Labour and the Decolonization Struggle in Trinidad and Tobago.* New York: Palgrave Macmillan.

TUNISIA

The North African country of Tunisia is bordered by Algeria, Libya, and the Mediterranean Sea. Its climate is desert in the south, where the terrain becomes part of the Sahara Desert. The interior is flat and semi-arid. It is mountainous in the north.

In the north, the summers are hot and dry and the winters mild and rainy. Natural resources include oil, lead, phosphates, zinc, and salt.

Altogether, 10.8 million people reside on Tunisia's 163,610 km² of land and 1,148 km of coastline. Sixty-five percent of the population is urbanized, and 30 percent lives in a city having more than 100,000 inhabitants. There are additionally many small communities.

Current Waste Practices

The Ministry of Environment and Sustainable Development develops sanitation, wastewater and environmental planning. The Ministry of Agriculture and Hydraulic Resources develops water management policies. Most urban areas have sewer and water systems. Connection to central sewers is very high, and connections continue to increase. About 80 percent of urban populations are connected. Drinking water is monitored by the national water distribution utility and the Ministry of Health from production until consumption. Freshwater is a scarce commodity, making Tunisia a water-stressed nation. Tunisia is a regional leader in integrated water management. There are about fifteen desalination plants, with many more planned. Tunisia has researched ways to reuse wastewater since the 1960s. There are about eighty-five wastewater treatment plants. Most of the urban population has access to improved drinking water sources and sanitation facilities, but only 84 percent of the rural population has access to an improved drinking water sources, and 64 percent has access to an improved sanitation facility. Tunisia collected 1,316,000 tons of municipal waste in 2004, almost all of it landfilled. Most trash is not collected outside urban areas.

Emissions and Industry

In 2000, Tunisia generated 25,140.8 metric tons of greenhouse gases, a 36 percent increase from 1994.

There is a substantial amount of arable land. Agricultural products include olives, grain, dates, fruits, vegetables, beef, and dairy products. Agricultural emissions accounted for 22 percent of all emissions. Within this sector, agricultural soils accounted for 50.6 percent of emissions, enteric fermentation 29.7 percent, manure management 19.4 percent, and field burning of agricultural residues 0.14 percent. This is an unusually high amount of greenhouse gas emissions from manure, indicating the presence of large amounts of untreated feces.

Tunisia produces crude oil and maintains proven reserves. Energy emissions accounted for 60.6 percent of all emissions. Within this sector, energy industries accounted for 27 percent of emissions, transportation 25 percent, manufacturing and construction industries 21 percent, and fugitive emissions 10 percent. Fugitive emissions are essentially unaccounted waste streams into the air. Fugitive emissions can affect regional ecosystems and the public health, because they can fall from the air to the land and water. Industrial emissions accounted for 12 percent of all emissions. Within this sector, mineral products accounted for 82 percent of emissions, metal production 9 percent, and chemical industries 9 percent.

Waste emissions from wastes accounted for 5.5 percent of all emissions. Within this sector, solid waste disposal on land accounted for 70 percent of emissions and wastewater management 30 percent.

Major Waste Issues

Although Tunisia has one of the most advanced waste management policies in the region, there are still problems with water pollution, especially from industrial wastes. Mining phosphate is a large and growing industry, and Tunisia is the fifth largest producer of phosphate in the world. It is used in agriculture and food preservatives after it is refined. One waste product from the process used to refine phosphate is phosphogypsum. This is a toxic material that contains small amounts of uranium and radium-226. Much of the phosphorus produced is transported via ships through the Gulf of Gabe. That is where the Tunisian Chemical Company is located and where significant amounts phosphate refining takes place. The phosphogypsum is stacked in column and piles outside the factory. The waste materials used in the processes are discharged directly into the gulf. Currently other methods of final disposal are being explored, such as an underground storage chamber 25 km away from the factory. There is community concern that these wastes will affect the groundwater. Groundwater is protected, so other options are being developed.

Further Reading

Feki, J., et al. 2013. "Application of Membrane Bioreactor Technology for Urban Wastewater Treatment in Tunisia: Focus on Treated Water Quality." *Sustainable Sanitation Practice* 14: 49–54.

Tunisia Government. www.tunisie.gov.tn.

Zawahri, N., et al. 2011. "The Politics of Assessment: Water and Sanitation Millennium Development Goals in the Middle East." *Development and Change* 42: 1154–1178.

TURKEY

Turkey borders Armenia, Azerbaijan, Bulgaria, Georgia, Greece, Iran, Iraq, Syria, the Black Sea, the Aegean Sea, and the Mediterranean Sea. Its terrain is varied, with a number of mountain ranges. The interior is primarily a high plateau. It is flat along the coasts. The climate is temperate, with hot, dry summers and wet winters. At higher altitudes in the interior plateau and mountains, the weather is harsher. There are many natural resources, such as iron ore, copper, coal, hydropower, mercury, gold, marble, feldspar, emery, and strontium.

Altogether, 73.2 million people reside on Turkey's 783,562 km^2 of land and 7,200 km of coastline. Sixty-seven percent of the population is urbanized, and 61 percent lives in a city having more than 100,000 inhabitants.

Current Waste Practices

Most communities have modern sewer and water systems, but not all wastewater is fully treated before being discharged into freshwater. Water quality is poor.

Although access to improved drinking water sources and sanitation facilities is generally very good, only about 75 percent of the rural population has access to improved sanitation facilities. About 6,500 deaths a year are attributed to unsafe water. Sixteen percent of the population suffers malnutrition. Turkey collected 28,006,000 tons of municipal waste in 2009, almost 85 percent of it landfilled and 1 percent recycled. Eighty-two percent of the population receives municipal waste collection. In 2008, Turkey generated 1,024,000 tons of hazardous wastes.

Turkey is developing its waste infrastructure with help from the European Union (EU). Turkey seeks admission to the EU but needs help to achieve EU standards. The "ascension" process is the long process of applying for membership to the EU. The EU offers an Instrument for Pre-Accession Assistance to candidate and potential candidate countries, such as Turkey.

Emissions and Industry

Turkey generated 439,874 metric tons of greenhouse gas in 2012, a 133 percent increase from 1990.

Agricultural products include cotton, tobacco, citrus, grains, livestock, and beets. Agricultural emissions accounted for 7 percent of all emissions. Within this sector, enteric fermentation accounted for 60 percent of emissions, agricultural soils 25 percent, manure management 14 percent, and rice cultivation and field burning of agricultural residues about 1 percent. This is a high amount of greenhouse gas emissions from manure, indicating the presence of large amounts of untreated feces.

Turkey produced 56,650 bbl/day of crude oil, with proven reserves of 270.4 million bbl, in 2012. There are large reserves of natural gas. Energy emissions accounted for 70 percent of all emissions within this sector, energy industries 39 percent, transportation 20 percent, and manufacturing and construction 18 percent.

Industrial emissions accounted for 14 percent of the overall emissions. Within this sector, mineral products accounted for 55 percent of emissions, metal production 32 percent, and chemical industries 1 percent.

Waste emissions accounted for 8 percent of all emissions within this sector, solid waste disposal on land 91 percent, and wastewater handling 9 percent.

Major Waste Issues

One of the primary environmental issues in Turkey is water pollution. Industrial, commercial, agricultural and municipal wastes are discharged into waterways. The major waste issue is the protection of public health both in the country and the region. There are many infectious diseases—hepatitis A, hepatitis B, typhoid, malaria, and schistosomiasis. More than 2 percent of the population is persistently infected with hepatitis B.

Turkey is preparing for climate change effects on water. It is the first country to benefit from the World Bank's climate investment funds. Climate change observers note increased temperatures, decreased winter precipitation, and sea level rises. Projected effects include temperature increases, loss of surface water, soil degradation, shifts from snowfall to rainfall, risks of saltwater intrusion, eutrophication and salination of inland water bodies, increases in severe weather events, and loss of biodiversity. The key vulnerability is water supply and quality. Primary concerns are about water quality, quantity, and sanitation. Surface waters are the primary source of water for all domestic use. There are also concerns about extreme weather events and damages to ecosystems. In response to these concerns and projections, the Turkish government developed policies, regulatory instruments, and economic instruments under the National Climate Change Adaptation Strategy and Action Plan, focusing on increased water use efficiency. There is continuing research on the effects of climate change on the river basins. The Gediz and the Buyuk Menderes basins are predicted to lose 20 percent of their surface water by 2030. Other ongoing research includes study of climate change effects on the Euphrates River. The National Climate Change Adaption plan is also assessing the vulnerability of groundwater sources to climate change.

Further Reading

Climate Change Impacts on Water Systems. www.oecd.org.

Gunes, K., et al. 2013. "Large Scale Constructed Wetland Implementation Projects in Turkey in Salt Lake Special Environmental Protection Area." *Desalinization and Water* 51: 22–24.

President's Office. www.tccb.gov.tr.

Yalcin, S., et al. 2013. "Changes and Determinants in under Five Mortality Rate in Turkey Since 1988." *Central European Journal of Public Health* 21: 80–87.

TURKMENISTAN

The Caspian Sea, Afghanistan, Kazakhstan, and Uzbekistan border the central Asian nation of Turkmenistan. The western and central regions are part of the Karakum Desert. It is mountainous in the south, subject to earthquakes. The Garabil Plateau dominates the east. The climate of Turkmenistan is subtropical desert, with very hot summers and cold winters. Rainfall is sparse in most of the country. Natural resources include oil, gas, sulfur, and salt.

Five million people live on Turkmenistan's 488,100 km^2 of land. Forty-six percent of the population is urbanized, and 18 percent lives in a city having more than 100,000 inhabitants. There are many small communities. The capital and largest city is Ashgabat, having a population of about 730,000 people. Twenty-eight percent of the whole population suffers malnutrition. The life expectancy is 69 years.

Current Waste Practices

Water management is a key issue in Turkmenistan, water being scarce—and almost 90 percent of it going to agricultural uses. Inefficient irrigation techniques have caused 60 percent of agricultural land to become salinized. Waste management is fairly new as national policy, and there are significant regulatory gaps. There is no national integrated water resources plan, and there is very little water monitoring. There are few, if any, municipal wastewater treatment plants, and the drinking water is becoming saline in some areas.

Ninety-seven percent of the urban population has access to an improved source of drinking water, and 99 percent has access to improved sanitation facilities. Seventy-two percent of rural populations have access to an improved drinking water source, and 97 percent have access to improved sanitation facilities. There is basic municipal waste collection supplemented by private waste collection services. Not all trash is collected. Trash is taken from communities to nearby landfills and dumpsites. These dumpsites are very close to many neighborhoods, because both the dumpsite and the community grew. In rural areas, trash is either moved to a communal dumpsite or, in many households, burned on site.

Emissions and Industry

Turkmenistan generated 75,408 tons of greenhouse gases in 2004, a 116 percent increase from 1994. It is likely that greenhouse gas emissions are higher now because of increased population and petrochemical production.

Agricultural products include cotton, grain, and livestock. Agricultural emissions accounted for 9 percent of all emissions in 2004. Within this sector, enteric fermentation accounted for 80 percent of emissions, agricultural soils almost 19 percent, and rice cultivation less than 1 percent.

Turkmenistan produces substantial amounts of crude oil and maintains proven reserves. Energy emissions accounted for 70 percent of all emissions in 2004. Within this sector, fugitive emissions accounted for almost 52 percent of emissions, energy industries almost 16 percent, transportation almost 5 percent, and manufacturing and construction industries almost 2 percent. The high levels of fugitive emissions for such a dominant sector may have the potential to affect the environment and public health. Fugitive emissions are essentially unaccounted waste streams into the air. Fugitive emissions can affect regional ecosystems and the public health, because they can fall from the air to the land and water.

Industrial emissions accounted for 20 percent of all emissions in 2004. Within this sector, consumption of halocarbons accounted for 95 percent of emissions, the chemical industry almost 4 percent, and mineral products less than 1 percent.

Waste emissions accounted for less than 1 percent of all emissions in 2004. Within this sector, solid waste disposal on land accounted for all emissions.

Major Waste Issues

Agricultural chemical fertilizer runoff is a major waste issue, often causing significant water pollution. In the cotton farms of the most productive areas around the middle and lower Amu Darya and Murgap oases, massive amounts of chemical fertilizers are applied. They are also poorly applied, so cotton absorbs only 15 percent to 40 percent of them. Use of these chemicals has declined, but primarily for economic, not environmental, reasons. There are also significant issues with oil pollution in almost all surrounding waterways. Both oil pollution and chemical runoff pollute the Caspian Sea. Water draws for irrigation have also helped drain the Aral Sea, which is actually a lake. The Aral was once the fourth-largest lake in the world, but excessive water withdrawals in the region have reduced it to 10 percent of its former size.

Waste management lacks legislation and a regulatory structure. A 2009 medical waste management strategy defined methods of collection, sorting, transportation, treatment, and disposal. Industries and municipal solid wastes do not have waste management strategies.

Further Reading

Church, J. 2014. "International Cooperation of Turkmenistan in the Water Sector." *The Handbook of Environmental Chemistry* 28: 291–310.

Sorenson, S., et al. 2011. "Safe Access to Safe Water in Low Income Countries: Water Fetching in Current Times." *Social Science and Medicine* 72: 1522–1526.

Turkmenistan Government. www.turkmenistan.gov.tm.

UGANDA

Uganda is an African nation bordered by the Democratic Republic of the Congo, Kenya, Rwanda, South Sudan, and Tanzania. The terrain is mostly flat, with mountains in the west and east. The climate is tropical—hot and humid. There are two rainy seasons that last from December to February and from June to August. Natural resources include gold, copper, cobalt, salt, and hydropower.

Approximately 35 million people live on Uganda's 241,000 km^2 of land. Only 13 percent of the population is urbanized, and just 5 percent lives in a city having more than 100,000 inhabitants. There are many small communities away from urban areas. Uganda has among the fastest growing population rates in the world.

Current Waste Practices

Ninety-five percent of the urban population of Uganda has access to an improved source of drinking water, and only 34 percent has access to improved sanitation facilities. Sixty-eight percent of rural populations have access to an improved drinking water source, and 34 percent have access to improved sanitation facilities. About 27,000 deaths a year are attributed to unsafe water. Uganda has the tenth-dirtiest water in the world, as measured by BOD (biological oxygen demand). Malaria is a major health concern. Uganda collected 224,000 tons of municipal waste in 2006, all of it landfilled. Collection is through urban municipal waste collection, supplemented by private waste services. Only about 40 percent of the waste is collected. The dumps and waste heaps are generally uncontrolled. Communities of waste pickers perform any recycling done. Uganda is home to many illegal dumpsites. Small communities may dispose of waste in communal dumps or burn it at home.

Emissions and Industry

In 1994, Uganda generated 41,547.2 metric tons of greenhouse gases. It is likely that greenhouse gases are higher now because of population increases and reliance on agriculture.

There is a large amount of arable land. Agricultural products include coffee, tea, tobacco, cotton, cassava, potatoes, corn, and meat. Agricultural emissions accounted for 90 percent of all emissions. Within this sector, prescribed burning of the savannas accounted for 87 percent of emissions, enteric fermentation 11 percent, rice cultivation 1 percent, and field burning of agricultural residues and manure management 0.39 percent. The burning of the savannas accounted for unusually large amounts greenhouse gas emissions.

Uganda has little crude oil production but maintains massive proven oil reserves. Oil consumption per capita is low. There are seventy-one days a year without electrical power. Energy emissions accounted for 9 percent of all emissions. Within this sector, "other sectors" account for 82 percent of emissions, transportation 17 percent and manufacturing, and construction industries 0.53 percent. Industrial emissions accounted for 10 percent of all emissions. Within this sector, mineral products accounted for 99.8 percent of emissions.

Waste emissions accounted for 0.23 percent of all emissions. Within this sector, solid waste disposal on land accounted for 65 percent of emissions and wastewater management 35 percent.

Major Waste Issues

Although there is a basic legal structure for waste management, waste practices are still not managed well. There are big challenges at every stage—from collection and transportation to storage, treatment, and final disposition. Wastes are not separated, so the current method of partial landfilling mixes municipal wastes with hazardous wastes. The dumpsites provide breeding grounds for mosquitoes that carry diseases. Infectious diseases pose a threat to Uganda, stemming from waste management issues. These diseases include yellow fever, cholera, hepatitis A, hepatitis B, meningococcal meningitis, typhoid, dengue fever, and schistosomiasis. Two percent or more of the population is persistently infected with hepatitis B. There is a high risk of malaria.

Further Reading

Foeken, D. W. J., et al. 2013. *Sanitation in Africa: Access to Improved Sanitation Facilities and Improvement Index*. Leiden, The Netherlands: African Studies Center.

Stringer, Lindsay C., et al. 2009. "Adaptations to Climate Change Drought and Desertification: Local Insights to Enhance Policy in Southern Africa." *Environmental Science and Policy* 12: 748–765.

Tumwebaze, I., et al. 2013. "Sanitation Facilities in Kampala Slums, Uganda: User's Satisfaction and Determinant Factors." *International Journal of Environmental Health Research* 23: 191–204.\

Uganda President's Office. www.statehouse.go.ug.

UKRAINE

Ukraine is an eastern European nation bordered by Belarus, Hungary, Moldova, Poland, Romania, Russia, Slovakia, the Sea of Azov, and the Black Sea. The border with Russia is politically tense now, and the Crimean area was recently ceded to Russia. The terrain is varied in Ukraine, made up mainly of steppes and plateaus. The Carpathian Mountains are in the west and the Crimean Peninsula is in the south. The climate is varied from coast to steppes and to mountains. Winters are cold in the mountains and cool along the coast. Summers are hot along the coast and cool in the mountains. Natural resources include coal, iron ore, gas, oil, sulfur, magnesium, and woodlands.

Altogether, 44.5 million people live on Ukraine's 603,500 km² of land and 2,782 km of coastline. Sixty-eight percent of the population is urbanized, and 42 percent lives in a city having more than 100,000 inhabitants. Twenty-three percent of the population is malnourished.

Current Waste Practices

Overall waste generation is more than 750 million tons a year, including about 70 million tons of hazardous wastes. It is estimated that there is an accumulation of 35 billion tons, including 1.6 billion tons of toxic wastes. Before the present conflict with Russia, Ukraine had a comprehensive waste management policy and was planning for further development. In 2010, Ukraine's president signed off on a basic principles of waste management strategy. This strategy included implementation of the latest technologies of solid waste utilization, an increase in re-use and use of recyclable materials, an increase of municipal waste collection to 70 percent by 2015 and to 100 percent by 2020, and a decrease of municipal wastes by separating out biodegradable wastes.

Actual waste infrastructure is in disrepair at many locations. There is little recycling. Municipal wastes are collected and taken one of the more than 4,000 landfills. Landfills cover 7 percent of the land mass. Eighty-five percent to 90 percent of the landfills are not environmentally sound. In a survey by the Ukrainian State Sanitary Inspectorate, it was discovered that 43 percent are potentially dangerous in terms of air pollution, 34 percent in terms of soil pollution, and 28 percent in terms of water table pollution and that 23 percent risk polluting the groundwater. Many landfills are very old, and most have been over capacity for years. There is growing public concern about chemicals leaching into soil and water. There are two incineration sites that burn about 2 percent to 5 percent of the trash. In 2011, there were early plans for a Clean City initiative that would cover ten of the largest cities. This was designed to handle 2.5 million tons of waste, increase recycling rates to about 15 percent, and increase incineration capacity. It was based on public/private partnerships that did not develop, and the initiative is stalled.

Most communities have modern sewer and water systems, but not all wastewater is fully treated before being discharged into freshwater. Most of the population has access to improved drinking water sources and sanitation facilities, though water quality is poor. Ukraine generated 2,301,000 tons of hazardous wastes in 2008.

Emissions and Industry

Ukraine generated 401,019 tons of greenhouse gases in 2012, a 4 percent decrease from 1990. Recent border clashes with Russia may affect greenhouse gas emissions and will affect sewer and water systems.

Much of the land is arable. Agricultural products include wheat, sunflower seeds, sugar beets, vegetables, meat, and milk. Agricultural emissions accounted for 9 percent of all emissions. Within this sector, agricultural soils accounted for 60 percent of emissions, enteric fermentation 25 percent, manure management 13 percent, and field burning of agricultural residues and rice cultivation 1 percent.

Ukraine produces some crude oil and maintains proven reserves. Oil production per capita is moderate. Oil consumption and electricity production and consumption per capita are high. Energy emissions accounted for 77 percent of all emissions, which is high. Within this sector, energy industries accounted for 39 percent of emissions, manufacturing and construction industries 21 percent, fugitive emissions 15 percent, and transport 11 percent. For such a dominant source of emissions, the amount of fugitive emissions indicates airborne wastes that are not accounted for. These wastes can enter the land and water through rain, flooding, and wind, distributing their environmental and public health effects over a region. Fugitive emissions are essentially unaccounted waste streams into the air. Fugitive emissions can affect regional ecosystems and the public health, because they can fall from the air to the land and water.

Industrial emissions accounted for 11 percent of overall emissions. Within this sector, metal production accounts for 54 percent of emissions, mineral products 22 percent, and chemical industries 22 percent.

Waste emissions accounted for 3 percent of overall emissions. Within this sector, solid waste disposal on land accounted for 67 percent of emissions and wastewater handling 33 percent.

Major Waste Issues

During control by the Soviet Union, little consideration was given to the environment. There were no waste treatment plants or pollution controls. Zaporizhzhya and other industrial cities experienced severe air pollution. Because the Soviet Union was focused on increasing agricultural productivity, there was little regard for environmental effects of chemical fertilizers, banned pesticides, or efficient irrigation processes. Agricultural pollution permeated the formerly fertile arable land in the south. None of the ecological damage was remediated or cleaned up.

The major waste issue is cleaning radioactive and hazardous waste from the Chernobyl nuclear accident in 1986. Northern Ukraine and southern Belarus were the most severely affected by the radiation plume. About 10 percent of the land mass was affected by the radiation, and about 1 million people were affected by radioactive food. Today the main waste issue is cleaning and remediating contaminated sites and decreasing the ongoing industrial pollution. Water management for safety is a challenge. In some areas, leaching landfills and illegal wastes sites taint the water supply. Water pollution is a large problem. It also affects the region because Ukraine discharges water polluted with sewage, industrial chemicals, and hazardous wastes into the Black Sea.

Ukraine is currently in a conflict with Russia. In 2014, it ceded the Crimea to Russia. There have been violent border conflicts since then. Most waste management processes have slowed, and there is little planning for the extensive waste cleanup and remediation required in the north and south. The human toll of exposure to wastes is still being evaluated and will not be complete until the land-fill situation is under control.

Further Reading

Liedel, M., et al. 2014. "Supporting Decisions in Water Management by Exploring Information and Capacity Gaps: Western Bug River Basin, Ukraine." *Environmental Earth Sciences* 72: 4771–4786.

Nazariv, N., et al. 2001. "Environmental Issues in the Post-Communist Ukraine." *Journal of Environmental Management* 63: 71–86.

Shestopalov, V., ed. 2002. *Chernobyl Disaster and Groundwater*. New York: Taylor & Francis.

Ukraine Government. www.kmu.gov.ua.

UNITED ARAB EMIRATES

The United Arab Emirates (UAE) are bordered by Oman, Saudi Arabia, the Gulf of Oman and the Persian Gulf. The terrain is mainly flat with sand dunes. There are mountains in the east. The climate is desert—hot and dry. It is cooler in the mountains. Natural resources include large amounts gas and oil.

Altogether, 5.5 million people live on the UAE's 83,600 km^2 of land and 1,318 km of coastline.

Current Waste Practices

UAE is very arid and water is scarce. It is estimated that 75 percent of the rainfall evaporates, 15 percent runs off the surface, and only 10 percent makes it to an aquifer. Groundwater supplies more than half the water, most of this used for irrigation. Desalinization plants provide 40 percent of the water supply and are used mainly as potable water. Treated wastewater provides 9 percent of the water and is used for industrial purpose.

Most communities in the UAE have modern sewer and water systems, but not all wastewater is fully treated before being discharged into freshwater. Most of the population has access to improved drinking water sources and sanitation facilities. Altogether, 10,875,000 tons of municipal wastes were collected in 2009. Additionally, 273,000 tons of hazardous wastes were generated in 2008.

Emissions and Industry

In 2005, the United Arab Emirates generated 195,308 metric tons of greenhouse gases, a 50 percent increase from 1994.

There is little arable land. Agricultural products include dates, vegetables, melons, poultry, dairy products, and fish. Agricultural emissions accounted for 2 percent of all emissions. Within this sector, agricultural soils accounted for 50 percent of emissions, enteric fermentation 38 percent, and manure management 11 percent.

The United Arab Emirates produces large amounts of crude oil and maintains massive proven reserves. Oil and electricity production and consumption per capita are high. Energy emissions accounted for 89 percent of all emissions. Within this sector, manufacturing and construction accounted for 30 percent of emissions, energy industries 28 percent, and transportation 17 percent. Fugitive emissions were 24 percent of this sector's emissions. In light of the overall effect of this sector, a high number of fugitive emissions indicates unaccounted wastes. Airborne wastes can affect regional ecosystems and public health. Fugitive emissions are essentially unaccounted waste streams into the air. Fugitive emissions can affect regional ecosystems and the public health, because they can fall from the air to the land and water. These effects accumulate far faster than the capacity of regional ecosystems to handle them. Overwhelmed ecosystems essentially become dead zones having low resilience to climate change effects. They do continue to accumulate in the land and water, permeating fragile ecosystems.

Industrial emissions accounted for 5 percent of the overall emissions. Within this sector, mineral products accounted for 68 percent of emissions, metal production 25 percent, and chemical industries 6 percent.

Waste emissions accounted for 4 percent of the overall emissions. Within this sector, solid waste disposal on land accounted for 89 percent of emissions and wastewater management 11 percent.

Major Waste Issues

Although a well-financed and comprehensive waste management system is in place, the UAE faces significant challenges in a harsh environment and rapidly increasing population. Most of the increase in population is from migrant laborers. Between 1995 and 2005, the population increased 75 percent and still continues to grow. Water demand is predicted to double by 2030. Decreasing freshwater forces the UAE to rely on large desalinization plants both along the coast and inland. Most of these plants run on fossil fuels and emit greenhouse gases. Water concerns exist over extraction of groundwater that can deplete freshwater for a whole region. There is broad concern about saltwater intrusion. Saltwater intrusion can come from the sea along the coast, from the upwelling of saline water from underground, and from lateral movement of saline water to freshwater aquifers. There is also concern about expanding desertification and coastal pollution from numerous oil spills.

Further Reading

El-Khoury, Gabi. 2014. "Water Indicators in Arab Countries: Selected Indicators." *Contemporary Arab Affairs* 7: 339–349.

Emirates and the Environment. www.emirates.com.

Howidi, M., et al. 2014. "Burden and Genotyping of Rotavirus Disease in the United Arab Emirates." *Human Vaccines and Immunotherapeutics* 10: 2284–2289.

United Arab Emirates Ministry of Environment. www.moew.gov.ae.

UNITED KINGDOM

Ireland, the North Sea, and the North Atlantic Ocean border the United Kingdom (UK). The terrain of the United Kingdom's island of Great Britain is made up of hills and low mountains in the west and north. The eastern and western parts of the island are mostly rolling plains. The climate is a temperate maritime climate. The warmer Gulf Stream current moderates the land temperature, especially in the east, where it is closer to shore. It rains all year long. The north gets about twice as much rainfall as the south. Summers are cool and winters mild and cloudy. Natural resources include oil, coal, gas, lead, zinc, gold, tin, chalk, potash, and slate.

Altogether, 63.1 million people live on the UK's 242,495 km² of land and 12,429 km of coastline. Ninety percent of the population is urbanized, and 53 percent lives in a city having more than 100,000 inhabitants.

Current Waste Practices and Recycling

Most communities have modern sewer and water systems, but not all wastewater is fully treated before being discharged into freshwater. Most of the population has access to improved drinking water sources and sanitation facilities. Reducing, reusing, and recycling are a high priority in many local government agencies. For example, to reduce greenhouse gas emissions, London installed air monitors. If the readings get too high, non-essential vehicle traffic is not allowed in the central business district and other areas. The UK collected 32,600,000 tons of municipal waste in 2009, almost 49 percent of it landfilled, 11 percent incinerated, 27 percent recycled, and about 14 percent composted. The UK generated 7,285,000 tons of hazardous wastes in 2008.

The amounts of landfill wastes have been dramatically reduced. Roughly 600 million tons of products enter the UK annually, and about 115 million tons is recycled. The UK developed many programs for waste prevention. The Waste Prevention Program for England encourages waste reduction in the design of products

---

Fatbergs in the Sewer: A Source of Energy?

Fatbergs are very large globs of coagulated fats, oil, and most other sewer wastes. Diapers, grease from restaurants, paper, and plastics help them form. Some have been as large as 15 tons. Left in place, they clog large sewers lines and continue to grow as long as the sewer is used. Eventually they damage sewer infrastructure and cause backups of sewer sludge that can reach the surface. From there, they can block normal drainage routes and cause flooding. They can be dangerous to work with, because they absorb oxygen, radiate heat, and emit large amounts of methane.

London's sewer system sees about 55,000 fatbergs a year. Similarly, Scotland had to remove 40,000 fatberg blockages in 2014. It takes powerful water jets, shovels, and hard labor to remove them.

There is early commercial interest in reclaiming fatbergs and using them for biofuel. A big obstacle is the cost of pretreating them, which would require removing a variety of unknown materials. Low-grade fuels need to go through an additional process of acid esterification.

and packaging. It also seeks to develop a culture of valuing resources, including by making it easier to reduce waste. Products can be used longer, repaired, or transferred to other uses before disposed.

The UK approaches waste structurally. There are a number of measures of the framework conditions related to the generation of waste. One is the use of planning and economic instruments to promote the efficient use of resources. Other measures include promotion of research and development in waste reduction and results dissemination, development of indicators of environmental stresses from waste effects, and ecodesign, the systematic integration of environmental aspects into product design with the aim to improve the environmental performance of the product through out the whole life cycle. They are also examining the use of extra waste charges on nonrecyclable materials, promotion of credible ecolabels, and assistance to accredited repair and reuse centers and networks in densely populated areas.

The UK also approaches waste from an international perspective. In 2012, it recognized sanitation as a human right. Altogether, 2.5 billion people in the world do not have access to safe and clean sanitation facilities. Moreover, 1.4 million children die annually from diarrheal disease. These facts pushed the UK to examine global waste issues in the context of the United Nations Millennium Development Goal targets. It concluded that at the 2012 rate of progress, the sanitation goals would not be met until 2026. In 2012, the UK committed to increased support for this, with a goal of reaching 60 million people. Part of this goal is empowering poor people from developing countries to claim their right to sanitation. Increasing transparency and accountability in waste management decisions by government is also a goal.

Emissions and Industry

The UK generated 584,304.3 metric tons of greenhouse gases in 2012, a 25 percent decrease from 1990.

Cremation and Air Pollution

Cremation is the incinerating of bodily remains; it is practiced all over the world. Cremation accounts for 16 percent of the United Kingdom's mercury pollution. More than 70 percent of deaths in the United Kingdom result in the use of cremation to dispose of bodily remains. Wastes from cremation can affect the air, land, and water. Crematoriums emit carbon dioxide, carbon monoxide, nitrous oxide, sulfur oxide, hydrogen chloride, hydrogen fluoride, and mercury. The process also generates carcinogens such as polychlorinated dibenzofurans. The remains of burning are ashes that have toxic chemicals in them. These are often spread on land or in water.

Embalming fluids, coffin styles, dental fillings, and temperature of incineration all affect waste emissions from cremation. Reducing or changing embalming fluids, making fewer coffin requirements and biodegradable coffins, removing dental filings, and optimizing the temperature of incineration could reduce wastes.

Agricultural products include potatoes, cereals, vegetables, livestock, fish, and poultry. Agricultural emissions accounted for 9 percent of overall emissions. Within this sector, agricultural soils accounted for 52 percent of emissions, enteric fermentation 30 percent, and manure management 18 percent. This is a high amount of greenhouse gas emissions from manure, indicating the presence of large amounts of untreated feces.

The United Kingdom produces substantial amounts of crude oil and maintains large proven reserves. Consumption and production of electricity and oil is roughly equal. Energy emissions accounted for 83 percent of overall emissions. Within this sector, energy industries accounted for 40 percent of emissions, transport 24 percent, manufacturing and construction industries 14 percent, and fugitive emissions 2 percent.

Industrial emissions accounted for 4 percent of overall emissions. Within this sector, consumption of halocarbons accounted for 58 percent of emissions, mineral products 26 percent, chemical industry emissions 12 percent, and metal production 5 percent.

Waste emissions accounted for almost 4 percent of overall emissions. Within this sector, solid waste disposal on land accounted for 86 percent of emissions, wastewater handling almost 13 percent, and incineration almost 2 percent.

Major Waste Issues

Waste is a major issue in the UK. As a modern industrialized nation, the United Kingdom also has a history of centuries of large-scale industrialization.

The United Kingdom is preparing for climate change effects on water systems. Climate observers note increased temperatures, regions having increased rainfall, and more winter rainfall overall from heavy precipitation. Projected effects include increased temperatures, changes in the seasonal distribution of precipitation, decreased snowfall, increases in extreme weather events, more winter flooding, and ecosystem damages. The key vulnerability is water supplies and flood control. Primary concerns are over water quality, quantity, and sanitation. There is also concern about extreme weather events and flooding. In response to these concerns and projections, the UK developed policies, regulatory instruments, and economic instruments, as well as processes that local government must follow to assess risks from climate change and construct adaptation plans. The Adapting to Climate Change Program is designed to focus on climate change adaptation and mitigation. One economic instrument is an agreement between the government and the Association of British Insurers to make flood insurance widely available and affordable. The UK supports a range of research and tools in climate change effects. They have developed a tool known as the Adaption Wizard that assesses vulnerability to climate change, identifies key risks, and develops an adaption strategy.

Further Reading

Brown, A., et al. 2013. "Developing Novel Approaches to Tracking Domestic Water Demand under Uncertainty—A Reflection in the Up Scaling of Social Science Approaches in the United Kingdom." *Water Resources Management* 27: 1013–1035.

Climate Change Impacts on Water Systems. www.oecd.org.

United Kingdom Climate Projections. www.ukcip.org.uk.

Wolfer, T. 2014. "Community-Led Sanitation: A 'New Frontier' for International Social Work Practice." *Social Development Issues* 36: 67–77.

UNITED STATES

The United States is bordered by Canada, Mexico, the Atlantic Ocean, and the Pacific Ocean. The terrain is varied. In the continental forty-eight states, it is mountainous in the west and flat in the interior, with lower mountains in the east. The southwest is desert in places. In Alaska, the terrain is mountainous, with glaciated valleys. The climate is more arctic. There is a very cold winter in the interior. Warmer ocean currents moderate the coastal climate. The winters are long and the summers short and mild. In Hawaii, the terrain is mountainous. All the islands are the product of volcanic eruptions and are still changing. The climate is tropical. Natural resources for the United States include oil, gas, coal, uranium, gold, copper, lead, iron, potash, silver, zinc, timber, and hydropower.

Altogether, 317 million people reside on the United States' 9,629,091 km² of land and 19,924 km of coastline. Eighty-one percent of the population is urbanized, and 72 percent lives in a city having more than 1,000,000 people. Life expectancy is 78 years.

Current Waste Practices

Most communities have modern sewer and water systems, but not all wastewater is fully treated before it is discharged into freshwater. Six percent of the rural population does not have access to an improved drinking water source. The rest of the population has access to safe sanitation and improved drinking water sources.

Geographic Information Systems (GIS) Improve Sewer Systems

Aging sewer infrastructure often results in broken and blocked sewer and water pipes. This can cause waste backups and damages to nearby electrical and gas infrastructure. The current process is to respond to a complaint, set up a work order, and send a crew out to contain and fix it if they can. They need to determine exactly what and where the problem is. This can occur in freezing and flooding conditions. It takes an indeterminate time to get it fixed, increasing risks from wastes and damage from other nearby infrastructure.

San Francisco is using a GIS system to decrease response and problem evaluation time. It can create work orders directly from service complaints and aggregate duplicate service calls, access real location information in the field, and access main structures in the sewer system. Field conditions are reflected in GIS maps. This system will also help understand sewer system conditions, pinpoint life cycle costs, and decrease worker exposure time to dangerous conditions.

In 2013, the United States generated 251 million tons of garbage and recycled about 35 percent of it. About 1.5 pounds of the per-capita waste generation of 4.4 pounds was recycled in 2012. Not all this waste entered the waste collection and treatment process. The United States collected 32.6 million tons of municipal waste in 2009, almost 55 percent of it landfilled, 14 percent incinerated, and about 8 percent composted. Everyone receives municipal waste collection. Most of the municipal solid wastes comprise paper and paperboard, at 27 percent. Food wastes make up 15 percent, yard trimmings 14 percent, plastics 12 percent, rubber and leathers 9 percent, and wood 6 percent—though there are significant regional differences. Paper, yard wastes, metals, and gall are the primary materials recycled. Community composting programs have decreased from 3,227 in 2002 to 3,120 in 2012, though many informal community-composting arrangements may not have been included. There are about eighty-six waste-to-energy facilities in the United States that burn 28 millions tons of waste a year to produce 2,720 megawatts. About 29 million tons of municipal solid waste was burned for energy recovery, primarily methane gas.

The United States generated 39,027,000 tons of hazardous wastes in 2001. Several new programs seek to recycle hazardous wastes primarily through metals and solvent recovery. Emissions of air toxics declined by 62 percent from 1990 to 2008.

Water pollution is an issue, especially in urban and coastal areas. More than 67 percent of estuaries and bays are degraded because of chemical runoff of phosphorus and nitrogen. These chemicals can facilitate toxic algae blooms in warmer waters and when other conditions are favorable. Almost half of lakes and streams are polluted, unsafe for swimming and fishing. More and more beaches are closed every year because of waste issues in the water. Septic systems are not maintained, cesspools eventually become full, and leach fields are beginning to contaminate nearby water more frequently. An estimated more than 1.2 trillion gallons of untreated sewage and industrial wastes are discharged into water every year. This is often beyond the ecological carrying capacity of the body of water and can create favorable conditions for infectious diseases.

There are long-standing controversies around illegal dumping of trash. As recycling rates increased and control of trash tighten, more people have illegally disposed of trash rather than pay to do so at the landfill or recycling center. In many U.S. indigenous reservations, the primary environmental concern is midnight dumping, or the secret dumping of wastes that are expensive to dispose off—usually hazardous.

Emissions and Industry

In 2008, the United States generated 19 percent of global carbon dioxide emissions, the second most after China. This does not include changes in land use, such as deforestation. It does include emissions from sources such as fossil fuel combustion, cement manufacturing, and gas flaring.

The United States generated 94 million tons of greenhouse gases in 2012, a 4 percent increase from 1990.

Sewage into Drinking Water: The San Diego Experience

San Diego, California, is suffering drought—again. Growing populations, agricultural irrigation, decreasing rain, shrinking rivers, and less snow in the nearby mountains create stress on all water systems.

In need of drinking water and water for other purposes, San Diego purifies wastewater for drinking. The purification program was scrutinized with a six-year research project to closely monitor water quality. The project concluded that the water was cleaner than regular tap water and cheaper to produce than water sourced from desalinization plants. By converting wastewater into drinking water, San Diego could meet increasing water demand and decrease wastewater water pollution.

The process is called indirect potable reuse. The wastewater is purified and discharged into a drinking water reservoir. Direct potable reuse goes from purification to drinking water.

The sewage receives primary municipal waste treatment that removes most of the solids, chemicals, and biological organisms. This water can be used for agricultural or industrial uses. The sludge can be used as biosolids. This aspect of waste disposal and recycling can be controversial, because some communities do not consider it safe. The San Diego process takes the water to be used as drinking water to another water processing plant. The first step in the advanced purification process is microfiltration. Then the water is pressurized and shot through smaller filtered tubes. This process is reverse osmosis. In the last step, the water is mixed with hydrogen peroxide and exposed to ultraviolet light. This process holds promise for many countries that do not have ocean access or that cannot afford to build and operate desalination plants. It can also decrease infectious disease exposures by purifying the water.

There is a substantial amount of arable land—175 million ha. Agricultural products include corn, wheat, fruits, vegetables, cotton, meat, dairy products, and fish. High use of pesticides and fertilizers facilitate agricultural productivity. Agricultural emissions accounted for 8 percent of all emissions. Within this sector, agricultural soils accounted for 58 percent of emissions, enteric fermentation 26.7 percent, manure management 13.5 percent, and rice cultivation 1.4 percent.

The United States produces a large amount of crude oil and maintains robust proven reserves. Oil and electricity production are high, and so is their consumption. Energy emissions accounted for 85 percent of all emissions. Within this sector, energy industries accounted for 37 percent of emissions, transportation 31.5 percent, manufacturing and construction 14 percent, and fugitive emissions 4.7 percent.

Industrial emissions accounted for 5 percent of all emissions. Within this sector, consumption of halocarbons accounted for 47 percent of emissions, metal production 19.8 percent, mineral products 18 percent, and chemical industries 14 percent.

Waste emissions accounted for 2 percent of all emissions. Within this sector, solid waste disposal on land accounted for 83 percent of emissions, and wastewater handling 14.3 percent, and other 2.7 percent.

An NOAA worker prepares air sample canisters for the May 2014 shipment going to monitoring sites all over the world. March 2014 was the first time in about 2 million years that the global monthly average for carbon dioxide hit 400.83 parts per million. Carbon dioxide traps heat and increases the rate of global warming, causing climatic changes. (Will Von Dauster/ NOAA via AP Photo)

Major Waste Issues

The major waste issues are also the main environmental issues in the United States. Air pollution from burning fossil fuels pollutes the air and causes acid rain in other parts of the environment. Agricultural runoff of pesticides and fertilizers creates pollution problems. Infectious diseases are present, including hepatitis A and hepatitis B. Dengue fever and other tropical diseases may increase their ranges to the southern United States.

The United States is preparing for climate change effects on water systems. Climate observers note regional changes in temperatures, precipitation, and extreme weather events. Projected effects include increased temperatures, floods, droughts, wildfires, widespread tree mortality in the Southwest, reduced ice cover on the Great Lakes, and heavy runoff from heavy rain events. An increased amount of waste is projected to come from heavy rains washing sediment, pollutants, trash, animal wastes, sewer overflows, and other materials into water supplies. Key vulnerabilities are water supplies and coastal saltwater intrusion. Primary concerns are over water quality, quantity, and sanitation. There is also concern about extreme weather events, especially drought in the west. In response to these concerns and projections, the United States developed policies and regulatory instruments. The U.S. Environmental Protection Agency (EPA) developed the Climate Ready Water

Climate Change Adaptation Planning and Infectious Disease Preparation: Washington State

Washington State has a multifaceted climate change adaption plan. Its strategy for infectious diseases is to increase and improve monitoring of disease outbreaks and events. The plan is to enhance laboratory-reporting requirements and follow through with investigations. Washington also plans to increase electronic reporting and training of human and animal healthcare workers on the expanded range of notifiable infectious diseases (by law, the department of health must be notified). The strategy also includes a research on the effects of increased temperatures and high humidity on diseases pathogenesis and on the continued refinement of climate change parameters in modeling infectious diseases.

Utilities Initiative to help water and wastewater facilities become climate-ready. It seeks to the implementation of climate change water adaptation strategies at water and wastewater facilities that include potential change effects and build water sector resilience to these effects. There are also watershed protection policies that offer guidance and support for local and state government. The Interagency Climate Change Task Force began in 2009 and includes twenty federal agencies. Its purpose is to develop a report with recommendations on how the federal government can strengthen policies. The EPA also issued more stormwater protection rules to prevent runoff from federal projects. The United States supports many research efforts. The U.S. Global Change Research Program coordinates and integrates federal research on global changes and social implications and develops programs to prepare to adapt to the effects of climate change. Many climate change effects have been analyzed in numerous large river basins—the Colorado, Klamath, Missouri, Rio Grande, Sacramento, San Joaquin, and Truckee river basins, for example. In addition to national approaches, many states and local governments have their own approaches to dealing with climate change effects.

An emerging environmental and waste issue is the increasing number of hazardous waste sites. The worst sites are often called Superfund sites. There are other illegal toxic and hazardous waste sites from a period of rapid industrialization and urbanization that occurred without enforced environmental or land use regulation. Nuclear power has created wastes that have no certain final disposition location. Some of these have leaked, being stored on site.

Further Reading

Climate Change Impacts on Water Systems. www.oecd.org.

Collin, Robert. 2005. *The Environmental Protection Agency: Cleaning Up America's Act.* Westport, CT: Greenwood Press.

Interagency Climate Change Adaption Task Force. www.whitehouse.gov/administration/eop/ceq/initiatives/adaptation.

Municipal Solid Waste Decision Support Tool. www.mswds.rtl.org.

State of Garbage in America. www.seas.columbia.edu.
U.S. Global Change Research Program. www.globalchange.gov.
Zero Waste Recycling Data, Maps, and Graphs. www.zerowasteamarica.org.

URUGUAY

Argentina, Brazil, and the South Atlantic Ocean border the South American country of Uruguay. The terrain is mostly rolling plains and small hills. There are wetlands along the coast. The climate is temperate with warm summers and cool winters. Precipitation is evenly distributed and ranges from 950 to 1,235 millimeters a year. Natural resources include fish, some minerals, and hydropower.

Altogether, 3.3 million people reside on Uruguay's 176,215 km² of land and 660 km of coastline. Ninety-two percent of the population is urbanized, and 44 percent lives in cities of 100,000. Overcrowded living conditions affect about 22 percent of the population. The capital and largest city is Montevideo, having about 2 million people. About 14 percent of the total population suffers malnutrition.

Current Waste Practices

Waste recyclers are recognized by law, which helps protect them from dangerous working conditions and stabilizes income. Recycling is a business. In 2004, a packaging recycling law went into effect. Part of expanding that law is to explicitly recognize the role the informal workers in the waste management processes. Uruguay is very concerned about e-wastes and has monitored their rapid increase in the waste stream. There is legislation that proposes to set up an e-waste management plan where the manufacturers of e-wastes sources would be liable for the products final disposition, known as extended producer responsibility.

Most communities have modern sewer and water systems, but not all wastewater is fully treated before being discharged into freshwater. Fifteen percent of urban sewage is treated before discharge into water. Of this, 50 percent receives primary treatment, 28 percent receives secondary waste treatment, and 22 percent receives tertiary waste treatment. Most of the population has access to improved drinking water sources and sanitation facilities. Altogether, 910,000 tons of municipal wastes were collected in 2000. However, not all wastes were collected. There is some municipal collection supplemented by informal waste workers and waste cooperatives. The trash is trucked out town to a landfill. Many landfills are uncontrolled and over capacity. Periodically the wastes are burned to make more space. They are surrounded by waste picking communities.

Emissions and Industry

Uruguay generated 36,278.4 metric tons of greenhouse gases in 2004.

There is a substantial amount of arable land. Agricultural products include wheat, rice, soybeans, meat, dairy products, and fish. Agricultural emissions accounted for 80 percent of all emissions in 2004. Within this sector, enteric

Lead: More Dangerous Than Previously Known

Lead is pervasive in the environment, in the air, water, and land. It is included in paint, metal, and many other products used by consumers. It can cause cognitive impairment by mimicking necessary calcium in brain neural networks. Earlier public health efforts focused on prenatal care and children aged up to 5, because these ages see rapid neural development. There is still a high level of concern that lead exposure in this developmental timeframe can cause irreversible effects. Lead exposure is linked to anger management issues, hyperactivity, attention deficits, behavioral issues of development, high blood pressure, and heart attacks.

Lead also disrupts the hemoglobin in the blood, decreasing its ability to carry oxygen. This can be a precondition for other medical problems, many of them causally controversial. Some effects of lead are well accepted, such as neurological damage in children. Until recently lead was accepted in the workplace, toxic waste cleanups, and the regulation of hazardous chemicals because its effects were not as well known and cumulative effects were discounted. Now that the effects of small exposures are known to be risky and that they accumulate, lead as a precondition or as linked to other medical issues will now receive more public health attention to examine causality from a rigorous cause and effect model.

Consumers and workers are exposed to lead through the products they consume and the work they do. Workers are often more exposed to lead as an occupational safety hazard. Air and water pollution also expose people to lead.

Recent research shows that much lower dosages can cause damage to cognitive abilities. Long-term research started after lead was taken out gas in 1996. It is estimated that this single act reduced American exposure substantially, but not below recently announced danger levels. In 2010, the Centers for Disease Control and Prevention made lower lead limits a condition reported to federal authorities when exceeded.

fermentation accounted for 55 percent of emissions, agricultural soils 41 percent, rice cultivation almost 3 percent, and manure management more than 1 percent.

Energy emissions accounted for 14 percent of all emissions in 2004. Within this sector, transportation accounted for 43 percent of emissions, energy industries almost 26 percent, and manufacturing and construction industries almost 11 percent. Industrial emissions accounted for almost 1 percent of all emissions in 2004. Within this sector, mineral products accounted for 93 percent of emissions.

Waste emissions accounted for almost 4 percent of all emissions in 2004. Within this sector, solid waste disposal on land accounted for 79 percent of emissions, wastewater handling 15 percent, and other almost 6 percent. Generally, a significant source of other greenhouse gas emissions from wastes can indicate the presence of untreated and possibly hazardous wastes.

Major Waste Issues

One of the major waste issues is lead contamination. The first reports of lead poisoning came in 2001. The lead came from a degraded lead piping system having between 300,000 and 600,000 connections. The waste management priority at the time was to expand sewer and water connections. Lead contamination is now widespread, and lead poisoning helped drive a political movement against dismantling the previous social welfare based government. Wealth disparities increased, and poor areas experienced more lead poisoning.

The major environmental problems are also waste issues. Wastes from meat processing and poor hazardous waste disposal pollute major waterways. Though a functional waste management regulatory system is in place, the waste infrastructure is challenged by industrial pollution, illegal hazardous wastes, and lack of environmental enforcement.

Further Reading

Boeni, A., et al. 2008. E-waste Recycling in Latin America: Overview, Challenges, and Potential. www.Ewasteguide.info.

Ellis, K., and L. Feris. 2014. "The Right to Sanitation: Time to Delink from Right to Water." *Human Rights Quarterly* 36: 607–629.

Presidents Office of Uruguay. www.presidentia.gub.uy.

Renfrew, D. 2013. "We Are Not Marginals: Cultural Politics of Lead Poisoning in Montevideo, Uruguay." *Latin America Perspectives* 40: 202–217.

UZBEKISTAN

Afghanistan, Kazakhstan, Kyrgyzstan, Tajikistan, and Turkmenistan border the landlocked central Asian country of Uzbekistan. Uzbekistan's summers are long and very hot. It is generally warmer in the south and colder in the north. It is mountainous along the Tajikistan and Kyrgyzstan. The tallest mountain is Adelunga Toghi, at 4,301 m. In the north and central region is the Kyzyl Kum, a large desert. Natural resources include oil, gas, uranium, coal, gold, silver, lead, copper, and zinc.

Almost 29 million people live on Uzbekistan's 447,400 km^2 of land. Thirty-seven percent of the population is urbanized, and 21 percent lives in a city having more than 100,000 inhabitants. Twenty percent suffers malnutrition. Approximately 35 million people live on 241,000 km^2 of land. Only 13 percent of the population is urbanized, and just 5 percent lives in a city having more than 100,000 inhabitants. There are many small communities. The capital and largest city is Tashkent, having a population of more than 2.2 million people. The life expectancy is 68 years.

Current Waste Practices

The Law of Waste Management was implemented as policy in 2002. The National Waste Management Strategy and Action Plan was developed to address deficiencies in waste collection, recycling, and treatment.

The sewer system is basic. Only about half of urban populations and 3 percent of rural populations have sewer connections. Rural waste practices can be basic—pit toilets, latrines, drainage ditches, cesspools, and open defecation.

Twenty-nine percent of rural populations do not have access to improved sanitation facilities, but most other populations do. There are about 160 municipal solid waste landfills and dumpsites, which handle about 30 million m³ of wastes annually. It is estimated that 10 million tons of hazardous wastes are created per year. However this is based on 5 percent of the large industrial businesses self-reported data.

Industrial regulation of wastes has not stopped pollution. More than 80 percent of industrial pollutants discharged directly into rivers from the Tashkent, Fergana, Navoiy, and Samarkand regions.

Emissions and Industry

Uzbekistan generated 199,837.1 metric tons of greenhouse gases in 2005, a 9.3 percent increase from 1990.

There is a substantial amount of arable land. Agricultural products include cotton, grain, fruits, vegetables, and livestock. Agricultural emissions accounted for 8 percent of all emissions. Within this sector, enteric fermentation accounted for 48 percent of emissions, agricultural soils 45 percent, and manure management 5 percent.

Uzbekistan produces crude oil and maintains proven reserves. Oil and electricity per capita consumption is higher than oil and electricity per capita consumption. Large amounts of natural gas are produced and consumed and large proven reserves of natural gas maintained. Energy emissions accounted for 86 percent of all emissions. Within this sector, energy industries accounted for 21 percent of emissions, transportation 5.5 percent, and manufacturing and construction industries 3 percent. Fugitive emissions accounted for 44 percent of emissions and other sectors 25 percent. With such a large part of overall emissions, unaccounted and other emissions can affect environmental and public health. Fugitive emissions are essentially unaccounted waste streams into the air. Fugitive emissions can affect regional ecosystems and the public health, because they can fall from the air to the land and water. Industrial emissions accounted for 3 percent of all emissions. Within this sector, chemical industries accounted for 47 percent of emissions, mineral products 15 percent, and metal production 15 percent

Waste emissions accounted for 2 percent of all emissions. Within this sector, solid waste disposal on land accounted for 81 percent of emissions and wastewater handling 19 percent.

Major Waste Issues

The waste management system is not comprehensive so that waste issues are becoming clean up and remediation issues. There are many old, illegal, and overcapacity landfill sites. The most pressing concern is to clean up the sites that are radioactive. The open pit mining of uranium has dotted the country with at least 800 radioactive dumpsites. Uranium ore, radioactive rocks, ashes with uranium or radionuclides, and radioactive dyes characterizes these sites. Some of these sites have had other industrial and municipal wastes added to them over the years. About 400 of these sites have been deactivated.

One of the major environmental problems is also a waste issue. The Aral Sea is actually a saltwater lake. Owing to climate changes, it is rapidly decreasing and becoming more concentrated. Untreated sewage, industrial discharges, and pesticide and fertilizer agricultural runoff polluted the sea for years. When the sea begins to dry up, these chemicals become dust and create significant environmental effects, ultimately creating more desertification of the landscape. Dangerous soil pollution results from disposed radioactive and chemical wastes.

Further Reading

Herbst, S., D. Fayzieva, and T. Kistemann, eds. 2012. *Water and Sanitation Related Health Aspects in Khorem, Uzbekistan*. Dordrecht, Netherlands: Springer Netherlands.

Neumann, L., et al. 2014. "Water Use, Sanitation, and Health in a Fragmented Urban Water System: Case Study and Household Survey." *Urban Water Journal* 11: in press.

Republic of Uzbekistan Government. www.gov.uz.

Shodieva, D., et al. 2014. "Promoting Women's Capacity Building to Adapt to Climate Change in Uzbekistan." *Asian Journal of Women's Studies* 9: 132–144.

VANUATU

Vanuatu is a nation at great risk from rising ocean levels. Vanuatu is a country made of about eighty low-lying islands is the South Pacific. In 1980, it became an independent member of the British Commonwealth. Altogether, 262,000 people reside on more than 12,300 km² of land in the South Pacific. Twenty-three percent live in urbanized areas, and 14 percent live in a city having more than 100,000 inhabitants. There many small communities spread out among the many islands.

Vanuatu's terrain is mountainous.. The climate is tropical, with rainfall from November to April and hurricane season from December to April. Natural resources include woodlands, manganese, and fish.

Current Waste Practices

There is no comprehensive environmental or waste policy in Vanuatu. In 2002, the Environment Management and Conservation Act was passed. By 2008 the country had developed 16,259 Community Conservation Areas. Water pollution now threatens tourism, the main source of economic development.

Many of the towns on the islands lack the basic infrastructure to handle wastes. About 80 percent of the people live in villages. There is a plan to improve waste management in some towns, especially those visited by tourists. This plan includes official town garbage bags, more garbage trucks, and opening another landfill. There is also a composting effort under way. Ninety-eight percent of the urban population has access to improved drinking water, and 64 percent has access to improved sanitation facilities. Eighty-seven percent of the rural population has access to improved drinking water facilities, and about half has access to improved sanitation facilities.

Waste collection is poor, and trash piles accumulate in the capital city of Port Vila. Tourist areas do not receive municipal trash collection but are served by private waste services. The municipality collects about 60 percent of the trash in the main urban area of the capital. All collected wastes are brought to the Bouffa dump. Other wastes are burned or dumped near where they are generated. Three recycling businesses collect scrap metal, but otherwise there is no recycling or waste separation.

Emissions and Industry

Vanuatu generated 299.4 metric tons of greenhouse gases in 1994. It is likely that greenhouse gases are higher now because of population increases and reliance on agriculture.

There is a small amount of arable land. Agricultural products include coconuts, fish, coffee, taro, fruits, vegetables, and meat. Agricultural emissions accounted for 78.5 percent of all emissions.

Oil, electricity and natural gas production and consumption per capita were all low. Energy emissions accounted for 21 percent of all emissions. Within this sector, transportation accounted for 70.5 percent of these emissions, and energy production accounted for 20 percent.

Major Waste Issues

Solid waste management and water pollution are serious waste management challenges. About seventy tons of solid waste and five tons of ship wastes per day is generated now, a figure expected to reach 145 tons per day by 2034. The landfill has been over capacity for decades and is often not in compliance with environmental regulations, such as those requiring the covering of the site or the compacting of its wastes. Although there a waste collection fee is assessed, very few households pay it.

Vanuatu is one of the most vulnerable nations in the world to natural disasters such as volcanic emissions, cyclones, droughts, flooding, and coral bleaching. Overfishing has led to loss of mangrove and fishing breeding areas. Land and marine pollution are growing problems as population continues to increase. Climate change and rising ocean levels are major concerns and are an obstacle to waste management development, deterring private or public investment in waste infrastructure.

Untreated waste accumulation can create breeding areas for mosquitoes that carry diseases. Public health can be an issue as well, with infectious diseases such as hepatitis A, hepatitis B, typhoid, and dengue fever. Two percent or more of the population is persistently infected with hepatitis B. There is a high risk of malaria.

Further Reading

Clarke, M., et al. 2014. "Water, Sanitation and Hygiene Interventions in the Pacific: Defining, Assessing and Improving 'Sustainability.'" *European Journal of Development Research* 26: 692–706.

Government of Vanuatu. www.governmentofvanatua.gov.vu.

Management of Wastes in Small Island Developing States. www.islands.unep.ch.

Poustie, M., and A. Deletic. 2014. "Modeling Integrated Urban Water Systems in Developing Countries: A Case Study of Port Vila, Vanuatu." *AMBIO* 43: 1093–1111.

VENEZUELA

Venezuela is bordered by Colombia, Brazil, Guyana, and the Atlantic Ocean. Its terrain is varied, with mountains in the northwest. The tallest mountain is Pico Bolivar, at 5,007 m. The climate is tropical—hot and humid. Natural resources include oil, gas, gold, iron ore, diamonds, and hydropower.

Twenty-nine million people reside on Venezuela's 912,050 km² of land and 2,800 km of coastline. Ninety-three percent of the population is urbanized, and 62 percent lives in a city having more than 100,000 inhabitants. The largest and capital city is Caracas, with about 5.3 million people in its metropolitan region. The second largest city is Maracaibo, having more than 2.3 million people. There are four other cities with populations greater than 1 million.

Current Waste Practices

Most cities have modern sewer and water systems, but not all wastewater is fully treated before being discharged into freshwater. Ninety-four percent of the urban population has access to an improved source of drinking water, and 94 percent has access to improved sanitation facilities. Waste practices in rural areas are very basic—pit toilets, latrines, drainage ditches, cesspools, and open defecation. Seventy-five percent of rural populations have access to an improved drinking water source, and 57 percent have access to improved sanitation facilities.

In 2010, Venezuela began a program to increase its management of municipal solid wastes. The International Development Bank extended a $140 million line of credit that year for projects reducing and preventing environmental and health effects of improper waste management. Venezuela provided matching funds of about $60 million. It is focused on increasing waste management decision-making through development of technical skills and training. Currently most wastes are collected in open dumps, often near waste picker communities. Another part of the line of credit is to finance basic infrastructure for the transfer and disposal of municipal solid waste. The goal is to reduce open dumps and illegal dumping with sanitary landfills having a capacity of 1,100 tons of solid waste per day. Urban areas currently produce about 3.6 millions tons of solid wastes annually. Another goal of the project is to increase the rate of recycling to 20 percent by 2020.

Emissions and Industry

In 1999, Venezuela generated 192,192.2 metric tons of greenhouse gases. It is likely that greenhouse gases are much higher now because of population increase, the rapid rate population growth and industrialization, and the growth in petrochemical development.

Agricultural products include coffee, sugar cane, rice, bananas, vegetables, sorghum, dairy products, and fish. Agricultural emissions accounted for 17 percent of all emissions. Within this sector, enteric fermentation accounted for 48 percent emissions, agricultural soils 45 percent, manure management 3.5 percent, and rice cultivation 2 percent.

Venezuela produces large amounts of crude oil and maintains massive proven reserves. Oil and electricity production per capita are high. Energy emissions accounted for 75 percent of emissions. Within this sector, energy industries accounted for 33 percent of emissions, transportation 23.6 percent, and manufacturing and construction industries 10 percent. Twenty-eight percent of emissions in this sector are fugitive emissions. The large amount of fugitive emissions from this sector can affect the environment and public health. Fugitive emissions are essentially unaccounted waste streams into the air. Fugitive emissions can affect regional ecosystems and the public health, because they can fall from the air to the land and water.

Industrial emissions accounted for 5 percent of all emissions. Within this sector, mineral products accounted for 73 percent of emissions, chemical industries 14 percent, and metal production 12 percent.

Waste emissions accounted for 3.3 percent of emissions. Within this sector, solid waste disposal on land accounted for 90.5 percent of emissions and wastewater management 9.5 percent.

Major Waste Issues

The major waste issue is the lack of financial investment because of economic and political instability. The environment is challenging for basic waste infrastructure such as pipes, pumps, and treatment plants because of earthquakes, volcanic eruptions, landslides, floods, and unpredictable droughts. Without significant financial investment, it will continue to degrade. Water pollution is a symptom of a failed waste management system. Gold mining, coal mining, oil and gas exploration and drilling, aggressive deforestation, and soil erosion create wastes that are directly discharged into internal waterways and along the coasts. Water pollution along the coast is also affected by the numerous oil spills.

Further Reading

Griffing, S., et al. 2014. "Malaria Control and Elimination, Venezuela 1800s–1970s." *Emerging Infectious Diseases* 20: 1691–1696.
McMillan, R., et al. 2014. "Water Participation, Equity, and Coproduction of Water and Sanitation Services in Caracas, Venezuela." *Water International* 39: 201–215.
Venezuelan Government Agencies. www.embavenez_is.org.

VIETNAM

Vietnam is a southeast Asian country bordered by China, Laos, Cambodia, and the South China Sea. Its climate is tropical in the south and monsoonal in the north. From May to January, there are occasional typhoons, which cause extensive flooding and damage. The Mekong River Delta, where much of the population lives, is vulnerable to flooding. More than half the population lives within 10 meters of sea level. Agricultural practices contribute to soil degradation and desertification. Eighty-nine million people live on Vietnam's 330,957 km² with a 3,444 km coastline. Twenty-six percent of the population is urbanized, and 21 percent lives in a city having more than 100,000 inhabitants. After a history of war and conflict, North and South Vietnam were reunified in 1976. There are many small communities outside of the urban centers.

Current Waste Practices

Ninety-eight percent of the urban population and 90 percent of the rural population has access to improved drinking water sources, which involves separating drinking water from wastewater. Eighty-eight percent of the urban population and 56 percent of the rural population has access to improved sanitation facilities. Waste practices can be basic—pit toilets, latrines, drainage ditches, cesspools, and open defecation. The first reported cholera outbreak was in 1964. The open defecation rate in 2012 was 2 percent, down from 39 percent in 1990. In 2008, there were 377 confirmed cases of cholera and no reported deaths. Water quality is poor.

About 13 million tons of municipal wastes and 2.2 million tons of industrial and agricultural wastes are generated per year. Waste collection practices are basic. The municipality collects about 70 percent of the urban wastes, which is taken to a landfill without separation, toxic and hazardous wastes mixed with solid wastes. There are almost 100 large open and controlled landfills overall, and almost twenty of them are sanitary landfills. A few of the landfills incorporate the latest technology. The Go Cat landfill covers 25 ha, has a total capacity of 3.65 million tons and a daily capacity of 2,500 tons, and includes a waste treatment system for leachates collection and treatment that can handle 400 m³ a day. It also has a methane extraction system that extracts gas from a 7 ha part of the landfill. Illegal waste dumping in rivers and lakes, burning at home, and burying are common waste disposal methods.

Street sweepers clean the streets near the Ho Chi Minh Mausoleum in Hanoi, Vietnam. Many cities use street sweepers to keep the main public streets clean. Street sweepers are often exposed to unhealthy work conditions and should always wear gloves, shoes, and a mask, as seen here. (Richard Van Der Woude/Dreamstime.com)

Recycling is part of the culture of Vietnam but is just becoming part of the official waste treatment process. There are few recycling plants opening, and some NGOs are helping communities develop their own recycling efforts. E-wastes are considered a major problem and a good economic opportunity. Although specific regulations do not yet exist, proposed regulations are in development.

Emissions and Industry

In 2000, Vietnam generated 55,905.7 metric tons of greenhouse gas emissions, a 61 percent increase from 1990. It is likely that greenhouse gases are higher now because of population increases, rate of population growth and industrialization, and reliance on agriculture.

Agricultural emissions accounted for 48 percent of all emissions. Within this sector, rice cultivation accounted for 58 percent of emissions, agricultural soils 22 percent, enteric fermentation 12 percent, and manure management 5 percent.

Energy emissions accounted for 39 percent of all emissions. Within this sector, manufacturing and construction industries accounted for 28.6 percent of emissions, transportation 22.6 percent, and energy industries 21 percent. Industrial emissions accounted for 7 percent of all emissions. Within this sector, mineral products accounted for 74.5 percent of emissions and metal production 25 percent.

Waste emissions from solid wastes accounted for 5.8 percent of all emissions. Within this sector, solid waste disposal on land accounted for 70 percent of emissions and wastewater handling 29 percent.

Major Waste Issues

The waste management system has some fundamental challenges. A regulatory issue is that the 1999 law on water resources has not been implemented. Lack of technology and human resources, lack of infrastructure, and insufficient funding prevent the implementation of national waste management policies. Water supply is an issue and with a rapidly growing population will become a problem. Lack of waste treatment and industrial discharges into water could affect the quality of remaining water.

Infectious diseases pose a major threat in Vietnam, stemming from waste management issues. These include yellow fever, cholera, hepatitis A, hepatitis B, typhoid, malaria, dengue fever, and Japanese encephalitis. More than 2 percent of the population is persistently infected with hepatitis B.

Further Reading

Anh, Le Vu. Van. 2014. "Public Health in Vietnam and Diseases." *Vietnam Journal of Public Health* 2: 1–2.

Drunen, Michiel A., B. Lasage, and C. Dorland. 2006. *Climate Change in Developing Countries.* Oxfordshire, UK: CAB International North America.

Vietnam Government. www.gov.vnm.tel.

Y

YEMEN

Yemen is bordered by Oman, Saudi Arabia, the Arabian Sea, and the Red Sea. The terrain is varied. In from the coast, it becomes mountainous. From the dry interior are slopes down into the Arabian Peninsula. The climate is mainly desert—very hot and dry. The west coast is hot and humid. The mountains do get precipitation in the form of seasonal monsoons. Natural resources include oil, coal, marble, gold, lead, copper, fish, and salt.

Altogether, 25.4 million people live on Yemen's 527,970 km^2 of land and 1,906 km of coastline. There are many small communities in more rural areas, some of which are nomadic. Seven percent of the population is urbanized, and 15 percent lives in a city having more than 100,000 inhabitants. Fifty-four percent of the population lives in overcrowded conditions.

Current Waste Practices

Yemen's Waste Management Plan and facilities development were set to start in 2001, but civil conflict has probably put them off. The plan identified principles, key components, and specific waste management procedures. The principles were enhanced record keeping and creation of inventory. Waste was to be first recycled, then used to create energy if possible. The plan also created buffer zones around agricultural areas, houses, and sensitive desert ecosystems. One major concern about the plan was its financing.

About 1,410,000 tons of municipal wastes were collected in Yemen in 2009. Only 19 percent of the population receives municipal waste collection. All collected wastes were landfilled. Altogether, 738,000 tons of hazardous wastes were generated in 1995 and mixed in with municipal solid wastes. Most of these wastes are dumped outside the major cities in open and uncontrolled areas. Communities of waste pickers recycle and use what they can.

Waste practices are very basic—pit toilets, latrines, drainage ditches, cesspools, and open defecation. Two percent of the urban population has access to an improved source of drinking water, and 93 percent has access to improved sanitation facilities. Seventy-two percent of rural populations have access to an improved drinking water source, and 34 percent have access to improved sanitation facilities. Yemen has the sixth-dirtiest water in the world, as measured by BOD (biological oxygen demand).

Emissions and Industry

In 2000, Yemen generated 25,742.1 metric tons of greenhouse gases, a 44 percent increase from 1995.

Agricultural products include bananas, grain, fruit, vegetables, qat, coffee, cotton, livestock, dairy, poultry, and fish. The leaves of the qat shrub are ingested for stimulating effects. Agricultural emissions accounted for 23 percent of all emissions. Within this sector, agricultural soils accounted for 62 percent of emissions, enteric fermentation 35.6 percent, and manure management 2 percent.

Yemen produced substantial amounts of crude oil and has large proven reserves. Oil and electricity production per capita is very high, but oil and electricity consumption per capita is much lower. Energy emissions accounted for 69 percent of all emissions. Within this sector, transportation accounted for 28 percent of emissions, energy industries 28 percent, manufacturing and construction industries 9.6 percent, and fugitive emissions 11 percent. Fugitive emissions are essentially unaccounted waste streams into the air. Fugitive emissions can affect regional ecosystems and the public health, because they can fall from the air to the land and water.

Industrial emissions accounted for 3 percent of all emissions. Within this sector, mineral products accounted for all emissions.

Emissions from solid wastes accounted for 5 percent of all emissions. Within this sector, solid waste disposal on land accounted for 90 percent of emissions and wastewater management 10 percent.

Major Waste Issues

Waste management is very difficult now because of violent civil conflict. An intensely arid desert environment also challenges it. An integrated solid waste management plan in Yemen has no in-country contractors or local knowledge of recycling or hazardous or solid wastes. Water is very scarce, so communities that generate wastes are often near water. Waste sites near these communities are not easily accepted. Yemen faces enormous logistical challenges of then transporting the waste over long distances, often in dangerous environments having no roads.

Most current issues pertain to the lack of freshwater and increasing desertification. Without wastewater treatment or environmental regulation and increasing population, the existing water quality will risk contamination. Public health is also a concern as diseases such as cholera, hepatitis A, hepatitis B, typhoid, malaria, dengue fever, and schistosomiasis are spread through poor waste management. Two percent or more of the population is persistently infected with hepatitis B.

Further Reading

Sabahi, E., et al. 2015. "Evaluation of Groundwater Quality for Drinking Water by Using Physio-Chemical Analysis in the City of Ibb, Yemen." *British Journal of Applied Science and Technology* 5: 5.

Verner, Dort, and Clemens Breisinger, eds. 2013. *Economics of Climate Change in the Arab World*. Washington, DC: The World Bank.

Yemeni Government. www.yemen.gov.ye.

Zawahri, N., et al. 2011. "The Politics of Assessment: Water and Sanitation Millennium Development Goals in the Middle East." *Development and Change* 42: 1154–1178.

Z

ZAMBIA

Zambia is a landlocked African nation bordered by Angola, the Democratic Republic of Congo, Tanzania, Malawi, Mozambique, Zimbabwe, Botswana, and Namibia. The climate is tropical, but it is cooler in higher mountains. Most of the country consists of a large high plateau. Floods occur regularly throughout the country. Natural resources include coal, lead, zinc, gold, silver, uranium, and hydropower.

Altogether, 14.3 million people reside on Zambia's 752,614 km^2 of land. Thirty-five percent of the population is urbanized, and 29 percent lives in a city having more than 100,000 inhabitants. Zambia has among the fastest-growing population rates in the world. There are additionally many small communities outside of the cities. About three-quarters of the population live beneath the international poverty line of $1 per day.

Current Waste Practices

Waste practices in rural areas and parts of urban areas are very basic—pit toilets, latrines, drainage ditches, cesspools, and open defecation. Eighty-seven percent of the urban population has access to an improved source of drinking water, and only 57 percent has access to improved sanitation facilities. Forty-six percent of rural populations have access to an improved drinking water source, and 43 percent have access to improved sanitation facilities. About 20 percent suffer chronic malnutrition. In 2010, there were about 6,804 cases of cholera. Most cases are recorded in rural fishing camps and in the semi-urban areas of Lusaka and Copperbelt provinces. After the rainy season, cholera outbreaks start in October and end around the end of June. The life expectancy is about 43 years, and infant mortality is just under 20 percent.

Only 20 percent of the population receives municipal waste collection. Altogether, 389,000 tons of municipal wastes were collected in 2005. Eighty thousand tons of hazardous wastes were generated in 2005, most dumped in trash heaps on the edge of cities.

Emissions and Industry

In 1994, Zambia generated 32,770.1 metric tons of greenhouse gases. It is likely that greenhouse gases are higher now because of population increases, rate of population growth, and reliance on agriculture.

Agricultural products include corn, rice, tobacco, cotton, peanuts, coffee, livestock, and eggs. Agricultural emissions accounted for 41.5 percent of all emissions.

Within this sector, prescribed burning of savannas accounted for 54 percent of emissions, agricultural soils 33 percent, and enteric fermentation 12 percent.

Energy emissions accounted for 53 percent of all emissions. Within this sector, manufacturing and construction industries accounted for 13 percent of emissions, transportation 7 percent, and other sectors 80 percent. Given the size of this sector, a large amount of unaccounted emissions can mean significant environmental and public health effects. Industrial emissions accounted for 1 percent of all emissions. Within this sector, mineral products accounted for 90 percent of emissions, and chemical industries 10 percent.

Waste emissions accounted for 4.3 percent of all emissions. Within this sector, wastewater management accounted for 73.5 percent of emissions and solid waste disposal on land 26.4 percent.

Major Waste Issues

Mining wastes are a significant waste challenge. Mining contributes about 65 percent of earning from exports. Copper is the main mineral that is mined. There are massive tailings, air pollution, and slag produced in the copper refining processes. There are about forty-five tailing ponds, containing almost 800 million tons of tailing and covering almost 10,000 ha. There about ten slag dumps, containing about 40 million tons of slag and covering about 300 ha. Most of the copper mining wastes migrate to the Kafue River, the drinking water source for 40 percent of urban areas. Along with processing wastes, there are waste oil and other lubricants discharged into the river from mining operations. Although there is a basic regulatory structure for mining operations, actual environmental enforcement seldom occurs.

Because of the lack of adequate waste management there is an accumulation of trash and sewage sludge in urban areas. Public health is a major waste issue, there being many infectious diseases in Zambia. These include yellow fever, cholera, hepatitis A, hepatitis B, meningococcal meningitis, typhoid, dengue fever, and schistosomiasis. Two percent or more of the population is persistently infected with hepatitis B. There is a high risk of malaria.

Further Reading

Gutierrez, Eric. 2007. "Delivering Pro-Poor Water and Sanitation Services: The Technical and Political Challenges in Malawi and Zambia." *Geoforum*: 5: 886–900.

Stringer, Lindsay C., et al. 2009. "Adaptations to Climate Change Drought and Desertification: Local Insights to Enhance Policy in Southern Africa." *Environmental Science and Policy* 12: 748–765.

Zambia Ministry of Health. www.moh.gov.zm.

ZIMBABWE

Zimbabwe is a landlocked nation in south-central Africa. It became a nation in 1965. From 1965 to 1979, internal civil war dominated the nation. Millions of people have fled to neighboring nations. These bordering nations are Botswana, Mozambique, South Africa, and Zambia.

The government agencies responsible for national waste policy are the Ministry of Environment and Tourism and the Ministry of Science and Technology Development. In 2000, Zimbabwe passed a Water Act designed to set up catchment areas, institute a permit system for use of water, and provide for the protection of the environment and control of water pollution.

Zimbabwe's climate is tropical, with a rainy season from November to March. There are reoccurring droughts but floods are rare. The land is mainly a high plateau, with mountains in the east. Natural resources include coal, chromium, asbestos, gold, diamonds, nickel, copper, vanadium, iron ore, lithium, tin, and platinum. Altogether, 13.8 million people reside on Zimbabwe's 390,580 kilometers of land. Thirty-seven percent of the population is urbanized, and 26 percent lives in a city having more than 100,000 inhabitants. There are many small communities outside of urban areas. The capital and largest city is Harare, with a population of about 1.6 million people.

Current Waste Practices

Waste practices are very basic and include pit toilets, latrines, drainage ditches, cesspools, and open defecation. Ninety-eight percent of urban populations have access to improved drinking water sources, and about half have access to improved sanitation facilities. Sixty-nine percent of rural populations have access to an improved drinking water source, and only 32 percent have access to improved sanitation facilities. Water quality is poor. In 2009, there were 98,592 reported cases of cholera, including 4,288 deaths.

The underlying factors were identified as no toilets/latrines, sewage in the streets, limited access to health care, limited supplies, lack of education about cholera, and cultural practices around burials. There was a concentrated national and international effort to contain cholera outbreaks. Forty-seven percent of the population suffers chronic malnutrition. There is a chronic and severe food shortage. Zimbabwe generated 17,000 tons of hazardous wastes in 2008. This waste is mixed with all other wastes. Some of the trash is taken to open pit landfills. Waste picker communities often reside nearby. Trash often builds up in piles and is sometimes burned.

Emissions and Industry

Zimbabwe generated 68,540 tons of greenhouse gases in 2000, a 148 percent increase from 1990. It is likely that greenhouse gas emissions are higher now because of increases in population, rapid population and urbanization growth, and reliance on agriculture.

Agricultural products include bananas, corn, coffee, cotton, tobacco, sugar cane, peanuts, sheep, goats, and pigs. Between 8 percent and 11 percent of land is arable. Agricultural emissions accounted for 58 percent of all emissions. Agricultural soils accounted for 88 percent of emissions within this sector, enteric fermentation 11 percent, and manure management accounted for 2.6 percent.

Zimbabwe produces 120 bbl/day of crude oil and consumes 11,000 bbl/day. Energy emissions accounted for 39 percent of overall emissions. Within this sector, energy production accounted for 28 percent of emissions, manufacturing industries and construction 49 percent, transportation 4 percent, and fugitive emissions 2 percent.

Manufacturing growth is in decline, but mining remains a steady source of economic development. Industrial emissions accounted for 2 percent of overall emissions. Within this sector, metal production accounted for 73 percent emissions and metal production 27 percent.

Waste emissions accounted for 2 percent of overall emissions. Solid waste disposal on land accounted for 83 percent of emissions and wastewater handling 17 percent.

Major Waste Issues

Civil war destroyed most urban waste systems. Rampant unregulated mining created toxic waste and heavy metal water pollution. Deforestation, soil erosion, land degradation, and air and water pollution contribute to desertification. Mining exerts strong political force. The diamond industry alone paid $684.5 million in taxes in 2013. Mining wastes are discharged directly into rivers, causing significant water pollution. Without an adequate waste management infrastructure, and with a rapidly increasing population, wastes can accumulate and facilitate the transfer of wasteborne diseases.

The major waste issue is the protection of public health both in the country and the region. There are many infectious diseases here—cholera, hepatitis A, hepatitis B, typhoid, malaria, dengue fever, and schistosomiasis. Two percent or more of the population is persistently infected with hepatitis B.

There are long droughts and desertification that have substantial environmental and public health effects. With increasing temperatures, desertification will increase and increase these effects.

Further Reading

Central Africa Regional Program for the Environment, Regional Development Strategy 2012–2020, U.S. Agency for International Development. www.usaid.gov.

Mosler, H., et al. 2013. "Achieving Long Term Use of Solar Water Disinfection in Zimbabwe." *Public Health* 127: 92–98.

Van Drunen, M., et al. 2006. *Climate Change in Developing Countries.* Oxfordshire, UK: CAB International North America.

Zimbabwe Parliament. www.parlzim.gov.zw.

Glossary

Aarhus Convention and Protocol

The United Nations Economic Commission for Europe Convention on Access to Information, Public Participation in Decision-Making and Access to Justice in Environmental Matters was adopted on June 25, 1998, in Aarhus, Denmark. This convention sets a new standard for environmental processes, fairness, and public engagement.

Acid Stabilization

A process to balance the pH of animal manure, generally to create methane gas.

African Trypanosomiasis

A disease transmitted to humans via the tsetse fly that carries the parasitic protozoa *Trypanosomes*. Symptoms include malaise and irregular fevers. If the parasites get into the central nervous system, coma and death can occur. It is endemic in thirty-six sub- Saharan African countries.

Anaerobic Lagoon

A waste treatment process. The lagoon or treatment pond or ditch is ideally water-filled to a depth of at least five feet. Depending on environmental conditions, most manure takes from a month to more than 200 days to decompose. If left over capacity, it can become a cesspool.

Bamako Convention

The Bamako Convention on the Ban on the Import into Africa and the Control of Transboundary Movement and Management of Hazardous Wastes within Africa went into effect in 1991. Only African countries can become parties to this convention.

Basel Convention on the Control of Transboundary Movements of Hazardous Wastes and Their Disposal

The Basel Convention requires the environmentally sound management of hazardous wastes or other wastes. This means taking all practicable steps to ensure that hazardous wastes or other wastes are managed in a manner that will protect human health and the environment against the adverse effects that may result from such wastes.

Carbon Dioxide Equivalent

The amount of carbon by weight emitted that produces the same radioactive forcing as a given weight of a similar gas. The formula for equivalency is to multiply the carbon dioxide equivalent number by the carbon content of carbon dioxide.

Cesspool

A method of liquid waste storage. Usually underground, but can be open. When septic systems and sewer lines clog, cesspools of wastes can form.

Chikungunya

A virus transmitted by mosquitoes. It causes the sudden onset of fever and severe joint pain. Other symptoms include fatigue, muscle pain, nausea, headache, and rash. There is no vaccine or antiviral treatment. It is seldom deadly, but older adults are at greater risk of the disease, meaning that symptoms can last much longer and possibly affect other health issues. Until recently, it was only found in tropical areas of Africa, Asia, and India. In 2007, Italy reported an outbreak. In 2013, an outbreak was reported on the Caribbean islands. Because it is spread by a species of mosquito found in North and Central America, it is likely that this disease will spread to the United States.

Cholera

A bacterial disease spread through contaminated water, found in all oceans and occurring naturally in coastal water. Raw shellfish, uncooked fruits and vegetables, and other foods can harbor cholera. Where cholera is widespread, uncomposted manure fertilizers or irrigation water containing raw sewage con introduce cholera into the produce. Cooked grains that are allowed to stand for several hours at room temperature can become a vector for cholera. Cholera causes severe dehydration and, if untreated, can be fatal in hours for anyone, including healthy adults. It can cause vomiting for hours. Severe dehydration is the loss of more than 10 percent of body weight. It is easily remedied through modern rehydration treatments. This is not available in many places. Most people exposed to cholera do not become ill. About one in ten infected people develop symptoms in a few days of the infection. Cholera bacteria remain active in feces for one to two weeks and can infect others. In most countries, water is involved in waste treatment, formally or informally. If wastewater is contaminated with cholera and becomes mixed with any drinking, bathing, cooking, or washing water, then many people can become quickly exposed. Cholera can remain dormant for a long time in wells and other water sources. Urbanization and overcrowding can create cholera-friendly environments.

Climate Change

Climate change is defined by the United Nation Framework Convention on Climate Change as a change of climate attributed directly or indirectly to human activity that alter the composition of the global atmosphere, and that is in addition to natural climate variability observed over comparable time periods.

Climate Vulnerability

The susceptibility and resilience to climate changes of the environment. The degree of vulnerability is dependent on the kind of climate change and the adaptive capacity of the environment.

Composting

Composting requires a biological process that exposes biodegradable waste to anaerobic or aerobic decomposition and that results in a product that can be used to increase soil fertility.

Crimean–Congo Hemorrhagic Fever

A tick-borne viral disease. Exposure to infected animal blood or tissue can also spread it. Symptoms include headache, sudden onset of fever, muscle aches, and hemorrhaging in the bowels, nose, and gums. The disease is widely distributed through Africa, Asia, the Middle East, and eastern Europe.

Cutaneous Leishmaniasis

A disease transmitted via the bites of sandflies that carry the parasitic protozoa *Leishmania*. Symptoms include skin rashes that may become chronic. It is endemic to eighty-eight countries. Most cases occur in Afghanistan, Syria, Saudi Arabia, Brazil, and Peru.

Dengue

A mosquito-borne tropical disease caused by the dengue virus. It is often found in cities and rapidly urbanizing countries. Symptoms are fever, headache, and muscle and joint pains, with a skin rash. In rare cases, the disease can develop into dengue hemorrhagic fever. It can come on so quickly that it causes shock and hemorrhage and death in 5 percent of cases. This results in bleeding, decreased number of blood platelets, and blood plasma leakage. There is no vaccine. The main preventative effort is to reduce mosquito contact by reducing habitat and limiting exposure to bites.

Drainage Ditch

A trench or small creek used for human wastes. Some drain into water systems, especially with heavy rains. Most are not sanitary.

Endemic Disease

The continuous occurrence of the disease at an expected frequency over a certain period of time in a certain geographical area. When it is restricted to a small geographic area or population, it is called an outbreak. If the epidemic is restricted to a nonhuman population, it is called epizootic.

Epidemic Diseases

Diseases that occur more than expected in a geographical area.

Enteric Fermentation

A process of digestion in animals that can produce methane, a greenhouse gas. Mammals with multiple stomachs, like cattle and deer, use microbial fermentation to break down their food. A byproduct of this digestion process is methane, emitted as flatulence.

EU Standards

Standards of waste treatment necessary to join the European Union, inaugurated in 1973 to protect and improve Europe's environment for the future. These waste standards are the highest in the world.

E-Wastes

E-waste describes end-of-life or otherwise disposed-of appliances that use electricity. It includes computers, refrigerators, cell phones, shop tools, lighting, televisions, coffee machines, toasters, and vacuum cleaners. Some e-waste contains hazardous materials. Some e-waste also contains recyclable metals.

Greenhouse Gases

Those gases, listed in many international treaties and agreements, generally include carbon dioxide, methane, nitrous oxide, perfluorocarbons, and sulfur hexafluoride. They trap heat around the Earth and increase global warming.

Helminth Infections

A disease from parasitic worms transmitted via dirt. Their eggs are laid in human feces. Children can suffer irreparable physical and mental damage from the infections caused. More than a billion people globally are infected.

Hepatitis A

A viral disease that interferes with liver function, usually spread via consumption of food or water having fecal contamination. Symptoms include fever, jaundice, abdominal pain, and diarrhea.

Hepatitis B

A waterborne virus that interferes with liver functioning. Symptoms include jaundice, abdominal pain, and dark urine.

Holoendemic Diseases

Diseases that register high levels of infection at a young age.

Hydrofluorocarbons

A group of very long-lasting manmade chemicals that can persist in the environment and cause damage to ecosystems. These chemicals are a combination of carbon, hydrogen, and fluorine.

Hygiene

The science of preserving and promoting health of the individual and of the community. Domestic hygiene includes food preparation and food and kitchen cleanliness. Personal hygiene includes healthy food and body and clothing cleanliness. Public hygiene includes controls over food and water supply, infectious diseases, waste and sewage disposal, and air and water pollution.

Hyperendemic Diseases

Diseases affecting all age groups.

Improved Sanitation Facilities

Minimally adequate access to excreta disposal facilities that prevent contact with humans, animals, and insects. This includes pit toilet and latrines. It does not include 24-hour access or safety.

Improved Water Source

Improved water sources are those safe from waste contamination. They generally include most residential connections, public standpipes, protected wells and springs, boreholes, and rainwater. If waste is not far enough from the source, the source will become contaminated. Unimproved sources are contaminated sources, vendors, tanker trucks and unprotected wells, springs, or boreholes. Access means the availability for one person to get twenty liters of water within 1 km per day. It does not include 24-hour access or safety.

Internally Displaced Person

An internally displaced person (IDP) is someone who is unwillingly displaced from his or her home but within the country's borders. Conflict, natural disasters, and the need for water and food can cause displacement. IDP camps can suffer unsanitary conditions for drinking water and facilities. They are usually not counted in public health programs in most countries. It is estimated that 2011 there were 26.4 million internally displaced people.

Japanese Encephalitis

A viral disease carried by a mosquito. Acute encephalitis is characterized by paralysis, coma, and death. The mortality rate is about 30 percent. It is found in many rural parts of Asia.

Landfill

A method of waste storage, treatment, and disposal. Open landfills are pits or trenches where waste is disposed. They are not lined, covered with soil, or compacted. Sometimes the trash is burned to make room for more trash. Sanitary landfills use a clay liner to keep trash away from the environment until it decomposes. Municipal solid waste landfills use a plastic liner to do the same thing. There are specialized landfills for industrial, radioactive, and hazardous wastes. Landfills can leach concentrated wastes into surrounding areas.

Lassa Fever

A viral disease acquired through aerosolized dust or soil contact and carried by rats. It is endemic in parts of west Africa and is transmitted by direct contact or consumption of food with rat feces or urine. Mortality rates can be as high as 50 percent during epidemics.

Latrine

A pit or trench in the ground used for human wastes. A pit latrine is the most basic form of improved sanitation when there is a floor separating wastes from the user. Pit latrines should be covered and downhill from water sources to minimize drinking water contamination.

Leptospirosis

A bacterial disease spread through contact with water, food, or soil contaminated with animal urine. Symptoms include severe headache, high fever, jaundice, vomiting, and diarrhea. Without treatment, kidney damage, liver failure, meningitis, and respiratory problems can occur.

Long-Range Transboundary Air Pollution Convention

This 1979 convention was implemented in 1983. Between twenty-five and forty-two nations have agreed to various protocols. It establishes measurements and responsibility for air pollution. United Nations Economic Commission for Europe. www.unece.org.

Malaria

The parasitic protozoon *Plasmodium* causes malaria. It is transmitted via the female *Anopheles* mosquito. The parasite reproduces in the liver. Symptoms include cycles of fever, chills, sweats, and anemia. Death is caused by damage to vital organs and inadequate blood to the brain. Malaria is endemic in 100 countries. Approximately 1.5–2.5 million people die annually. Most cases and most deaths are in sub-Saharan Africa.

Meningococcal Meningitis

A bacterial disease that causes inflammation of the brain lining and the spinal cord. Symptoms include stiff neck, headaches, high fever, and vomiting. Transmission is facilitated by overcrowded living conditions, because respiratory droplets from one person to the next transmit it. Some strains can cause rapid epidemics, such as *Neisseria meningitides*. The mortality rate varies from 5 percent to 15 percent. Death comes very quickly, usually within one or two days. The Meningitis Belt is a region of sub-Saharan Africa from Ethiopia to eastern Senegal that has a high concentration of meningitis.

Methane

A regulated greenhouse gas. It occurs in many unregulated forms, such as in the arctic. As the arctic warms, some fear that even more methane will be released, increasing the rate of global warming. Methane is the main ingredient in natural gas and the source of hydrogen in some industrial process. It is one of the main gases recovered from waste decomposition and is often called biogas.

Municipal Solid Waste

All residential solid wastes, plus all nonhazardous commercial and industrial solid wastes.

Municipal Waste Collection

Collection of all residential solid wastes, plus all nonhazardous commercial and industrial solid wastes, by the local government. It includes waste collection, separation, transfer, storage, treatment, and disposal.

Open Defecation

Defecation outside, often with little or no privacy, such as behind bushes or in alleys. It can be unsafe and unsanitary. About 1 billion people globally practice open defecation, usually because for lack of any other option.

Organic Waste

Waste from a plant or animal. Food wastes, human and animal wastes, and agricultural wastes constitute organic wastes. Organic wastes are biodegradable and can be recycled and sometimes used as sources of biogas.

Plague

A bacterial disease transmitted by fleas usually found on rats. Symptoms include fever, headache, and very swollen lymph glands. Plague moves quickly through its victims and without treatment develops into pneumonia, with mortality rate greater than 50 percent.

Pit Toilet

A hole in the ground used for human wastes, generally with no water. Pour flush pit latrines use water per flush. Unless cleaned and maintained with a sanitary floor or concrete slab, most pit toilets are unsanitary.

Recycling

Recycling is a broad term having many nuances and undergoing constant change. Recycling is the reprocessing of waste material in a production process that diverts it from the waste stream. It is part of integrated waste management approaches. It is also part of the existence of waste pickers, people who scavenge the dump and trash for anything that can be sold or used. In some countries, recycling is new, and in other countries, recycling borne of necessity is part of history and culture. A primary purpose of recycling is to decrease the need for landfill space and suppress illegal dumping.

Refugee

Someone who flees a country to escape armed conflict, generalized violence, or human rights violations.

Stockholm Convention on Persistent Organic Pollutants (POPs)

In 2001, ninety countries agreed to reduce POPs, which are toxic, don't break down, bioaccumulate in food chains, and can travel long distances. The parties agreed to reduce or eliminate production of POPs. See Stockholm Convention (www.chm.pop.int).

The Rotterdam Convention

The objective of this convention is to promote shared responsibility and cooperative efforts among parties in the international trade of certain hazardous chemicals to protect human health and the environment from potential harm and to contribute to their environmentally sound use by facilitating information exchange about their characteristics, by providing for a national decision-making process on their import and export, and by disseminating these decisions.

Safely Managed Sanitation Services

The United Nations defines safely managed sanitation services as access to a sanitation facility, with excreta transported to a disposal/treatment site or treated in place before being reused or returned to the environment. Basic sanitation facilities move excreta through a sewer network to a specific location or hygienically remove it from septic tank, cesspools, and latrine pits. This definition does not take into account personal safety.

Sanitation

The hygienic disposal or recycling of waste materials focusing on excrement and other bodily fluids, domestic wastewater, and solid wastes. Sanitation is a public health strategy to prevent disease.

Schistosomiasis

Schistosomiasis is caused by a parasitic trematode carried by freshwater snails. These snails are hosts that release the parasite larvae that penetrate the skin of people exposed to contaminated water. From there, the larvae mature and reproduce in the body. Symptoms include malaise, urinary and intestinal diseases. Schistosomiasis is endemic in seventy-four countries. Eighty percent of infected people live in sub-Saharan Africa. It is found in lakes, ponds, cesspools, dams, canals, and irrigation ditches.

Septic Tank

A common method of sewage treatment whereby bacteria digest sewage as it flows along a tank or series of pipes and tanks. It effectiveness is dependent on environmental conditions and maintenance. Tanks can fill or become clogged and become a cesspool.

Typhoid Fever

A bacterial disease spread via food or water contaminated by feces or sewage. Symptoms include a high fever. If untreated, the mortality rate is 20 percent.

United Nations: Framework Convention on Climate Change

This convention set the standards for greenhouse gas emissions monitoring and regulation. United Nations: Framework Convention on Climate Change (www.unfccc.int).

UN Millennium Development Goals (MDG)

Goals set by the United Nation per country to increase the quality of human life and protect the environment. In the area of sanitation and drinking water, the goal for 2015 is half of the population's having safe access to sanitation and drinking water. These are minimal thresholds and often access requires traveling long distances, with only hygiene separating waste from water. Water quality and continuous water supply are not necessarily included in United Nations methods.

Vectors

Vectors are the paths of a disease. Some vectors are not necessary to the functioning of the organism that carries them. Some vectors are biological, being part of the functioning of the organism. Vectorial capacity is a measurement of the vector in terms of disease presence, survival rates, building structure and waste systems infestation, and other measures of the capacity of the disease to spread.

Wadi

A dry riverbed or channel that is dry except for the rainy season.

Waigani Convention

This convention applies mainly to the South and Central Pacific countries. It aims for cleaner production, meaning a conceptual and procedural approach to production that demands that all phases of the life cycle of a product or process be addressed with the objective of preventing or minimizing short- and long-term risks to humans and to the environment.

Waste picker

An individual who scavenges trash for recyclable materials and sustenance without the support or protection of government. Waste pickers are relied upon in many cities where hazardous and toxic wastes are not separated from municipal wastes. Waste from urban trash heaps and landfills can support waste picker communities.

Wastewater

Used water that contains liquid and solid wastes. It is essentially sewage.

Waste and Water Diseases

Infectious diarrhea, cholera, salmonellosis, shigellosis, amebiasis, typhoid, schistosomiasis, trachoma, ascariasis, trichuriasis, and hookworm.

Yellow Fever

A virus spread via the *Culex tritaeniorhyncus* mosquito. The severity can range from influenza symptoms to severe hepatitis and hemorrhagic fever. So far, it occurs only in tropical South American and sub-Saharan Africa. The mortality rate is less than 20 percent.

Zoonotic Disease

An infectious disease of an animal that can cause disease when transmitted to humans.

Bibliography

Angelakis, Andreas N., and Joan B. Rose. 2014. *Evolution of Sanitation and Wastewater Technologies through the Centuries.* London, UK: IWA Publishing.

Black, Maggie, and Ben Fawcett. 2008. *The Last Taboo: Opening the Door on the Global Sanitation Crisis.* New York: Taylor & Francis.

Blum, Deborah, and Richard G. Feachem. 1983. "Measuring the Impact of Water Supply and Sanitation Investments in Diarrheal Diseases: Problems of Methodology." *International Journal of Epidemiology* 12, iss. 3: 357–365.

Bourke, John G. 1891. *Scatalogic Rites of All Nations.* Washington DC: W.H. Lowdermilk & Co.

Clasen, Thomas, et al. 2007. "Interventions to Improve Water Quality for Preventing Diarrhea: Systematic Review and Meta-Analysis." *British Medical Journal (BMJ)* (April) 334: 782–795.

Collin, Robert. 2005. *The Environmental Protection Agency: Cleaning Up America's Act.* Westport, CT: Greenwood Press.

Collin, Robert. 2008. *Battleground Environment.* Westport, CT, Greenwood Press.

Collin, Robert, and Robin Collin. 2010. *The Encyclopedia of Sustainability.* Santa Clara, CA: ABC-CLIO.

Collin, Robert, and Robin Collin. 2014. *The Encyclopedia of Energy: Choices for the Future.* Westport, CT: Praeger Press.

George, Rose. 2008. *The Big Necessity: The Unmentionable World of Human Waste and Why It Matters.* New York: Metropolitan Books.

Grossman, Elizabeth. 2006. *High-Tech Trash: Digital Devices, Hidden Toxics, and Human Health.* Washington, DC: Island Press.

Harris, Christopher, William L. Want, and Morris A. Ward. 1987. *Hazardous Waste: Confronting the Challenge.* Westport, CT: Praeger.

Humes, Edward. 2012. *Garbology: Our Dirty Love Affair with Trash*, London, UK: Penguin Books.

Hutton, Guy, and Laurence Haller. 2004. *Evaluation of the Costs and Benefits of Water and Sanitation Improvements at the Global Level.* Geneva, Switzerland: World Health Organization.

Jamieson, Dale. 2014. *Reason in a Dark Time: Why the Struggle against Climate Change Failed—and What It Means to Our Future.* New York: Oxford University Press.

Johansen, Bruce E. 2003. *Indigenous Peoples and Environmental Issues.* Westport, CT: Greenwood Press.

Kang, Manjit S., and Surinder S. Banga. 2013. *Combatting Climate Change: An Agricultural Perspective.* Danvers, MA: CRC Press.

Klein, Naomi. 2014. *This Changes Everything: Capitalism vs. the Climate.* New York: Simon and Schuster.

Landrigan, Philip J., and Ruth A. Etzel. 2014. *Textbook of Children's Environmental Health.* New York: Oxford University Press.

Leonard, Annie. 2010. *The Story of Stuff*. New York: Free Press.

Mara, Duncan, et al. 2012. "Selection of Sustainable Sanitation Arrangements." *Water Policy* 9: 305–318.

Melosi, Martin V. 2008. *The Sanitary City: Environmental Services in Urban America from Colonial Times to the Present*. Pittsburgh, PA: University of Pittsburgh Press.

Nagle, Robin. 2013. *On the Streets and behind the Trucks with the Sanitation Workers of New York City*. New York: Farrar, Straus & Giroux.

Onda, Kyle, et al. 2014. "Country Clustering Applied to the Waste and Sanitation Sector: A New Tool with Potential Applications in Research and Policy." *International Journal of Hygiene and Environmental Health* 217: 379–385.

Royte, Elizabeth. 2005. *Garbage Land: On the Secret Trail of Trash*. New York: Little, Brown and Company.

Teague, J., et al. 2014. "Water, Sanitation, Hygiene and Nutrition: Successes, Challenges and Implications for Integration." *International Journal of Public Health* 59: 913–921.

Thomson, Vivian E. 2009. *Garbage In, Garbage Out: Solving the Problems with Long-Distance Trash Transport*. Charlottesville: University of Virginia Press.

Tremmel, Joerg Chet, and Katherine Robinson. 2014. *Climate Ethics: Environmental Justice and Climate Change*. London, UK: I.B. Tauris & Co., Ltd.

Pellow, Naguib David. 2007. *Resisting Global Toxics: Transnational Movements for Environmental Justice,* Cambridge, MA: MIT Press.

Peterson, A. Townsend. 2014. *Mapping Disease Transmission Risk: Enriching Models Using Biogeography and Ecology*. Baltimore, MD: Johns Hopkins University Press

Riddell, Robert. 2014. *Resilience, Adaptation, and Sustainability*. Auckland, NZ: Mary Egan Publishing.

Sato, T. 2013. "Global, Regional, and Country Level Need for Data on Wastewater Generation, Treatment and Use." *Agricultural Water Management* 130: 1–13.

Selendy, Janine M. H., ed. 2011. *Waste and Sanitation Related Diseases and the Environment: Challenges, Interventions, and Preventative Measures*. Hoboken, NJ: Wiley.

Strasser, Susan. 1999. *Waste and Want: A Social History of Trash*. New York: Holt and Company, LLC.

Vaughn, Jacqueline. 2008. *Waste Management*. Santa Barbara, CA: ABC-Clio.

Winblad, Uno. 1985. *Sanitation without Water*. New York: Macmillan Education.

Wise, A. F. E., and J. A. Swaffield. 2002. *Water, Sanitary, and Waste Services for Buildings*. New York: Taylor & Francis.

Woolley, Leslie. 1990. *Sanitation Details*. New York: Taylor & Francis.

World Health Organization. 2006. *WHO Guidelines for the Safe Use of Wastewater, Excreta and Greywater: Policy and Regulatory Aspects*. Geneva, Switzerland: WHO Publications.

World Health Organization and UNICEF. 2010. *Progress on Sanitation and Drinking Water 2014 Update*. Geneva, Switzerland: World Health Organization.

Online Resources

Adaptation Policy Framework. United Nations Development Program 2004. www.who.int.

Basel Convention Data Visualization Tool on the Generation, Export and Import of Hazardous Wastes and Other Wastes. www.basel.int/Countries/NationalReporting/DataVisualizationTool/.

Basel Convention On-Line Reporting Database. Data and Information on Hazardous and Other Wastes. www.basel.int/Countries/NationalReporting/ReportingDatabase/tabid/1494/Default.aspx.

Centre for Climate Adaptation. www.climateadaptation.eu.

Climate Change and African Political Stability. www.ccaps.aiddata.org/aid.

Climate Change and Infectious Disease. www.chgnharvard.org.

Compact of Mayors for Greenhouse Gas Emissions. www.un.org.

Countries and Their Cultures. www.everyculture.com.

Freeman, Matthew C., et al. 2013. "Integration of Water, Sanitation, and Hygiene for the Prevention and Control of Neglected Tropical Diseases: A Rationale for Inter-Sectoral Collaboration." www.plosntds.org.

Global Footprint Network. www.footprintnetwork.org.

Microdiversity of Public Health. www.indiegogo.com/americangut.

National Oceanic and Atmospheric Administration Realtime Data and Climate Indices. www.artic.noaa.gov.

Near Real Time Monitoring of Algal Blooms. www.spie.org.

Ocean Trash Index. www.oceanconservancy.or.

Organization for Economic Development and Cooperation. www.oecd.org.

Pan American Health Organization. www.paho.org.

RadNet Map Interface for Near Real Time Radiation Monitoring Data. www.catalog.data.gov.

Sulabh International Social Service Organization. www.sulabhinternational.org.

The World Bank. www.worldbank.org.

United Nations Framework Convention on Climate Change. www.unfccc.int/ghg-emissions-data/items/3800.php.

UN High Commissioner for Refugees. www.unhcr.org.

UN Statistics Division Millennium Development Goals Indicator Database. www.unstats.un.org/unsd/environment/qindicators.

Water, Sanitation, and Hygiene: Strategy Overview. www.gatesfoundation.org.

WHO/UNICEF Joint Monitoring Program Hygiene. www.wssinfor.org/post-2015-monitoring/working-groups/hygiene/.

WHO/UNICEF Joint Monitoring Program Sanitation. www.wssinfor.org/post-2015-monitoring/working-groups/sanitation/.

U.S. Centers for Disease Control and Prevention. www.cdc.gov.

U.S. Environmental Protection Agency Waste Reduction Model. www.epa.gov/epawaste/conserv/tools/warm/.

Zero Waste Recycling Data, Maps, and Graphs. www.zerowasteamarica.org.

About the Author and Contributors

Robert William Collin, the author of this encyclopedia, is a senior research scholar at Willamette University. He is the author of *The Environmental Protection Agency: Cleaning Up America's Act* (2005) and *Battleground Environment: 101 Most Controversial Environmental Issues* (2008, 2 vols.). He is a co-author of the *Encyclopedia of Sustainability* (2010, 3 vols.) and a co-editor and author of *Energy Choices: How to Power the Future* (2014, 2 vols.). He is a co-author of "Sustainability and Environmental Justice," in Michael Redding, ed., *The Sustainability Handbook* (New York: Routledge Press, 2015).

Faduma Ali is a community organizer with Groundworks, Portland, and is also a poet.

Susan Lea Collin has been a registered nurse of 34 years and hold a master's of science in nursing from the University of North Carolina, Chapel Hill. She is nurse executive board–certified by the American Nurses Association. Her nursing practice has embraced all aspects of healthcare over the years, and she currently works in nursing administration. Her research assistant is Morganne Staring, a student at the University of North Carolina, Chapel Hill.

Robin Morris Collin is the Norma Paulis professor of law at Willamette University School of Law. She is a co-author of the *Encyclopedia of Sustainability* (2010, 3 vols.) and a co-editor and author of *Energy Choices: How to Power the Future* (2014, 2 vols.). She is a co-author of "Sustainability and Environmental Justice," in Michael Redding, ed., *The Sustainability Handbook* (New York: Routledge Press, 2015).

Ben Duncan is the equity and public health coordinator for Multnomah County, Oregon. He has served as the chair of the environmental justice task force in Oregon.

Michael Lytton is a writer and an organizational management consultant.

Brent Merrill is a member of the Grand Rhonde Tribe, a writer, and an economic development consultant.

Index

Science waste training 130; nuclear waste storage 18; public health roles 8

Security issues: historical defense xxii, global infectious diseases xxxiv, in a refugee camp 13; information on waste in Cuba; landfill control in Marshall Islands 291; sanitation security 28; sustainable development in Myanmar 306; see also food security

Sewers: fatberg clogs in London 423; effects of war in Palestine 329, Syria 392, Timor-Leste 403; experimental jet spray cleaning in Austria 64; generally xxii, xxvi–xxvii; groundwater wells and disease vectors in Mali 289; pharmaceutical residues in Germany xix, 199; sewer sludge xix; source tracking leaky sewers in Greece 206; workers and manual scavengers in India 11; without sewers in Latin America 210; see country entries

Skull Valley Band of the Goshute Reservation: nuclear waste siting controversy 15

Slavery: in Antigua and Barbuda 50, Central African Republic 117

Snow: see country entries

Social class: caste system in India 10–12, Indonesia 234; consumerism trash effects 125; inequality and sustainability 29; loss of working class from Plague xxii; public health 3, 7; rising middle class in China 126; Social determinants of health 4

Soil: climate change projected effects in Turkey 413; food wastes in Taiwan; erosion and conservation in Angola 48; Argentina 51, Bhutan 88, Guinea 210, Lesotho 274, Hungary 223, Venezuela 440, Vietnam 440, Zimbabwe 448; pollution in Belarus 78, Bulgaria 101, Czech Republic 147, Eritrea 170, Haiti 219, Moldova 295, Russia 353, Senegal 361, Ukraine 419, Uzbekistan 435; Persistent Organic Pollutants in China 128;

radioactivity in Austria 65; recycling phosphorous in Algeria 44, Sweden 387: 395; refugees 14; salinization in Australia 62, Kyrgyzstan 267; soil transmitted Helminthiasis in Belize 84, Cambodia 109, Laos 270, Myanmar 306, South America 133, Sri Lanka 380; sustainability 32

Solid wastes: caste system in India 10, 11; contamination free and reusable xviii; generally xv, hazardous chemicals not counted as solid wastes in Texas xviii; municipal solid wastes landfill in US xvi; public health concerns 6; urbanization impacts xx; see country entries

Space waste: 389

Superfund: generally xxiii–xxiv; hazardous waste clean up in US 430

Sustainability: Agenda 21 of the Rio Declaration 32; bioaccumulation 97; ecological challenges from waste xii; environmental benchmarks in Ireland; global focus xi, xxi, 26; persistent organic pollution 97; precautionary principle xxi; production and consumption 28; President Obama 21; production lifecycle in Switzerland 390; reuse of waste in Australia 59; risk management and perception 34; sewer waste monitoring xix; tourism in Monaco 298; waste and pollution 28, 30, 35; waste plan in Denmark 155, Finland 184, Germany 198, New Zealand 314, Norway 322, Sweden 387; water in Algeria 46

Texas: deep well injection waste treatment xviii; University of Texas Climate Change and African Political Stability 135

Toilets: clogged toilets and public health 6; history generally xxii; right to privacy in South Africa 34; right to sanitation 33; toilet wars in South Africa 374

Tourism: cruise ships and wastes 84; ecotourism assessment in the